THE MEMOIRS OF EMMA COURTNEY
by Mary Hays

and

ADELINE MOWBRAY; OR THE MOTHER AND THE DAUGHTER
by Amelia Alderson Opie

Eighteenth-Century Literature Series
by College Publishing

Laura L. Runge, Series Editor

This series brings into print significant eighteenth-century literature in pairs or groups that speak to each other. In an age when coffee-houses and salons hummed with the talk of culture, conversation provided a key to urban growth and civilization. Combined with an unprecedented boom in print, the age also witnessed the first widespread success of women and middle class authors. For various reasons, women's part in the cultural conversation became muted over the course of time. The Eighteenth-Century Literature series by College Publishing focuses on restoring that dynamic by making the work of men and women available to today's student in a format that stresses their intertextuality. With informative introductions based in current research and several aids to guide the undergraduate to further reading, this unique series creates an opportunity for a rich and historically based discussion of the work of well-known authors together with their important, but frequently overlooked, contemporaries.

Published Titles

Clara Reeve's *The Old English Baron*
and Horace Walpole's *The Castle of Otranto*,
edited by Laura Runge of the University of South Florida

Mary Wollstonecraft's *The Wrongs of Woman; or Maria*
and William Godwin's *Memoirs of Mary Wollstonecraft Godwin*,
edited by Cynthia Richards of Wittenberg University

Mary Hays's *The Memoirs of Emma Courtney*
and Amelia Alderson Opie's *Adeline Mowbray;*
or the Mother and the Daughter

THE MEMOIRS OF EMMA COURTNEY
by Mary Hays

and

ADELINE MOWBRAY; OR THE MOTHER AND THE DAUGHTER
by Amelia Alderson Opie

Edited by Miriam L. Wallace
New College of Florida

College Publishing
Glen Allen, Virginia

College Publishing books are printed on acid-free paper.

ISBN 0-9679121-9-9
Library of Congress Card Number: 2004102757

College Publishing
12309 Lynwood Drive, Glen Allen, Virginia 23059
T (800) 827-0723   (804) 364-8410   F (804) 364-8408
collegepub@mindspring.com

TABLE OF CONTENTS

ACKNOWLEDGEMENTS

Many people have been instrumental in helping this edition to reach its conclusion. First, I would like to thank my editor, Laura L. Runge, for her perceptive eye and quick responses to my questions, and my publisher, Stephen Mosberg, whose excitement over this project and interest in these novels was truly encouraging. R. L. Silver deserves my most grateful thanks for crucial editing work, a patient eye, and unfailing support of the most important yet intangible kinds. My student assistant for one semester, Ya'el Morowati, did important service helping me get the original text of *Adeline Mowbray* from page to electronic form. Thanks also go to New College of Florida's Humanities Division and our Chair, Glenn Cuomo, who provided material support in the shape of student assistance, and to the New College Faculty Development Fund for research travel at a crucial stage in this project. New College President Mike Michalson put me in touch with John Wetenhall, the Director of the John and Mabel Ringling Museum of Art; Heidi Taylor at the Ringling Museum of Art was friendly and efficient: Together, they made it possible to reproduce the image for the cover from the Museum's collection. I thank the John and Mabel Ringling Museum for permission to reproduce this wonderful portrait. The British Library supplied Gillray's "New Morality," and the National Portrait Gallery of Britain provided John Opie's portrait of Amelia Alderson Opie from their collection. My colleagues in the 2003 NEH Summer Seminar on "Rethinking the British Romantic Fiction" were important for inspirational conversation and general wisdom: Stephen Behrendt, Margaret Case Croskery, Joy Currie, Chris Flynn, Anne Frey, Daniella Mallinick, Julie Schaffer, Daniel Schierenbeck, Sandra Sherman, Brian Trinque, Dawn Van Epp, Samantha Webb, Lisa Wilson, and Margaret Wye. I would particularly like to thank Julie Schaffer, whose prior work on the Corvey Project's website originally led me to track the reviews of both *Emma* and *Adeline*, and Dan Schierenbeck for his help with the English Dissenters. Samantha Kirby's reviews on the Corvey Project website were also helpful locators. The library staff at the University of Nebraska-Lincoln were immensely helpful in the final stages of tracking down period documents, particularly Kate Kane and the folks in Microfilm; Melissa Sinner in Electronic Text Services helped procure a copy of the title page from *Adeline*. Stephen Wagner at the New York Public Library's Pforzheimer Collection and Gina Luria Walker at the New School University were both helpful in determining that there is no extant image of Mary Hays known to any of us—itself a fascinating detail. As promised, I would also like to thank the students in my "Romantic-Era Novel" class of Fall 2002, for their generosity in serving as guinea pigs in my first attempt to teach these novels and for reading both of these works with high seriousness and detailed attention. Editions of *Emma Courtney* prepared by Eleanor Ty and Marilyn Brooks blazed the trail, and set a high standard for efforts to identify Hays's citations, which are particularly challenging because of her extensive reading, citing from memory sometimes with important changes, and the relative obscurity for us of some of her sources. I have found both editions helpful at various stages in my own work on Hays. Shelley King and John B. Pierce's edition of *Adeline Mowbray*, which I consulted only at the very last stage, also pushed me to rethink some attributions and footnotes in helpful ways.

Finally, I would like to dedicate this project to Miriam Bradley Sidle, my grandmother, who provided books, piano music, and an independent female exemplar to her daughters and their daughters. In many ways my own interest in the lives of women who came before me is a gift from her.

LIST OF ILLUSTRATIONS

FOR FURTHER EXPLORATION

A NOTE ON THE TEXTS

This edition was prepared from the first London editions of *Emma Courtney* (1796) and of *Adeline Mowbray* (1804). Comparisons were made with the late edition of *Adeline Mowbray* from *The Works of Mrs. Opie*, overseen by Amelia Alderson Opie in 1834, but the earlier variant was preferred because of its closer proximity to the period in which *Emma Courtney* appeared. A final edition, the Grove edition, was prepared in 1844, which omits several scenes and is taken by Shelley King and John Pierce to be a more conservative variation, thus providing a further reason for preferring the earliest edition. The American edition of *Emma Courtney* from 1802 was also compared, but no substantive changes appear in that edition, and it is the 1796 edition that Amelia Alderson read and to which she responded at the time.

Some obvious typographical errors in both texts have been silently corrected, but much of the period's inconsistencies in spelling and capitalization have been purposefully retained. A few particularly confusing ones such as "desert" for "dessert" have been silently corrected throughout *Emma Courtney*. Proper names of estates such as Morton Park and the Lawn have been capitalized consistently as well in both works. Quotation marks have been regularized in accordance with modern American practice. Alderson Opie uses dialect extensively in the dialog of Savanna and of Mary, and apparent grammatical and spelling errors are the result of Opie's efforts at transcribing non-standard English speech, some of which were softened mildly in the 1834 edition.

In the footnotes, *The Oxford English Dictionary* has been abbreviated as OED throughout when it served as a significant source.

INTRODUCTION

Reading *Emma*, Reading *Adeline*

Reading *Memoirs of Emma Courtney* and *Adeline Mowbray* together highlights points of similarity and differentiation between these two end-of-the-century novels. Both works are indebted to the particularly tense decade of the 1790s when the British public was engaged with ongoing debates about the status of family, state, government, and national identity. Even in the apparently "new" approaches and ideas raised, like other novels of the 1790s each is also indebted to the traditions of the eighteenth-century English novel that precedes it. Most scholars agree that eighteenth-century British novels were an important vehicle for imagining the kind of heroic, psychological, modern "subject" or self necessary for modern literature.[1] An individuated character, capable of growth and education, changing over time in ways which seem probable and coherent, is developed importantly in canonical novels from Daniel Defoe's *Robinson Crusoe* (1719) to Samuel Richardson's *Pamela* (1740), and Henry Fielding's *Tom Jones* (1749). In her contribution to this discussion, Nancy Armstrong provocatively argued that the "subject" or core self of modern literature, formulated in the eighteenth century, was centrally a female subjectivity.[2] Armstrong was not arguing that the eighteenth-century British novel is seldom

---

[1] See for example, Ian Watt, *Rise of the Novel*, Michael McKeon, *Origins of the English Novel*, Terry Lovell, *Consuming Fiction*, Nancy Armstrong, *Desire and Domestic Fiction*, Helene Moglen, *Trauma of Gender*, and Lennard Davis, *Factual Fictions* for different but important accounts of the English novel and the modern subject.

[2] Nancy Armstrong, *Desire and Domestic Fiction: A Political History of the Novel.* (New York: Oxford UP, 1987), 8.

concerned with male heroes—many important novels throughout the century are centrally concerned with male characters: Beside those already named, *Joseph Andrews, David Simple, Humphrey Clinker, Tristram Shandy* and *The Man of Feeling* are evidently centered on a male protagonist from their very titles. Rather, Armstrong was suggesting that, surprisingly, when one looks at the eighteenth-century foundations of the English novel, one is struck by the sense that the development of a protagonist with complexly rendered internal psychological self corresponds best to a feminine or feminized figure. Important novels focused on the adventures of female characters are common: *Moll Flanders, Roxana, Fantomina, The History of Miss Betsy Thoughtless, Clarissa, Amelia, Evelina, Cecelia, Miss Sidney Bidulph, Maria; or the Wrongs of Woman,* including the novels represented here, *Memoirs of Emma Courtney* and *Adeline Mowbray, or the Mother and the Daughter.* Even novels ostensibly focused on male heroes such as Sarah Fielding's *David Simple,* Laurence Sterne's *Life and Opinions of Tristram Shandy, Gentleman,* and Henry MacKenzie's *The Man of Feeling* are so concerned with their characters' internal emotional states that they intersect importantly with Armstrong's claim for the centrality of a feminized self. Explorations of psychological states, emotional life, and particularly the state of one's heart were claimed in the eighteenth century as the special arena in which feminine and female characters and writers shone. The two novels considered here are deeply concerned with how their heroine's sense of themselves come to be formed through their intersection with the world of action and event. Hays's and Opie's interest in the psychological and emotional lives of their heroines, Emma's and Adeline's negotiations with love, family, and social expectations, and the reactions these heroines provoke in other characters and in their readers are central to the project of British fiction, rather than merely peripheral to it.

Mary Hays's first novel and Amelia Alderson Opie's third, *Emma Courtney* and *Adeline Mowbray* represent late entries into the eighteenth-century exploration of the importance of feeling and sensibility, and the complex negotiation between one's duty to one's self and to one's larger community—family and nation. Both novels respond in different ways to the sea change in European social order and political thought fomented by the "Age of Revolution"—the period of the American (1776), French (1789), and Haitian (1797-1804) Revolutions, Naval mutinies, and of popular uprisings in Ireland and in Eastern Europe. Hays's *Emma Courtney* both cautions against the over-development of female sensibility and celebrates the importance of affect as a form of particularly feminine knowledge.[3] Alderson Opie's *Adeline Mowbray* is ambivalently coded, apparently attacking the radical arguments for female liberty associated with Mary Wollstonecraft, and for open marriages associated with William Godwin, and yet also valuing its own vision of female autonomy.

Historically, as the reviews of each novel in the appendices show, *Emma Courtney* was strongly associated with arguments for "the rights of women," while *Adeline Mowbray* was taken as strongly critical of revolutionary ideas of modern womanhood. By British conservatives or "church and king" loyalists, *Emma Courtney* was understood as a "Jacobin" novel, or one that, in sympathy with French philosophical ideas, recommended unfeminine and especially un-British behavior and values. In contrast, *Adeline Mowbray* was mostly praised by those who believed that traditional British reverence for marriage, the monarchy, feminine modesty, and the sentimentalized family were the foundations of British national greatness. Modern-day critics often replicate these categories, classifying *Emma* as a "Jacobin" novel, or a revolutionary novel supportive of Wollstonecraftian ideas, and designating *Adeline* as an "Anti-Jacobin" novel, or one that supports the status quo of British society and social order.[4]

---

[3] For a fuller version of this argument, see Miriam L. Wallace, "Mary Hays's 'Female Philosopher': Constructing Revolutionary Subjects in *Memoirs of Emma Courtney*," in *Rebellious Hearts: British Women and the French Revolution*, Eds. Adriana Cracuin and Kari Lokke, (New York: SUNY Press), 2001, 233-260.

[4] See Claudia Johnson, *Equivocal Beings: Politics, Gender and Sentimentality in the 1790s*, Gary Kelly, *The English Jacobin Novel* and *Women, Writing, and Revolution*, Matthew Grenby, *The Anti-Jacobin Novel*, Eleanor Ty, *Unsex'd Revolutionaries: Five*

Reading these two novels side by side, it becomes more difficult to oversimplify them as representatives of "radical" and proto-feminist work on the side of Hays and of "conservative" and anti-feminist fiction on that of Alderson Opie. Rather, each novel's complex contradictions are made more evident by this pairing. Hays appears to value Emma's feelings even though the preface to her novel argues for self-restraint, while Alderson Opie's representation of Adeline's sufferings at first appears as a warning, but also reminds the reader that Adeline suffers because her principles are too refined for the crass and self-interested world in which she lives. Both novels are hard to resolve into a simple didactic point; both resist easy resolution into modern-day oppositional terms such as "feminist" and "conservative," and for this reason they are valuable. They remind us that literary-cultural negotiations are complex. A careful reading militates against reading them simply in terms of twenty-first century "feminist" or "anti-feminist" agendas or liberal versus conservative traditions, with Hays as the liberal, feminist foremother and Alderson Opie as the conservative proponent of an idealized and proper femininity. Both novels assume that marriage and love are central concerns for women, and both novels offer us heroines who are too high-minded to function well in their own social contexts.

Reading/Writing/Rewriting

Despite critical suspicion since the "death of the author" about depending heavily on the author's life for interpreting their literary work,[5] readers of women's writing have often felt

Women Novelists of the 1790s and *Empowering the Feminine: The Narratives of Mary Robinson, Jane West, and Amelia Opie,* and Anne K. Mellor, *Mothers of the Nation: Women's Political Writing in England* for examples and discussion.

[5]Suspicion about the usefulness of biographical information in interpreting literature runs across theoretical camps beginning in the mid-twentieth century. In the 1950s, W. K. Wimsatt and Monroe C. Beardsley published "The Intentional Fallacy," arguing that searching for an author's intentions as a key to understanding his or her work is an erroneous critical premise, and that a work's meaning lies solely in the writing itself. Roland Barthe's famous essay, "Death of the Author"

that the author's biography was essential. Feminist critics often argue that gender does make a difference, and that the life and struggles of the woman writer are marked visibly in the text.[6] But if the specifics of Mary Hays's and Amelia Alderson Opie's lives, their intellectual circles and experiences, their successes and disappointments are significant for reading these two novels, we ought also to be cautious about the historical tendency to interpret their novels solely in terms of their own lives. These two novels, in particular, tempt the reader to do just that.

Mary Hays's *Memoirs of Emma Courtney* was read in its own day as a thinly veiled account of Hays's own love life and her unsuccessful pursuit of William Frend, detailed partially in her philosophical letters to William Godwin and an open secret in London when *Emma Courtney* was published. Reading the novel as engaged with Hays's personal experience is not wholly mistaken, but to read the novel as *merely* autobiographical misses the distinction between a confessional biography and a fictionalized narrative with an explicit didactic agenda. Hays's novel *is* autobiographical—going so far as to incorporate sections of actual letters written by and to Hays—but it is also a carefully crafted *fictional* work. Hays invites her reader to respond to her

problematized authorial intention even further, arguing that not only was depending on the author's intentions fallacious, but that the reader has taken the place of the "author" as the source of meaning and significance in modern literature and criticism. Following Barthes's announcement of the author's death, Michel Foucault's "What Is An Author" argued that rather than historical authors, critics discuss "an author function" when they use writers' names to refer to their work— so, for instance "Freud" and "Shakespeare" stand for far more than the writing produced by the actual historical authors "Sigmund Freud" and "William Shakespeare."

[6] Foundational texts in early feminist literary criticism which take women writers' lives and experiences seriously include Elaine Showalter, *A Literature of Their Own: British Women Novelists from Bronte to Lessing.* (Princeton: Princeton UP, 1977); Tillie Olsen, *Silences*, (New York: Delacorte, 1978); Sandra Gilbert and Susan Gubar, *The Madwoman in the Attic*, (New Haven: Yale UP, 1985); and Janet Todd, *Feminist Literary History: A Defence*, (Cambridge: Polity, 1988). For an early critique of this approach as "bourgeois realism," see Toril Moi, *Sexual/Textual Politics*, (New York: Methuen, 1985).

story emotionally at first; just as the heroine learns that her feelings are important but limited as a lens through which to understand her life and the world in which she lives, the reader is asked to consider the larger consequences of the actions and beliefs which drive personal and domestic life.

Significantly, *Emma Courtney* traces the education and growth of Emma's mind in great detail. We see how her mind works in her extensive and detailed letters to Augustus Harley, as she struggles with the problem of how a woman ought to deal with a romantic passion for a man she deems worthy of her affection, but who refuses to speak of his own feelings. In most novels of the eighteenth and nineteenth centuries, well-bred young ladies do not confess love to young men before the men declare themselves. They are allowed a "prepossession" in favor of a particular suitor, but the kind of blended passion and esteem that Emma confesses to Augustus is well beyond what is considered permissible. Emma herself is represented as self-consciously choosing to break with romantic conventions in the interest of something more important. Emma's intellectual and emotional development is carefully tracked through childhood and adolescent experiences, and particularly through her own reading. Her early years are formed by social interaction with her cousins and light reading. It is not until she begins to pay extended visits to her father, who guides her reading, choosing her books for her (as most educators agreed a father ought to do) that she begins to read more "serious" literature—from classical works such as tragedies to non-fiction such as histories.

Importantly, Hays herself argued that for women, emotional and intellectual interest lead into each other. Thus, the interest aroused in female readers by light fiction could be productively channeled into progressively reading more serious and intellectual writing. Hays's concern that women should study history in particular was so strong that she published *Female Biography; or, Memoirs of Illustrious and Celebrated Women, of all Ages and Countries* (1803), *Historical Dialogues for Young Persons* (1806-08), *Memoirs of Queens, Illustrious and Celebrated* (1821), and wrote the third volume of *History of England, from the Earliest Records, to the Peace of Amiens; in a Series of Letters to a Young Lady at School* (1806). Both *Female Biography* and *Memoirs of Queens* attempt to engage specifically female readers in the study of history through the palatable mode of biography and women's lives. As Hays explains in the Preface to *Female Biography*:

My pen has been taken up in the cause, and for the benefit, of my own sex. For their improvement, and to their entertainment, my labours have been devoted. Women, unsophisticated by the pedantry of the schools, read not for dry information, to load their memories with uninteresting facts, or to make a display of vain erudition....they require pleasure to be mingled with instruction, lively images, the graces of sentiments, and the polish of language. Their understandings are principally accessible through their affections: they delight in minute delineation of character; nor must the truths which impress them be either cold or unadorned. I have at heart the happiness of my sex, and their advancement in the grand scale of rational and social existence. I perceive, with mingled concern and indignation, the follies and vices by which they suffer themselves to be degraded. If, through prudence or policy, the generous contention between the sexes for intellectual equality must be waived, be not, my amiable country-women, poorly content with the destination of the slaves of an Eastern haram [sic], with whom the season of youth forms the whole of life! A woman who, to the graces and gentleness of her own sex, adds the knowledge and fortitude of the other, exhibits the most perfect combination of human excellence....

To excite a worthy emulation, the following memorial of those women, whose endowments, or whose conduct, have reflected lustre upon the sex, is presented more especially to the rising generation, who have not grown old in folly, whose hearts have not been seared by fashion, and whose minds prejudice has not yet warped.[7]

Hays is concerned that if women do not develop their intellectual powers, they fail to develop their full potential as rational contributors to society. Further, she wants for them the combination of "graces" and "fortitude" that she thinks will see women beyond their youthful beauty and provide resources for them in their old age. That Hays chose to write biographies of powerful and admirable *women* for a primarily female audience, suggests her strong belief that later generations can learn from the experiences, successes, and errors of earlier generations, and that personal stories are more likely to catch the interest of a woman reader and so lead her on to study more generalized history and political philosophy. These principles are also at work in *Emma Courtney*. The tale is told ostensibly to the young Augustus, son of Emma's flawed beloved, to help him through the emotional distress of losing his first love. The reader, like Augustus, is invited to learn from the sufferings and experiences of Emma Courtney, becoming like him, part of the next generation. The novel attempts to draw the reader in emotionally, and to teach us to use our judgment to distinguish between what is admirable and worthy of emulation in Emma, and what is erroneous.

Alderson Opie's *Adeline Mowbray* is a slippery novel, telling the tale of a principled and innately modest woman who is influenced by "the new philosophy" first to live with a man outside of marriage, then to repent and suffer through a disastrous marriage with an incompatible mate. It goes beyond the controversy over women's sexual behavior, however, tracing also the relationships between mothers and daughters, men and women, and white British women and black women. Adeline's tale of principled suffering is *both* a reference to Mary Wollstonecraft's life *and* a more broad-ranging engagement with the complex questions of women's social position, their need for paid work, and the different social pressures under which differently situated women must live.

---

[7] Hays, *Female Biography*, Philadelphia, 1807, Vol. I, p.iii-v.

The story of Mary Wollstonecraft's life and loves has tended to overshadow many novels in the last decade of the eighteenth century and the first of the nineteenth, particularly *Adeline Mowbray*. Mary Wollstonecraft (1759-1797) became a symbol of the intellectual Englishwoman when she published *A Vindication of the Rights of Man* (1790) in response to Edmund Burke's anti-revolutionary tract *Reflections on the Revolution in France* (1790). Although hers was not the most famous response, it was among the very first and garnered a good deal of public attention. She attracted even more attention when in 1792 she published *A Vindication of the Rights of Woman*, arguing against many conventional beliefs about female nature. Living in France during the tempestuous years from 1792-1795, Wollstonecraft returned to England, where she continued to write. She produced a first-hand account of the French Revolution, an account of her travels in Scandinavia, and a final, incomplete novel before her untimely death from complications in childbirth in 1797. She eventually married the philosopher and reformist, William Godwin (1756-1836) in 1797 when they discovered that she was pregnant. After her death, however, Wollstonecraft's personal life became more notorious than her writings, which were more often referred to than actually read by her critics. Her sexual relationship with American Gilbert Imlay while she was living in France, her child by him, her two suicide attempts after he broke off the relationship and moved in with another woman, her relationship with William Godwin, and their marriage only on discovering her pregnancy, were all recounted in detail by Godwin in *Memoirs of the Author of A Vindication of the Rights of Woman* in 1798. In 1797 when they announced their marriage, even some former friends like Elizabeth Inchbald dropped Wollstonecraft socially, because after their marriage the irregularity of her relationship with Imlay could not be ignored. Until then Wollstonecraft had been able to pass under the fiction that she was actually married to Imlay, believing that because she considered their relationship inviolable, it was as much a marriage as any sanctioned by church or state. After her death,

Mary Wollstonecraft came to stand for everything that opponents of the "new philosophy" and revolutionary ideas rejected. By focusing on Wollstonecraft's irregular sexual relations with two men outside of marriage, her impious attempts to commit suicide, and the arguments for rethinking female virtue as more than mere bodily chastity in her writings, critics were able to paint anyone associated with reform as immodest, unfeminine, and immoral. Heroines who are seduced by false philosophers, posing as revolutionaries but often actually French hairdressers, libertines, or worse, became a stock image in loyalist propaganda and novels after 1798.[8]

In *Adeline Mowbray*, then, Adeline's conversion to "new philosophy" and her choice to live with Glenmurray outside of marriage were immediately associated by readers with the public image of Mary Wollstonecraft. However, even contemporary reviewers noted that Adeline's subsequent marriage to Berrendale did not really represent legal and religious marriage in a salutary light. If Adeline's story is one of education and growth, it is not entirely clear into *what* she is educated, despite her later statements in support of marriage. This novel is more than a conventional loyalist, "church and king" screed supporting British nationalism, loyalty to the monarchy, duty to one's parents, and adherence to the Church of England (to which Alderson Opie never belonged in any case). Roxane Eberle has argued that:

> By confounding two familiar narratives—the sentimental bildungsroman and the seduction plot—the novel highlights essential questions about property, freedom of the individual, and female sexuality. Opie draws on elements of the philosophical novel—specifically Rousseau's *La Nouvelle Héloïse*—as well as the conventions of the domestic tale in her characterization of Adeline, but her novel does not idealize either genre. By situating the debate between "radicals" and "conser-

---

[8] See the textbox on "Anti-Jacobinism" and Gillray's illustration of *New Morality*, particularly the figure of Sensibility.

vatives" directly over the heroine's desirable—and commodifiable—female form, Opie exposes the self-interest implicit in both radical and conservative prescriptions about female education and citizenship. Ultimately the novel critiques rather than proselytizes.[9]

Thus, *Adeline Mowbray* is critical of the Wollstonecraftian idea that the "individuality of an affection constitutes its chastity," or that legal and religiously sanctioned marriage is not necessarily more virtuous than an exclusive and sincere commitment outside of those terms. But Alderson Opie's novel is also critical of the notion that marriage is so necessary to a woman's social position that she should accept it, even if the man is himself unchaste and vice-ridden. In *Adeline*, then, the reader is invited to recognize that *both* the radical philosophy of Glenmurray and the conventional notion of domestic virtue seek to dominate and control the female body. In *Adeline Mowbray*, Adeline suffers in ways that Glenmurray, but not she, foresees from their allegiance; Glenmurray is self-interested in accepting Adeline's offer to live with him outside of marriage. His later interest in marrying her is also necessarily self-interested, rather than motivated purely by concern for her and her needs. Despite his love for her, Glenmurray does not put his own social position in jeopardy by attempting to convince friends and relatives that they ought to accept Adeline's company, and on his deathbed he engages in emotional blackmail to pass Adeline on to his cousin as if she were his property to leave. On the other hand, Berrendale is even more guilty of selfishness than Glenmurray, marrying Adeline largely to secure a nurse for his gout and a cook for his household. His treatment of her as a kind of upper servant precisely illustrates Wollstonecraft's criticism of middling women's social position despite the discourse of gallantry that masks their servitude. A weak-willed and selfish husband is not only no better than none, but actually *worse*.

---

[9] "Amelia Opie's Adeline Mowbray: Diverting the Libertine Gaze; or, the Vindication of a Fallen Woman." *Studies in the Novel.* 26:2 (1994): 121-54. See pp. 123-4.

If the novel suggests that Wollstonecraft's experiment was a failure, like Adeline making vice attractive because she was herself so admirable in other ways, it does not mock Wollstonecraft's concern that many marriages may constitute merely legalized prostitution. There is nothing in *Adeline Mowbray* that does not appear to support Wollstonecraft's contention that "highly as I respect marriage, as the foundation of every social virtue, I cannot avoid feeling the most lively compassion for those unfortunate females who are broken off from society, and by one error torn from all those affections and relationships that improve the heart and mind....Asylums and Magdalens[10] are not the proper remedies for these abuses. It is justice, not charity, that is wanting in the world!."[11] In fact, Adeline's suffering, her social isolation, and the self-satisfied judgments passed upon her by women who are less virtuous than she provide an excellent illustration of Wollstonecraft's analysis here. Further, like *Emma Courtney*, *Adeline Mowbray* raises the problem for middling women of financial self-support which might free them from the necessity of making bad marriages.

Both *Emma Courtney* and *Adeline Mowbray* engage in important ways with women's lives, both those of their authors and other famous women's lives. By incorporating not only her own letters, but those of William Frend and William Godwin into her novel, Mary Hays uses *Emma Courtney* to remake and re-present Hays's own disappointments and intellectual education.[12] *Adeline Mowbray*, likewise, enables Amelia Alderson Opie to recast and revisit obliquely the debates of the 1790s and her own participation in the radical ideas stemming from the circles of William Godwin and Mary Wollstonecraft. Each of these writers recasts her own mentors and teachers, using a virtuous but erring heroine to trace the implications and concerns of these earlier versions

---

[10] I.e., Charitable homes for unwed mothers and prostitutes.
[11] *A Vindication of the Rights of Woman*, in *The Works of Mary Wollstonecraft*, Eds. Janet Todd and Marilyn Butler, 7 Vols., Vol. 5, (New York: New York UP, 1989), 140.
[12] See Wallace, "Mary Hays's Female Philosopher."

of themselves. *Emma Courtney* and *Adeline Mowbray* each in a different sense provides an opportunity to remake and revise past history, leaving Mary Hays and Amelia Alderson Opie in control of these fictional versions. The wise mentor figure of Mr. Francis and the beloved Augustus Harley represent revised versions of real-life dominating figures for Hays, while the Wollstonecraftian Adeline, the Godwinian Glenmurray, and even Savanna are fictional recastings for Alderson Opie.[13] Rewriting through fictionalizing serves the purposes of these women writers, granting them authority denied in their lives. Importantly, by fictionalizing biography and history, both novels move beyond the mode of *roman à clef,* or a "novel with a key." Knowing the biographical details of the authors' lives and their acquaintance with the London radicals is helpful, but not sufficient, for interpreting their works. Biographical and historical background must be carefully sifted and examined, recognized as significant but also as suspect in the act of interpretation.

Mary Hays (1759-1843)

Mary Hays grew up in the Southwark area of London where most of her neighbors were "Dissenters," or Protestants who "dissented" from the beliefs of the Church of England—the only state-sanctioned religion.[14] Dissenters included Unitarians, Baptists, Methodists, Lutherans, Quakers, and other non-Church of England protestants. Male dissenters, like Catholics and non-Christians, were barred from holding political office and from voting for parliamentary representation, even if they met the

---

[13] Carol Howard explains, in "The Story of the Pineapple," that Amelia Alderson Opie's mother had had a Bengali servant woman named "Savannah." For Alderson Opie, as for many European British people, the native peoples of both South Asia and of Africa were understood as belonging to the rubric "Black." Since Alderson Opie's mother died while she was yet a girl, the association between this Black servant and her mother seems important in considering Alderson Opie's own adult abolitionism as well. See Carol Howard, " 'The Story of the Pineapple': Sentimental Abolitionism and Moral Motherhood in Amelia Opie's *Adeline Mowbray,*" *Studies in the Novel* 30:3. (Fall 1998): 355-76.

[14] See textbox on "Religion and Politics in 1790s Britain," p. 54.

property requirements to do so. Thus, Dissenters as a group were strongly critical of the British government, and many joined reformist organizations such as the Society for Constitutional Information and the London Corresponding Society. During the late eighteenth century and early nineteenth century many political reformers argued for lowering the amount of landed property necessary for enfranchisement, for better representation of the well-populated and growing urban areas, for reforming "rotten boroughs" where a single land-owner was the sole voter and so could essentially sell seats in Parliament to the highest bidder, and for lessening the restrictions on "non-conforming" or non-Church of England communicants. Dissenters had also founded academies for educating their own clergy and young men, since admission to Oxford and Cambridge Universities was usually barred to those who were not members of the state religion. William Godwin, for example, had been educated at one of these and originally trained to become a dissenting minister. Another, "New College" at Hackney, was located near to where Hays's family lived.

While dissenting women like Mary Hays in London and Amelia Alderson in Norwich were not particularly engaged by debates about male suffrage or admission to Parliament, they *were* steeped in the traditions of public argumentation and debate and a sense of being important yet excluded members of the nation. Hays began her professional writing career at the age of 30 under the pen-name "Eusebia"[15] with *Cursory Remarks*

---

[15] This appears to be a reference to the Roman Empress Eusebia, second wife of Constantius II, and who is associated with the "Arian controversy" or the roots of Unitarianism. Arius, a Presbyter or church Elder in Alexandria in the 4th century A.D., along with Eusebius, the Bishop of Nicomedia, believed that God the father preceded God the son, and that although the two were of like substances they were not the same. Early supporters of the Trinity found this anathema, arguing that both God the father and God the son must be consubstantial and coexistent. Hays sets herself up both as an echo of an early important and educated woman (with a classical background) and identifying herself as a "dissenter" or as the Unitarians would put it, a true monotheist. Because male scholars turned so often to Classical Greek and Roman texts and shared a base education in the Classics to

on an Enquiry into the Expediency and Propriety of Public or Social Worship (1791), responding to Gilbert Wakefield's attack on the appropriateness of public worship. Her response brought her to the attention of William Frend, a dissenting intellectual recently dismissed from Cambridge University for publishing his non-conformist views. After Frend wrote an admiring letter to "Eusebia," Hays and Frend began a regular correspondence. He became the second love of her life[16] until he made it clear that he was not as interested in her as she was in him. Apparently, Hays believed he had been less direct and honest with her about his feelings and reasons for rejecting her than he ought to have been as a "philosopher," and it was on this failed relationship that she based *The Memoirs of Emma Courtney*.

In October 1794, Hays also began a correspondence with William Godwin. After reading his recently published novel, *Things as They Are, or Caleb Williams*, Hays wrote to Godwin to ask if she could borrow his copy of his earlier work of political philosophy, *An Enquiry Concerning Political Justice*, which was too expensive for her to acquire on her own. Godwin loaned her the book, and encouraged her to write to him and use him as a kind of mentor/teacher for her continuing self-education. Their letters reveal a close friendship; Godwin frequently stopped by for tea and philosophical conversation, while Hays wrote him long missives containing her responses to her readings and de-

---

authorize their own writings, Hays's use of a Roman figure here asserts her claims to being a learned lady. Hays significantly included an entry on Eusebia in her *Female Biography*:

> Eusebia, wife of Constance, was the protectrix of Julian, whom she raised to the rank of emperor; and, by the influence which her talents and beauty gave to her, saved him from the political fury of a prince who murdered without scruple those whom he distrusted or feared. Julian, indebted to Eusebia for life and empire, composed her eulogium. (368)

[16] Hays had been engaged to John Eccles, a neighbor also from a dissenting family, in her youth. Initially their families opposed the match; their clandestine correspondence is published in *The Love Letters of Mary Hays*, Ed. A. F. Wedd, (London, Metheun, 1925). The families finally were persuaded to allow the pair to marry and the wedding was imminent, when Eccles tragically became ill and died of a fever.

tailing her emotional state. Like many of the dissenting reformers of this period, Godwin and Hays believed strongly in the power of conversation and debate to develop correct philosophical and political ideas.

Emma Courtney, likewise, is a woman who is mostly self-educated through broad reading and through educating conversation at the dinner table. Men like Godwin and his friend, Thomas Holcroft, could belong to political societies dedicated to debating political and social issues, such as the Society for Constitutional Information to which Holcroft belonged, and where Godwin may have attended some meetings. However, women like Hays and Alderson Opie had to find other venues for such self-education. For Hays, personal friendships, exchanges of letters, reading, and responding to debates in the newly important periodical press were particularly important. Many of her letters and essays show her reading to be broad, including not just English but also continental European sources. While she lamented her inability to read Greek, Latin, and French in her letters to her fiancé John Eccles in the 1770s, her published *Letters and Essays: Moral and Miscellaneous* (1793) shows wide reading among important thinkers in English, French, and German. She was particularly strongly connected to Mary Wollstonecraft, having met her shortly after Wollstonecraft published *A Vindication of the Rights of Woman* in 1792.

Just as she had solicited Godwin's advice, Hays solicited Wollstonecraft's opinion of her writing and entered into extended discussions on the situation of women, their education, and the difficulties of being a female author. While Hays has frequently been represented as a secondary figure, a follower of Wollstonecraft rather than a thinker in her own right, this version of Hays is in part the effect of satirical portraits from *The Anti-Jacobin* and other conservative propaganda. Hays was, in fact, the one who introduced Godwin and Wollstonecraft after Wollstonecraft's return from France, and a letter from Godwin to Hays the day after he and Wollstonecraft were married shows that Hays was influential in determining the two to seek legal married status. Both Hays and Wollstonecraft appear to have offered each other advice and criticism freely. On November 20, 1792, Wollstonecraft wrote to Hays critiquing her preface to *Letters and Essays*:

...I do not approve of your preface—and I will tell you why. If your work should deserve attention it is a blur on the very face of it. —Disadvantages of education etc. ought, in my opinion, never to be pleaded (with the public) in excuse for defects of any importance, because if the writer has not sufficient strength of mind to overcome the common difficulties which lie in his way, nature seems to command him, with a very audible voice, to leave the task of instructing others to those who can. This kind of vain humility has ever disgusted me—and I should say to an author, who humbly sued for forbearance, 'if you have not a tolerably good opinion of your own production, why intrude it on the public? We have plenty of bad books already, that have just gasped for breath and died.'

The last paragraph I particularly object to, it is so full of vanity. Your male friends will still treat you like a woman—and many a man, for instance Dr. Johnson, Lord Littleton, and even Dr. Priestley have insensibly been led to rather warm elogiums in private that they would be sorry openly to avow without some cooling explanatory ifs. An author, especially a woman, should be cautious lest she too hastily swallows the...praises which partial friends and polite acquaintance bestow thoughtfully when the supplicating eye looks for them. In short, it requires great resolution to try rather to be useful than to please....Rest on yourself,—if your essays have merit they will stand alone, if not the *shouldering up* of Dr. this or that will not long keep them from falling to the ground....let me remind you that when weakness claims indulgence it seems to justify the despotism of strength.[17]

Wollstonecraft's tone, although it sounds harsh to modern ears, is typical of the kind of sincere and frank criticism that Hays and her colleagues valued. This is intended as a friendly and supportive letter from Wollstonecraft; she begins by telling Hays that she has put in a good word for her with the publisher Joseph Johnson, and that he will likely commission Hays to write paid book reviews. In the context of such strong and personal criticism of Hays by her close friend, even Alderson Opie's representation of a couple modeled partly on Wollstonecraft and Godwin in *Adeline Mowbray* seems less clearly a hostile attack than some reviewers assumed. Writers associated with the circles of Wollstonecraft and Godwin read and evaluated works by writers of quite different political and religious persuasions, believing strongly in the improving powers of active and informed public debate. Strongly worded, even harsh criticisms were a sign of respect, as distinct from the superficial, parodic, or intentional misrepresentations of some political enemies such as *The Anti-Jacobin Magazine and Review* (see textbox on "Anti-Jacobinism"). It is important to remember the shared dissenting belief in rigorous debate as a path to religious truth and the rejection of polite social lies shared by both Hays and Alderson Opie throughout their lives in considering how far Alderson Opie rejected her youthful mentors in *Adeline*.

Hays wrote likewise to Godwin on all topics that interested her, including her disappointment with William Frend's response to her openly avowed affection. While Godwin had, in *Political Justice*, apparently validated rational control over human passions, Hays argued in her letters to him that passionate feeling was an important spur to action and self-development. For her, it was from the strength of her desires and sorrows that she turned to philosophical writing in the first place. While her letters

[17] Cited with permission, from the Carl H. Pforzheimer Collection of Shelley and His Circle; The New York Public Library; Astor, Lennox, and Tilden Foundations, MW Letter 35, November 25, 1792.

appear sometimes deferential, she argues forcefully with this se-
nior male intellectual about the importance of her womanly feeling, the inadequacies of her education which makes attention to
initial passions important, and for the unfairness of expecting
women to behave exactly as reasonable men do without having
had the same education or breadth of experience. Gina Luria
Walker documents Hays's engagement in the first issues of the
liberal publication, the *Monthly Magazine* of 1796, with debates over "the relative importance of environment over heredity
in determining intelligence."[18] Hays's belief in the formational
impact of nurture and education is explored in *Emma Courtney*,
as if Emma herself were a test case for Hays's idea of the likely
fate of a brilliant, talented, unevenly educated, and powerfully
emotional woman in the England of the 1790s.

Because Emma Courtney, like Mary Hays, suffers from an
unrequited passion for a man who will not openly explain to her
that he is either unavailable or unable to love her, and because it
was an open secret that the novel was based on actual biographical events, readers from 1796 onward have tended to read the
novel as a kind of *roman à clef* about Hays and Frend. However,
there are important differences between the imaginary Emma
and the historical Mary. Emma is born to a higher social class
than Mary Hays herself. While Mary Hays was born into a
dissenting mercantile family in south London, the fictional Emma
Courtney is the daughter of a landed gentleman with a university education and inherited wealth. Emma's cousins the
Melmoths, who initially raise her, are an idealized version of the
rational bourgeois merchant family, further removed from the
libertine life of Emma's father. While Mary's first romance was
with the son of a neighboring dissenting family, John Eccles,
Emma first develops a friendship with Mrs. Harley, and then
falls in love in the abstract with the "portrait"— both the painting and the mother's representation—of Augustus Harley. Mary's

---

[18] Gina Luria Walker, "Introduction," *Memoirs of Emma Courtney*, NY: Garland,
1974, p. 11.

relationship with William Frend did begin through textual self-representations and was intellectualized in a manner somewhat parallel to Emma's, but Mary was in her thirties when she began corresponding with Frend, while Emma is imagined as much younger, in her late teens, when she falls in love with Augustus Harley. Emma's education is more haphazard than Hays's was; Emma is first educated by her adoptive family who allow her to read sentimental novels, and then by her father's more extensive and challenging selections from his library. Hays, by contrast, was both self-educated and exposed to the atmosphere of a dissenting circle, where reading not only the Bible, but works of philosophy and theology and debating them publicly was a matter of course. Hays also made a lifelong effort to seek out educated men as mentors, guides, and debating opponents throughout her life.[19] While Hays began publishing after she reached thirty, she continued to publish until the 1820s, spanning three decades of public writing and continuing as a public figure through the British backlash to the decade of revolution and well into the nineteenth century. She died in 1843, after seeing many of the reforms called for by male political radicals in the 1790s passed in the Reform Bill of 1832, but without achieving the universal recognition of women as rational and co-equal beings for which she and Wollstonecraft had argued.

By creating Emma as a vehicle for exploring the possible experience of a young, beautiful, intelligent, and philosophically progressive woman dealing with a romantic passion, Mary Hays was able to explore her own concerns about the education of women, the need to balance reason and passion, and the seductive power of abstract philosophy. She was even able to raise questions about the function of sexual desire in romantic relationships. While Godwin initially encouraged Hays to write about her experiences in a novel, Hays replied that she needed to base her writing on material which was powerfully emotional,

---

[19]See Gina Luria Walker, *Mary Hays (1759-1843): The Growth of A Woman's Mind*, (Brookfield, VT: Ashgate Press, forthcoming 2004).

and so with his encouragement, she decided to draw directly on her own real letters.[20] One thing she accomplished in so doing, was to remake her less than satisfying experiences with William Frend and William Godwin, both of whom were her seniors and better known publicly, into a situation where Hays-the-writer was in control of both Emma and her lover.[21]

Hays's detailed exploration of Emma's multiple educations reflects her own version of Godwin's philosophy of "necessarianism," holding that one's character is formed by one's experiences and situation. This amounts to an early form of the liberal argument that nurture is more significant than nature in forming the adult, which stems from John Locke's arguments that children are born *tabula rasa* or as "blank slates," rather than possessed of "innate ideas" of the good or of God. In contrast to supporters of aristocratic hereditary rights, most explicitly Edmund Burke, Hays aligned herself with radicals who argued for the importance of experience and education in developing innate abilities, and for merit as opposed to birth-rank as the true measure of a human being. Emma is "naturally" bright and beautiful, but it is nurture that teaches her to be thoughtful, to judge of other's feelings by her own, to respect herself and her own judgment, and to seek for a mate who will love her enough to treat her as a rational being who deserves a truthful, honest answer. Her love for Augustus Harley is both a sign of her ideal conception of manhood and a mistake, since Harley is proved to be an equivocator who cannot tell her either why he will not propose marriage or that he does not love her. The novel raises the question of whether Emma is unable to find an appropriate mate because the only figures who value her correctly are other women, like Mrs. Harley. Even Mr. Francis, usually assumed to be an idealized portrait of William Godwin, underestimates Emma because he cannot properly value her feelings—a debate

---

[20] See Mary Hays to William Godwin, MH 12, 6 February 1796, MS Pforzheimer Collection.

[21] See Wallace, "Mary Hays's Female Philosopher" for further discussion.

shown in Hays's letters to Godwin as well.

Emma ostensibly tells her story in an effort to share her experience and hard-earned knowledge with her impetuous adopted son, Augustus, who is threatening to reproduce his father's and Emma's mistakes. Emma recounts her own growth and development in great detail because Hays believed that it was through experiences—including reading—that human beings developed and were educated into the adults they became. Addressing her tale through the frame narrative to her adoptive son, Emma gestures to the possibility that the next generation may learn from the errors and sufferings of the previous one. Hays, likewise, is suggesting that we are not doomed to repeat the errors of the past, but that, rather, learning from previous mistakes, new generations may move beyond those errors. Godwinians argued that all we call "evil" is in actuality merely "error" stemming from the failure of human rationality, knowledge, and education to prepare us to live just and benevolent lives. Thus, Hays's call to correct the errors of the past generation in the next resonates with a call to learn from and study human history. The reader is invited to extrapolate from individual to general, from Emma's story to the situation of women, from young Augustus to him or herself.

Amelia Alderson Opie (1769-1853)

As a young and unmarried woman, Amelia Alderson was part of Wollstonecraft and Godwin's circle.[22] In 1798 she married the well-known portrait painter, John Opie; most biographers date her growing distance from the radical circles of Godwin and Wollstonecraft from that period. Mary Wollstonecraft had died in childbirth late the preceding year (September 10, 1797), and Alderson Opie's distance from Godwin and Holcroft seems

---

[22] See Janet Todd, *Mary Wollstonecraft: A Revolutionary Life*, (Oxford: Oxford UP, 2000); Cecilia Lucy Brightwell, *Memorials of the Life of Amelia Opie: Selected and arranged from her letters, diaries, and other manuscripts* (London, 1854); Gertrude Townshend Mayer, "Amelia Opie," in *Women of Letters*, Vol. I, (London, 1894, 59-114).

likely to have stemmed from the combined death of her friend and her own newlywed status. Additionally, despite general acceptance and even popularity in the early years of the 1790s, English radicalism and "New Philosophy" had become less socially respectable since England had declared war on France in 1793 (see textbox "English Jacobins and Jacobinism"). Amelia Alderson Opie, recently married and moving in her new husband's social circles and no longer connected by her affection for Wollstonecraft, might well have welcomed a chance to distance herself from her old role and acquaintances. Since Godwin and Holcroft were reputed to have been romantically interested in her, her husband may have encouraged such distancing for practical reasons.[23]

Later critics and biographers have often emphasized Amelia Opie's distance from the young Amelia Alderson, attempting to elide her close connection with unfashionable radical ideas and remake her into an ideal feminine type. Cecilia Lucy Brightwell, Alderson Opie's earliest biographer, emphasized her conversion to Quakerism in 1825 and downplayed her involvement with the circles of Godwin and Wollstonecraft:

> Her own good sense and firm rectitude of principle, happily preserved her from the follies and errors into which not a few around her were led, by their extravagant zeal for a liberty which speedily degenerated into license. She too, was enthusiastic, ardent, perhaps imprudent, at least so she seems to have judged in cooler moments; but there was too much of the pure womanly character in her, to suffer her ever to sympathize with the assertors of "woman's rights," (so called;) and she

---

[23] Mayer cites a letter from Amelia Alderson in which she writes "Mrs. [Elizabeth] Inchbald says the report of the world is that Mr. Holcroft is in love with her, *she* with Mr. Godwin, Mr. Godwin with *me*, and I with Mr. Holcroft"(67). She goes on to blame the story on Mrs. Inchbald's jealousy, attempting to make Godwin believe that Alderson preferred Holcroft. Whatever the facts may have been, the circle of men and women associated with Godwin and Wollstonecraft was bound by emotional attractions as powerfully as by radical ideas.

was not to be spoiled even though exposed to the influence of philosophising serpents, the Paines, the Tookes, and the Wollstonecrofts.[24]

Brightwell's effort to protect Alderson Opie's reputation from association with Wollstonecraft was followed by most nineteenth-century biographies and by reviews of her writing. However, Amelia Alderson's relationship with Wollstonecraft was indeed quite close. When Wollstonecraft's marriage to William Godwin made it impossible to maintain the polite fiction that she was in fact legally "Mrs. Imlay," she wrote to her friend, Amelia Alderson, about her effort to maintain her own principles in the face of public criticism and social ostracism by some former friends:

> I shall be sorry to resign the acquaintance of Mrs. and Mr. F. Twiss, because I respect their characters, and feel grateful for their attention; but my conduct in life must be directed by my own judgment and moral principles....I wished, while fulfilling the duty of a mother, to have some person with similar pursuits, bound to me by affection; and beside, I earnestly desired to resign a name which seemed to disgrace me [i.e., that of Imlay]. I am proud perhaps, conscious of my own purity and integrity; and many circumstances in my life have contributed to excite in my bosom an indignant contempt for the forms of a world I should have bade a long good night to, had I not been a mother. Condemned then to toil my hour out, I wish to live as rationally as I can.[25]

This frank letter makes it clear that Amelia Alderson was well aware of Wollstonecraft's past relationship with Gilbert Imlay,

---

[24] Cecilia Lucy Brightwell, *Memorials of the Life of Amelia Opie: Selected and Arranged From Her Letters, Diaries, and Other Manuscripts*, London, 1854, p. 55. "Tooke" is John Horne Tooke, a radical reformer and leader of the London Corresponding society. "Paine" is Thomas Paine, author of *The Rights of Man* and a friend of William Godwin and Thomas Holcroft.

[25] *Collected Letters of Mary Wollstonecraft*, Ed. Ralph Wardle, (Ithaca: Cornell UP, 1979), 389-90.

and understood Wollstonecraft's marriage to Godwin in the context of wanting support in raising her child and giving the new child a legitimate birth. It further reveals that while Alderson knew that other acquaintances were cutting Wollstonecraft for social propriety's sake, she herself had no thoughts of doing so, but was rather acting as a confidant in discussing this problem with her friend.

There is considerable evidence that from her trip to London in 1794 until after Wollstonecraft's death in 1797 Amelia Alderson was strongly affiliated with the London radicals, as one might expect from her dissenting upbringing in Norwich. Gertrude Mayer reminds us that "Dr. Alderson, like nearly all his contemporary notabilities in 'that city of sedition, Norwich,' was a Liberal, and at that time to be a Liberal meant to be a strong sympathizer with the revolutionary spirit stirring throughout Europe—which had then very real tyrannies to combat and wrongs to redress ..."(65). Amelia Alderson on her arrival in London attended the 1794 Trials for High Treason of thirteen London political radicals, all members of the Society for Constitutional Information, including Thomas Holcroft, Thomas Hardy, John Thelwall, and John Horne Tooke. Later, the widowed Amelia Alderson Opie wrote of those days, remembering:

Not only hearing the first pleaders at the bar, but beholding the first magnates of the land, and knowing in my secret heart that my own prospects for life might probably have been darkened by the result. To such a height had party spirit reached on both sides in my native city and elsewhere that even innocent men were accused of treasonable intentions and practices who *talked* when excited by contradiction the fearful things they would never have thought of acting; and I had reason to believe that if the 'felons' about to be tried should not be acquitted, certain friends of mine would have emigrated to America, and my beloved father would have been induced to accompany them.[26]

Fear of government overreaching in the period was such that Amelia Alderson's letters home to her father were carefully burned by him, and so none of her original accounts of the Treason Trials remain. It seems likely that had the trials ended in convictions, Alderson's father and herself would have emigrated to the new United States, fleeing political persecution. Like most Londoners, when the trials ended in dismissal, she celebrated.[27] Her letters to Wollstonecraft from this period are admiring and laudatory, and she was particularly enthusiastic about Wollstonecraft's *Letters Written During a Short Residence in Sweden, Norway, and Denmark*, a sentimental travel narrative based on Wollstonecraft's letters to her faithless lover, Gilbert Imlay, written as she traveled through Scandinavia with their very young daughter to settle his financial affairs. Even more interesting, Amelia Alderson read and responded extremely positively to *Memoirs of Emma Courtney*: "I am delighted with Miss Hays's novel! I would give a great deal to have written it" she wrote in a letter to Wollstonecraft.[28]

Encouraged by her husband to publish her writing, Alderson Opie's first novel, *The Father and the Daughter* was published in 1801 and went through five editions. Like *Adeline*, *The Father and the Daughter* deals with the familial and social repercussions caused by a daughter's sexual "fall" and includes the birth of a child out of wedlock. Her second novel, *Adeline Mowbray, or the Mother and the Daughter* (1804), did not go through so many editions, but was widely reviewed in periodical literature. Readers

[26] Cited in Gertrude Mayer, "Amelia Opie," in *Women of Letters*, Vol. I, (London, 1894), 59-114, p. 68.

[27] There is a story that, at the end of Horne Tooke's trial, when he was found "not guilty" of High Treason, she climbed down from the gallery and kissed him. Alderson Opie later hotly denied that such a thing had happened, although it fits well with other accounts of the public joy on the occasion (Mayer, 69).

[28] Cited in Janet Todd, *Mary Wollstonecraft: A Revolutionary Life*, (Oxford: Oxford UP, 2000), p. 411. Todd does not indicate the date or source of this citation.

immediately understood Adeline's first relationship with the philosopher Glenmurray outside of marriage as a coded fictionalization of Mary Wollstonecraft's romantic relationships with Gilbert Imlay and William Godwin. The very year after Wollstonecraft died, William Godwin had published her posthumous works, including her unfinished masterpiece, *Maria; or the Wrongs of Woman*. In the spirit of philosophical frankness and believing that her life was an exemplary one, he also published *Memoirs of the Author of a Vindication of the Rights of Woman*, in which he detailed Wollstonecraft's attempt to live "platonically" with Henry Fuseli, her romantic and sexual liaison with Gilbert Imlay by whom she had her first daughter, her despondent attempts at suicide after Imlay deserted her, and the beginning of his own intimate relationship with Wollstonecraft before their marriage. To make matters even worse, Godwin's 1793 *Political Justice* had argued openly against marriage as a legal and religious state, suggesting that enlightened adults ought to base their relationships upon rational pleasure in each others' society. While his vision of such rational relationships included sexual contact, in *Political Justice* Godwin had not considered sexual desire a particularly significant aspect of adult relationships. Godwin argued, perhaps naively, that a man should be expected to:

> assiduously cultivate the intercourse of that woman whose moral and intellectual accomplishments strike me in the most powerful manner. But "it may happen that other men will feel for her the same preference that I do." This will create no difficulty. We may all enjoy her conversation; and her choice being declared, we shall all be wise enough to consider the sexual commerce as unessential to our regard. It is a mark of the extreme depravity of our present habits, that we are inclined to suppose the sexual commerce necessary to the advantages arising from the purest friendship. It is by no means indispensable that the female to whom each man attaches himself in that matter, should appear to each

the most deserving and excellent of her sex.[29]

This claim followed Godwin's argument that his ideal of marriage ought be based solely on the acquiescence and desire of the two people concerned, and that the true foundation of rational enjoyment was destroyed by the presumption of eternal attachment based on youthful delusions and sanctioned by church and government (see Appendix I). Godwin's concern with the irrevocable nature of legal marriage gains force if we remember that divorce in the 1790s and well into the 1800s was difficult, if not impossible for most couples to attain; it required money, cause, and usually an Act of Parliament. (In fact, Amelia Alderson Opie had personal knowledge of this problem; John Opie's first marriage was dissolved by Act of Parliament before they were wed.) Alderson Opie's depiction of Glenmurray responded directly to Godwin's belief that a more ideal form of heterosexual pairing would be initiated by the abolition of legal, religious marriage in favor of a more personal and rational manner. Glenmurray the philosopher misjudges his own abilities as a human being to live by pure rationality rather than "natural feeling," as the duel he fights with Sir Patrick O'Carroll and his growing desire to marry Adeline reveal. Moreover, the social stigma under which Adeline suffers limits her ability to be useful to others, and even to engage in improving social intercourse, a foundational concern for Godwin and other rational dissenters.

Although Wollstonecraft's own *Vindication of the Rights of Woman* had supported marriage as a necessary state for human affection, her relationship with Imlay during the French Revolution, and her definition of marriage as more significantly based on sensibility and respect than on religious doctrine was seen as dangerous. Moreover, some of Wollstonecraft's critics did not actually read her work, but developed their ideas about her philosophy from the revelations of Godwin's *Memoirs* and the at-

---

[29] Godwin, *Enquiry Concerning Political Justice*, Appendix: "Of Co-Operation, Cohabitation and Marriage," Book VIII, Chapter VIII, (London, 1798), Third Edition, 511.

tacks of anti-Jacobin propaganda. *The Anti-Jacobin Review and Magazine* for July 1798-December 1799 reviewed Wollstonecraft's *Maria; or the Wrongs of Woman* and Godwin's *Memoirs* consecutively, thus collapsing the novel's story into Wollstonecraft's life. The *Anti-Jacobin* recounts the story of Maria's appearance in court to dispute her husband's legal accusation of "criminal conversation"[30] against her lover, Darnford. Because of her husband's appalling treatment, Maria has declared that she no longer holds herself obligated to recognize their marriage as still in force. She believes that she is then free to accept another as her "husband," and she declares that her former husband, George Venables, is likewise free. By prosecuting Darnford for "criminal conversation," or illicit sexual access to his wife, Venables hopes to collect "damages" in the form of a monetary payment, a common recourse at the time. Maria's insistence that she can represent herself, and that his quarrel is with her, and not the man who "stole" his sexual property in his wife, undercuts the legal system under which a wife is the property of her husband, and particularly offended the reviewers of the *Anti-Jacobin Review and Magazine*:

> The lady appears in court herself, and pleads her feelings, not as her apology, but as her justification. This was indeed a conduct, according to Godwin's own heart. It avowed a disregard for the institution of marriage, an institution so strongly reprobated in the new system of political justice; it banished concealment, the only evil according to the philosopher, that can detract from the political and moral blessings of a promiscuous intercourse of the sexes, guided by the feelings of the parties. On the trial, the judge ... retains the old form of morals;

---

[30] Because under English law, wives were considered one person with their husband and because sexual access to his wife was among the legal rights marriage gave the man, a husband could prosecute any man who committed adultery with his wife of "criminal conversation" and sue the adulterous man for theft of the husband's property. Under this rubric, the wife's own actions and desire are rendered invisible and non-existent.

and does not admit Maria's plea of her feelings as a vindication of her adultery, however conformable it may be to the new philosophy. *The restrictions upon adultery* constitute, in Maria's opinion, A MOST FLAGRANT WRONG TO WOMEN. Such is the moral tendency of the work, such are the lessons which may be learned from the writings of Mrs. Wollstonecraft; such the advantages which the public may derive from this performance given to the world by Godwin, celebrated by him, and perfectly consonant to the principles of *his* political justice.—But as there have been writers, who have in theory promulgated opinions subversive of morality, yet in their conduct have not been immoral; Godwin has laboured to inform the world, that the theory of Mrs. Wollstonecraft was reduced to practice; that she lived and acted, as she wrote and taught. (July 1798-Dec. 1799, Art. VI, 93)

In the atmosphere created by Godwin's *Memoirs* and the attacks of *The Anti-Jacobin Magazine*, novels were reviewed and judged primarily with an eye to their affiliation or difference from the "new philosophy." Not only *The Anti-Jacobin Magazine*, but other more mainstream publications used "Wollstonecraft" as shorthand for unfeminine, improper, and licentious behavior. In such an atmosphere, subtle distinctions were lost. It is in this context that Alderson Opie married, began to distinguish herself from the Godwin-Wollstonecraft circle, and drafted *Adeline Mowbray.* Some contemporary reviewers read the novel as a condemnation of "new philosophy," and modern day critics have often followed suit. However, remembering the young Amelia Alderson's admiration for her friend Mary Wollstonecraft, her upbringing as a rational dissenter and conversion to Quakerism, and noting the complexity of her representation of marriage in this novel significantly complicates the supposed "anti-Jacobin" tendency of the novel.

Countering the conservative insistence that female sexual chastity is all, *Adeline Mowbray* stresses rather the ideal of partnership in marriage, the importance of social usefulness in women's lives, and depicts Adeline as an idealized chaste woman *despite* her sexual relationship with Glenmurray. Rather than being saved by her marriage to Berrendale, Adeline's sufferings only change character: she is neglected, impoverished, and significantly not restored to her social position or usefulness. One telling detail in the novel is that after her mother's marriage and her own, Adeline's ability to perform the charitable duties of her station is limited; although she frequently deprives herself to aid others, husbands in the book seldom show concern for the sufferings of others. Adeline's principled refusal to tell a lie, even when it might make her life easier, is emphasized consistently throughout the novel and is one of her most admirable traits. At several points in the novel the narrator remarks that "never was Adeline so tempted to lie," pointing carefully to the many temptations to falsehood that beset Adeline. The absolute refusal to lie or even mislead was a shared value among the rational dissenters and Quakers, and remained a central concern for Alderson Opie even after she ceased writing novels as the titles of two late works, *Illustrations of Lying in All Its Branches* (1825) and *White Lies* (1845), show.

Women and Professional Writing

Finally, both *Emma Courtney* and *Adeline Mowbray* represent heroines whose opportunities for financially supporting themselves are severely curtailed, and who are led to make bad marriage choices as a result. Importantly, however, both novels were written by thoroughly professional women writers. Hays never married, and supported herself by her writing and with a small annuity from her family. She lived modestly and self-sufficiently, although her publishing record suggests a need for supplemental income. Her turn to juvenile literature and to historical biography in the early nineteenth century shows that Hays understood that the market for her literary work was changing, and that she sought both to continue her didactic messages and to write profitably.

Both *Emma Courtney* and *Victim of Prejudice* were reprinted once, suggesting moderate sales, even if the first print runs were small ones. Mary Hays, however, was not particularly well off. She continued to live in less fashionable areas of London after her mother's death, and there is a story that she was once embarrassed when William Godwin called and found her dressing by the fire in her parlour, there being no fire in the bedroom to save money. Hays reviewed books for money as well, although it is not clear if this continued beyond the 1790s.

Married in 1798, Alderson Opie lost her husband in 1807 and never remarried. The evidence of biographers suggests that her marriage to the portrait painter John Opie was a happy one, and she was no child, but a woman of twenty-nine at their wedding. Alderson Opie had an income on the principle of £10,000 left her by John Opie's death, which she supplemented by writing until the early 1820s. She produced eleven novels, three books of poetry, and several volumes of moral "Tales" over thirty years of writing. There is also evidence that Alderson Opie was a good businesswoman, wisely managing the risks of the publishing world, even though she often borrowed advances when she could get good terms.[31] Opie's novels were published in runs of 2000 copies, midway between the more cautious 1000 for an uncertain sale and 3000 for the most popular writers, according to Fergus and Thaddeus. This also allowed her publishers to identify some of this first run falsely as a second edition, thus making the works look even more popular and saving the cost of actually reprinting them unless demand was very great. When she became a Quaker in 1825, Alderson Opie ceased writing fiction, which was not an acceptable practice for a member of the Society of Friends, as Quakers call themselves. Many critics have suggested that her Quakerism destroyed her role as professional author, since she wrote mostly religious and abolitionist

---

[31] See Jan Fergus and Janice Farrar Thaddeus, "Women, Publishers, and Money, 1790-1820," in *Studies in Eighteenth-Century Culture*, Vol. 17 (1987), especially pp. 197-201, which discusses Alderson Opie's publishing career and financial status in detail.

literature after this point. However, Jan Fergus and Janice Thaddeus point out that her novel, *Madeline*, was rejected by her publisher in 1821, and that her popularity as a writer had declined to a degree that she lost little by ceasing to write fiction and turning instead to moral tales in Christian publications.[32]

Despite the youth and naïveté of their heroines, both Hays and Opie were established, published authors when *Emma Courtney* and *Adeline Mowbray* were published. Hays was 37 and Alderson Opie 35 at the time each published her work— these are not novels by young ladies like their heroines, but by mature writers, adept at negotiating in the public sphere of publishing and the literary marketplace. Curiously, of the two heroines only Adeline turns to writing as a possible source for supporting herself, although Emma is certainly portrayed as a prolific writer of letters. Contrasting the professional writerly life of each author with the narrow options for paid work of each heroine suggests that it would be wise to exercise a certain skepticism toward collapsing real women of the late eighteenth and early nineteenth centuries with the heroines of novels.

Slavery, Abolition, and English Women

In 1792, Mary Wollstonecraft used the metaphor of slavery to attack the social position of British women in *A Vindication of the Rights of Woman*, echoing Jean-Jacques Rousseau's famous opening to Book One of *The Social Contract*: "Man is born free, and everywhere in chains" (*Le Contrat Social; ou Principes du Droit Politique*, Amsterdam, 1762).[33] This was not a new argument when Wollstonecraft made it, but it took on a particular resonance in the late eighteenth and early nineteenth centuries. The Rational Dissenters to whom Wollstonecraft, Hays, and Amelia Alderson belonged, were generally sympathetic to abolitionist arguments, if not strongly abolitionist themselves. Both *Emma*

---

[32] 197-8.
[33] "L'homme est né libre, et partout il est dans les fers" (see http://un2sq4.unige.ch/athena/ for *Le Contrat Social*, from the original 1762 Amsterdam edition).

Courtney and *Adeline Mowbray* reveal abolitionist sympathies. *Emma* utilizes references to West Indian slavery and its effects on the European planters at the dinner party where the eldest son of Mr. Melmoth, recently returned from Jamaica, debates the policies of slavery and "amelioration" with Augustus Harley. The scene partly indicates the political sympathies of Augustus with the more moderate party of amelioration, that stressed improving the condition of enslaved Africans and gradually preparing them for freedom, rather than with the planters' complaints about their enslaved laborers' "natural" vicious propensities.

It is important to remember that while "amelioration" of the condition of enslaved African laborers in the British West Indies does not look particularly liberal to our eyes, it was feared as the thin edge of the wedge which might abolish not only the *trade* in new slaves (abolition of the slave trade), but eventually the practice of enslaved labor altogether (abolition of slavery). In 1795, because of the new Seditious Meetings Act, the British Abolition movement had ceased all public meetings. Meetings were reinstated only in 1806, and the slave trade, though not slavery itself, was abolished in 1807. However, amelioration was also the express policy of a group of planters, represented most famously by Bryan Edwards, whose *The History, Civil and Commercial, of the British Colonies in the West Indies* (1793) represented the problem of slavery as primarily one of occasional bad masters and infantilized enslaved blacks. Arguments that could be considered "abolitionist" thus cover a wide range: while some thought enslaved blacks were better off under white management than free in their own "degenerate" countries, others claimed that it would be both more efficient and more moral to abolish West Indian slavery and simply colonize Africa directly.

Emma Courtney invokes West Indian slavery, however, primarily as a symbol of a more generalized oppressive attitude, and does not develop the full abolitionist positions implicit in the conversation. Mr. Melmoth's attitude toward West Indian slavery reveals much about his character. From the childhood playmate Emma remembers, he has degenerated, suggesting the inherently deleterious effects of the decadent West Indies on English youth. Unsympathetic portrayals of British West Indian colonists also allowed British writers back home to claim moral superiority to their colonial cousins. Just as some believed that Africans became paler and more civilized by living in Europe,[34] so they assumed that white English people living in hot climates degenerated and became racially tainted. Reformers like Wollstonecraft and freed slaves like Olaudah Equiano had also argued that the system of slavery itself ended by brutalizing even would-be benevolent slave-owners as well as the enslaved, exemplified in the white master who beat his own half-blood offspring and the white ladies who tolerated this. Finally, patronizing or unsympathetic attitudes to Blacks, children, Jews, and animals were often coded in novels of this period as indicative of likely attitudes toward women as well, and this is largely the manner in which *Emma Courtney* uses the motif of decadent white West Indians.

Adeline Mowbray makes more explicit use of the language of what Carol Howard denominates "sentimental abolitionism." Because the novel includes mixed-race characters—Savanna, her husband George, and her son the "tawny boy"—it goes somewhat beyond a metaphorical symmetry between white British women and black African slaves. Several aspects of Alderson Opie's representation of Savanna are interesting and have sparked much critical commentary. First, Savanna's strong emotionality and her willingness to voice anger on Adeline's behalf both contrasts with Adeline's ladylike self-control and also gives the novel a voice to express rage openly. Secondly, Savanna speaks in dialect (as does the "Black Man" in Alderson Opie's narrative poem *How to Make Sugar*). The reader must ask whether this represents an effort to render an often unrepresented voice in litera-

---

[34] See Carol Howard's "The Story of the Pineapple" and Moira Ferguson, *Subject to Others: British Women Writers and Colonial Slavery*, *1670-1834*, (New York: Routledge, 1992), for further discussion of the complex theories of racial identity and colorism in this period.

ture of the period, or whether it tends to demean and undermine the authority with which Opie's black characters speak.
Moira Ferguson reminds us that enslaved Africans in the Caribbean spoke different native languages, and that creole languages
and pidgins were created to enable multi-lingual communities
to communicate.[35] Alderson Opie had some first-hand experience with non-white people in England: as a child she remembered being frightened at meeting a local black man, but was
encouraged by her parents to overcome this fear and make friends.
Alderson Opie's mother had had a Bengali woman servant named
"Savannah," who was understood as black and yet not the same
as African "negroes." Thus, Alderson Opie's representation of
the mixed-race Savanna is complexly tied to both the real situation of black people and the construction of racial difference in
the early nineteenth century, making efforts to locate *Adeline* as
implicitly either racist or anti-racist quite complex.

In Opie's novel Adeline saves Savanna from losing her family, in an eerie echo of the colonial slave market where families
were routinely broken apart. British abolitionist writers, including black abolitionists, frequently argued that among the
most heinous and unchristian practices of the slave trade was
disregarding family ties and selling children from parents and
wives from husbands. In the course of Alderson Opie's novel,
Savanna becomes a central part of Adeline's family, but her own
original family oddly vanishes in the process. The final family of
the novel, Mrs. Mowbray, Adeline's daughter, the Quaker Rachel
Pemberton, and Savanna might represent an idealized vision of
an all female, nurturing community which supersedes the unhappy and bad marriages of both Adeline and her mother. However, it seems significant that this new women-only family is
constructed by dissolving Savanna's original family unit, even in
a book that seems to validate domestic life as strongly as *Adeline
Mowbray*. Some families seem to represent idealized rational
British domesticity better than others.

[35] Ferguson, 102-3.

Conclusion

Reading these two novels together highlights both their continuities and their differences. *Emma Courtney* is recognized as carrying a more radical agenda for female autonomy, while *Adeline Mowbray* is overtly a more conventional celebration of domestic life and maternal love. Yet both novels work to reveal the ways in which middling women's lives are constrained by poor education, a lack of possible modes for financial independence, and the limitations of centering one's life on love and marriage. In both novels there is an absence of rational maternal figures in each heroine's childhood which leaves Emma and Adeline unprepared for the complexities and challenges of the social world they must negotiate. Both novels are either overtly or implicitly critical of social mores and conventional expectations placed on young women. Emma is misunderstood, liable to having her virtuous and highly rarified intellectual interests misinterpreted as low, lustful desires. Even her love for Augustus, which becomes a true passion, is open to misrepresentation as merely sexual. Adeline, likewise, is misread as a kept mistress and a fallen woman because her real position fails to correspond with any available social script. Although Adeline is chastised by Rachel Pemberton for making vice look so like virtue, the novel leaves the reader with the nagging suspicion that Adeline's actions *were* virtuous, but that those around her were incapable of understanding her particularly elevated virtue as the reader does. Both novels permit reading through a more conventional lens, for example by emphasizing Emma's errors of passion or by noting Adeline's penitent deathbed as warnings against imitating these heroines. But both novels are finally unsatisfying as merely cautionary tales. The energy of these two novels is engaged with the large questions of their era about the relation of the family to the state, the need to discover and define virtue for oneself, and the complex negotiation between the self and one's society. Interpreting them solely as warning against excessive feeling and independent thought, or as counseling restrained and conventional modesty leaves to the side all that is engaging, intriguing, and admirable in these two heroines's tales. Likewise, interpreting these merely as *romans à clef* oversimplifies both the lives and the novels of Mary Hays and Amelia Alderson Opie.

SELECT BIBLIOGRAPHY

Mary Hays

Cursory Remarks on an Enquiry into the Expediency and Propriety of Public or Social Worship. Inscribed to Gilbert Wakefield, by "Eusebia," London, 1791.

Letters and Essays, Moral and Miscellaneous. London, 1793.

The Memoirs of Emma Courtney. London, 1796.

An Appeal to the Men of Great Britain in Behalf of Women, Anonymous, London. 1798.

The Victim of Prejudice. London, 1799.

Female Biography; or, Memoirs of Illustrious and Celebrated Women, of all Ages and Countries. London, 1803.

Harry Clinton: A Tale of Youth. London, 1804.

The Brothers; or Consequences: A Story of What Happens Every Day; Addressed to that Most Useful Part of the Community, the Labouring Poor. Bristol, 1815.

Family Annals; or the Sisters. London, 1817.

Amelia Alderson Opie

Dangers of Coquetry. London, 1790.

The Father and the Daughter. London, 1801.

Poems. London,1803.

Adeline Mowbray; or the Mother and the Daughter. London, 1804.

Simple Tales. London, 1806.

The Warrior's Return and Other Poems. London, 1808.

Temper, or Domestic Scenes. London, 1813.

New Tales. London, 1818.

Madeline. London, 1822.

Illustrations of Lying in all its branches. London, 1825.

The Black Man's Lament; Or, How To Make Sugar. London, 1826.

Lays for the Dead. London, 1834.

White Lies. Boston, 1845.

All Is Not Gold That Glitters. London, 1846.

Suggested Reading

Behrendt, Stephen. "Questioning the Romantic Novel." *Studies in the Novel,* 26.2 (1994): 5-25.

Butler, Marilyn. *Jane Austen and the War of Ideas.* Oxford: Clarendon, 1975.

Coleman, Deirdre. "Conspicuous Consumption: White Abolitionism and English Women's Protest Writing in the 1790s." *ELH* 61.2 (1994): 341-62.

Colley, Linda. *Britons: Forging the Nation 1707-1837.* New Haven: Yale University Press, 1992.

Cone, Carl. *The English Jacobins: Reformers in Late 18th Century England.* New York: Scribners, 1968.

Eberle, Roxanne. *Chastity and Transgression in Women's Writing, 1792-1897: Interrupting the Harlot's Progress.* New York: Palgrave, 2002.

—. ""Tales of Truth?": Amelia Opie's Antislavery Poetics." *Romanticism and Women Poets: Opening the Doors of Reception.* Eds. Harriet Kramer Linkin and Stephen C. Behrendt. Lexington: University of Kentucky Press, 1999. 71-98.

Garside, Peter. "The English Novel in the Romantic Era: Consolidation and Dispersal." *The English Novel, 1770-1829 : a bibliographical survey of prose fiction published in the British Isles.* 2 Vols. Vol. 2: 1800-1829. Eds. Peter Garside, James Raven, and Rainer Shöwerling. 15-103.

Gatens, Moira. "'The Oppressed of My Sex': Wollstonecraft on Reason, Feeling and Equality." *Feminist Interpretations and Political Theory.* Eds. Mary Lyndon Shanley and Carole Pateman. University Park, PA: Pennsylvania State University Press, 1991. 112-28.

Goodwin, Albert. *The Friends of Liberty: The English Democratic Movement in the Age of the French Revolution.* Cambridge, MA: Harvard University Press, 1979.

Grenby, M. O. *The Anti-Jacobin Novel: British Conservatism and the French Revolution.* Cambridge Studies in Romanticism.

Eds. Marilyn Butler and James Chandler. New York: Cambridge University Press, 2001.

Johnson, Claudia. *Equivocal Beings: Politics, Gender and Sentimentality in the 1790s; Wollstonecraft, Radcliffe, Burney, Austen.* Chicago: University of Chicago Press, 1995.

—. *Jane Austen: Women, Politics, and the Novel.* Chicago: Chicago University Press, 1989.

Jones, Vivien. "Women Writing Revolution: Narratives of History and Sexuality in Wollstonecraft and Williams." *Beyond Romanticism: New Approaches to Texts and Contexts 1780-1832.* Eds. Stephen Copley and John Whale. New York: Routledge, 1992. 178-99.

Kelly, Gary. *Women, Writing and Revolution: 1790-1827.* Oxford: Clarendon Press, 1993.

Mellor, Anne K. *Mothers of the Nation: Women's Political Writing in England, 1780-1830.* Bloomington: Indiana University Press, 2000.

Poovey, Mary. *The Proper Lady and the Woman Writer: Ideology as Style in the Works of Mary Wollstonecraft, Mary Shelley, and Jane Austen.* Chicago: University of Chicago Press, 1984.

Ty, Eleanor. *Empowering the Feminine: The Narratives of Mary Robinson, Jane West, and Amelia Opie, 1796-1812.* Toronto: University of Toronto Press, 1998.

—. *Unsex'd Revolutionaries: Five Women Novelists of the 1790s.* Toronto: University of Toronto Press, 1993.

Watson, Nicola. *Revolution and the Form of the British Novel, 1790-1825: Intercepted Letters, Interrupted Seductions.* Oxford: Clarendon Press, 1994.

Wedd, A. F., ed. *The Love Letters of Mary Hays (1779-1780),* London: Methuen, 1925.

MEMOIRS

OF

EMMA COURTNEY.

By *MARY HAYS*.

" *The preceptions of persons in retirement are very different from those of people in the great world : their passions, being differently modified, are differently expressed ; their imaginations, constantly impressed by the same objects, are more violently affected. The same small number of images continually return, mix with every idea, and create those strange and false notions, so remarkable in people who spend their lives in solitude.*"

ROUSSEAU.

TWO VOLUMES IN ONE.

VOL. I.

NEW-YORK:

PRINTED FOR HUGH M. GRIFFITH, NO. 88, WATER-STREET, 1802.

Title page of *Memoirs of Emma Courtney*, Philadelphia, 1802. This edition is closer in time to *Adeline Mowbray*, and appeared in a single volume. (By permission of the General Research Division, The New York Public Library, Astor, Lenox and Tilden Foundations.)

Illustration to poem "New Morality" for *The Anti-Jacobin Review and Magazine.* By James Gillray, July 1798. Gillray's image satirically represents a wide range of French revolutionaries and English radical reformers: the donkey (see very small figures near center front) holding *Political Justice* represents William Godwin; the spectacled man next to him represents Thomas Holcroft. The publications pouring from the "Cornucopia of Ignorance" include Wollstonecraft's *Wrongs of Woman* and Godwin's *Enquirer*, and is made up of journals like *The Analytical Review, The Monthly Review,* and *The Critical Review* for which Hays wrote or which reviewed her work favorably. (By permission of the British Library.)

MEMOIRS
OF
EMMA COURTNEY.

BY MARY HAYS.

"The perceptions of persons in retirement are very different from those of people in the great world: their passions, being differently modified, are differently expressed; their imaginations, constantly impressed by the same objects, are more violently affected. The same small number of images continually return, mix with every idea, and create those strange and false notions, so remarkable in people who spend their lives in solitude."

ROUSSEAU.[1]

IN TWO VOLUMES.
VOL. I.
LONDON:

Printed for G. G. and J. Robinson, Paternoster-Row.
1796.

[1] Jean-JacquesRousseau (1712-1778), *Julie ou la Nouvelle Heloise*, 1759, from the Second Preface, which was written before the publication of the novel. Hays quotes extensively throughout *Emma Courtney* from Rousseau in English translation of her period. Because there was no international copyright and the original author had little control over how his or her work was translated, there are frequently significant differences between English translations and original French and German texts. For a searchable electronic French text, see: http://c18.net/pr/ rousseau/julie/1018.html.

PREFACE.

THE most interesting, and the most useful, fictions, are, perhaps, such, as delineating the progress, and tracing the consequences, of one strong, indulged, passion, or prejudice, afford materials, by which the philosopher may calculate the powers of the human mind, and learn the springs which set it in motion —— "Understanding, and talents," says Helvetius, "being nothing more, in men, than the produce of their desires, and particular situations."[2] Of the passion of terror Mrs. Radcliffe[3] has made admirable use in her ingenious romances. — In the novel of *Caleb Williams*,[4] curiosity in the hero, and the love of reputation in the soul-moving character of Falkland, fostered into ruling passions, are drawn with a masterly hand.

For the subject of these Memoirs, a more universal sentiment is chosen — a sentiment hackneyed in this species of composition, consequently more difficult to treat with any degree of originality; — yet, to accomplish this, has been the aim of the author; with what success, the public will, probably, determine.

Every writer who advances principles, whether true or false,

---

[2] Claude Adrien Helvétius (1715-71), Swiss-French Enlightenment philosopher, considered an important influence for British utilitarian philosophy. His *De l'esprit* was translated as *Essays on the Mind* in 1759, and his *De l'homme, de ses facultés intellectuelles et de son éducation* appeared in 1772 as *A Treatise on Man; his Intellectual Faculties and his Education.* Hays quotes primarily from the second in English translation of the *Treatise* throughout *Emma Courtney*.

[3] Ann Radcliffe (1764-1823), author of popular gothic novels such as *Mysteries of Udolpho (1794)*, and *Romance of the Forest* (1791). In 1797 she published *The Italian* partially in response to Matthew Lewis's *The Monk* (1796).

[4] Novel by William Godwin (1756-1836), published in 1794, immediately following his political magnum opus, *An Enquiry Concerning Political Justice.* Hays read *Caleb Williams* first, and then wrote to Godwin introducing herself and asking to borrow his copy of the rather expensive *Political Justice.*

that have a tendency to set the mind in motion, does good. Innumerable mistakes have been made, both moral and philosophical: — while covered with a sacred and mysterious veil, how are they to be detected? From various combinations and multiplied experiments, truth, only, can result. Free thinking, and free speaking, are the virtue and the characteristics of a rational being: — there can be no argument which militates against them in one instance, but what equally militates against them in all; every principle must be doubted, before it will be examined and proved.

It has commonly been the business of fiction to pourtray characters, not as they really exist, but, as, we are told, they ought to be — a sort of *ideal perfection*, in which nature and passion are melted away, and jarring attributes wonderfully combined.

In delineating the character of Emma Courtney, I had not in view these fantastic models: I meant to represent her, as a human being, loving virtue while enslaved by passion, liable to the mistakes and weaknesses of our fragile nature. — Let those readers, who feel inclined to judge with severity the extravagance and eccentricity of her conduct, look into their own hearts; and should they there find no record, traced by an accusing spirit, to soften the asperity of their censures — yet, let them bear in mind, that the errors of my heroine were the offspring of sensibility; and that the result of her hazardous experiment is calculated to operate as a *warning*, rather than as an example. — The philosopher — who is not ignorant, that light and shade are more powerfully contrasted in minds rising above the common level; that, as rank weeds take strong root in a fertile soil, vigorous powers not unfrequently produce fatal mistakes and pernicious exertions; that character is the produce of a lively and constant affection — may, possibly, discover in these Memoirs traces of reflection, and of some attention to the phænomena of the human mind.

Whether the incidents, or the characters, are copied from life, is of little importance — The only question is, if the *circum-*

stances, and situations, are altogether improbable? If not — whether the consequences *might* not have followed from the circumstances? —— This is a grand question, applicable to all the purposes of education, morals, and legislation —— *and on this I rest my moral* — "Do men gather figs of thorns, or grapes of thistles?"[5] asked a moralist and a reformer.

Every *possible* incident, in works of this nature, might, perhaps, be rendered *probable*, were a sufficient regard paid to the more minute, delicate, and connecting links of the chain. Under this impression, I chose, as the least arduous, a simple story — and, even in that, the fear of repetition, of prolixity, added, it may be, to a portion of indolence, made me, in some parts, neglectful of this rule: — yet, in tracing the character of my heroine from her birth, I had it in view. For the conduct of my hero, I consider myself less responsible — it was not *his* memoirs that I professed to write.

I am not sanguine respecting the success of this little publication. It is truly observed, by the writer of a late popular novel[6] —— "That an author, whether good or bad, or between both, is an animal whom every body is privileged to attack; for, though all are not able to write books, all conceive themselves able to judge them. A bad composition carries with it its own punishment — contempt and ridicule: — a good one excites envy, and (frequently) entails upon its author a thousand mortifications."[7]

To the feeling and the thinking few, this production of an active mind, in a season of impression, rather than of leisure, is presented.

---

[5] A biblical citation from memory, as Hays's slight misquoting shows, from Matthew 7:16. Jesus asks, "Do men gather grapes of thorns or figs of thistles?"

[6] "*The Monk.*" [M.H.] Matthew Lewis's popular and shocking gothic novel published in 1796.

[7] *The Monk*, Vol. II.

Memoirs of Emma Courtney

To Augustus Harley.

Rash young man! —— why do you tear from my heart the affecting narrative, which I had hoped no cruel necessity would ever have forced me to review? — Why do you oblige me to recall the bitterness of my past life, and to renew images, the remembrance of which, even at this distant period, harrows up my soul with inconceivable misery? — But your happiness is at stake, and every selfish consideration vanishes. — Dear and sacred deposit of an adored and lost friend! —— for whose sake I have consented to hold down, with struggling, suffocating reluctance, the loathed and bitter portion of existence; — shall I expose your ardent mind to the incessant conflict between truth and error — shall I practise the disingenuousness, by which my peace has been blasted — shall I suffer you to run the wild career of passion — shall I keep back the recital, written upon my own mind in characters of blood, which may preserve the child of my affections from destruction?

Ah! why have you deceived me? — Has a six months' absence obliterated from your remembrance the precept I so earnestly and incessantly laboured to inculcate — the value and importance of unequivocal sincerity? A precept, which I now take shame to myself for not having more implicitly observed! Had I supposed your affection for Joanna more than a boyish partiality; had I not believed that a few months' absence would entirely erase it from your remembrance; had I not been assured that her heart was devoted to another object, a circumstance of which she had herself frankly informed you; I should not now have distrusted your fortitude, when obliged to wound your feelings with the intelligence — that the woman, whom you

48

have so wildly persecuted, was, yesterday, united to another.

To the Same.

I RESUME my pen. Your letter, which Joanna a few days since put into my hands, has cost me —— Ah! my Augustus, my friend, my son —— what has it not cost me, and what impressions has it not renewed? I perceive the vigour of your mind with terror and exultation. But you are mistaken! Were it not for the insuperable barrier that separates you, for ever, from your hopes, perseverance itself, however active, however incessant, may fail in attaining its object. Your ardent reasoning, my interesting and philosophic young friend, though not unconsequential, is a finely proportioned structure, resting on an airy foundation. The science of morals is not incapable of demonstration, but we want a more extensive knowledge of particular facts, on which, in any given circumstance, firmly to establish our data. — Yet, be not discouraged; exercise your understanding, think freely, investigate every opinion, disdain the rust of antiquity, raise systems, invent hypotheses, and, by the absurdities they involve, seize on the clue of truth. Rouse the nobler energies of your mind; be not the slave of your passions, neither dream of eradicating them. Sensation generates interest, interest passion, passion forces attention, attention supplies the powers, and affords the means of attaining its end: in proportion to the degree of interest, will be that of attention and power. Thus are talents produced. Every man is born with sensation, with the aptitude of receiving impressions; the force of those impressions depends on a thousand circumstances, over which he has little power; these circumstances form the mind, and determine the future character. We are all the creatures of education; but in that education, what we call chance, or accident, has so great a share, that the wisest preceptor, after all his cares, has reason to tremble: one strong affection, one ardent incitement, will turn, in an instant, the whole current of our thoughts, and introduce a new train of ideas and associations.

You may perceive that I admit the general truths of your

reasoning; but I would warn you to be careful in their particular application; a long train of patient and laborious experiments must precede our deductions and conclusions. The science of mind is not less demonstrative, and far more important, than the science of Newton; but we must proceed on similar principles. The term *metaphysics* has been, perhaps, justly defined — *the first principles of arts and sciences*.[8] Every discovery of genius, resulting from a fortunate combination of circumstances, may be resolved into simple facts: but in this investigation we must be patient, attentive, indefatigable; we must be content to arrive at truth through many painful mistakes and consequent sufferings. —— Such appears to be the constitution of man!

To shorten and meliorate your way, I have determined to sacrifice every inferior consideration. I have studied your character: I perceive, with joy, that its errors are the ardent excesses of a generous mind. I loved your father with a fatal and unutterable tenderness: time has softened the remembrance of his faults. — Our noblest qualities, without incessant watchfulness, are liable insensibly to shade into vices — but his virtues and *misfortunes*, in which my own were so intimately blended, are indelibly engraven on my heart.

A mystery has hitherto hung over your birth. The victim of my own ardent passions, and the errors of one whose memory will ever be dear to me, I prepare to withdraw the veil — a veil, spread by an importunate, but, I fear, a mistaken tenderness. Learn, then, from the incidents of my life, entangled with those of his to whom you owe your existence, a more striking and affecting lesson than abstract philosophy can ever afford.

Chap. I.

THE events of my life have been few, and have in them nothing very uncommon, but the effects which they have produced on my mind; yet, that mind they have helped to form, and this

[8]"Helvetius." [M.H.] From *Treatise on Man.*

in the eye of philosophy, or affection, may render them not wholly uninteresting. While I trace them, they convince me of the irresistible power of circumstances, modifying and controuling our characters, and introducing, mechanically, those associations and habits which make us what we are; for without outward impressions we should be nothing.

I know not how far to go back, nor where to begin; for in many cases, it may be in all, a foundation is laid for the operations of our minds, years — nay, ages — previous to our birth. I wish to be brief, yet to omit no one connecting link in the chain of causes, however minute, that I conceive had any important consequences in the formation of my mind, or that may, probably, be useful to your's.

My father was a man of some talents, and of a superior rank in life, but dissipated, extravagant, and profligate. My mother, the daughter of a rich trader, and the sole heiress of his fortunes, allured by the specious address and fashionable manners of my father, sacrificed to empty shew the prospect of rational and dignified happiness. My father courted her hand to make himself master of her ample possessions: dazzled by vanity, and misled by self-love, she married him; — found, when too late, her error; bitterly repented, and died in child bed the twelfth month of her marriage, after having given birth to a daughter, and commended it, with her dying breath, to the care of a sister (the daughter of her mother by a former marriage), an amiable, sensible, and worthy woman, who had, a few days before, lost a lovely and promising infant at the breast, and received the little Emma, as a gift from heaven, to supply its place.

My father, plunged in expence and debauchery, was little moved by these domestic distresses. He held the infant a moment in his arms, kissed it, and willingly consigned it to the guardianship of its maternal aunt.

It will here be necessary to give a sketch of the character, situation, and family, of this excellent woman; each of which had an important share in forming the mind of her charge to those dispositions, and feelings, which irresistibly led to the subsequent events.

CHAP. II.

MR. and Mrs. Melmoth, my uncle and aunt, married young, purely from motives of affection. Mr. Melmoth had an active, ardent, mind, great benevolence of heart, a sweet and chearful temper, and a liberal manner of thinking, though with few advantages of education: he possessed, also, a sanguine disposition, a warm heart, a generous spirit, and an integrity which was never called in question. Mrs. Melmoth's frame was delicate and fragile; she had great sensibility, quickness of perception, some anxiety of temper, and a refined and romantic manner of thinking, acquired from the perusal of the old romances, a large quantity of which, belonging to a relation, had, in the early periods of her youth, been accidentally deposited in a spare room in her father's house. These qualities were mingled with a devotional spirit, a little bordering on fanaticism. My uncle did not exactly resemble an Orlando, or an Oroondates, [9] but he was fond of reading; and having the command of a ship in the West India trade, had, during his voyages in fine weather, time to indulge in this propensity; by which means he was a tolerable proficient in the belles lettres, and could, on occasion, quote Shakespeare, scribble poetry, and even philosophize with Pope and Bolingbroke. [10]

Mr. Melmoth was one-and-twenty, his bride nineteen, when they were united. They possessed little property; but the one was enterprizing and industrious, the other careful and œconomical; and both, with hearts glowing with affection for

---

[9] Romantic literary heroes from courtly continental Romances. Orlando is an alternate version of the name Roland, subject of *Chanson de Roland* (11th century), and also the hero of Ludovico Ariosto's *Orlando Furioso* (1516). Oroondates is the hero of Gaultier de Coste, Seigneur de la Calprenède's *Cassandre* (translated into English in 1676).

[10] Alexander Pope (1688-1744), an important eighteenth-century poet, satirist, and intellectual, and Henry St. John, first Viscount Bolingbroke, who was associated with Pope and Jonathan Swift, and wrote political works in the first half of the eighteenth century.

each other, saw cheering hope and fairy prospects dancing before their eyes. Every thing succeeded before their most sanguine expectations. My uncle's cheerful and social temper, with the fairness and liberality of his dealings, conciliated the favour of the merchants. His understanding was superior, and his manners more courteous, than the generality of persons in his line of life: his company was eagerly courted, and no vessel stood a chance of being freighted till his had its full cargo.

His voyages were not long, and frequent absences and meetings kept alive between him and my aunt, the hopes, the fears, the anxieties, and the transports of love. Their family soon increased, but this was a new source of joy to Mr. Melmoth's affectionate heart. A walk or a ride in the country, with his wife and little ones, he accounted his highest relaxation: — on these occasions he gave himself up to a sweet and lively pleasure; would clasp them alternately to his breast, and, with eyes overflowing with tears of delight, repeat Thomson's charming description of the joys of virtuous love —

"Where nothing strikes the eye but sights of bliss,
All various nature pressing on the heart!"[11]

This was the first picture that struck my young imagination, for I was, in all respects, considered as the adopted child of the family.

This prosperity received little other interruption than from my uncle's frequent absences, and the pains and cares of my aunt in bringing into the world, and nursing, a family of children. Mr. Melmoth's successful voyages, at rather earlier than forty years of age, enabled him to leave the sea, and to carry on an extensive mercantile employment in the metropolis. — At this period his health began to be injured by the progress of a threatening internal disorder; but it had little effect either on his spirits or activity. His business every day became wider, and his attention to it was unremitted, methodical, and indefati-

---

[11] James Thomson, "Spring" from *The Seasons*, a long, sentimental, and highly regarded poem written from 1726-1730.

gable. His hours of relaxation were devoted to his family and social enjoyment; at these times he never suffered the cares of the counting house to intrude; — he was the life of every company, and the soul of every pleasure.

He at length assumed a more expensive style of living; took a house in the country (for the charms of which he had ever a peculiar taste) as a summer residence; set up an equipage, increased the number of his servants, and kept an open and hospitable, though not a luxurious, table.

The hours fled on downy pinions; his wife rested on him, his children caught sunshine from his smiles; his domestics adored him, and his acquaintance vied with each other in paying him respect. His life, he frequently repeated, had been a series of unbroken success. His religion, for he laid no stress on forms, was a sentiment of grateful and fervent love. — "*God is love*," he would say, "and the affectionate, benevolent heart is his temple."

RELIGION AND POLITICS IN 1790s BRITAIN

Late eighteenth-century Britain, like most nations at the time, ascribed to a state religion, the Anglican Church or the Church of England. While Great Britain offered a certain amount of religious tolerance, those who were not "conforming" members of the dominant religious group were routinely excluded from some of the privileges of citizenship. The Test and Corporation Acts of the late 1600s required those who wanted to hold public office to show "conformity" to the Church of England by taking the sacrament and subscribing to the core doctrinal principles as set out in the Thirty-Nine Articles of 1563. Those who would not and could not subscribe to the Thirty-Nine Articles of the established church included not only non-Christians, such as Jews, and non-Protestant Christians (Roman Catholics), but also Protestant Christians such as Quakers, Wesleyans (or Methodists), Baptists, Presbyterians, and Unitarians. These "dissenting" Protestants were commonly called "Non-Conformists" or "Dissenters."

Some of the major doctrinal differences between the established Church of England and the Dissenters included the appropriate balance between revelation (scripture) and reason in discovering God's will, the role of good works versus that of faith alone in attaining salvation, belief either in the innate sinfulness of humankind or the innate benevolence and goodness of humankind, the status of the sacraments (and their number), and the authority of the Church fathers' writings. Many, though not all, Dissenters in the later eighteenth century were more likely to value good works and a reasoned belief in God over faith in scriptural revelation; others accepted the Calvinist doctrine of predestination for the elect. Albert Goodwin tells us that:

> The chief characteristic of English Dissent in the eighteenth century was the diversity of its sects and their divergent responses to the challenging doctrinal issues raised by biblical scholarship, scientific progress and philosophical speculation. Of the three denominations of old Dissent, it was the Presbyterians who were the most flexible in allowing their theological doctrines to be reformulated in accordance with the findings of Socinian exegesis, Newtonian physics, and Locke's 'sensational' psychology. Whereas the Independents (or Congregationalists) and the Baptists still continued to profess, in different degrees, the traditional Calvinist doctrines of election and predestination, the Presbyterians (partly as a result of their contact with Dutch theologians) abandoned both these dogmas and the doctrine of the Trinity as irrational. Early in the eighteenth century they were converted to the Arian interpretation of the scriptures, according to which Christ himself was not regarded as divine, although divinely instructed....In the second half of the century Arianism itself was abandoned by the majority of Presbyterians in favour of the more explicit theology of Socinianism or Unitarianism.

Rejecting the Calvinist belief that humanity was by nature totally depraved, and claiming for all unrestricted freedom of speculation, the group of 'Rational Dissenters'—a Nonconformist intellectual elite—substituted for the doctrine of the Trinity the Socinian concept of the homogeneity of God. (Goodwin, 69-70)

Thus, Dissenters were likely to harbor reservations about the Trinity, a major dogma of the Church of England, but one which was held to be revealed through scripture rather than the operation of reason or innate knowledge.

The Thirty-Nine Articles were explicitly aimed to differentiate the English Church from the Catholic Church, but some of the articles also make important differentiations from other forms of Protestant Christianity. The articles explicitly support the doctrine of the trinity and the divinity of Jesus and his resurrection, they lay out exactly which books of the Bible are accepted as Scripture, qualify belief in original sin, free will, the "justification" of man (or belief in an afterlife for those who meet the obligations of faith and are forgiven by God), and that faith alone and not good works is sufficient for salvation. They clarify the idea of Predestination, reject "Romish" doctrines such as Purgatory, demand that church prayer be conducted in the common language, specify two necessary sacraments (Baptism and the Lord's Supper) and their purposes, accept a married priesthood, express some tolerance for changing traditions and practices in those Church ceremonies which are human conventions, offer some clarification of the role of princes and civil laws (for instance, that it is acceptable for practitioners to wear weapons and go to war), support private ownership of property and recommend charity, and accept the taking of oaths as a legitimate practice. The articles which proclaim only two official sacraments, reject belief in Purgatory, call for prayer in English, disallow any authority to the "Bishop of Rome" (or the Pope), provide for a married priesthood, and reject the notion of transubstantiation are explicitly aimed against Catholicism. The articles which allow the swearing of oaths, bearing arms in secular wars, and emphasize the authority of the church fathers and the episcopal hierarchy (priests, bishops, archbishops, and so forth) are aimed more directly at Dissenters like the Quakers, who believed in the "inner light" or internal voice of God available to each human, rather than to a tradition of sacred text and its interpreters. The articles on Predestination and the Fall are replies to Calvinism. The article of belief in the Trinity — God the father, God the son, and God the Holy Spirit — was a particular point of dissention between the established Church and various Dissenters.

Both Mary Hays and Amelia Opie came from "Rational Dissenting" backgrounds. Their families and their neighborhoods were predominantly composed of those who "dissented" from the Thirty-Nine Articles and saw themselves as seeking truth through reason. They tended to reject the doctrine of the "fall," and believed instead that humankind was innately good, only sinning through "error." Rational Dissenters were associated with a strong belief in human reason as a vehicle through which one could reach godliness, and stressed a benevolent deity and the progress of virtue through the right use of reason. Coming most often from trading and mercantile families, they also valued labor and social usefulness and were critical of what they regarded as frivolous or socially reprehensible fashions. Rational Dissenters joined many other groups in condemning dueling, gambling, wet-nursing, and "dissipation" in general. They had a strong value for education, and argued that adult character was formed through one's experience and education as a child. Thus, education stressing modesty, self-control, independent thought, and practical skills appropriate to one's station was a shared value.

SOURCES

Albert Goodwin, *The Friends of Liberty: The English Democratic Movement in the Age of the French Revolution* (Cam-

bridge, MA: Harvard University Press, 1979).
William Speck, *Stability and Strife: England 1714-1760* (Cambridge, MA: Harvard University Press, 1977).
Emma Vincent Macleod, *A War of Ideas: British Attitudes to the Wars Against Revolutionary France, 1792-1802*. Brookfield, VT: Ashgate, 1998.
<http://www.historyguide.org/intellect/dissenter.html> (5/ 31/03)
<http://dspace.dial.pipex.com/town/terrace/adw03/peel/religion/39articles.htm> (5/31/03)

Chap. III.

It will now be necessary, for the developement of my own particular character, again to revert to earlier periods. —— A few days before my birth, my aunt had lost (as already related) a lovely female infant, about four months old, and she received me, from the hands of my dying mother, as a substitute. — From these tender and affecting circumstances I was nursed and attended with peculiar care. My uncle's ship (it being war time) was then waiting for a convoy at Portsmouth, where he was joined by his wife: she carried me with her, and, tenderly watchful over my safety, took me on all their little excursions, whether by sea or land: I hung at her breast, or rested in her arms, and her husband, or attendant, alternately relieved her. —— Plump, smiling, placid, happy, I never disturbed her rest, and the little Emma was the darling of her kind guardians, and the plaything of the company.

At the age at which it was thought necessary to wean me, I was sent from my tender nurse for that purpose, and consigned to the care of a stranger, with whom I quickly pined myself into a jaundice and bilious fever. My aunt dared not visit me during this short separation, she was unable to bear my piercing cries of anguish at her departure. If a momentary sensation, at that infantine period, deserve the appellation, I might call this my first affectionate sorrow. I have frequently thought that the tenderness of this worthy woman generated in my infant disposition that susceptibility, that lively propensity to attachment, to which I have through life been a martyr. On my return to my friends, I quickly regained my health and spirits; was active, blythsome, ran, bounded, sported, romped; always light, gay, alert, and full of glee. At church, (whither on Sunday I was accustomed to accompany the family) I offended all the pious ladies in our vicinity by my gamesome tricks, and avoided the reprimands of my indulgent guardians by the drollery and good humour which accompanied them.

When myself and my little cousins had wearied ourselves with play, their mother, to keep us quiet in an evening, while her husband wrote letters in an adjoining apartment, was accustomed to relate (for our entertainment) stories from the Arabian Nights, Turkish Tales, and other works of like marvellous import.[12] She recited them circumstantially, and these I listened to with ever new delight: the more they excited vivid emotions, the more wonderful they were, the greater was my transport: they became my favourite amusement, and produced, in my young mind, a strong desire of learning to read the books which contained such enchanting stores of entertainment.

Thus stimulated, I learned to read quickly, and with facility. My uncle took pleasure in assisting me; and, with parental partiality, thought he discovered, in the ardour and promptitude with which I received his instructions, the dawn of future talents. At six years old I read aloud before company, with great applause, my uncle's favourite authors, Pope's Homer,[13] and Thomson's *Seasons*, little comprehending either. Emulation was roused, and vanity fostered: I learned to recite verses, to modulate my tones of voice, and began to think myself a wonderful scholar.

Thus, in peace and gaiety, glided the days of my childhood.

---

[12] The *Arabian Nights* or the *1001 Nights* was first translated into French in 1704, and various English Grub street versions circulated under various names such as "Turkish Tales" throughout the eighteenth century.

[13] Alexander Pope's translation of Homer's *Iliad* and *Odyssey*.

Caressed by my aunt, flattered by her husband, I grew vain and self-willed; my desires were impetuous, and brooked no delay; my affections were warm, and my temper irascible; but it was the glow of a moment, instantly subsiding on conviction, and, when conscious of having committed injustice, I was ever eager to repair it, by a profusion of caresses and acknowledgements. Opposition would always make me vehement, and coercion irritated me to violence; but a kind look, a gentle word, a cool expostulation — softened, melted, arrested, me, in the full career of passion. Never, but once, do I recollect having received a blow; but the boiling rage, the cruel tempest, the deadly vengeance it excited, in my mind, I now remember with shuddering.

Every day I became more attached to my books; yet, not less fond of active play; stories were still my passion, and I sighed for a romance that would never end. In my sports with my companions, I acted over what I had read: I was alternately the valiant knight — the gentle damsel — the adventurous mariner — the daring robber — the courteous lover — and the airy coquet. Ever inventive, my young friends took their tone from me. I hated the needle: — my aunt was indulgent, and not an hour passed unamused: — my resources were various, fantastic, and endless. Thus, for the first twelve years of my life, fleeted my days in joy and innocence. I ran like the hind, frisked like the kid, sang like the lark, was full of vivacity, health, and animation; and, excepting some momentary bursts of passion and impatience, awoke every day to new enjoyment, and retired to rest fatigued with pleasure.

Chap. IV.

At this period, by the command of my father, I was sent to boarding school. — Ah! never shall I forget the contrast I experienced. I was an alien and a stranger; — no one loved, caressed, nor cared for me; — my actions were all constrained; — I was obliged to sit poring over needle work, and forbidden to prate; — my body was tortured into forms, my mind coerced, and tasks imposed upon me, grammar and French, mere words, that conveyed to me no ideas. I loved my guardians with passion — my tastes were all passions — they tore themselves from my embraces with difficulty. I sat down, after their departure, and wept — bitter tears — sobbed convulsively — my griefs were unheeded, and my sensibility ridiculed — I neither gave nor received pleasure. After the rude stare of curiosity, ever wounding to my feelings, was gratified, I was left to sob alone.

At length, one young lady, with a fair face and a gentle demeanour, came and seated herself beside me. She spoke, in a soft voice, words of sympathy —— my desolate heart fluttered at the sound. I looked at her —— her features were mild and sweet; I dried my tears, and determined that she should be my friend. — My spirits became calmer, and for a short time I indulged in this relief; but, on enquiry, I found my fair companion had already a selected favourite, and that their amity was the admiration of the school. — Proud, jealous, romantic — I could not submit to be the second in her esteem — I shunned her, and returned her caresses with coldness.

The only mitigation I now felt to the anguish that seized my spirits, was in the hours of business. I was soon distinguished for attention and capacity; but my governess being with-held, by an infirm constitution, from the duties of her office, I was consigned, with my companions, to ignorant, splenetic, teachers, who encouraged not my emulation, and who sported with the acuteness of my sensations. In the intervals from school hours I sought and procured books. — These were often wantonly taken from me, as a punishment for the most trivial offence; and, when my indignant spirit broke out into murmurs and remonstrance, I was constrained to learn, by way of penance, chapters in the Proverbs of Solomon, or verses from the French testament.[14] To revenge myself, I satirized my tyrants in doggrel rhymes: my writing master also came in for a share of this little malice; and my productions, wretched enough, were handed

---

[14] Emma is forced to memorize Bible passages in English and French as punishment for less pious reading.

round the school with infinite applause. Sunk in sullen melancholy, in the hours of play I crept into corners, and disdained to be amused: — home appeared to me to be the Eden from which I was driven, and there my heart and thoughts incessantly recurred.

My uncle from time to time addressed to me — with little presents — kind, pleasant, affectionate notes — and these I treasured up as sacred relics. A visit of my guardians was a yet more tumultuous pleasure; but it always left me in increased anguish. Some robberies had been committed on the road to town. — After parting with my friends, I have laid awake the whole night, conjuring up in my imagination all the tragic accidents I had ever heard or read of, and persuading myself some of them must have happened to these darling objects of my affections.

Thus passed the first twelvemonth of my exile from all I loved; during which time it was reported, by my school-fellows, that I had never been seen to smile. After the vacations, I was carried back to my prison with agonizing reluctance, to which in the second year I became, however, from habit, better reconciled. I learned music, was praised and encouraged by my master, and grew fond of it; I contracted friendships, and regained my vivacity; from a forlorn, unsocial, being, I became, once more, lively, active, enterprising, — the soul of all amusement, and the leader of every innocently mischievous frolic. At the close of another year I left school. I kept up a correspondence for some time with a few of my young friends, and my effusions were improved and polished by my paternal uncle.

Chap. V.

This period, which I had anticipated with rapture, was soon clouded by the gradual decay, and premature death, of my revered and excellent guardian. He sustained a painful and tedious sickness with unshaken fortitude; — with more, with chearfulness. I knelt by his bedside on the day of his decease; and, while I bathed his hand with my tears, caught hope from the sweet, the placid, serenity of his countenance, and could not believe the terrors of dissolution near.

"The last sentiment of my heart," said he, "is gratitude to the Being who has given me so large a portion of good; and I resign my family into his hands with confidence."

He awoke from a short slumber a few minutes before his death. —— "Emma," said he, in a faint voice, (as I grasped his cold hand between both mine) turning upon me a mild, yet dying, eye, "I have had a pleasant sleep —— Be a good girl, and comfort your aunt!" —

He expired without a groan, or a struggle —— "His death was the serene evening of a beautiful day!"[15] I gazed on his lifeless remains, the day before their interment, and the features still wore the same placid, smiling benignity. I was then about fourteen years of age, — this first emotion of real sorrow rent my heart asunder!

The sensations of Mrs. Melmoth were those of agonizing, suffocating anguish: —— the fair prospect of domestic felicity was veiled for ever! This was the second strong impression which struck my opening mind. Many losses occurred, in consequence of foreign connections, in the settlement of Mr. Melmoth's affairs. — The family found their fortunes scanty, and their expectations limited: — their numerous fair-professing acquaintance gradually deserted them, and they sunk into œconomical retirement; but they continued to be respectable, because they knew how to contract their wants, and to preserve their independence.

My aunt, oppressed with sorrow, could be roused only by settling the necessary plans for the future provision of her family. Occupied with these concerns, or absorbed in grief, we were left for some time to run wild. Months revolved ere the tender sorrows of Mrs. Melmoth admitted of any mitigation: they at length yielded only to tender melancholy. My wonted amusements were no more; a deep gloom was spread over our once cheerful residence; my avidity for books daily increased: I sub-

---

[15] Helvétius says this of the death of Baucis, Vol. ii.

scribed to a circulating library,[16] and frequently read, or rather devoured — little careful in the reflection — from ten to fourteen novels in a week.

Chap. VI.

My father satisfied himself, after the death of my beloved uncle, with making a short and formal visit of condolence to the family, and proposing either my return to school, or to pay an annual stipend (which Mr. and Mrs. Melmoth had hitherto invariably refused) for defraying the expences of my continuance and board with the amiable family by which I had been so kindly nurtured. I shrunk from the cold and careless air of a man whom I had never been able to teach my heart either to love or honour; and, throwing my arms round the neck of my maternal aunt, murmured a supplication, mingled with convulsive sobs, that she would not desert me. She returned my caresses affectionately, and entreated my father to permit me to remain with her; adding, that it was her determination to endeavour to rouse and strengthen her mind, for the performance of those pressing duties — the education of her beloved children, among whom she had ever accounted her Emma — which now devolved wholly upon her.

My father made no objection to this request; but observed, that notwithstanding he had a very favourable opinion of her heart and understanding, and considered himself indebted to her, and to her deceased husband, for their goodness to Emma, he was nevertheless apprehensive that the girl had been weakened and spoiled by their indulgence; — that his own health was at present considerably injured; — that it was probable he might not survive many years; — in which case, he frankly confessed, he had enjoyed life too freely to be able to make much

---

[16] Circulating libraries bought new books and made them available to their paying members; free public libraries were unknown. They were particularly known for offering light reading and novels, and frequently attacked as a source of dangerous reading for young women. See textbox "Sensibility and Novel Reading," p. 71.

provision for his daughter. It would therefore, he conceived, be more judicious to prepare and strengthen my mind to encounter, with fortitude, some hardships and rude shocks, to which I might be exposed, than to foster a sensibility, which he already perceived, with regret, was but too acute. For which purpose, he desired I might spend one day in every week at his house in Berkley-square, when he should put such books into my hands (he had been informed I had a tolerable capacity) as he judged would be useful to me; and, in the intervals of his various occupations and amusements, assist me himself with occasional remarks and reflections. Any little accomplishments which Mrs. Melmoth might judge necessary for, and suitable to, a young woman with a small fortune, and which required the assistance of a master, he would be obliged to her if she would procure for me, and call upon him to defray the additional expence.

He then, looking on his watch, and declaring he had already missed an appointment, took his leave, after naming Monday as the day on which he should constantly expect my attendance in Berkley-square.

Till he left the room I had not courage to raise my eyes from the ground — my feelings were harrowed up — the tone of his voice was discordant to my ears. The only idea that alleviated the horror of my weekly punishment (for so I considered the visits to Berkley-square) was the hope of reading new books, and of being suffered to range uncontrouled through an extensive and valuable library, for such I had been assured was Mr. Courtney's. I still retained my passion for adventurous tales, which, even while at school, I was enabled to gratify by means of one of the day-boarders, who procured for me romances from a neighbouring library, which at every interval of leisure I perused with inconceivable avidity.

CHAP. VII.

THE following Monday I prepared to attend Mr. Courtney. On arriving at his house, and announcing my name, a servant conducted me into his master's dressing-room. I appeared before him with trembling steps, downcast eyes, and an averted face.

"Look up, child!" said my father, in an imperious tone. "If you are conscious of no crime, why all this ridiculous confusion?"

I struggled with my feelings: the tone and manner in which I was addressed gave me an indignant sensation: — a deeper suffusion than that of modesty, the glow of wounded pride, burnt in my cheeks: — I turned quick, gazed in the face of Mr. Courtney with a steady eye, and spoke a few words, in a firm voice, importing — that I attended by his desire, and waited his direction.

He regarded me with somewhat less *hauteur*; and, while he finished dressing, interrogated me respecting the books I had read, and the impression they had left on my mind. I replied with simplicity, and without evasion. He soon discovered that my imagination had been left to wander unrestrained in the fairy fields of fiction; but that, of historical facts, and the science of the world, I was entirely ignorant.

"It is as I apprehended," said he: — "your fancy requires a *rein* rather than a *spur*. Your studies, for the future, must be of a soberer nature, or I shall have you mistake my valet for a prince in disguise, my house for a haunted castle, and my rational care for your future welfare for barbarous tyranny."

I felt a poignant and suffocating sensation, too complicated to bear analyzing, and followed Mr. Courtney in silence to the library. My heart bounded when, on entering a spacious room, I perceived on either side a large and elegant assortment of books, regularly arranged in glass cases, and I longed to be left alone, to expatiate freely in these treasures of entertainment. But I soon discovered, to my inexpressible mortification, that the cases were locked, and that in this intellectual feast I was not to be my own purveyor. My father, after putting into my hands the lives of Plutarch, left me to my meditations; informing me, that he should probably dine at home with a few friends, at five o'clock, when he should expect my attendance at the table.

I opened my book languidly, after having examined through

the glass doors the titles of those which were with-held from me. I felt a kind of disgust to what I considered as a task imposed, and read a few pages carelessly, gazing at intervals through the windows into the square. — But my attention, as I proceeded, was soon forcibly arrested, my curiosity excited, and my enthusiasm awakened. The hours passed rapidly — I perceived not their flight — and at five o'clock, when summoned to dinner, I went down into the dining-room, my mind pervaded with republican ardour, my sentiments elevated by a high-toned philosophy, and my bosom glowing with the virtues of patriotism.

I found with Mr. Courtney company of both sexes, to whom he presented me on my entrance. Their easy compliments disconcerted me, and I shrunk, abashed, from the bold and curious eyes of the gentlemen. During the repast I ate little, but listened in silence to every thing that passed.

The theatres were the first topic of conversation, *Venice Preserved*[17] had been acted the preceding evening, and from discussing the play, the conversation took a political turn. A gentleman that happened to be seated next me, who spoke fluently, looking around him every moment for approbation, with apparent self-applause, gave the discourse a tone of gallantry, declaring — "Pierre to be a noble fellow, and that the loss of a mistress was a sufficient excuse for treason and conspiracy, even though the country had been deluged in blood and involved in conflagration."

"And the mistresses of all his fellow citizens destroyed of course;" — said a gentleman coolly, on the opposite side of the table.

Oh! that was not a consideration, every thing must give place when put in competition with certain feelings. "What, young lady, (suddenly turning to me) do you think a lover would not risque, who was in fear of losing you?"

Good God! what a question to an admirer of the grecian heroes! I started, and absolutely shuddered. I would have re-

---

[17] Thomas Otway's tragedy *Venice Preserved, or a Plot Discovered*, 1682.

plied, but my words died away upon my lips in inarticulate murmurs. My father observed and enjoyed my distress.

"The worthies of whom you have been reading, Emma, lived in ancient times: Aristides the just, would have made but a poor figure among our modern men of fashion!"

"This lady reads, then" — said our accomplished coxcomb — "Heavens, Mr. Courtney! you will spoil all her feminine graces; knowledge and learning, are insufferably masculine in a woman — born only for the soft solace of man! The mind of a young lady should be clear and unsullied, like a sheet of white paper, or her own fairer face: lines of thinking destroy the dimples of beauty; aping the reason of man, they lose the exquisite, *fascinating* charm, in which consists their true empire; — Then strongest, when most weak —

"Loveliest in their fears —
And by this silent adulation, soft,
To their protection more engaging man."[18]

"Pshaw!" replied Mr. Courtney, a little peevishly — "you will persuade Emma, that the age of chivalry is not yet over; and that giants and ravishers are as common now, as in the time of Charlemagne: a young woman of sense and spirit needs no other protection; do not flatter the girl into affectation and imbecility. If blank paper be your passion, you can be at no loss; the town will supply quires and reams."

"There I differ from you," said the gentleman on the oppo-site side of the table; "to preserve the mind a blank, we must be both deaf and blind, for, while any inlet to perception remains, your paper will infallibly contract characters of some kind, or be blotted and scrawled!"

"For God's sake! do not let us begin to philosophise," re-torted his antagonist, who was not to be easily silenced.

"I agree with you" — rejoined the other — "*thinking* is un-doubtedly very laborious, and *principle* equally troublesome and impertinent."

---

[18] James Thomson, "Autumn," from *The Seasons*, 1726-1730.

I looked at him as he finished speaking, and caught his eye for a moment; its expression methought was doubtful. The man of fashion continued to expatiate in rhetorical periods — He informed us, that he had fine feelings, but they never extended beyond selfish gratification. For his part, he had as much humanity as any man, for which reason he carefully avoided the scene or the tale of distress. He, likewise, had his opinions, but their pliability rendered them convenient to himself, and accommodating to his friends. He had courage to sustain fatigue and hardship, when, not his country, but vanity demanded the exertion. It was glorious to boast of having travelled two hundred miles in eight and forty hours, and sat up three nights, to be present, on two succeeding evenings, at a ball in distant counties.

"This man," said I to myself, while I regarded him with a look of ineffable scorn — "takes a great deal of pains to render himself ridiculous, he surely must have a vile heart, or a contemptible opinion of mankind: if he be really the character he describes, he is a compound of atrocity and folly, and a pest to the world: if he slanders himself, what must be that state of society, the applause of which he persuades himself is to be thus acquired?" I sighed deeply; — in either case the reflection was melancholy; — my eyes enquired — "Am I to hate or to despise you?" I know not whether he understood their language, but he troubled me no more with his attentions.

I reflected a little too seriously: — I have since seen many a prating, superficial coxcomb, who talks to display his oratory — *mere words* — repeated by rote, to which few ideas are affixed, and which are uttered and received with equal apathy.

CHAP. VIII.

DURING three years, I continued my weekly visits to Berkley square; I was not always allowed to join the parties who assembled there, neither would it have been proper, for they were a motley groupe; when permitted so to do, I collected materials for reflection. I had been educated by my good aunt, in strict principles of religion; many of Mr. Courtney's friends were men of wit and talents, who, occasionally, discussed important subjects with freedom and ability: I never ventured to mingle in the conversations, but I overcame my timidity sufficiently to behave with propriety and composure; I listened attentively to all that was said, and my curiosity was awakened to philosophic enquiries.

Mr. Courtney now entrusted me with the keys of the bookcases, through which I ranged with ever new delight. I went through, by my father's direction, a course of historical reading, but I could never acquire a taste for this species of composition. Accounts of the early periods of states and empires, of the Grecian and Roman republics, I pursued with pleasure and enthusiasm: but when they became more complicated, grew corrupt, luxurious, licentious, perfidious, mercenary, I turned from them fatigued, and disgusted, and sought to recreate my spirits in the fairer regions of poetry and fiction.

My early associations rendered theology an interesting subject to me; I read ecclesiastical history, a detail of errors and crimes, and entered deeply into polemic divinity: my mind began to be emancipated, doubts had been suggested to it, I reasoned freely, endeavoured to arrange and methodize my opinions, and to trace them fearlessly through all their consequences: while from exercising my thoughts with freedom, I seemed to acquire new strength and dignity of character. I met with some of the writings of Descartes, and was seized with a passion for metaphysical enquiries. I began to think about the nature of the soul — whether it was a composition of the elements, the result of organized matter, or a subtle and etherial fire.

In the course of my researches, the Heloise of Rousseau fell into my hands. — Ah! with what transport, with what enthusiasm, did I peruse this dangerous, enchanting, work! — How shall I paint the sensations that were excited in my mind! — the pleasure I experienced approached the limits of pain — it was tumult — all the ardour of my character was excited. — Mr. Courtney, one day, surprised me weeping over the sorrows of the tender St Preux. He hastily snatched the book from my hand,

and, carefully collecting the remaining volumes, carried them in silence to his chamber: but the impression made on my mind was never to be effaced — it was even productive of a long chain of consequences, that will continue to operate till the day of my death.

SENSIBILITY AND NOVEL READING

In the late eighteenth century, public concern about appropriate reading material and the impact of novel reading in particular was common. One fear was that young adolescent middling girls who read highly emotional and sensational novels like Rousseau's *Julie, or the New Heloise* might be unable to recognize the difference between the fictional worlds portrayed in their reading material and the quite different reality in which they actually lived. Charlotte Lennox's *The Female Quixote* (1752) recounts the story of a young lady whose reading of French Romances leads her to make ridiculous and dangerous errors of judgement. Hays herself was concerned about the impact of novel reading, especially the "novel of sensibility" which sought to educate the reader into developing highly refined and strong feelings about fictional characters and situations. In an essay from *Letters and Essays, Moral and Miscellaneous*, the narrator-Hays writes to a mother who asks about appropriate reading material for her daughter:

> You ask if I would advise you to put Richardson's *Clarissa* into the hands of your daughters....If we may judge of the merit of a work by the effects which it produces on the mind, I confess, this is a book, which I would recommend to the attention of any young persons under my care. I read it repeatedly in very early life, and ever found my mind more pure, more chastened, more elevated after the perusal of it. The extreme youth and beauty, fine talents, and exalted piety of the heroine, render the character...something like the fine ideal beauty of

the ancients....in contemplating the perfect model [Clarissa herself], the imagination is raised, and the soul affected; we perceive the pencil of genius, and while we admire, catch the glorious enthusiasm.... Rousseau is not a writer equally pure. (Folger Collective on Early Women Critics, *Women Critics 1660-1820: An Anthology*, Bloomington: Indiana University Press, 1995, 298-9.)

Hays's warning about the dangers of reading the novels of Jean-Jacques Rousseau, particularly the immensely popular *Julie ou la Nouvelle Héloïse* (*Julie, or the New Heloise*), is a fairly common one in the last decades of the eighteenth century. *Julie* recounts the story of the love affair between Julie d'Étange, the daughter of a Swiss Baron, and her tutor, St. Preux, in imitation of the medieval romance of Heloise and Abelard. The delicate and elevated feelings of Julie and her lover allow their relationship to include sexual intimacy while both are still unmarried. Although Julie eventually marries the worthy Monsieur Wolmar in duty to her parents, the education of sentiment and delicacy which she provides to those who surround her and which the novel offers to its readers leaves the interpretation of the book's morals fluid. Rousseau's own Preface anticipates a small audience who will be pleased with the book, and warns explicitly against unmarried female readers: "Never did a chaste maiden read Novels; and I have affixed to this one a sufficiently clear title so that upon opening it anyone would know what to expect. She who, despite this title, dares to read a single page of it, is a maiden undone: but let her not attribute her undoing to this book; the harm was already done. Since she has begun, let her finish reading: she has nothing more to risk" (Rousseau, trans. Philip Stewart and Jean Vaché, Hanover, Vt: University of New England Press, 1997, 3).[19] Hays's essay emphasizes the elevation of mind which accompanies

[19] See for the original French, Rousseau, *Julie ou La Nouvelle Héloïse: Lettres de deux amants habitants d'une petite ville au pied des Alpes*, from the Preface, http://c18.net/pr/rousseau/julie/1018.html.

and supercedes strong sympathy with fictional characters.

Her ideas run counter to the conventional wisdom of eighteenth-century novelists such as Samuel Richardson and Samuel Johnson, who tended to argue that novels should show virtue rewarded and vice punished, and who feared that "mixed" characters, or those who combined some virtuous qualities with some flaws and weaknesses, would confuse and mislead susceptible readers. In 1798, Joseph Robertson's *Essay on the Education of Young Ladies* argued that: "A young woman who employs her time in reading novels, will never find amusement in other books. Her mind will be soon debauched by licentious descriptions and lascivious images; ...her mind will become a magazine of trifles and follies, or rather impure and wanton ideas" (cited in John Brewer, "Reconstructing the Reader" in *The Practice and Representation of Reading in England*, Ed. James Raven, 233; 44-5 original). In a later essay, Hays insisted that literature can and ought to educate readers to move from a feeling response to pathetic narrative to a more judicious stance of serious reflection:

> The business of familiar narrative should be to describe life and manners in real or probable situations, to delineate the human mind in its endless varieties, to develop the heart, to paint the passions, to trace the springs of action, to interest the imagination, exercise the affections, and awaken the powers of the mind. A good novel ought to be subservient to the purposes of truth and philosophy: such are the novels of Fielding and Smollet. ... The language of the novelist should be simple, unaffected, perspicuous, yet energetic, touching, and impressive. It is not necessary that we should be able to deduce from a novel, a formal and didactic moral; it is sufficient if it has a tendency to raise the mind by elevated sentiments, to warm the heart with generous affections, to enlarge our views, or to increase our stock of useful knowledge. A more effectual les-

son might perhaps be deduced from tracing the pernicious consequences of an erroneous judgment, a wrong step, an imprudent action, an indulged and intemperate affection, a bad habit, in a character in other respects amiable and virtuous, than in painting chimerical perfection and visionary excellence, which rarely, if ever, existed. How deep is our regret, how touching our sympathy, how generous our sorrow, while we contemplate the noble mind blasted by the ravages of passion, or withered by the canker of prejudice! Such examples afford an affecting and humiliating lesson of human frailty, they teach us to soften the asperity of censure, to appreciate the motives and actions of our fellow beings with candour, to distrust ourselves, and to watch with diffidence lest we should, even by the excess of our most amiable and laudable qualities, be precipitated into folly, or betrayed into vice. It is such examples that are the most calculated to be useful; they affect every heart, they are consistent with truth, for they do not calumniate the species....

Fictitious histories, in the hands of persons of talents and observation, might be made productive of incalculable benefit; by interesting curiosity, and addressing the common sympathies of our nature, they pervade all ranks; and judiciously conducted, would become a powerful and effective engine of truth and reform. (Hays, "On Novel Writing")

SOURCES

Mary Hays, "On Novel Writing," *Monthly Magazine.* 4 (September 1797): 180-81.

———. *Letters and Essays, Moral and Miscellaneous.* (Folger Collective on Early Women Critics, *Women Critics 1660-1820: An Anthology*, (Bloomington: Indiana University Press, 1995).

Joseph Robertson. *Essay on the Education of Young Ladies.*

London, 1798.
Jean-Jacques Rousseau, *Julie*. (1759). Trans. Philip Stewart
and Jean Vaché, (Hanover, VT: University of New England Press, 1997), 3.

My time at this period passed rapidly and pleasantly. My
father never treated me with affection; but the austerity of his
manner gradually subsided. He gave me, occasionally, useful hints
and instructions. Without feeling for him any tenderness, he
inspired me with a degree of respect. The library was a source of
lively and inexhaustible pleasure to my mind; and, when admitted to the table of Mr. Courtney, some new character or sentiment frequently sharpened my attention, and afforded me subjects for future enquiry and meditation. I delighted to expatiate,
when returning to the kind and hospitable mansion of my beloved aunt, (which I still considered as my home) on the various
topics which I had collected in my little emigrations. I was listened to by my cousins with a pleasure that flattered my vanity,
and looked up to as a kind of superior being; — a homage particularly gratifying to a young mind.

CHAP. IX.

THE excellent woman, who had been my more than mother,
took infinite pains to cure the foibles, which, like pernicious
weeds, entangled themselves with, and sometimes threatened to
choak, the embryo blossoms of my expanding mind. Ah! with
what pleasure do I recall her beloved idea to my memory! Fostered by her maternal love, and guided by her mild reason, how
placid, and how sweet, were my early days! — Why, my first,
my tenderest friend, did I lose you at that critical period of life,
when the harmless sports and occupations of childhood gave
place to the pursuits, the passions, and the errors of youth? —
With the eloquence of affection, with gentle, yet impressive persuasion, thou mightest have checked the wild career of energetic

feeling, which thou hast so often remarked with hope and terror.

As I entered my eighteenth year, I lost, by a premature death, this tender monitor. Never shall I forget her last emphatic, affectionate, caution.

"Beware, my dear Emma" said this revered friend, "beware of strengthening, by indulgence, those ardent and impetuous sensations, which, while they promise vigour of mind, fill me with apprehension for the virtue, for the happiness of my child. I wish not that the canker-worm, Distrust, should blast the fair fruit of your ripening virtues. The world contains many benevolent, many disinterested, spirits; but civilization is yet distempered and imperfect; the inequalities of society, by fostering artificial wants, and provoking jealous competitions, have generated selfish and hostile passions. Nature has been vainly provident for her offspring, while man, with mistaken avidity, grasping more than he has powers to enjoy, preys on his fellow man: — departing from simple virtues, and simple pleasures, in their stead, by common consent, has a wretched semblance been substituted. Endeavour to contract your wants, and aspire only to a rational independence; by exercising your faculties, still the importunate suggestions of your sensibility; preserve your sincerity, cherish the ingenuous warmth of unsophisticated feeling, but let discernment precede confidence. I tremble even for the excess of those virtues which I have laboured to cultivate in your lively and docile mind. If I could form a wish for longer life, it is only for my children, and that I might be to my Emma instead of reason, till her own stronger mind matures. I dread, lest the illusions of imagination should render those powers, which would give force to truth and virtue, the auxiliaries of passion. Learn to distinguish, with accuracy, the good and ill qualities of those with whom you may mingle: while you abhor the latter, separate the being from his errors; and while you revere the former, the moment that your reverence becomes personal, that moment, suspect that your judgement is in danger of becoming the dupe of your affections."

Would to God that I had impressed upon my mind — that

I had recalled to my remembrance more frequently — a lesson so important to a disposition like mine! — a continual victim to the enthusiasm of my feelings; incapable of approving, or disapproving, with moderation — the most poignant sufferings, even the study of mankind, have been insufficient to dissolve the powerful enchantment, to disentangle the close-twisted associations! —— But I check this train of overwhelming reflection, that is every moment on the point of breaking the thread of my narration, and obtruding itself to my pen.

CHAP. X.

MR. Courtney did not long survive the guardian of my infancy: — his constitution had for some years been gradually impaired; and his death was hastened by a continuance of habitual dissipation, which he had not the resolution to relinquish, and to which his strength was no longer equal. It was an event I had long anticipated, and which I contemplated with a sensation of solemnity, rather than of grief. The ties of blood are weak, if not the mere chimeras of prejudice, unless sanctioned by reason, or cemented by habits of familiar and affectionate intercourse. Mr. Courtney refusing the title of father, from a conviction that his conduct gave him no claim to this endearing appellation, had accustomed me to feel for him only the respect due to some talents and good qualities, which threw a veil over his faults. Courage and truth were the principles with which he endeavoured to inspire me; — precepts, which I gratefully acknowledge, and which forbid me to adopt the language of affection, when no responsive sympathies exist in the heart.

My eyes were yet moist with the tears that I had shed for the loss of my maternal friend, when I received a hasty summons to Berkley-square. A servant informed me, that his master was, at length, given over by his physicians, and wished to speak to Miss Courtney, before his strength and spirits were too much exhausted.

I neither felt, nor affected, surprise at this intelligence, but threw myself, without reply, into the carriage which had been dispatched for my conveyance.

On entering the house, a gloomy silence seemed to reign throughout the late festive apartments; but, as I had seldom been a partaker of the festivity, the contrast struck me less forcibly than it might otherwise have done. My name was announced, and I was conducted, by the housekeeper, to the chamber of her dying master, who, supported on pillows, breathed with difficulty, but appeared to be free from pain, and tolerably composed. I met the physician in the ante-chamber; who, on my requesting earnestly to know the situation of his patient, informed me — That an internal mortification had taken place, and that he could not survive many hours.

Approaching the bed, considerably shocked at the intelligence I had received, Mr. Courtney, in a low and faint voice, desired me to draw a chair near him. I obeyed in silence.

"Emma," said he, "I am about to quit a world, in which I have experienced little sincere enjoyment; yet, I leave it reluctantly. Had I been more temperate in my pleasures, perhaps, they might have been less destructive, and more protracted. I begin to suspect, that I have made some great mistakes; but it is now too late for retraction, and I will not, in my last moments, contradict, by my example, the lesson of fortitude, with which it has been a part of my plan to inspire you. You have now, unprotected, the world to encounter; for, I will frankly confess, that my affection for you has not been strong enough to induce me to forego my own more immediate gratification: but I have never deceived you. Your mother, when she married, reserved for her private expences a thousand pounds, which, on her deathbed, she desired might be invested in the funds on your account. This request I religiously complied with, and there it has remained untouched; and, being purchased in your name, you may claim it whenever you please. I have appointed you no guardians; for, already in your nineteenth year, and possessing an understanding superior to your sex and age, I chose to leave you unfettered, at your own discretion. I spared from my pleasures what money was requisite to complete your education; for having no fortune to give you, and my health being precarious, I thought it just to afford you every advantage for the improvement of those talents which you evidently possess, and which must now enable you to make your way in the world; for the scanty pittance, that the interest of your fortune will produce, is, I doubt, insufficient for your support. Had I lived, it was my intention to have established you by marriage; but that is a scheme, to which, at present, I would not advise you to trust. Marriage, generally speaking, in the existing state of things, must of necessity be an affair of *finance*. My interest and introduction might have availed you something; but mere merit, wit, or beauty, stand in need of more powerful auxiliaries. My brother, Mr. Morton,[20] called on me this morning: — he has agreed, for the present, to receive you into his family, where you must endeavour to make yourself useful and agreeable, till you can fix on a better and more independent plan. Finding me in so low a state, your uncle would have waited a few days in town, to have seen the result, and, in case of the worst, to have taken you down with him, but pressing business urged his departure. I would advise you, immediately after my decease, to set out for Morton Park. Proper persons are appointed to settle my affairs: — when every thing is turned into money, there will, I trust, be sufficient to discharge my just debts; but do not flatter yourself with the expectation of a surplus. Your presence here, when I am no more, will be equally unnecessary and improper."

This was said at intervals, and with difficulty; when, seeming quite exhausted, he waved his hand for me to leave the room, and sunk into a sort of dose, or rather stupor, which continued till within some minutes of his decease.

Mr. Courtney had been, what is called, a man of pleasure: — he had passed thro' life without ever loving anyone but himself — intent, merely, on gratifying the humour of the moment. A superior education, and an attentive observance, not of ratio-

[20] "Mr. Courtney's brother had taken the name of Morton, to qualify himself for the inheritance of an estate, bequeathed to him by a distant relation." [M.H.]

nal, but, of social man, in an extensive commerce with the world, had sharpened his sagacity; but he was inaccessible to those kindlings of the affections — those glowings of admiration — inspired by real, or fancied, excellence, which never fail to expand and advance the minds of such as are capable of sketching, with a daring hand, the dangerous picture: — or of those philosophic and comprehensive views, which teach us to seek a reflected happiness in benevolent exertions for the welfare of others. My mother, I suspected, had been the victim of her husband's unkindness and neglect: wonder not, then, that my heart revolted when I would have given him the tender appellation of father! If he coldly acknowledged any little merits which I possessed, he regarded them rather with jealousy than approbation; for he felt that they tacitly reproached him.

I will make no comment on the closing scene of his life. Among the various emotions which had rapidly succeeded each other in my mind, during his last address, surprize had no place; I had not then his character to learn.

Chap. XI.

THE small pittance bequeathed to me was insufficient to preserve me from dependence. — *Dependence!* — I repeated to myself, and I felt my heart die within me. I resolved in my mind various plans for my future establishment. — I might, perhaps, be allowed to officiate, as an assistant, in the school where I had been placed in my childhood, with the mistress of which I still kept up an occasional correspondence; but this was a species of servitude, and my mind panted for freedom, for social intercourse, for scenes in motion, where the active curiosity of my temper might find a scope wherein to range and speculate. What could the interest of my little fortune afford? It would neither enable me to live alone, nor even to board in a family of any respectability. My beloved aunt was no more; her children were about to be dispersed, and to form various connections.

Cruel prejudices! — I exclaimed — hapless woman! Why was I not educated for commerce, for a profession, for labour?

Why have I been rendered feeble and delicate by bodily constraint, and fastidious by artificial refinement? Why are we bound, by the habits of society, as with an adamantine chain? Why do we suffer ourselves to be confined within a magic circle, without daring, by a magnanimous effort, to dissolve the barbarous spell?

A child in the drama of the world, I knew not which way to turn, nor on what to determine. I wrote to Mr. Morton, to enquire on what terms I was to be received by his family. If merely as a visitor for a few weeks, till I had time to digest my plans, I should meet, with pleasure, a gentleman whose character I had been taught to respect; but I should not consider myself as subject to controul. I ought, perhaps, to have been satisfied with Mr. Morton's answer to my interrogatories.

He wished to embrace the daughter of his brother, his family would be happy to render Morton Park agreeable to her, as long as she should think proper to favour them by making it her residence. The young ladies expected both pleasure and improvement from the society of their accomplished kinswoman, &c.

I believe I was unreasonable, the style of this letter was civil, nay kind, and yet it appeared, to me, to want the vivifying principle — what shall I say? — dictated merely by the head, it reached not the heart.

The trials of my mind, I foreboded, were about to commence, I shrunk from the world I had been so willing to enter, for the rude storms of which I had been little fitted by the fostering tenderness of my early guardians. Those ardent feelings and lively expectations, with all the glowing landscapes which my mind had sketched of the varied pleasures of society, while in a measure secluded from its enjoyments, gradually melted into one deep, undistinguished shade. That sanguine ardour of temper, which had hitherto appeared the predominant feature of my character, now gave place to despondency. I wept, I suffered my tears to flow unrestrained: the solemnity of the late events had seized my spirits, and the approaching change filled me with solicitude. I wandered over the scenes of my past pleasures, and recalled to my remembrance, with a sad and tender luxury, a thousand little incidents, that derived all their importance from the impossibility of their renewal. I gazed on every object, *for the last time* — What is there in these words that awakens our fanaticism? I could have done homage to these inanimate, and, till now, uninteresting objects; merely because I should *see them no more.*

How fantastic and how capricious are these sentiments! Ought I, or ought I not, to blush while I acknowledge them? My young friends, also, from whom I was about to separate myself! — how various might be our destinies, and how unconscious were we of the future! Happy ignorance, that by bringing the evils of life in succession, gradually inures us to their endurance.

"Had I beheld the sum of ills, which one
By one, I have endured — my heart had broke."[21]

Chap. XII.

The hour at length came, when, harrassed in body and mind, I set out for Morton Park. I travelled alone, and reached the end of my journey at the close of day. I entreated Mr. Morton, who hastened to hand me from the carriage, and welcome my arrival, that I might be permitted to retire to my apartment, pleading fatigue, and wishing to wave the ceremony of an introduction to the family till the next morning. My request was obligingly granted, and a servant ordered to attend me to my chamber.

Many years had elapsed since I had seen this family, and my judgment was then so immature, that our meeting at the breakfast table had with each of us, I believe, the force of a first impression. You know my *fanaticism* on these occasions. I will attempt an imperfect sketch of the groupe, assembled in the saloon, to whom I was severally presented on my entrance, by the lord of the domain. Mr. Morton, himself, to whom precedence is due, seemed to be about fifty years of age, was of the middle stature, his features regular, and his countenance placid: he spoke but little, but that little was always mild and often judicious.

---

[21] John Home, *Douglas, A Tragedy*, Act I, lines 281-82.

He appeared not to be void of benevolent affections, and had the character of a humane landlord, but his virtues were, in a great measure, sunk in an habitual indolence of temper; he would sometimes sacrifice his principles to his repose, though never to his interest. His lady — no, I will not describe her; her character will, it may be, unfold itself to you in future — Suffice it to say, that her person was gross, her voice loud and discordant, and her features rugged: she affected an air of openness and pleasantry; I may be prejudiced, perhaps she did not *affect it*. Sarah Morton, the eldest of the daughters, was about my own age, she was under the middle height, fair, plump, loquacious; there was a childish levity in her accent and manners, which impressed strangers with an unfavourable opinion of her understanding, but it was an acquired manner, for she was shrewd and sensible. Ann, the second daughter, was a little lively brunette, with sharp features and sparkling black eyes; volatile, giddy, vain and thoughtless, but good humoured and pretty. The other children were much younger.

Two gentlemen joined us at our repast, visitors at Morton Park. Mr. Francis, the elder, was in his fortieth year, his figure slender and delicate, his eye piercing, and his manner impressive. It occurred to me, that I had somewhere seen him before, and, after a few minutes recollection, I recognized in him a gentleman who had occasionally visited at my father's, and whom I have already mentioned as the antagonist of the man of fashion, whose sentiments and volubility excited my youthful astonishment and indignation. Mr. Montague the younger, the son of a medical gentleman residing in a neighbouring county, seemed about one and twenty, tall, elegantly formed, full of fire and vivacity, with imperious manners, an impetuous temper, and stubborn prejudices.

The introduction of a stranger generally throws some kind of restraint over a company; a break is made in their usual topics and associations, till the disposition and habits of the intruder have, in some degree, unfolded themselves. Mrs. Morton took upon herself to entertain; she exhibited her talents on various subjects, with apparent self-approbation, till a few keen remarks from Mr. Francis arrested the torrent of her eloquence. The young ladies scrutinized me with attention; even the lively Ann, while she minutely observed me, ceased to court play from Mr. Montague, who attended to me with the air, and addressed me in the language of gallantry. I sometimes caught the penetrating eye of Mr. Francis, and his glance seemed to search the soul.

After breakfast, Mr. Morton having retired to his dressing-room, and the younger part of the company strolling into the pleasure grounds, whither I declined accompanying them, I took an opportunity, being ever desirous of active and useful employment, of offering my assistance to Mrs. Morton, in the education of her younger children; proposing to instruct them in the rudiments either of music, drawing, French, or any other accomplishment, for which my own education had capacitated me. Mr. Francis remained standing in a window, his back towards us, with a book in his hand, on which he seemed intent.

"If," replied Mrs. Morton, "it is your wish, Miss Courtney, to procure the situation of governess in any gentleman's family, and it is certainly a very laudable desire in a young woman of your *small fortune*, Mr. Morton will, I have no doubt, have it in his power to recommend you: but in the education of my family, I desire no interference; it is an important task, and I have my peculiar notions on the subject: their expectations are not great, and your *elegant* accomplishments might unfit them for their future, probable, stations."

The manner in which this speech was uttered spoke yet more forcibly than the words. — I felt my cheeks glow.

"I was not asking favours, Madam, I was only desirous of being useful."

"It is a pity, then, that your discernment had not corrected your vanity."

The housekeeper entering, to consult her mistress on some domestic occasion, Mrs. Morton quitted the room. Mr. Francis closed his book, turned round, and gazed earnestly in my face: before sufficiently mortified, his observation, which I felt at this moment oppressive, did not relieve me. I attempted to escape, but, seizing my hand, he detained me by a kind of gentle violence.

"And why this confusion, my dear Miss Courtney; do you blush for having acted with propriety and spirit?" I burst into tears — I could not help it — "How weak is this, how unworthy of the good sense you have just manifested."

"I confess it, but I feel myself, at this moment, a poor, a friendless, an unprotected being."

"What prejudices! poverty is neither criminal, nor disgraceful; you will not want friends, while you continue to deserve them; and as for protection, (and he smiled) I had not expected from Emma Courtney's spirited letter to Mr. Morton, and equally proper retort to his lady's impertinence, so plaintive, so feminine a complaint. — You have talents, cultivate them, and learn to rest on your own powers."

"I thank you for your reproof, and solicit your future lessons."

"Can you bear the truth?"

"Try me."

"Have you not cherished a false pride?"

It is too true, thought I, and I sighed.

"How shall I cure this foible?"

"By self-examination, by resolution, and perseverance."

"Be to me instead of a conscience."

"What, then, is become of your own?"

"Prejudice, I doubt, has blinded and warped it."

"I suspect so; but you have energy and candor, and are not, I hope, of a temper to despond."

The return of the family terminated this singular conversation. The young ladies rallied me, on being found *tête-à-tête* with the philosopher; Mr. Montague, I thought looked displeased. I stole out, while the party were dressing for dinner, and rambled into the gardens, which were extensive, and laid out with taste.

Chap. XIII.

I judged my visit here would not be very long. I scarcely

knew whether I was most inclined to like or to fear Mr. Francis, but I determined, if possible, to cultivate his friendship. I interrogated myself again and again — From whence this restlessness, this languor, this disgust, with all I hear and see? — Why do I feel wayward, querulous, fastidious? Mr. Morton's family had no hearts; they appeared to want a *sense*, that preyed incessantly on mine; I could not love them, and my heart panted to expand its sensations.

Sarah and Ann became jealous of me, and of each other; the haughty, yet susceptible, Montague addressed each in turn, with a homage equally fervent for the moment, and equally transient. This young man was bold, ardent, romantic, and enterprizing, but blown about by every gust of passion, he appeared each succeeding moment a different character: with a glowing and rapid imagination, he had never given himself time to reason, to compare, to acquire principles: following the bent of a raised, yet capricious fancy, he was ever in pursuit of meteors, that led him into mischief, or phantoms, that dissolved at his approach.

Had my mind been more assured and at ease, I could have amused myself with the whimsical flights of this eccentric being — One hour, attracted by the sportive graces of Ann, he played with and caressed her, while the minutes flew rapidly on the light wing of amusement, and, till reminded by the grave countenance of Mr. Morton, seemed to forget that any other person was present. The next minute, disgusted with her frivolity, all his attention was absorbed by the less fascinating, but more artful and ingenious, Sarah. Then, quitting them both, he would pursue my steps, break in upon my meditations, and haunt my retreats, from whence, when not disposed to be entertained by his caprice, I found it not difficult to drive him, by attacking some of his various prejudices: — accustomed to feel, and not to reason, his tastes and opinions were vehement and uncontroulable.

From this society, so uncongenial to my reflecting, reasoning, mind, I found some resource in the conversation of Mr. Francis. The pride of Montague was evidently piqued by the decided preference which I gave to the company of his friend; but his homage, or his resentment, were alike indifferent to me: accustomed to speak and act from my convictions, I was but little solicitous respecting the opinion of others. My understanding was exercised by attending to the observations of Mr. Francis, and by discussing the questions to which they led; yet it was exercised without being gratified: he opposed and bewildered me, convicted me of error, and harrassed me with doubt.

Mr. Francis soon after prepared to return to town. I was affected at the idea of his departure; and felt, that in losing his society, I should be deprived of my only rational recreation, and should again be exposed to Mrs. Morton's illiberal attacks, who appeared to have marked me out for her victim, though at present restrained by the presence of a man, who had found means to inspire, even her, with some degree of respect.

Mr. Francis, on the evening preceding the day on which he purposed leaving Morton Park, passing under the open window of my chamber, in which I was sitting with a book to enjoy the refreshing breeze, invited me to come down, and accompany him in a ramble. I immediately complied with his request, and joined him in a few minutes, with a countenance clouded with regret at the idea of his quitting us.

"You are going," said I, as I gave him my hand (which he passed under his arm), "and I lose my friend and counsellor."

"Your concern is obliging; but you are capable of standing alone, and your mind, by so doing, will acquire strength."

"I feel as if this would not be the case: the world appears to me a thorny and a pathless wilderness; I step with caution, and look around me with dread. — That I require protection and assistance, is, I confess, a proof of weakness, but it is nevertheless true."

"Mr. Montague," replied he, with some degree of archness in his tone and manner, "is a gallant knight, a pattern of chivalry, and appears to be particularly calculated for the defender of distressed damsels!"

"I have no inclination to trust myself to the guidance of one, who seems himself entangled in an inextricable maze of error, and whose versatile character affords little basis for confidence."

"Tell me what it is you fear; —— are your apprehensions founded in reason?"

"Recollect my youth, my sex, and my precarious situation."

"I thought you contemned the plea of *sex*, as a sanction for weakness!"

"Though I disallow it as a natural, I admit it as an artificial, plea."

"Explain yourself."

"The character, you tell me, is modified by circumstances: the customs of society, then, have enslaved, enervated, and degraded woman."

"I understand you: there is truth in your remark, though you have given it undue force."

I hesitated — my heart was full — I felt as if there were many things which I wished to say; but, however paradoxical, the manners of Mr. Francis repressed, while they invited, confidence. I respected his reason, but I doubted whether I could inspire him with sympathy, or make him fully comprehend my feelings. I conceived I could express myself with more freedom on paper; but I had not courage to request a correspondence, when he was silent on the subject. That it would be a source of improvement to me, I could not doubt, but prejudice with-held me from making the proposal. He looked at me, and perceived my mind struggling with a suggestion, to which it dared not give utterance: he suspected the truth, but was unwilling to disturb the operations of my understanding. We walked for some time in silence: — my companion struck into a path that led towards the house — listened to the village clock as it struck nine — and observed, the hour grew late. He had distinguished me, and I was flattered by that distinction; he had supported me against the arrogance of Mrs. Morton, retorted the sly sarcasms of Sarah, and even helped to keep the impetuous Montague in awe, and obliged him to rein in his offensive spirit, every moment on the brink of outrage. My heart, formed for grateful attachment, taking, in one instant, a hasty retrospect of the past, and a rapid glance into futurity, experienced at that moment so desolating a pang, that I endeavoured in vain to repress its sensations, and burst into a flood of tears. Mr. Francis suddenly stopped, appeared moved, and, with a benevolent aspect and soothing accents, enquired into the cause of an emotion so sudden and unexpected. I wept a few minutes in silence, and my spirits seemed, in some measure relieved.

"I weep, (said I,) because I am *friendless*; to be esteemed and cherished is necessary to my existence; I am an alien in the family where I at present reside, I cannot remain here much longer, and to whom, and whither, shall I go?"

He took my hand — "I will not, at present, say all that it might be proper to say, because I perceive your mind is in a feeble state; — My affairs call me to London; — yet, there is a method of conversing at a distance."

I eagerly availed myself of this suggestion, which I had wished, without having the courage to propose.

"Will you, then, allow me, through the medium of pen and paper, to address, to consult you, as I may see occasion?"

"Will I? yes, most cheerfully! Propose your doubts and state your difficulties, and we shall see, (smiling) whether they admit of a solution."

Thanking him, I engaged to avail myself of this permission, and we proceeded slowly to the house, and joined the party in the supper room. I never once thought of my red and swoln eyes, till Sarah, glancing a look half curious, half sarcastic, towards me, exclaimed from Shakespear, in an affected tone,

"Parting is such sweet sorrow!"[22]

Mr. Francis looked at her sternly, she blushed and was silent; Mr. Montague was captious; Ann mortified, that she could not by her little tricks gain his attention. Mrs. Morton sat wrapped in mock dignity; while Mr. Morton, and his philosophic friend, canvassed the principles upon which an horizon-

---

[22] *Romeo and Juliet*, II.3.184-5.

tal mill was about to be constructed on the estate of the former. After a short and scanty meal, I retired to my apartment, determined to rise early the next morning, and make breakfast for my friend before his departure.

CHAP. XIV.

MR. Francis had ordered his horse to be ready at five o'clock. I left my chamber at four, to have the pleasure of preparing for him the last friendly repast, and of saying *farewel*. He was serene and chearful as usual, I somewhat more pensive; we parted with great cordiality, he gave me his address in town, and engaged me to write to him shortly. I accompanied him through the park to the porter's lodge, where the servant and horses waited his coming. My eyes glistened as I bade him adieu, and reiterated my wishes for his safety and prosperity, while his features softened into a more than usual benignity, as he returned my salutation.

I wandered thoughtfully back towards the house, but the rich purple that began to illumine the east, the harbinger of the rising sun, the freshness of the morning air, the soft dews which already glittered on every fragrant plant and flower, the solemn stillness, so grateful to the reflecting mind, that pervaded the scene, induced me to prolong my walk. Every object appeared in unison with my feelings, my heart swelled with devotional affections, it aspired to the Author of nature. After having bewildered ourselves amid systems and theories, religion, in such situations, returns to the susceptible mind as a *sentiment* rather than as a principle. A passing cloud let fall a gentle, drizzling shower; sheltered beneath the leafy umbrage of a spreading oak, I rather heard than felt it; yet, the coolness it diffused seemed to quench those ardent emotions, which are but too congenial with my disposition, while the tumult of the passions subsided into a delicious tranquillity.

How mutable are human beings! — A very few hours converted this sublime complacency into perturbation and tumult. Having extended my walk beyond its accustomed limits, on my return, I retired, somewhat fatigued to my apartment, and devoted the morning to my studies. At the dinner hour I joined the family, each individual of which seemed wrapped up in reserve, scarcely deigning to practise the common ceremonies of the occasion. I was not sufficiently interested in the cause of these appearances to make any enquiries, and willingly resigned myself, in the intervals of the entertainment, to meditation.

When the table was cleared, and the servants had withdrawn, perceiving the party not sociably inclined, I was about to retire — when Mrs. Morton observed, with features full of a meaning which I did not comprehend, that —

"Their guest, Mr. Francis, had, no doubt, left Morton Park gratefully impressed by the *kindness* of Miss Courtney."

Montague reddened — bit his lips — got up — and sat down again. The young ladies wore an air not perfectly good humoured, and a little triumphant. Mr. Morton looked very solemn.

"I hope so, Madam," I replied, somewhat carelessly. "I felt myself indebted to Mr. Francis for his civilities, and was solicitous to make him all the return in my power — I wish that power had been enlarged."

She held up her hands and eyes with an affected, and ridiculous, gesture.

"Mr. Francis," said Montague, abruptly, "is very happy in having inspired you with sentiments *so partial.*"

"I am not partial — I am merely just. Mr. Francis appeared to me a rational man, and my understanding was exercised and gratified by his conversation."

I was about to proceed, but my uncle (who seemed to have been tutored for the occasion) interrupted me with much gravity.

"You are but little acquainted, Emma, with the customs of society; there is a great indecorum in a young lady's making these distinctions."

"What distinctions, my dear Sir! — in prefering a reasonable man to fools and coxcombs?"

"Forgive me, my dear — you have a quick wit, but you want

experience. I am informed, that you breakfasted with Mr. Francis this morning, and attended him through the Park: — this, with your late walk yesterday evening, and evident emotion on your return, let me tell you, child, wears an indecorous appearance: — the world is justly attentive to the conduct of young women, and too apt to be censorious."

I looked round me with unaffected surprize — "Good God! — did I suppose, in this family, it was necessary to be upon my guard against malicious constructions?"

"Pray," — interrupted Sarah, pertly — "would you not have expressed some surprize, had I shewed Mr. Montague similar attentions?"

I looked at her, I believe, a little too contemptuously — "Whatever sentiments might have been excited in my mind by the attentions of Miss Morton to Mr. Montague, *surprize*, assuredly, would not have been among them."

She coloured, and Montague's passions began to rise. I stopped him in the beginning of an impertinent harangue, by observing —

"That I did not think myself accountable to him for my conduct; — before I should be solicitous respecting his opinions, he must give me better reasons, than he had hitherto done, to respect his judgment."

Ann wept, and prattled something, to which nobody thought it worth while to attend.

"Well, Sir" continued I, turning to Mr. Morton, "be pleased to give me, in detail, what you have to alledge, that I may be enabled to justify myself."

"Will you allow me to ask you a question?"

"Most certainly."

"Has Mr. Francis engaged you to correspond with him?"

I was silent a few moments.

"You hesitate!"

"Only, Sir, *how* to answer your question. —— I certainly intend myself the pleasure of addressing Mr. Francis on paper; but I cannot strictly say *he engaged* me so to do, as it was a proposal he was led to make, by conjecturing my wishes on the subject."

Again, Mrs. Morton, with uplifted hands and eyes — "What effrontery!"

I seemed not to hear her. —— "Have you any thing more to say, my dear uncle?"

"You are a strange girl. It would not, perhaps, be proper before this company to enquire" — and he stopped.

"Any thing is proper, Sir, to enquire of me, and in any company — I have no reserves, no secrets."

"Well, then, I think it necessary to inform you, that, though a sensible, well educated, liberal-minded, man, Mr. Francis has neither estate nor fortune, nor does he practise any lucrative profession."

"I am sorry for it, on his own account, and for those whom his generosity might benefit. But, what is it to me?"

"You affect to misunderstand me."

"I *affect* nothing."

"I will speak more plainly: — Has he made you any proposals?"

The purport of this solemn, but ludicrous, preparation, at once flashed upon my mind, the first time the thought had ever occurred. I laughed — I could not help it.

"I considered Mr. Francis as a *philosopher*, and not as a *lover*. Does this satisfy you, Sir?"

My uncle's features, in spite of himself, relaxed into a half-smile.

"Very platonic — sweet simplicity!" — drauled out Mrs. Morton, in ironical accents.

"I will not be insulted, Mr. Morton!" quitting my seat, and rising in temper. — "I consider myself, merely, as your visitant, and not as responsible to any one for my actions. Conscious of purity of intention, and superior to all disguise or evasion, I was not aware of these feminine, indelicate, unfriendly suggestions. If this behaviour be a specimen of what I am to expect in the world — the world may do its will — but I will never be its

slave: while I have strength of mind to form principles, and courage to act upon them, I am determined to preserve my freedom,
and trust to the general candour and good sense of mankind to
appreciate me justly. As the brother of my late father, and as
entitled to respect from your own kind intentions, I am willing
to enter into any explanations, which *you, Sir,* may think necessary: — neither my motives, nor my actions, have ever yet shrunk
from investigation. Will you permit me to attend you in your
library? It is not my intention to intrude longer on your hospitality, and I could wish to avail myself of your experience and
counsels respecting my future destination."

Mr. Morton, at my request, withdrew with me into the library, where I quickly removed from his mind those injurious
suspicions with which Mrs. Morton had laboured to inspire him.
He would not hear of my removal from the Park — apologized
for what had passed — assured me of his friendship and protection — and entreated me to consider his house as my home.
There was an honest warmth and sincerity in his manner, that
sensibly affected me; I could have wept; and I engaged, at his
repeated request, not to think, at present, of withdrawing myself from his protection. Thus we separated.

How were the virtues of this really good man tarnished by
an unsuitable connection! In the giddy hours of youth, we
thoughtlessly rush into engagements, that fetter our minds, and
affect our future characters, without reflecting on the important
consequences of our conduct. This is a subject on which I have
had occasion to reflect deeply; yet, alas! my own boasted reason
has been, but too often, the dupe of my imagination.

Chap. XV.

Nothing, here, occupied my heart — a heart to which it
was necessary to love and admire. I had suffered myself to be
irritated — the tumult of my spirits did not easily subside — I
was mortified at the reflection — I had believed myself armed
with patience and fortitude, but my philosophy was swept before the impetuous emotions of my passions like chaff before the

whirlwind. I took up my pen to calm my spirits, and addressed myself to the man who had been, unconsciously, the occasion of these vexations. — My swelling heart needed the relief of communication.

TO MR. FRANCIS.

"I SOUGHT earnestly for the privilege of addressing you on paper. My mind seemed to overflow with a thousand sentiments, that I had not the courage to express in words; but now, when the period is arrived, that I can take up my pen, unawed by your penetrating glance, unchecked by your poignant reply, and pour out my spirit before you, I feel as if its emotions were too wayward, too visionary, too contradictory, to merit your attention.

"Every thing I see and hear is a disappointment to me: — brought up in retirement — conversing only with books — dwelling with ardour on the great characters, and heroic actions, of antiquity, all my ideas of honour and distinction were associated with those of virtue and talents. I conceived, that the pursuit of truth, and the advancement of reason, were the grand objects of universal attention, and I panted to do homage to those superior minds, who, teaching mankind to be wise, would at length lead them to happiness. Accustomed to think, to feel, to kindle into action, I am at a loss to understand the distinction between theory and practice, which every one seems eager to inculcate, as if the degrading and melancholy intelligence, which fills my soul with despondency, and pervades my understanding with gloom, was to them a subject of exultation.

"Is virtue, then, a chimera — does it exist only in the regions of romance? — Have we any interest in finding our fellow creatures weak and miserable? — Is the Being who formed them unjust, capricious, impotent, or tyrannical?

"Answer these questions, that press heavily on my mind, that dart across it, in its brightest moments, clouding its sun-shine with a thick and impenetrable darkness. Must the benevolent emotions, which I have hitherto delighted to cherish, turn into misanthropy — must the fervent and social affections of my heart give place to inanity, to apathy — must the activity of a curious and vigorous mind sink into torpor and abhorred vacuity?

"While they teach me to distrust the existence of virtue, they endeavour to impose on me, in its stead, a fictitious semblance; and to substitute, for the pure gold of truth, a paltry tinsel. It is in vain I ask — what have those to do with '*seeming*,' who still retain 'that which *passeth shew*?'[23] However my actions may be corrupted by the contagious example of the world, may I still hold fast my integrity, and disdain to wear the *appearance* of virtue, when the substance shall no longer exist.

"To admire, to esteem, to love, are congenial to my nature — I am unhappy, because these affections are not called into exercise. To venerate abstract perfection, requires too vigorous an exertion of the mental powers — I would see virtue exemplified, I would love it in my fellow creatures — I would catch the glorious enthusiasm, and rise from created to uncreated excellence.

"I am perplexed with doubts; relieve the wanderings of my mind, solve the difficulties by which it is agitated, prepare me for the world which is before me. The prospect, no longer beaming with light, no longer glowing with a thousand vivid hues, is overspread with mists, which the mind's eye vainly attempts to penetrate. I would feel, again, the value of existence, the worth of rectitude, the certainty of truth, the blessing of hope! Ah! tell me not — that the gay expectations of youth have been the meteors of fancy, the visions of a romantic and distempered imagination! If I must not live to realize them, I would not live at all.

"My harrassed mind turns to you! You will not ridicule its scruples — you will, at least, deign to reason with me, and, in the exercise of my understanding, I shall experience a temporary relief from the sensations which devour me, the suspicions that distress me, and which spread over futurity a fearful veil.

"EMMA."

I walked to the next market town, and left my letter at the

---

[23] *Hamlet*, I.2.86-87. "But I have that within which passeth shew."

post-house. — I waited impatiently for a reply; my mind wanted *impression*, and sunk into languor. The answer, which arrived in a few days, was kind, because it was prompt, my sickly mind required a speedy remedy.

TO EMMA COURTNEY.

"Why will you thus take things in masses, and continually dwell in extremes? You deceive yourself; instead of cultivating your reason, you are fostering an excessive sensibility, a fastidious delicacy. It is the business of reason to compare, to separate, to discriminate. Is there no medium — extraordinary exertions are only called forth by extraordinary contingencies; — because every human being is not a hero, are we then to distrust the existence of virtue?

"The mind is modified by the circumstances in which it is placed, by the accidents of birth and education; the constitutions of society are all, as yet, imperfect; they have generated, and perpetuated, many mistakes — the consequences of those mistakes will, eventually, carry with them their antidote, the seeds of reproduction are, even, visible in their decay. The growth of reason is slow, but not the less sure; the increase of knowledge must necessarily prepare the way for the increase of virtue and happiness.

"Look back upon the early periods of society, and, taking a retrospective view of what has been done, amidst the interruptions of barbarous inroads, falling empires, and palsying despotism, calculate what yet may be atchieved: while the causes, which have hitherto impeded the progress of civilization, must continue to decrease, in an accelerated ratio, with the wide, and still wider, diffusion of truth.

"We may trace most of the faults, and the miseries of mankind, to the vices and errors of political institutions, their permanency having been their radical defect. Like children, we have dreamt, that what gratifies our desires, or contributes to our convenience, to-day, will prove equally useful and satisfactory to-morrow, without reflecting on the growth of the body, the change of humours, the new objects, and the new situations, which every succeeding hour brings in its train. That immutability, which constitutes the perfection of what we (from poverty of language) term the *divine mind*, would inevitably be the bane of creatures liable to error; it is of the constancy, rather than of the fickleness, of human beings, that we have reason to complain.

"Every improvement must be the result of successive experiments, this has been found true in natural science, and it must be universally applied to be universally beneficial. Bigotry, whether religious, political, moral, or commercial, is the cankerworm at the root of the tree of knowledge and of virtue. The wildest speculations are less mischievous than the torpid state of error: he, who tamely resigns his understanding to the guidance of another, sinks at once, from the dignity of a rational being, to a mechanical puppet, moved at pleasure on the wires of the artful operator. — *Imposition* is the principle and support of every varied description of tyranny, whether civil or ecclesiastical, moral or mental; its baneful consequence is to degrade both him who is imposed on, and him who imposes. *Obedience*, is a word, which ought never to have had existence: as we recede from conviction, and languidly resign ourselves to any foreign authority, we quench the principle of action, of virtue, of reason; — we bear about the semblance of humanity, but the spirit is fled.

"These are truths, which will slowly, but ultimately, prevail; in the splendour of which, the whole fabric of superstition will gradually fade and melt away. The world, like every individual, has its progress from infancy to maturity — How many follies do we commit in childhood? how many errors are we precipitated into by the fervor and inexperience of youth! Is not every stable principle acquired through innumerable mistakes — can you wonder, that in society, amidst the aggregate of jarring interests and passions, reformation is so tardy? Though civilization has been impeded by innumerable obstacles, even these help to carry on the great work: empires may be overturned, and the arts scattered, but not lost. The hordes of barbarians, which overwhelmed ancient Rome, adopted at length the religion, the laws, and the improvements of the vanquished, as Rome had before done those of Greece. As the stone, which, thrown into the water, spreads circles still more and more extended; — or (to adopt the gospel similitude) as the grain of mustard seed, growing up into a large tree, shelters the fowls of heaven in its branches[24] — so will knowledge, at length, diffuse itself, till it covers the whole earth.

"When the minds of men are changed, the system of things will also change; but these changes, though active and incessant, must be gradual. Reason will fall softly, and almost imperceptibly, like a gentle shower of dews, fructifying the soil, and preparing it for future harvests. Let us not resemble the ambitious shepherd, who, calling for the accumulated waters of the Nile upon his lands, was, with his flock, swept away in the impetuous torrent.[25]

"You ask, whether — because human beings are still imperfect — you are to resign your benevolence, and to cherish misanthropy? What a question! Would you hate the inmates of an hospital for being infected with a pestilential disorder? Let us remember, that vice originates in mistakes of the understanding, and that, he who seeks happiness by means contradictory and destructive, *is emphatically the sinner.* Our duties, then, are obvious — If selfish and violent passions have been generated by the inequalities of society, we must labour to counteract them, by endeavouring to combat prejudice, to expand the mind, to give comprehensive views, to teach mankind their true interest, and to lead them to habits of goodness and greatness. Every prejudice conquered, every mistake rectified, every individual improved, is an advance upon the great scale of virtue and happiness.

---

[24] Matthew 13:31.

[25] This may be a reference to a Biblical tale, likely from the Jewish scriptures or Christian Old testament. Anne Finch, Countess of Winchilsea has a curiously relevant poem, "The Shepherd and the Calm" in which an ambitious shepherd changes his profession, goes to sea, and loses everything in a storm.

"Let it, then, be your noblest ambition to co-operate with, to join your efforts, to those of philosophers and sages, the benefactors of mankind. To waste our time in useless repinings is equally weak and vain; every one in his sphere may do something; each has a little circle where his influence will be availing. Correct your own errors, which are various — weeds in a luxuriant soil — and you will have done something towards the general reformation. But you are able to do more; — be vigilant, be active, beware of the illusions of fancy! I suspect, that you will have much to suffer — may you, at length, reap the fruits of a wholesome, though it should be a bitter, experience.

" ——Francis."

I perused the letter, I had received, again and again; it awakened a train of interesting reflections, and my spirits became tranquillized.

English Jacobins and Jacobinism

Mr. Francis's letter, taken in part from the writings and letters of William Godwin, advocates reforms and philosophical views proposed by the so-called English "Jacobins." English reformers were inspired by the ideals of the French *Philosophes*—such as Voltaire, Montesquieu, and Rousseau— and energized by the Revolution in France to promote social and political reforms in Britain.

The French Revolution began officially in 1789 with the fall of the Bastille prison, an infamous and ancient building where political prisoners were immured and often forgotten. English people generally celebrated the beginnings of the French Revolution, viewing France's long history of tension between the monarch and the aristocracy and lack of a substantial "middling sort," as exemplifying extreme and arbitrary rule. Particularly abhorrent to the British was the system of *lettres de cachet*, or secret letters by which a person could be accused of a political crime and imprisoned for life with no trial or hearing required. The Bastille, significantly, held just such political prisoners, and was thus symbolic of the despotism of the *lettres de cachet*. By contrast, Britain was proud of its legal trial system and its conception of a constitutional balance between Parliament and monarch. Eighteenth-century Britain understood itself through John Locke's version of the "social contract," which based government in the agreement of the people to be so governed to the benefit of all. Locke's conception of the purpose of government is the guarantee of "life, liberty, and property," a phrase familiar to Americans in Thomas Jefferson's reworking in the American Declaration of Independence as the right to "life, liberty, and the pursuit of happiness." By contrast, as the British saw it, the French government was autocratic, secretive, unbalanced, and ripe for a change.

In 1790, Edmund Burke disassociated himself from mainstream British opinion when he wrote *Reflections on the Revolution in France*, ostensibly in the form of an extended letter to a young Frenchman who, knowing that Burke had supported the rebellion of the American colonists, assumed that he must also support the uprisings in France. To the contrary, Burke argued that the French Revolution was an insidious and destructive event, and that he feared that the heady and ill-conceived ideas of the "rights of man" would destroy all that was admirable about the British system of governance as well. Burke's opposition elicited several responses, among the most famous being Thomas Paine's *Rights of Man* published in 1792. Mary Wollstonecraft wrote one of the very first responses, *A Vindication of the Rights of Man* in 1790. Both Paine and Wollstonecraft took issue with key points of Burke's *Reflections*. Paine argued that it was ludicrous to suppose that the contract between subject and state presumed by Britain's constitution could be a perpetual contract, made for each subject before his (or her) birth and established for all time. Paine argued that no man can make a contract for another, especially not before his birth, and so the social contract must be renewed and remade with each successive generation. If a government fails to live up to its part of the contract, the people under it have the right and even the duty to resist and to refuse their allegiance. Wollstonecraft particularly attacked Burke's sentimental glorification of Marie Antoinette, his chivalrous defense of her beauty and modesty, and his disgust with the French peasants and prostitutes he imagined as the leaders of the Revolutionary faction. All three works were widely read and debated in both public meetings and more domestic settings.

By 1793 the French Revolution had become increasingly violent, and England was terrified of the possible consequences. The beheading of first King Louis XVI, and later his wife, Marie Antoinette, in 1792 after more than a year's imprisonment, reminded Britons unpleasantly of their own regicide in 1649, and popular opinion began to swing against the French Revolution. 1793 was also the year of the "Terror" in France, a particularly bloody period of mass beheadings by guillotine in public squares, instigated by the infamous Robespierre and the other members of the French "Jacobins" or Montagnard faction. Further, France declared war on Britain and made explicit their intention to export Revolution to other countries in Europe as the champions of the "rights of man."

English sympathizers of the original principles of the French Revolution were thus caught in a precarious position. On the one hand, Burke's *Reflections* alarmed readers and came to seem prescient as events in France became progressively more violent and antagonistic to their monarchical neighbors. On the other hand, works by firsthand observers like Mary Wollstonecraft (*Moral History of the French Revolution*) and Helen Maria Williams (*Letters Written in France*) offered English readers a more complex and optimistic view of the ultimate outcome of the revolutionary struggle. But beginning in 1792, the more moderate political party in France, the Girondins (with whom most English reformers were connected), was losing power to the more extreme Jacobins. Many prominent Girondins were guillotined, and even English radicals like Helen Maria Williams and Mary Wollstonecraft were either imprisoned or fled Paris to live in less politically volatile towns. Wollstonecraft passed for the wife of her American lover, Gilbert Imlay, in part to avoid imprisonment as a citizen of a hostile nation. As the decade progressed and as French nobles emigrated to Britain with tales of losing lands and privileges, popular sentiment emphasized the instability and poverty of France in opposition to a stable, balanced, and common-sensical British character.

The nuances of different factions in France were mostly lost in Britain, particularly after war between the two nations was declared in 1793. Thus, British reformers who were associated with a sympathetic view of the French Revolution, even with an abstract interest in the ideas of human liberty with which it had begun, came to be known derogatorily as "English Jacobins" rather than as associates of the Girondin party. This terminology is still common among scholars of the period. The "English Jacobins" were really a diverse and eclectic group of writers, speakers, and political figures who were concerned with various kinds of political reform. Male political figures like Thomas Hardy,[26] John Thelwall, and John Horne Tooke were best known for their activities with political groups such as the London Corresponding Society and the Society for Constitutional Information, both groups agitating for parliamentary reform and seeking to educate the general public. Male writers like William Godwin, Thomas Holcroft, and Thomas Paine were known for writing, publishing, and popularizing political and economic ideas, and in the case of Godwin and Holcroft, for their novels and plays as well. Women writers like Mary Wollstonecraft, Elizabeth Inchbald, and Mary Hays wrote in many genres, including fiction, political tracts, educa-

---

[26] No relation to the important later nineteenth-century novelist of the same name.

tional works, letters and essays, and histories. Women also were particularly liable to becoming known for their personal lives; their misadventures could be and were used to discredit their writings and their propriety as public figures.

Among British radical men's groups, issues for reform ranged from calling for annual elections to Parliament (the current term of 7 years, they felt, was too open to abuse), seeking to expand the franchise by lowering property requirements and even moving from requirements for land ownership to include wealthy merchants who did not own country estates, agitating for salaries for members of the House of Commons (so that men who were not independently wealthy could consider political office as a career), and doing away with so-called "rotten boroughs" or areas in which a single land-owner essentially had the gift of seats in Parliament and could sell them to the highest bidder. More radical proposals were mooted in political philosophical works such as William Godwin's *Enquiry Concerning Political Justice* (1793), which argued that when men were wholly rational and no longer motivated by self-interest and irrational prejudices, government would cease to be necessary. Godwin was opposed to promises and oaths, arguing that one's duty to do right superceded any oath: if one ought to do something, an oath could not make it more binding, and if one ought not to do something an oath was itself a sign of error. Women radicals like Mary Hays and Mary Wollstonecraft drew on the idea that all people are born with natural rights to education, productive labor, and self-determination to examine the situation of women, barred from most real education, many kinds of labor, and legally subject to their husbands as property after marriage and to their fathers before marriage. While male radicals questioned whether a son always owed a duty to his father, even if the father behaved in a tyrannical and oppressive manner, female radicals expanded this concern to argue that women ought likewise to be allowed to exercise their own rational capabilities in making their own choices about their "partner for life" in marriage.

While questioning the extent to which a child owes implicit obedience to his or her parents seems on the surface an exclusively domestic issue, and thus the proper subject of women's novels dealing with familial arrangements and romantic love, because the conception of the nation-state drew an analogy between the structure of the patriarchal family and the monarchical nation, such topics were politically loaded. If British subjects ought properly to think of their king as like the father of his nation, then novels which questioned the duty of a daughter to her father (or even her mother) were implicitly questioning national political arrangements. That British readers in the late 1700s and early 1800s understood this, is clear by the strong reactions and debates such novels provoked.

SOURCES

Edmund Burke, *Reflections on the Revolution in France* (1790). Vol. 2, *Select Works of Edmund Burke*. New Imprint of the Payne Edition (1875) (Indianapolis, IN: Liberty Fund, 1999).

Marilyn Butler, *Burke, Paine, Godwin, and the Revolution Controversy* (Cambridge: Cambridge University Press, 1984).

Carl B. Cone, *The English Jacobins: Reformers in Later 18th Century England* (NY: Charles Scribner's Sons, 1968).

Albert Goodwin, *The Friends of Liberty: The English Democratic Movement in the Age of the French Revolution* (Cambridge, MA: Harvard University Press, 1979).

Gary Kelly, *The English Jacobin Novel 1780-1805* (Oxford: Clarendon Press, 1976).

CHAP. XVI.

EARLY one fine morning, Ann tapped gently at the door of my chamber; I had already risen, and invited her to enter.

"Would I accompany her to breakfast, with a widow lady, who resided in a village about two miles from Morton Park, an occasional visitant in the family, a lady with whom, she was certain, I should be charmed."

I smiled at her ardour, thanked her for her kindness, and readily agreed to her proposal. We strolled together through an adjacent wood, which, by a shady and winding path, conducted us towards the residence of this vaunted favourite of my little companion.

On our way, she entertained me with a slight sketch of the history of Mrs. Harley and her family. She was the widow of a merchant, who was supposed to possess great property; but, practising occasionally as an underwriter, a considerable capture by the enemy (during war time) of some rich ships, reduced his fortune;[27] and, by the consequent anxiety, completely destroyed a before debilitated constitution. He died in a few weeks after the confirmation of his loss, and, having neglected to make a will, a freehold estate of some value,[28] which was all that remained of his effects, devolved of course to his eldest son; his two younger sons and three daughters being left wholly unprovided for. Augustus Harley, the heir, immediately sold the estate, and divided the produce, in equal shares, between each individual of the family. His brothers had been educated for commerce, and were enabled, through the generous kindness of Augustus, to carry on, with advantage and reputation, their respective occupations; the sisters were, soon after, eligibly married. Augustus, who had been educated for the law, disgusted with its chicanery, relinquished the profession, content to re-

---

[27] Mr. Harley uses his capital to insure the outcomes of other merchants' expeditions, a risky but potentially very profitable way to make money without himself venturing on dangerous sea voyages. Dangers to mercantile ventures included not only shipwreck or storms which might force a crew to throw cargo overboard, but also piracy by sailors of hostile countries, something in which English sailors also engaged.

[28] A freehold estate could be inherited with no obligation to any other possible heirs. Thus, Augustus, as the eldest son by the law of primogeniture, inherits the estate and its incomes entirely for himself, with no obligation to share any of it with his siblings or his father's widow.

strain his expenses within the limits of a narrow income. This income had since received an increase, by the bequest of a distant relation, a man of a whimsical character, who had married, early in life, a beautiful woman, for love; but his wife having eloped from him with an officer, and, in the course of the intrigue, practised a variety of deceptions, he had retired disgusted from society, cherishing a misanthropical spirit: and, on his decease, bequeathed an annual sum of four hundred pounds to Augustus Harley, (to whom in his childhood he had been particularly attached) on condition of his remaining unmarried. On his marriage, or death, this legacy passed into another branch of the family. On this acquisition Augustus determined on making the tour of Europe; and, after travelling on the continent for three years, on his return to his native country, alternately resided, either in the village of ——, with his mother, or in the metropolis, where he divided his time, between liberal studies, and rational recreation. His visits to the country had, of late, been shorter and less frequent: he was the idol of his mother, and universally respected by his acquaintance, for his noble and generous conduct. — "Ah!" (added the lively narrator) "could you but see Augustus Harley, you would, infallibly, lose your heart — so frank, so pleasant, so ingenuous are his manners, so intrepid, and yet so humane! Montague is a fine gentleman, but Augustus Harley is more — *he is a man!*"

She began to grow eloquent on this, apparently, exhaustless theme, nor did she cease her panegyric till we came in view of Mrs. Harley's mansion.

"You will love the mother as well as the son," continued this agreeable prattler, "when you come to know her; she is very good and very sensible."

Drawing near the house, she tripped from me, to enquire if its mistress had yet risen.

A small white tenement, half obscured in shrubbery, on a verdant lawn, of dimensions equally modest, situated on the side of a hill, and commanding an extensive and variegated prospect, was too interesting and picturesque an object, not to engage for some moments my attention. The image of Augustus, also, which my lively companion had pourtrayed with more than her usual vivacity, played in my fancy — my heart paid involuntary homage to virtue, and I entered the mansion of Mrs. Harley with a swelling emotion, made up of complicated feelings — half respectful, half tender — sentiments, too mingled to be distinctly traced. I was introduced into a room that overlooked a pleasant garden, and which the servant called a library. It was hung with green paper, the carpet the same colour, green venetian blinds to the windows, a sopha and chairs covered with white dimity; some drawings and engravings hung on the walls, arranged with exact symmetry; on one side of the room stood a grand piano-forte, opposite to which, was a handsome book-case, filled with books, elegantly bound; in the middle of the apartment was placed a table, covered with a green cloth, on which was a reading desk, some books and pamphlets, with implements for writing and drawing. Nothing seemed costly, yet neatness, order, and taste, appeared through the whole apartment, bespeaking the elegant and cultivated mind of the owner.

After amusing myself for a short time, in this charming retirement, I was summoned by Ann to the breakfast room, where Mrs. Harley awaited me. I was interested, at the first glance, in favour of this amiable woman — she appeared to be near fifty, her person agreeable, her countenance animated, her address engaging, and her manners polished. Mutually pleased with each other, the hours passed rapidly; and, till reminded by a significant look from my little friend, I was unconscious, that I had made my visit of an unreasonable length.

Mrs. Harley spoke much of her son, he was the darling and the pride of her heart; she lamented the distance that separated them, and wished, that her health, and his tenderness, would allow of her residence with him in London. When conversing on this favourite topic, a glow enlivened her countenance, and her eyes sparkled with a humid brightness. I was affected by her maternal love — tender remembrances, and painful comparisons, crouded into my mind — a tear fell, that would not be twinkled away — she observed it, and seemed to feel its meaning; she held out her hand to me, I took it and pressed it to my lips. At parting, she entreated me speedily to renew my visit, to come often without ceremony — I should cheer her solitude — my sympathy, for she perceived I had a feeling heart, would help to console her in the absence of her Augustus.

Chap. XVII.

On our way home, Ann was in high spirits, congratulating herself upon her sagacity.

"Mrs. Harley," (said she, archly leering in my face) "will console you for the departure of Mr. Francis."

I smiled without replying. At dinner our visit of the morning was canvassed (Ann had wished me to conceal it, but this I positively refused). Mr. Morton spoke of Mrs. Harley and her son with great respect, Mrs. Morton with a sarcastic sneer, accompanied with a reprimand to her daughter, for the improper liberty she had taken.

I quitted the table, immediately after the dessert, to stifle my disgust, and, taking a book, wandered into the pleasure grounds, but incapable of fixing my attention, I presently shut my book, and, sauntering slowly on, indulged in a reverie. My melancholy reflections again returned — How could I remain in a house, where I was every day marked out for insult by its mistress — and where was I to dispose of myself? My fortune was insufficient to allow of my boarding in a respectable family. Mrs. Harley came across my mind —— Amiable woman! — Would she, indeed, accept of my society, and allow me to soften her solitude! — But her income was little less limited than my own — it must not be thought of. I reflected on the inequalities of society, the source of every misery and of every vice, and on the peculiar disadvantages of my sex. I sighed bitterly; and, clasping my hands together, exclaimed, unconsciously —

"Whither can I go — and where shall I find an asylum?"

"Allow me to propose one," said a voice, in a soft accent,

suddenly, behind me.

I started, turned, and beheld Mr. Montague. After some expressions of sympathy for the distress which he had witnessed, apologies for his intrusion, and incoherent expressions of respect and regard, he somewhat abruptly offered his hand and heart to my acceptance, with the impetuosity which accompanied all his sentiments and actions; yet, he expressed himself with the air of a man who believes he is conferring an obligation. I thanked him for his generous proposal —

But, as my heart spake not in his favour — "I must be allowed to decline it."

"That heart," said he, rudely, "is already bestowed upon another."

"Certainly not, Mr. Montague; if it were, I would frankly tell you."

He pronounced the name of Mr. Francis —

"Mr. Francis is a man for whom I feel a sincere respect and veneration — a man whom I should be proud to call my friend; but a thought beyond that, I dare venture to say, has never occurred to either of us."

He knew not how to conceive — that a woman in my situation, unprepossessed, could reject so advantageous an establishment!

This, I told him, was indelicate, both to me and to himself. Were my situation yet more desolate, I would not marry any man, merely for an *establishment*, for whom I did not feel an affection.

Would I please to describe to him the model of perfection which I should require in a husband?

It was unnecessary; as I saw no probability of the portrait bearing any resemblance to himself.

He reddened, and turned pale, alternately; bit his lips, and muttered to himself. — "Damned romantic affectation!"

I assumed a firmer tone — methought he insulted me. — "I beg you will leave me, Sir — I chuse to be alone — By what right do you intrude upon my retirements?"

My determined accent abashed him: — he tried, but with an ill grace, to be humble; and entreated me to take time for consideration.

"There is no need of it. It is a principle with me, not to inflict a moment's suspence on any human being, when my own mind is decided."

"Then you absolutely refuse me, and prefer the being exposed to the mean and envious insults of the vulgar mistress of this mansion!"

"Of the two evils, I consider it as the least, because it involves no permanent obligation."

His countenance was convulsed with passion. His love, he told me, was converted into vengeance by my scorn: he was not to be contemned with impunity; and he warned me to beware.

I smiled, I believe, a little too contemptuously. "You love me not, Sir: I am glad, for your own sake, that you never loved me."

"My hatred may be more terrible!"

"You cannot intimidate me —— I am little accustomed to fear."

I turned from him somewhat disdainfully: but, instantly recollecting myself, I stepped back, and apologized for the harsh manner into which I had been betrayed by his abrupt address, vehement expostulation, and the previous irritated state of my mind.

"I acknowledge," said I, "the disinterestedness of your proposal, and the *distinction* which it implies. Will you allow my own wounded feelings to be an excuse for the too little consideration with which I have treated *your's*? Can you forgive me?" added I, in a conciliating tone, holding out my hand.

The strong emotions, which rapidly succeeded each other in his mind, were painted in his countenance. After a moment's hesitation, he snatched the hand I offered him, pressed it to his lips, and, murmuring a few incoherent words, burst into tears. My spirits were already depressed — affected by these marks of his sensibility, and still more distressed by the recollection of the pain I had occasioned him by my inconsiderate behaviour, I wept with him for some minutes in silence.

"Let us no more," resumed I, making an effort to recover myself, "renew these impressions. I thank you sincerely for the sympathy you have manifested for my situation. I am sensible that I have yielded to weak and wayward feelings. — I have youth, health, and activity — I ought not — neither do I despair. — The mortifications I have experienced, since my residence here, will afford me a useful lesson for the future — they have already taught me, what I before merely conjectured, *the value of independence!*"

"Why, then," interrupted he with quickness, "do you reject an opportunity of placing yourself out of the reach of insult?"

"Stop, my good friend," replied I, smilingly looking in his face; "there is a possibility of exchanging evils. You are yet too young, and too unstable, maturely to have weighed the importance of the scheme you propose. Remember, likewise, that you are, yourself, in a great measure, dependent on the will of your father; and that much reflection is requisite before we fetter ourselves with engagements, that, once entered into, are not easily dissolved."

"You allow me, then, to hope!"

"Indeed I meant not to imply any such thing. I wish to soften what I have already expressed — but, there are a variety of reasons which oblige me to assure you, that I see no probability of changing my sentiments on the subject."

"Why, then, this cruel ostentation? I would either love or hate, bless or curse you."

"You shall do neither, if I can prevent it. If my esteem is of any value to you, you must learn to respect both me and yourself."

"Esteem! — Is that to be my frigid reward!"

"If *mine* be worthless, propose to yourself *your own* as a recompense."

"I have already forfeited it, by seeking to move a heart, that triumphs in its cold inflexibility."

"Is this just — is it kind? Is it, indeed, *my welfare* you seek, while you can thus add to the vexations and embarrassment, which were before sufficiently oppressive? I would preserve you from an act of precipitation and imprudence; — in return, you load me with unmerited reproaches. But it is time to put an end to a conversation, that can answer little other purpose than vain recrimination."

He was about to speak —— "Say no more — I feel myself, again, in danger of losing my temper — my spirits are agitated — I would not give you pain — Allow me to retire, and be assured of my best wishes."

Some of the family appearing in sight, as if advancing towards us, favoured my retreat. I quitted the place with precipitation, and retired to my chamber, where I sought, by employing myself, to calm the perturbation of my heart.

CHAP. XVIII.

IN a few days I renewed my visit to Mrs. Harley: — a strong sympathy united us, and we became almost inseparable. Every day I discovered in this admirable woman a new and indissoluble tie, that bound me to her. Her cultivated understanding afforded an inexhaustible fund of instruction and entertainment; and her affectionate heart spread a charm over her most indifferent actions. We read, we walked, we conversed together; but, with whatever subjects these conversations commenced, some associated idea always led them to terminate in an eulogium on the virtues and talents, or an expression of regret, for the absence of Augustus. There was a portrait of him (drawn by a celebrated artist, which he had lately sent from town as a present to his mother) hung up in the library. I accustomed myself to gaze on this resemblance of a man, in whose character I felt so lively an interest, till, I fancied I read in the features all the qualities imputed to the original by a tender and partial parent.

Cut off from the society of mankind, and unable to expound my sensations, all the strong affections of my soul seemed concentrated to a single point. Without being conscious of it myself, my grateful love for Mrs. Harley had, already, by a transition easy to be traced by a philosophic mind, transferred itself to her son. He was the St. Preux, the Emilius,[29] of my sleeping and waking reveries. I now spent almost my whole time in the cottage of my friend, returning to Morton Park late in the evening, and quitting it early in the morning, and sometimes being wholly absent for weeks together.

Six months thus passed away in tranquillity, with but little variation. Mr. Montague, during this period, had several times left Mr. Morton's, and returned again abruptly: his manners became sullen, and even, at times, ferocious. I carefully avoided encountering him, fearful of exasperating a spirit, that appeared every moment on the verge of excess.

Hastening one evening to my friend, after a longer separation than common, (having been prevailed on by Mr. Morton and his daughters to accompany them on a distant visit, where business of Mr. Morton's detained us for some days) I ran into the library, as usual, and threw myself into the arms of Mrs. Harley, that opened spontaneously to receive me.

"Ah! you little truant," said she, in a voice of kindness, "where have you been so long? My son has visited me in your absence; he passed through this part of this country, in his way to the seat of a friend. He staid with me two days, during which I sent half a dozen messages to Morton Park, but you were flown away, it seems, nor could I learn any tidings of you. Augustus," continued she, without observing the emotions she excited, "had scarcely quitted the house an hour when you arrived."

I made no reply; an unaccountable sensation seized, and oppressed, my heart — sinking on the sopha, I burst into a convulsive flood of tears.

My friend was struck: all the indiscretion of her conduct (as she has since told me) flashed suddenly into her mind; she felt that, in indulging her own maternal sensations, she had, per-

---

[29] The idealized heroes of Jean-Jacques Rousseau's *Julie* and *Émile* respectively.

haps, done me an irreparable injury, and she shuddered at the probable consequences. It was some moments before either of us recovered; — our conversation was that evening, for the first time, constrained, reserved, and painful; and we retired at an early hour to our respective apartments.

I spent the night in self-examination. I was compelled to acknowledge, to myself, that solitude, the absence of other impressions, the previous circumstances that had operated on my character, my friendship for Mrs. Harley, and her eloquent, affectionate, reiterated, praises of her son, had combined to awaken all the exquisite, though dormant, sensibilities of my nature; and, however romantic it might appear to others, and did appear even to myself, I felt, that I loved an ideal object (for such was Augustus Harley to me) with a tender and fervent excess; an excess, perhaps, involving all my future usefulness and welfare. 'People, in general,' says Rousseau, 'do not sufficiently consider the influence which the first attachments, between man and woman, have over the remainder of their lives; they do not perceive, that an impression so strong, and so lively, as that of love, is productive of a long chain of effects, which pass unobserved in a course of years, yet, nevertheless, continue to operate till the day of their deaths.'[30] It was in vain I attempted to combat this illusion; my reason was but an auxiliary to my passion, it persuaded me, that I was only doing justice to high and uncommon worth; imagination lent her aid, and an importunate sensibility, panting after good unalloyed, completed the seduction.

From this period Mrs. Harley was more guarded in her conduct; she carefully avoided the mention of her son. — Under pretence of having an alteration made in the frame, she removed his picture from the library; but the constraint she put upon herself was too evident and painful; we no longer sought, with equal ardour, an interchange of sentiment, reserve took place of the tender confidence of friendship; a thousand times, while I

[30] Rousseau, *Émile*, transl. Barbara Foxley (Rutland, VT: Everyman, 1974), Book V, p. 378.

gazed upon her dear averted countenance, I yearned to throw myself upon her bosom, to weep, to unfold to her the inmost recesses of my mind — that ingenuous mind, which languished for communication, and preyed upon itself! Dear and cruel friend, why did you transfix my heart with the barbed and envenomed arrow, and then refuse to administer the only healing balsam?

My visits to Mrs. Harley became less frequent; I shut myself up whole days in my apartment, at Morton Park, or wandered through its now leafless groves, absorbed in meditation — fostering the sickly sensibility of my soul, and nursing wild, improbable, chimerical, visions of felicity, that, touched by the sober wand of truth, would have 'melted into thin air.'[31] 'The more desires I have (observes an acute, and profound French Philosopher[32]) the less ardent they are. The torrents that divide themselves into many branches, are the least dangerous in their course. A strong passion is a solitary passion, that concentrates all our desires within one point.'

Chap. XIX.

I had not seen my friend for many days, when, on a dark and stormy night, in the month of January, between nine and ten o'clock, the family at Morton Park were alarmed, by a loud and violent knocking at the hall door.

On opening it, a servant appeared — and a chaise, the porter having unbolted the great gates, drew up to the door. The man delivered a note addressed to Miss Courtney. I was unacquainted with the hand writing, and unfolded it with trepidation. It contained but a few lines, written in a female character, and signed with the name of a lady, who resided about twelve miles from Morton Park, at whose house Mrs. Harley sometimes made a visit of a few days. It stated —

'That my friend was seized at the mansion of this lady with an apoplectic fit, from which she had been restored, after some

[31] William Shakepeare, *The Tempest*, IV.i.150.
[32] "Helvetius." [M.H.] from *The Treatise on Man*.

hours of insensibility: that the physicians were apprehensive of a relapse, and that Mrs. Harley had expressed a desire of seeing Miss Courtney — A carriage and servants were sent for her conveyance.'

Mr. Morton was from home, his lady made no offer of any of her own domestics to accompany me. Montague, who had been at the Park for some days past, solicited permission to be my escort. I hesitated a moment, and would willingly have declined this proposal, but he repeated and enforced it with a vehemence, that, in the present hurried state of my mind, I had not spirits to oppose. Shocked, alarmed, distressed, I wrapped a shawl round me, and sprang into the chaise. Montague stepped in after me, and seated himself by my side; the horses galloped, or rather flew down the avenue, that led to the high road.

We travelled with great swiftness, and in uninterrupted silence, for some miles: the darkness was so thick and profound, that I could not discover the road we took, and I began to feel very impatient to arrive at the place of our destination. I questioned my companion respecting his knowledge of our situation, and expressed an apprehension, that we might possibly have missed the way. He made no reply to my interrogation, but, starting as if from a reverie, seized my hand, while his own trembled with a visible agitation, and began once more to urge a suit, which I had hoped the steadiness and consistency of my conduct had induced him entirely to relinquish.

"Is this a time, Mr. Montague, for an address of this nature — do you believe, that my favour is to be gained by these proofs of inconsideration? Have some respect for the claims of humanity and friendship, and, in seeking my affection, do not forfeit my esteem."

He was about to reply, and I could perceive by the few words which he uttered, and by the tone of his voice, that he struggled, in vain, to rein in his quick and irascible spirit; when, in turning a sharp angle of the road, the horses took fright at some object, indistinctly seen, and ran precipitately down a steep hill, with a velocity that threatened destruction.

My companion, forcing open the door, seemed inclined to leap from the carriage, but hesitated, as if unwilling to desert me in so imminent a danger; I exhorted him to think only of providing for his own safety, and, letting down the glasses on the side on which I sat, I resigned myself to my fate. In springing from the chaise, by some means, Montague entangled his coat in the step — he fell, without clearing it, and I felt, with a horror that congealed my blood, the wheel go over him. In a few minutes, I perceived a traveller, at the risque of his own life, endeavouring to stop the horses — the pole of the chaise striking him with great force, he was obliged to relinquish his humane efforts — but this impediment occasioning the restive animals to turn out of the road, they ran furiously up a bank, and overset the carriage. I felt it going, and sitting, with my arms folded, close in the lower corner, fell with it, without attempting to struggle, by which means I escaped unhurt.

The stranger, once more, came to our assistance, and, the mettle of the horses being now pretty well exhausted, my deliverer was enabled to cut the traces,[33] and then hastened to extricate me from my perilous situation. It was some time before I recovered myself sufficiently to thank him for his humanity, and to assure him, that I had received no other injury than from my fears. I then mentioned to him, my apprehensions for the fate of my fellow traveller, entreating that he would return with me in search of him. With this request he immediately complied, leaving the horses in the care of the servants, neither of which had received any material hurt.

We soon discovered the unfortunate Montague, lying in the road, in a melancholy situation: the wheel had gone over one of his legs, the bone of which was broken and splintered in a terrible manner, and, having fainted from the pain, we were at first apprehensive that he was already dead. Turning from this shocking spectacle, a faint sickness overspread my heart, the stranger

---

[33] He cuts the leather straps which bind the horses to the carriage.

supported me in his arms, while a violent burst of tears preserved me from swooning. My companion examining the body, perceived signs of life, and, by our united efforts, sense and recollection were soon restored.

I remained with Montague while the stranger returned to the carriage, to enquire what damages it had received, and whether it was in a condition to proceed to the next village, which, the postilion[34] informed him, was near two miles from the spot where the accident had happened, and we were, yet, five miles from the place whither we were going. The axle-tree and one of the hind wheels, upon examination, were found broken, the traces had been cut in pieces, and the horses, had the chaise been in a better condition, were so unmanageable, in consequence of their late fright, that it would have been dangerous to have attempted putting them again into harness.

With this intelligence our kind friend came back to us — We held a short consultation, on the means most proper to be adopted, and, at length it was determined, that, after placing Montague in the carriage, where he would be sheltered from the inclemency of the elements, and leaving him in the charge of the servants, the traveller and myself should walk onward to the village, and send a chaise, or litter, for the conveyance of our unfortunate companion.

To this proposal Montague assented, at the same time, declaring it to be his intention, to proceed directly across the country, to the house of his father, which could not, he conjectured, be at any great distance, and where he should be assured of meeting with greater attention, and more skilful assistance, than at a petty inn, in a paltry village. Having thus adjusted our plan, and, with the help of the servants, carefully placed Montague in the chaise, we proceeded towards the village.

---

[34] One of the drivers of a carriage who usually rides one of the horses pulling the carriage. On a small chaise such as this with only two horses, the postilion might be the sole driver.

Chap. XX.

THE night was tempestuous, and, though the moon was now rising, her light was every moment obscured by dark clouds, discharging frequent and heavy showers of rain, accompanied by furious gusts of wind. After walking near a mile we entered upon a wide heath, which afforded no shelter from the weather. I perceived my companion's steps began to grow feeble, and his voice faint. The moon suddenly emerging from a thick cloud, I observed his countenance, and methought his features seemed familiar to me; but they were over-spread by a palid and death-like hue. He stopped suddenly ——

"I am very ill," said he, in a tone of voice that penetrated into my soul, "and can proceed no further."

He sunk upon the turf. Seating myself beside him, while his head fell on my shoulder, I threw around him my supporting arms. His temples were bedewed with a cold sweat, and he appeared to be in expiring agonies. A violent sickness succeeded, followed by an hemorrhage.

"Gracious God!" I exclaimed, "you have broken a blood vessel!"

"I fear so," he replied. "I have felt strangely disordered since the blow I received from the pole of the carriage; but, till this moment, I have not been at leisure to attend to my sensations."

"Do not talk," cried I, wildly; "do not exhaust yourself."

Again the clouds gathered; an impetuous gust of wind swept over the heath, and the rain fell in torrents. Unconscious what I did, I clasped the stranger to my throbbing bosom, — the coldness of death seemed upon him — I wrapped my shawl around him, vainly attempting to screen him from the piercing blast. He spake not; my terrified imagination already represented him as a lifeless corpse; I sat motionless for some minutes, in the torpor of despair.

From this horrible situation, I was, at length, roused, by the sound of a distant team: breathless, I listened for a few moments; I again distinctly heard it wafted upon the wind; when, gently reclining my charge on the grass, I started from the ground, and ran swiftly towards the highway. The sound approached, and the clouds once more breaking, and discovering a watery moon-light gleam, I perceived, with joy, a waggon loaded with hay. I bounded over a part of the turf that still separated me from the road, and accosting the driver, explained to him, in a few words, as much of my situation as was necessary; and, entreating his assistance, allured him by the hope of a reward.

We returned together to my patient: he raised his head on my approach, and attempted to speak; but, enjoining him silence, he took my hand, and, by a gentle pressure, expressed his sense of my cares more eloquently than by words. I assisted the countryman in supporting him to the road. We prepared for him, in the waggon, a soft bed of hay, upon which we placed him; and, resting his head on my lap, we proceeded gently to the nearest village. On our arrival at an indifferent inn, I ordered a bed to be immediately prepared for him, and sent a man and horse express, to the next town, for medical assistance: at the same time, relating in brief the accidents of the night, I dispatched a carriage for the relief of Montague, who was conveyed, according to his wishes, to the house of his father.

Notwithstanding all my precautions, the moving brought on a relapse of the alarming symptoms; the discharge of blood returned with aggravated violence, and, when the physician arrived, there appeared in the unfortunate sufferer but little signs of life; but by the application of styptics and cordials he once more began to revive; and, about five in the morning, I was prevailed on, by the joint efforts of the landlady and the humane Dr. —— , to resign my seat at the bed's head to a careful servant, and to recruit my exhausted strength by a few hours' repose.

The vivid impressions, which had so rapidly succeeded each other in my mind, for some time kept me waking, in a state of feverish agitation; but my harrassed spirits were at length relieved by wearied nature's kind restorer, and I slept for four hours profoundly.

On waking, my first enquiry was after my companion, in

whose fate I felt an unusual degree of interest; and I heard, with pleasure, that the hemorrhage had not returned; that he had rested with apparent tranquillity, and appeared revived. I dressed myself hastily, and passed into his apartment: he faintly smiled on perceiving my approach, and gave me his hand. — The physician had ordered him to be kept quiet, and I would not suffer him to speak; but, contemplating more attentively his countenance, which had the night before struck me with a confused recollection — what were my emotions, on tracing the beloved features of Augustus Harley! His resemblance, not only to the portrait, but to his mother, could not, as I thought, be mistaken. A universal trembling seized me — I hastened out of the apartment with tottering steps, and shutting myself into my chamber, a tide of melancholy emotions gushed upon my heart. I wept, without knowing wherefore, tears half delicious, half agonizing! Quickly coming to myself, I returned to the chamber of my patient, (now more tenderly endeared) which, officiating as a nurse for five days, I never quitted, except to take necessary rest and refreshment.

I had written to Mr. Morton a minute account of all that happened, merely suppressing the name of my deliverer: to this letter I received no reply; but had the pleasure of hearing, on the return of my messenger (who was commissioned to make enquiries), that Mrs. Harley had suffered no return of her disorder, and was daily acquiring health and strength. — I feared, yet, to acquaint her with the situation of her son; not only on the account of her own late critical situation, but, also, lest any sudden agitation of spirits from the arrival of his mother, might, in his present weak state, be fatal to Augustus.

I now redoubled for him my cares and attentions: he grew hourly better; and, when permitted to converse, expressed in lively terms his grateful sense of my kindness. Ah! why did I misconstrue these emotions, so natural in such circumstances — why did I flatter my heart with the belief of a sympathy which did not, could not, exist!

CHAP. XXI.

As my patient began to acquire strength, I demanded of him his name and family, that I might inform his friends of his situation. On his answering "Harley," I enquired, smiling —

If he remembered hearing his mother speak of a little *Protegé*, Emma Courtney, whom she favoured with her partial friendship?

"Oh, yes!" — and his curiosity had been strongly awakened to procure a sight of this lady.

"Behold her, then, in your nurse!"

"Is it possible!" he exclaimed, taking my hand, and pressing it with his lips — "My sister! — my friend! — how shall I ever pay the debt I owe you?"

"We will settle that matter another time; but it is now become proper that I should inform your excellent mother of what has happened, which I have hitherto delayed, lest surprise should be prejudicial to you, and retard your recovery."

I then recounted to him the particulars of the late occurrences, of which he had before but a confused notion; adding my surprise, that I had neither seen, nor heard, any thing from Mr. Morton.

He informed me, in his turn, that, having received an express, informing him of his mother's alarming situation, he immediately quitted the seat of his friend, where he was on a visit, to hasten to her; that, for this purpose, riding late, he by some means bewildered himself through the darkness of the evening, by which mistake he encountered our chaise, and he hoped was, in some measure, notwithstanding the accidents which ensued, accessory to my preservation.

I quitted him to write to my friend, whom I, at length, judged it necessary to acquaint with his situation. On the receipt of my letter, she flew to us on the wings of maternal tenderness — folded her beloved Augustus, and myself, alternately to her affectionate bosom, calling us "her children — her darling children! —— I was her guardian angel — *the preserver of her son!* — and *he* only could repay my goodness!" I ventured to raise my eyes to him — they met his — mine were humid with tears of tenderness: a cloud passed over his brow — he entreated his mother to restrain her transports — he was yet too enfeebled to bear these emotions. She recollected herself in an instant; and, after again embracing him, leaning on my arm, walked out into the air, to relieve the tumultuous sensations that pressed upon her heart.

Once more she made me recite, minutely, the late events — strained me in her arms, repeatedly calling me —

"Her beloved daughter — the meritorious child of her affections — the preserver of her Augustus!"

Every word she uttered sunk deep into my soul, that greedily absorbed the delicious poison, prepared for me by the cruel hand of more than maternal fondness.

I mentioned to her my having written to Mr. Morton, and my astonishment at his silence.

He had not yet returned, she informed me, to Morton Park; and intimated, that some malicious stories, respecting my sudden disappearance, had been circulated by Mrs. Morton through the neighbourhood. She had herself been under extreme solicitude on my account. It was generally believed, from the turn Mrs. Morton's malice had given to the affair, that I had eloped with Mr. Montague: — the accident which had befallen him had been rumoured; but the circumstances, and the occasion of it, had been variously related. Confiding in my principles, she had waited with anxiety for the elucidation of these mysterious accounts; lamenting herself as the innocent occasion of them, yet assured they would, eventually, prove to my honour. She commended the magnanimity, which her partial friendship imputed to my behaviour, with all the enthusiasm of affection, and execrated the baseness of Mrs. Morton, who, having received my letter, must have been acquainted with the real truth.

Her narration gave me many complicated, and painful, sensations; but the good opinion of the world, however desirable it may be, as connected with our utility, has ever been with me but a secondary consideration. Confiding in the rectitude of my conduct, I composed my spirits; depending on that rectitude, and time, for removing the malignant aspersions which at present clouded my fame. The tale of slander, the basis of which is falsehood, will quietly wear away; and should it not — how unfounded, frequently, are the censures of the world — how confused its judgments! I entreated my friend to say nothing, at present, to her son on this subject; it was yet of importance that his mind should be kept still and tranquil.

We rejoined Augustus at the dinner hour, and spent the day together in harmony and friendship. The physician calling in the evening, Mrs. Harley consulted him, whether it would be safe to remove her son, as she was impatient to have him under her own roof. To this the doctor made no objection, provided he was conveyed in an easy carriage, and by short stages. On Mrs. Harley's thanking him for his polite and humane attention to his patient, smilingly pointing to me, he replied — "Her thanks were misplaced." His look was arch and significant; it called a glow into my cheeks. I ventured, once more, to steal a glance at Augustus: his features were again overspread with a more than usual seriousness, while his eyes seemed designedly averted. Mrs. Harley sighed, and, abruptly changing the subject, asked the physician an indifferent question, who soon after took his leave.

Chap. XXII.

In a few days we returned to the peaceful mansion of my maternal friend. Augustus seemed revived by the little journey, while every hour brought with it an increase of health and spirits. Mrs. Harley would not suffer me to speak of going to Morton Park in the absence of its master; neither could Augustus spare his kind nurse: — "I must stay," he added, and methought his accents were softened, "and complete my charitable purpose." My appearance again in the village, the respectability, and the testimony, of my friends, cleared my fame; and it was only at Morton Park, that any injurious suspicions were affected to be entertained.

The hours flew on downy pinions: — my new *brother*, for so he would call himself, endeavoured to testify his gratitude, by encouraging and assisting me in the pursuit of learning and science: he gave us lectures on astronomy and philosophy —

"While truths divine came mended from his
tongue."[35]

I applied myself to the languages, and, aided by my preceptor, attained a general knowledge of the principles, and philosophy, of criticism and grammar, and of the rules of composition. Every day brought with it the acquisition of some new truth; and our intervals from study were employed in music, in drawing, in conversation, in reading the *belles lettres* — in —

"The feast of reason, and the flow of souls."[36]

The spring was advancing: — we now made little excursions, either on horse-back, in a chaise, or in a boat on the river, through the adjacent country. The fraternal relation, which Augustus had assumed, banished restraint, and assisted me in deceiving myself. I drank in large and intoxicating draughts of a delicious poison, that had circulated through every vein to my heart, before I was aware of its progress. At length, part of a conversation, which I had accidentally overheard between Mrs. Harley and her son, recalled me to a temporary recollection.

I was seeking them in the garden, towards the dusk of the evening, and a filbert hedge separated us. I heard the voice of my friend, as speaking earnestly, and I unconsciously stopped.

"It would be a comfort to my declining years to see you the husband of a woman of virtue and sensibility: domestic affections meliorate the heart; no one ought to live wholly to himself."

"Certainly not, neither does any one; but, in the present state of society, there are many difficulties and anxieties attending these connections: they are a lottery, and the prizes are few. I think, perhaps, nearly with you, but my situation is, *in many*

---

[35] Alexander Pope, "Eloise to Abelard," "And truths divine came mended from that tongue," line 66.

[36] Alexander Pope, "Satire I," from *The Works of Alexander Pope*, Vol. I, 1736. "There [in the Grotto], my retreat the best companions grace,/ Chiefs out of ward, and Statesmen out of place. There St. John mingles with my friendly bowl,/ The Feast of Reason and the Flow of soul." (lines 127-130).

respects, a peculiar one," — and he sighed deeply: —— "Need I enumerate these peculiarities to you? Neither do I pretend to have lived so long in the world without imbibing many of its prejudices, and catching the contagion of its habits."

"They are unworthy of you."

"Perhaps so — but we will, if you please, change the subject; this to me is not a pleasant one. What is become of my pupil? It is likely to be a clear night; let us go in, and prepare for some astronomical observations."

My heart reproved me for listening, I crept back to my chamber — shed one tear — heaved a convulsive, struggling sigh — breathed on my handkerchief, applied it to my eyes, and joined my friends in the library.

Four months had passed rapidly — "the spot of azure in the cloudy sky"[37] — of my destiny. Mr. Morton, I was informed, had returned to the Park, and Augustus, whose health was now thoroughly restored, talked of quitting the country. I advised with my friends, who agreed with me, that it was now become proper for me to visit my uncle, and, explaining to him the late events, justify my conduct.

Mrs. Harley and her son offered to accompany me; but this, for many reasons, I declined; taking my leave of them with a heavy heart, and promising, if I were not kindly received, an immediate return.

CHAP. XXIII.

ON my arrival at Mr. Morton's, the porter informed me, he was ordered, by his lady, to deny my entrance. My swelling heart! — a sentiment of indignation distended it almost to suffocation. — At this moment, Ann tripped lightly through the court-yard, and, seeing me, ran to embrace me. I returned her caresses with warmth.

"Ah!" said she, "you are not, you cannot be, guilty. I have been longing to see you, and to hear all that has happened, but

---

[37] John Scott (1730-83), "Elegy; Written at Amwell in Hertfordshire," 1758.

it was not permitted me." She added, in a whisper, "I cannot love my mother, for she torments and restrains me — my desire of liberty is stronger than my duty — but I shall one day be able to outwit her."

"Will not your father, my love, allow me to speak to him? I have a right to be heard, and I demand his attention."

"He is in his dressing-room," said Ann, "I will slide softly, to him, and tell him you are here."

Away she flew, and one of the foot-men presently returned, to conduct me to his master. I found him alone, he received me with a grave and severe aspect. I related to him, circumstantially, the occurrences which had taken place during his absence. My words, my voice, my manner, were emphatic — animated with the energy of truth — they extorted, they commanded, they, irresistibly, compelled assent. His features softened, his eyes glistened, he held out his hand, he was about to speak — he hesitated a moment, and sighed. At this instant, Mrs. Morton burst into the room, with the aspect of a fury — her bloated countenance yet more swelled and hideous — I shrunk back involuntarily — she poured forth a torrent of abuse and invective. A momentary recollection reassured me — waiting till she had exhausted her breath, I turned from her, and to her husband, with calm dignity —

"I thank you, Sir, for all the kindness I have received from you — I am convinced you do me justice — *for this I do not thank you*, it was a duty to which I had a claim, and which you owed, not only to me, but, to yourself. My longer continuance in this house, I feel, would be improper. For the present, I return to Mrs. Harley's, where I shall respectfully receive, and maturely weigh, any counsels with which you may in future think proper to favour me."

Mr. Morton bowed his head; poor man! his mild spirit was overborne, he dared not assert the dictates of his own reason. I hurried out of the apartment, and hastily embracing Ann, who awaited me in the hall, charging myself with a hundred kisses for Mrs. Harley, I took the way to the hospitable mansion of my friend.

I had proceeded about half a mile, when I beheld Augustus, advancing towards me; he observed my tremulous emotions, and pallid countenance; he took my hand, holding it with a gentle pressure, and, throwing his other arm round me, supported my faultering steps. His voice was the voice of kindness — his words spake assurance, and breathed hope — *fallacious hope!* — My heart melted within me — my tremor encreased — I dissolved into tears.

"A deserted outcast from society — a desolate orphan — what was to become of me — to whom could I fly?"

"Unjust girl! have I then forfeited all your confidence — have you not a mother and a friend, who love you — " he stopped — paused — and added "with maternal, with *fraternal*, tenderness? to whom would you go? — remain with us, your society will cheer my mother's declining years" — again he hesitated — "I am about to return to town, assure me, that you will continue with Mrs. Harley — it will soften the pain of separation."

I struggled for more fortitude — hinted at the narrowness of my fortune — at my wish to exert my talents in some way, that should procure me a less dependent situation — spoke of my active spirit — of my abhorrence of a life of indolence and vacuity.

He insisted on my waving these subjects for the present. "There would be time enough, in future, for their consideration. In the mean while, I might go on improving myself, and whether present, or absent, might depend upon him, for every assistance in his power."

His soothing kindness, aided by the affectionate attentions of my friend, gradually, lulled my mind into tranquillity. My bosom was agitated, only, by a slight and sweet emotion — like the gentle undulations of the ocean, when the winds, that swept over its ruffled surface, are hushed into repose.

Chap. XXIV.

ANOTHER month passed away — every hour, I imbibed, in large draughts, the deceitful poison of hope. A few days before that appointed for the departure of Augustus, I received a visit from Mr. Montague, of whose situation, during his confinement, I had made many enquiries, and it was with unaffected pleasure that I beheld him perfectly restored to health. I introduced him to my friends, who congratulated him upon his recovery, and treated him with that polite and cordial hospitality which characterized them. He was on his way to Morton Park, and was particular in his enquiries respecting the late conduct of the lady of the mansion, of which he had heard some confused reports. I could not conceal from him our final separation, but, aware of his inflammable temper, I endeavoured to soften my recital as far as was consistent with truth and justice. It was with difficulty, that our united persuasions induced him to restrain his fiery spirit, which broke out into menaces and execrations. I represented to him —

"That every thing had been already explained; that the affair had now subsided; that a reconciliation was neither probable nor desirable; that any interference, on his part, would only tend to mutual exasperation, from which I must eventually be the sufferer."

I extorted from him a promise — that, as he was necessitated to meet Mr. Morton on business, he would make no allusion to the past — I should be mortified, (I added) by having it supposed, that I stood in need of a *champion*. — Mr. Morton had no doubts of the rectitude of my conduct, and it would be barbarous to involve him in a perpetual domestic warfare.

Mr. Montague, at the request of Augustus, spent that day, and the next, with us. I thought, I perceived, that he regarded Mr. Harley with a scrutinizing eye, and observed my respect for, and attention to, him, with jealous apprehension. Before his departure, he requested half an hour's conversation with me alone, with which request I immediately complied, and withdrew with him into an adjoining apartment. He informed me —

"That he was going to London to pursue his medical studies — that, on his return, his father had proposed to establish him in his profession — that his prospects were very favourable, and that he should esteem himself completely happy if he might, yet, hope to soften my heart in his favour, and to place me in a more assured and tranquil situation."

I breathed a heavy sigh, and sunk into a melancholy reverie.

"Speak to me, Emma," said he, with impatience, "and relieve the anxiety I suffer."

"Alas! What can I say?"

"Say, that you will try to love me, that you will reward my faith and perseverance."

"Would to God, I could" — I hesitated — my eyes filled with tears — "Go to London," resumed I; "a thousand new objects will there quickly obliterate from your remembrance a romantic and ill-fated attachment, to which retirement, and the want of other impression, has given birth, and which owes its strength merely to opposition."

"As that opposition," retorted he, "is the offspring of pride and insensibility — "

I looked at him with a mournful air — "Do not reproach me, Montague, my situation is far more pitiable than yours. *I am, indeed, unhappy*," — added I, after a pause; "I, like you, am the victim of a raised, of, I fear, a distempered imagination."

He eagerly entreated me to explain myself.

"I will not attempt to deceive you — I should accuse myself, were I to preserve any sentiment, however delicate its nature, that might tend to remove your present illusion. It is, I confess, with extreme reluctance — with real pain" — I trembled — my voice faultered, and I felt my colour vary — "that I constrain myself to acknowledge a hopeless, an extravagant" — I stopped, unable to proceed.

Fire flashed from his eyes, he started from his seat, and took two or three hasty strides across the room.

"I understand you, but too well — Augustus Harley shall dispute with me a prize" —

"Stop, Sir, be not unjust — make not an ungenerous return to the confidence I have reposed in you. Respect the violence which, on your account, I have done to my own feelings. I own, that I have not been able to defend my heart against the accomplishments and high qualities of Mr. Harley — I respected his virtues and attainments, and, by a too easy transition — at length — *loved his person.*[38] But my tenderness is a secret to all the world but yourself — It has not met with" — a burning blush suffused my cheek — "It has little hope of meeting, a return. To your *honor* I have confided this cherished *secret* — dare you betray my confidence? I know, you dare not!"

He seemed affected — his mind appeared torn by a variety of conflicting emotions, that struggled for victory — he walked towards me, and again to the door, several times. I approached him — I gave him my hand ——

"Adieu, Montague," said I, in a softened accent — "Be assured of my sympathy — of my esteem — of my best wishes! When you can meet me with calmness, I shall rejoice to see you — as a *friend.* Amidst some excesses, I perceive the seeds of real worth in your character, cultivate them, they may yield a noble harvest. I shall not be forgetful of the distinction you have shewn me, *when almost a deserted orphan* — Once again — farewel, my friend, and — may God bless you!"

I precipitately withdrew my hand from his, and rushed out of the room. I retired to my chamber, and it was some hours before my spirits became sufficiently composed to allow me to rejoin my friends. On meeting them, Mrs. Harley mentioned, with some surprize, the abrupt departure of Montague, who had quitted the house, without taking leave of its owners, by whom he had been so politely received.

"He is a fine young man" added she, "but appears to be very eccentric."

Augustus was silent, but fixed his penetrating eyes on my face, with an expression that covered me with confusion.

---

[38] I.e., physical person or body, in addition to a more intellectual admiration. Compare this to Miss Milner's confession in Elizabeth Inchbald's 1790 *A Simple Story*, "I love [Mr. Dorriforth] with all the passion of a mistress, and with all the tenderness of a wife" (New York: Oxford UP, 1988), 72.

CHAP. XXV.

THE day fixed for the departure of Mr. Harley, for London, now drew near — I had anticipated this period with the most cruel inquietude. I was going to lose, perhaps for ever, my preceptor, my friend! He, from whom my mind had acquired knowledge, and in whose presence my heart had rested satisfied. I had hitherto scarcely formed a wish beyond that of daily beholding, and listening to him — I was now to gaze on that beloved countenance, to listen to those soothing accents, no longer. He was about to mix in the gay world — to lose in the hurry of business, or of pleasure, the remembrance of those tender, rational, tranquil, moments, sacred to virtue and friendship, that had left an indelible impression on my heart. Could I, indeed, flatter myself, that the idea of the timid, affectionate, Emma, would ever recur to his mind in the tumultuous scenes of the crouded metropolis, it would doubtless quickly be effaced, and lost in the multiplicity of engagements and avocations. How should I, buried in solitude and silence, recall it to his recollection, how contrive to mingle it with his thoughts, and entangle it with his associations? Ah! did he but know my tenderness — *the desire of being beloved*, of inspiring sympathy, is congenial to the human heart — why should I hesitate to inform him of my affection — why do I blush and tremble at the mere idea? It is a false shame! It is a pernicious system of morals, which teaches us that hypocrisy can be virtue! He is well acquainted with the purity, and with the sincerity, of my heart — he will at least regard me with esteem and tender pity — and how often has 'pity melted the soul to love!'[39] The experiment is, surely, innocent, and little hazardous. What have I to apprehend? Can I distrust, for a moment, those principles of rectitude, of honour, of goodness, which gave birth to my affection? Have I not witnessed his humanity, have I not experienced his delicacy, in a thousand instances? Though he should be obliged to wound, he is incapable of insulting, the heart that loves him;

---

[39] John Dryden, "Alexander's Feast; The Power of Musique" (1697). "For pity melts the Mind to Love," line 96.

and that, loving him, believed, alas! for a long time, *that it loved only virtue!*

The morning of our separation, at last, arrived. My friend, too much indisposed to attend the breakfast table, took leave of her son in her own apartment. I awaited him, in the library, with a beating heart, and, on his departure, put into his hands a paper. —

"Read it not," said I, in a low and almost inarticulate tone of voice, "till arrived at the end of your journey; or, at least, till you are ten miles from hence."

He received it in silence; but it was a silence more expressive than words.

"Suffer me," it said," for a few moments, to solicit your candour and attention. You are the only man in the world, to whom I could venture to confide sentiments, that to many would be inconceivable; and by those, who are unacquainted with the human mind, and the variety of circumstances by which characters are variously impressed and formed — who are accustomed to consider mankind in masses — who have been used to bend implicitly, to custom and prescription — the deviation of a solitary individual from *rules* sanctioned by usage, by prejudice, by expediency, would be regarded as romantic. I frankly avow, while my cheeks glow with the blushes of *modesty*, not of shame, that your virtues and accomplishments have excited in my bosom an affection, as pure as the motives which gave it birth, and as animated as it is pure. — This ingenuous avowal may perhaps affect, but will scarcely (I suspect) surprise, you; for, incapable of dissimulation, the emotions of my mind are ever but too apparent in my expressions, and in my conduct, to deceive a less penetrating eye than yours — neither have I been solicitous to disguise them.

"It has been observed, that, 'the strength of an affection is generally in the same proportion, as the character of the species, in the object beloved, is lost in that of the individual,'[40] and,

---

[40] "Woolstonecraft's *Rights of Woman*." [M.H.] I.e., Mary Wollstonecraft, *Vindication of the Rights of Woman*, (1792) in *Works of Mary Wollstonecraft*, Ed. Janet Todd

that individuality of character is the only fastener of the affections. It is certain, however singular it may appear, that many months before we became personally acquainted, the report of your worth and high qualities had generated in my mind, an esteem and reverence, which has gradually ripened into a tenderness, that has, at length, mixed itself with all my associations, and is become interwoven with every fibre of my heart.

"I have reflected, again and again, on the imprudence of cherishing an attachment, which a variety of circumstances combine to render so unpromising, and ———— What shall I say? —— So peculiar is the constitution of my mind, that those very circumstances have had a tendency directly opposite to what might reasonably have been expected; and have only served to render the sentiment, I have delighted to foster, more affecting and interesting. — Yes! I am aware of the tenure upon which you retain your fortunes — of the cruel and unnatural conditions imposed on you by the capricious testator: neither can I require a sacrifice which I am unable to recompense. But while these melancholy convictions deprive me of hope, they encourage me, by proving the disinterestedness of my attachment, to relieve my heart by communication. — Mine is a whimsical pride, which dreads nothing so much as the imputation of sordid, or sinister motives. Remember, then — should we never meet again — if in future periods you should find, that the friendship of the world is — 'a shade that follows wealth and fame;'[41] — if, where you have conferred obligation, you are repaid with ingratitude — where you have placed confidence, with treachery — and where you have a claim to zeal, with coldness! Remember, *that you have once been beloved, for yourself alone,* by

and Marilyn Butler, 5 Vols. Vol. 5 (Washington Square, NY: New York University Press, 1989). This quote is from Wollstonecraft's note on the individuality of character, Chapter IV, p. 138, note 10.
[41] Oliver Goldsmith (1730-74), "Edwin and Angelina," (1796) "And what is friendship but a name,/A charm that lulls to sleep;/A shade that follows wealth or fame,/But leaves the wretch to weep?" lines 73-76.

one, who, in contributing to the comfort of your life, would have found the happiness of her own.

"Is it possible that a mind like yours, neither hardened by prosperity, nor debased by fashionable levity — which vice has not corrupted, nor ignorance brutalized — can be wholly insensible to the balmy sweetness, which natural, unsophisticated, affections, shed through the human heart?

> 'Shall those by heaven's own influence join'd,
> By feeling, sympathy, and mind,
> The sacred voice of truth deny,
> And mock the mandate of the sky?'[42]

"But I check my pen: — I am no longer —
> 'The hope-flush'd enterer on the stage of life.'[43]

"The dreams of youth, chaced by premature reflection, have given place to soberer, to sadder, conclusions; and while I acknowledge, that it would be inexpressibly soothing to me to believe, that, in happier circumstances, my artless affection might have awakened in your mind a sympathetic tenderness: — this is the extent of my hopes! ——— I recollect you once told me 'It was our duty to make our reason conquer the sensibility of our heart.' Yet, why? Is, then, apathy the perfection of our nature — and is not that nature refined and harmonized by the gentle and social affections? The Being who gave to the mind its reason, gave also to the heart its sensibility.

"I make no apologies for, because I feel no consciousness of, weakness. An attachment sanctioned by nature, reason, and virtue, ennobles the mind capable of conceiving and cherishing it: of such an attachment a corrupt heart is utterly incapable.

"You may tell me, perhaps, 'that the portrait on which my fancy has dwelt enamoured, owes all its graces, its glowing colouring — like the ideal beauty of the ancient artists — to the imagination capable of sketching the dangerous picture.' — Al-

---

[42] Mary Robinson (1758-1800), "Anselmo, the Hermit of the Alps." From *Poetical Works*, Vol. II, pp. 34-5, 1806.

[43] John Scott of Amwell, "Elegy IV: Written at the Approach of Winter." (1782).

lowing this, for a moment, *the sentiments it inspires are not the less genuine*; and without some degree of illusion, and enthusiasm, all that refines, exalts, softens, embellishes, life — genius, virtue, love itself, languishes. But, on this subject, my opinions have not been lightly formed: — it is not to the personal graces, though 'the body charms, because the mind is seen,'[44] but to the virtues and talents of the individual (for without intellect, virtue is an empty name), that my heart does homage; and, were I never again to behold you — were you even the husband of another — my tenderness (a tenderness as innocent as it is lively) would never cease!

"But, methinks, I hear you say, — 'Whither does all this tend, and what end does it propose?' Alas! this is a question I scarcely dare to ask myself! — Yet, allow me to request, that you will make me one promise, and resolve me one question: — ah! do not evade this enquiry; for much it imports me to have an explicit reply, lest, in indulging my own feelings, I should, un-consciously, plant a thorn in the bosom of another: — *Is your heart, at present, free?* Or should you, in future, form a tender engagement, tell me, that I shall receive the first intimation of it from yourself; and, in the assurance of your happiness, I will learn to forget my own.

"I aspire to no higher than that of the most faithful of your friends, and the wish of becoming worthy of your esteem and confidence shall afford me a motive for improvement. I will learn of you moderation, equanimity, and self-command; and you will, perhaps, continue to afford me direction, and assistance, in the pursuit of knowledge and truth.

"I have laid down my pen, again and again, and still taken it up to add something more, from an anxiety, lest even you, of

---

[44] Edward Young (1683-1765), "Satire VI; On Women" from *The Complete Works*, Vol. 1, 1854, line 154. Cited also in *Adeline Mowbray*, page 586, this edition: "What's female beauty, but an air divine,/ Through which the mind's all-gentle graces shine?/ They, like the sun, irradiate all between;/ The body charms because the soul is seen. (lines 151-154).

whose delicacy I have experienced repeated proofs, should misconstrue me. — 'Oh! what a world is this! —— into what false habits has it fallen! Can hypocrisy be virtue? Can a desire to call forth all the best affections of the heart, be misconstrued into something too degrading for expression?'[45] But I will banish these apprehensions; I am convinced they are injurious.

"Yes! — I repeat it — I relinquish my pen with reluctance. A melancholy satisfaction, from what source I can scarcely define, diffuses itself through my heart while I unfold to you its emotions. — Write to me; *be ingenuous*; I desire, I call for, truth!"

"EMMA."

MARRIAGE AND COURTSHIP

The complex rules governing courtship with the goal of marriage were detailed in many conduct manuals of the eighteenth century. Emma's letter confessing her passion to Augustus runs directly counter to most beliefs about the female role in courtship, and even about feminine nature. In 1774, John Gregory published the widely read *A Father's Legacy to His Daughters* as a posthumous guide for his orphaned and unmarried daughters' future behavior. He specifically addresses the nature of female love and courtship, and how a young lady ought to behave should she discover in herself a "preference" for a specific eligible man. Most particularly, a proper lady did not allow herself to develop preferences, let alone passion, for a man prior to certain knowledge of his honorable interest in her.

It is a maxim laid down among you, and a very prudent one it is, That love is not to begin on your part, but is entirely to be the consequence of our attachment to you. Now, supposing a woman to have sense and taste, she will not find many men to

---

[45] "Holcroft's *Anna St. Ives*." [MH]. The 1792 novel by Thomas Holcroft, identified by Gary Kelly as the first English Jacobin novel. See Vol. III, letter XLIV, ed. Peter Faulkner (Oxford: Oxford University Press, 1970), p. 146.

whom she can possibly be supposed to bear any considerable share of esteem. Among these few, it is a very great chance if any of them distinguishes her particularly. Love, at least with us, is exceedingly capricious, and will not always fix where reason says it should. But supposing one of them should become particularly attached to her, it is still extremely improbable that he should be the man in the world her heart most approved of.

As, therefore, Nature has not given you that unlimited range in your choice which we enjoy, she has wisely and benevolently assigned to you a greater flexibility of taste on this subject. Some agreeable qualities recommend a gentleman to your liking and friendship. In the course of his acquaintance, he contracts an attachment to you. When you perceive it, it excites your gratitude; this gratitude rises into a preference, and this preference perhaps at last advances to some degree of attachment, especially if it meets with crosses and difficulties; for these, and a state of suspense, are very great incitements to attachment, and are the food of love in both sexes. If attachment was not excited in your sex in this manner, there is not one of a million of you that could ever marry with any degree of love.

A man of taste and delicacy marries a woman because he loves her more than any other. A woman of equal taste and delicacy marries him because she esteems him, and because he gives her that preference.

...When you observe in a gentleman's behavior these marks which I have described above, reflect seriously on what you are to do. If his attachment is agreeable to you, I leave you to do as nature, good sense, and delicacy, shall direct you. If you love him, let me advise you never to discover to him the full extent of your love, no not although you marry him. That sufficiently shews your preference, which is all he is intitled to know. If he has delicacy, he will ask for no stronger proof of your affection for your sake; if he has sense, he will not ask it for his own. This is an unpleasant truth, but it is my duty to let you know it. Violent love cannot subsist, at least cannot be expressed, for any time together, on both sides; otherwise the certain consequence, however concealed, is satiety and disgust. Nature in the case has laid the reserve on you. (Gregory, 36-37 and 39-40)

Hester Chapone, in a series of letters ostensibly to her niece, stresses the "Regulation of Heart and the Affections" in Letter IV. Although Chapone was an evangelical, usually associated with a more conservative, conventional religiousity than Wollstonecraft or Hays, she emphasizes like them, rational choice in a marriage partner, warns against romantic notions of love and passion, and suggests that it is better to remain single than to make a bad marriage. On the other hand, her emphasis on duty to parental wisdom and wishes is more conventional than the skepticism about parental self-interest in some English Jacobin novels.

Whatever romantic notions you may hear, or read of, depend upon it, those matches are the happiest which are made on rational grounds—on suitableness of character, degree, and fortune—on mutual esteem, and the prospect of a real and permanent friendship. Far be it from me to advise you to marry where you do not love;—a mercenary marriage is a detestable prostitution:—But, on the other hand, a union formed upon mere personal liking, without the requisite foundation of esteem, without the sanction of parental approbation, and, consequently, without the blessing of God, can be productive of nothing by misery and shame. [...]

From an act like this, I trust, your duty and gratitude to your kind parents—the first of duties next to that we owe God, and inseparably connected with it—will effectually preserve you. But most young people think they have fulfilled their duty, if they refrain from actually marrying against prohibition: They suffer their affections, and even perhaps their word of honour, to be engaged, without consulting their parents; yet satisfying themselves with resolving not to marry without their consent: not considering that, beside the wretched, useless, and uncomfortable state they plunge themselves into, when they contract an hopeless engagement, they must likewise involve a parent in the miserable dilemma of either giving a forced consent against his judgement, or of seeing his beloved child pine away her prime of life in fruitless anxiety—seeing her accuse him of tyranny, because he restrains her from certain ruin—seeing her affections alienated from her family—and all her thoughts engrossed by one object, to the destruction of her health and spirits, and of all improvements and occupations. What a cruel alternative for parents, whose happiness is bound up with that of their child!—The time to consult them is before you have given a lover the least encouragement; nor ought you to listen a moment to the man who would wish you to keep his addresses secret; since he thereby shews himself conscious that they are not fit to be encouraged.

But perhaps I have said enough on this subject at present; though, if ever advice on such a topic can be of use, it must be before passion has got possession of the heart, and silenced both reason and principle.

...But, if this happy lot [marriage] should be denied you, do not be afraid of a single life. A worthy woman is never destitute of valuable friends, who in a great measure supply to her the want of nearer connections. She can never be slighted or disesteemed, while her good temper and benevolence render her a blessing to her companions. Nay, she must be honoured by all persons of sense and virtue, for preferring the single state to an union unworthy of her. The calamities of an unhappy marriage are so much greater than can befal a single person, that the unmarried woman may find abundant argument to be contented with her condition, when pointed out to her by Providence. Whether married or single, if your first care is to please God, you will undoubtedly be a blessed creature.... (Chapone, "On the Regulation of the Affections," 94-96 and 97-98)

Sources

Hester Chapone, *Letters on the Improvement of the Mind. Addressed to a Lady*, London, 1773.

John Gregory, *A Father's Legacy to His Daughters*, Third Edition, Dublin, 1774.

Chap. XXVI.

I had not courage to make my friend a confident[46] of the step I had taken; so wild, and so romantic, did it appear, even to myself — a false pride, a false shame, with-held me. I brooded in silence over the sentiment, that preyed on the bosom which cherished it. Every morning dawned with expectation, and every evening closed in disappointment. I walked daily to the post-office, with precipitate steps and a throbbing heart, to enquire for letters, but in vain; and returned slow, dejected, spiritless. *Hope*, one hour, animated my bosom and flushed my cheek; the next, pale *despair* shed its torpid influence through my languid frame. Inquietude, at length, gradually gave place to despondency, and I sunk into lassitude.

My studies no longer afforded me any pleasure. I turned

---

[46] I.e., confidante.

over my books, incapable of fixing my attention; took out my drawings, threw them aside; moved, restless and dissatisfied, from seat to seat; sought, with unconscious steps, the library, and throwing myself on the sopha, with folded arms, fixed my eyes on the picture of Augustus, which had lately been replaced, and sunk into waking dreams of ideal perfection and visionary bliss. I gazed on the lifeless features, engraven on my heart in colours yet more true and vivid — but where was the benignant smile, the intelligent glance, the varying expression? Where the pleasant voice, whose accents had been melody in my ear; that had cheered me in sadness, dispelled the vapours of distrust and melancholy, and awakened my emulation for science and improvement? Starting from a train of poignant and distressing emotions, I fled from an apartment once so dear, presenting now but the ghosts of departed pleasures — fled into the woods, and buried myself in their deepest recesses; or, shutting myself in my chamber, avoided the sight of my friend, whose dejected countenance but the more forcibly reminded me —

'That such things were, and were most dear.'[47]

In this state of mind, looking one day over my papers, without any known end in view, I accidentally opened a letter from Mr. Francis (with whom I still continued, occasionally, to correspond), which I had recently received. I eagerly seized, and re-perused it. My spirits were weakened; the kindness which it expressed affected me — it touched my heart — it excited my tears. I determined instantly to reply to it, and to acknowledge my sense of his goodness.

My mind was overwhelmed with the pressure of its own

[47] Henry Fielding's *Joseph Andrews* seems likely to be the source of the citation in this form. Joseph cites the lines thus: "Yes, I will bear my Sorrows like a Man,/But I must also feel them as a Man. I cannot but remember such things were,/ And were most dear to me—." (Vol II, Book III, Chapter X, p. 152, London, 1742.) Joseph acknowledges to Parson Adams that he is citing a play, and the source is likely one of the various eighteenth-century variants from William Shakespeare's *Macbeth*: "I must also feel it as a man:/ I cannot but remember such things were,/ That were most precious to me" (IV.iii.225-227).

thoughts; a gleam of joy darted through the thick mists that pervaded it; communication would relieve the burthen. I took up my pen, and, though I dared not betray the fatal secret concealed, as a sacred treasure, in the bottom of my heart, I yet gave a loose to, I endeavoured to paint, its sensations.

After briefly sketching the events that had driven me from Morton Park (of which I had not hitherto judged it necessary to inform him), without hinting the name of my deliverer, or suffering myself to dwell on the services he had rendered me, I mentioned my present temporary residence at the house of a friend, and expressed an impatience at my solitary, inactive, situation.

I went on ———— "To what purpose should I trouble you with a thousand wayward, contradictory, ideas and emotions, that I am, myself, unable to disentangle — which have, perhaps, floated in every mind, that has had leisure for reflection — which are distinguished by no originality, and which I may express (though not feel) without force? I sought to cultivate my understanding, and exercise my reason, that, by adding variety to my resources, I might increase the number of my enjoyments: for *happiness* is, surely, the only desirable *end* of existence! But when I ask myself, Whether I am yet nearer to the end proposed? — I dare not deceive myself — sincerity obliges me to answer in the negative. I daily perceive the gay and the frivolous, among my sex, amused with every passing trifle; gratified by the insipid *routine* of heartless, mindless, intercourse; fully occupied, alternately, by domestic employment, or the childish vanity of varying external ornaments, and 'hanging drapery on a smooth block.'[48] I do not affect to despise, and I regularly practise, the necessary avocations of my sex; neither am I superior to their vanities. The habits acquired by early precept and example ad-

[48] Wollstonecraft, *Rights of Woman*, Chapter IX, page 216, suggesting that women are degraded by mindless occupation such as "merely fitting drapery upon a smooth block." Hays also uses the phrase in her letter to William Godwin of 28 July, 1795, held in the Pforzheimer collection of the New York Public Library.

here tenaciously, and are never, perhaps, entirely eradicated. But all these are insufficient to engross, to satisfy, the active, aspiring, mind. Hemmed in on every side by the constitutions of society, and not less so, it may be, by my own prejudices — I perceive, indignantly perceive, the magic circle, without knowing how to dissolve the powerful spell. While men pursue interest, honor, pleasure, as accords with their several dispositions, women, who have too much delicacy, sense, and spirit, to degrade themselves by the vilest of all interchanges, remain insulated beings, and must be content tamely to look on, without taking any part in the great, though often absurd and tragical, drama of life. Hence the eccentricities of conduct, with which women of superior minds have been accused — the struggles, the despairing though generous struggles, of an ardent spirit, denied a scope for its exertions! The strong feelings, and strong energies, which properly directed, in a field sufficiently wide, might — ah! what might they not have aided? forced back, and pent up, ravage and destroy the mind which gave them birth!

"Yes, I confess, *I am unhappy*, unhappy in proportion as I believe myself (it may be, erringly) improved. Philosophy, it is said, should regulate the feelings, but it has added fervor to mine! What are passions, but another name for powers? The mind capable of receiving the most forcible impressions is the sublimely improveable mind! Yet, into whatever trains such minds are accidentally directed, they are prone to enthusiasm, while the vulgar stupidly wonder at the effects of powers, to them wholly inconceivable: the weak and the timid, easily discouraged, are induced, by the first failure, to relinquish their pursuits. 'They make the impossibility they fear!' But the bold and the persevering, from repeated disappointment, derive only new ardor and activity. 'They conquer difficulties, by daring to attempt them.'[49]

---

[49] Nicholas Rowe, *The Ambitious Stepmother. A Tragedy*, 1700, I.i: "The Wise and Active conquer Difficulties,/ By daring to attempt 'em: Sloth and Folly/Shiver and shrink at sight of Toil and Hazard,/And make the Impossibility they fear."

"I feel, that I am writing in a desultory manner, that I am unable to crowd my ideas into the compass of a letter, and, that could I do so, I should perhaps only weary you. There are but few persons to whom I venture to complain, few would understand, and still fewer sympathise with me. You are in health, they would say, in the spring of life, have every thing supplied you without labour (so much the worse) nature, reason, open to you their treasures! All this is, partly, true — but, with inexpressible yearnings, my soul pants for something more, something higher! The morning rises upon me with sadness, and the evening closes with disgust — Imperfection, uncertainty, is impressed on every object, on every pursuit! I am either restless or torpid, I seek to-day, what to-morrow, wearies and offends me.

"I entered life, flushed with hope — I have proceeded but a few steps, and the parterre of roses, viewed in distant prospect, nearer seen, proves a brake of thorns. The few worthy persons I have known appear, to me, to be struggling with the same half suppressed emotions. — Whence is all this? Why is intellect and virtue so far from conferring happiness? Why is the active mind a prey to the incessant conflict between truth and error? Shall I look beyond the disorders which, *here*, appear to me so inexplicable? — shall I expect, shall I demand, from the inscrutable Being to whom I owe my existence, in future unconceived periods, the *end* of which I believe myself capable, and which capacity, like a tormenting *ignis fatuus*, has hithero served only to torture and betray? The animal rises up to satisfy the cravings of nature, and lies down to repose, undisturbed by care — has man superior powers, only to make him pre-eminently wretched? — wretched, it seems to me, in proportion as he rises? Assist me, in disentangling my bewildered ideas — write to me — reprove me — spare me not!"

"EMMA."

To this letter I quickly received a kind and consolatory reply, though not unmingled with the reproof I called for. It afforded me but a temporary relief, and I once more sunk into inanity; my faculties rusted for want of exercise, my reason grew feeble, and my imagination morbid.

CHAP. XXVII.

A PACQUET of letters, at length, arrived from London — Mrs. Harley, with a look that seemed to search the soul, put one into my hands — The superscription bore the well known characters — yes, it was from Augustus, and addressed to Emma — I ran, with it, into my chamber, locked myself in, tore it almost asunder with a tremulous hand, perused its contents with avidity — scarce daring to respire — I reperused it again and again.

"I had trusted my confessions (it said) to one who had made the human heart his study, who could not be affected by them improperly. It spoke of the illusions of the passions — of the false and flattering medium through which they presented objects to our view. He had answered my letter earlier, had it not involved him in too many thoughts to do it with ease. There was a great part of it to which he knew not how to reply — perhaps, on some subjects, it was not necessary to be explicit. And now, it may be, he had better be silent — he was dissatisfied with what he had written, but, were he to write again, he doubted if he should please himself any better. — He was highly flattered by the favourable opinion I entertained of him, it was a grateful proof, not of his merit, but of the warmth of my friendship, &c. &c."

This letter appeared to me vague, obscure, enigmatical. Unsatisfied, disappointed, I felt, I had little to hope — and, yet, had no *distinct* ground of fear. I brooded over it, I tortured its meaning into a hundred forms — I spake of it to my friend, but in general terms, in which she seemed to acquiesce: she appeared to have made a determination, not to enquire after what I was unwilling to disclose; she wholly confided both in my principles, and in those of her son: I was wounded by what, entangled in prejudice, I conceived to be a necessity for this reserve.

Again I addressed the man, whose image, in the absence of

all other impressions, I had suffered to gain in my mind this dangerous ascendancy.

To Augustus Harley.

"I, once more, take up my pen with a mind so full of thought, that I foresee I am about to trespass on your time and patience — yet, perhaps, to one who makes 'the human heart his study,' it may not be wholly uninteresting to trace a faithful delineation of the emotions and sentiments of an ingenuous, uncorrupted, mind — a mind formed by solitude, and habits of reflection, to some strength of character.

"If to have been more guarded and reserved would have been more discreet, I have already forfeited all claim to this discretion — to affect it now, would be vain, and, by pursuing a middle course, I should resign the only advantage I may ever derive from my sincerity, the advantage of expressing my thoughts and feelings with freedom.

"The conduct, which I have been led to adopt, has been the result of a combination of peculiar circumstances, *and is not what I would recommend to general imitation* — To say nothing of the hazards it might involve, I am aware, generally speaking, arguments might be adduced, to prove, that certain customs, of which I, yet, think there is reason to complain, may not have been unfounded in nature — I am led to speak thus, because I am not willing to spare myself, but would alledge all which you might have felt inclined to hint, had you not been with-held by motives of delicate consideration.

"Of what then, you may ask, do I complain? — Not of the laws of nature! But when mind has given dignity to natural affections; when reason, culture, taste, and delicacy, have combined to chasten, to refine, to exalt (shall I say) to sanctify them — Is there, then, no cause to complain of rigor and severity, that such minds must either passively submit to a vile traffic, or be content to relinquish all the endearing sympathies of life? Nature has formed woman peculiarly susceptible of the tender affections. 'The voice of nature is too strong to be silenced by artificial precepts.'[50] To feel these affections in a supreme degree, a mind enriched by literature and expanded by fancy and reflection, is necessary — for it is intellect and imagination only, that can give energy and interest to ——

'The thousand soft sensations —
Which vulgar souls want faculties to taste,
Who take their good and evil in the gross.'[51]

"I wish we were in the vehicular state, and that you understood the sentient language;[52] you might then comprehend the whole of what I mean to express, but find too delicate for *words*. But I do you injustice.

"If the affections are, indeed, generated by sympathy, where the principles, pursuits, and habits, are congenial — where the *end*, sought to be attained, is —

'Something, than beauty dearer,'[53]

"You may, perhaps, agree with me, that it is *almost* indifferent on which side the sentiment originates. Yet, I confess, my frankness has involved me in many after thoughts and inquietudes; inquietudes, which all my reasoning is, at times, insufficient to allay. The shame of being singular, it has been justly

---

[50] Not found, though similar statements about the strength of the "voice of nature" run through later eighteenth-century British literature.

[51] Not found. A similar sentiment is expressed in Henry Fielding's play *The Miser* from 1733: "how is the/ noble Passion of Love abus'd by vulgar Souls, who are/ incapable of tasting its Delicacies. When Love is great/as mine,/ None can its Pleasures, or its Pains declare;/ We can but feel how exquisite they are." (Act 1, Scene IX).

[52] "See Light of Nature pursued. An entertaining philosophical work." [M.H.] Abraham Tucker, *The Light of Nature Pursued* (1768) Chapter 21, vol. ii, pp 135-6. In this work, the pseudonymous author "Ned Search" encounters John Locke in a vision and discovers that after death the spirit is transported from the body by a refined "vehicle," and communicates via a new "sentient" language that is more reliable than our embodied "vocal"language. Like other radical reformers, Hays is concerned with the difficulty for Emma of communicating precisely her thoughts and feelings without misunderstanding or suspicion of her desires.

[53] James Thomson, *The Seasons*, "Spring:" "Something than beauty dearer, should they look/ Or on the mind, or mind-illuminated face;...." (lines 1138-39).

observed,[54] requires strong principles, and much native firmness of temper, to surmount. — Those who deviate from the beaten track must expect to be entangled in the thicket, and wounded by many a thorn — my wandering feet have already been deeply pierced.

"I should vainly attempt to describe the struggles, the solicitudes, the doubts, the apprehensions, that alternately rend my heart! I feel, that I have "put to sea upon a shattered plank, and placed my trust in miracles for safety."[55] I dread, one moment, lest, in attempting to awaken your tenderness, I may have forfeited your respect; the next, that I have mistaken a delusive meteor for the sober light of reason. In retirement, numberless contradictory emotions revolve in my disturbed mind: — in company, I start and shudder from accidental allusions, in which no one but myself could trace any application. The end of doubt is the beginning of repose. Say, then, to me, that it is a principle in human nature, however ungenerous, to esteem lightly what may be attained without difficulty. — Tell me to make distinctions between love and friendship, of which I have, hitherto, been able to form no idea. — Say, that the former is the caprice of fancy, founded on external graces, to which I have little pretension, and that it is vain to pretend, that —

'Truth and good are one,
And beauty dwells with them.'[56]

"Tell me, that I have indulged too long the wild and extravagant chimeras of a romantic imagination. Let us walk together into the palace of Truth, where (it is fancifully related by an ingenious writer,[57] that) every one was compelled by an irresist-

---

[54] "Aikin's *Letters*." [M.H.] John Aikins, *Letters from a Father to his Son, On Various Topics Relative to Literature and the Conduct of Life*, 1793.

[55] Edward Young, *The Revenge*, 1721. "The Maid that loves/Goes out to Sea upon a shatter'd Plank/And puts her trust in Miracles for Safety."

[56] Mark Akenside, *The Pleasures of Imagination*, 1757.

[57] "Madame de Genlis's *Tales of the Castle*." [M.H.] Stéphanie Félicité, Comtesse de Genlis (1746-1830), wrote *Les Veillées de Chateau*, translated as *Tales of the Castle* by Thomas Holcroft in 1793.

ible, controuling, power, to reveal his inmost sentiments! All this I will bear, and will still respect your integrity, and confide in your principles; but I can no longer sustain a suspense that preys upon my spirits. It is not the Book of Fate — it is your mind, only, I desire to read. A sickly apprehension overspreads my heart —— I pause here, unable to proceed."

"EMMA."

CHAP. XXVIII.

WEEK after week, month after month, passed away in the anguish of vain expectation: my letter was not answered, and I again sunk into despondency. — Winter drew near. I shuddered at the approach of this dreary and desolate season, when I was roused by the receipt of a letter from one of the daughters of the maternal aunt, under whose care I had spent the happy, thoughtless, days of childhood. My cousin informed me —

"That she had married an officer in the East India service; that soon after their union he was ordered abroad, and stationed in Bengal for three years, during which period she was to remain in a commodious and pleasant house, situated in the vicinity of the metropolis. She had been informed of my removal from Morton Park, and had no doubt but I should be able to give a satisfactory account of the occasion of that removal. She purposed, during the absence of her husband, to let out a part of her house; and should I not be fixed in my present residence, would be happy to accommodate me with an apartment, on terms that should be rather dictated by friendship than interest. She also hinted, that a neighbouring lady, of respectable character, would be glad to avail herself of the occasional assistance of an accomplished woman in the education of her daughters; that she had mentioned me to her in advantageous terms, conceiving that I should have no objection, by such a means, to exercise my talents, to render myself useful, and to augment my small income."

This intelligence filled me with delight: the idea of change, of exertion, of new scenes — shall I add, *of breathing the same air with Augustus,* rushed tumultuously through my imagination. Flying eagerly to my friend, to impart these tidings, I was not aware of the ungrateful and inconsiderate appearance which these exultations must give me in her eyes, till I perceived the starting tear. — It touched, it electrified, my heart; and, throwing myself into her arms, I caught the soft contagion, and wept aloud.

"Go, Emma — my daughter," said this excellent woman; "I banish the selfish regret that would prompt me to detain thee. I perceive this solitude is destructive to thy ardent mind. Go, vary your impressions, and expand your sensations; gladden me only from time to time with an account of your progress and welfare."

I had but little preparation to make. I canvassed over, with my friend, a thousand plans, and formed as many expectations and conjectures; but they all secretly tended to one point, and concentrated in one object. I gave my cousin notice that I should be with her in a few days — settled a future correspondence with my friend — embraced her, at parting, with unfeigned, and tender sorrow — and, placing myself in a stage-coach, that passed daily through the village, took the road, once more, with a fluttering heart, to London. We travelled all night — it was cold and dreary — but my fancy was busied with various images, and my bosom throbbing with lively, though indistinct sensations.

The next day, at noon, I arrived, without accident, at the residence of my relation, Mrs Denbeigh. She received me with unaffected cordiality: our former amity was renewed; we spent the evening together, recalling past scenes; and, on retiring, I was shewn into a neat chamber, which had been prepared for me, with a light closet[58] adjoining. The next day, I was introduced to the lady, mentioned to me by my kind hostess, and agreed to devote three mornings in the week to the instruction of the young ladies (her daughters), in various branches of education.

END OF THE FIRST VOLUME.

---

[58] A small room for private reading and writing.

MEMOIRS
OF
EMMA COURTNEY.

VOL. II.

To Augustus Harley.

"My friend, my son, it is for your benefit, that I have determined on reviewing the sentiments, and the incidents, of my
past life. Cold declamation can avail but little towards the reformation of our errors. It is by tracing, by developing, the passions
in the minds of others; tracing them, from the seeds by which
they have been generated, through all their extended consequences, that we learn, the more effectually, to regulate and to
subdue our own.

"I repeat, it will cost me some pain to be ingenuous in the
recital which I have pledged myself to give you; even in the
moment when I resume my pen, prejudice continues to struggle
with principle, and I feel an inclination to retract. While unfolding a series of error and mortification, I tremble, lest, in
warning you to shun the rocks and quicksands amidst which my
little bark has foundered, I should forfeit your respect and esteem, the pride, and the comfort, of my declining years. But
you are deeply interested in my narrative, you tell me, and you
entreat me to proceed."

Chap. I.

Change of scene, regular employment, attention to my pupils, and the conscious pride of independence, afforded a temporary relief to my spirits. My first care, on my arrival in town,
was to gladden the mind of my dear benefactress, by a minute
detail of my present comforts and occupations.

She had charged me with affectionate remembrance and letters to her son. I enclosed these letters; and, after informing him (in the cover) of the change in my situation, and the incident which had occasioned it, complained of the silence he had observed towards my last letter.

— "If," said I, "from having observed the social and sympathetic nature of our feelings and affections, I suffered myself to yield, involuntarily, to the soothing idea, that the ingenuous avowal of an attachment so tender, so sincere, so artless, as mine, could not have been unaffecting to a mind with which my own proudly claimed kindred: — if I fondly believed, that simplicity, modesty, truth — the eye beaming with sensibility, the cheek mantling with the glow of affection, the features softened, the accents modulated, by ineffable tenderness, might, in the eyes of a virtuous man, have supplied the place of more dazzling accomplishments, and more seductive charms: if I over-rated my own merit, and my own powers — surely my mistakes were sufficiently humiliating! You should not, indeed you should not, have obliged me to arrive at the conviction through a series of deductions so full of mortification and anguish. You are too well acquainted with the human heart not to be sensible, that no certainty can equal the misery of conjecture, in a mind of ardour — the agonizing images which *suspense* forces upon the tender and sensible heart! You should have written, in pity to the situation of my mind. I would have thanked you for being ingenuous, even though, like Hamlet, you had *spoke daggers*,[59] I expected it, from your character, and I had a claim to your sincerity.

"But it is past! — the vision is dissolved! The barbed arrow is not extracted with more pain, than the enchantments of hope from the ardent and sanguine spirit! But why am I to lose your friendship? My heart tells me, I have not deserved this! Do not suspect, that I have so little justice, or so little magnanimity, as

[59] William Shakespeare, *Hamlet*, III.2.386.

to refuse you the privilege, the enviable privilege, of being master of your own affections. I am unhappy, I confess; the principal charm of my life is fled, and the hopes that should enliven future prospects are faint: melancholy too often obscures reason, and a heart, perhaps too tender, preys on itself.

"I suspect I had formed some vain and extravagant expectations. I could have loved you, had you permitted it, with no mean, nor common attachment. — My words, my looks, my actions, betrayed me, ere I suffered my feelings to dictate to my pen. Would to God I had buried this fatal secret in the bottom of my soul! But repentance is, now, too late. Yet the sensible heart yearns to disclose itself — and to whom can it confide its sentiments, with equal propriety, as to him who will know how to pity the errors, of which he feels himself, however involuntarily, the cause? The world might think my choice in a confident singular; it has been my misfortune seldom to think with the world, and I ought, perhaps, patiently to submit to the inconveniences to which this singularity has exposed me.

"I know not how, without doing myself a painful violence, to relinquish your society; and why, let me again ask, should I? I now desire only that repose which is the end of doubt, and this, I think, I should regain by one hour's frank conversation with you; I would compose myself, listen to you, and yield to the sovereignty of reason. After such an interview, my mind — no longer harrassed by vague suspicion, by a thousand nameless apprehensions and inquietudes — should struggle to subdue itself — at least, I would not permit it to dictate to my pen, not to bewilder my conduct. I am exhausted by perturbation. I ask only certainty and rest.

"EMMA."

A few days after I had written the preceding letter, Mr. Harley called on me, Mrs. Denbeigh was with me on his entrance; I would have given worlds to have received him alone, but had not courage to hint this to my relation. Overwhelmed by a variety of emotions, I was unable for some time to make any reply to his friendly enquiries after my health, and congratulations on my amended prospects. My confusion and embarrassment were but too apparent; perceiving my distress, he kindly contrived to engage my hostess in discourse, that I might have time to rally my spirits. By degrees, I commanded myself sufficiently to join in the conversation — I spoke to him of his mother, expressed the lively sense I felt of her goodness, and my unaffected regret at parting with her. Animated by my subject, and encouraged by the delicacy of Augustus, I became more assured: we retraced the amusements and studies of H —— shire, and two hours passed delightfully and insensibly away, when Mrs. Denbeigh was called out of the room to speak to a person who brought her letters and intelligence from the India House. Mr. Harley, rising at the same time from his seat, seemed about to depart, but hesitating, stood a few moments as if irresolute.

"You leave me," said I, in a low and tremulous tone, "and you leave me still in suspense?"

"Could you," replied he, visibly affected, "but have seen me on the receipt of your last letter, you would have perceived that my feelings were not enviable — Your affecting expostulation, added to other circumstances of a vexatious nature, oppressed my spirits with a burthen more than they were able to sustain."

He resumed his seat, spoke of his situation, of the tenure on which he held his fortune, — "I am neither a stoic nor a philosopher" added he, — "I knew not how — *I could not answer your letter*. What shall I say? — I am with-held from explaining myself further, by reasons — *by obligations* — Who can look back on every action of his past life with approbation? Mine has not been free from error! I am distressed, perplexed — *Insuperable obstacles* forbid what otherwise" ——

"I feel," said I, interrupting him, "that I am the victim of my own weakness and vanity — I feel, that I have been rushing headlong into the misery which you kindly sought to spare me — I am sensible of your delicacy — of your humanity! — And is it with the full impression of your virtues on my heart that I must teach that heart to renounce you — renounce, for ever, the man with whose pure and elevated mind my own panted to mingle? My reason has been blinded by the illusions of my self-love — and, while I severely suffer, I own my sufferings just — yet, the sentiments you inspired were worthy of you! I understand little of — I have violated common forms — seeking your tenderness, I have perhaps forfeited your esteem!"

"Far, *very far*, from it — I would, but cannot, say more."

"Must we, then, separate for ever — will you no longer assist me in the pursuit of knowledge and truth — will you no more point out to me the books I should read, and aid me in forming a just judgment of the principles they contain — Must all your lessons be at an end — all my studies be resigned? How, without your counsel and example, shall I regain my strength of mind — to what *end* shall I seek to improve myself, when I dare no longer hope to be worthy of him — "

A flood of tears choked my utterance; hiding my face with my hands, I gave way to the kindly relief, but for which my heart had broken. I heard footsteps in the passage, and the voice of Mrs. Denbeigh as speaking to her servant — covered with shame and grief, I dared not in this situation appear before her, but, rushing out at an opposite door, hid myself in my chamber. A train of confused recollections tortured my mind, I concluded, that Augustus had another, a prior attachment; I felt, with this conviction, that I had not the fortitude, and that perhaps I ought not, to see him again. I wrote to him under this impression; I poured out my soul in anguish, in sympathy, in fervent aspirations for his happiness. These painful and protracted conflicts affected my health, a deep and habitual depression preyed upon my spirits, and, surveying every object through the medium of a distempered imagination, I grew disgusted with life.

Chap. II.

I BEGAN, at length, to think, that I had been too precipitate, and too severe to myself. — Why was I to sacrifice a friend, from whose conversation I had derived improvement and pleasure? I repeated this question to myself, again and again; and I blushed and repented. But I deceived myself. I had too frequently acted with precipitation, I determined, now, to be more prudent — I waited three months, fortified my mind with many reflections, and resumed my pen ——

TO AUGUSTUS HARLEY.

"NEAR three months have elapsed, since I last addressed you. I remind you of this, not merely to suppress, as it arises, any apprehension which you may entertain of further embarrassment or importunity: for I can no longer afflict myself with the idea, that my peace, or welfare, are indifferent to you, but will rather adopt the sentiment of Plato[60] — who on being informed, that one of his disciples, whom he had more particularly distinguished, had spoken ill of him, replied, to the slanderer — 'I do not believe you, for it is impossible that I should not be esteemed by one whom I so sincerely regard.'

"My motive, for calling to your remembrance the date of my last, is, that you should consider what I am now about to say, as the result of calmer reflection, the decision of judgment after having allowed the passions leisure to subside. It is, perhaps, unnecessary to premise, that I am not urged on by pride, from an obscure consciousness of having been betrayed into indiscretion, to endeavour to explain away, or to extenuate, any part of my former expressions or conduct. To a mind like yours, such an attempt would be impertinent; from one like mine, I hope, superfluous. I am not ashamed of being a human being, nor blush to own myself liable to 'the shakes and agues of his fragile nature.'[61] I have ever spoken, and acted, from the genuine dictates of a mind swayed, at the time, by its own views and propensities, nor have I hesitated, as those views and propensities have changed, to avow my further convictions — 'Let not the

---

[60] Greek philosopher 428-348 B.C.E, with Aristotle foundational to western European thought.
[61] Thomas Holcroft, *Anna St. Ives* (1792). Vol. III, Letter XLII, Ed. Peter Faulkner, 1970, p. 139.

coldly wise exult, that their heads were never led astray by their hearts.'[62] I have all along used, and shall continue to use, the unequivocal language of sincerity.[63]

"However *romantic* (a vague term applied to every thing we do not understand, or are unwilling to imitate) my views and sentiments might appear to many, I dread not, from you, this frigid censure. 'The ideas, the associations, the circumstances of each man are properly his own, and it is a pernicious system, that would lead us to require all men, however different their circumstances, to act in many of the common affairs of life, by a precise, general rule.'[64] The genuine effusions of the heart and mind are easily distinguished, by the penetrating eye, from the vain ostentation of sentiment, lip deep, which, causing no emotion, communicates none — Oh! how unlike the energetic sympathies of truth and feeling — darting from mind to mind, enlightening, warming, with electrical rapidity!

"My ideas have undergone, in the last three months, many fluctuations. My *affection* for you (why should I seek for vague, inexpressive phrases?) has not ceased, has not diminished, but it has, in some measure, changed its nature. It was originally generated by the report, and cemented by the knowledge, of your virtues and talents; and to virtue and talents my mind had ever paid unfeigned, enthusiastic, homage! It is somewhere said by Rousseau — 'That there may exist such a suitability of moral, mental, and personal, qualifications, as should point out the propriety of an union between a prince and the daughter of an

---

[62]Not found.

[63]The "language of sincerity" is strongly associated with William Godwin, who argued in a letter to his friend Joseph Gerrald upon his trial for Treason in 1793, that if he spoke calmly and truthfully his evident sincerity was certain to persuade the jury to find for him. Gerrald was, however, found guilty, imprisoned on a brig and deported to Botany Bay Australia, where he died a few months after his arrival. (See Appendix to *Caleb Williams.*, ed. Maurice Hindle, New York: Penguin, 1988.)

[64] "Godwin's *Political Justice*." [MH]. From Appendix "Of Co-operation, Cohabitation, and Marriage," Book VIII, Chapter VIII, London, 1798, p. 501. See textbox "Female Sexuality and Desire," page 311.

executioner.'[65] Vain girl that I was! I flattered myself that between us this sympathy really existed. I dwelt on the union between mind and mind — sentiments of nature gently insinuated themselves — my sensibility grew more tender, more affecting — and my imagination, ever lively, traced the glowing
picture, and dipped the pencil in rainbow tints! Possessing one
of those determined spirits, that is not easily induced to relinquish its purposes — while I conceived that I had only your
pride, or your insensibility, to combat, I wildly determined to
persevere. — A further recapitulation would, perhaps, be unnecessary: — my situation, alas! is now changed.

"Having then examined my heart, attentively and deliber-
ately, I suspect that I have been unjust to myself, in supposing it
incapable of a disinterested attachment. — Why am I to deprive
you of a faithful friend, and myself of all the benefits I may yet
derive from your conversation and kind offices? I ask, why? And
I should, indeed, have cause to blush, if, after having had time
for reflection, I could really think this necessary. Shall I, then,
sign the unjust decree, that women are incapable of energy or
fortitude? Have I exercised my understanding, without ever intending to apply my principles to practice? Do I mean always to
deplore the prejudices which have, systematically, weakened the
female character, without making any effort to rise above them?
Is the example you have given me, of a steady adherence to honour
and principle, to be merely respected, without exciting in my
bosom any emulation? Dare I to answer these questions in the
affirmative, and still ask your esteem — the esteem of the wise
and good? — I dare not! No longer weakened by alternate hopes
and fears, like the reed yielding to every breeze, I believe myself
capable of acting upon firmer principles; and I request, with
confidence, the restoration of your friendship! Should I afterwards find, that I have over-rated my own strength, I will frankly

---

[65] See Rousseau's *Émile*, transl. Barbara Foxley, Everyman, p. 369. Significantly,
Rousseau first imagines his ideal woman, Sophia, falling in love with the fictional
hero of Fénélon's *Telemachus*.

tell you so, and expect from your humanity those allowances, which are but a poor substitute for respect.

"Believe, then, my views and motives to be simply such as I state them; at least, such, after severely scrutinizing my heart, they appear to myself; and reply to me with similar ingenuousness. My expectations are very moderate: answer me with simplicity — my very soul sickens at evasion! You have, undoubtedly, a right to judge and to determine for yourself; but it will be but just to state to me the reasons for, and the result of, that judgment; in which case, if I cannot obviate those reasons, I shall be bound, however reluctantly, to acquiesce in them. Be assured, I will never complain of any consequences which may ensue, even, from the utterance of all truth.

"EMMA."

CHAP. III.

THIS letter was succeeded by a renewal of our intercourse and studies. Mrs. Denbeigh, my kind hostess, was usually of our parties. We read together, or conversed only on general topics, or upon subjects of literature. I was introduced by Mr. Harley to several respectable families, friends of his own and of his mother's. I made many indirect enquiries of our common acquaintance, with a view to discover the supposed object of my friend's attachment, but without success. All that he had, himself, said, respecting such an engagement, had been so vague, that I began to doubt of the reality of its existence. — When, in any subsequent letters (for we continued occasionally to correspond) I ventured to allude to the subject, I was warned 'not to confound my own conceptions with real existences.' When he spoke of a susceptibility to the tender affections, it was always in the past time, 'I *have* felt,' — 'I *have* been — ' Once he wrote — 'His situation had been rendered difficult, by a combination of *peculiar circumstances*; circumstances, with which but few persons were acquainted.' Sometimes he would affect to reflect upon his past conduct, and warn me against appreciating him too highly. In fine, he was a perfect enigma, and every thing which he said or wrote tended to increase the mystery.

A restless, an insatiable, curiosity, devoured me, heightened by feelings that every hour became more imperious, more uncontroulable. I proposed to myself, in the gratification of this curiosity, a satisfaction that should compensate for all the injuries I might suffer in the career. This inquietude prevented my mind from resting; and, by leaving room for conjecture, left room for the illusions of fancy, and of hope. Had I never expressed this, he might have affected ignorance of my sensations; he might have pleaded guiltless, when, in the agony of my soul, I accused him of having sacrificed my peace to his disingenuousness — but vain were all my expostulations!

"If," said I, "I have sought, too earnestly, to learn the state of your affections, it has been with a view to the more effectually disciplining of my own — of stifling every *ignis fatuus*[66] of false hope, that making, even, impossibilities possible, will still, at times, continue to mislead me. Objects seen through obscurity, imperfectly discerned, allow to the fancy but too free a scope; the mind grows debilitated, by brooding over its apprehensions; and those apprehensions, whether real or imaginary, are carried with accumulated pain to the heart. I have said, on this subject, you have a right to be free; but I am, now, doubtful of this right: the health of my mind being involved in the question, has rendered it a question of *utility* — and on what other basis can morals rest?"

I frequently reiterated these reasonings, always with encreased fervor and earnestness: represented — "that every step I took in advance would be miles in return — every minute that the blow was suspended, prepared it to descend with accumulated force." I required no particulars, but merely requested to be assured of *a present, existing, engagement.* I continued, from time to time, to urge this subject.

---

[66] Literally "fool's fire," a reference to the lights seen over marshy land that betray travelers into dangerous swamps believing that they are traveling towards human habitation.

"Much" said I, "as I esteem you, and deeply as a thousand associations have fixed your idea in my heart — in true candour of soul, I, yet, feel myself, your superior. —— I recollect a sentiment of Richardson's Clarissa that always pleased me, and that may afford a test, by which each of us may judge of the integrity of our own minds — 'I should be glad that you, and all the world, knew my heart; let my enemies sit in judgment upon my actions; fairly scanned, I fear not the result. Let them ask me my most secret thoughts; and, whether they make for me, or against me, I will reveal them.'[67]

"This is the principle, my friend, upon which I have acted towards you. I have said many things, I doubt not, which make against me; but I trusted them to one, who told me, that he had made the human heart his study: and it is only in compliance with the prejudices of others, if I have taken any pains to conceal all I have thought and felt on this, or on any other, subject, from the rest of the world. Had I not, in the wild career of fervent feeling, had sufficient strength of mind to stop short, and to reason calmly, how often, in the bitterness of my spirit, should I have accused you of sporting with my feelings, by involving me in a hopeless maze of conjecture — by leaving me a prey to the constant, oppressive, apprehension of hearing something, which I should not have the fortitude to support with dignity; which, in proportion as it is delayed, still contributes to harrass, to weaken, to incapacitate, my mind from bearing its disclosure.

"I know you might reply — and more than nine-tenths of the world would justify you in this reply — 'That you had already said, what ought to have been sufficient, and would have been so to any other human being; — that you had not sought the confidence I boast of having reposed in you; — and that, so far from affording you any satisfaction, it has occasioned you only perplexity. If my own destiny was not equivocal, of what

[67] Samuel Richardson, *Clarissa; or the History of a Young Lady* (1747-8), Ed. Angus Ross (New York: Penguin, 1985), p. 822. From Clarissa's letter to Captain Tomlinson.

importance could it be to me, and what right had I to enquire after circumstances, in which, however affecting, I could have no real concern.'

"You may think all this, perhaps — I will not spare myself — and it may be reasonable. *But could you say it* — and have you, indeed, studied the human heart — *have you, indeed, ever felt the affections?* — Whatever may be the event — and it is in the mind of powers only that passions are likely to become fatal — and however irreproachable every other part of your conduct may have been, I shall, *here*, always say, you were culpable!"

I changed my style. "I know not," said I, "the nature of those stern duties, which oblige you to with-hold from me your tenderness; neither do I any longer enquire. I dread, only, lest I should acquire this knowledge when I am the least able to support it. Ignorant, then, of any reasons which should prevent me from giving up my heart to an attachment, now become interwoven with my existence, I yield myself up to these sweet and affecting emotions, so necessary to my disposition — to which apathy is abhorrent. 'The affections (truly says Sterne) must be exercised on something; for, not to love, is to be miserable. Were I in a desart, I would find out wherewith in it to call forth my affections. If I could do no better, I would fasten them upon some sweet myrtle, or seek some melancholy cypress to connect myself to — I would court their shade, and greet them kindly for their protection. I would cut my name upon them, and swear they were the loveliest trees throughout the desart. If their leaves withered, I would teach myself to mourn; and, when they rejoiced, I would rejoice with them.'[68]

"An attachment, founded upon a full conviction of worth, must be both safe and salutary. My mind has not sufficient strength to form an abstract idea of perfection. I have ever found

---

[68] Laurence Sterne, *A Sentimental Journey Through France and Italy.* Ed. Ian Jack (New York: Oxford University Press, 1987), p. 28. Hays is also citing her own letters to Godwin especially that of 4 April 1796, as she does throughout this novel.

it stimulated, improved, advanced, by its affections. I will, then, continue to love you with fervor and purity; I will see you with joy, part from you with regret, grieve in your griefs, enter with zeal into your concerns, interest myself in your honour and welfare, and endeavour, with all my little power, to contribute to your comfort and satisfaction. — Is your heart so differently constituted from every other human heart, that an affection, thus ardent and sincere, excites in it no grateful, and soothing, emotions? Why, *then*, withdraw yourself from me, and by that means afflict, and sink into despondency, a mind that entrusts its peace to your keeping.

"EMMA."

We met the next day at the house of a common friend. My accents, involuntarily, were softened, my attentions pointed. — Manifestly agitated, embarrassed, even distressed, Augustus quitted the company at an early hour.

It would be endless to enumerate all the little incidents that occurred; which, however trifling they might appear in the recital, continued to operate in one direction. Many letters passed to the same purport. My curiosity was a consuming passion; but this inflexible, impenetrable, man, was still silent, or alternately evaded, and resented, my enquiries.[69] We continued, occasionally, to meet, but generally in company.

CHAP. IV.

DURING the ensuing summer, Mr. Harley proposed making a visit to his mother, and, calling to take his leave of me, on the evening preceding his journey, accidentally found me alone. — We entered into conversation on various subjects: twilight stole upon us unperceived. The obscure light inspired me with cour-

---

[69] Emma's curiosity to know the secret reason for Augustus's resistance to her proposals echoes Godwin's Caleb Williams, whose "fatal curiosity" leads him to discover a criminal secret which ultimately destroys both the guilty murderer and the curious Caleb.

age: I ventured to resume a subject, so often discussed; I complained, gently, of his reserve.

"Could I suppose," he asked, "that he had been without *his share* of suffering?"

I replied something, I scarce know what, adverting to his stronger mind.

"Strength!" said he, turning from me with emotion, "rather say, weakness!"

I reiterated the important, the so often proposed, enquiry — "Had he, or had he not, a *present, existing, engagement?*"

He endeavoured to evade my question — I repeated it — He answered, with a degree of impatience, "*I cannot tell you*; if I could, do you think I would have been silent so long?" — as once, before, he spoke of the circumstances of his past life, as being of '*a singular, a peculiar, nature.*'

At our separation, I asked, if he would write to me during his absence. 'Certainly, he would.' The next morning, having some little commissions to execute for Mrs. Harley, I sent them, accompanied by a few lines, to her son.

"Why is it," said I, "that our sagacity, and penetration, frequently desert us on the most interesting occasions? I can read any mind with greater facility than I can read your's; and, yet, what other have I so attentively studied? This is a problem I know not how to solve. One conclusion will force itself upon me — if a mistaken one, whom have you to blame? — That an *honourable*, suitable, engagement, could have given no occasion for mystery." I added, "I should depend on hearing from him, according to his promise."

Week after week, month after month, wore away, and no letter arrived. Perturbation was succeeded by anxiety and apprehension; but hearing, through my maternal friend, Mrs. Harley, of the welfare of this object of our too tender cares, my solicitude subsided into despondency. The pressure of one corroding train of ideas preyed, like a canker-worm, upon my heart, and destroyed all its tranquillity.

In the beginning of the winter, this mysterious, inexplicable, being, again returned to town. I had undertaken a little business, to serve him, during his absence. — I transmitted to him an account of my proceedings; subjoining a gentle reproach for his unkind silence.

"You promised you would write to me," said I, "during your residence in —— shire. I therefore depended upon hearing from you; and, yet, I was disappointed. You should not, indeed you should not, make these experiments upon my mind. My sensibility, originally acute, from having been too much exercised, has become nearly morbid, and has almost unfitted me for an inhabitant of the world. I am willing to believe, that your conduct towards me has originated in good motives, nevertheless, you have made some sad mistakes — you have *deeply*, though undesignedly, wounded me: I have been harassed, distressed, mortified. You know not, neither will I attempt to describe, all I have suffered! language would be inadequate to paint the struggles of a delicate, susceptible, mind, in some peculiar and interesting situations.

"You may suspect me of wanting resolution, but strong, persevering affections, are no mark of a weak mind. To have been the wife of a man of virtue and talents was my dearest ambition, and would have been my glory: I judged myself worthy of the confidence and affection of such a man — I felt, that I could have united in his pursuits, had shared his principles — aided the virtuous energies of his mind, and assured his domestic comfort. I earnestly sought to inspire you with tenderness, from the conviction, that I could contribute to your happiness, and to the worth of your character. And if, from innumerable associations, I at length loved your person, it was the magnanimity of your conduct, it was your virtues that first excited my admiration and esteem. But you have rejected an attachment originating in the highest, the purest, principles — you have thrown from you a heart of exquisite sensibility, and you leave me in doubt, whether you have not sacrificed that heart to prejudice. Yet, contemned affection has excited in my mind no resentment; true tenderness is made up of gentle and amiable emotions; nothing hostile, nothing severe, can mix with it: it may gradually subside, but it will continue to soften the mind it has once subdued.

"I see much to respect in your conduct, and though, it is probable, some parts of it may have originated in mistaken principles, I trust, that their source was pure! I, also, have made many mistakes — have been guilty of many extravagances. Yet, distrust the morality, that sternly commands you to pierce the bosom that most reveres you, and then to call it virtue — *Yes! distrust and suspect its origin!*" I concluded with expressing a wish to see him — '*merely as a friend*' — requesting a line in reply.

He wrote not, but came, unexpectedly came, the next evening. I expressed, in lively terms, the pleasure I felt in seeing him. We conversed on various subjects, he spoke affectionately of his mother, and of the tender interest she had expressed for my welfare. He enquired after my pursuits and acquirements during his absence, commending the progress I had made. Just before he quitted me, he adverted to the reproach I had made him, for not having written to me, according to his engagement.

"Recollect," said he, "in the last letter I received from you, before I left London, you hinted some suspicions — " I looked at him, "and what," added he, "could I reply?"

I was disconcerted, I changed colour, and had no power to pursue the subject.

CHAP. V.

FROM this period, he continued to visit me (I confess at my solicitation) more frequently. We occasionally resumed our scientific pursuits, read together, or entered into discussion on various topics. At length he grew captious, disputatious, gloomy, and imperious — the more I studied to please him, the less I succeeded. He disapproved my conduct, my opinions, my sentiments; my frankness offended him. This change considerably affected me. In company, his manners were studiously cold and distant; in private capricious, yet reserved and guarded. He seemed to overlook all my efforts to please, and, with a severe and penetrating eye, to search only for my errors — errors, into which I was but too easily betrayed, by the painful, and delicate, situation, in which I had placed myself.

We, one day, accompanied Mrs. Denbeigh on a visit of congratulation to her brother (eldest son of my deceased uncle Mr. Melmoth), who had, when a youth, been placed by his father in a commercial house in the West Indies, and who had just returned to his native country with an ample fortune. His sister and myself anticipated the pleasure of renewing our early, fraternal, affection and intimacy, while I felt a secret pride in introducing to his acquaintance a man so accomplished and respectable as Mr. Harley. We were little aware of the changes which time and different situations produce on the character, and, with hearts and minds full of the frank, lively, affectionate, youth, from whom we had parted, seven years since, with mutual tears and embraces, shrunk spontaneously, on our arrival at Mr. Melmoth's elegant house in Bedford square, from the cold salutation, of the haughty, opulent, purse-proud, Planter,[70] surrounded by ostentatious luxuries, and evidently valuing himself upon the consequence which he imagined they must give him in our eyes.

Mr. Harley received the formal compliments of this favourite of fortune with the easy politeness which distinguishes the gentleman and the man of letters, and the dignified composure which the consciousness of worth and talents seldom fails to inspire. Mr. Melmoth, by his awkward and embarrassed manner, tacitly acknowledged the impotence of wealth, and the real superiority of his guest. We were introduced by our stately relation to his wife, the lady of the mansion, a young woman whom he had accidentally met with in a party of pleasure at Jamaica, whither she had attended a family in the humble office of companion or

---

[70] I.e., plantation owner. The British West Indies or Caribbean colonies were largely plantations where exotic cash crops were raised by slave labor. Planters were usually assumed to possess great wealth, and to be made proud and autocratic by their position as slave-masters.

chief attendant to the lady. Fascinated by her beauty and lively manner, our trader had overlooked an empty mind, a low education, and a doubtful character, and, after a very few interviews, tendered to her acceptance his hand and fortune; which, though not without some affectation of doubt and delay, were in a short time joyfully accepted.

A gentleman joined our party in the dining-room, whom the servant announced by the name of Pemberton, in whom I presently recognized, notwithstanding some years had elapsed since our former meeting, the man of fashion and gallantry who had been the antagonist of Mr. Francis, at the table of my father. He had lately (we were informed by our host) been to Jamaica, to take possession of an estate bequeathed to him, and had returned to England in the same vessel with Mr. and Mrs. Melmoth. After an elegant dinner of several courses had been served up and removed for the dessert, a desultory conversation took place.

Mr. Pemberton, it appeared, held a commission in the militia, and earnestly solicited Mrs. Melmoth, on whom he lavished a profusion of compliments, to grace their encampment, which was to be stationed in the ensuing season near one of the fashionable watering places, with her presence.

This request the lady readily promised to comply with, expressing, in tones of affected softness, her admiration of military men, and of the

'Pride, pomp, and circumstance of glorious war!'[71]

"Do you not think, Miss Courtney," said she, turning to me, "that soldiers are the most agreeable and charming men in the world?"

"Indeed I do not, Madam; their trade is *murder*, and their trappings, in my eyes, appear but as the gaudy pomp of sacrifice."

"*Murder*, indeed! What a harsh word — I declare you are a shocking creature — There always have been wars in the world,

---

[71] William Shakespeare, *Othello*, III.3.358.

and there always must be: but surely you would not confound the brave fellows, who fight to protect their King and Country; and *the ladies*, with common ruffians and housebreakers!"

"All the difference between them is, that the one, rendered desperate by passion, poverty, or injustice, endeavours by *wrong* means to do himself *right*, and through this terrible and pitiable mistake destroys the life or the property of a fellow being — The others, wantonly and in cold blood, cut down millions of their species, ravage whole towns and cities, and carry devastation through a country."

"What *odd notions!* Dear, Mr. Pemberton, did you ever hear a lady talk so strangely?"

Thus called upon, Mr. Pemberton thought it incumbent upon him to interfere — "*Courtney*, I think, Madam, your name is! The daughter of an old friend of mine, if I am not mistaken, and who, I remember, was, when a very young lady, a great admirer of *Roman virtues*."

"Not of *Roman virtues*, I believe, Sir; they had in them too much of the destructive spirit which Mrs. Melmoth thinks so admirable."

"Indeed, I said nothing about *Roman virtues*, nor do I trouble myself with such subjects — I merely admired the soldiers because they are so brave and so polite; besides, the military dress is so very elegant and becoming — Dear, Mr. Pemberton, how charmingly you must look in your regimentals!"

Mr. Pemberton, bowing in return to the compliment, made an animated eulogium on the taste and beauty of the speaker.

"Pray, Sir," resumed she, addressing herself to Mr. Harley, whose inattention seemed to pique her, and whose notice she was determined to attract, "are you of Miss Courtney's opinion —— do you think it right to call soldiers *murderers?*"

"Upon my word, Madam," with an air of irony, "you must excuse me from entering into such *nice distinctions* — when *ladies* differ, who shall presume to decide?"

Mr. Melmoth interposed, by wishing, "that they had some thousands more of these *murderers* in the West Indies, to keep the slaves in subordination, who, since absurd notions of liberty had been put into their heads, were grown very troublesome and refractory, and, in a short time, he supposed, would become as insolent as the English servants."[72]

"Would you believe it, Mrs. Denbeigh," said the Planter's lady, addressing the sister of her husband, "Mr. Melmoth and I have been in England but a month, and have been obliged three times to change our whole suit of servants?"

"This is a land of freedom, my dear sister; servants, here, will not submit to be treated like the slaves in Jamaica."

"Well, I am sure it is very provoking to have one's will disputed by such low, ignorant, creatures. How should they know what is right? It is enough for them to obey the orders of their superiors."

"But suppose," replied Mrs. Denbeigh, "they should happen to think their superiors unreasonable!"

"*Think!* sister," said the lordly Mr. Melmoth, with an exulting laugh, "what have *servants*, or *women*, to do with *thinking?*"

"Nay, now" interrupted Mr. Pemberton, "you are too severe upon the ladies — how would the elegant and tasteful arrangement of Mrs. Melmoth's ornaments have been produced without thinking?"

"Oh, you flatterer!" said the lady.

"Let them think only about their dress, and I have no objection, but don't let them plague us with *sermonizing*."

"Mrs. Melmoth," said I, coolly, "does not often, I dare say, offend *in this way*. That some of the gentlemen, present, should object to a woman's exercising her discriminating powers, is not wonderful, since it might operate greatly to their disadvantage."

---

[72] Slave rebellions were becoming common in the late 1700s, the most famous case being that of San Domingue, which won its freedom and became Haiti in 1804 after thirteen years of strife. British colonies including Jamaica also experienced slave revolts. White Planters were badly outnumbered in the West Indies, and feared uprisings, especially as Revolutionary France early on declared slavery abolished in the French colonies (but reinstated it under Napoleon). See textbox "Slavery and the Abolition Movement" p. 174.

"A blow on the right cheek, from so fair a hand," replied Mr. Pemberton, affectedly bending his body, "would almost induce one to adopt the christian maxim, and turn the left, also.[73] What say you, Mr. Harley?"

"Mr. Harley, I believe, Sir, does not feel himself included in the reflection."

"He is a happy man then."

"No, Sir, merely a *rational one!*"

"You are pleased to be severe; of all things I dread a female wit."

"It is an instinctive feeling of self-preservation — nature provides weak animals with timidity as a guard."

Mr. Pemberton reddened, and, affecting a careless air, hummed a tune. Mr. Melmoth again reverted to the subject of English servants, which gave rise to a discussion on the Slave Trade. Mr. Harley pleaded the cause of freedom and humanity with a bold and manly eloquence, expatiating warmly on the iniquity as well as impolicy of so accursed a traffic. Melmoth was awed into silence. Mr. Pemberton advanced some trite arguments in opposition, respecting the temporary mischiefs which might ensue, in case of an abolition, to the planters, landholders, traders, &c. Augustus explained, by contending only for the gradual emancipation, after their minds had been previously prepared, of the oppressed Africans. The conversation grew interesting. Pemberton was not devoid of talents when he laid aside his affectation; the subject was examined both in a moral and a political point of view. I listened with delight, while Augustus exposed and confuted the specious reasoning and sophistry of his antagonist: exulting in the triumph of truth and justice, I secretly gloried — 'with more than selfish vanity'[74] — in the virtue and abilities of my friend. Though driven from all his resources, Mr.

[73] See Matthew 5:39 and Luke 6.29.

[74] James Thomson, *Tancred and Sigismunda. A Tragedy* (1745), I.1: "The Heart of Woman tastes no truer Joy,/ Is never flatter'd with such dear Endearment—/'Tis more than selfish Vanity—as when/ She hears the Praises of the Man she loves—...."

Pemberton was too much the courtier to be easily disconcerted, but, complimenting his adversary on his eloquence, declared he should be happy to hear of his having a seat in Parliament.

SLAVERY AND THE ABOLITION MOVEMENT

By the 1780s, Abolition had become a popular movement in Britain. The most widespread support was for the abolition of the trade in newly enslaved Africans, while some supported the more radical attempt to abolish slave-labor itself in the British colonies. English Jacobins, along with many kinds of dissenting protestants, were mostly abolitionists because of their concern with the concept of "the rights of man" and their belief in a universal moral code.

Most Britains believed that slavery was illegal in Britain itself since Justice Mansfield had ruled against a West Indian planter's attempt to reclaim his former slave in 1774. The planter had traveled on business to Britain accompanied by his slave who then became ill. Abandoned by his master, the slave was rescued and taken in by William Wilberforce, an important and well-known anti-slavery advocate. Once cured, the planter tried to reclaim his "property," but lost the case in court. The "Mansfield Decision" came to be understood to mean that there was no slavery on the isles of Great Britain, and this popularly was taken to mean that enslaved Africans and West Indians who reached the shores of Britain proper were emancipated. In 1787, the Abolition Society was formed in Britain, and through the late 1780s and early 1790s multiple petitions were presented to Parliament for the Abolition of the Slave Trade, arguing along socio-political lines that slavery was an inefficient system of labor and farming, along spiritual lines that if Black Africans and their descendants could be converted to Christianity then they were fellow humans with souls rather than chattels, and along political lines that like other peoples they were possessed of individual rights which could not justifiably be abridged.

British colonies were self-ruled, thus, British planters could establish laws that held only in the colonies. Because so much of Britain's wealth depended upon the colonies, Parliamentarians were usually reluctant to meddle in the internal affairs of the colonists. Moreover, the colonial land-owners had powerful connections to Parliament, and in some cases, had themselves been members or came from families of members. The disjunction between a rejection of slavery in Britain itself and a complex system of slave labor and birth into slavery in the West Indian colonies helped to make slavery and the slave trade unpopular at home. Further, Britain's involvement in the triangulated slave trade, shipping West Indian goods such as sugar and rum to Britain, shipping manufactured goods to the West Indies and for trade in Africa, and shipping newly enslaved Africans from West Africa to the West Indies led abolitionists to boycott West Indian goods, going so far as to compare taking sugar in one's tea to cannibalism.

Slave-produced sugar became the target of a na-tionwide boycott mounted by the London Aboli-tion Committee in 1791. Thomas Clarkson claimed that some 300,000 families were involved in the boycott. … William Fox, distinguished philanthro-pist and associate of William Wilberforce, set a pub-lishing record (50,000 copies in four months) for the time with the circulation of his *Address to the People of Great Britain on the Utility of Refraining from the Use of West Indian Sugar and Rum* (1791). His shocking identification of sugar consumption with cannibalism ('with every pound of sugar we may be considered as consuming two ounces of hu-man flesh,' he wrote) canonized the pattern of im-agery that was to be widely reproduced by other authors. The once mystical body of sugar was here-after, on the authority of abolitionist writings by Samuel Taylor Coleridge, Robert Southey and Mary Wollstonecraft (among others), shamefully demystified as containing the blood, sweat, tears, and other assorted bodily secretions of slaves. (Sandiford 124)

The prevalence of strong emotions on the subject, the importance of religious and spiritual objections to the slave trade, and an imagined similarity between enslaved Africans and British women—both treated as property bound to the interests of others—drew British women strongly to the call for abolition. Comparisons between the "enslavement" of English women by marriage and social etiquette and slave labor on the plantations were common throughout the literature of the 1790s, although such parallels began before the eighteenth century.

British abolitionist women tended to emphasize the emotional revulsion produced by the idea of tearing family members, particularly mothers and children, and husbands and wives away from each other. They also tended to object to the difficulty for slaves of practicing true Christianity, since under the rule of slavery, families were often broken, marriage was frequently impossible or meaningless, and even church attendance could be a rare privilege, since most slaves used Sundays to tend their own garden plots from which much of their food came. Finally, most women writers and abolitionists decried the tendency for the system of slavery to brutalize not just the enslaved but the slave-owners as well. Accounts of the brutality of slave-mistresses are common, and the idea that languid, delinquent, enervated West Indian white ladies, who appeared incapable of useful work, could rouse themselves to beat their erring slaves savagely was promoted in white British women's writing. Hinted at as well, was the problem of planters impregnating their own slaves, leaving their wives silently to condone the enslavement of illegitimate half-siblings to their own legitimate progeny. Thus, slavery was inherently anti-Christian, destroyed the family integrity of both blacks and whites, and was particularly pernicious to feminine delicacy and virtue. Women writers across the political spectrum were united in opposing slavery on these grounds.

On the one hand, as Moira Ferguson and others have argued, the metaphor of slavery enabled white British women to engage their own position of exclusion and domination in ways which revitalized and complicated old debates on the question of "woman." On the other hand, following Ferguson's critique, white British women's appropriation of colonial slavery as a figure for their own rather different concerns, tended to ill-serve enslaved Blacks in British territories, often representing them as at best, the sentimental objects of benevolent white concern rather than as active agents in their own interests. Nevertheless, the positive, if sentimental representation of black people as worthy objects of charity, as rights bearing human subjects, and as capable of affection and human connection did help to create an audience for the writings produced by Black Britons themselves and ultimately helped the cause of abolishing the slave trade in 1807, and finally slavery itself in 1833.

The abolition movement in Britain largely went underground in the later 1790s; in an attempt to silence reformist and radical sentiment, the government in 1795 passed the Seditious Meetings Act, which prohibited public meetings of political groups. At the same time, the government broadened its power to prosecute publishers and writers for works the government thought seditious. Abolitionist groups ceased meeting in 1795 with the passage of the Seditious Meetings Act and the Treasonable Practices Act; they did not hold meetings again until after 1805. Also, in 1794 France had outlawed slavery in its own colonies, putting pressure on the British colonies in the West Indies which depended upon slave labor, particularly for the production of sugar. British colonials, who had powerful ties to Parliament, were terrified that their slaves would rebel and overthrow the white planters' rule, following the example of French San Domingue, where enslaved people had begun rebelling in 1791, and which won its independence as Haiti in 1804 after years of bloody war. It was only in 1806 that the issue of abolition could again be broached publicly in Britain and the Abolition Society was reformed. In 1807 Britain ended the slave trade, making it illegal to import newly enslaved Africans to its colonies as laborers, but it was not until 1833 that Britain abolished slave labor itself in its colonies.

SOURCES

Seymour Drescher, *Capitalism and Antislavery: British Mobilization in Comparative Perspective* (New York: Oxford University Press, 1987).

Moira Ferguson, *Subject to Others: British Women Writers and Colonial Slavery, 1670-1834* (New York: Routledge, 1992).

Keith Sandiford, *The Cultural Politics of Sugar: Caribbean Slavery and Narratives of Colonialism* (New York: Cambridge University Press, 2000).

Mrs. Melmoth, who had yawned and betrayed various symptoms of weariness during the discussion, now proposed the adjournment of the ladies into the drawing-room, whither I was compelled, by a barbarous and odious custom, reluctantly to follow, and to submit to be entertained with a torrent of folly and impertinence.[75]

"I was ill-natured," she told me. — "How could I be so severe upon the *charming* and *elegant* Mr. Pemberton?"

It was in vain I laboured to convince her, that to be treated like *ideots* was no real compliment; and that the men who condescend to flatter our foibles, despised the weak beings they helped to form.[76]

My remonstrances were as fatiguing, and as little to be com-

[75] It was customary for ladies to leave the dinner table while the men smoked, drank port, and discussed topics such as politics.
[76] Similar sentiments run through Wollstonecraft's *Vindication of the Rights of Woman*. Hays's own published writings express this idea consistently as well.

prehended by this *fine lady*, as the arguments respecting the Slave Trade: — she sought refuge from them in interrogating Mrs. Denbeigh respecting the last new fashions, and in consulting her taste on the important question — whether blue or violet colour was the most becoming to a brunette complexion? The gentlemen joined us, to our great relief, at the tea-table: — other company dropped in, and the evening was beguiled with cards and the chess-board; — at the latter Mr. Melmoth and Mr. Harley were antagonists; — the former was no match for Augustus. I amused myself by observing their moves, and overlooking the game.

During our return from this visit, some conversation occurred between Mr. Harley, my cousin, and myself, respecting the company we had quitted. I expressed my disappointment, disgust, and contempt, in terms, it may be, a little too strong.

"I was *fastidious*," Augustus told me, "I wanted a world made on purpose for me, and beings formed after one model. It was both amusing, and instructive, to contemplate varieties of character. I was a romantic enthusiast — and should endeavour to become more like an inhabitant of the world."

Piqued at these remarks, and at the tone and manner in which they were uttered, I felt my temper rising, and replied with warmth; but it was the glow of a moment; for, to say truth, vexation and disappointment, rather than reason, had broken and subdued my spirit. Mrs. Denbeigh, perceiving I was pained, kindly endeavoured to give a turn to the conversation; yet she could not help expressing her regret, on observing the folly, levity, and extravagance, of the woman whom her brother had chosen for a wife.

"No doubt," said Augustus, a little peevishly, "he is fond of her — she is a fine woman — there is no accounting for the *caprices* of the affections."

I sighed, and my eyes filled with tears — "Is, then, affection so *capricious* a sentiment — is it possible to love what we despise?"

"I cannot tell," retorted Mr. Harley, with quickness. "Triflers can give no *serious* occasion for uneasiness: — the humours of superior women are sometimes still less tolerable."

"Ah! how unjust. If gentleness be not *the perfection of reason*, it is a quality which I have never, yet, properly understood."

He made no reply, but sunk into silence, reserve, and reverie. On our arrival at my apartments, I ventured (my cousin having left us) to expostulate with him on his unkind behaviour; but was answered with severity. Some retrospection ensued, which gradually led to the subject ever present to my thoughts. — Again I expressed a solicitude to be informed of the real state of his heart, of the nature of those mysterious obstacles, to which, when clearly ascertained, I was ready to submit. — "Had he, or had he not, an attachment, that looked to, as its *end*, a serious and legal engagement?" He appeared ruffled and discomposed. — "I ought not to be so urgent — he had already sufficiently explained himself." He then repeated to me some particulars, apparently adverse to such a supposition — asking me, in his turn, "If these circumstances bespoke of his having any such event in view?"

CHAP. VI.

FOR some time after this he absented himself from me; and, when he returned, his manners were still more unequal; even his sentiments, and principles, at times, appeared to me equivocal, and his character seemed wholly changed. I tried, in vain, to accommodate myself to a disposition so various. My affection, my sensibility, my fear of offending — a thousand conflicting, torturing, emotions, threw a constraint over my behaviour. — My situation became absolutely intolerable — time was murdered, activity vain, virtue inefficient: yet, a secret hope inspired me, that *indifference* could not have produced the irritations, the inequalities, that thus harrassed me. I thought, I observed a conflict in his mind; his fits of absence, and reflection, were unusual, deep, and frequent: I watched them with anxiety, with terror, with breathless expectation. My health became affected, and my mind disordered. I perceived that it was impossible to proceed, in the manner we had hitherto done, much longer — I felt that it would, inevitably, destroy me.

I reflected, meditated, reasoned, with myself — 'That one channel, into which my thoughts were incessantly impelled, was destructive of all order, of all connection.' New projects occurred to me, which I had never before ventured to encourage — I revolved them in my mind, examined them in every point of view, weighed their advantages and disadvantages, in a moral, in a prudential, scale. — Threatening evils appeared on all sides — I endeavoured, at once, to free my mind from prejudice, and from passion; and, in the critical and *singular* circumstances in which I had placed myself, coolly to survey the several arguments of the case, and nicely to calculate their force and importance.

"If, as we are taught to believe, the benevolent Author of nature be, indeed, benevolent," said I, to myself, "he surely must have intended the *happiness* of his creatures. Our morality cannot extend to him, but must consist in the knowledge, and practice, of those duties which we owe to ourselves and to each other. — Individual happiness constitutes the general good: — *happiness* is the only true *end* of existence; — all notions of morals, founded on any other principle, involve in themselves a contradiction, and must be erroneous. Man does right, when pursuing interest and pleasure — it argues no depravity — this is the fable of superstition: he ought only to be careful, that, in seeking his own good, he does not render it incompatible with the good of others — that he does not consider himself as standing alone in the universe. The infraction of established *rules* may, it is possible, in some cases, be productive of mischief; yet, it is difficult to state any *rule* so precise and determinate, as to be alike applicable to every situation: what, in one instance, might be a *vice*, in another may possibly become a *virtue*: — a thousand imperceptible, evanescent, shadings, modify every thought, every motive, every action, of our lives — no one can estimate the sensations of, can form an exact judgment for, another.

"I have sometimes suspected, that all mankind are pursuing

phantoms, however dignified by different appellations. — The healing operations of time, had I patience to wait the experiment, might, perhaps, recover my mind from its present distempered state; but, in the meanwhile, the bloom of youth is fading, and the vigour of life running to waste. —— Should I, at length, awake from a delusive vision, it would be only to find myself a comfortless, solitary, shivering, wanderer, in the dreary wilderness of human society. I feel in myself the capacities for increasing the happiness, and the improvement, of a few individuals — and this circle, spreading wider and wider, would operate towards the grand end of life — *general utility.*"

Again I repeated to myself — "Ascetic virtues are equally barbarous as vain; — the only just morals, are those which have a tendency to increase the bulk of enjoyment. My plan tends to this. The good which I seek does not appear to me to involve injury to any one — it is of a nature, adapted to the disposition of my mind, for which every event of my life, the education both of design and accident, have fitted me. If I am now put out, I may, perhaps, do mischief: — the placid stream, forced from its channel, lays waste the meadow. I seem to stand as upon a wide plain, bounded on all sides by the horizon: — among the objects which I perceive within these limits, some are so lofty, my eyes ache to look up to them; others so low, I disdain to stoop for them. *One*, only, seems fitted to my powers, and to my wishes —— *one, alone*, engages my attention! Is not its possession worthy an arduous effort? *Perseverance* can turn the course of rivers, and level mountains! Shall I, then, relinquish my efforts, when, perhaps, on the very verge of success?

"The mind must have an object: — should I desist from my present pursuit, after all it has cost me, for what can I change it? I feel, that I am neither a philosopher, nor a heroine — but a *woman, to whom education has given a sexual character.* It is true, I have risen superior to the generality of my *oppressed sex*; yet, I have neither the talents for a legislator; nor for a reformer, of the world. I have still many female foibles, and shrinking delicacies, that unfit me for rising to arduous heights. Ambition cannot stimulate me, and to accumulate wealth, I am still less fitted. Should I, then, do violence to my heart, and compel it to resign its hopes and expectations, what can preserve me from sinking into, the most abhorred of all states, *languor and inanity?* — Alas! that tender and faithful heart refuses to change its object — it can never love another. Like Rousseau's Julia, my strong individual attachment has annihilated every man in the creation: — him I love appears, in my eyes, something more — every other, something less.

"I have laboured to improve myself, that I might be worthy of the situation I have chosen. I would unite myself to a man of worth — I would have our mingled virtues and talents perpetuated in our offspring — I would experience those sweet sensations, of which nature has formed my heart so exquisitely susceptible. My ardent sensibilities incite me to love — to seek to inspire sympathy — to be beloved! My heart obstinately refuses to renounce the man, to whose mind my own seems akin! From the centre of private affections, it will at length embrace — like spreading circles on the peaceful bosom of the smooth and expanded lake — the whole sensitive and rational creation. Is it virtue, then, to combat, or to yield to, my passions?"

I considered, and reconsidered, these reasonings, so specious, so flattering, to which passion lent its force. One moment, my mind seemed firmly made up on the part I had to act; — I persuaded myself, that I had gone too far to recede, and that there remained for me no alternative: — the next instant, I shrunk, gasping, from my own resolves, and shuddered at the important consequences which they involved. Amidst a variety of perturbations, of conflicting emotions, I, at length, once more, took up my pen.

WOMEN AND EDUCATION I
Emma's conflicting debate between what her reason urges and what passion desires touches on a central issue of education in the 1790s. The debate over how women should be

educated and to what ends was complex in late eighteenth-century Britain. Jean-Jacques Rousseau's *Émile*, a philosophical narrative suggesting an ideal educational system which depended upon working with the child's natural instincts, was written in 1762. Émile's education exemplifies Rousseau's model of masculine education, while his idealized wife, Sophie, is educated in accordance with Rousseau's conception of female "nature." Rousseau argued that men and women were constituted differently, each with particular abilities and powers such that they complement each other. Believing that children ought to be educated in accordance with their natural tendencies, he suggested widely varied approaches for the two sexes, stressing for girls the development of taste and the ability to charm and please, in contrast to a boy's need to refine and train his intellectual abilities.

> [T]he woman who is both virtuous, wise, and charming, she who, in a word, combines love and esteem, can send them at her bidding to the ends of the earth, to war, to glory, and to death at her behest....
>
> This is the spirit in which Sophy has been educated, she has been trained carefully rather than strictly, and her taste has been followed rather than thwarted....
>
> Sophy is well born and she has a good disposition; she is very warm-hearted, and this warmth of heart sometimes makes her imagination run away with her. Her mind is keen rather than accurate, her temper is pleasant but variable, her person pleasing though nothing out of the common, her countenance bespeaks a soul and it speaks true; you may meet her with indifference, but you will not leave her without emotion. Others possess good qualities which she lacks; others possess her good qualities in a higher degree, but in no one are these qualities better blended to form a happy disposition. She

knows how to make the best of her very faults, and if she were more perfect she would be less pleasing.

Sophy is not beautiful; but in her presence men forget the fairer women, and the latter are dissatisfied with themselves. At first sight she is hardly pretty; but the more we see her the prettier she is; she wins where so many lose, and what she wins she keeps. Her eyes might be finer, her mouth more beautiful, her stature more imposing; but no one could have a more graceful figure, a finer complexion, a whiter hand, a daintier foot, a sweeter look, and a more expressive countenance. She does not dazzle; she arouses interest; she delights us, we know not why.

Sophy is fond of dress, and she knows how to dress; her mother has no other maid; she has taste enough to dress herself well; but she hates rich clothes; her own are always simple but elegant. ...

Sophy has natural gifts; she is aware of them, and they have not been neglected; but never having had a chance of much training she is content to use her pretty voice to sing tastefully and truly; her little feet step lightly, easily, and gracefully, she can always make an easy graceful courtesy. She has had no singing master but her father, no dancing mistress but her mother; a neighbouring pianist has given her a few lessons in playing accompaniments on the spinet, and she has improved herself by practice. At first she only wanted to show off her hand on the dark keys; then she discovered that the thin clear tone of the spinet made her voice sound sweeter; little by little she recognised the charms of harmony; as she grew older she at last began to enjoy the charms of expression, to love music for its own sake. But she has taste rather than talent; she cannot read a simple air from notes.

Needlework is what Sophy likes best; and the

feminine arts have been taught her most carefully, even those you would not expect, such as cutting out and dressmaking. There is nothing she cannot do with her needle, and nothing that she does not take a delight in doing; but lacemaking is her favourite occupation, because there is nothing which requires such a pleasing attitude, nothing which calls for such grace and dexterity of finger. She has also studied all the details of housekeeping; she understands cooking and cleaning; she knows the prices of food, and also how to choose it; she can keep accounts accurately, she is her mother's housekeeper. Some day she will be the mother of a family; by managing her father's house she is preparing to manage her own; she can take the place of any of the servants and she is always ready to do so. You cannot give orders unless you can do the work yourself; that is why her mother sets her to do it. Sophy does not think of that; her first duty is to be a good daughter, and that is all she thinks about for the present. (Rousseau, *Émile*, 356-7)

Wollstonecraft, Hays, and other early proponents of women's rights objected to Sophie's education, arguing that educating women only as charming companions to men left them unprepared for life. Women who were educated solely to attract a mate were, they argued, unable to function as useful and rational companions, liable to lose their husband's affection and even respect, vulnerable when their husbands died, and unable to deal competently with their own lives or the education of their children. Worse, as Wollstonecraft argued, a woman educated only to please men by her beauty and simplicity would be unable to make a rational, educated man a good partner. Wives who were trained only to be pleasing, who suffered through long stints at their needle to produce useless decorative work, who had no interests with which to entertain themselves nor skills to support themselves and their families in financial troubles were unlikely, thought some, to hold their husbands' interest or to be proper mothers and model women. Rousseau's belief that women were born with an innate concern for dress, finery, and tending their looks offended many eighteenth-century women, who aspired to the status of rational beings and thought of themselves as useful members of society. While writers like Hays and Wollstonecraft admired Rousseau's conception of an education in accordance with children's "natural" tendencies, affections, and interests, they rejected his designation of women to second class status, seeking to expand the Enlightenment value for rationality and Rousseau's appreciation for natural human feeling to include their sex.

SOURCES

Jean-Jacques Rousseau, *Émile, ou de l'Éducation* (1762), as *Émile*, Trans. Barbara Foxley, (Rutland, VT: Everyman, 1974).

Mary Wollstonecraft, *Vindication of the Rights of Woman* (1792), in *Works of Mary Wollstonecraft*, Ed. Janet Todd and Marilyn Butler, 5 Vols. Vol. 5, (Washington Square, NY: New York University Press, 1989).

Mary and Elizabeth Hays, *Letters and Essays, Moral and Miscellaneous* (1794). Ed. Gina Luria Walker (New York: Garland, 1974).

CHAP. VII.

TO AUGUSTUS HARLEY.

"I BLUSH, when I reflect what a weak, wavering, inconsistent, being, I must lately have appeared to you. I write to you on important subjects — I forbid you to answer me on paper; and, when you seem inclined to put that period to the present, painful, high-wrought, and trying, state of my feelings, which is now become so necessary, I appear neither to hear, nor to com_ prehend you. I fly from the subject, and thicken the cloud of mystery, of which I have so often, and, I still think, so justly

complained. — These are some of the effects of the contradictory systems, that have so long bewildered our principles and
conduct. A combination of causes, added to the conflict between
a thousand delicate and nameless emotions, have lately conspired
to confuse, to weaken, my spirits. You can conceive, that these
acute, mental, sensations, must have had a temporary effect on
the state of my health. To say truth (and, had I not said it, my
countenance would have betrayed me), I have not, for some time
past, been so thoroughly disordered.

"Once more, I have determined to rally my strength; for I
feel, that a much longer continuance in the situation, in which
my mind has been lately involved, would be insupportable: —
and I call upon you, *now*, with a resolution to summon all my
fortitude to bear the result, for the *written* state of your mind, on
the topic become so important to my future welfare and usefulness.

"You may suppose, that a mind like mine must have, repeatedly, set itself to examine, on every side, all that could possibly have a relation to a subject affecting it so materially. You
have hinted at *mysterious* obstacles to the wish, in which every
faculty of my soul has been so long absorbed — the wish of
forming with you, a connection, nearer, *and more tender*, than
that of friendship. This mystery, by leaving room for conjecture
(and how frequently have I warned you of this!), left room for
the illusions of imagination, and of hope — left room for the
suspicion, that you might, possibly, be sacrificing *your own feelings*, as well as mine, to a mistaken principle. Is it possible that
you were not aware of this — you, who are not unacquainted
with the nature of mind! Still less were you ignorant of the nature of my mind — which I had so explicitly, so unreservedly,
laid open! I had a double claim upon your confidence — a confidence, that I was utterly incapable of abusing, or betraying —
a confidence, which must have stopped my mind in its career —
which would have saved me the bitter, agonizing, pangs I have
sustained. Mine were not common feelings — It is *obscurity* and
mystery which has wrought them up to frenzy — *truth* and *cer-*

tainty would, long ere this, have caused them temperately to subside into their accustomed channels. You understand little of the human heart, if you cannot conceive this — 'Where the imagination is vivid, the feelings strong, the views and desires not bounded by common rules; — in such minds, passions, if not subdued, become ungovernable and fatal: where there is much warmth, much enthusiasm, there is much danger. — My mind is no less ardent than yours, though education and habit may have given it a different turn — it glows with equal zeal to attain its end.'[77] Yes, I must continue to repeat, there has been in your conduct *one grand mistake*; and the train of consequences which may, yet, ensue, are uncertain, and threatening. — But, I mean no reproach —— we are all liable to errors; and my own, I feel, are many, and various. But to return ——

"You may suppose I have revolved, in my thoughts, every possible difficulty on the subject alluded to; balancing their degrees of probability and force: — and, I will frankly confess, such is the sanguine ardour of my temper, that I can conceive but one obstacle, that would be *absolutely invincible*; which is, supposing that you have already contracted a *legal, irrevocable*, engagement. Yet, this I do not suppose. I will arrange, under five heads, (on all occasions, I love to class and methodize) every other possible species of objection, and subjoin all the reasonings which have occurred to me on the subjects.

"And, first, I will imagine, as the most serious and threatening difficulty, that you love another. I would, then, ask — Is she capable of estimating your worth — does she love you — has she the magnanimity to tell you so — would she sacrifice to that affection every meaner consideration — has she merit to secure, as well as accomplishments to attract, your regard? —— You are too well acquainted with the human heart, not to be aware, that what is commonly called love is of a fleeting nature, kept alive only by hopes and fears, if the qualities upon which it is

---

[77] "Holcroft's *Anna St Ives*." [M.H.] ed. Peter Faulkner, 1970, Vol. III, Letter LIII, p. 171.

founded afford no basis for its subsiding into tender confidence, and rational esteem. Beauty may inspire a transient desire, vivacity amuse, for a time, by its sportive graces; but the first will quickly fade and grow familiar — the last degenerate into impertinence and insipidity. Interrogate your own heart — Would you not, when the ardour of the passions, and the fervor of the imagination, subsided, wish to find the sensible, intelligent, friend, take place of the engaging mistress? — Would you not expect the economical manager of your affairs, the rational and judicious mother of your offspring, the faithful sharer of your cares, the firm friend to your interest, the tender consoler of your sorrows, the companion in whom you could wholly confide, the discerning participator of your nobler pursuits, the friend of your virtues, your talents, your reputation — who could understand you, who was formed to pass the ordeal of honour, virtue, friendship? — Ask yourself these questions — ask them closely, without sophistry, and without evasion. You are not, now, an infatuated boy! Supposing, then, that you are, at present, entangled in an engagement which answers not this description — Is it virtue to fulfill, or to renounce, it? Contrast with it my affection, with its probable consequences, and weigh our different claims! *Would you have been the selected choice, of this woman from all mankind* — would no other be capable of making her equally happy — would nothing compensate to her for your loss — are you the only object that she beholds in creation — might not another engagement suit her equally well, or better — is her whole soul absorbed but by one sentiment, that of fervent love for you — is her future usefulness, as well as peace, at stake — does she understand your high qualities better than myself — will she emulate them more? — Does the engagement promise a favourable issue, or does it threaten to wear away the best period of life in protracted and uncertain feeling — *the most pernicious, and destructive, of all states of mind?* Remember, also, that the summer of life will quickly fade; and that he who has reached the summit of the hill, has no time to lose — if he seize not the present moment, age is approaching, and life melting fast away.

— I quit this, to state my second hypothesis —

"That you esteem and respect me, but that your heart has hitherto refused the sympathies I have sought to awaken in it. If this be the case, it remains to search for the reason; and, I own, I am at a loss to find it, either in moral, or physical, causes. Our principles are in unison, our tastes and habits not dissimilar, our knowledge of, and confidence in, each other's virtues is reciprocal, tried, and established — our ages, personal accomplishments, and mental acquirements do not materially differ. From such an union, I conceive, mutual advantages would result. I have found myself distinguished, esteemed, beloved, by others, where I have not sought for this distinction. How, then, can I believe it compatible with the nature of mind, that so many strong efforts, and reiterated impressions, can have produced no effect upon yours? Is your heart constituted differently from every other human heart? — I have lately observed an inequality in your behaviour, that has whispered something flattering to my heart. Examine yourself — Have you felt no peculiar interest in what concerns me — would the idea of our separation affect you with no more than a slight and common emotion? ———— One more question propose to yourself, as a test — Could you see me form a new, and a more fortunate, attachment, with indifference? If you cannot, without hesitation, answer these questions, I have still a powerful pleader in your bosom, though unconscious of it yourself, that will, ultimately, prevail. If I have, yet, failed of producing an unequivocal effect, it must arise from having mistaken the *means* proper to produce the desired *end*. My own sensibility, and my imperfect knowledge of your character may, here, have combined to mislead me. The first, by its suffocating and depressing powers, clouding my vivacity, incapacitating me from appearing to you with my natural advantages — these effects would diminish as assurance took place of doubt. The last, every day would contribute to correct. Permit me, then, *to hope for*, as well as to seek your affections, and if I do not, at length, gain and secure them, it will be a phenomenon in the history of mind!

"But to proceed to my third supposition — The peculiar, pecuniary, embarrassments of your situation — Good God! did this barbarous, insidious, relation, allow himself to consider the pernicious consequences of his absurd bequest? — threatening to undermine every manly principle, to blast every social virtue! Oh! that I had the eloquence to rouse you from this tame and unworthy acquiescence — to stimulate you to exercise your talents, to trust to the independent energies of your mind, to exert yourself to procure the honest rewards of virtuous industry. In proportion as we lean for support on foreign aid, we lose the dignity of our nature, and palsey those powers which constitute that nature's worth. Yet, I will allow, from my knowledge of your habits and associations, this obstacle its full force. But there remains one method of obviating, even this! I will frankly confess, that could I hope to gain the interest in your heart, which I have so long and so earnestly sought — my confidence in your honour and integrity, my tenderness for you, added to the wish of contributing to your happiness, would effect, what no lesser considerations could have effected — would triumph, not over my principles, (*for the individuality of an affection constitutes its chastity*)[78] but over my prudence. I repeat, I am willing to sacrifice every inferior consideration — retain your legacy, so capriciously bequeathed — retain your present situation, and I will retain mine. This proposition, though not a violation of modesty, certainly involves in it very serious hazards — *It is, wholly, the triumph of affection!* You cannot suppose, that a transient engagement would satisfy a mind like mine; I should require a reciprocal faith plighted and returned — an after separation,

---

[78]The notion that chastity depends more on the exclusiveness of love than the legal marital status was Mary Wollstonecraft's argument. As William Godwin explained in *Memoirs of the Author of A Vindication of the Rights of Woman*, "It was her [Wollstonecraft's] maxim, 'that the imagination should awaken the senses, and not the senses the imagination.' In other words, that whatever related to the gratification of the senses, ought to arise, in a human being of a pure mind, only as the consequences of an individual affection" (Godwin, *Memoirs*, Glen Allen, VA: College Publishing, 249-50). See also *Adeline Mowbray*, p. 317.

otherwise than by mutual consent, would be my destruction — I should not survive your desertion. My existence, then, would be in your hands. Yet, having once confided, your affection should be my recompense — my sacrifice should be a cheerful and a voluntary one; I would determine not to harass you with doubts nor jealousies, I would neither reflect upon the past, not distrust the future: I would rest upon you, I would confide in you fearlessly and entirely! but, though I would not enquire after the past, my delicacy would require the assurance of your present, undivided, affection.

"The fourth idea that has occurred to me, is the probability of your having formed a plan of seeking some agreeable woman of fortune, who should be willing to reward a man of merit for the injustice of society. Whether you may already have experienced some disappointments of this nature, I will not pretend to determine. I can conceive, that, by many women, a coxcomb might be preferred to you —— however this may be, the plan is not unattended with risque, nor with some possible degrading circumstances — and you may succeed, and yet be miserable: happiness depends not upon the abundance of our possessions.

"The last case which I shall state, and on which I shall lay little comparative stress, is the possibility of an engagement of a very inferior nature — a mere affair of the senses. The arguments which might here be adduced are too obvious to be repeated. Besides, I think highly of your refinement and delicacy — Having therefore just hinted, I leave it with you.

"And now to conclude — After considering all I have urged, you may, perhaps, reply — That the subject is too nice[79] and too subtle for reasoning, and that the heart is not to be compelled. These, I think, are mistakes. There is no subject, in fact, that may not be subjected to the laws of investigation and reasoning. What is it that we desire — *pleasure* — *happiness?* I allow, pleasure is the supreme good: but it may be analyzed — it

[79] I.e., delicate.

must have a stable foundation — to this analysis I now call you! This is the critical moment, upon which hangs a long chain of events — This moment may decide your future destiny and mine — it may, even, affect that of unborn myriads! My spirit is pervaded with these important ideas — my heart flutters — I breathe with difficulty — *My friend* — *I would give myself to you* — the gift is not worthless. Pause a moment, ere you rudely throw from you an affection so tried, so respectable, so worthy of you! The heart may be compelled — compelled by the touching sympathies which bind, with sacred, indissoluble ties, mind to mind! Do not prepare for yourself future remorse — when lost, you may recollect my worth, and my affection, and remember them with regret — Yet mistake me not, I have no intention to intimidate — I think it my duty to live, while I may possibly be useful to others, however bitter and oppressive may be that existence. I will live *for duty*, though peace and enjoyment should be for ever fled. You may rob me of my happiness, you may rob me of my strength, but, even, you cannot destroy my principles. And, if no other motive with-held me from rash determinations, my tenderness for you (it is not a selfish tenderness), would prevent me from adding, to the anxieties I have already given you, the cruel pang, of feeling yourself the occasion, however unintentionally, of the destruction of a fellow creature.

"While I await your answer, I summon to my heart all its remaining strengths and spirits. Say to me, in clear and decisive terms, that the obstacles which oppose my affection *are absolutely, and altogether, insuperable* — Or that there is a possibility of their removal, but that time and patience are, yet, necessary to determine their force. In this case, I will not disturb the future operations of your mind, assuring myself, that you will continue my suspence no longer than is proper and requisite — or frankly accept, and return, the faith of her to whom you are infinitely dearer than life itself!

"Early to-morrow morning, a messenger shall call for the paper, which is to decide the colour of my future destiny. Every moment, that the blow has been suspended, it has acquired additional force — since it must, at length, descend, it would be weakness still to desire its protraction — We have, already, refined too much — *I promise to live — more, alas! I cannot promise.*

"*Farewel!* dearest and most beloved of men — whatever may be my fate — *be happiness yours!* Once more, my lingering, foreboding heart, repeats *farewel!*

"Emma."

It would be unnecessary to paint my feelings during the interval in which I waited a reply to this letter — I struggled to repress hope, and to prepare my mind for the dissolution of a thousand air-built fabrics. The day wore tediously away in strong emotion, and strong exertion. On the subsequent morning, I sat, waiting the return of my messenger, in a state of mind, difficult even to be conceived — I heard him enter — breathless, I flew to meet him — I held out my hand — I could not speak.

"Mr. Harley desired me to tell you, *he had not had time to write.*"

Gracious God! I shudder, even now, to recall the convulsive sensation! I sunk into a chair — I sat for some time motionless, every faculty seemed suspended. At length, returning to recollection, I wrote a short incoherent note, entreating ——

"To be spared another day, another night, like the preceding — I asked only *one single line!* In the morning I had made up my mind to fortitude — it was now sinking — another day, I could not answer for the consequences."

Again an interval of suspense — again my messenger returned with a verbal reply — "*He would write to-morrow.*" Unconsciously, I exclaimed — "*Barbarous, unfeeling, unpitying, man!*" A burst of tears relieved — no — *it did not relieve me.* The day passed — I know not how — I dare not recollect.

The next morning, I arose, somewhat refreshed; my exhausted strength and spirits had procured me a few hours of profound slumber. A degree of resentment gave a temporary firmness to my nerves. "What happiness (I repeated to myself) could I have expected with a man, thus regardless of my feelings?" I composed my spirits — *hope was at an end* — into a sort of sullen resignation to my fate — a half stupor!

At noon the letter arrived, coldly, confusedly written; methought there appeared even a degree of irritation in it.

"*Another, a prior attachment* — His behaviour had been such, as necessarily resulted from such an engagement — unavoidable circumstances had prevented an earlier reply." My swollen heart — but it is enough — "He blamed my impatience — he would in future, perhaps, when my mind had attained more composure, make some remarks on my letter."

CHAP. VIII.

To write had always afforded a temporary relief to my spirits — The next day I resumed my pen.

TO AUGUSTUS HARLEY.

"If, after reflecting upon, and comparing, many parts of your past conduct, you can acquit yourself, at the sacred bar of humanity — it is well! How often have I called for — urged, with all the energy of truth and feeling — but in vain — such a letter as you have at length written — and, *even, now*, though somewhat late, I thank you for it. Yet, what could have been easier, than to repeat so plain and so simple a tale? The vague hints, you had before given, I had repeatedly declared to be insufficient. Remember, all my earnestness, and all my simplicity, and *learn the value of sincerity!* 'Oh! with what difficulty is an active mind, once forced into any particular train, persuaded to desert it as hopeless!'[80]

"This recital, then, was not to be confirmed, till the whole moral conformation of my mind was affected — till the barbed

---

[80] "Godwin's *Caleb Williams*." [MH] "An active mind, which has once been forced into any particular train, can scarcely be persuaded to desert it as hopeless." Ed. Maurice Hindle (New York: Penguin, 1988), p. 199.

arrow had fixed, and rankled in, and poisoned, with its envenomed point, every vein, every fibre, of my heart. This, I confess, is now the case — Reason and self-respect sustain me — but the wound you have inflicted *is indelible* — it will continue to be the corroding canker at the root of my peace. My youth has been worn in anguish — and the summer of life will probably be overshadowed by a still thicker and darker cloud. But I mean not to reproach you — it is not given me to contribute to your happiness — the dearest and most ardent wish of my soul — I would not then inflict unnecessary pain — yet, I would fix upon your mind, the value of *unequivocal sincerity.*

"Had the happiness of any human being, the meanest, the vilest, depended as much upon me, as mine has done upon you, I would have sacrificed, for their relief, the dearest secret of my heart — the secret, even upon which my very existence had depended. It is true, you did not directly deceive me — but is that enough for the delicacy of humanity? May the past be an affecting lesson to us both — it is written upon my mind in characters of blood. I feel, and acknowledge, my own errors, in yielding to the illusion of vague, visionary, expectation; but my faults have originated in a generous source — they have been the wild, ardent, fervent, excesses, of a vigorous and an exalted mind!

"I checked my tears, as they flowed, and they are already dried — uncalled, unwished, for — why do they, thus, struggle to force their way? my mind has, I hope, too much energy, utterly to sink — I know what it is to suffer, and to combat with, if not to subdue, my feelings — and *certainty*, itself, is some relief. I am, also, supported by the retrospect of my conduct; with all its mistakes, and all its extravagances, it has been that of a virtuous, ingenuous, uncorrupted, mind. You have contemned a heart of no common value, you have sported with its exquisite sensibilities — but it will, still, know how to separate your virtues from your errors.

"You reprove, perhaps justly, my impatience — I can only say, that circumstanced as you were, I should have stolen an hour from rest, from company, from business, however important, to have relieved and soothed a fellow-creature in a situation, so full of pain and peril. Every thought, during a day scarcely to be recollected without agony, *was a two-edged sword* — but some hours of profound and refreshing slumber recruited my exhausted spirits, and enabled me, yesterday, to receive my fate, with a fortitude but little hoped for.

"You would oblige me exceedingly by the remarks you allow me to hope for, on my letter of the ——— th. You know, I will not shrink from reproof — that letter afforded you the last proof of my affection, and I repent not of it. I loved you, first, for what, I conceived, high qualities of mind — from nature and association, my tenderness became personal — till at length, I loved you, not only rationally and tenderly — *but passionately* — it became a pervading and a devouring fire! And, yet, I do not blush — my affection was modest, if intemperate, *for it was individual* — it annihilated in my eyes every other man in the creation. I regret these natural sensations and affections, their forcible suppression injures the mind — it converts the mild current of gentle, and genial sympathies, into a destructive torrent. This, I have the courage to avow it, has been one of the miserable mistakes in morals, and, like all other partial remedies, has increased the evil, it was intended to correct. From monastic institutions and principles have flowed, as from a polluted source, streams, that have at once spread through society a mingled contagion of dissoluteness and hypocrisy.

"You have suddenly arrested my affections in their full career — in all their glowing effervescence — you have taken

'The rose
From the fair forehead of an innocent love,
And placed a blister there.'[81]

"And, yet, I survive the shock, and determine to live, not for future enjoyment — that is now, for ever, past — *but for future usefulness* — Is not this virtue?

---

[81] Shakespeare, *Hamlet*, III.4.42-4.

"I am sorry your attachment has been, and I fear is likely to be, protracted — I know, too well, the misery of these situations, and I should, now, feel a melancholy satisfaction in hearing of its completion — In that completion, may you experience no disappointment! I do not wish you to be beloved, as I have loved you; this, perhaps, is unnecessary; such an affection, infallibly, enslaves the heart that cherishes it; and slavery is the tomb of virtue and of peace.

"I believe it would not be proper for us to meet again — at least at present — should I hear of sickness, or calamity, befalling you, I shall, I suspect, be impelled, by an irresistible impulse to seek you — but I will no more interrupt your repose — Though you have contemned my affection, my friendship will still follow you.

"If you really *love*, I think you ought to make some sacrifices, and not render yourself, and the happy object of your tenderness, the victims of factitious notions. — Remember — youth and life will quickly fade. Relinquish, call upon her to relinquish, her prejudices — should she refuse, she is unworthy of you, and you will regret, too late, the tender, faithful, ingenuous, heart, that you have pierced through and through — *that you have almost broken!* Should she make you happy, I will esteem, though I may never have an opportunity of thanking, her — Were she informed of my conduct, she might rejoice in the trial of your affection — though I should not.

"The spirits, that had crouded round my heart, are already subsiding — a flood of softness, a tide of overwhelming reflection, gushes upon it — and I feel sinking into helpless, infantine, distress! Hasten to me your promised remarks — they will rouse, they will strengthen, me. — *Truth* I will never call either indelicate or inhuman — it is only the virtuous mind can dare to practise, to challenge, it: — simplicity is true refinement.

"Let us reap from the past all the good we can — a close, and searching, knowledge of the secret springs and foldings of our hearts. Methinks, I could wish you justified, *even at my own expence.* — I ask, unshrinking, a frank return.

"A heart-rending sigh accompanies my *farewel* — the last struggles of expiring nature will be far less painful — but my philosophy, now, *sternly* calls upon me to put its precepts in practice —— trembling — shuddering — I obey!

"*Farewel!*

"EMMA."

Perhaps it cost me some efforts to make the preceding letter so moderate — yet, every victory gained over ourselves is attended with advantages. But this apparent calm was the lethargy of despair —— it was succeeded by severer conflicts, by keener anguish. A week passed, and near a second — I received no answer.

CHAP. IX.

A LETTER from the country made it necessary for me, again, to address Mr. Harley, to make some enquiries which respected business of his mother's. It may be, that I felt a mixture of other motives; —— it is certain, that when I wrote, I spoke of more than business.

"I had hoped," I told him, "ere this, to have received the promised letter — Yet, I do not take up my pen," said I, "either to complain of, or to importune, you. If I have already expressed myself with bitterness, let the harrassed state of my mind be my excuse. My own conduct has been too erroneous, too eccentric, to enable me to judge impartially of your's. Forgive me, if, by placing you in an embarrassed situation, I have exposed you to consequent mistake or uneasiness. I feel, that whatever errors we may either of us have committed, *originated only with myself,* and I am content to suffer all the consequences. It is true, had you reposed in me an early, generous, confidence, much misery would have been avoided — I had not been wounded

'There, where the human heart most exquisitely feels!'[82]

[82] James Thomson, *Tancred and Sigismunda* (1745), II.8: "This murderous stroke

"You had been still my friend, and I had been comparatively happy. Every passion is, in a great measure, the growth of indulgence: all our desires are, in their commencement, easily suppressed, when there appears no probability of attaining their object; but when strengthened, by time and reflection, into habit, in endeavouring to eradicate them, we tear away part of the mind. In my attachments there is a kind of savage tenacity — they are of an elastic nature, and, being forced back, return with additional violence.

"My affection for you has not been, altogether, irrational or selfish. While I felt that I loved you, as no other woman, I was convinced, would love you — I conceived, could I once engage your heart, I could satisfy, and, even, purify it. While I loved your virtues, I thought I saw, and I lamented, the foibles which sullied them. I suspected you, perhaps erroneously, of pride, ambition, the love of distinction; yet your ambition could not, I thought, be of an ignoble nature — I feared that the gratifications you sought, if, indeed, attainable, were factitious — I even fancied I perceived you, against your better judgment, labouring to seduce yourself! 'He is under a delusion,' said I, to myself; — 'reason may be stunned, or blinded, for awhile; but it will revive in the heart, and do its office, when sophistry will be to no avail.' I saw you struggling with vexations, that I was assured might be meliorated by tender confidence — I longed to pour its balms into your bosom. My sensibility disquieted you, and myself, only *because it was constrained*. I thought I perceived a conflict in your mind — I watched its progress with attention and solicitude. A thousand times has my fluttering heart yearned to break the cruel chains that fettered it, and to chace the cloud, which stole over your brow, by the tender, yet chaste, caresses and endearments of ineffable affection! My feelings became too high wrought, and altogether insupportable. Sympathy for your situation, zeal for your virtues, love for your mind, tenderness

that stabs my peace forever!/ That wounds me there—there! where the human Heart/Most exquisitely feels...."

for your person — a complication of generous, affecting, exquisite, emotions, impelled me to make one great effort — [83]'The world might call my plans absurd, my views romantic, my pretensions extravagant — Was I, or was I not, guilty of any crime, when, in the very acme of the passions, I so totally disregarded the customs of the world?' Ah! what were my sensations — what did I not suffer, in the interval? — and you prolonged that cruel interval — and still you suffer me to doubt, whether, at the moment in my life when I was actuated by the highest, the most fervent, the most magnanimous, principles — whether, at that moment when I most deserved your respect, I did not for ever forfeit it.

"I seek not to extenuate any part of my conduct — I confess that it has been wild, extravagant, romantic — I confess, that, even for your errors, I am justly blameable — and yet I am unable to bear, because I feel they would be unjust, your hatred and contempt. I cherish no resentment — my spirit is subdued and broken — your unkindness sinks into my soul.

"EMMA."

Another fortnight wore away in fruitless expectation — the morning rose, the evening closed, upon me, in sadness. I could not, yet, think the mystery developed: on a concentrated view of the circumstances, they appeared to me contradictory, and irreconcileable. A solitary enthusiast, a child in the drama of the world, I had yet to learn, that those who have courage to act upon advanced principles, must be content to suffer moral martyrdom.[84] In subduing our own prejudices, we have done little, while assailed on every side by the prejudices of others. My own heart acquitted me; but I dreaded that distortion of mind, that should wrest guilt out of the most sublime of its emanations.

---

[83] "Holcroft's *Anna St. Ives*." [M.H.] Ed. Peter Faulkner, 1970, Vol. IV, Letter LXXIX, p. 264 and Vol. III, Letter XLI, p. 138.

[84] "This sentiment may be just in some particular cases, but it is by no means of general application, and must be understood with great limitations." [M.H.]

I ruminated, in gloomy silence, on my forlorn, and hopeless, situation. "If there be not a future state of being," said I to
myself, "what is this! — Tortured in every stage of it, 'Man cometh
forth like a flower, and is cut down — he fleeth, as a shadow, and
continueth not!'[85] —— I looked backward on my past life, and
my heart sickened — its confidence in humanity was shaken —
I looked forward, and all was cheerless. I had certainly committed many errors! —— Who has not — who, with a fancy as
lively, feelings as acute, and a character as sanguine, as mine?"
'What, in fact,' says a philosophic writer,[86] 'is character? — the
production of a lively and constant affection, and, consequently,
of a strong passion:' — eradicate that passion, that ferment, that
leaven, that exuberance, which raises and makes the mind what
it is, and what remains? Yet, let us beware how we wantonly
expend this divine, this invigorating, power. Every grand error,
in a mind of energy, in its operation and consequences, carries us
years forward — *precious years, never to be recalled!* I could find no
substitute for the sentiment I regretted — for that sentiment
formed my character; and, but for the obstacles which gave it
force, though I might have suffered less misery, I should, I suspect, have gained less improvement; still adversity *is a real evil*;
and I foreboded that this improvement had been purchased too
dear.

CHAP. X.

WEEKS elapsed ere the promised letter arrived — a letter still
colder, and more severe, than the former. I wept over it, bitter
tears! It accused me "of adding to the vexations of a situation,
before sufficiently oppressive." — Alas! had I known the nature
of those vexations, could I have merited such a reproof? The
Augustus, I had so long and so tenderly loved, no longer seemed
to exist. Some one had, surely, usurped his signature, and imitated those characters, I had been accustomed to trace with de-

[85] Job 14.2
[86] "Helvetius." [M.H.]

light. He tore himself from me, *nor would he deign to soften the pang of separation.* Anguish overwhelmed me — my heart was pierced. Reclining my head on my folded arms, I yielded myself up to silent grief. Alone, sad, desolate, no one heeded my sorrows — no eye pitied me — no friendly voice cheered my wounded spirit! The social propensities of a mind forbidden to expand itself, forced back, preyed incessantly upon that mind, secretly consuming its powers.

I was one day roused from these melancholy reflections by the entrance of my cousin, Mrs. Denbeigh. She held in her hand a letter, from my only remaining friend, Mrs. Harley. I snatched it hastily; my heart, lacerated by the seeming unkindness of him in whom it had confided, yearned to imbibe the consolation, which the gentle tenderness of this dear, maternal, friend, had never failed to administer. The first paragraph informed me

"That she had, a few days since, received a letter from the person to whom the legacy of her son devolved, should he fail in observing the prescribed conditions of the testator: that this letter gave her notice, that those conditions had already been infringed, Mr. Harley having contracted a marriage, three years before, with a foreigner, with whom he had become acquainted during his travels; that this marriage had been kept a secret, and, but very lately, by an accidental concurrence of circumstances, revealed to the person most concerned in the detection. Undoubted proofs of the truth of this information could be produced; it would therefore be most prudent in her son to resign his claims, without putting himself, and the legal heir, to unnecessary expence and litigation. Ignorant of the residence of Mr. Harley, the writer troubled his mother to convey to him these particulars."

The paper dropped from my hand, the colour forsook my lips and cheeks; — yet I neither wept, nor fainted. Mrs. Denbeigh took my hands — they were frozen — the blood seemed congealed in my veins — and I sat motionless — my faculties suspended, stunned, locked up! My friend spake to me — embraced, shed tears over, me — but she could not excite mine; —

my mind was pervaded by a sense of confused misery. I remained many days in this situation — it was a state, of which I have but a feeble remembrance; and I, at length, awoke from it, as from a troublesome dream.

With returning reason, the tide of recollection also returned. Oh! how complicated appeared to me the guilt of Augustus! Ignorant of his situation, I had been unconsciously, and perseveringly, exerting myself to seduce the affections of a *husband* from his *wife*. He had made me almost criminal in my own eyes — he had risqued, at once, by a disingenuous and cruel reserve, the virtue and the happiness of three beings. What is virtue, but a calculation of *the consequences of our actions?* Did we allow ourselves to reason on this principle, to reflect on its truth and importance, we should be compelled to shudder at many parts of our conduct, which, *taken unconnectedly*, we have habituated ourselves to consider as almost indifferent. Virtue can exist only in a mind capable of taking comprehensive views. How criminal, then, is ignorance!

During this sickness of the soul, Mr. Francis, who had occasionally visited me since my residence in town, called, repeatedly, to enquire after my welfare; expressing a friendly concern for my indisposition. I saw him not — I was incapable of seeing any one — but, informed by my kind hostess of his humane attentions, soothed by the idea of having yet a friend who seemed to interest himself in my concerns, I once more had recourse to my pen (Mrs. Denbeigh having officiously placed the implements of writing in my way), and addressed him in the wild and incoherent language of despair.

To Mr. Francis.

"You once told me, that I was incapable of heroism; and you were right — yet, I am called to great exertions! a blow that has been suspended over my head, days, weeks, months, years, has at length fallen — still I live! My tears flow — I struggle, in vain, to suppress them, but they are not tears of blood! — My heart, though pierced through and through, is not broken!

"My friend, come and teach me how to acquire fortitude — I am wearied with misery — All nature is to me a blank — an envenomed shaft rankles in my bosom — philosophy will not heal the festering wound — *I am exquisitely wretched!*

"Do not chide me till I get more strength — I speak to you of my sorrows, for your kindness, while I was yet a stranger to you, inspired me with confidence, and my desolate heart looks round for support.

"I am indebted to you — how shall I repay your goodness? Do you, indeed, interest yourself in my fate? Call upon me, then, for the few incidents of my life — I will relate them simply and without disguise. There is nothing uncommon in them, but the effect which they have produced upon my mind — yet, that mind they formed.

"After all, my friend, what a wretched farce is life! Why cannot I sleep, and, close my eyes upon it for ever? But something whispers, '*this would be wrong.*' — How shall I tear from my heart all its darling, close-twisted, associations? — And must I live — *live for what?* God only knows! Yet, how am I sure that there is a God — is he wise — is he powerful — is he benevolent? If he be, can he sport himself in the miseries of poor, feeble, impotent, beings, forced into existence, without their choice — impelled, by the iron hand of necessity, through mistake, into calamity? — Ah! my friend, who will condemn the poor solitary wanderer,[87] whose feet are pierced with many a thorn, should he turn suddenly out of the rugged path, seek an obscure shade to shroud his wounds, his sorrows, and his indignation, from the scorn of a pitiless world, and accelerate the hour of repose.[88] Who would be born if they could help it? You would perhaps —

---

[87] The "solitary wanderer" is an important figure in turn-of-the-century Britain. See for example Rousseau's *Les Reveries du Promeneur Solitaire (Memoirs of a Solitary Wanderer)* (1776-8), Charlotte Smith's *Wanderings of Warwick* (1794) and *Letters of a Solitary Wanderer* (1802), and Frances Burney's novel *The Wanderer; or Female Difficulties* (1814).

[88] "This is the reasoning of a mind distorted by passion. Even in the moment of disappointment, our heroine judged better. See page 69." [M.H.] See Emma's

you may do good — But on me, the sun shines only to mock my woes — Oh! that I had never seen the light.

"Torn by conflicting passions — wasted in anguish — life is melting fast away — A burthen to myself, a grief to those who love me, and worthless to every one. Weakened by long suspence — preyed upon, by a combination of imperious feelings — I fear, I greatly fear, *the irrecoverable blow is struck!* But I blame no one — I have been entangled in error — *who is faultless?*

"While pouring itself out on paper, my tortured mind has experienced a momentary relief: If your heart be inaccessible to tender sympathies, I have only been adding one more to my numberless mistakes!

"EMMA."

Mr. Francis visited me, and evinced for my situation the most humane and delicate consideration. He reminded me of the offer I had made him, and requested the performance of my engagement. In compliance with this request, and to beguile my melancholy thoughts, I drew up a sketch of events of my past life, and unfolded a history of the sentiments of my mind (from which I have extracted the preceding materials) reserving only any circumstance which might lead to a detection of the name and family of the man with whom they were so intimately blended.

CHAP. XI.

AFTER having perused my manuscript, Mr. Francis returned it, at my desire, accompanied by the following letter.

TO EMMA COURTNEY.

"Your narrative leaves me full of admiration for your quali-

---

letter, Vol. 2, Chapt. VII, "we are too liable to errors" for the original reference. The author appears to be reflecting on Emma's earlier understanding of the importance of self-improvement and learning to escape and correct "error." Here Emma allows feeling passion to overwhelm her previous wisdom.

ties, and compassion for your insanity.

"I entreat however your attention to the following passage, extracted from your papers. 'After considering all I have urged, you may perhaps reply, that the subject is too nice, and too subtle, for reasoning, and that the heart is not to be compelled. This, I think, is a mistake. There is no topic, in fact, that may not be subjected to the laws of investigation and reasoning. What is it we desire? pleasure, happiness. What! the pleasure of an instant, only; or that which is more solid and permanent? I allow, pleasure is the supreme good! but it may be analysed. To this analysis I now call you.'

"Could I, if I had studied for years, invent a comment on your story, more salutary to your sorrows, more immoveable in its foundation, more clearly expressed, or more irresistibly convincing to every rational mind?

"How few real, substantial, misfortunes there are in the world! how few calamities, the sting of which does not depend upon our cherishing the viper in our bosom, and applying the aspic to our veins! The general pursuit of all men, we are frequently told, is happiness. I have often been tempted to think, on the contrary, that the general pursuit is misery. It is true, men do not recognize it by its genuine appellation; they content themselves with the pitiful expedient of assigning it a new denomination. But, if their professed purpose were misery, could they be more skilful and ingenious in the pursuit?

"Look through your whole life. To speak from your own description, was there ever a life, to its present period, less chequered with substantial *bona fide* misfortune? The whole force of every thing which looks like a misfortune was assiduously, unintermittedly, provided by yourself. You nursed in yourself a passion, which, taken in the degree in which you experienced it, is the unnatural and odious invention of a distempered civilization, and which in almost all instances generates an immense overbalance of excruciating misery. Your conduct will scarcely admit of any other denomination than moon-struck madness, hunting after torture. You addressed a man impenetrable as a rock, and the smallest glimpse of sober reflection, and common sense, would have taught you instantly to have given up the pursuit.

"I know you will tell me, and you will tell yourself, a great deal about constitution, early association, and the indissoluble chain of habits and sentiments. But I answer with small fear of being erroneous, 'It is a mistake to suppose, that the heart is not to be compelled. There is no topic in fact, that may not be subjected to the laws of investigation and reasoning. Pleasure, happiness, is the supreme good; and happiness is susceptible of being analysed.'[89] I grant, that the state of a human mind cannot be changed at once; but, had you worshipped at the altar of reason but half as assiduously as you have sacrificed at the shrine of illusion, your present happiness would have been as enviable, as your present distress is worthy of compassion. If men would but take the trouble to ask themselves, once every day, Why should I be miserable? how many, to whom life is a burthen, would become chearful and contented.

"Make a catalogue of all the real evils of human life; bodily pain, compulsory solitude, severe corporal labour, in a word, all those causes which deprive us of health, or the means of spending our time in animated, various, and rational pursuits. Aye, these are real evils! But I should be ashamed of putting disappointed love into my enumeration. Evils of this sort are the brood of folly begotten upon fastidious indolence. They shrink into non-entity, when touched by the wand of truth.

"The first lesson of enlightened reason, the great fountain of heroism and virtue, the principle by which alone man can become what man is capable of being, is *independence*. May every power that is favourable to integrity, to honour, defend me from leaning upon another for support! I will use the world, I will use my fellow men, but I will not abuse these invaluable benefits of

---

[89] Loosely cited from Godwin's *Political Justice* and reiterated by Hays in other private writings. Compare Emma's previous letter to Augustus Harley, "pleasure is the supreme good: but it may be analyzed...." (p. 193 this volume).

the system of nature. I will not be weak and criminal enough, to make my peace depend upon the precarious thread of another's life or another's pleasure. I will judge for myself; I will draw my support from myself — the support of my existence and the support of my happiness. The system of nature has perhaps made me dependent for the means of existence and happiness upon my fellow men taken collectively; but nothing but my own folly can make me dependent upon individuals. Will these principles prevent me from admiring, esteeming, and loving such as are worthy to excite these emotions? Can I not have a mind to understand, and a heart to feel excellence, without first parting with the fairest attribute of my nature?

"You boast of your sincerity and frankness. You have doubtless some reason for your boast — Yet all your misfortunes seem to have arisen from concealment. You brooded over your emotions, and considered them as a sacred deposit — You have written to me, I have seen you frequently, during the whole of this transaction, without ever having received the slightest hint of it, yet, if I be a fit counsellor now, I was a fit counsellor then; your folly was so gross, that, if it had been exposed to the light of day, it could not have subsisted for a moment. Even now you suppress the name of your hero: yet, unless I know how much of a hero and a model of excellence he would appear in my eyes, I can be but a very imperfect judge of the affair.

"—— FRANCIS."

CHAP. XII.

To the remonstrance of my friend, which roused me from the languor into which I was sinking, I immediately replied —

TO MR. FRANCIS.

"You retort upon me my own arguments, and you have cause. I felt a ray of conviction dart upon my mind, even, while I wrote them. But what then? — 'I seemed to be in a state, in which reason had no power; I felt as if I could coolly survey the several arguments of the case — perceive, that they had prudence, truth, and common sense on their side — And then answer — I am under the guidance of a director more energetic than you!'[90] I am affected by your kindness — I am affected by your letter. I could weep over it, bitter tears of conviction and remorse. But argue with the wretch infected with the plague — will it stop the tide of blood, that is rapidly carrying its contagion to the heart? I blush! I shed burning tears! But I am still desolate and wretched! And how am I to help it? The force which you impute to my reasoning was the powerful frenzy of a high delirium.

"What does it signify whether, abstractedly considered, a misfortune be worthy of the names real and substantial, if the consequences produced are the same? That which embitters all my life, that which stops the genial current of health and peace is, whatever be its nature, a real calamity to me. There is no end to this reasoning — what individual can limit the desires of another? The necessaries of the civilized man are whimsical superfluities in the eye of the savage. Are we, or are we not (as you have taught me) the creatures of sensation and circumstance?

"I agree with you — and the more I look into society, the deeper I feel the soul-sickening conviction — 'The general pursuit is misery' — necessarily — excruciating misery, from the source to which you justly ascribe it — '*The unnatural and odious inventions of a distempered civilization.*' I am content, you may perceive, to recognize things by their genuine appellation. I am, at least, a reasoning maniac: perhaps the most dangerous species of insanity. But while the source continues troubled, why expect the streams to run pure?

"You know I will tell you — 'about the indissoluble chains of association and habit:' and you attack me again with my own weapons! Alas! while I confess their impotence, with what consistency do I accuse the flinty, impenetrable, heart, I so earnestly sought, in vain, to move? What materials does this stubborn mechanism of the mind offer to the wise and benevolent legisla-

---

[90] "Godwin's *Caleb Williams.*" [M.H.]. Ed. Maurice Hindle (New York: Penguin, 1988), p. 154.

tor!

"Had I, you tell me, 'worshipped at the altar of reason, but half as assiduously as I have sacrificed at the shrine of illusion, my happiness might have been enviable.' But do you not perceive, that my reason was the auxiliary of my passion, or rather my passion the generative principle of my reason? Had not these contradictions, these oppositions, roused the energy of my mind, I might have domesticated, tamely, in the lap of indolence and apathy.

"I do ask myself, every day — 'Why should I be miserable?' — and I answer, 'Because the strong, predominant, sentiment of my soul, close twisted with all its cherished associations, has been rudely torn away, and the blood follows from the lacerated wound.' You would be ashamed of placing disappointed love in your enumeration of evils! Gray was not ashamed of this —

> 'And pining love shall waste their youth,
> And jealousy, with the rankling tooth,
> That inly gnaws the secret heart!'

> ———

> 'These shall the stings of falsehood try,
> And hard unkindness' alter'd eye,
> That mocks the tear it forc'd to flow.'[91]

"Is it possible that you can be insensible of all the mighty mischiefs which have been caused by this passion — of the great events and changes of society, to which it has operated as a powerful, though secret, spring? That Jupiter shrouded his glories beneath a mortal form; that he descended yet lower, and crawled as a reptile — that Hercules took the distaff, and Sampson was shorn of his strength, are, in their spirit, no fables.[92] Yet, these

---

[91] Thomas Gray, "Ode on a Distant Prospect of Eton College" 1747. Lines 65-67 and 75-77.

[92] All classical or biblical tales of gods and heroes reduced by love. Jupiter or Zeus, king of the gods, frequently took on different forms to pursue women. Hercules, half-god, was reduced to women's work by his love for Omphale. Samson in the

were the legends of ages less degenerate than this, and states of society less corrupt. Ask your own heart — whether some of its most exquisite sensations have not arisen from sources, which, to nine-tenths of the world, would be equally inconceivable? Mine, I believe, is a *solitary madness in the eighteenth century: it is not on the altars of love, but of gold, that men, now, come to pay their offerings.*

"Why call woman, miserable, oppressed, and impotent, woman — *crushed, and then insulted* — why call her to *independence* — which not nature, but the barbarous and accursed laws of society, have denied her? *This is mockery!* Even you, wise and benevolent as you are, can mock the child of slavery and sorrow![93] 'Excluded, as it were, by the pride, luxury, and caprice, of the world, from expanding my sensations, and wedding my soul to society, I was constrained to bestow the strong affections, that glowed consciously within me, upon a few.'[94] Love, in minds of any elevation, cannot be generated but upon a real, or fancied, foundation of excellence. But what would be a miracle in architecture, is true in morals — the fabric can exist when the foundation has mouldered away. *Habit* daily produces this wonderful effect upon every feeling, and every principle. Is not this the theory which you have taught me?

"Am I not sufficiently ingenuous? — I will give you a new proof of my frankness (though not the proof you require). — From the miserable consequences of wretched moral distinctions, from chastity having been considered as a sexual virtue, all these calamities have flowed. Men are thus rendered sordid and dissolute in their pleasures; their affections vitiated, and their feelings petrified; the simplicity of modest tenderness loses its charm; they become incapable of satisfying the heart of a woman of sensibility and virtue. — Half the sex, then, are the wretched,

biblical tale was ensnared by Delilah who cut his hair while he slept, magically depriving him of his astonishing strength.
[93] Hays's letters to Godwin make precisely this argument.
[94] "Godwin's *Caleb Williams*." [M.H.] Hays's version is unique.

degraded, victims of brutal instinct: the remainder, if they sink
not into mere frivolity and insipidity, are sublimed into a sort of
—— (what shall I call them?) —— refined, romantic, factitious, unfortunate, beings; who, for the sake of the present moment, dare not expose themselves to complicated, inevitable,
evils; evils, that will infallibly overwhelm them with misery and
regret! Woe be, more especially, to those who, possessing the
dangerous gifts of fancy and feeling, find it as difficult to discover a substitute for the object as for the sentiment! You, who
are a philosopher, will you still controvert the principles founded
in truth and nature? 'Gross as is my folly' (and I do not deny it)
you may perceive I was not wholly wandering in darkness. But
while the wintry sun of hope illumined the fairy frost-work with
a single, slanting, ray — dazzled by the transient brightness, I
dreaded the meridian fervors that should dissolve the glittering
charm. Yes! it was madness — but it was the pleasurable madness which none but madmen know.

"I cannot answer your question — Pain me not by its repetition; neither seek to ensnare me to the disclosure. Unkindly, severely, as I have been treated, I will not risque, even, the possibility of injuring the man, whom I have so tenderly loved, in the
esteem of any one. Were I to name him, you know him not; you
could not judge of his qualities. He is not 'a model of excellence.'
I perceive it, with pain — and if obliged to retract my judgment
on some parts of his character —— I retract it with agonizing
reluctance! But I could trace the sources of his errors, and candour
and self-abasement imperiously compel me to a mild judgment,
to stifle the petulant suggestions of a wounded spirit.

"Ought not our principles, my friend, to soften the asperity
of our censures? — Could I have won him to my arms, I thought
I could soften, and even elevate, his mind — a mind, in which I
still perceive a great proportion of good. I weep for him, as well
as for myself. He will, one day, know my value, and feel my loss.
Still, I am sensible, that, by my extravagance, I have given a
great deal of vexation (possibly some degradation), to a being,
whom I had no right to persecute, or to compel to chuse happi-

ness through a medium of my creation. I cannot exactly tell the extent of the injury I may have done him. A long train of consequences succeed, even, our most indifferent actions. —— Strong energies, though they answer not the end proposed, must yet produce correspondent effects. Morals and mechanics are here analogous. No longer, then, distress me by the repetition of a question I ought not to answer. I am content to be the victim — Oh! may I be the only victim — of my folly!

"One more observation allow me to make, before I conclude. That we can 'admire, esteem, and love,' an individual — (for love in the abstract, loving mankind collectively, conveys to me no idea) — which must be, in fact, depending upon that individual for a large share of our felicity, and not lament his loss, in proportion to our apprehension of his worth, appears to me a proposition, involving in itself an absurdity; therefore demonstrably false.

"Let me, my friend, see you ere long — your remonstrance has affected me — save me from myself!"

————

TO THE SAME.

(In Continuation.)

"My letter having been delayed a few days, through a mistake — I resume my pen; for, running my eye over what I had written, I perceive (confounded by the force of your expressions) I have granted you too much. My conduct was not, altogether, so insane as I have been willing to allow. It is certain, that could I have attained the end proposed, my happiness had been encreased. 'It is necessary for me to love and admire, or I sink into sadness.'[95] The behaviour of the man, whom I sought to move, appeared to me too inconsistent to be the result of *indifference*. To be roused and stimulated by obstacles — obstacles admitting hope, because obscurely seen — is no mark of weak-

---

[95] Mary Wollstonecraft, *Letters Written During a Short Residence in Sweden, Norway, and Denmark,* "I must love and admire with warmth, or I sink into sadness" in *Works,* ed. Janet Todd and Marilyn Butler, Vol 6, p. 280.

ness. Could I have subdued, what I, *then*, conceived to be the *prejudices* of a worthy man, I could have increased both his happiness and my own. I deeply reasoned, and philosophized, upon the subject. Perseverance, with little ability, has effected wonders; — with perseverance, I felt, that, I had the power of uniting ability — confiding in that power, I was the dupe of my own reason. No other man, perhaps, could have acted the part which this man has acted: — how, then, was I to take such a part into my calculations?

"Do not misconceive me — it is no miracle that I did not inspire affection. On this subject, the mortification I have suffered has humbled me, it may be, even, unduly in my own eyes — but to the emotions of my pride, I would disdain to give words. Whatever may have been my feelings, I am proud to express the rage of slighted love! — Yet, I am sensible to all the powers of those charming lines of Pope——

'Unequal task, a passion to resign,
For hearts so touch'd, so pierc'd, so lost, as mine!
Ere such a soul regains its peaceful state,
How often must it love, how often hate;
How often hope, despair, resent, regret,
Conceal, disdain, *do all things but forget!*[96]

"But to return. I pursued, comparatively, (as I thought) a certain good; and when, at times, discouraged, I have repeated to myself — What! after all these pains, shall I relinquish my efforts, when, perhaps, on the very verge of success? — To say nothing of the difficulty of forcing an active mind out of its trains — if I desisted, what was to be the result? The sensations I now feel — apathy, stagnation, abhorred vacuity!

"You cannot resist the force of my reasoning — you, who are acquainted with, who know how to paint, in colours true to nature, the human heart — you, who admire, as a proof of power,

---

[96] "Eloisa to Abelard," 1717, pp. 195-200. Note that not only Pope's retelling of the medieval tale of Heloise and Abelard, but Rousseau's in *Julie*, runs through Hays's novel.

the destructive courage of an Alexander, even the fanatic fury of a Ravaillac — you, who honour the pernicious ambition of an Augustus Caesar, as bespeaking the potent, energetic, mind![97] — why should *you* affect to be intolerant to a passion, though differing in nature, generated on the same principles, and by a parallel process. The capacity of perception, or of receiving sensation, is (or generates) the power; into what channel that power shall be directed, depends not on ourselves. Are we not the creatures of outward impressions? Without such impressions, should we be any thing? Are not passions and powers synonymous — or can the latter be produced without the lively interest that constitutes the former? Do you dream of annihilating the one — and will not the other be extinguished? With the apostle, Paul, permit me to say — 'I am not mad, but speak the words of truth and soberness.'[98]

"To what purpose did you read my confessions, but to trace in them a character formed, like every other human character, by the result of unavoidable impressions, and the chain of necessary events. I feel, that my arguments are incontrovertible: — I suspect that, by affecting to deny their force, you will endeavour to deceive either me or yourself. — I have acquired the power of reasoning on this subject at a dear rate — at the expence of inconceivable suffering. Attempt not to deny me the miserable, expensive, victory. I am ready to say (ungrateful that I am) — Why did you put me upon calling forth my strong reasons?

"I perceive there is no cure for me — (apathy is, not the restoration to health, but, the morbid lethargy of the soul) but

---

[97] Alexander the Great (356-323 B.C.E.) is referenced in mixed terms in English radical writings and Rousseau's *Émile*, as one both brave and murderous. François Ravaillac (1578-1610) is cited in Godwin's *Political Justice* as an example of an assassin for his murder of the prostestant-raised French King, Henri de Navarre in Book II, Chapter III, "Of the Equality of Mankind." Augustus Caesar (63-14 BCE), heir to Julius Caesar, was one of the triumvirate with Mark Anthony and Lepedus, and after victory against Cleopatra sole ruler of the Roman Empire. (Cambridge Biographical Dictionary)

[98] Acts 26:25.

by a new train of impressions, of whatever nature, equally forcible with the past. — You will tell me, It remains with myself whether I will predetermine to resist such impressions. Is this true? Is it philosophical? Ask yourself. What! — can *even you* shrink from the consequences of your own principles?

"One word more — You accuse me of brooding in silence over my sensations — of considering them as a 'sacred deposit.' Concealment is particularly repugnant to my disposition — yet a thousand delicacies — a thousand nameless solicitudes, and apprehensions, sealed my lips! — He who inspired them was, alone, the depositary of my most secret thoughts! — my heart was unreservedly open before him — I covered my paper with its emotions, and, transmitted it to him — like him who whispered his secret into the earth, to relieve the burden of uncommunicated thought.[99] My secret was equally safe, and received in equal silence! Alas! he was not then ignorant of the effects it was likely to produce!

"EMMA."

Mr. Francis continued his humane and friendly attentions; and, while he opposed my sentiments, as conceiving them destructive of my tranquillity, mingled with his opposition a gentle and delicate consideration for my feelings, that sensibly affected me, and excited my grateful attachment. He judged right, that, by stimulating my mind into action, the sensations, which so heavily oppressed it, might be, in some measure, mitigated — by diverting the course of my ideas into different channels, and by that means abating their force. His kindness soothed and

---

[99] Classical Greek tale of King Midas's barber who, forbidden to reveal that the King had long, donkey's ears, whispered it into a hole in the ground. Reeds grew from the hole, and, when the wind blew through them, told the secret to the whole kingdom. The story was told in many forms in the seventeenth and early eighteenth centuries, including in John Dryden's *Translations from Persius*, "First Satire of Persius," lines 242-45: "At least, I'll dig a hole within the ground,/And to the trusty earth commit the sound;/ the reeds shall tell you what the poet fears,/ 'King Midas has a snout and ass's ears.'" (*Works of John Dryden*, London: 1882-1892.)

flattered me, and communication relieved my thoughts.

CHAP. XIII.

THE period which succeeded these events, though tedious in wearing away, marked by no vicissitude, has left little impression behind. The tenor of my days resembled the still surface of a stagnant lake, embosomed in a deep cavern, over which the refreshing breezes never sweep. Sad, vacant, inactive — the faculties both of mind and body seemed almost suspended. I became weak, languid, enervated —— my disorder was a lethargy of soul. This was gradually succeeded by disease of body: — an inactivity, so contrary to all the habits of my past life, generated morbid humours, and brought on a slow, remitting, fever. I recovered, by degrees, from this attack, but remained for some time in a debilitated, though convalescent, state. A few weeks after my disorder returned, lasted longer, and left me still more weakened and depressed. A third time it assailed me, at a shorter interval; and, though less violent, was more protracted, and more exhausting.

Mrs. Denbeigh, alarmed by my situation, wrote to Mrs. Harley, expressing the apprehensions which she entertained. From this dear friend, who was herself in a declining state of health, I received a pressing invitation to visit, once more the village of F ——— ; and to seek, from change of air, change of scene, and the cordial endearments of friendship, a restoration for my debilitated frame, and a balm for my wounded mind.

My relation, at this period, had letters from her husband, informing her, that the term of his residence in India was prolonged; pressing her to join him there, and to come over in the next ship. To this request she joyfully acceded; and, hearing that a packet was about to sail for Bengal, secured her passage, and began immediately to make preparations for her departure. I no longer hesitated to comply with the entreaties of my friend; besides the tie of strong affection, which drew me to her, I had, at present, little other resource.

After affectionately embracing Mrs. Denbeigh, wishing a happy issue to her voyage, thanking her for all her kindness, and leaving a letter of grateful acknowledgment for Mr. Francis, I quitted the metropolis, with an aching heart, and a wasted frame. My cousin accompanied me to the inn, from whence the vehicle set out that was to convey me to Mrs. Harley. We parted in silence — a crowd of retrospective ideas of the past, and solicitudes respecting the future, occupied our thoughts — our sensations were too affecting for words.

The carriage quitted London at the close of the evening, and travelled all night: — it was towards the end of the year. At midnight we passed over Hounslow and Bagshot heaths. 'The moon,' to adopt the language of Ossian, 'looked through broken clouds, and brightened their dark-brown sides.'[100] A loud November blast howled over the heath, and whistled through the fern. — There was a melancholy desolation in the scene, that was in unison with my feelings, and which overwhelmed my spirits with a tide of tender recollections. I recalled to my imagination a thousand interesting images — I indulged in all the wild enthusiasm of my character. My fellow-travellers slept tranquilly, while my soul was awake to agonizing sorrow. I adopted the language of the tender Eloisa — 'Why,' said I, 'am I indebted for life to his care, whose cruelty has rendered it insupportable? Inhuman, as he is, let him fly from me for ever, and deny himself the savage pleasure of being an eye-witness to my sorrows! — But why do I rave thus? — He is not to be blamed — *I, alone, am guilty* — I, alone, am the author of my own misfortunes, and should, therefore, be the only object of anger and resentment.'[101]

---

[100] Hays cites both from "Canthon" lines 11-14 and from "Dar-Thula: A Poem" lines 3-4, from *Fingal: An Ancient Epic Poem in Six Books: Together with Several Other Poems Composed by Ossian, Son of Fingal,* Translated by James Macpherson, London, 1762. In fact, the Ossian cycle was later revealed to be a forgery composed, rather than translated, by Macpherson.

[101] "Rousseau." [M.H.] From *Julie,* Vol. 1, letter XXIX. The French original importantly emphasizes the heroine's progression from accusing her lover to self-critique, noting that it is one of the effects of vice to accuse another of one's own faults.

Weakened by my late indisposition, fatigued by the rough motion of the carriage, and exhausted by strong emotion, when arrived at the end of my journey, I was obliged to be lifted from the coach, and carried into the cottage of my friend. The servant led the way to the library — the door opened —— Mrs. Harley advanced, to receive me, with tottering steps. The ravages of grief, and the traces of sickness, were visible in her dear, affectionate, countenance. I clasped my hands, and, lifting up my eyes, beheld the portrait of Augustus — beheld again the resemblance of those features so deeply engraven on my heart! My imagination was raised — methought the lively colours of the complexion had faded, the benignant smile had vanished, and an expression of perplexity and sternness usurped its place. I uttered a faint shriek, and fell lifeless into the arms of my friend. It was some time before I returned to sense and recollection, when I found myself on the bed, in the little chamber which had formerly been appropriated to my use. My friend sat beside me, holding my hand in her's, which she bathed with her tears. 'Thank God!' she exclaimed, in a rapturous accent, (as, with a deep sigh, I raised my languid eyes, and turned them mournfully towards her) — 'she lives! — My Emma! — child of my affections!' — Sobs suppressed her utterance. I drew the hand, which held mine, towards me — I pressed it to my bosom —— '*My mother!*' —— I would have said; but the tender appellation died away upon my lips, in inarticulate murmurs.

These severe struggles were followed by a return of my disorder. Mrs. Harley would scarcely be persuaded to quit my chamber for a moment — her tenderness seemed to afford her new strength; — but these exertions accelerated the progress of an internal malady, which had for some time past been gaining ground, and gradually undermining her health.

Youth, and a good constitution, aided by the kind solicitudes of friendship, restored me, in a few weeks, to a state of convalescence. I observed the declining strength of my friend with terror — I accused myself of having, though involuntarily, added to these alarming symptoms, by the new fatigues and anxieties which I had occasioned her. Affection inspired me with those energies, that reason had vainly dictated. I struggled to subdue myself — I stifled the impetuous suggestions of my feelings, in exerting myself to fulfill the duties of humanity. My mind assumed a firmer tone — I became, once more, the cheerful companion, the tender consoler, the attentive nurse, of this excellent woman, to whose kindness I was so much indebted — and, if I stole a few moments in the day, while my friend reposed, to gaze on the resemblance of Augustus, to weep over the testimonies of his former respect and friendship, I quickly chased from my bosom, and my countenance, every trace of sadness, when summoned to attend my friend.

CHAP. XIV.

THE winter came on severe and cold. Mrs. Harley was forbidden to expose herself to the frosty air, which seemed to invigorate my languid frame. I was constituted her almoner, to distribute to the neighbouring poor the scanty portion, which she was enabled, by a rigid œconomy, to spare from her little income: yet the value of this distribution had been more than redoubled, by the gentler charities of kind accents, tender sympathy, and wholesome counsels. To these indigent, but industrious, cottagers, I studied to be the worthy representative of their amiable benefactress, and found my reward in their grateful attachment, and the approving smiles of my friend.

By degrees, she ventured to converse with me on the subject nearest her heart — the situation of her son. He had been obliged to yield to the proofs produced of his marriage, which he had, at first, seemed desirous of evading. He had written, with reserve, upon the subject to his mother; but, from the enquiries of a common friend, she had reason to apprehend, that his engagement had been of an imprudent nature. Two children were, already, the fruits of it: the mother, with a feminine helplessness of character, had a feeble constitution. The small fortune, which Augustus had originally shared with his family, was greatly reduced. His education and habits had unfitted him for those exertions which the support of an encreasing family necessarily required: — his spirits (her friend had informed her) seemed broken, and his temper soured. Some efforts had been made to serve him, which his lofty spirit had repelled with disdain.

This narration deeply affected my heart — I had resigned myself to his loss — but the idea of his suffering, I felt, was an evil infinitely severer. It was this conviction that preyed incessantly on the peace and health of his mother. My fortitude failed, when I would have tried to sustain her; and I could only afford the melancholy satisfaction of mingling my sorrows with her's.

The disorder of my friend rapidly increased —— her mind became weakened, and her feelings wayward and irritable. I watched her incessantly — I strove, by every alleviating care, to soften her pains. Towards the approach of spring the symptoms grew more threatening; and it was judged, by her physician, necessary to apprize her family of her immediate danger. What a trial for my exhausted heart! I traced, with a trembling hand, a line to this melancholy purpose — addressed it to Mr. Harley, and through him to his younger brother and sisters.

In a few days they arrived in the village — sending from the inn a servant, to prepare their mother for their approach. I gently intimated to her the visitants we might expect. The previous evening, a change had taken place, which indicated approaching dissolution; and her mind (not uncommon in similar cases) seemed, almost instantaneously, to have recovered a portion of its original strength. She sighed deeply, while her eyes, which were fixed wistfully on my face, were lighted with a bright, but transient, lustre.

"My dear Emma" said she, "this is a trying moment for us both. I shall soon close my eyes, for ever, upon all wordly cares —— Still cherish, in your pure and ingenuous mind, a friendship for my Augustus — the darling of my soul! He may, in future, stand in need of consolation. I had formed hopes — vain hopes! — in which you and he were equally concerned. In the happiness of this partially-favoured child — this idol of my affections — all mine was concentrated. He has disappointed me,

and I have lost the desire of living — Yet, he has noble qualities!
— Who, alas! is perfect? Summon your fortitude, collect your
powers, my child, for this interview!"

She sunk upon her pillow — I answered her only with my
tears. A servant entered —— but spoke not —— her look
announced her tidings — It caught the eye of Mrs. Harley ——

"Let them enter," said she; and she raised herself, to receive
them, and assumed an aspect of composure.

I covered my face with my handkerchief — I heard the sound
of footsteps approaching the bed — I heard the murmurs of
filial sorrow — The voice of Augustus, in low and interrupted
accents, struck upon my ear — it thrilled through my nerves —
I shuddered, involuntarily —— What a moment! My friend
spoke a few words, in a faint tone.

"My children" she added, "repay to this dear girl," laying
her hand upon mine, "the debt of kindness I owe her — she has
smoothed the pillow of death — she is an orphan — she is
tender and unfortunate."

I ventured to remove for a moment the handkerchief from
my eyes — they met those of Augustus — he was kneeling by
the bed-side — his countenance was wan, and every feature sunk
in dejection; a shivering crept through my veins, and chilled my
heart with a sensation of icy coldness — he removed his eyes,
fixing them on his dying mother.

"My son," she resumed, in still fainter accents, "behold in
Emma, your sister — *your friend!* — confide in her — she is
worthy of your confidence?" — "Will you not love him, my
child," — (gazing upon me,) — "with a sisterly affection?"

I hid my face upon the pillow of my friend — I threw my
arms around her — "Your request is superfluous, my friend, my
more than parent, *ah, how superfluous!*"

"Forgive me, I know the tenderness of your nature — yielding, in these parting moments, to the predominant affection of
my heart — I fear, I have wounded that tender nature." 'Farewell, my children! Love and assist each other — Augustus, where
is your hand? — my sight fails me — God bless you and your

little ones — *God bless you all!* My last sigh — my last prayer — is yours.'

Exhausted by these efforts, she fainted — Augustus uttered a deep groan, and raised her in his arms — but life was fled.

At the remembrance of these scenes, even at this period, my heart is melted within me.

What is there of mournful magic in the emotions of virtuous sorrow, that in retracing, in dwelling upon them, mingles with our tears a sad and sublime rapture? Nature, that has infused so much misery into the cup of human life, has kindly mixed this strange and mysterious ingredient to qualify the bitter draught.

CHAP. XV.

AFTER the performance of the last melancholy duties, this afflicted family prepared to separate. I received from them, individually, friendly offers of service, and expressions of acknowledgment, for my tender attentions to their deceased parent. I declined, for the present, their invitations, and proffered kindness, though uncertain how to dispose of myself, or which way to direct my course. Augustus behaved towards me with distant, cold, respect. I observed in his features, under a constrained appearance of composure, marks of deep and strong emotion. I recalled to my mind the injunctions of my deceased friend — I yearned to pour into his bosom the balm of sympathy, but, with an aspect bordering on severity, he repressed the expression of those ingenuous feelings which formed my character, and shunned the confidence I so earnestly sought. Unfortunate love had, in my subdued and softened mind, laid the foundation of a fervent and durable friendship — But my love, my friendship, were equally contemned! I relinquished my efforts — I shut myself in my chamber — and, in secret, indulged my sorrows.

The house of my deceased friend was sold, and the effects disposed of. On the day previous to their removal, and the departure of the family for London, I stole into the library, at the close of the evening, to view, for *the last time*, the scene of so many delightful, so many afflicting, emotions. A mysterious and sacred enchantment is spread over every circumstance, even every inanimate object, connected with the affections. To those who are strangers to these delicate, yet powerful sympathies, this may appear ridiculous — but the sensations are not the less genuine, nor the less in nature. I will not attempt to analyse them; it is a subject upon which the language of philosophy would appear frigid, and on which I feel myself every moment on the verge of fanaticism. Yet, affections like these are not so much weakness, as strength perhaps badly exerted. Rousseau was, right, when he asserted, that, 'Common men know nothing of violent sorrows, nor do great passions ever break out in weak minds. Energy of sentiment is the characteristic of a noble soul.'[102]

I gazed from the windows on the shrubbery, where I had so often wandered with my friends — where I had fondly cherished so many flattering, so many visionary, prospects. Every spot, every tree, was associated with some past pleasure, some tender recollection. The last rays of the setting sun, struggling from beneath a louring cloud, streamed through its dark bosom, illumined its edges, played on the window in which I was standing, and gilding the opposite side of the wainscot, against which the picture of Augustus still hung, shed a soft and mellow lustre over the features. I turned almost unconsciously, and contemplated it with a long and deep regard. It seemed to smile benignly — it wore no traces of the cold austerity, the gloomy and inflexible reserve, which now clouded the aspect of the original. I called to my remembrance a thousand interesting conversations — when

> 'Tuned to happy unison of soul, a fairer world of
> which the vulgar never had a glimpse, displayed,
> its charms.'[103]

Absorbed in thought, the crimson reflection from the western clouds gradually faded, while the deep shades of the evening, thickened by the appearance of a gathering tempest, involved in

---

[102] From *Julie*, Book 1.
[103] Thomson, *The Seasons*, Summer, lines 1385-8.

obscurity the object on which, without distinctly perceiving it, I still continued to gaze.

I was roused from this reverie by the sudden opening of the door. Some person, whom the uncertain light prevented me from distinguishing, walked across the room, with a slow and solemn pace, and, after taking several turns backwards and forwards, reclined on the sopha, remaining for some time perfectly still. A tremor shook my nerves — unable either to speak, or to move, I continued silent and trembling — my heart felt oppressed, almost to suffocation — at length, a deep, convulsive sigh, forced its way.

"My God!" exclaimed the person, whose meditations I had interrupted, "what is that?"

It was the voice of Mr. Harley, he spoke in a stern tone, though with some degree of trepidation, and advanced hastily towards the window against which I leaned.

The clouds had for some hours been gathering dark and gloomy. Just as Augustus had reached the place where I stood, a flash of lightning, pale, yet vivid, glanced suddenly across my startled sight, and discovered to him the object which had alarmed him.

"Emma," said he, in a softened accent, taking my trembling and almost lifeless hand, "how came you here, which way did you enter?"

I answered not — Another flash of lightning, still brighter, blue and sulphurous, illuminated the room, succeeded by a loud and long peal of thunder. Again the heavens seem to rend asunder and discover a sheet of livid flame — a crash of thunder, sudden, loud, short, immediately followed, bespeaking the tempest near. I started with a kind of convulsive terror. Augustus led me from the window, and endeavoured, in vain, to find the door of the library — the temporary flashes, and total darkness by which they were succeeded, dazzled and confounded the sight. I stumbled over some furniture, which stood in the middle of the room, and unable to recover my feet, which refused any longer to sustain me, sunk into the arms of Augustus, suffering him to lift me to the sopha. He seated himself beside me, the storm continued; the clouds, every moment parting with a horrible noise, discovered an abyss of fire, while the rain descended in a deluge. We silently contemplated this sublime and terrible scene. Augustus supported me with one arm, while my trembling hand remained in his. The tempest soon exhausted itself by its violence — the lightning became less fierce, gleaming at intervals — the thunder rolled off to a distance — its protracted sound, lengthened by the echoes, faintly died away; while the rain continued to fall in a still, though copious, shower.

My spirits grew calmer, I gently withdrew my hand from that of Mr. Harley. He once more enquired, but in a tone of greater reserve, how I had entered the room without his knowledge? I explained, briefly and frankly, my situation, and the tender motives by which I had been influenced.

"It was not possible," added I, "to take leave of this house *for ever*, without recalling a variety of affecting and melancholy ideas — I feel, that I have lost *my only friend*."

"This world," said he, "may not unaptly be compared to the rapids on the American rivers — We are hurried, in a frail bark, down the stream — It is in vain to resist its course — happy are those whose voyage is ended!"

"My friend," replied I in a faultering voice, "I could teach my heart to bear your loss — though, God knows, the lesson has been sufficiently severe — but I know not how, with fortitude, to see you suffer."

"Suffering is the common lot of humanity — but, pardon me, when I say, your conduct has not tended to lessen my vexations!"

"My errors have been the errors of *affection* — Do they deserve this rigor?"

"Their source is not important, their consequences have been the same — you make not the allowances you claim."

"Dear, and severe, friend! — Be not unjust — the confidence which I sought, and merited, would have obviated" —

"I know what you would alledge — that confidence, you

had reason to judge, was of a painful nature — it ought not to have been extorted."

"If I have been wrong, my faults have been severely expiated — if the error has been *only mine*, surely my sufferings have been in proportion; seduced by the fervor of my feelings; ignorant of your situation, if I wildly sought to oblige you to chuse happiness through a medium of my creation — yet, to have assured *yours*, was I not willing to risque all my own? I perceive my extravagance, my views were equally false and romantic — dare I to say — they were the ardent excesses of a generous mind? Yes! my wildest mistakes had in them a dignified mixture of virtue. While the institutions of society war against nature and happiness, the mind of energy, struggling to emancipate itself, will entangle itself in error" —

"Permit me to ask you" interrupted Augustus, "whether, absorbed in your own sensations, you allowed yourself to remember, and to respect, the feelings of others?"

I could no longer restrain my tears, I wept for some moments in silence — Augustus breathed a half-suppressed sigh, and turned from me his face.

"The pangs which have rent my heart," resumed I, in low and broken accents, "have, I confess, been but too poignant! That lacerated heart still bleeds — we have neither of us been guiltless — *Alas! who is?* Yet in my bosom, severe feelings are not more painful than transient — already have I lost sight of your unkindness, (God knows how little I merited it!) in stronger sympathy for your sorrows — whatever be their nature! We have both erred — why should we not exchange mutual forgiveness? Why should we afflict each other? Friendship, like charity, should suffer all things and be kind!"

"My mind," replied he coldly, "is differently constituted."

"*Unpitying man!* It would be hard for us, if we were all to be judged at so severe a tribunal — you have been a *lover*," added I, in a softer tone, "and can you not forgive the faults of *love?*"

He arose, visibly agitated — I also stood up — my bosom deeply wounded, and, unknowing what I did, took his hand

and pressed it to my lips.

"You have rudely thrown from you a heart of exquisite sensibility — you have contemned my love, and you disdain my friendship — is it brave, is it manly," added I wildly — almost unconscious of what I said — forgetting at the moment his situation and my own — "thus to triumph over a spirit, subdued by its affections into unresisting meekness?"

He broke from me, and precipitately quitted the room.

I threw myself upon the floor, and, resting my head on the seat which Augustus had so lately occupied, passed the night in cruel conflict — a tempest more terrible than that which had recently spent its force, shook my soul! The morning dawned, ere I had power to remove myself from the fatal spot, where the measure of my afflictions seemed filled up. — Virtue may conquer weakness, but who can bear to be despised by those they love. The sun darted its beams full upon me, but its splendour appeared mockery — hope and joy were for ever excluded from my benighted spirit. The contempt of the world, the scoffs of ignorance, the contumely of the proud, I could have borne without shrinking — but to find myself rejected, contemned, scorned, by him with whom, of all mankind, my heart claimed kindred; by him for whom my youth, my health, my powers, were consuming in silent anguish — who, instead of pouring balm into the wound he had inflicted, administered only corrosives! — *It was too painful.* I felt, that I had been a lavish prodigal — that I had become a wretched bankrupt; that there was but *one way* to make me happy and *a thousand* to make me miserable! Enfeebled and exhausted, I crawled to my apartment, and, throwing myself on the bed, gave a loose to the agony of my soul.

Chap. XVI.

UNDER pretence of indisposition, I refused to meet the family. I heard them depart. Too proud to accept of obligation, I had not confided to them my plans, if plans they could be called, where no distinct end was in view.

A few hours after their departure, I once more seated myself in a stage coach, in which I had previously secured a place, and took the road to London. I perceived, on entering the carriage, only one passenger, who had placed himself in the opposite corner, and in whom, to my great surprize, I immediately recognized Mr. Montague. We had not met since the visit he had paid me at Mrs. Harley's, the result of which I have already related: since that period, it had been reported in the village, that he addressed Sarah Morton, and that they were about to be united. Montague manifested equal surprize at our meeting: the intelligence of my friend's death (at which he expressed real concern) had not reached him, neither was he acquainted with my being in that part of the country. He had not lately been at Mr. Morton's, he informed me, but had just left his father's, and was going to London to complete his medical studies.

After these explanations, absorbed in painful contemplation, I for some time made little other return to his repeated civilities, than by cold monosyllables: till at length, his cordial sympathy, his gentle accents, and humane attentions, awakened me from my reverie. Ever accessible to the soothings of kindness, I endeavoured to exert myself, to prove the sense I felt of his humanity. Gratified by having succeeded in attracting my attention, he redoubled his efforts to cheer and amuse me. My dejected and languid appearance had touched his feelings, and, towards the end of our journey, his unaffected zeal to alleviate the anxiety under which I evidently appeared to labour, soothed my mind and inspired me with confidence.

He respectfully requested to know in what part of the town I resided, and hoped to be permitted to pay his respects to me, and to enquire after my welfare? This question awakened in my bosom so many complicated and painful sensations, that, after remaining silent for a few minutes, I burst into a flood of tears.

"I have no home;" said I, in a voice choaked with sobs — "I am an alien in the world — and alone in the universe."

His eyes glistened, his countenance expressed the most lively, and tender, commiseration, while, in a timid and respectful voice, he made me offers of service, and entreated me to permit him to be useful to me.

"I then mentioned, in brief, my present unprotected situation, and hinted, that as my fortune was small, I could wish to procure a humble, but decent, apartment in a reputable family, till I had consulted one friend, who, I yet flattered myself, was interested in my concerns, or till I could fix on a more eligible method of providing for myself."

He informed me — "That he had a distant relation in town, a decent, careful, woman, who kept a boarding house, and whose terms were very reasonable. He was assured, would I permit him to introduce me to her, she would be happy, should her accommodation suit me, to pay me every attention in her power."

In my forlorn situation, I confided, without hesitation, in his recommendation, and gratefully acceded to the proposal.

Mr. Montague introduced me to this lady in the most flattering terms, she received me with civility, but, I fancied, not without a slight mixture of distrust. I agreed with her for a neat chamber, with a sitting room adjoining, on the second floor, and settled for the terms of my board, more than the whole amount of the interest of my little fortune.

Chap. XVII.

I took an early opportunity of addressing a few lines to Mr. Francis, informing him of my situation, and entreating his counsel. I waited a week, impatiently, for his reply, but in vain: well acquainted with his punctuality, and alarmed by this silence, I mentioned the step I had taken, and my apprehensions, to Montague, who immediately repaired, himself, to the house of Mr. Francis; and, finding it shut up, was informed by the neighbours, that Mr. Francis had quitted England, a short time before, in company with a friend, intending to make a continental tour.

This intelligence was a new shock to me. I called on some of my former acquaintance, mentioning to them my wish of procuring pupils, or of engaging in any other occupation fitted to my talents. I was received by some with civility, by others with coldness, but every one appeared too much engrossed by his own affairs to give himself the trouble of making any great exertion for others.

I returned dispirited — I walked through the crowded city, and observed the anxious and busy faces of all around me. In the midst of my fellow beings, occupied in various pursuits, I seemed, as if in an immense desart, a solitary outcast from society. Active, industrious, willing to employ my faculties in any way, by which I might procure an honest independence, I beheld no path open to me, but that to which my spirit could not submit — the degradation of servitude. Hapless woman! — crushed by the iron hand of barbarous despotism, pampered into weakness, and trained the slave of meretricious folly! — what wonder, that, shrinking from the chill blasts of penury (which the pernicious habits of thy education have little fitted thy tender frame to encounter) thou listenest to the honied accents of the spoiler; and, to escape the galling chain of servile dependence, rushest into the career of infamy, from whence the false and cruel morality of the world forbids thy return, and perpetuates thy disgrace and misery! When will mankind be aware of the uniformity, of the importance, of truth? When will they cease to confound, by sexual, by political, by theological, distinctions, those immutable principles, which form the true basis of virtue and happiness? The paltry expedients of combating error with error, and prejudice with prejudice, in one invariable and melancholy circle, have already been sufficiently tried, have already been demonstrated futile: —— they have armed man against man, and filled the world with crimes, and with blood. — How has the benign and gentle nature of Reform been mistated! 'One false idea,' justly says an acute and philosophic writer,[104] 'united with others, produces such as are necessarily false; which, combining again with all those the memory retains, give to all a tinge of falsehood. One error, alone,

---

[104] "Helvetius." [M.H.] From *A Treatise on Man*, Chapter 13: "Of the Evils Produced by an Indifference for the Truth."

is sufficient to infect the whole mass of the mind, and produce an infinity of capricious, monstrous, notions. — Every vice is the error of the understanding; crimes and prejudices are brothers; truth and virtue sisters. These things, known to the wise, are hid from fools!'

Without a sufficiently interesting pursuit, a fatal torpor stole over my spirits — my blood circulated languidly through my veins. Montague, in the intervals from business and amusement, continued to visit me. He brought me books, read to me, chatted with me, pressed me to accompany him to places of public entertainment, which (determined to incur no pecuniary obligation) I invariably refused.

I received his civilities with the less scruple, from the information I had received of his engagement with Miss Morton; which, with his knowledge of my unhappy attachment, I thought, precluded every idea of a renewal of those sentiments he had formerly professed for me.

In return for his friendship, I tried to smile, and exerted my spirits, to prove my grateful sensibility of his kindness: but, while he appeared to take a lively interest in my sorrows, he carefully avoided a repetition of the language in which he had once addressed me; yet, at times, his tender concern seemed sliding into a sentiment still softer, which obliged me to practise more reserve: he was not insensible of this, and was frequently betrayed into transient bursts of passion and resentment, which, on my repelling with firmness, he would struggle to repress, and afterwards absent himself for a time.

Unable to devise any method of increasing my income, and experiencing the pressure of some daily wants and inconveniencies, I determined, at length, on selling the sum vested, in my name, in the funds, and purchasing a life annuity.[105]

Recollecting the name of a banker, with whom my uncle, the friend of my infancy, had formerly kept cash, I learned his

---

[105] Emma plans to withdraw her principle from the volatile market and to buy an account that will pay her a yearly, regular income.

residence, and, waiting upon him, made myself known as the niece of an old and worthy friend; at the same time acquainting him with my intentions. — He offered to transact the affair for me immediately, the funds being, then, in a very favourable position; and to preserve the money in his hands till an opportunity should offer of laying it out to advantage. I gave him proper credentials for the accomplishing of this business, and returned to my apartment with a heart somewhat lightened. This scheme had never before occurred to me. The banker, who was a man of commercial reputation, had assured me, that my fortune might now be sold out with little loss; and that, by purchasing an annuity, on proper security, at seven or eight per cent, I might, with œconomy, be enabled to support myself decently, with comfort and independence.

CHAP. XVIII.

SOME weeks elapsed, and I heard no more from my banker. A slight indisposition confined me to the house. One evening, Mr. Montague, coming to my apartment to enquire after my health, brought with him a newspaper (as was his frequent custom), and, finding me unwell, and dispirited, began to read some parts from it aloud, in the hope of amusing me. Among the articles of home intelligence, a paragraph stated — 'The failure of a considerable mercantile house, which had created an alarm upon the Exchange, as, it was apprehended, some important consequences would follow in the commercial world. A great banking-house, it was hinted, not many miles from ———— , was likely to be affected, by some rumours, in connection with this business, which had occasioned a considerable run upon it for the last two or three days.'

My attention was roused — I eagerly held out my hand for the paper, and perused this alarming paragraph, again and again, without observing the surprize expressed in the countenance of Montague, who was at a loss to conceive why this intelligence should be affecting to me. — I sat, for some minutes, involved in thought, till a question from my companion, several times

repeated, occasioned me to start. I immediately recollected myself, and tried to reason away my fears, as vague and groundless.
I was about to explain the nature of them to my friend — secretly accusing myself for not having done so sooner, and availed
myself of his advice, when a servant, entering, put a letter into
his hand.

Looking upon the seal and superscription, he changed colour,
and opened it hastily. Strong emotion was painted in his features while he perused it. I regarded him with anxiety. He rose
from his seat, walked up and down the room with a disordered
pace — opened the door, as if with an intention of going out —
shut it — returned back again — threw himself into a chair —
covered his face with his handkerchief — appeared in great agitation — and burst into tears. I arose, went to him, and took his
hand — "*My friend!*" said I —— I would have added something
more —— but, unable to proceed, I sunk into a seat beside
him, and wept in sympathy. He pressed my hand to his lips —
folded me wildly in his arms, and attempted to speak — but his
voice was lost in convulsive sobs. I gently withdrew myself, and
waited, in silence, till the violence of his emotions should subside. He held out to me the letter he had received. I perused it.
It contained an account of the sudden death of his father, and a
summons for his immediate return to the country, to settle the
affairs, and to take upon him his father's professional employment.

"You leave me, then!" said I — "I lose my only remaining
friend!"

"*Never!*" — he replied, emphatically.

I blushed for having uttered so improper, so selfish, a remark; and endeavoured to atone for it by forgetting the perils of
my own situation, in attention to that of this ardent, but affectionate, young man. — His sufferings were acute and violent for
some days, during which he quitted me only at the hours of
repose — I devoted myself to sooth and console him. I felt, that
I had been greatly indebted to his friendship and kindness, and
I endeavoured to repay the obligation. He appeared fully sen-

sible of my cares, and mingled with his acknowledgments expressions of a tenderness, so lively, and unequivocal, as obliged me, once more, to be more guarded in my behaviour.

In consideration for the situation of Mr. Montague —— I had forgotten the paragraph in the paper, till an accidental intelligence of the bankruptcy of the house, in which my little fortune was entrusted, confirmed to me the certainty of this terrible blow. Montague was sitting with me when I received the unwelcome news.

"Gracious God!" I exclaimed, clasping my hands, and raising my eyes to heaven —— "What is to become of me now? — The measure of my sorrows is filled up!"

It was some time before I had power to explain the circumstances to my companion.

"Do not distress yourself, my lovely Emma," said he; "I will be your friend — your guardian ——" (and he added, in a low, yet fervent, accent) — "*your husband!*"

"No — no — no!" answered I, shaking my head, "that must not, cannot, be! I would perish, rather than take advantage of a generosity like yours. I will go to service — I will work for my bread — and, if I cannot procure a wretched sustenance — *I can but die!* Life, to me, has long been worthless!"

My countenance, my voice, my manner, but too forcibly expressed the keen anguish of my soul. I seemed to be marked out for the victim of a merciless destiny — *for the child of sorrow!* The susceptible temper of Montague, softened by his own affliction, was moved by my distress. He repeated, and enforced, his proposal, with all the ardour of a youthful, a warm, an uncorrupted, mind.

"You add to my distress," replied I. "I have not a heart to bestow —— I lavished mine upon one, who scorned and contemned it. Its sensibility is now exhausted. Shall I reward a faithful and generous tenderness, like yours, with a cold, a worthless, an alienated, mind? No, no! —— Seek an object more worthy of you, and leave me to my fate."

At that moment, I had forgotten the report of his engagement with Miss Morton; but, on his persisting, vehemently, to urge his suit, I recollected, and immediately mentioned, it, to him. He confessed —

'That, stung by my rejection, and preference of Mr. Harley, he had, at one period, entertained a thought of that nature; but that he had fallen out with the family, in adjusting the settlements. Mrs. Morton had persuaded her husband to make, what he conceived to be, ungenerous requisitions. Miss Morton had discovered much artifice, but little sensibility, on the occasion. Disgusted with the apathy of the father, the insolence of the mother, and the low cunning of the daughter, he had abruptly quitted them, and broken off all intercourse with the family.'

It is not necessary to enlarge on this part of my narrative. Suffice it to say, that, after a long contest, my desolate situation, added to the persevering affection of this enthusiastic young man, prevailed over my objections. His happiness, he told me, entirely depended on my decision. I would not deceive him: — I related to him, with simplicity and truth, all the circumstances of my past conduct towards Mr. Harley. He listened to me with evident emotion — interrupted me, at times, with execrations; and, once or twice, vowing vengeance on Augustus, appeared on the verge of outrage. But I at length reasoned him into greater moderation, and obliged him to do justice to the merit and honour of Mr. Harley. He acquiesced reluctantly, and with an ill grace, yet, with a lover-like partiality, attributed his conduct to causes, of which I had discerned no traces. He assured himself, that the affections of a heart, tender as mine, would be secured by kindness and assiduity — and I at last yielded to his importunity. We were united in a short time, and I accompanied my husband to the town of ———, in the county of ——— , the residence of his late father.

WOMEN AND WORK I
A common concern throughout the eighteenth century was what ought to be done about middling women who

could not find husbands, and who were dependent upon their extended families for financial support. Suggestions for a kind of Protestant convent, or for communities of women working together have a long history as a suggested solution. Sarah Scott's *Millenium Hall* (1762) portrays a community of gentlewomen, each with her own story, who form a community together where they live productively without men, pursuing painting, music, and other ladylike arts, and providing charitable work and sustenance for a mixed community of poor and laboring folk under their care. Samuel Richardson's *Sir Charles Grandison* (1753-4), his novel about a virtuous and manly man, also touches on the possibility for a kind of retirement community for virtuous and unmarried or widowed Protestant English women. However, for middling women without fortunes and whose families were unable or unwilling to support them, such options did not really exist. Their situation was dire, and they were often unable or barely able to support themselves in genteel poverty.

For the middling woman, some fine needlework, educating small children as a governess, or if she could find the money, opening a day-school or boarding school for girls were among the very few options available. To become a teacher, such a woman would need a better education than most women, including needlework, some music, some art, and probably a polite knowledge of the French language. Acting as the companion or "toad-eater" to a wealthier woman was another unpalatable possibility. Respectable but dependent women (and men) often spent their lives attending to the needs, entertainment, and whims of those wealthier than they, who provided bed and board in exchange for companionship and good temper. By the late century, writing for money had become another option, and it is no accident that in the 1790s the majority of British novel writers and many respectable poets were women. Other genres were more mixed, with theology, philosophy, politics, and sometimes poetry considered more appropriate for men. Finally, acting on stage was an option, but a complicated one to negotiate. Elizabeth Simpson Inchbald, for instance, a member of the radical circle surrounding William Godwin in which both Mary Hays and Amelia Alderson initially moved, had successfully negotiated the difficulty in being a "public" woman appearing on stage and remaining a respected citizen by marrying a much older actor, Joseph Inchbald, when she ran away to join the stage in 1772. By the time Amelia Alderson reached London in 1794 and when Hays wrote *Emma Courtney* in 1796, Inchbald was both widowed and retired from the stage, and had an active career translating German drama and writing her own plays. She was later responsible for selecting and writing critical introductions for a twenty-five volume *British Theatre*, followed by a ten-volume *Modern Theatre* and a seven-volume *Collection of Farces*, thus taking on the role of literary critic. The career of Sarah Siddons, arguably the most popular and famous actress of the later eighteenth century is a better known example. In the 1790s then, women writers were engaged in ongoing debates with their male colleagues on the position of women, the significance of literary works, matters of religious practice, governmental structures, and their own position as professional women.

Marriage was the most common, if not a wholly satisfactory career for most women, particularly in the middle ranks of society. However, there were public examples of women whose marriages had not provided adequate protection and support, and several of them made their experiences public rationales for their entry into letters. Charlotte Turner Smith, for example, wrote poetry and novels, and made no secret of her husband's inability to support her and her children and his theft of her inheritance. Smith used her public self-representation as a writer to conduct a public relations campaign that made her a popular author and has left modern scholars with invariably negative impressions of her ne'er-do-well husband. Eliza Fenwick, another friend of the Wollstonecraft and Godwin circle, was married to a radical, John Fenwick, who also became unable to support his family. Striking out on her own, Eliza Fenwick eventually moved to the British West Indies to help with her daughter's career as an actress and manage her household. Thus, familial arrangements and women's work were changing in the late eighteenth and early nineteenth centuries. However, not only was a middling woman unlikely to take up a trade associated with women of the working class, such as laundering, or selling goods on the street, but even if she had tried, she would likely have been suspect, marked by her accent, manners, and education as not belonging. Charlotte Brontë's 1840 novel, *Jane Eyre*, shows this possibility when Jane, destitute, begs for work as a servant and is sent away by a suspicious servant who recognizes by her hands, clothes, and accent that she is not bred to servitude.

Mary Wollstonecraft's *Vindication of the Rights of Woman* (1792) rails against the masculinization of professions such as mantua-maker or milliner which might offer women a profitable living. (Thomas Paine was often mocked as a staymaker, another profession which one might have assumed would be open to women, as they were the ones who wore stays.) Nor was advocating for appropriate trades for poor women and polite modes of self-subsistence for middling women exclusively a concern of radical reformers. Hannah More, an evangelical writer strongly associated with Anti-Jacobin arguments in her *Cheap Repository Tracts*, was a powerful proponent of work for poor women as conducive to virtue and a protection against drunkenness and prostitution. Middling support for laissez-faire employment practices (derived from the economic arguments of Adam Smith) ran counter to laboring and artisan male efforts to protect their specialized labor, Anna Clark tells us. Women were generally relegated to tasks considered lower, such as winding thread rather than fine weaving, binding books rather than the finer labor of printing, or binding the soles of shoes to uppers rather than manufacturing the uppers themselves. However, as a genre associated most strongly with the middle classes, the novel seldom addresses the work of poor women. One exception from the late 1790s is Mary Wollstonecraft's *Maria; or the Wrongs of Woman*, which famously includes a history of the character Jemima. Jemima is working as a jailer in a madhouse when we first meet her in that novel. As she tells her story to the imprisoned middling Maria, we learn that Jemima began life as an unwanted, illegitimate child who was sent out as a servant at a young age to do the dirty jobs of household maintenance such as scullery work, laundering, and so on. Raped by her master and then thrown out by her mistress as a whore, Jemima indeed becomes a prostitute, and eventually is lucky enough to become the kept woman of an educated and older gentleman. When he dies, however, she is dispossessed of the little he meant to leave her by the man's legitimate family. Working as a laundress, she persuades a fellow servant to marry her and desert his pregnant lover, until she is struck with remorse for the child who will be left fatherless as she herself was. Finally Jemima accepts the degrading and unpleasant work as jailer in the madhouse, having lost all sympathy with her fellow creatures. Prostitution appears to have been the only trade which truly ran across class boundaries.

SOURCES

Anna Clark, *The Struggle for the Breeches: Gender and the Making of the British Working Class* (Berkeley: University of California Press, 1995).

Mary Wollstonecraft, *Vindication of the Rights of Woman*, (1792), in *Works of Mary Wollstonecraft*, Ed. Janet Todd and Marilyn Butler, 5 Vols. Vol. 5 (Washington Square, NY: New York University Press, 1989).

—. *Wrongs of Woman; or Maria*. Ed. Cynthia Richards (Glen Allen, VA: College Publishing, 2003).

CHAP. XIX.

MR. Montague presented me to his relations and friends, by

whom I was received with a flattering distinction. My wearied spirits began now to find repose. My husband was much occupied in the duties of his profession. We had a respectable circle of acquaintance: In the intervals of social engagement, and domestic employment, ever thirsting after knowledge, I occasionally applied myself to the study of the physic, anatomy, and surgery, with the various branches of science connected with them; by which means I frequently rendered myself essentially serviceable to my friend; and, by exercising my understanding and humanity, strengthened my mind, and stilled the importunate suggestions of a heart too exquisitely sensible.

The manners of Mr. Montague were kind and affectionate, though subject, at times, to inequalities and starts of passion; he confided in me, as his best and truest friend — and I deserved his confidence: — yet, I frequently observed the restlessness and impetuosity of his disposition with apprehension.

I felt for my husband a rational esteem, and a grateful affection: — but those romantic, high-wrought, frenzied, emotions, that had rent my heart during its first attachment — that enthusiasm, that fanaticism, to which opposition had given force, the bare recollection of which still shook my soul with anguish, no longer existed. Montague was but too sensible of this difference, which naturally resulted from the change of circumstances, and was unreasonable enough to complain of what secured our tranquillity. If a cloud, at times, hung over my brow — if I relapsed, for a short period, into a too habitual melancholy, he would grow captious, and complain.

"You esteem me, Emma: I confide in your principles, and I glory in your friendship — but, you have never *loved* me!"

"Why will you be so unjust, both to me, and to yourself?"

"Tell me, then, sincerely — I know you will not deceive me —— Have you ever felt for me those sentiments with which Augustus Harley inspired you?"

"Certainly not — I do not pretend to it — neither ought you to wish it. My first attachment was the morbid excess of a distempered imagination. Liberty, reason, virtue, usefulness, were the offerings I carried to its shrine. It preyed incessantly upon my heart, it drank up its vital spirit, it became a vice from its excess — it was a pernicious, though a sublime, enthusiasm — its ravages are scarcely to be remembered without shuddering — all the strength, the dignity, the powers, of my mind, melted before it! Do you wish again to see me the slave of my passions — do you regret, that I am restored to reason? To you I owe every thing — life, and its comforts, rational enjoyment, and the opportunity of usefulness. I feel for you all the affection that a reasonable and a virtuous mind ought to feel — that affection which is compatible with the fulfilling of other duties. We are guilty of vice and selfishness when we yield ourselves up to unbounded desires, and suffer our hearts to be wholly absorbed by one object, however meritorious that object may be."

"Ah! how calmly you reason, — while I listen to you I cannot help loving and admiring you, but I must ever hate that accursed Harley — No! *I am not satisfied* — and I sometimes regret that I ever beheld you."

Many months glided away with but little interruption to our tranquillity. — A remembrance of the past would at times obtrude itself, like the broken recollections of a feverish vision. To banish these painful retrospections, I hastened to employ myself; every hour was devoted to active usefulness, or to social and rational recreation.

I became a mother; in performing the duties of a nurse, my affections were awakened to new and sweet emotions. — The father of my child appeared more respectable in my eyes, became more dear to me: the engaging smiles of my little Emma repayed me for every pain and every anxiety. While I beheld my husband caress his infant, I tasted a pure, a chaste, an ineffable pleasure.

CHAP. XX.

ABOUT six weeks after my recovery from childbed, some affairs of importance called Mr. Montague to London. Three days after he had quitted me, as, bending over the cradle of my babe, I contemplated in silence its tranquil slumbers, I was alarmed by an uncommon confusion in the lower part of the house. Hastening down stairs, to enquire into the cause, I was informed — that a gentleman, in passing through the town, had been thrown from his horse, that he was taken up senseless, and, as was customary in cases of accident, had been brought into our house, that he might receive assistance.

Mr. Montague was from home, a young gentleman who resided with us, and assisted my husband in his profession, was also absent, visiting a patient. Having myself acquired some knowledge of surgery, I went immediately into the hall to give the necessary directions on the occasion. The gentleman was lying on the floor, without any signs of life. I desired the people to withdraw, who, crowding round with sincere, but useless sympathy, obstructed the circulation of air. Approaching the unfortunate man, I instantly recognised the well-known features, though much altered, wan and sunk, of *Augustus Harley*. Staggering a few paces backward — a death-like sickness overspread my heart — a crowd of confused and terrible emotions rushed through my mind. — But a momentary reflection recalled my scattered thoughts. Once before, I had saved from death an object so fatal to my repose. I exerted all my powers, his hair was clotted, and his face disfigured with blood; I ordered the servants to raise and carry him to an adjoining apartment, wherein was a large, low sopha, on which they laid him. Carefully washing the blood from the wound, I found he had received a dangerous contusion in his head, but that the scull, as I had at first apprehended, was not fractured. I cut the hair from the wounded part, and applied a proper bandage. I did more — no other assistance being at hand, I ventured to open a vein:[106] the blood presently flowed freely, and he began to revive. I bathed his temples, and sprinkled the room with vinegar, opened the win-

---

[106] Letting blood or bleeding was a normative medical practice into the nineteenth century.

dows to let the air pass freely through, raised his head with the pillows of the sopha, and sprinkled his face and breast with cold water. I held his hand in mine — I felt the languid and wavering pulse quicken — I fixed my eyes upon his face — at that moment every thing else was forgotten, and my nerves seemed firmly braced by my exertions.

He at length opened his eyes, gazed upon me with a vacant look, and vainly attempted, for some time, to speak. At last, he uttered a few incoherent words, but I perceived his senses were wandering, and I conjectured, too truly, that his brain had received a concussion. He made an effort to rise, but sunk down again.

"Where am I," said he, "every object appears to me double."

He shut his eyes, and remained silent. I mixed for him a cordial and composing medicine, and entreating him to take it, he once more raised himself, and looked up. — Our eyes met, his were wild and unsettled.

"That voice," — said he, in a low tone, — "that countenance — Oh God! where am I?"

A strong, but transient, emotion passed over his features. With a trembling hand he seized and swallowed the medicine I had offered, and again relapsed into a kind of lethargic stupor. I then gave orders for a bed to be prepared, into which I had him conveyed. I darkened the room, and desired, that he might be kept perfectly quiet.

I retired to my apartment, my confinement was yet but recent,[107] and I had not perfectly recovered my strength. Exhausted by the strong efforts I had made, and the stronger agitation of my mind, I sunk into a fainting fit, (to which I was by no means subject) and remained for some time in a state of perfect insensibility. On my recovery, I learnt that Mr. Lucas, the assistant of my husband, had returned, and was in the chamber of the stranger; I sent for him on his quitting the apartment, and eagerly interrogated him respecting the state of the patient. He

---

[107] That is, she is only recently up and about after giving birth to her daughter.

shook his head — I related to him the methods I had taken, and enquired whether I had erred? He smiled —

"You are an excellent surgeon," said he, "you acted very properly, but," observing my pallid looks, "I wish your little nursery may not suffer from your humanity" —

"I lay no claim," replied I with emotion — "to extraordinary humanity — I would have done the same for the poorest of my fellow creatures — but this gentleman is an old acquaintance, *a friend*, whom, in the early periods of my life, I greatly respected."

"I am sorry for it, for I dare not conceal from you, that I think him in a dangerous condition."

I changed countenance — "There is no fracture, no bones are broken." —

"No, but the brain has received an alarming concussion — he is also, otherwise, much bruised, and, I fear, has suffered some internal injury."

"You distress and terrify me," said I, gasping for breath — "What is to be done — shall we call in further advice?"

"I think so; in the mean time, if you are acquainted with his friends, you would do well to apprize them of what has happened."

"I know little of them, I know not where to address them — Oh! save him," continued I, clasping my hands with encreased emotion, unconscious what I did, "for God's sake save him, if you would preserve me from dis —— "

A look penetrating and curious from Lucas, recalled me to reason. Commending his patient to my care, he quitted me, and rode to the next town to procure the aid of a skilful and experienced Physician. I walked up and down the room for some time in a state of distraction.

"He will die" — exclaimed I — "die in my house — fatal accident! Oh, Augustus! *too tenderly beloved*, thou wert fated to be the ruin of my peace! But, whatever may be the consequences, I will perform, for thee, the last tender offices. — I will not desert my duty!"

The nurse brought to me my infant, it smiled in my face —

I pressed it to my bosom — I wept over it. — How could I, from that agitated bosom, give it a pernicious sustenance?[108]

Chap. XXI.

In the evening, I repaired to the chamber of Mr. Harley, I sat by his bed-side, I gazed mournfully on his flushed, but vacant countenance — I took his hand — it was dry and burning — the pulse beat rapidly, but irregularly, beneath my trembling fingers. His lips moved, he seemed to speak, though inarticulately — but sometimes raising his voice, I could distinguish a few incoherent sentences. In casting my eyes round the room, I observed the scattered articles of his dress, his cloaths were black, and in his hat, which lay on the ground, I discovered a crape hatband. I continued to hold his burning hand in mine.

"She died," — said he — "and my unkindness killed her — unhappy Emma — thy heart was too tender!" — I shuddered — "No, no," — continued he, after a few minutes pause, "she is not married — she dared not give her hand without her heart, *and that heart was only mine!*" he added something more, in a lower tone, which I was unable to distinguish.

Overcome by a variety of sensations, I sunk into a chair, and, throwing my handkerchief over my face, indulged my tears.

Sometimes he mentioned his wife, sometimes his mother. —— At length, speaking rapidly, in a raised voice — "My son," — said he, — "thou hast no mother — but Emma will be a mother to thee — she will love thee — *she loved thy father* — her heart was the residence of gentle affections — yet, I pierced that heart!"

I suspected, that a confused recollection of having seen me on recovering from the state of insensibility, in which he had been brought, after the accident, into our house, had probably recalled the associations formerly connected with this idea. The scene became too affecting: I rushed from the apartment. All the

[108] Emma fears to pass her own emotional distress on to her child through her breastmilk. See textbox on "Appetite and Temperance," p. 521 in *Adeline*.

past impressions seemed to revive in my mind — my thoughts, with fatal mechanism, ran back into their old and accustomed channels. — For a moment, conjugal, maternal, duties, every consideration *but for one object* faded from before me!

In a few hours, Mr. Lucas returned with the physician; — I attended them to the chamber, heedfully watching their looks. The fever still continued very high, accompanied with a labouring, unsteady pulse, a difficult respiration, and strong palpitations of the heart. The doctor said little, but I discovered his apprehensions in his countenance. The patient appeared particularly restless and uneasy, and the delirium still continued. On quitting the apartment, I earnestly conjured the gentlemen to tell me their opinion of the case. They both expressed an apprehension of internal injury.

"But a short time" they added, "would determine it; in the mean while he must be kept perfectly still."

I turned from them, and walked to the window — I raised my eyes to heaven — I breathed an involuntary ejaculation — I felt that the crisis of my fate was approaching, and I endeavoured to steel my nerves — to prepare my mind for the arduous duties which awaited me.

Mr. Lucas approached me, the physician having quitted the room. — "*Mrs. Montague*," said he, in an emphatic tone — "in your sympathy for a *stranger*, do not forget other relations."

"I do not need, sir, to be reminded by you of my duties; were not the sufferings of a fellow being a sufficient claim upon our humanity, this gentleman has *more affecting claims* — I am neither a stranger to him, nor to his virtues."

"So I perceive, madam," said he, with an air a little sarcastic, "I wish, Mr. Montague were here to participate your cares."

"I wish he were, sir, his generous nature would not disallow them." I spoke haughtily, and abruptly left him.

I took a turn in the garden, endeavouring to compose my spirits, and, after visiting the nursery, returned to the chamber of Mr. Harley. I there found Mr. Lucas, and in a steady tone, declared my intention of watching his patient through the night.

"As you please, madam," said he coldly.

I seated myself in an easy chair, reclining my head on my hand. The bed curtains were undrawn on the side next me. Augustus frequently started, as from broken slumbers; his respiration grew, every moment, more difficult and laborious, and, sometimes, he groaned heavily, as if in great pain. Once he suddenly raised himself in the bed, and, gazing wildly round the room, exclaimed in a distinct, but hurried tone ——

"Why dost thou persecute me with thy ill-fated tenderness? A fathomless gulf separates us! — Emma!" added he, in a plaintive voice, "*dost thou, indeed, still love me?*" and, heaving a convulsive sigh, sunk again on his pillow.

Mr. Lucas, who stood at the feet of the bed, turned his eye on me. I met his glance with the steady aspect of conscious rectitude. About midnight, our patient grew worse, and, after strong agonies, was seized with a vomiting of blood. The fears of the physician were but too well verified, he had again ruptured the blood-vessel, once before broken.

Mr. Lucas had but just retired, I ordered him to be instantly recalled, and, stifling every feeling, that might incapacitate me for active exertion, I rendered him all the assistance in my power — I neither trembled, nor shed a tear — I banished the *woman* from my heart — I acquitted myself with a firmness that would not have disgraced the most experienced, and veteran surgeon. My services were materially useful, my solicitude vanquished every shrinking sensibility, *affection had converted me into a heroine!* The hæmorrhage continued, at intervals, all the next day: I passed once or twice from the chamber to the nursery, and immediately returned. We called in a consultation, but little hope was afforded.

The next night, Mr. Lucas and myself continued to watch — towards morning our exhausted patient sunk into an apparently tranquil slumber. Mr. Lucas intreated me to retire and take some repose, on my refusal, he availed himself of the opportunity, and went to his apartment, desiring to be called if any change should take place. The nurse slept soundly in her chair, I alone remained watching — I felt neither fatigue nor languor — my strength seemed preserved as by a miracle, so omnipotent is the operation of moral causes!

Silence reigned throughout the house; I hung over the object of my tender cares — his features were serene — but his cheeks and lips were pale and bloodless. From time to time I took his lifeless hand — a low, fluttering, pulse, sometimes seeming to stop, and then to vibrate with a tremulous motion, but too plainly justified my fears — his breath, though less laborious, was quick and short — a cold dew hung upon his temples — I gently wiped them with my handkerchief, and pressed my lips to his forehead. Yet, at that moment, that solemn moment — while I beheld the object of my virgin affections — whom I had loved with a tenderness, 'passing the love of woman'[109] — expiring before my eyes — I forgot not that I was a wife and a mother. — The purity of my feelings sanctified their enthusiasm!

The day had far advanced, though the house still remained quiet, when Augustus, after a deep drawn sigh, opened his eyes. The loss of blood had calmed the delirium, and though he regarded me attentively, and with evident surprize, the wildness of his eyes and countenance had given place to their accustomed steady expression. He spoke in a faint voice.

"Where am I, how came I here?"

I drew nearer to him — "An unfortunate accident has thrown you into the care of kind friends — you have been very ill — it is not proper that you should exert yourself — rely on those to whom your safety is precious."

He looked at me as I spoke — his eyes glistened — he breathed a half smothered sigh, but attempted not to reply. He continued to doze at intervals throughout the day, but evidently grew weaker every hour — I quitted him not for a moment, even my nursery was forgotten.[110] I sat, or knelt, at the bed's head,

---

[109] Samuel 1.26: "I am distressed for thee, my brother Jonathan, very pleasant hast thou been unto me: thy love to me was Wonderfull, passing the love of women."

[110] Emma here forgets to breastfeed and care for her newborn child.

and, between his short and broken slumbers, administered cordial medicines. He seemed to take them with pleasure from my hand, and a mournful tenderness at times beamed in his eyes. I neither spake nor wept — my strength appeared equal to every trial.

In the evening, starting from a troubled sleep, he fell into convulsions — I kept my station — our efforts were successful — he again revived. I supported the pillows on which his head reclined, sprinkled the bed cloaths, and bathed his temples, with hungary water,[111] while I wiped from them the damps of death. A few tears at length forced their way, they fell upon his hand, which rested on the pillow — he kissed them off, and raised to mine his languid eyes, in which death was already painted.

The blood forsaking the extremities, rushed wildly to my heart, a strong palpitation seized it, my fortitude had well nigh forsaken me. But I have been habituated to subdue my feelings, and should I suffer them to disturb the last moments of him, *who had taught me this painful lesson?* He made a sign for a cordial, an attendant offering one — he waved his hand and turned from her his face — I took it — held it to his lips, and he instantly drank it. Another strong emotion shook my nerves — once more I struggled and gained the victory. He spoke in feeble and interrupted periods — kneeling down, scarce daring to breathe, I listened.

"I have a son" — said he, — "I am dying — he will have no longer a parent — transfer to him a portion of — "

"I comprehend you — say no more — *he is mine* — I adopt him — where shall I find ———?"

He pointed to his cloaths — "a pocket book" — said he, in accents still fainter.

"Enough! — I swear, in this awful moment, never to forsake him."

---

[111] A kind of fragrance or eau de toilette, often used to revive the victim of illness or a fainting fit. Strong scents were also used as a prophylactic against disease believed to be carried by noxious smells.

He raised my hand to his lips — a tender smile illumined his countenance — "Surely," said he, "I have sufficiently fulfilled the dictates of a rigid honour! — In these last moments — when every earthly tie is dissolving — when human institutions fade before my sight — I may, without a crime, tell you — *that I have loved you.* — Your tenderness early penetrated my heart — aware of its weakness — I sought to shun you — I imposed on myself those severe laws of which you causelessly complained. — Had my conduct been less rigid, I had been lost — I had been unjust to the bonds which I had voluntarily contracted; and which, therefore, had on me indispensible claims. I acted from good motives, but no doubt, was guilty of some errors — yet, my conflicts were, even, more cruel than yours — I had not only to contend against my own sensibility, but against yours also. — The fire which is pent up burns the fiercest!" —

He ceased to speak — a transient glow, which had lighted up his countenance, faded — exhausted, by the strong effort he had made, he sunk back — his eyes grew dim — they closed — *their last light beamed on me!* — I caught him in my arms — and — *he awoke no more.* The spirits, that had hitherto supported me, suddenly subsided. I uttered a piercing shriek, and sunk upon the body.

Chap. XXII.

MANY weeks passed of which I have no remembrance, they were a blank in my life — a long life of sorrow! When restored to recollection, I found myself in my own chamber, my husband attending me. It was a long time before I could clearly retrace the images of the past. I learned ——

'That I had been seized with a nervous fever, in consequence of having exerted myself beyond my strength; that my head had been disordered; that Mr. Montague on his return, finding me in this situation, of which Mr. Lucas had explained the causes, had been absorbed in deep affliction; that, inattentive to every other concern, he had scarcely quitted my apartment; that my child had been sent out to nurse;[112] and that my recovery had been despaired of.'

My constitution was impaired by these repeated shocks. I continued several months in a low and debilitated state. — With returning reason, I recalled to my remembrance the charge which Augustus had consigned to me in his last moments. I enquired earnestly for the pocket-book he had mentioned, and was informed, that, after his decease, it had been found, and its contents examined, which were a bank note of fifty pounds, some letters, and memorandums. Among the letters was one from his brother, by which means they had learned his address, and had been enabled to transmit to him an account of the melancholy catastrophe, and to request his orders respecting the disposal of the body. On the receipt of this intelligence, the younger Mr. Harley had come immediately into ——shire, had received his brother's effects, and had his remains decently and respectfully interred in the town where the fatal accident had taken place, through which he was passing in his way to visit a friend.

As soon as I had strength to hold a pen, I wrote to this gentleman, mentioning the tender office which had been consigned to me; and requesting that the child, or children, of Mr. Augustus Harley might be consigned to my care. To this letter I received an answer, in a few days, hinting —

'That the marriage of my deceased friend had not been more imprudent than unfortunate; that he had struggled with great difficulties and many sorrows; that his wife had been dead near a twelve-month; that he had lost two of his children, about the same period, with the small-pox, one only surviving, the younger, a son, a year and a half old; that it was, at present, at nurse, under his (his brother's) protection; that his respect for me, and knowledge of my friendship for their family, added to his wish

---

[112] I.e., to wetnurse. Poor women, who had children of their own young enough to be still nursing, took in the nursing children of wealthier mothers and fed them. The practice was becoming unacceptable in the late 1700s, and was associated with the decadence of aristocratic women and French women in particular.

of complying with every request of his deceased brother, prevented him from hesitating a moment respecting the propriety of yielding the child to my care; that it should be delivered to any person whom I should commission for the purpose; and that I might draw upon him for the necessary charges towards the support and education of his nephew.'

I mentioned to Mr. Montague these particulars, with a desire of availing myself of his counsel and assistance on the occasion.

"You are free, madam," he replied, with a cold and distant air, "to act as you shall think proper; but you must excuse me from making myself responsible in the affair."

I sighed deeply. I perceived, but too plainly, that *a mortal blow was given to my tranquillity*; but I determined to persevere in what I considered to be my duty. On the retrospect of my conduct, my heart acquitted me; and I endeavoured to submit, without repining, to my fate.

I was, at this period, informed by a faithful servant, who attended me during my illness, of what I had before but too truly conjectured — That in my delirium I had incessantly called upon the name of Augustus Harley, and repeated, at intervals, in broken language, the circumstances of our last tender and fatal interview: this, with some particulars related by Mr. Lucas to Mr. Montague on his return, had, it seems, at the time, inflamed the irascible passions of my husband, almost to madness. His transports had subsided, by degrees, into gloomy reserve: he had watched me, till my recovery, with unremitting attention; since which his confidence and affection became, every day, more visibly alienated. Self-respect suppressed my complaints — conscious of deserving, even more than ever, his esteem, I bore his caprice with patience, trusting that time, and my conduct, would restore him to reason, and awaken in his heart a sense of justice.

I sent for my babe from the house of the nurse, to whose care it had been confided during my illness, and placed the little Augustus in its stead. "It is unnecessary, my friend, to say, that you were that lovely and interesting child. — Oh! with what emotion did I receive, and press, you to my care-worn bosom; retracing in your smiling countenance the features of your unfortunate father! Adopting you for my own, I divided my affection between you and my Emma. Scarce a day passed that I did not visit the cottage of your nurse. I taught you to call me by the endearing name of *mother!* I delighted to see you caress my infant with fraternal tenderness —— I endeavoured to cherish this growing affection, and found a sweet relief from my sorrows in these tender, maternal, cares."

CHAP. XXIII.

MY health being considerably injured, I had taken a young woman into my house, to assist me in the nursery, and in other domestic offices. She was in her eighteenth year — simple, modest, and innocent. This girl had resided with me for some months. I had been kind to her, and she seemed attached to me. One morning, going suddenly into Mr. Montague's dressing-room, I surprised Rachael sitting on a sopha with her master: — he held her hand in his, while his arm was thrown round her waist; and they appeared to be engaged in earnest conversation. They both started, on my entrance: —— Unwilling to encrease their confusion, I quitted the room.

Montague, on our meeting at dinner, affected an air of unconcern; but there was an apparent constraint in his behaviour. I preserved towards him my accustomed manner, till the servants had withdrawn. I then mildly expostulated with him on the impropriety of his behaviour. His replies were not more unkind than ungenerous — they pierced my heart.

"It is well, sir, I am inured to suffering; but it is not of *myself* that I would speak. I have not deserved to lose your confidence — this is my consolation; — yet, I submit to it: —— but I cannot see you act in a manner, that will probably involve you in vexation, and intail upon you remorse, without warning you of your danger. Should you corrupt the innocence of this girl, she is emphatically *ruined*. It is the strong mind only, that, firmly resting on its own powers, can sustain and recover itself amidst the world's scorn and injustice. The morality of an uncultivated understanding, is that of *custom*, not of reason: — break down the feeble barrier, and there is nothing to supply its place —— you open the flood-gates of infamy and wretchedness. Who can say where the evil may stop?"

"You are at liberty to discharge your servant, when you please, madam."

"I think it my duty to do so, Mr. Montague — not on my own, but on *her*, account. If I have no claim upon your affection and principles, I would disdain to watch your conduct. But I feel myself attached to this young woman, and would wish to preserve her from destruction!"

"You are very generous; but as you thought fit to bestow on me your *hand*, when your *heart* was devoted to another —— "

"It is enough, sir! — To your justice, only, in your cooler moments, would I appeal!"

I procured for Rachel a reputable place, in a distant part of the county. — Before she quitted me, I seriously, and affectionately, remonstrated with her on the consequences of her behaviour. She answered me only with tears and blushes.

In vain I tried to rectify the principles, and subdue the cruel prejudices, of my husband. I endeavoured to shew him every mark of affection and confidence. I frequently expostulated with him, upon his conduct, with tears — urged him to respect himself and me — strove to convince him of the false principles upon which he acted — of the senseless and barbarous manner in which he was sacrificing my peace, and his own, to a romantic chimera. Sometimes he would appear, for a moment, melted with my tender and fervent entreaties.

"Would to God!" he would say, with emotion, "the last six months of my life could be obliterated for ever from my remembrance!"

He was no longer active, and chearful: he would sit, for hours, involved in deep and gloomy silence. When I brought the little Emma, to soften, by her engaging caresses, the anxieties by which his spirits appeared to be overwhelmed, he would gaze wildly upon her — snatch her to his breast — and then, suddenly throwing her from him, rush out of the house; and, inattentive to the duties of his profession, absent himself for days and nights together: — his temper grew, every hour, more furious and unequal.

He by accident, one evening, met the little Augustus, as his nurse was carrying him from my apartment; and, breaking rudely into the room, overwhelmed me with a torrent of abuse and reproaches. I submitted to his injustice with silent grief — my spirits were utterly broken. At times, he would seem to be sensible of the impropriety of his conduct — would execrate himself, and entreat my forgiveness; —— but quickly relapsed into his accustomed paroxysms, which, from having been indulged, were now become habitual, and uncontroulable. These agitations seemed daily to encrease — all my efforts to regain his confidence — my patient, unremitted, attentions — were fruitless. He shunned me — he appeared, even, to regard me with horror. I wept in silence. The hours which I passed with my children afforded me my only consolation — they became painfully dear to me. Attending to their little sports, and innocent gambols, I forgot, for a moment, my griefs.

Chap. XXIV.

Some months thus passed away, with little variation in my situation. Returning home one morning, early, from the nurse's, where I had left my Emma with Augustus (whom I never, now, permitted to be brought to my own house) as I entered, Mr. Montague shot suddenly by me, and rushed up stairs towards his apartment. I saw him but transiently, as he passed; but his haggard countenance, and furious gestures, filled me with dismay. He had been from home the preceding night; but to these absences I had lately been too much accustomed to regard them as any thing extraordinary. I hesitated a few moments, whether I should follow him. I feared, lest I might exasperate him by so doing; yet, the unusual disorder of his appearance gave me a thousand terrible and nameless apprehensions. I crept towards the door of his apartment — listened attentively, and heard him walking up and down the room, with hasty steps — sometimes he appeared to stop, and groaned heavily: ——once I heard him throw up the sash, and shut it again with violence.

I attempted to open the door, but, finding it locked, my terror increased. — I knocked gently, but could not attract his attention. At length I recollected another door, that led to this apartment, through my own chamber, which was fastened on the outside, and seldom opened. With trembling steps I hurried round, and, on entering the room, beheld him sitting at a table, a pen in his hand, and paper before him. On the table lay his pistols — his hair was dishevelled — his dress disordered — his features distorted with emotion — while in his countenance was painted the extreme of horror and despair.

I uttered a faint shriek, and sunk into a chair. He started from his seat, and, advancing towards me with hurried and tremulous steps, sternly demanded, Why I intruded on his retirement? I threw myself at his feet, — I folded my arms round him — I wept — I deprecated his anger — I entreated to be heard — I said all that humanity, all that the most tender and lively sympathy could suggest, to inspire him with confidence — to induce him to relieve, by communication, the burthen which oppressed his heart. — He struggled to free himself from me — my apprehensions gave me strength — I held him with a strenuous grasp — he raved — he stamped — he tore his hair — his passion became frenzy! At length, forcibly bursting from me, I fell on the floor, and the blood gushed from my nose and lips. He shuddered convulsively — stood a few moments, as if irresolute — and, then, throwing himself beside me, raised me from the ground; and, clasping me to his heart, which throbbed tumultuously, burst into a flood of tears.

"I will not be thy *murderer*, Emma!" said he, in a voice of agony, interrupted by heart-rending sobs —— "I have had enough of blood!"

I tried to sooth him — I assured him I was not hurt — I besought him to confide his sorrows to the faithful bosom of his wife! He appeared softened — his tears flowed without controul.

"Unhappy woman! — you know not what you ask! To be ingenuous, belongs to purity like yours! —— Guilt, black as hell! — conscious, aggravated, damnable, guilt! — *Your fatal attachment* — my accursed jealousy! — Ah! Emma! I have injured you — but you are, indeed, revenged!"

Every feature seemed to work — seemed pregnant with dreadful meaning — he was relapsing into frenzy.

"Be calm, my friend — be not unjust to yourself — you can have committed no injury that I shall not willingly forgive — you are incapable of persisting in guilt. The ingenuous mind, that avows, has already made half the reparation. Suffer me to learn the source of your inquietude! I may find much to extenuate — I may be able to convince you, that you are too severe to yourself."

"Never, never, never! — nothing can extenuate — *the expiation must be made!* — Excellent, admirable, woman! — Remember, without hating, the wretch who has been unworthy of you — who could not conceive, who knew not how to estimate, your virtues! — Oh! do not — do not" — straining me to his bosom — "curse my memory!"

He started from the ground, and, in a moment, was out of sight.

I raised myself with difficulty — faint, tottering, gasping for breath, I attempted to descend the stairs. I had scarcely reached the landing-place, when a violent knocking at the door shook my whole frame. I stood still, clinging to the balustrade, unable to proceed. I heard a chaise draw up — a servant opening the door — a plain-looking countryman alighted, and desired instantly to speak to the lady of the house — his business was, he said, of life and death! I advanced towards him, pale and trembling!

"What is the matter, my friend — whence came you?"

"I cannot stop, lady, to explain myself — you must come with me — I will tell you more as we go along."

"Do you come," enquired I, in a voice scarcely articulate,

"from my husband?"

"No — no — I come from a person who is dying, who has somewhat of consequence to impart to you —— Hasten, lady — there is no time to lose!"

"Lead, then, I follow you."

He helped me into the chaise, and we drove off with the rapidity of lightning.

Chap. XXV.

I ASKED no more questions on the road, but attempted to fortify my mind for the scenes which, I foreboded, were approaching. After about an hour's ride, we stopped at a small, neat, cottage, embosomed in trees, standing alone, at a considerable distance from the high-road. A decent-looking, elderly, woman, came to the door, at the sound of the carriage, and assisted me to alight. In her countenance were evident marks of perturbation and horror. I asked for a glass of water; and, having drank it, followed the woman, at her request, up stairs. She seemed inclined to talk, but I gave her no encouragement —— I knew not what awaited me, nor what exertions might be requisite — I determined not to exhaust my spirits unnecessarily.

On entering a small chamber, I observed a bed, with curtains closely drawn. I advanced towards it, and, unfolding them, beheld the unhappy Rachel lying in a state of apparent insensibility.

"She is dying," whispered the woman, "she had been in strong convulsions; but she could not die in peace without seeing Madam Montague, and obtaining her forgiveness."

I approached the unfortunate girl, and took her lifeless hand. — A feeble pulse still trembled — I gazed upon her, for some moments, in silence. —— She heaved a deep sigh — her lips moved, inarticulately. She, at length, opened her eyes, and, fixing them upon me, the blood seemed to rush through her languid frame — reanimating it. She sprung up in the bed, and, clasping her hands together, uttered a few incoherent words.

"Be pacified, my dear — I am not angry with you — I feel

only pity."

She looked wildly. "Ah! my dear lady, I am a wicked girl — but not — Oh, no! — *not a murderer!* I did not —— indeed, I did not —— murder my child!"

A cold tremor seized me — I turned heart-sick — a sensation of horror thrilled through my veins!

"My dear, my kind mistress," resumed the wretched girl, "can you forgive me? —— Oh! that cruel, barbarous, man! — It was *he* who did it — indeed, it was *he* who did it!" Distraction glared in her eyes.

"I do forgive you," said I, in broken accents. "I will take care of you — but you must be calm."

"I will — I will" — replied she, in a rapid tone of voice — "but do not send me to prison — *I did not murder it!* — Oh! my child, my child!" continued she, in a screaming tone of frantic violence, and was again seized with strong convulsions.

We administered all the assistance in our power. I endeavoured, with success, to stifle my emotions in the active duties of humanity. Rachel once more revived. After earnestly recommending her to the care of the good woman of the house, and promising to send medicines and nourishment proper for her situation, and to reward their attentions — desiring that she might be kept perfectly still, and not be suffered to talk on subjects that agitated her — I quitted the place, presaging but too much, and not having, at that time, the courage to make further enquiries.

Chap. XXVI.

On entering my own house my heart misgave me. I enquired, with trepidation, for my husband, and was informed — 'That he had returned soon after my departure, and had shut himself in his apartment; that, on being followed by Mr. Lucas, he had turned fiercely upon him, commanding him, in an imperious tone, instantly to leave him; adding, he had affairs of importance to transact; and should any one dare to intrude on him, it would be at the peril of their lives.' All the family appeared in consternation, but no one had presumed to disobey the orders of their master. — They expressed their satisfaction at my return — Alas! I was impotent to relieve the apprehensions which, I too plainly perceived, had taken possession of their minds.

I retired to my chamber, and, with a trembling hand, traced, and addressed to my husband, a few incoherent lines — briefly hinting my suspicions respecting the late transactions — exhorting him to provide for his safety, and offering to be the companion of his flight. I added — "Let us reap wisdom from these tragical consequences of *indulged passion!* It is not to atone for the past error, by cutting off the prospect of future usefulness — Repentance for what can never be recalled, is absurd and vain, but as it affords a lesson for the time to come — do not let us wilfully forfeit the fruits of our dear-bought experience! I will never reproach you! Virtuous resolution, and time, may yet heal these aggravated wounds. Dear Montague, be no longer the slave of error; inflict not on my tortured mind new, and more insupportable, terrors! I await your directions — let us fly — let us summon our fortitude — let us, at length, bravely stem the tide of passion — let us beware of the criminal pusillanimity of despair!"

With faultering steps, I sought the apartment of my husband. I listened a moment at the door — and hearing him in motion, while profound sighs burst every instant from his bosom, I slid my paper under the door, unfolded, that it might be more likely to attract his attention. Presently, I had the satisfaction of hearing him take it up. After some minutes, a slip of paper was returned, by the same method which I had adopted, in which was written, in characters blotted, and scarcely legible, the following words —

"Leave me, one half hour, to my reflections: at the end of that period, be assured, I will see, or write, to you."

I knew him to be incapable of falsehood — my heart palpitated with hope. I went to my chamber, and passed the interval in a thousand cruel reflections, and vague plans for our sudden departure. Near an hour had elapsed, when the bell rang. I started, breathless, from my seat. A servant passed my door, to take his master's orders. He returned instantly, and, meeting me in the passage, delivered to me a letter. I heard Montague again lock the door. —— Disappointed, I re-entered my chamber. In my haste to get at the contents of the paper, I almost tore it in pieces — the words swam before my sight. I held it for some moments in my hand, incapable of deciphering the fatal characters. I breathed with difficulty — all the powers of life seemed suspended — when the report of a pistol roused me to a sense of confused horror. — Rushing forward, I burst, with preternatural strength, into the apartment of my husband —— What a spectacle! — Assistance was vain! —— Montague — the impetuous, ill-fated, Montague — *was no more — was a mangled corpse!* — Rash, unfortunate, young, man!

But, why should I harrow up your susceptible mind, by dwelling on these cruel scenes? *Ah! suffer me to spread a veil over this fearful catastrophe!* Some time elapsed ere I had fortitude to examine the paper addressed to me by my unfortunate husband. Its contents, which were as follows, affected me with deep and mingled emotions.

To Mrs. Montague.

"Amidst the reflections which press, by turns, upon my burning brain, an obscure consciousness of the prejudices upon which my character has been formed, is not the least torturing — because I feel *the inveterate force of habit* — I feel, that my convictions come too late!

"I have destroyed myself, and you, dearest, most generous, and most unfortunate, of women! I am a monster! — I have seduced innocence, and embrued my hands in blood! —— Oh, God! — Oh, God! —— *'Tis there distraction lies!* — I would, circumstantially, retrace my errors; but my disordered mind, and quivering hand, refuse the cruel task — yet, it is necessary that I should attempt a brief sketch.

"After the cruel accident, which destroyed our tranquillity, I nourished my senseless jealousies (the sources of which I need not, now, recapitulate), till I persuaded myself — injurious wretch that I was! — that I had been perfidiously and ungenerously treated. Stung by false pride, I tried to harden my heart, and foolishly thirsted for revenge. Your meekness, and magnanimity, disappointed me. — I would willingly have seen you, not only suffer the PANGS, but express the *rage*, of a slighted wife. The simple victim of my baseness, by the artless affection she expressed for me, gained an ascendency over my mind; and, when you removed her from your house, we still contrived, at times, to meet. The consequences of our intercourse could not long be concealed. It was, then, that I first began to open my eyes on my conduct, and to be seized with remorse! — Rachel, now, wept incessantly. Her father, she told me, was a stern and severe man; and should he hear of her misconduct, would, she was certain, be her destruction. I procured for her an obscure retreat, to which I removed the unhappy girl (Oh, how degrading is vice!), under false pretences. I exhorted her to conceal her situation — to pretend, that her health was in a declining state — and I visited her, from time to time, as in my profession.

"This poor young creature continued to bewail the disgrace she anticipated — her lamentations pierced my soul! I recalled to my remembrance your emphatic caution. I foresaw that, with the loss of her character, this simple girl's misfortune and degradation would be irretrievable; and I could, now, plainly distinguish the morality of *rule* from that of *principle*. Pursuing this train of reasoning, I entangled myself, for my views were not yet sufficiently clear and comprehensible! Bewildered, amidst contending principles — distracted by a variety of emotions — in seeking a remedy for one vice, I plunged (as is but too common), into others of a more scarlet dye. With shame and horror, I confess, I repeatedly tried, by medical drugs, to procure an abortive birth: the strength and vigour of Rachel's constitution defeated this diabolical purpose. Foiled in these attempts, I became hardened, desperate, and barbarous!

"Six weeks before the allotted period, the infant saw the light — for a moment — to close its eyes on it for ever! I, only, was with the unhappy mother. I had formed no deliberate purpose — I had not yet arrived at the acme of guilt — but, perceiving, from the babe's premature birth, and the consequences of the pernicious potions which had been administered to the mother, that the vital flame played but feebly — that life was but as a quivering, uncertain, spark — a sudden and terrible thought darted through my mind. I know not whether my emotion betrayed me to the ear of Rachel — but, suddenly throwing back the curtain of the bed, she beheld me grasp — with savage ferocity — *with murderous hands!* — Springing from the bed, and throwing herself upon me — her piercing shrieks —

"*I can no more* — of the rest you seem, from whatever means, but too well informed!

"I need not say — protect, if she survive, the miserable mother! — To you, whose heavenly goodness I have so ill requited, it would be injurious as unnecessary! I read, too late, the heart I have insulted!

"I have settled the disposal of my effects — I have commanded my feelings to give you this last, sad, proof of my confidence. — *Kneeling*, I entreat your forgiveness for the sufferings I have caused you! I found your heart wounded — and into those festering wounds I infused a deadly venom — curse not my memory — *We meet no more.*

"Farewel! first, and last, and only, beloved of women! — a long — a long farewel!"

"Montague."

These are the consequences of confused systems of morals — and thus it is, that minds of the highest hope, and fairest prospect, are blasted!

Chap. XXVII.

The unhappy Rachel recovered her health by slow degrees. I had determined, when my affairs were settled, to leave a spot, that had been the scene of so many tragical events. I proposed to the poor girl to take her again into my family, to which she acceded with rapture. She has never since quitted me, and her faithful services, and humble, grateful attachment, have repaid my protection an hundred fold.

Mr. Montague left ten thousand pounds, the half of which was settled on his daughter, the remainder left to my disposal. This determined me to adopt you wholly for my son. I wrote to your uncle to that purport, taking upon myself the entire charge of your education, and entreating, that you might never know, unless informed by myself, to whom you owed your birth. That you should continue to think me *your mother*, flattered my tenderness, nor was my Emma, herself, more dear to me.

I retired in a few months to my present residence, sharing my heart and my attentions between my children, who grew up under my fostering care, lovely and beloved.

"While every day, soft as it roll'd along,
Shew'd some new charm"[113]

I observed your affection for each other with a flattering presage. With the features of your father, you inherited his intrepidity, and manly virtues — even, at times, I thought I perceived the seeds of his inflexible spirit: but the caresses of my Emma, more fortunate than her mother — yet, with all her mother's sensibility — could, in an instant, soften you to tenderness, and melt you into infantine sweetness.

I endeavoured to form your young minds to every active virtue, to every generous sentiment. — You received, from the same masters, the same lessons, till you attained your twelfth year; and my Emma emulated, and sometimes outstripped your progress. I observed, with a mixture of hope and solicitude, her lively capacity — her enthusiastic affections; while I laboured to moderate and regulate them.

It now became necessary that your educations should take a somewhat different direction; I wished to fit you for a commercial line of life; but the ardor you discovered for science and literature occasioned me some perplexity, as I feared it might

[113] Thomson, *Seasons*, "Spring," lines 1147-8.

unfit you for application to trade, in the pursuit of which so many talents are swallowed up, and powers wasted. Yet, to the professions my objections were still more serious. — The study of law, is the study of chicanery. — The church, the school of hypocrisy and usurpation! You could only enter the universities by a moral degradation,[114] that must check the freedom, and contaminate the purity, of the mind, and, entangling it in an inexplicable maze of error and contradiction, *poison virtue at its source*, and lay the foundation for a duplicity of character and a perversion of reason, destructive of every manly principle of integrity. For the science of physic you expressed a disinclination. A neighbouring gentleman, a surveyor, a man high in his profession, and of liberal manners, to whose friendship I was indebted, offered to take you. You were delighted with this proposal, (to which I had no particular objection) as you had a taste for drawing and architecture.

Our separation, though you were to reside in the same town, cost us many tears — I loved you with more than a mother's fondness — and my Emma clung round the neck of her beloved brother, her Augustus, her playfellow, and sobbed on his bosom. It was with difficulty that you could disentangle yourself from our embraces. Every moment of leisure you flew to us — my Emma learned from you to draw plans, and to study the laws of proportion. Every little exuberance in your disposition, which, generated by a noble pride, sometimes wore the features of asperity, was soothed into peace by her gentleness and affection: while she delighted to emulate your fortitude, and to rise superior to the feebleness fostered in her sex, under the specious name of delicacy. Your mutual attachment encreased with your years, I renewed my existence in my children, and anticipated their more perfect union.

---

[114] Likely a reference to the Test Act and the practice of occasional conformity, by which non-Church of England members could gain access restricted to practicing members by taking communion occasionally, fulfilling the letter, if not the spirit of the requirement.

Ah! my son, need I proceed? Must I continually blot the page with the tale of sorrow? Can I tear open again, can I cause to bleed afresh, in your heart and my own, wounds scarcely closed? In her fourteenth year, in the spring of life, your Emma and mine, lovely and fragile blossom, was blighted by a killing frost — After a few days illness, she drooped, faded, languished, and died!

It was now that I felt — 'That no agonies were like the agonies of a mother.'[115] My broken spirits, from these repeated sorrows, sunk into habitual, hopeless, dejection. Prospects, that I had meditated with ineffable delight, were for ever veiled in darkness. Every earthly tie was broken, except that which bound you to my desolated heart with a still stronger cord of affection. You wept, in my arms, the loss of her whom you, yet, fondly believed your sister. — I cherished the illusion lest, by dissolving it, I should weaken your confidence in my maternal love, weaken that tenderness which was now my only consolation.

To Augustus Harley.

My Augustus, *my more than son*, around whom my spirit, longing for dissolution, still continues to flutter! I have unfolded the errors of my past life — I have traced them to their source — I have laid bare my mind before you, that the experiments which have been made upon it may be beneficial to yours! It has been a painful, and a humiliating recital — the retrospection has been marked with anguish. As the enthusiasm — as the passions of my youth — have passed in review before me, long forgotten emotions have been revived in my lacerated heart — it has been again torn with *the pangs of contemned love* — the disappointment of rational plans of usefulness — the dissolution of the darling hopes of maternal pride and fondness. The frost of a premature age sheds its snows upon my temples, the ravages of a sickly mind shake my tottering frame. The morning dawns, the evening closes upon me, the seasons revolve, without hope; the

[115] Not found.

sun shines, the spring returns, but, to me, it is mockery.

And is this all of human life — this, that passes like a tale that is told? Alas! it is a tragical tale! Friendship was the star, whose cheering influence I courted to beam upon my benighted course. The social affections were necessary to my existence, but they have been only inlets to sorrow — *yet, still, I bind them to my heart!*

Hitherto there seems to have been something strangely wrong in the constitutions of society — a lurking poison that spreads its contagion far and wide — a canker at the root of private virtue and private happiness — a principle of deception, that sanctifies error — a Circean cup that lulls into a fatal intoxication.[116] But men begin to think and reason; reformation dawns, though the advance is tardy. Moral martyrdom may possibly be the fate of those who press forward, yet, their generous efforts will not be lost. — Posterity will plant the olive and the laurel, and consecrate their mingled branches to the memory of such, who, daring to trace, to their springs, errors the most hoary, and prejudices the most venerated, emancipate the human mind from the trammels of superstition, and teach it, *that its true dignity and virtue, consist in being free.*

Ere I sink into the grave, let me behold *the son of my affections*, the living image of him, whose destiny involved mine, who gave an early, but a mortal blow, to all my worldly expectations — let me behold my Augustus, escaped from the tyranny of the passions, restored to reason, to the vigor of his mind, to self controul, to the dignity of active, intrepid, virtue!

The dawn of my life glowed with the promise of a fair and bright day; before its noon, thick clouds gathered; its mid-day was gloomy and tempestuous. — It remains with thee, my friend, to gild with a mild radiance the closing evening; before the scene shuts, and veils the prospect in impenetrable darkness.

FINIS.

---

[116] Reference to the sorceress Circe from Homer's *Odyssey*, whose potions turned Odysseus's men into swine.

Portrait of Amelia Opie. By John Opie, 1798. (By courtesy of the National Portrait Gallery.)

ADELINE MOWBRAY,

OR THE

MOTHER AND DAUGHTER:

𝔄 𝔗𝔞𝔩𝔢,

IN THREE VOLUMES.

BY MRS. OPIE.

VOL. I.

LONDON:

PRINTED FOR LONGMAN, HURST, REES, & ORME,
PATERNOSTER ROW ;
AND A. CONSTABLE AND CO. EDINBURGH.

1805.

Title page of the first edition of *Adeline Mowbray; or the Mother and the Daughter*, 1804. (By courtesy of the University of Nebraska - Lincoln Love Library.)

Adeline Mowbray
Or the
Mother and Daughter:
A Tale,
In Three Volumes
By Mrs. Opie

Vol. I.

Chapter I.

In an old family mansion, situated on an estate in Gloucestershire known by the name of Rosevalley, resided Mrs. Mowbray, and Adeline her only child.

Mrs. Mowbray's father, Mr. Woodville, a respectable country gentleman, married, in obedience to the will of his mother, the sole surviving daughter of an opulent merchant in London, whose large dower paid off some considerable mortgages on the Woodville estates, and whose mild and unoffending character soon gained that affection from her husband after marriage, which he denied her before it.

Nor was it long before their happiness was increased, and their union cemented, by the birth of a daughter; who continuing to be an only child, and the probable heiress of great possessions, became the idol of her parents, and the object of unremitted attention to those who surrounded her. Consequently, one of the first lessons which Editha Woodville learnt was that of egotism, and to consider it as the chief duty of all who approached her, to study the gratification of her whims and caprices.

But, though rendered indolent in some measure by the blind folly of her parents, and the homage of her dependents, she had a taste above the enjoyments which they offered her.

She had a decided passion for literature, which she had acquired from a sister of Mrs. Woodville, who had been brought up amongst literary characters of various pursuits and opinions; and this lady had imbibed from them a love of free inquiry, which she had little difficulty in imparting to her young and enthusiastic relation.

But, alas! that inclination for study, which, had it been directed to proper objects, would have been the charm of Miss Woodville's life, and the safeguard of her happiness, by giving her a constant source of amusement within herself, proved to her, from the unfortunate direction which it took, the abundant cause of misery and disappointment.

For her, history, biography, poetry, and discoveries in natural philosophy, had few attractions, while she pored with still unsatisfied delight over abstruse systems of morals and metaphysics, or new theories in politics; and scarcely a week elapsed in which she did not receive, from her aunt's bookseller in London, various tracts on these her favourite subjects.

Happy would it have been for Miss Woodville, if the merits of the works which she so admired could have been canvassed in her presence by rational and unprejudiced persons; but, her parents and friends being too ignorant to discuss philosophical opinions or political controversies, the young speculator was left to the decisions of her own inexperienced enthusiasm.[1] To her, therefore, whatever was bold and uncommon seemed new and wise; and every succeeding theory held her imagination captive till its power was weakened by one of equal claims to singularity.

She soon, however, ceased to be contented with reading, and was eager to become a writer also. But, as she was strongly imbued with the prejudices of an antient family, she could not

---

[1] Enthusiasm throughout the eighteenth century carried connotations of extreme fervor, often fanatical or religious fervor, rather than merely heightened interest.

think of disgracing that family by turning professed author: she therefore confined her little effusions to a society of admiring friends, secretly lamenting the loss which the literary world sustained in her being born a gentlewoman.[2]

Nor is it to be wondered at, that, as she was ambitious to be, and to be thought, a deep thinker, she should have acquired habits of abstraction, and absence, which imparted a look of wildness to a pair of dark eyes, that beamed with intelligence, and gave life to features of the most perfect regularity.

To reverie, indeed, she was from childhood inclined; and her life was long a life of reverie. To her the present moment had scarcely ever existence; and this propensity to lose herself in a sort of ideal world, was considerably increased by the nature of her studies.

Fatal and unproductive studies! While, wrapt in philosophical abstraction, she was trying to understand a metaphysical question on the mechanism of the human mind, or what constituted the true nature of virtue, she suffered day after day to pass in the culpable neglect of positive duties; and while imagining systems for the good of society, and the furtherance of general philanthropy, she allowed individual suffering in her neighborhood to pass unobserved and unrelieved. While professing her unbounded love for the great family of the world, she suffered her own family to pine under the consciousness of her neglect; and viciously devoted those hours to the vanity of abstruse and solitary study, which might have been better spent in amusing the declining age of her venerable parents, whom affection had led to take up their abode with her.

Let me observe, before I proceed further, that Mrs. Mowbray scrupulously confined herself to theory, even in her wisest speculations; and being too timid, and too indolent, to illustrate

---

[2] As a gentlewoman, Miss Woodville lacks the financial need which was often understood to excuse the immodesty for women writers of publishing and selling their literary work. Circulating her writing "privately" among an exclusive circle of polite acquaintance is a more genteel option, and often how women writers began their careers in the seventeenth through early nineteenth centuries.

by her conduct the various and opposing doctrines which it was her pride to maintain by turns, her practice was ever in opposition to her opinions.

Hence, after haranguing with all the violence of a true whig on the natural rights of man,[3] or the blessings of freedom, she would "turn to a tory in her elbow chair,"[4] and govern her household with despotic authority; and after embracing at some moments the doubts of the sceptic, she would often lie motionless in her bed, from apprehension of ghosts, a helpless prey to the most abject superstition.

Such was the mother of ADELINE MOWBRAY! such was the woman who, having married the heir of Rosevalley, merely to oblige her parents, saw herself in the prime of life a rich widow, with an only child, who was left by Mr. Mowbray, a fond husband, but an ill-judging parent, entirely dependent on her!

At the time of Mr. Mowbray's death, Adeline Mowbray was ten years old, and Mrs. Mowbray thirty; and like an animal in an exhausted receiver,[5] she had during her short existence been tormented by the experimental philosophy of her mother.

Now it was judged right that she should learn nothing, and now that she should learn every thing. Now, her graceful form and well-turned limbs were to be free from any bandage, and any clothing save what decency required,—and now they were

---

[3] One of the two primary political parties in eighteenth-century Britain, Whigs were associated with the interests of the merchant class and in favor of moderate constitutional reform. They were strongly opposed to Catholicism and sought to weaken the powers of the monarch.

[4] Opposing the Whigs was the Tory political party, associated most strongly with the traditional rights of the monarch and landed classes, and historically associated with Catholicism and Royalism. Tories were particularly hostile to ideas of reforming Parliament, granting more power to the House of Commons over the House of Lords, and to more republican notions of representation.

[5] Experiments with vacuum chambers at the end of the eighteenth century were popular; birds and small animals, even dogs, could be placed in such a chamber or "receiver," the air withdrawn, and then as the animal was apparently dead, it could be resuscitated by allowing air to enter the chamber. Joseph Wright of Derby illustrates this in his painting "Experiment on a Bird in the Air Pump" (1768), currently in the National Gallery in London. See <www.nationalgallery.org.uk.>

to be tortured by stiff stays, and fettered by the stocks and the backboard.[6]

All Mrs. Mowbray's ambition had settled in one point, one passion, and that was EDUCATION. For this purpose she turned over innumerable volumes in search of rules on the subject, on which she might improve, anticipating with great satisfaction the moment when she should be held up as a pattern of imitation to mothers, and be prevailed upon, though with graceful reluctance to publish her system, without a name, for the benefit of society.

But, however good her intentions were, the execution of them was continually delayed by her habits of abstraction and reverie. After having over night arranged the tasks of Adeline for the next day,—lost in some new speculations for the good of her child, she would lie in bed all the morning, exposing that child to the dangers of idleness.[7]

At one time Mrs. Mowbray had studied herself into great nicety with regard to the diet of her daughter; but, as she herself was too much used to the indulgencies of the palate to be able to set her in reality an example of temperance, she dined in appearance with Adeline at one o'clock on pudding without butter, and potatoes without salt; but while the child was taking her afternoon's walk, her own table was covered with viands fitted for the appetite of opulence.

Unfortunately, however, the servants conceived that the daughter as well as the mother had a right to regale clandestinely;

---

[6] Stays, often whalebone or reinforced fabric, were used in women's bodices to shape and constrict the female figure, though they were out of fashion in the late 1700s and early 1800s when a more "natural" figure was fashionable. The stock and backboard are form-fitting devices used to force young girls' bodies into correct and proper posture, attacked in educational treatises in the later 1700s which emphasized exercise and freedom of movement.

[7] Similarly, in Laurence Sterne's *The Life and Opinions of Tristram Shandy, Gentleman* (1759-67), Walter Shandy attempts to write a "Tristrapaedia" to provide the proper instruction for his son. Like Tristram's own account of his life, however, Walter's Tristrapaedia is always lagging behind Tristram's actual age, and so is of no practical use in educating his son (see Vol. V, Chapt XXX).

and the little Adeline used to eat for her supper, with a charge not to tell her mamma, some of the good things set by from Mrs. Mowbray's dinner.

It happened that, as Mrs. Mowbray was one evening smoothing Adeline's flowing curls, and stroking her ruddy cheek, she exclaimed triumphantly, raising Adeline to the glass, "See the effect of temperance and low living! If you were accustomed to eat meat, and butter, and drink any thing but water, you would not look so healthy, my love, as you do now. O the excellent effects of a vegetable diet!"

The artless girl, whose conscience smote her during the whole of this speech, hung her blushing head on her bosom:—it was the confusion of guilt; and Mrs. Mowbray perceiving it earnestly demanded what it meant, when Adeline, half crying, gave a full explanation.

Nothing could exceed the astonishment and mortification of Mrs. Mowbray; but, though usually tenacious of her opinions, she in this case profited by the lesson of experience. She no longer expected any advantage from clandestine measures:—but Adeline, her appetites regulated by a proper exertion of parental authority, was allowed to sit at the well-furnished table of her mother, and was precluded, by a judicious and open indulgence, from wishing for a secret and improper one; while the judicious praises which Mrs. Mowbray bestowed on Adeline's ingenuous confession endeared her to the practice of truth, and laid the foundation of a habit of ingenuousness which formed through life one of the ornaments of her character..... Would that Mrs. Mowbray had always been equally judicious!

Another great object of anxiety to her was the method of clothing children; whether they should wear flannel, or no flannel; light shoes, to give agility to the motions of the limbs; or heavy shoes, in order to strengthen the muscles by exertion;—when one day, as she was turning over a voluminous author on this subject, the nursery-maid hastily entered the room, and claimed her attention, but in vain; Mrs. Mowbray went on reading aloud:—

"Some persons are of opinion that thin shoes are most beneficial to health; others, equally worthy of respect, think thick ones of most use: and the reasons for these different opinions we shall class under two heads...."

"Dear me, ma'am!" cried Bridget, "and in the mean time miss Adeline will go without shoes at all."

"Do not interrupt me, Bridget," cried Mrs. Mowbray, and proceeded to read on. "In the first place, it is not clear, says a learned writer, whether children require any clothing at all for their feet."

At this moment Adeline burst open the parlour door, and crying bitterly, held up her bleeding toes to her mother.

"Mamma, mamma!" cried she, "you forget to send for a pair of new shoes for me; and see, how the stones in the gravel have cut me!"

This sight, this appeal, decided the question in dispute. The feet of Adeline bleeding on a new Turkey carpet proved that some clothing for the feet was necessary; and even Mrs. Mowbray for a moment began to suspect that a little experience is better than a great deal of theory.[8]

CHAPTER II.

MEANWHILE, in spite of all Mrs. Mowbray's eccentricities and caprices, Adeline, as she grew up, continued to entertain for her the most perfect respect and affection.

Her respect was excited by the high idea which she had formed of her abilities,—an idea founded on the veneration which all the family seemed to feel for her on that account,—and her affection was excited even to an enthusiastic degree by the tenderness with which Mrs. Mowbray had watching over her during an alarming illness.

---

[8] Associating abstract "theory" and "philosophy" with republican, French sentiments, and opposing them to practical "common sense" Englishness was a conventional criticism through the 1790s and early 1800s. The theme of "experience" versus "theory" runs importantly through *Adeline Mowbray*.

For twenty-one days Adeline had been in the utmost danger; nor is it probable that she would have been able to struggle against the force of the disease, but for the unremitting attention of her mother. It was then, perhaps, for the first time that Mrs. Mowbray felt herself a mother:— all her vanities, all her systems, were forgotten in the danger of Adeline,—she did not even hazard an opinion on the medical treatment to be observed. For once she was contented to obey instructions in silence; for once she was never caught in a reverie; but, like the most common-place woman of her acquaintance, she lived to the present moment:— and she was rewarded for her cares by the recovery of her daughter, and by that daughter's most devoted attachment.

Not even the parents of Mrs. Mowbray, who, because she talked on subjects which they could not understand, looked up to her as a superior being, could exceed Adeline in deference to her mother's abilities; and when, as she advanced in life, she was sometimes tempted to think her deficient in maternal fondness, the idea of Mrs. Mowbray bending with pale and speechless anxiety over her sleepless pillow used to recur to her remembrance, and in a moment the recent indifference was forgotten.

Nor could she entirely acquit herself of ingratitude in observing this seeming indifference: for, whence did the abstraction and apparent coldness of Mrs. Mowbray proceed? From her mind's being wholly engrossed in studies for the future benefit of Adeline. Why did she leave the concerns of her family to others? why did she allow her infirm but active mother to superintend all the household duties? and why did she seclude herself from all society, save that of her own family, and Dr. Norberry, her physician and friend, but that she might devote every hour to endeavours to perfect a system of education for her beloved and only daughter, to whom the work was to be dedicated? "And yet," said Adeline mentally, "I am so ungrateful sometimes as to think she does not love me sufficiently."

But while Mrs. Mowbray was busying herself in plans for Adeline's education, she reached the age of fifteen, and was in a manner educated; not, however, by her,—though Mrs. Mowbray would, no doubt, have been surprised to have heard this assertion.

Mrs. Mowbray, as I have before said, was the spoiled child of rich parents; who, as geniuses were rarer in those days than they are now, spite of their own ignorance, rejoiced to find themselves the parents of a genius; and as their daughter always disliked the usual occupations of her sex, the admiring father and mother contented themselves with allowing her to please herself; saying to each other, "She must not be managed in a common way; for you know, my dear, she is one of your geniuses,—and they are never like other folks."

Mrs. Woodville, the mother, had been brought up with all the ideas of œconomy and housewifery which at that time of day prevailed in the city, and influenced the education of the daughters of citizens.

"My dear," said she one day to Adeline, "as you are no genius, you know, like your mother, (and God forbid you should! for one is quite enough in a family,) I shall make bold to teach you every thing that young women in my young days used to learn, and my daughter may thank me for it some time or other: for you know, my dear, when I and my good man die, what in the world would become of my poor Edith, if so be she had no one to manage for her! for, Lord love you! she knows no more of managing a family, and suchlike, than a new-born babe."

"And can you, dear grandmother, teach me to be of any use to my mother?" said Adeline.

"To be sure, child; for, as you are no genius, no doubt you can learn all them there sort of things that women commonly know:—so we will begin directly."

In a short time Adeline, stimulated by the ambition of being useful, (for she had often heard her mother assert that utility was the foundation of all virtue,) became as expert in household affairs as Mrs. Woodville herself: even the department of making pastry was given up to Adeline, and the servants always came to her for orders, saying, that 'as their mistress was a learned lady, and that, and so could not be spoken with except here and there on occasion, they wished their young mistress, who was more easy spoken, would please to order:' and as Mr. and Mrs. Woodville's infirmities increased every day, Adeline soon thought it right to assume the entire management of the family.

She also took upon herself the office of almoner[9] to Mrs. Woodville, and performed it with an activity unknown to her; for she herself carried the broth and wine that were to comfort the infirm cottager; she herself saw the medicine properly administered that was to preserve his suffering existence: the comforts the poor required she purchased herself; and in sickness she visited, in sorrow she wept with them. And though Adeline was almost unknown personally to the neighboring gentry, she was followed with blessings by the surrounding cottagers; while many a humble peasant watched at the gate of the park to catch a glimpse of his young benefactress, and pray God to repay to the heiress of Rosevalley the kindness which she had shewn to him and his offspring.

Thus happy, because usefully employed, and thus beloved and respected, because actively benevolent, passed the early years of Adeline Mowbray; and thus was she educated, before her mother had completed her system of education.

WOMEN AND EDUCATION II

In late eighteenth-century Britain, education was a particularly hotly debated topic. Education for the aristocracy had depended for centuries on private tutors for boys followed by a University education (though not necessarily a degree) for young men, in contrast to less formal tutoring for girls and young women. Education for the middling sort and the working poor was less established. Since Shakespeare's day, the male children of gentlemen and well-to-do merchants had had access to Grammar Schools or in town to Town

---

[9] One who gives or, in this case, distributes alms to the poor.

Schools. The common base of male education was the Classics, with a heavy stress on Latin literature and history, some theology, art, and Ancient cultures. By the eighteenth century, travel on the "Grand Tour" was an expected and significant portion of any young gentleman's education, particularly for children of mercantile families seeking to elide their roots in trade. However, the sons of Dissenting families (and Catholics as well) were excluded explicitly from Public Schools (the elite schools which feed into Cambridge and Oxford) and the Universities, as well as from public and government office. In response, Dissenting Academies were founded which stressed, in addition to religious instruction and philosophy, the newly developing natural sciences. The Dissenting Academies arguably provided a stronger education in the period, being less focused on producing fashionable and well-connected gentlemen than the Universities of the time. Among the English Jacobin circle, for example, William Godwin attended Hindolvestan day school, studied with a tutor at Norwich (the town with a strong Dissenting tradition where Amelia Alderson grew up), and was educated at Hoxton Dissenting academy.

For women, educational options were considerably more limited. Education outside the home except for some day schools were explicitly closed to them, and while some women made good use of access to their brother's tutors, most were expressly forbidden from learning subjects considered too masculine, such as theology, Latin and Greek, Ancient History, Mathematics, and Natural Philosophy (or the Natural Sciences). In 1773, Hester Chapone published a collection of letters ostensibly to her neice, detailing an ideal gentlewoman's education:

> With regard to accomplishments, the chief of these is a competent share of reading, well chosen and properly regulated....Dancing and the knowledge of the French tongue are now so universal

that they cannot be dispensed with in the education of a gentlewoman; and indeed they both are useful as well as ornamental; the first, by forming and strengthening the body, and improving the carriage; the second, by opening a large field of entertainment and improvement for the mind....

To write a free and legible hand, and to understand common arithmetic, are indispensable requisites.

As to music and drawing, I would only wish you to follow as Genius leads: you have some turn for the first, and I should be sorry to see you neglect a talent, which will at least afford you an innocent amusement...: I think the use of both these arts is more for yourself than for others...it is of great consequence to have the power of filling up agreeably those intervals of time, which too often hang heavily on the hands of a woman, if her lot be cast in a retired situation. Besides this, it is certain that even a small share in these arts will heighten your pleasure in the performance of others: the taste must be improved before it can be susceptible of an exquisite relish for any of the imitative arts: an unskilful ear is seldom capable of comprehending *Harmony*, or of distinguishing the most *delicate* charms of *Melody*. The pleasure of seeing fine paintings, or even of contemplating the beauties of Nature, must be greatly heightened by our being conversant with the rules of drawing, and by the habit of considering the most picturesque objects. As I look upon taste to be an inestimable fund of innocent delight, I wish you to lose no opportunity to improving it, and of cultivating in yourself the relish of such pleasures as will not interfere with a rational scheme of life, nor lead you into dissipation, with all its attendant evils of vanity and luxury.

As to the learned languages, though I respect the abilities and application of those ladies, who have attained them, and who make a modest and proper use of them, yet I would by no means advise you— or any other woman who is not strongly impelled by a particular genius—to engage in such studies. The labour and time which they require are generally incompatible with our natures and proper employments: the real knowledge which they supply is not essential, since the English, French, or Italian tongues afford tolerable translations of all the most valuable productions of antiquity, besides the multitude of original authors which they furnish; and these are much more than sufficient to store your mind with as many ideas as you will know how to manage. The danger of pedantry and presumption in a woman—of her exciting envy in one sex and jealousy in the other—of her exchanging the graces of imagination for the severity and preciseness of a scholar, would be, I own, sufficient to frighten me from the ambition of seeing my girl remarkable for learning. Such objections are perhaps stronger with regard to the abstruse science....

Though *religion* is the most important of all your pursuits, there are not many *books* on that subject, which I should recommend to you at present. Controversy is wholly inappropriate at your age, and it is also too soon for you to enquire into the evidence of the truth of revelation, or to study the difficult parts of scripture: when these shall come before you, there are many excellent books, from which you may receive great assistance. At present, practical divinity—clear of superstition and enthusiasm, but addressed to the heart, and written with a warmth and spirit capable of exciting in it pure and rational piety—is what I wish you to meet with.

The principal study I would recommend, is *history*. I know of nothing equally proper to entertain and improve at the same time, or that is so likely to form and strengthen your judgement, and, by giving you a liberal and comprehensive view of human nature, in some measure to supply the defect of that experience, which is usually acquired too late to be of much service to us. Let me add, that more materials for conversation are supplied by this kind of knowledge, than by almost any other....

The faculty, in which women usually most excel, is that of imagination; and, when properly cultivated, it becomes the source of all that is most charming in society. Nothing you can read will so much contribute to the improvement of this faculty as *poetry*; which, if applied to its true ends, adds a thousand charms to those sentiments of religion, virtue, generosity, and delicate tenderness, by which the human soul is exalted and refined. I hope...that you will find it one of your greatest pleasures to be conversant with the best poets, whom our language can bring you acquainted with, particularly those immortal ornaments of our nation, *Shakespear* and *Milton*. (Hester Chapone, *Letters on the Improvement of the Mind, addressed to a Young Lady*, 1773, 'Letter VIII: On Politeness and Accomplishments,' 154-9)

In the late eighteenth century, a vogue for botany among women did help to introduce women to some scientific information and methods, but even this was disputed as perhaps too sexual for proper ladies. Mary Wollstonecraft was among those who argued strenuously that women were debilitated by inadequate education, and that many of the characteristically "feminine" traits such as illogical thinking, extreme sensibility, frivolous concern with dress and self-decoration, coquettishness, ill-temper and poor health were derived not from women's natural inability to function as rational creatures, but from a lack of education. Wollstonecraft argued not only that women were rational beings, capable of learning and thus of being better mothers and wives, but also that they needed physical exercise to develop into strong and self-reliant companions, and some sexual education to become good mothers. However, Wollstonecraft's novel notion that women might learn the proper function of their bodies, including their reproductive function, by studying flowers came under strong attack, notably in Richard Polwhele's satirical poem, "The Unsex'd Females":

I shudder at the new unpictur'd scene,
Where unsex'd woman vaunts the imperious mien;
… With bliss botanic as their bosoms heave,
Still pluck forbidden fruit, with mother Eve,
For puberty in sighing florets pant,
Or point the prostitution of a plant;
Dissect its organ of unhallow'd lust,
And fondly gaze the titillating dust;
With liberty's sublimer views expand,
And o'er the wreck of kingdoms sternly stand;
And, frantic, midst the democratic storm,
Pursue, Philosophy! thy phantom-form.
Far other is the female shape and mind,
By modest luxury heighten'd and refin'd;
…
See Wollstonecraft, whom no decorum checks,
Arise, the intrepid champion of her sex;
O'er humbled man assert the sovereign claim,
And slight the timid blush of virgin fame. (lines 15-66)

SOURCES

"William Godwin." *Cambridge Biographical Dictionary.* Ed.

Magnus Mangusson, (New York: Cambridge University Press, 1990).

Richard Polwhele, "The Unsex'd Females" *The Anti-Jacobin Review and Magazine*, Vol. III. (April-August 1799): 1-20.

Hester Chapone, *Letters on the Improvement of the Mind, addressed to a Young Lady*, 'On Politeness and Accomplishments,' London, 1773.

Mary Wollstonecraft, *Vindication of the Rights of Woman* (1792), in *Works of Mary Wollstonecraft*, Ed. Janet Todd and Marilyn Butler, 5 Vols. Vol. 5, (Washington Square, NY: New York University Press, 1989).

It was not long before Adeline took on herself a still more important office. Mrs. Mowbray's steward was detected in very dishonest practices; but, as she was too much devoted to her studies to like to look into her affairs with a view to dismiss him, she could not be prevailed upon to discharge him from her service. Fortunately, however, her father on his deathbed made it his request that she would do so; and Mrs. Mowbray pledged herself to obey him.

"But what shall I do for a steward in Davison's place?" said she soon after her father died.

"Is one absolutely necessary?" returned Adeline modestly. "Surely farmer Jenkins would undertake to do all that is necessary for half the money; and, if he were properly overlooked—"

"And pray who can overlook him properly?" asked Mrs. Mowbray.

"My grandmother and I," replied Adeline timidly: "we both like business, and—"

"Like business ... but what do you know of it?"

"Know!" cried Mrs. Woodville, "why, daughter, Lina is very clever at it, I assure you!"

"Astonishing! She knows nothing yet of accounts."

"Dear me! how mistaken you are, child! She knows accounts perfectly."

"Impossible!" replied Mrs. Mowbray: "who should have taught her? I have been inventing an easy method of learning arithmetic, by which I was going to teach her in a few months."

"Yes, child: but I, thinking it a pity that the poor girl should learn nothing, like, till she was to learn every thing, taught her according to the old way; and I cannot but say she took to it very kindly. Did not you, Lina?"

"Yes, grandmother," said Adeline; "and as I love arithmetic very much, I am quite anxious to keep all my mother's accounts, and overlook the accounts of the person whom she shall employ to manage her estates in future."

To this Mrs. Mowbray, half pleased and half mortified, at length consented; and Adeline and farmer Jenkins entered upon their occupations. Shortly after Mrs. Woodville was seized with her last illness; and Adeline neglected every other duty, and Mrs. Mowbray her studies, "to watch, and weep, beside a parent's bed."[10]

But watch and weep was all Mrs. Mowbray did: with every possible wish to be useful, she had so long given way to habits of abstraction, and neglect of everyday occupations, that she was rather a hindrance than a help in the sick-room.

During Adelines' illness, excessive fear of losing her only child had indeed awakened her to unusual exertion; and as all that she had to do was to get down, at stated times, a certain quantity of wine and nourishment, her task though wearisome was not difficult: but to sooth the declining hours of an aged parent, to please the capricious appetite of decay, to assist with ready and skilful alacrity the shaking hand of the invalid, jealous of waiting on herself and wanting to be cheated into being waited upon;— these trifling yet important details did not suit the habits of Mrs. Mowbray. But Adeline was versed in them all; and her

---

[10] Anna Letitia Barbauld (1743-1825), "To Miss R—, On Her Attendance Upon Her Mother at Buxton," line 7.

mother, conscious of her superiority in these things, was at last contented to sit by inactive, though not unmoved.

One day, when Mrs. Mowbray had been prevailed upon to lie down for an hour or two in another apartment, and Adeline was administering to Mrs. Woodville some broth which she had made herself, the old lady pressed her hand affectionately, and cried, "Ah! child, in a lucky hour I made bold to interfere, and teach you what your mother was always too clever to learn. Wise was I to think one genius enough in a family,—else, what should I have done now? Lord bless me! my daughter, though the best child in the world, could never have made such nice broth as this to comfort me, so hot, and boiled it to a minute like! Lord bless her! she'd have tried, that she would, but ten to one she'd have smoked it, overturned it, and scalt her fingers into the bargain.—Ah, Lina, Lina! mayhap the time will come when you, should you have a sick husband or child to nurse, may bless your poor grandmother for having taught you to be useful."

"Dear grandmother," said Adeline tenderly, "the time is come: I am, you see, useful to you; and therefore I bless you already for having taught me to be so."

"Good girl, good girl! just what I would have you! And God forgive me, and you too, Lina, when I own that I have often thanked God for not making you a genius! Not but what no child can behave better than mine; for, with all her wit and learning, she was always so respectful, and so kind to me and my dear good man, that I am sure I could not but rejoice in such a daughter; though, to be sure, I used to wish she was more conversible like; for, as to the matter of a bit of chat, Lord help us as save us! We never gossiped together in our lives. And though, to be sure, the squires' ladies about are none of the brightest, and not to compare with my Edith, yet still they would have done very well for me and my dear good man to gossip a bit with. So I was vexed when my daughter declared she wanted all her time for her studies, and would not visit any body, no, not even Mrs. Norberry, who is to be sure a very good sort of woman, though a little given to speak ill of her neighbors. But then so we are all, you know: and, as I say, why, if one spoke well of all alike, what would be the use of one person's being better than his neighbors, except for conscience's sake? But, as I was going to say, my daughter was pleased to compliment me, and declare she was sure I could amuse myself without visiting women so much inferior to me; and she advised my beginning a course of study, as she called it."

"And did you?" asked Adeline with surprise.

"Yes. To oblige her, my good man and I began to read one Mr. Locke on the conduct of the human understanding; which my daughter said would teach us to think."[11]

"To think?" said Adeline.

"Yes.—Now, you must know, my poor husband did not look upon it as very respectful like in Edith to say that, because it seemed to say that we had lived all these years without having thought at all; which was not true, to be sure, because we were never thoughtless like, and my husband was so staid when a boy that he was called a little old man."

"But I am sure," said Adeline, half smiling, "that my mother did not mean to insinuate that you wanted[12] proper thought."

"No, I dare say not," resumed the old lady, "and so I told my husband, and so we set to study this book: but, dear me! it was Hebrew Greek to us—and so dull!"

"Then you did not get through it, I suppose?"

"Through it, bless your heart! No—not three pages! So my good man says to Edith, says he, 'You gave us this book, I think, child, to teach us to think?' 'Yes, sir' says she. 'And it has taught us to think,' says he:—'it has taught us to think that it is very dull and disagreeable.' So my daughter laughed, and said her father was witty; but, poor soul! he did not mean it.

"Well, then: as, to amuse us, we liked to look at the stars

---

[11] John Locke (1632-1704), English philosopher and author of *An Essay Concerning Human Understanding* (1690), which argued against the belief that humans are born with innate ideas, and for a concept of the infant as *tabula rasa*, or a blank slate upon which experience and the association of ideas creates knowledge.
[12] I.e., lacked.

sometimes, she told us we had better learn their names, and study astronomy; and so we began that: but that was just as bad as Mr. Locke; and we knew no more of the stars and planets, than the man in the moon. Yet that's not right to say, neither; for, as he is so much nearer the stars, he must know more about them than any one whosomever. So at last my daughter found out that learning was not our taste: so she left us to please ourselves, and play cribbage and draughts in an evening as usual."[13]

Here the old lady paused, and Adeline said affectionately, "Dear grandmother, I doubt[14] you exert yourself too much: so much talking can't be good for you."

"O! yes, child!" replied Mrs. Woodville: "it is no trouble at all to me, I assure you, but quite natural and pleasant like: besides, you know I shall not be able to talk much longer, so let me make the most of my time now."

This speech brought tears into the eyes of Adeline; and seeing her mother re-enter the room, she withdrew to conceal the emotion which she felt, lest the cheerful loquacity of the invalid, which she was fond of indulging, should be checked by seeing her tears. But it had already received a check from the presence of Mrs. Mowbray, of whose superior abilities Mrs. Woodville was so much in awe, that, concluding her daughter could not bear to hear her nonsense, the old lady smiled kindly on her when with a look of tender anxiety she hastened to her bedside, and then, holding her hand, composed herself to sleep.

In a few days more, she breathed her last on the supporting arm of Adeline; and lamented in her dying moments that she had nothing valuable in money to leave, in order to show Adeline how sensible she was of her affectionate attentions: "but you are an only child," she added, "and all your mother has will be yours."

"No doubt," observed Mrs. Mowbray eagerly; and her mother died contented.

---

[13] Cribbage is a game using a deck of cards and a board with pegs to keep score, while draughts is a board game similar to American checkers.

[14] I.e., fear that, or worry that.

CHAPTER III.

AT this period Adeline's ambition had led her to form new plans, which Mrs. Woodville's death left her at liberty to put in execution. Whenever the old lady reminded her that she was no genius, Adeline had felt as much degraded as if she had said that she was no conjurer; and though she was too humble to suppose that she could ever equal her mother, she was resolved to try to make herself more worthy of her, by imitating her in those pursuits and studies on which were founded Mrs. Mowbray's pretensions to superior talents.

She therefore made it her business to inquire what those studies and pursuits were; and finding that Mrs. Mowbray's noted superiority was built on her passion for abstruse speculations, Adeline eagerly devoted her leisure hours to similar studies: but, unfortunately, these new theories, and these romantic reveries, which only served to amuse Mrs. Mowbray's fancy, her more enthusiastic daughter resolved to make conscientiously the rules of her practice.[15] And while Mrs. Mowbray expended her eccentric philosophy in words, as Mr. Shandy did his grief,[16] Adeline carefully treasured up hers in her heart, to be manifested only by its fruits.

One author in particular, by a train of reasoning captivating though sophistical, and plausible though absurd, made her a delighted convert to his opinions, and prepared her young and impassioned heart for the practice of vice, by filling her mind, ardent in the love of virtue, with new and singular opinions on the subject of moral duty. On the works of this writer Adeline had often heard her mother descant in terms of the highest praise; but she did not feel herself so completely his convert on her own conviction, till she had experienced the fatal fascination of his

---

[15] See footnote 1, page 274 this volume. Enthusiasm in this context and time refers to ideological excess, particularly in religion or political philosophy. Adeline is an enthusiast, or someone whose theoretical beliefs overly influence her actions.
[16] Laurence Sterne, *Life and Opinions of Tristram Shandy, Gentleman*, 1759-67. Walter Shandy, an amateur philosopher, responds to multiple disappointments throughout the book by developing further his idiosyncratic philosophical notions.

style, and been conveyed by his bewitching pen from the world as it is, into a world as it *ought* to be.

This writer, whose name was Glenmurray, amongst other institutions, attacked the institution of marriage; and after having elaborately pointed out its folly and its wickedness, he drew so delightful a picture of the superior purity, as well as happiness, of an union cemented by no ties but those of love and honour, that Adeline, wrought to the highest pitch of enthusiasm for a new order of things, entered into a solemn compact with herself to act, when she was introduced into society, according to the rules laid down by this writer.[17]

Unfortunately for her, she had no opportunity of hearing these opinions combated by the good sense and sober experience of Dr. Norberry then their sole visitant; for at this time the American war[18] was the object of attention to all Europe: and as Mrs. Mowbray, as well as Dr. Norberry, were deeply interested in this subject, they scarcely ever talked on any other; and even Glenmurray and his theories were driven from Mrs. Mowbray's remembrance by political tracts and the eager anxieties of a politician. Nor had she even leisure to observe, that while she was feeling all the generous anxiety of a citizen of the world for the sons and daughters of American independence, her own child was imbibing, through her means, opinions dangerous to her well-being as a member of any civilized society, and laying, perhaps, the foundation to herself and her mother of future misery and disgrace. Alas! the astrologer in the fable was but too like Mrs. Mowbray![19]

---

[17] The philosopher Frederick Glenmurray is in part a fictional representation of William Godwin. Godwin's *Enquiry Concerning Political Justice* (1793) contains as an appendix an essay "Of Co-Operation, Cohabitation and Marriage" which argues against exclusive legal rights to a woman through the institution of marriage, and instead for affective relationships based on rational choice by both the man and the woman, to be dissolved at will by either. See textbox "Masculinity and Dueling," p. 319.

[18] I.e., the American Revolutionary War, 1775-1783.

[19] See Walter Pope, *Moral and Political Fables* (1698). "Fable LXXXVI: The Astrologer" tells the story of an astrologer who falls into a pit because he is so

But even had Adeline had an opportunity of discussing her new opinions with Dr. Norberry, it is not at all certain that she would have had the power.

Mrs. Mowbray was, if I may be allowed the expression, a showing-off woman, and loved the information which she acquired, less for its own sake than for the supposed importance which it gave her amongst her acquaintance, and the means of displaying her superiority over other women.[20] Before she secluded herself from society in order to study education, she had been the terror of the ladies in the neighborhood; since, despising small talk, she would always insist on making the gentlemen of her acquaintance (as much terrified sometimes as their wives) engage with her in some literary or political conversation. She wanted to convert every drawing-room into an arena for the mind, and all her guests into intellectual gladiators. She was often heard to interrupt two grave matrons in an interesting discussion of an accouchement,[21] by asking them if they had read a new theological tract, or a pamphlet against the minister? If they softly expatiated on the lady-like fatigue of body which they had endured, she discoursed in choice terms on the energies of the mind; and she never received or paid visits without convincing the company that she was the most wise, most learned, and most disagreeable of companions.

But Adeline, on the contrary, studied merely from the love of study, and not with a view to shine in conversation; nor dared she venture to expatiate on subjects which she had often heard Mrs. Woodville say were very rarely canvassed, or even alluded to, by women. She remained silent, therefore, on the subject nearest to her heart, from choice as well as necessity, in the presence of Dr. Norberry, till at length she imbibed the political

intent on watching the skies that he fails to attend to where he puts his feet, and must be rescued by a more practical farmer. The moral reads "They who can all things by the stars foretel,/May easily avoid an open well" (lines 16-17).
148

[21] French for "lying in," a euphemism for labor and giving birth.

mania herself, and soon found it impossible to conceal the interest which she took in the success of the infant republic.[22] She therefore one day put into the doctor's hands some bouts rimés[23] which she had written on some recent victory of the American arms; exclaiming with a smile, "I, too, am a politician!" and was rewarded by an exclamation of "Zounds![24] girl—I protest you are as clever as your mother!"

This unexpected declaration fixed her in the path of literary ambition: and though wisely resolved to fulfill, as usual, every feminine duty, Adeline was convinced that she, like her mother, had a right to be an author, a politician, and a philosopher; while Dr. Norberry's praises of her daughter convinced Mrs. Mowbray, that almost unconsciously she had educated her into a prodigy, and confirmed her in her intention of exhibiting herself and Adeline to the admiring world during the next season at Bath; for at Bath she expected to receive that admiration which she had vainly sought in London.

Soon after their marriage, Mr. Mowbray had carried his lovely bride to the metropolis, where she expected to receive the same homage which had been paid to her charms at the assize-balls[25] in her neighborhood. What then must have been her disappointment, when, instead of hearing as she passed, "That is miss Woodville, the rich heiress—or the great genius—or the great beauty"—or, "That is the beautiful Mrs. Mowbray," she

---

[22] I.e., the newly created United States, which was still an example in the 1790s of a new rational form of government such as reformers hoped to see emerge in France and Britain.

[23] Literally end-rhymes, or rhyming words from which verses might be composed. The sense here seems to be simple rhymed verses since Dr. Norberry extracts political meaning from them.

[24] "Zounds" is a light epithet, derived from the expression "by God's wounds," referring to the wounds of Jesus on the cross. Dr. Norberry's use of such an old-fashioned and inoffensive curse is a sign of his old-fashioned, rather gallant personality.

[25] Criminal and civil cases outside of London were scheduled for periodical legal trials and hearings called "assizes." The period of the assizes in rural areas was often marked as a holiday with special events in addition to the legal proceedings themselves, such as balls and social gatherings.

walked unknown and unobserved in public and in private, and found herself of as little importance in the wide world of the metropolis, as the most humble of her acquaintance in a country ball-room. True, she had beauty, but then it was unset-off by fashion; nay, more, it was eclipsed by unfashionable and tasteless attire; and her manner, though stately and imposing in an assembly where she was known, was wholly unlike the manners of the world, and in a London party appeared arrogant and offensive. Her remarks, too, wise as they appeared to her and Mr. Mowbray, excited little attention,—as the few persons to whom they were known in the metropolis were wholly ignorant of her high pretensions, and knew not that they were discoursing with a professed genius, and the oracle of a provincial circle. Some persons, indeed, surprised at hearing from the lips of eighteen, observations on morals, theology, and politics, listened to her with wonder, and even attention, but turned away, observing—

"Such things, 'tis true, are neither new nor rare,
The only wonder is, how they got there;"[26]

till at length, disappointed, mortified, and disgusted, Mrs. Mowbray impatiently returned to Rosevalley, where in beauty, in learning, and in grandeur she was unrivalled, and where she might deal out her dogmas, sure of exciting respectful attention, however she might fail of calling forth a more flattering tribute from her auditors. But in the narrower field of Bath she expected to shine forth with greater éclat than in London, and to obtain admiration more worthy of her acceptance than any which a country circle could offer.

To Bath, therefore, she prepared to go; and the young heart of Adeline beat high with pleasure at the idea of mixing with

---

[26] Alexander Pope, "Epistle to Dr. Arbuthnot": "Pretty! in amber to observe the forms/ Of hairs, or straws, or dirt, or grubs, or worms!/ The things, we know, are neither rich nor rare,/ But wonder how the devil they got there (lines 169-72). After 1805, the line is regularly cited as "neither new nor rare," for example, in works by Sydney Owenson (Lady Morgan) and both Percy Bysshe Shelley and Mary Godwin Shelley.

that busy world which her fancy had often clothed in the most winning attractions.

But her joy, and Mrs. Mowbray's, was a little overclouded at the moment of their departure, by the sight of Dr. Norberry's melancholy countenance. What was to be, as they fondly imagined, their gain, was his loss, and with a full heart he came to bid them adieu.

For Adeline he had conceived not only affection, but esteem amounting almost to veneration; for she appeared to him to unite various and opposing excellencies. Though possessed of taste and talents for literature, she was skilled in the minutest details of housewifery and feminine occupations; and at the same time she bore her faculties so meekly, that she never wounded the self-love of any one, by arrogating to herself any superiority.

Such Adeline appeared to her excellent old friend; and his affection for her was, perhaps, increased by the necessity which he was under of concealing it at home. The praises of Mrs. Mowbray and Adeline were odious to the ears of Mrs. Norberry and his daughters,—but especially the praises of the latter,—as the merit of Adeline was so uniform, that even the eye of envy could not at that period discover any thing in her vulnerable to censure: and as the sound of her name excited in his family a number of bad passions and corresponding expressions of countenance, the doctor wisely resolved to keep his feelings, with regard to her, locked up in his own bosom.

But he persisted in visiting at the Park daily; and it is no wonder, therefore, that the loss, even for a few months, of the society of its inhabitants should by him be anticipated as a serious calamity.

"Zounds!" cried he, as Adeline, with an exulting bound, sprung after her mother into the carriage, "how gay and delighted you are! though my heart feels devilish queer and heavy."

"My dear friend," cried Mrs. Mowbray, "I must miss your society wherever I go."— "I wish you were going too," said Adeline: "I shall often think of you." "Pshaw, girl! don't lie," replied Dr. Norberry, swallowing a sigh as he spoke: "you will soon forget an old fellow like me."— "Then I conclude that you will soon forget us."— "He! how! what! think so at your peril."— "I must think so, as we usually judge of others by ourselves."— "Go to—go, miss mal-a-pert.—Well, but, drive on, coachman—this taking leave is plaguy disagreeable, so shake hands and be off."

They gave him their hands, which he pressed very affectionately, and the carriage drove on.

"I am an old fool," cried the doctor, wiping his eyes as the carriage disappeared. "Well: God grant, sweet innocent, that you may return to me as happy and spotless as you now are!"

Mrs. Mowbray had been married at a very early age, and had accepted in Mr. Mowbray the first man who addressed her: consequently, that passion for personal admiration, so natural to women, had in her never been gratified, nor even called forth. But seeing herself, at the age of thirty-eight, possessed of almost undiminished beauty, she recollected that her charms had never received that general homage for which Nature intended them; and she who at twenty had disregarded, even to a fault, the ornaments of dress, was now, at the age of thirty-eight, eager to indulge in the extremes of decoration, and to share in the delights of conquest and admiration with her youthful and attractive daughter.

Attractive, rather than handsome, was the epithet best suited to describe Adeline Mowbray. Her beauty was the beauty of expression of countenance, not regularity of feature, though the uncommon fairness and delicacy of her complexion, the lustre of her hazel eyes, her long dark eyelashes, and the profusion of soft light hair which curled over the ever-mantling colour of her cheek, gave her some pretensions to what is denominated beauty. But her own sex declared she was plain—and perhaps they were right—though the other protested against the decision—and probably they were right also: but women criticize in detail, men admire in the aggregate. Women reason, and men feel, when passing judgement on female beauty: and when a woman declares another to be plain, the chances are that she is right in her opinion, as she cannot, from being a woman, feel the charm of that power to please, that "something than beauty dearer,"[27] which often throws a veil over the irregularity of features, and obtains, for even a plain woman, from men at least, the appellation of pretty.

Whether Adeline's face were plain or not, her form could defy even the severity of female criticism. She was indeed tall, almost to a masculine degree; but such were the roundness and proportion of her limbs, such the symmetry of her whole person, such the lightness and gracefulness of her movements, and so truly feminine were her look and manner, that her superior height was forgotten in the superior loveliness of her figure.

It is not to be wondered at, then, that miss Mowbray was an object of attention and admiration at Bath, as soon as she appeared, nor that her mother had her share of flattery and followers. Indeed, when it was known that Mrs. Mowbray was a rich widow, and Adeline dependent upon her, the mother became, in the eyes of some people, much more attractive than her daughter.

It was impossible, however, that, in such a place as Bath, Mrs. Mowbray and Adeline could make, or rather retain, a general acquaintance. Their opinions on most subjects were so very different from those of the world, and they were so little conscious, from the retirement in which they had lived, that this difference existed, or was likely to make them enemies, that not a day elapsed in which they did not shock the prejudices of some, and excite the contemptuous pity of others; and they soon saw their acquaintance coolly dropped by those who, as persons of family and fortune, had on their first arrival sought it with eagerness.

But this was not entirely owing to the freedom of their sentiments on politics, or on other subjects; but, because they associated with a well-known but obnoxious author;—a man whose speculations had delighted the inquiring but ignorant

---

[27] James Thomson, *The Seasons*, "Spring," lines 1138-9. The same line is cited in *Emma Courtney*, p. 149.

lover of novelty, terrified the timid idolater of antient usages, and excited the regret of the cool and rational observer:—regret, that eloquence so overwhelming, powers of reasoning so acute, activity of research so praise-worthy, and a love of investigation so ardent, should be thrown away on the discussion of moral and political subjects, incapable of teaching the world to build up again with more beauty and propriety, a fabric, which they were, perhaps, calculated to pull down: in short, Mrs. Mowbray and Adeline associated with Glenmurray, that author over whose works they had long delighted to meditate, and who had completely led their imagination captive, before the fascination of his countenance and manners had come in aid of his eloquence.

CHAPTER IV.

FREDERIC GLENMURRAY was a man of family, and of a small independent estate, which, in case he died without children, was to go to the next male heir; and to that heir it was certain to go, as Glenmurray on principle was an enemy to marriage, and consequently not likely to have a child born in wedlock.

It was an unfortunate circumstance for Glenmurray, that, with the ardour of a young and inexperienced mind, he had given his eccentric opinions to the world as soon as they were conceived and arranged,—as he, by so doing, prejudiced the world against him in so unconquerable a degree, that to him almost every door and every heart was shut; and he by that means excluded from every chance of having the errors of his imagination corrected by the arguments of the experienced and enlightened— and corrected, no doubt, they would have been, for he had a mild and candid spirit, and a mind open to conviction.

"I consider myself," he used to say, "as a sceptic, not as a man really certain of the truth of any thing which he advances. I doubt of all things, because I look upon doubt as the road to truth; and do but convince me what is the truth, and at whatever risk, whatever sacrifice, I am ready to embrace it."

But, alas! neither the blamelessness of his life, nor even his active virtue, assisted by the most courteous manners, were deemed sufficient to counteract the mischievous tendency of his works;[28] or rather, it was supposed impossible that his life could be blameless and his seeming virtues sincere:—and unheard, unknown, this unfortunate young man was excluded from those circles which his talents would have adorned, and forced to lead a life of solitude, or associate with persons unlike to him in most things, except in a passion for the bold in theory, and the almost impossible in practice.

Of this description of persons he soon became the oracle—the head of a sect, as it were; and those tenets which at first he embraced, and put forth more for amusement than from conviction, as soon as he began to suffer on their account, became as dear to him as the cross to the christian martyr: and deeming persecution a test of truth, he considered the opposition made to him and his doctrines, not as the result of dispassionate reason striving to correct absurdity, but as selfishness and fear endeavouring to put out the light which showed the weakness of the foundation on which were built their claims to exclusive respect.

When Mrs. Mowbray and Adeline first arrived at Bath, the latter had attracted the attention of colonel Mordaunt, an Irishman of fortune, and an officer in the guards; and Adeline had not been insensible to the charms of a very fine person and engaging manners, united to powers of conversation which displayed an excellent understanding improved by education and reading. But colonel Mordaunt was not a *marrying man*, as it is called: therefore, as soon as he began to feel the influence of

---

[28] The concern that a work's "tendency" might be immoral despite an overtly moral message was raised by William Godwin himself in his essay "Of Choice in Reading" published in *The Enquirer*, 1797. Godwin argued that "the moral of a work is a point of very subordinate consideration, and...the only thing worthy of much attention is the tendency" (p. 137). The mischievous tendency of Glenmurray's work seems to include his arguments against marriage and questioning of divine revelation, but may also indicate a concern with the dangers for women of reading philosophical debate and seeking to model their lives on abstract propositions.

Adeline growing too powerful for his freedom, and to observe that his attentions were far from unpleasing to her,—too honourable to excite an attachment in her which he was resolved to combat in himself, he resolved to fly from danger, which he knew he could not face and overcome; and after a formal but embarrassed adieu to Mrs. Mowbray and Adeline, he suddenly left Bath.

This unexpected departure both surprised and grieved Adeline; but, as her feelings of delicacy were too strong to allow her to sigh for a man who, evidently, had no thoughts of sighing for her, she dismissed colonel Mordaunt from her remembrance, and tried to find as much interest still in the ball-rooms, and the promenades, as his presence had given them: nor was it long before she found in them an attraction and an interest stronger than any which she had yet felt.

It is naturally to be supposed that Adeline had often wished to know personally an author whose writings delighted her as much as Glenmurray's had done, and that her fancy had often portrayed him in a form at once pleasing and respectable,—still, from an idea of his superior wisdom, she had imagined him past the meridian of life, and not likely to excite warmer feelings than those of esteem and veneration: and such continued to be Adeline's idea of Glenmurray, when he arrived at Bath, having been sent thither by his physicians for the benefit of his health.[29]

Glenmurray, though a sense of his unpopularity had long banished him from scenes of public resort in general, was so pleased with the novelties of Bath, that, though he walked wholly unnoticed except by the lovers of genius in whatsoever shape it shows itself, he frequented the pump-room,[30] and the

---

[29] The town of Bath, blessed with natural warm mineral springs, had been famous for health-cures since the Romans. In the eighteenth century fashionable people traveled to Bath not only to drink the waters and bathe in them, but to see and be seen in its fashionable social scene.

[30] A large, long public room where the mineral waters are pumped to the surface and are available for drinking. The Pump Room was also among the most important social scenes in Bath.

promenades;[31] and Adeline had long admired the countenance and dignified person of this young and interesting invalid, without the slightest suspicion of his being the man of all others whom she the most wished to see.

Nor had Glenmurray been slow to admire Adeline: and so strong, so irresistible was the feeling of admiration which she had excited in him, that, as soon as she appeared, all other objects vanished from his sight; and as women are generally quick-sighted to the effect of their charms, Adeline never beheld the stranger without a suffusion of pleasurable confusion on her cheek.

One morning at the pump-room, when Glenmurray, unconscious that Adeline was near, was reading the newspaper with great attention, and Adeline for the first time was looking at him unobserved, she heard the name of Glenmurray pronounced and turned her head towards the person who spoke, in hopes of seeing Glenmurray himself; when Mrs. Mowbray, turning round and looking at the invalid, said to a gentleman next her, "Did you say, sir, that that tall, pale, dark, interesting-looking young man is Mr. Glenmurray the celebrated author?"

"Yes, ma'am," replied the gentleman with a sneer: "that is Mr. Glenmurray, the celebrated author."

"Oh! how I should like to speak to him!" cried Mrs. Mowbray.

"It will be no difficult matter," replied her informant: "the gentleman is always quite as much at leisure as you see him now; for *all* persons have not the same taste as Mrs. Mowbray."

So saying, he bowed and departed, leaving Mrs. Mowbray, to whom the sight of a great author was new, so lost in contemplating Glenmurray, that the sarcasm with which he spoke entirely escaped her observation.

Nor was Adeline less abstracted: she too was contemplating Glenmurray, and with mixed but delightful feelings.

"So then he is young and handsome too!" said she mentally: "it is a pity he looks so *ill*," added she *sighing:* but the sigh was

---

[31] A walkway or public path, as much for fashionable display as for exercise or "taking the air."

caused rather by his looking so *well*—though Adeline was not conscious of it.[32]

By this time Glenmurray had observed who were his neighbors, and the newspaper was immediately laid down.

"Is there any news to-day?" said Mrs. Mowbray to Glenmurray, resolved to make a bold effort to become acquainted with him. Glenmurray, with a bow and a blush of mingled surprise and pleasure, replied that there was a great deal,—and immediately presented to her the paper which he had relinquished, setting chairs at the same time for her and Adeline.

Mrs. Mowbray, however, only slightly glanced her eye over the paper:—her desire was to talk to Glenmurray; and in order to accomplish this point, and prejudice him in her favour, she told him how much she rejoiced in seeing an author whose works were the delight and instruction of her life. "Speak, Adeline," cried she, turning to her blushing daughter; "do we not almost daily read and daily admire Mr. Glenmurray's writings?"— "Yes, certainly," replied Adeline, unable to articulate more, awed no doubt by the presence of so superior a being; while Glenmurray, more proud of being an author than ever, said internally, "Is it possible that that sweet creature should have read and admired my works?"

But in vain, encouraged by the smiles and even by the blushes of Adeline, did he endeavor to engage her in conversation. Adeline was unusually silent, unusually bashful. But Mrs. Mowbray made ample amends for her deficiency; and Mr. Glenmurray, flattered and amused, would have continued to converse with her and look at Adeline, had he not observed the impertinent sneers and rude laughter to which conversing so familiarly with him exposed Mrs. Mowbray. As soon as he observed this, he arose to depart; for Glenmurray was, according to Rochefoucault's maxim, so exquisitely selfish, that he always considered the welfare of others before his own;[33] and heroically sacrificing his own gratification

[32]I.e., looks so good, or physically attractive.
[33] François, Duc de la Rochefoucauld (1613-1680), known for somewhat cynical maxims often excerpted into quotes and popular in both France and Britain.

to save Mrs. Mowbray and Adeline from further censure, he bowed with the greatest respect to Mrs. Mowbray, sighed as he paid the same compliment to Adeline, and, lamenting his being forced to quit them so soon, with evident reluctance left the room.

"What an elegant bow he makes!" exclaimed Mrs. Mowbray. Adeline had observed nothing but the sigh; and on that she did not choose to make any comment.

The next day Mrs. Mowbray, having learned Glenmurray's address, sent him a card for a party at her lodgings. Nothing but Glenmurray's delight could exceed his astonishment at this invitation. He had observed Mrs. Mowbray and Adeline, even before Adeline had observed him; and, as he gazed upon the fascinating Adeline, he had sighed to think that she too would be taught to avoid the dangerous and disreputable acquaintance of Glenmurray. To him, therefore, this mark of attention was a source both of consolation and joy. But, being well convinced that it was owing to her ignorance of the usual customs and opinions of those with whom she associated, he was too generous to accept the invitation, as he knew that his presence at a rout[34] at Bath would cause general dismay, and expose the mistress to disagreeable remarks at least: but he endeavored to make himself amends for his self-denial, by asking leave to wait on them when they were alone.

CHAPTER V.

A DAY or two after, as Adeline was leaning on the arm of a young lady, Glenmurray passed them, and to his respectful bow she returned a most cordial salutation. "Gracious me! my dear," said her companion, "do you know who that man is?"

"Certainly:—it is Mr. Glenmurray."

"My good gracious! and do you speak to him?"

"Yes:—why should I not?"

"Dear me! Why, I am sure! Why... don't you know what he

---

[34] I.e., party or fashionable gathering (OED).

is?"

"Yes; a celebrated writer, and a man of genius."

"Oh, that may be, miss Mowbray: but they say one should not notice him, because he is— "

"He is what?" said Adeline eagerly.

"I do not exactly know what; but I believe it is a French spy, or a Jesuit."[35]

"Indeed?" replied Adeline laughing. But I am used to have better evidence against a person than a *they say* before I neglect an acknowledged acquaintance: therefore, with your leave, I shall turn back and talk a little to poor Mr. Glenmurray."

It so happened that *poor Mr. Glenmurray* heard every word of this conversation; for he had turned round and followed Adeline and her fair companion, to present to the former the glove which she had dropped; and as they were prevented from proceeding by the crowd on the parade,[36] which was assembling to see some unusual sight, he, being immediately behind them, could distinguish all that passed; so that Adeline turned round to go in search of him, before the blush of grateful admiration for her kindness had left his cheek.

"Then she seeks me because I am shunned by others!" said Glenmurray to himself. In a moment the world to him seemed to contain only two beings, Adeline Mowbray and Frederic Glenmurray; and that Adeline, starting and blushing with joyful surprise at seeing him so near her, was then coming in search of him!—of him, the neglected Glenmurray! Scarcely could he refrain catching the lovely and ungloved hand next him to his

[35] Anti-Jacobinism associated radical reformist ideas with anti-church, anti-king, and especially French sympathies. The speaker's misinformation and general conflation of Frenchness with being socially unacceptable is in part a critique of anti-French attitudes common in Britain and particularly heightened during the period of French Revolution. Although *Adeline* apparently predates the 1790s, many of the novel's concerns are driven by the debates of the 1790s and early 1800s. See textbox on "Anti-Jacobinism," p. 438.

[36] A parade-ground, or open area where military troops might organize for a display or any large public area where crowds could congregate (OED).

heart; but he contented himself with keeping the glove that he was before so eager to restore, and in a moment it was lodged in his bosom.

Nor could "I can't think what I have done with my glove," which every now and then escaped Adeline, prevail on him to own that he had found it. At last, indeed, it became unnecessary; for Adeline, as she glanced her eye towards Glenmurray, discovered it in the hiding-place: but, as delicacy forbade her to declare the discovery which she had made, he was suffered to retain his prize; though a deep and sudden blush which overspread her cheek, and a sudden pause which she made in her conversation, convinced Glenmurray that she had detected his secret. Perhaps he was not sorry—nor Adeline; but certain it is that Adeline was for the remainder of the morning more lost in reverie than ever her mother had been; and that from that day every one, but Adeline and Glenmurray, saw that they were mutually enamored.

Glenmurray was the first of the two lovers to perceive that they were so; and he made the discovery with a mixture of pain and pleasure. For what could be the result of such an attachment? He was firmly resolved never to marry; and it was very unlikely that Adeline, though she had often expressed to him her approbation of his writings and opinions, should be willing to sacrifice every thing to love, and become his mistress. But a circumstance took place which completely removed his doubts on this subject.

Several weeks had elapsed since the first arrival of the Mowbrays at Bath, and in that time almost all of their acquaintances had left them one by one; but neither Mrs. Mowbray nor Adeline had paid much attention to this circumstance. Mrs. Mowbray's habits of abstraction, as usual, made her regardless of common occurrences; and to these were added the more delightful reveries occasioned by the attentions of a very handsome and insinuating man, and the influence of a growing passion. Mrs. Mowbray, as we have before observed, married from duty, not inclination; and to the passion of love she had remained a total stranger, till she became acquainted at Bath with sir Patrick O'Carrol. Yes; Mrs. Mowbray was in love for the first time when she was approaching her fortieth year! and a woman is never so likely to be the fool of love, as when it assails her late in life, especially if a lover be as great a novelty to her as the passion itself. Though not, alas! restored to a second youth, the tender victim certainly enjoys a second childhood, and exhibits but too openly all the little tricks and *minauderies*[37] of a lovesick girl, without the youthful appearance that in a degree excuses them. This was the case with Mrs. Mowbray; and while, regardless of her daughter's interest and happiness, she was lost in the pleasing hopes of marrying the agreeable baronet, no wonder the cold neglect of her Bath associates was not seen by her.

Adeline, engrossed also by the pleasing reveries of a first love, was as unconscious of it as herself. Indeed she thought of nothing but love and Glenmurray; else, she could not have failed to see, that, while sir Patrick's attentions and flatteries were addressed to her mother, his ardent looks and passionate sighs were all directed to herself.

Sir Patrick O'Carrol was a young Irishman, of an old family but an encumbered estate; and it was his wish to set his estate free by marrying a rich wife, and one as little disagreeable as possible. With this view he came to Bath; and in Mrs. Mowbray he not only beheld a woman of large independent fortune, but possessed of great personal beauty, and young enough to be attractive. Still, though much pleased with the wealth and appearance of the mother, he soon became enamoured of the daughter's person; and had he not gone so far in his addresses to Mrs. Mowbray as to make it impossible she should willingly transfer him to Adeline, and give her a fortune at all adequate to his wants,[38] he would have endeavoured honourably to gain her

---

[37]The French verb *minauder* means to take on attitudes, to act in such a way as to attract attention, to attempt to please or seduce (*Micro-Robert*).
[38] I.e., needs.

affections, and entered the lists against the favoured Glenmurray.

But, as he wanted the mother's wealth, he resolved to pursue his advantage with her, and trust to some future chance for giving him possession of the daughter's person.[39] In his dealing with men, sir Patrick was a man of honour; in his dealings with women, completely the reverse: he considered them as a race of subordinate beings, formed for the service and amusement of men; and that if, like horses, they were well lodged, fed, and kept clean, they had no right to complain.

Constantly therefore did he besiege Mrs. Mowbray with his conversation, and Adeline with his eyes; and the very libertine gaze with which he often beheld her, gave a pang to Glenmurray which was but too soon painfully increased.

Sir Patrick was the only man of fashion who did not object to visit at Mrs. Mowbray's on account of her intimacy with Glenmurray; but he had his own private reasons for going thither, and continued to visit at Mrs. Mowbray's though Glenmurray was generally there, and sometimes he and the latter gentleman were the whole of their company.

One evening they and two ladies were drinking tea at Mrs. Mowbray's lodgings, when Mrs. Mowbray was unusually silent and Adeline unusually talkative. Adeline scarcely ever spoke in her mother's presence, from deference to her abilities; and whatever might be Mrs. Mowbray's defects in other respects, her conversational talents and her uncommon command of words were indisputable. But this evening, as I before observed, Adeline, owing to her mother's tender abstractions, was obliged to exert herself for the entertainment of the guests.

It so happened, also, that something was said by one of the party which led to the subject of marriage, and Adeline was resolved not to let so good an opportunity pass of proving to Glenmurray how sincerely she approved his doctrine on that subject. Immediately, with an unreserve which nothing but her

[39] In eighteenth-century usage, her physical body, as distinct from her mind or spirit.

ignorance of the world, and the strange education which she had received, could at all excuse, she began to declaim against marriage, as an institution at once absurd, unjust, and immoral, and to declare that she would never submit to so contemptible a form, or profane the sacred ties of love by so odious and unnecessary a ceremony.

FEMALE SEXUALITY AND DESIRE

Marriage with an appropriate mate was the goal for most women of the middling sort in late eighteenth- and early nineteenth-century Britain. Marriages served several purposes; most obviously a wife provided legitimate heirs for her husband; she also provided the services of a good household manager including cooking, cleaning, shopping, and managing any servants the household might contain. Most scholars agree that up until sometime in the eighteenth century, most marriages were primarily based on the needs of the families contracting the marriage; a marriage could create an alliance between important landed families, or could bring much needed cash into an impoverished landed family. Some scholars believe that there was a significant shift sometime in the eighteenth century, and that a new emphasis on companionship and affection became important for marriages among the landed and middling classes. Certainly in literary sources an interest in passionate love and romantic marriages has a long and significant history, with the novel as one of the most important literary forms exploring issues of love, marriage, duty, chastity, and family structure.

English Jacobins, particularly women writers, were keenly interested in reimagining relations between men and women given their belief that women were also rational creatures with innate "rights." Radical women writers often stress the importance of a marriage based on well-regulated affection and rational companionship in their writings. Mary Wollstonecraft in *A Vindication of the Rights of Woman* in 1792 had argued that a marriage based solely on romantic love was bound to disappoint, since such passions are by their nature, not long lived. Instead, she argued that women needed to have an education to suit them to become intelligent and rational companions to their husbands and good mothers and primary educators to their children. She was not alone in suggesting that marriage to further family property interests or even as a career move was tantamount to prostitution. Even more conventional and conservative women tended to represent marrying solely for an estate as next to prostitution and admonished women instead to marry in duty to their parents and to cultivate affection for their husbands. Wollstonecraft pressed the issue by suggesting that if women who accepted money in exchange for companionship and sex were social outcasts, how were women who married men solely for prestige and wealth different? Wollstonecraft famously shocked her contemporaries by arguing against basing female "virtue" solely in sexual chastity, but rather, that "virtue" ought to be for women, as for men, based in the acquisition of good principles and living by them. Although in 1792 she dismissed the sexual desires of both men and women as insignificant, after herself bearing a child to her lover, Gilbert Imlay in 1794, Wollstonecraft apparently began to take female sexuality and desire more seriously as intrinsic parts of women's humanity.

Wollstonecraft was not the only one to put forth revisionary ideas about female sexuality in the 1790s. Thomas Holcroft's novel *Anna St. Ives* (1792) argues that women have the right to choose their marriage partners based upon their own rational determination about what partner is most likely to make them happy and to enable them to do more social good. Robert Bage's *Hermsprong* (1796) likewise rewrites Richardson's *Clarissa* in suggesting that daughters owe no duty to marry according to the whims of tyrannical and proud fathers, but rather according to their own judgment and happiness. Charlotte Turner Smith's *Desmond* (1792) also explores the complex situation of a virtuous wife admired and loved by a man more worthy of her affections than her dissolute and libertine husband, and who struggles with her "duty" to her husband and her desire to reward her deserving lover. Mary Hays's *Emma Courtney* (1796) develops even further the Jacobin ideas that a woman ought, like a man, to exercise her own judgment, to speak truth rather than polite lies, and ought to be educated as a rational, intelligent being, the equal of her male companions.

William Godwin famously argued that men and women, as rational creatures, ought to determine themselves when they chose to come together without demanding a legal and religiously sanctioned right to the exclusive "enjoyment" of each other sexually. He went even further, suggesting that as rational, consenting adults, such men and women might legitimately break off such a relationship at its natural end, instead of contracting a marriage "till death do us part" (a position that Wollstonecraft would not have accepted). Godwin's argument in *Political Justice* attracted immediate attention for its refusal to recognize marriage as a sacred institution, rather than a flawed social one:

> The evil of marriage, as it is practised in European countries, extends further than we have yet described. The method is for a thoughtless and romantic youth of each sex to come together, to see each other, for a few times and under circumstances full of delusion, and then to vow eternal attachment....In almost every instance they find themselves deceived. They are reduced to make the best of an irretrievable mistake. They are led to conceive it their wisest policy to shut their eyes upon realities, happy, if, by any perversion of intellect, they can persuade themselves that they were right in their first crude opinion of each other. Thus the institution of marriage is made a system of fraud; and men who carefully mislead their judgements in the daily affair of their life must be expected to have a crippled judgement in every other concern.

Add to this that marriage, as now understood, is a monopoly, and the worst of monopolies. So long as two human beings are forbidden, by positive institution, to follow the dictates of their own mind, prejudice will be alive and vigorous. So long as I seek, by despotic and artificial means, to maintain my possession of a woman, I am guilty of the most odious selfishness. Over this imaginary prize, men watch with perpetual jealousy; and one man finds his desire, and his capacity to circumvent, as much excited as the other is excited to traverse his projects, and frustrate his hopes. As long as this state of society continues, philanthropy will be crossed and checked in a thousand ways, and the still augmenting stream of abuse will continue to flow.

The abolition of the present system of marriage appears to involve no evils. We are apt to represent that abolition to ourselves as the harbinger of brutal lust and depravity. But it really happens, in this, as in other cases, that the positive laws which are made to restrain our vices irritate and multiply them. Not to say that the same sentiments of justice and happiness which, in a state of equality, would destroy our relish for expensive gratifications might be expected to decrease our inordinate appetites of every kind, and to lead us universally to prefer the pleasures of intellect to the pleasures of sense.

...All these arguments are calculated to determine our judgement in favour of marriage as a salutary and respectable institution, but not of that species of marriage in which there is no room for repentance and to which liberty and hope are equally strangers. (William Godwin, "Of Co-operations, Cohabitation, and Marriage," 507-510)

Adeline's speech here is following the fictional Glenmurray's philosophy, and is related to Godwin's argument in *Political Justice*.

SOURCES

William Godwin, "Of Co-operations, Cohabitation, and Marriage," *An Enquiry Concerning Political Justice and Its Influence on Morals and Happiness*, Third Edition, London, 1798. 507-510.

Gary Kelly, *The Jacobin Novelists: 1780-1805* (Oxford: Oxford University Press, 1976).

Lawrence Stone, *The Family, Sex, and Marriage in England 1500-1800* (New York: Harper and Row, 1977).

Randolph Trumbach, *Sex and the Gender Revolution*. Vol 1. (Chicago: University of Chicago Press, 1998).

Eleanor Ty, *Unsex'd Revolutionaries: Five Women Novelists of the 1790s* (Toronto: University of Toronto Press, 1993).

Mary Wollstonecraft, *Vindication of the Rights of Woman* (1792), in *Works of Mary Wollstonecraft*, Ed. Janet Todd and Marilyn Butler, 5 Vols. Vol. 5 (Washington Square, NY: New York University Press, 1989).

This extraordinary speech, though worded elegantly and delivered gracefully, was not received by any of her hearers, except sir Patrick, with any thing like admiration. The baronet, indeed, clapped his hands, and cried, "Bravo! A fine spirited girl, upon my soul!" in a manner so loud, and so offensive to the feelings of Adeline, that, like the orator of old, she was tempted to exclaim, "What foolish thing can I have said, that has drawn forth this applause?"[40]

But Mrs. Mowbray, though she could not help admiring the eloquence of her daughter,—eloquence which she attributed to her example,—was shocked at hearing Adeline declare that her practice should be consonant to her theory; while Glenmurray, though Adeline had only expressed his sentiments, and his reason approved what she had uttered, felt his delicacy

---

[40] A reference to Phocian (402-318 B.C,E,), an Athenian military commander. The episode is recounted in *Plutarch's Lives*, volume 3.

and his feelings wounded by so open and decided an avowal of her opinions, and intended conduct in consequence of them: and he was still more hurt when he saw how much it delighted sir Patrick, and offended the rest of the company; who, after a silence the result of surprise and disgust, suddenly rose, and, coldly wishing Mrs. Mowbray good night, left the house.

By Mrs. Mowbray the cause of this abrupt departure was unsuspected: but Adeline, who had more observation, was convinced that she was the cause of it; and sighing deeply at the prejudices of the world, she sought to console herself by looking at Glenmurray, expecting to find in his eyes an expression of delight and approbation. To her great disappointment, however, his countenance was sad; while sir Patrick, on the contrary, had an expression of impudent triumph in his look, which made her turn blushing from his ardent gaze, and indignantly follow her mother, who was then leaving the room.

As she passed him, sir Patrick caught her hand rapturously to his lips (an action which made Glenmurray start from his chair), and exclaimed, "Upon my soul, you are the only honest little woman I ever knew! I always was sure that what you just now said was the opinion of all your sex, though they were so confoundedly coy they would not own it."

"Own what, sir?" asked the astonished Adeline.

"That they thought marriage a cursed bore, and preferred leading the life of honour, to be sure."

"The life of honour! What is that?" demanded Adeline, while Glenmurray paced the room in agitation.

"The life, my dear girl, which you mean to lead;—love and liberty with the man of your heart."

"Sir Patrick," cried Glenmurray impatiently, "this conversation is— "

"Prodigiously amusing to me," returned the baronet, "especially as I never could hold it to a modest woman before."

"Nor shall you now, sir," fiercely interrupted Glenmurray.

"Shall not, sir?" vociferated sir Patrick.

"Pray, gentlemen, be less violent," exclaimed the terrified

and astonished Adeline. "I can't think what could offend you, Mr. Glenmurray, in sir Patrick's original observation: the life of honour appears to me a very excellent name for the pure and honourable union which it is my wish to form; and—"

"There; I told you so;" triumphantly interrupted sir Patrick: "and I never was better pleased in my life: —sweet creature! at once so lovely, so wise, and so liberal!"

"Sir," cried Glenmurray, "this is a mistake: your life of honour and miss Mowbray's are as different as possible; you are talking of what you are grossly ignorant of."

"Ignorant! I ignorant! Look you, Mr. Glenmurray, do you pretend to tell me I know not of what the life of honour is, when I have led it so many times with so many different women?"

"How, sir!" replied Adeline: "many times? and with many different women? My life of honour can be led with one only."

"Well, my dear soul, I only led it with one at a time."

"O sir! you are indeed ignorant of my meaning," she rejoined: "it is the individuality of an attachment that constitutes its chastity; and—" [41]

"Ba-ba-bu, my lovely girl! What has chastity to do in the business?"

"Indeed, sir Patrick," meekly returned Adeline, "I—"

"Miss Mowbray," angrily interrupted Glenmurray, "I beg, I conjure you to drop this conversation: your innocence is no match for—"

"For what, sir?" furiously demanded sir Patrick.

"Your licentiousness," replied Glenmurray.

"Sir, I wear a sword," cried the baronet— "And I a cane,"

---

[41] See *Emma Courtney*, p. 192. The notion that chastity depends more on the exclusiveness of love than the legal marital status was Mary Wollstonecraft's argument. As William Godwin explained in *Memoirs of the Author of A Vindication of the Rights of Woman*, "It was her [Wollstonecraft's] maxim, 'that the imagination should awaken the senses, and not the senses the imagination.' In other words, that whatever related to the gratification of the senses, ought to arise, in a human being of a pure mind, only as the consequences of an individual affection." Godwin, *Memoirs*, ed. Cynthia Richards (Glen Allen, VA: College Publishing, 2003), p. 249-50.

said Glenmurray calmly, "either to defend myself or chastise insolence."

"Mr. Glenmurray! Sir Patrick!" exclaimed the agitated Adeline: "for my sake, for pity's sake, desist!"

"For the present I will, madam," faltered out sir Patrick;— "but I know Mr. Glenmurray's address, and he shall hear from me."

"Hear from you! Why, you do not mean to challenge him? you can't suppose Mr. Glenmurray would do so absurd a thing as fight a duel? Sir, he has written a volume to prove the absurdity of the custom. — No, no, thank God! you threaten his life in vain," she added, giving her hand to Glenmurray; who, in the tenderness of the action and the tone of her voice, forgot the displeasure which her inadvertency had caused, and, pressing her hand to his lips, secretly renewed his vows of unalterable attachment.

"Very well, madam," exclaimed sir Patrick in a tone of pique: "then, so as Mr. Glenmurray's life is safe, you care not what becomes of mine!"

"Sir," replied Adeline, "the safety of a fellow creature is always of importance in my eyes."

"Then you care for me as a fellow creature only," retorted sir Patrick, "not as sir Patrick O'Carrol? – Mighty fine, truly, you dear ungrateful—" seizing her hand; which he relinquished, as well as the rest of his speech, on the entrance of Mrs. Mowbray.

Soon after Adeline left the room, and Glenmurray bowed and retired; while sir Patrick, having first repeated his vows of admiration to the mother, returned home to muse on the charms of the daughter, and the necessity of challenging the moral Glenmurray.

Sir Patrick was a man of courage, and had fought several duels: but as life at this time had a great many charms for him, he resolved to defer at least putting himself in the way of getting rid of it; and after having slept late in the morning, to make up for the loss of sleep in the night, occasioned by his various cogitations, he rose, resolved to go to Mrs. Mowbray's, and, if he had an opportunity, indulge himself in some practical comments on the singular declaration made the evening before by her lovely daughter.

Glenmurray meanwhile had passed the night in equal watchfulness and greater agitation. To fight a duel would be, as Adeline observed, contrary to his principles; and to decline one, irritated as he was against sir Patrick, was repugnant to his feelings.

To no purpose did he peruse and reperuse nearly the whole of his own book against duelling; he had few religious restraints to make him resolve on declining a challenge, and he felt moral ones of little avail: but in vain did he sit at home till the morning was far advanced, expecting a messenger from sir Patrick;—no messenger came:—he therefore left word with his servant, that, if wanted, he might be found at Mrs. Mowbray's, and went thither, in hopes of enjoying an hour's conversation with Adeline; resolving to hint to her, as delicately as he could, that the opinions which she had expressed were better confined, in the present dark state of the public mind, to a select and discriminating circle.

MASCULINITY AND DUELING

Masculinity, like femininity, was particularly under pressure in the late 1790s and early 1800s. Republican masculinity, celebrated by writers like Wollstonecraft, was carefully imagined as a trait available to both sexes, and opposed to French and aristocratic "effeminacy." Thus, rational, strong-minded, independent, and virtuous women, such as radicals like Wollstonecraft and Hays had imagined, were positively coded as participating in a kind of Republican masculinity or were negatively portrayed as contrary to nature and usurping masculine prerogatives to the detriment of feminine virtues and delicacy. This put particular pressures on conceptions of masculinity.

The "duel of honor," nominally illegal since at least the

reign of Elizabeth I, was powerfully associated with elite masculinity. Dueling had been under attack for some time on the part of middling writers of all political persuasions. Even on the continent, Jean-Jacques Rousseau had attacked it in his novel *Julie, ou la nouvelle Héloïse* (1759), widely read in Britain. Significantly, Julie averts a duel between her lover, St. Preux ,and a hot-headed Englishman by confessing to Milord Edouard that she has admitted St. Preux to sexual intimacy, relying on Edouard's honor not to risk exposing her by a duel. Back in Britain and somewhat earlier, Samuel Richardson had criticized dueling in *Clarissa* (1748); Clarissa's fear that her brother's intemperate behavior will provoke her suitor, Lovelace, into a duel is partly responsible for the clandestine correspondence that enables Lovelace to abduct her. Richardson's *Sir Charles Grandison* (1752), his effort to portray a good and virtuous but manly man, is even more explicit in its engagement with dueling. Sir Charles carefully negotiates between the alternatives of being forced into a duel by insults, or being labeled cowardly and dishonorable by evading a duel altogether when Sir Hargrave attempts to call him out. Grandison carefully maneuvers Sir Hargrave Pollexfen not to provoke him so publicly that Grandison has no choice, and by his careful balance of Christian principle and manly assertion of his willingness to wield his sword in self-defense, wins Sir Hargrave's and his rakish associates' admiration of Grandison's manly control and bravery. As Grandison argues:

> Of what use are the Laws of society, if magistracy may be thus defied? Were I to accept your challenge, and were you to prevail against me, who is to challenge you; and if you fall, who him by whose sword you perish? Where, in short, is this evil to stop? But I will *not* meet you: My system is self-defence, and self-defence only. Put me upon *that*, and I question not that you will have cause to repent it. A *premeditated* revenge is that which I will not meet you to gratify. I will not dare to risque the

rushing into my Maker's presence from the consequences of an act, which cannot, in the man that falls, admit of repentance, and leaves for the survivor's portion nothing but bitter remorse....For your own sake, therefore, consider better of the matter; since it is not impossible, but, were we to meet, and both survive, you may exchange what you will think, a real disgrace for an imaginary one.

And thus, gentlemen, have I almost syllogistically argued with myself on this subject:

Courage is a virtue;

Passion is a vice:

Passion, therefore, cannot be Courage.

Does it not then, behove [sic] every man of true honor to shew, that reason has a greater share than resentment in the boldness of his resolves? (Vol 1, 265)

Thus, when Godwin wrote an explicit condemnation of dueling into his 1793 *Enquiry Considering Political Justice*, he was in tune with English mainstream opinion. However, while the common middling rationale against dueling relied upon Christian moral commandment to commit no murder, and less openly on the growing rejection of elite, aristocratic traditions by an emerging bourgeoisie, Godwin argued against dueling as irrational because it could produce nothing useful for the general good:

This despicable practice was originally invented by barbarians for the gratification of revenge. It was probably at that time thought a very happy project for reconciling the odiousness of malignity with the gallantry of courage.

But in this light it is now generally given up. Men of the best understanding who lend it their sanction are unwillingly induced to do so, and engage in single combat merely that their reputation may sustain no slander.

In examining this subject we must proceed upon

one of two suppositions. Either the lives of both the persons to be hazarded are worthless, or they are not. In the latter case, the question answers itself, and cannot stand in need of discussion. Useful lives are not to be hazarded, from a view to the partial and contemptible obloquy that may be annexed to the refusal of such a duel, that is, to an act of virtue....

'But the refusing a duel is an ambiguous action. Cowards may pretend to principle to shelter themselves from a danger they dare not meet.' This is partly true and partly false. There are few actions indeed that are not ambiguous, or that with the same general outline may not proceed from different motives. But the manner of doing them will sufficiently show the principle from which they spring....

If courage have any intelligible nature, one of its principle fruits must be the daring to speak truth at all times, to all persons, and in every possible situation in which a well informed sense of duty may prescribe it. What is it but want of courage that should prevent me from saying, 'Sir, I will not accept your challenge. Have I injured you? I will readily and without compulsion repair my injustice to the uttermost mite. Have you misconstrued me? State to me the particulars, and doubt not that what is true I will make appear to be true. I should be a notorious criminal were I to attempt your life, or assist you in an attempt upon mine. What compensation will the opinion of the world make for the recollection of so vile and brutal a proceeding? There is no true applause but where the heart of him that receives it beats in unison. There is no censure terrible while the heart repels it with conscious integrity. I am not the coward to do a deed that my soul detests because I cannot endure the scoffs of the mistaken. Loss of reputation is a serious evil. But I will act so that no man shall suspect me of irresolution and pusillanimity.' He that should firmly hold this language and act accordingly, would soon be acquitted of every dishonourable imputation. (Godwin, *Enquiry Concerning Political Justice*, Chapt 2 Appendix II, "Of Duelling," 179-80.)

Glenmurray's arguments against dueling, because they are not founded in Christian beliefs, are here represented as inadequate controls to his actual behavior once provoked. Godwin also refuses to ground his argument in Christianity, instead arguing for true courage as adherence to the abstract principle of general utility.

SOURCES

Robert Baldrick. *The Duel: A History of Duelling* (New York: Clarkson Potter, 1965).

William Godwin, *Enquiry Concerning Political Justice*, Third Edition, London, 1798.

V. G. Kiernan, *The Duel in European History: Honour and the Reign of Aristocracy* (Oxford: Oxford University Press, 1988).

Samuel Richardson, *Sir Charles Grandison*. Ed. Jocelyn Harris. (New York: Oxford University Press, 1972). Reprinted by Otago University Print, 2001.

——. *Clarissa, or the History of a Young Lady*. Ed. Angus Ross. (New York: Penguin, 1985).

Jean-Jacques Rousseau, *Julie*. (1759). Trans. Philip Stewart and Jean Vaché (Hanover, VT: University of New England Press, 1997).

CHAPTER VI.

SIR PATRICK had reached Mrs. Mowbray's some time before him, and had, to his great satisfaction, found Adeline alone; nor did it escape his penetration that her cheeks glowed, and her eyes sparkled with pleasure, at his approach.

But he would not have rejoiced in this circumstance, had he known that Adeline was pleased to see him merely because she considered his appearance as a proof of Glenmurray's safety; for, in spite of his having written against duelling, and of her confidence in his firmness and consistency, she was not quite convinced that the reasoning philosopher would triumph over the feeling man.

"You are welcome, sir Patrick!" cried Adeline, as he entered, with a most winning smile: "I am very glad to see you: pray sit down."

The baronet, who, audacious as his hopes and intentions were, had not expected so kind a reception, was quite thrown off his guard by it, and, catching her suddenly in his arms, endeavored to obtain a still kinder welcome. Adeline as suddenly disengaged herself from him, and, with the dignity of offended modesty, desired him to quit the room, as, after such an insolent attempt, she could not think herself justified in suffering him to remain with her.

But her anger was soon changed into pity, when she saw sir Patrick lay down his hat, seat himself, and burst into a long deliberate laugh.

"He is certainly mad!" she exclaimed; and, leaning against the chimney-piece, she began to contemplate him with a degree of fearful interest.

"Upon my soul! Now," cried the baronet, when his laugh was over, "you do not suppose, my dear creature, that you and I do not understand one another! Telling a young fellow to leave the house on such occasions, means, in the pretty no meaning of your sex, 'Stay, and offend again,' to be sure."

"He is certainly mad!" said Adeline, more confirmed than before in her idea of his insanity, and immediately endeavored to reach the door: but in so doing she approached sir Patrick, who, rather roughly seizing her trembling hand, desired her to sit down, and hear what he had to say to her. Adeline, thinking it not right to irritate him, instantly obeyed.

"Now, then, to open my mind to you," said the baronet,

drawing his chair close to hers: "From the very first moment I saw you, I felt that we were made for one another; though, being bothered by my debts, I made up to the old duchess, and she nibbled the bait directly,—deeming my clean inches (six feet one, without shoes) well worth her dirty acres."

"How dreadfully incoherent he is!" thought Adeline, not suspecting for a moment that, by the old duchess, he meant her still blooming mother.

"But, my lovely love!" continued sir Patrick, most ardently pressing her hand, "so much have your sweet person, and your frank and liberal way of thinking, charmed me, that I here freely offer myself to you, and we will begin the life of honour together as soon as you please."

Still Adeline, who was unconscious how much her avowed opinions had exposed her to insult, continued to believe sir Patrick insane; a belief which the wildness of his eyes confirmed. "I really know not,—you surprise me, sir Patrick,—I——."

"Surprise you, my dear soul! How could you expect anything else from a man of my spirit, after your honest declaration last night? ...All I feared was, that Glenmurray should get the start of me."

Adeline, though alarmed, bewildered, and confounded, had still recollection enough to know that, whether sane or insane, the words and looks of sir Patrick were full of increasing insult. "I believe, I think I had better retire," faltered out Adeline.

"Retire! ...Aye, by all means," exclaimed the baronet rudely seizing her.

This outrage restored Adeline to her usual spirit and self-possession; and bestowing on him the epithet of 'mean-soul'd ruffian!' she had almost freed herself from his grasp, when a quick step was heard on the stairs, and the door was thrown open by Glenmurray. In a moment Adeline, bursting into tears, threw herself into his arms, as if in search of protection.

Glenmurray required no explanation of the scene before him: the appearance of the actors in it was explanation sufficient; and while with one arm he fondly held Adeline to his bosom, he raised the other in a threatening attitude against sir Patrick, exclaiming as he did it, "Base, unmanly villain!"

"Villain!" echoed sir Patrick..... "but it is very well—very well for the present—Good morning to you, sir!" So saying, he hastily withdrew.

As soon as he was gone, Glenmurray for the first time declared to Adeline the ardent passion with which she had inspired him; and she, with equal frankness, confessed that her heart was irrevocably his.

From this interesting tête-à-tête Adeline was summoned to attend a person on business to her mother; and during her absence Glenmurray received a challenge from the angry baronet, appointing him to meet him that afternoon at five o'clock, about two miles from Bath. To this note, for fear of alarming the suspicions of Adeline, Glenmurray returned only a verbal message, saying he would answer it in two hours: but as soon as she returned he pleaded indispensable business; and before she could mention any fears respecting the consequences of what had passed between him and sir Patrick, he had left the room, having, to prevent any alarm, requested leave to wait on her early the next day.

As soon as Glenmurray reached his lodgings, he again revolved in his mind the propriety of accepting the challenge. "How can I expect to influence others by my theories to act right, if my practice sets them a bad example?" But then again he exclaimed, "How can I expect to have any thing I say attended to, when, by refusing to fight, I put it in the power of my enemies to assert I am a poltroon[42], and worthy only of neglect and contempt? No, no; I must fight:——even Adeline herself, especially as it is on her account, will despise me if I do not:"— and then, without giving himself any more time to deliberate, he sent an answer to sir Patrick, promising to meet him at the time appointed.

But after he had sent it he had found himself a prey to so

---

[42] I.e., coward.

much self-reproach, and after he had forfeited his claims to consistency of conduct, he felt himself so strongly aware of the value of it, that, had not the time of the meeting been near at hand, he would certainly have deliberated upon some means of retracting his consent to it.

Being resolved to do as little mischief as he could, he determined on having no second in the business; and accordingly repaired to the field accompanied only by a trusty servant, who had orders to wait his master's pleasure at a distance.

Contrary to Glenmurray's expectations, sir Patrick also came unattended by a second; while his servant, who was with him, was, like the other, desired to remain in the back ground.

"I wish, Mr. Glenmurray, to do every thing honourable," said the baronet, after they had exchanged salutations: "therefore, sir, as I concluded you would find it difficult to get a second, I am without one, and I *conclude* that I *concluded* right.—Aye, men of your principles can have but a few friends."

"And men of your practice ought to have none, sir Patrick," retorted Glenmurray: "but, as I don't think it worth while to explain to you my reasons for nor having a second, as I fear that you are incapable of understanding them, I must desire you to take your ground."

"With all my heart," replied his antagonist; and then taking aim, they agreed to fire at the same moment.

They did so; and the servants, hearing the report of the pistols, ran to the scene of action, and saw sir Patrick bleeding in the sword-arm, and Glenmurray, also wounded, leaning against a tree.

"This is cursed unlucky," said sir Patrick coolly: "as you have disabled my right arm I can't go on with this business at present; but when I am well again, command me. Your wound, I believe, is as slight as mine; but as I can walk, and you cannot, and as I have a chaise, and you not, you shall use it to convey you and your servant home, and I and mine will go on foot."

To this obliging offer Glenmurray was incapable of giving a denial; for he became insensible from loss of blood, and with the assistance of his antagonist was carried to the chaise, and, supported by his terrified servant, conveyed back to Bath.

It is not to be supposed that an event of this nature should be long unknown. It was soon told all over the city that sir Patrick O'Carrol and Mr. Glenmurray had fought a duel, and that the latter was dangerously wounded: the quarrel having originated in Mr. Glenmurray's scoffing at religion, king, and constitution, before the pious and loyal baronet.

This story soon reached the ears of Mrs. Mowbray, who, in an agony of tender sorrow, and in defiance of all decorum, went in person to call on her admired sir Patrick; and Adeline, who heard of the affair soon after, as regardless of appearances as her mother, and more alarmed, went in person to inquire concerning her wounded Glenmurray.

By the time that she had arrived at his lodgings, not only his own surgeon but sir Patrick's had seen him, as his antagonist thought it necessary to ascertain the true state of his wound, that he might know whether he ought to stay, or fly his country.[43]

The account of both the surgeons was, however, so favourable, and Glenmurray in all respects so well, that sir Patrick's alarms were soon quite at an end; and the wounded man was lying on a sopha, lost in no very pleasant reflections, when Adeline knocked at his door. Glenmurray at that very moment was saying to himself, "Well; —so much for principle and consistency! Now, my next step must be to marry, and then I shall have made myself a complete fool, and the worst of all fools,—a man presuming to instruct others by his precepts, when he finds them incapable even of influencing his own actions."

At this moment his servant came up with "miss Mowbray's compliments, and, if he was well enough to see her, she would come up and speak to him."

In an instant all his self-reproaches were forgotten; and when Adeline hung weeping and silent on his shoulder, he could not

---

[43] As dueling was illegal, an antagonist's death meant the winner had to leave Britain or risk trial for murder.

but rejoice in an affair which had procured him a moment of such heartfelt delight. At first Adeline expressed nothing but terror at the consequences of his wound, and pity for his sufferings; but when she found that he was in no danger, and in very little pain, the tender mistress yielded to the severe monitress, and she began to upbraid Glenmurray for having acted not only in defiance of her wishes and principles, but of his own; of principles laid down by him to the world in the strongest point of view, and in a manner convincing to every mind.

"Dearest Adeline, consider the provocation," cried Glenmurray;— "a gross insult offered to the woman I love!"

"But who ever fought a duel without provocation, Glenmurray? If provocation be a justification, your book was unnecessary; and did not you offer an insult to the understanding of the woman you love, in supposing that she could be obliged to you for playing the fool on her account?"

"But I should have been called a coward had I declined the challenge; and though I can bear the world's hatred, I could not its contempt:—I could not endure the loss of what the world calls honour."

"Is it possible," rejoined Adeline, "that I hear the philosophical Glenmurray talking thus, in the silly jargon of a man of the world?"

"Alas! I am a man, not a philosopher, Adeline!"

"At least be a sensible one;—consistent I dare not now call you. But have you forgotten the distinction which, in your volume on the subject of duels, you so strongly lay down between real and apparent honour? In which of the two classes do you put the honour of which, in this instance, you were so tenacious? What is there in common between the glory of risking the life of a fellow-creature, and the testimony of an approving conscience?"

"An excellent observation that of yours, indeed, my sweet monitress," said Glenmurray.

"An observation of mine! It is your own," replied Adeline: "but see, I have the book in my muff; and I will punish you for the badness of your practice, by giving you a dose of your theory."

"Cruel girl!" cried Glenmurray, "I am not ordered a sleeping draught!"

Adeline was however resolved; and, opening the book, she read argument after argument with unyielding perseverance, till Glenmurray, who, like the eagle in the song, saw on the dart that wounded him his own feathers, cried "Quarter!"[44]

"But tell me, dear Adeline," said Glenmurray, a little piqued at her too just reproofs, "you, who are so severe on my want of consistency, are you yourself capable of acting up in every respect to your precepts?"

"After your weakness," replied Adeline, smiling, "it becomes me to doubt my own strength; but I assure you that I make it a scruple of conscience, to show by my conduct my confidence in the truth of my opinions."

"Then, in defiance of the world's opinion, that opinion which I, you see, had not resolution to brave, you will be mine—not according to the ties of marriage, but with no other ties or sanction than those of love and reason?"

"I will," said Adeline: "and may that God when I worship (raising her fine eyes and white arms to heaven) desert me when I desert you!"

Who that had seen her countenance and gesture at that moment, could have imagined she was calling on heaven to witness an engagement to lead a life of infamy? Rather would they have thought her a sublime enthusiast breathing forth the worship of a grateful soul.

It may be supposed that Glenmurray's heart beat with exultation at this confession from Adeline, and that he forgot, in the promised indulgence of his passion, to confine himself within those bounds which strict decorum required. But Glenmurray did her justice; he beheld her as she was—all purity of feeling

---

[44] See Aesop's Fables for the original tale. Compare Thomas Moore, from "Corruption" (probably around 1808): "Like a young eagle who has lent his plume/ To fledge the shaft by which he meets his doom,/ See their own feathers pluck'd to wing the dart/ Which rank corruption destines for their heart."

and all delicacy; and, if possible, the slight favours by which true passion is long contented to be fed, though granted by Adeline with more conscious emotion, were received by him with more devoted respect: besides, he again felt that mixture of pain with pleasure, on this assurance of her love, which he had experienced before. For he knew, though Adeline did not, the extent of the degradation into which the step which her conscience approved would necessarily precipitate her; and experience alone could convince him that her sensibility to shame, when she was for the first time exposed to it, would not overcome her supposed fortitude and boasted contempt of the world's opinion, and change all the roses of love into the thorns of regret and remorse.

And could he who doted on her;—he, too, who admired her as much for her consummate purity as for any other of her qualities;—could he bear to behold this fair creature, whose open eye beamed with the consciousness of virtue, casting her timid glances to the earth, and shrinking with horror from the conviction of having in the world's eye forfeited all pretensions to that virtue which alone was the end of her actions! Would the approbation of her own mind be sufficient to support her under such a trial, though she had with such sweet earnestness talked to him of its efficacy! These reflections had for some time past been continually occurring to him, and now they came across his mind blighting the triumphs of successful passion:—nay, but from the dread of incurring yet more ridicule, on account of the opposition of his practice to his theory, and perhaps the indignant contempt of Adeline, he could have thrown himself at her feet, conjuring her to submit to the degradation of being a wife.

But, unknown to Glenmurray, perhaps, another reason prompted him to desire this concession from Adeline. We are never more likely to be in reality the slaves of selfishness, than when we fancy ourselves acting with most heroic disinterestedness.—Egotism loves a becoming dress, and is always on the watch to hide her ugliness by the robe of benevolence. Glenmurray thought that he was willing to marry Adeline merely for *her* sake; but I suspect it was chiefly for *his*. The true and delicate lover is always a monopolizer, always desirous of calling the woman of his affections his own: it is not only because he considers marriage as a holy institution that the lover leads his mistress to the altar; but because it gives him a right to appropriate the fair treasure to himself,—because it sanctions and perpetuates the dearest of all monopolies, and erects a sacred barrier to guard his rights,—around which, all that is respectable in society, all that is most powerful and effectual in its organization, is proud and eager to rally.[45]

But while Glenmurray, in spite of his happiness, was sensible to an alloy of it, and Adeline was tenderly imputing to the pain of his wound the occasionally mournful expression of his countenance, Adeline took occasion to declare that she would live with Glenmurray only on condition that such a step met with her mother's approbation.

"Then are my hopes for ever at an end," said Glenmurray:— "or,—or (and spite of himself his eyes sparkled as he spoke)—or we must submit to the absurd ceremony of marriage."

"Marriage!" replied the astonished Adeline: "can you think so meanly of my mother, as to suppose her practice so totally opposite to her principles, that she would require her daughter to submit to a ceremony which she herself regards with contempt?—Impossible. I am sure, when I solicit her consent to my being yours, she will be pleased to find that her sentiments and observations have not been thrown away on me."

Glenmurray thought otherwise: however, he bowed and was silent; and Adeline declared that, to put an end to all doubt on the subject, she would instantly go in search of Mrs. Mowbray and propose the question to her: and Glenmurray, feeling himself more weak and indisposed than he chose to own to her, allowed her, though reluctantly, to depart.

---

[45] See Godwin's *Political Justice*, "Of Co-operations, Cohabitation, and Marriage," 1798, 507-510. See also text box "Female Sexuality and Desire," p. 311, for an excerpt from Godwin on marriage as monopoly.

CHAPTER VII.

MRS. MOWBRAY was but just returned from her charitable visit when Adeline entered the room. "And pray, miss Mowbray, where have you been?" she exclaimed, seeing Adeline with her hat and cloak on.

"I have been visiting poor Mr. Glenmurray," she replied.

"Indeed!" cried Mrs. Mowbray: "and without my leave! and pray who went with you?"

"Nobody, ma'am."

"Nobody!—What! visit a man alone at his lodgings, after the education which you have received!"

"Indeed, madam," replied Adeline meekly, "my education never taught me that such conduct was improper; nor, as you did the same this afternoon, could I have dared to think it so."

"You are mistaken, miss Mowbray," replied her mother: "I did not do the same; for the terms which I am upon with sir Patrick made my visiting him no impropriety at all."

"If you think I have acted wrong," replied Adeline timidly, "no doubt I have done so; though you were quite right in visiting sir Patrick, as the respectability of your age and character, and sir Patrick's youth, warranted the propriety of the visit:—but, surely the terms which I am upon with Mr. Glenmurray——"

"The terms which you are upon with Mr. Glenmurray! and my age and character! what can you mean?" angrily exclaimed Mrs. Mowbray.

"I hoped, my dear mother," said Adeline tenderly, "that you had long ere this guessed the attachment which subsists between Mr. Glenmurray and me;—an attachment cherished by your high opinion of him and his writings; but which respect has till now made me hesitate to mention to you."

"Would to heaven!" replied Mrs. Mowbray, "that respect had made you for ever silent on the subject! Do you suppose that I would marry my daughter to a man of small fortune,—but more especially to one who, as sir Patrick informs me, is shunned for his principles and profligacy by all the world?"

"To what sir Patrick says of Mr. Glenmurray I pay no

attention," answered Adeline; "nor are you, my dear mother, capable, I am sure, of being influenced by the prejudices of the world.—But you are quite mistaken in supposing me so lost to consistency, and so regardless of your liberal opinions and the books which we have studied, as to think of *marrying* Mr. Glenmurray."

"Grant me patience!" cried Mrs. Mowbray: "why, to be sure you do not think of living with him *without* being married?"

"Certainly, madam; that you may have the pleasure of beholding one union founded on rational grounds and cemented by rational ties."

"How!" cried Mrs. Mowbray, turning pale. "I!—I have pleasure in seeing my daughter a kept mistress!—You are mad, quite mad.—*I* approve such unhallowed connections!"

"My dearest mother," replied Adeline, "your agitation terrifies me,—but indeed what I say is strictly true; and see here, in Mr. Glenmurray's book, the very passage which I have so often heard you admire." As she said this, Adeline pointed to the passage; but in an instant Mrs. Mowbray seized the book and threw it on the fire.

Before Adeline had recovered her consternation Mrs. Mowbray fell into a violent hysteric; and long was it before she was restored to composure. When she recovered she was so exhausted that Adeline dared not renew the conversation; but leaving her to rest, she made up a bed on her floor in her mother's room, and passed a night of wretchedness and watchfulness,—the first of the kind which she had ever known.—Would it had been the last!

In the morning Mrs. Mowbray awoke, refreshed and calm; and, affected at seeing the pale cheek and sunk eye of Adeline, indicative of a sleepless and unhappy night, she held her hand out to her with a look of kindness; Adeline pressed it to her lips, as she knelt by the bed-side, and moistened it with tears of regret for the past and alarm for the future.

"Adeline, my dear child," said Mrs. Mowbray in a faint voice, "I hope you will no longer think of putting a design in execution so fraught with mischief to you, and horror to me. Little did I think that you were so romantic[46] as to see no difference between amusing one's imagination with new theories and new systems, and acting upon them in defiance of common custom, and the received usages of society. I admire the convenient trowsers and graceful dress of the Turkish women; but I would not wear them myself, lest it should expose me to derision."

"Is there no difference," thought Adeline, "between the importance of a dress and an opinion!—Is the one to be taken up, and laid down again, with the same indifference as the other!" But she continued silent, and Mrs. Mowbray went on.

"The poetical philosophy which I have so much delighted to study, has served me to ornament my conversation, and make persons less enlightened than myself wonder at the superior boldness of my fancy, and the acuteness of my reasoning powers;—but I should as soon have thought of making this little gold chain round my neck fasten the hall-door, as act upon the precepts laid down in those delightful books. No; though I think all they say true, I believe the purity they inculcate too much for this world."

Adeline listened in silent astonishment and consternation. Conscience, and the conviction of what is right, she then for the first time learned, were not to be the rule of action; and though filial tenderness made her resolve never to be the mistress of Glenmurray, she also resolved never to be his wife, or that of any other man; while, in spite of herself, the great respect with which she had hitherto regarded her mother's conduct and opinions began to diminish.

"Would to heaven, my dear mother," said Adeline, when

[46] Note also the use of the term "romantic" throughout *Emma Courtney*. Earlier in the eighteenth century, "romantic" carried associations of old fashioned courtly Romances, of melancholia, or extravagant and absurd fantasies. With the newly developing artistic movement that came to be called "Romanticism," this formerly pejorative term was becoming a positive alternative to cold rationality associated with the Enlightenment. However, in these two novels the pejorative connotations dominate.

Mrs. Mowbray had done speaking, "that you had said all this to me ere my mind had been indelibly impressed with the truth of these forbidden doctrines; for now my conscience tells me that I ought to act up to them!"

"How!" exclaimed Mrs. Mowbray, starting up in her bed, and in a voice shrill with emotion, "are you then resolved to disobey me, and dishonour yourself?"

"Oh! never, never!" replied Adeline, alarmed at her mother's violence, and fearful of a relapse. "Be but the kind affectionate parent that you have ever been to me; and though I will never marry, out of regard to my own principles, I will also never contract any other union, out of respect to your wishes,—but will lead with you a quiet, if not a *happy*, life; for never, never can I forget Glenmurray."

"There speaks the excellent child I always thought you to be!" replied Mrs. Mowbray; "and I shall leave it to time and good counsels to convince you, that the opinions of a girl of eighteen, as they are not founded on long experience, may possibly be erroneous."

Mrs. Mowbray never made a truer observation; but Adeline was not in a frame of mind to assent to it.

"Besides," continued Mrs. Mowbray, "had I ever been disposed to accept of Mr. Glenmurray as a son-in-law, it is very unlikely that I should be so now; as the duel took place not only, I find, from the treasonable opinions which he put forth, but from some disrespectful language which he held concerning me."

"Who could dare to invent so infamous a calumny!" exclaimed Adeline.

"My authority is unquestionable, miss Mowbray: I speak from sir Patrick himself."

"Then he adds falsehood to his other villainies!" returned Adeline, almost inarticulate with rage:— "but what could be expected from a man who could dare to insult a young woman under the roof of her mother with his licentious addresses?"

"What mean you?" cried Mrs. Mowbray, turning pale.

"I mean that sir Patrick yesterday morning insulted me by

the grossest familiarities, and——"

"My dear child," replied Mrs. Mowbray laughing, "that is only the usual freedom of his manner; a manner which your ignorance of the world led you to mistake. He did not mean to insult you, believe me. I am sure that, spite of his ardent passion for me, he never, even when alone with me, hazarded any improper liberty."

"The ardent passion which he feels for you, madam!" exclaimed Adeline, turning pale in her turn.

"Yes, miss Mowbray! What, I suppose you think me too old to inspire one!—But, I assure you, there are people who think the mother handsomer than the daughter!"

"No doubt, dear mother, every one ought to think so,—and would to heaven sir Patrick were one of those! But he, unfortunately—— "

"Is of that opinion," interrupted Mrs. Mowbray angrily: "and to convince you—so tenderly does he love me, and so fondly do I return his passion, that in a few days I shall become his wife."

Adeline, on hearing this terrible information, fell insensible on the ground. When she recovered she saw Mrs. Mowbray anxiously watching her, but not with that look of alarm and tenderness with which she had attended her during her long illness; that look which was always present to her grateful and affectionate remembrance. No; Mrs. Mowbray's eye was cast down with a half-mournful, half-reproachful, and half-fearful expression, when it met that of Adeline.

The emotion of anguish which her fainting had evinced was a reproach to the proud heart of Mrs. Mowbray, and Adeline felt that it was so; but when she recollected that her mother was going to marry a man who had so lately declared a criminal passion for herself, she was very near relapsing into insensibility. She however struggled with her feelings, in order to gain resolution to disclose to Mrs. Mowbray all that had passed between her and sir Patrick. But as soon as she offered to renew the conversation, Mrs. Mowbray sternly commanded her to be silent; and insisting on her going to bed, she left her to her own reflections, till wearied and exhausted she fell into a sound sleep: nor, as it was late in the evening when she awoke, did she rise again till the next morning.

Mrs. Mowbray entered her room as she was dressing, and inquired how she did, with some kindness.

"I shall be better, dear mother, if you will but hear what I have to say concerning sir Patrick," replied Adeline, bursting into tears.

"You can say nothing that will shake my opinion of him, miss Mowbray," replied her mother coldly: "so I advise you to reconcile yourself to a circumstance which it is not in your power to prevent." So saying, she left the room; and Adeline, convinced that all she could say would be vain, endeavoured to console herself, by thinking that, as soon as sir Patrick became the husband of her mother, his wicked designs on her would undoubtedly cease; and that, therefore, in one respect, this ill-sorted union would be beneficial to her.

Sir Patrick, meanwhile, was no less sanguine in his expectations from his marriage. Unlike the innocent Adeline, he did not consider his union with the mother as a necessary check to his attempts on the daughter; but, emboldened by what to him appeared the libertine sentiments of Adeline, and relying on the opportunities of being with her, which he must infallibly enjoy under the same roof in the country, he looked on her as his certain prey. Though he believed Glenmurray to be at that moment preferred to himself, he thought it impossible that the superior beauty of his person should not, in the end, have its due weight; as a passion founded in esteem, and the admiration of intellectual beauty, could not, in his opinion, subsist: besides, Adeline appeared in his eyes not a deceived enthusiast, but a susceptible and forward girl, endeavoring to hide her frailty under fine sentiments and high-sounding theories. Nor was sir Patrick's inference an unnatural one. Every man of the world would have thought the same; and on very plausible grounds.

CHAPTER VIII.

As sir Patrick was not 'punctual as lovers to the moment sworn,'[47] Mrs. Mowbray resolved to sit down and write immediately to Glenmurray; flattering herself at the same time, that the letter which was designed to confound Glenmurray would delight the tender baronet;—for Mrs. Mowbray piqued herself on her talents for letter-writing, and was not a little pleased with an opportunity of displaying them to a celebrated author. But never before did she find writing a letter so difficult a task. Her eager wish of excelling deprived her of the means; and she who, in a letter to a friend or relation, would have written in a style at once clear and elegant, after two hours' effort produced the following specimen of the obscure, the pedantic, and affected.

"SIR,

"The light which cheers and attracts, if we follow its guidance, often leads us into bogs and quagmires:— *Verbum sapienti.*[48] Your writings are the lights, and the practice to which you advise my deluded daughter is the bog and the quagmire. I agree with you in all you have said against marriage;—I agree with the savage nations in the total uselessness of clothing; still I condescend to wear clothes, though neither becoming nor useful, because I respect public opinion; and I submit to the institution of marriage for reasons equally cogent. Such being my sentiments, sir, I must desire you never to see my daughter more. Nor could you expect to be received with open arms by me whom the shafts of your ridicule have pierced, though warded off by the shield of love and gallantry;—but for this I thank you! Now

---

[47] Edward Young (1683-1765), *Night Thoughts.* "Night III: Narcissa:" "and at the destined hour, /Punctual as lovers to the moment sworn, /keep my assignation with my woe" (lines 3-5).

[48] I.e., "a word to the wise."

[49] I.e., marriage. Hymen was the Roman god of wedlock.

shall I possess, owing to your baseness, at once a declared lover and a tried avenger; and the chains of Hymen[49] will be rendered more charming by gratitude's having blown the flame, while love forged the fetters.

"But with your writings I continue to amuse my imagination.—Lovely is the flower of the nightshade, though its berry be poison. Still shall I admire and wonder at you as an author, though I avoid and detest you as a man.

"EDITHA MOWBRAY."

This letter was just finished when sir Patrick arrived, and to him it was immediately shown.

"Heh! What have we here?" cried he laughing violently as he perused it. "Here you talk of being pierced by shafts which were warded off. Now, had *I* said that, it would have been called a bull.[50] As to the concluding paragraph—"

"O! that, I flatter myself," said Mrs. Mowbray, "will tear him with remorse."

"He must first understand it," cried sir Patrick: "I can but just comprehend it, and am sure it will be all botheration to him."

"I am sorry to find such is your opinion," replied Mrs. Mowbray; "for I think that sentence the best written of any."

"I did not say it was not fine writing," replied the baronet, "I only said it was not to be understood.—But, with your leave, you shall send the letter, and we'll drop the subject."

So said, so done, to the great satisfaction of sir Patrick, who felt that it was for his interest to suffer the part of Mrs. Mowbray's letter which alluded to Glenmurray's supposed calumnies against her to remain obscurely worded, as he well knew that what he had asserted on this subject was wholly void of foundation.

Glenmurray did not receive it with equal satisfaction. He

---

[50] A "bull" or particularly an "Irish Bull," from the early seventeenth century indicates a "contradiction in terms" or "a ludicrous inconsistency" (OED).

was indignant at the charge of having advised Adeline to become his mistress rather than his wife; and as so much of the concluding passage as he could understand seemed to imply that he had calumniated her mother, to remain silent a moment would have been to confess himself guilty: he therefore answered Mrs. Mowbray's letter immediately. The answer was as fellows:

"MADAM,

"To clear myself from the charge of having advised miss Mowbray to a step contrary to the common customs, however erroneous, of society at this period, I appeal to the testimony of miss Mowbray herself; and I here repeat to you the assurance which I made to her, that I am willing to marry her when and where she chooses. I love my system and my opinions, but the respectability of the woman of my affections *more*. Allow me, therefore, to make you a little acquainted with my situation in life:

"To you it is well known, madam, that wealth, honours, and titles have no value in my eyes; and that I reverence talents and virtues, though they wear the garb of poverty, and are born in the most obscure stations. But you, or rather those who are so fortunate as to influence your determinations, may consider my sentiments on this subject as romantic and absurd. It is necessary, therefore, that I should tell you, as an excuse in their eyes for presuming to address your daughter, that, by the accident of birth, I am descended from an antient family, and nearly allied to a noble one; and that my paternal inheritance, though not large enough for splendour and luxury, is sufficient for all the purposes of comfort and genteel influence. I would say more on this subject, but I am impatient to remove from your mind the prejudice which you seem to have imbibed against me. I do not perfectly understand the last paragraph in your letter. If you will be so kind as to explain it to me, you may depend on my being perfectly ingenuous: indeed, I have no difficulty in declaring, that I have neither encouraged a feeling, nor uttered a word, capable of giving the lie to the declaration which I am now going to make—That I am,

"With respect and esteem,
"Your obedient servant,

"F. GLENMURRAY"

This letter had an effect on Mrs. Mowbray's feelings so much in favor of Glenmurray, that she was almost determined to let him marry Adeline. She felt that she owed her some amends for contracting a marriage so suddenly, and without either her knowledge or approbation; and she thought that, by marrying her to the man of her heart, she should make her peace both with Adeline and herself. But, unfortunately, this design, as soon as it began to be formed, was communicated to sir Patrick.

"So, then!" exclaimed he, "you have forgotten and forgiven the impertinent things which the puppy said!— things which obliged me to wear this little useless appendage in a sling thus (pointing to his wounded arm)."

"O! no, my dear sir Patrick! But though what Mr. Glenmurray said might alarm the scrupulous tenderness of a lover, perhaps it was a remark which might only suit the sincerity of a friend. Perhaps, if Mr. Glenmurray had made it to me, I should have heard it with thanks, and with candour have approved it."

"My sweet soul!" replied sir Patrick, "you may be as candid and amiable as ever you please, but, 'by St. Patrick!' never shall sir Patrick O'Carrol be father-in-law to the notorious and infamous Glenmurray—that subverter of all religion and order, and that scourge of civilized society!"

So, saying, he stalked about the room; and Mrs. Mowbray, as she gazed on his handsome person, thought it would be absurd for her to sacrifice her own happiness to her daughter's, and give up sir Patrick as her husband in order to make Glenmurray her son. She therefore wrote another letter to Glenmurray, forbidding him any further intercourse with Adeline, on any pretence whatever; and delayed not a moment to send him her final decision.

"That is acting like the sensible woman I took you for," said sir Patrick: "the fellow has now gotten his quietus, I trust, and the dear little Adeline is reserved for a happier fate. Sweet soul! you do not know how fond she will be of me! I protest that I shall be so kind to her, it will be difficult for people to decide which I love best, the daughter or the mother."

"But I hope *I* shall always know, sir Patrick," said Mrs. Mowbray gravely.

"You!—O yes, to be sure. But I mean that my fatherly attentions shall be of the warmest kind. But now do me the favour of telling me at what hour to-morrow I may appoint the clergyman to bring the license?"

The conversation that followed, it were needless and tedious to describe. Suffice, that eight o'clock the next morning was fixed for the marriage; and Mrs. Mowbray, either from shame or compassion, resolved that Adeline should not accompany her to church, nor even know of the ceremony till it was over.

Nor was this a difficult matter. Adeline remained in her own apartment all the preceding day, endeavouring, but in vain, to reconcile herself to what she justly termed the degradation of her mother. She felt, alas! the most painful of all feelings, next to that of self-abasement,—the consciousness of the abasement of one to whom she had all her life looked up with love and veneration. To write to Glenmurray while oppressed by such contending emotions she knew to be impossible; she therefore contented herself with sending a verbal message, importing that he should hear from her the next day: and poor Glenmurray passed the rest of that day and the night in a state little better than her own.

The next morning Adeline, who had not closed her eyes till day-light, woke late, and from a sound but unrefreshing sleep. The first object she saw was her maid, smartly dressed, sitting by her bedside; and she also saw that she had been crying.

"Is my mother ill, Evans?" she exclaimed.

"O! no, miss Adeline, quite well," replied the girl, sighing.

"Thank God!" replied Adeline. The girl sighed still more deeply. "But why are you so much dressed?" demanded Adeline.

"I have been out," answered the maid.

"Not on unpleasant business?"

"That's as it may be," she cried, turning away; and Adeline, from delicacy, forbore to press her further.

"'Tis very late—is it not?" asked Adeline, "and time for me to rise?"

"Yes, miss—I believe you had better get up."

Adeline immediately rose.— "Give me the dark gown I wore yesterday," said she.

"I think, miss, you had better put on your new white one," returned the maid.

"My new white one!" exclaimed Adeline, astonished at an interference so new.

"Yes, miss—I think it will be taken kinder, and look better."

"At these words Adeline's suspicions were awakened. "I see, Evans," she cried, "you have something extraordinary to tell me:— I partly guess; I,— my mother—" Here, unable to proceed, she lay down on the bed which she had just quitted.

"Yes, miss Adeline— 'tis very true; but pray compose yourself. I am sure I have cried enough on your account, that I have."

"What is true, my good Evans?" said Adeline faintly.

"Why, miss, my lady was married this morning to sir Patrick O'Carrol!— Mercy on me, how pale you look! I am sure I wish the villain was at the bottom of the sea, so I do."

"Leave me," said Adeline faintly, struggling for utterance.

"No—that I will not," bluntly replied Evans; "you are not fit to be left; and they are rejoicing below with sir Pat's great staring servant. But, for my part, I had rather stay here and cry with you than laugh with them."

Adeline hid her face in the pillow, incapable of further resistance, and groaned aloud.

"Who should ever have thought my lady would have done

so!" continued the maid.— "Only think, miss! they say, and I
doubt it is too true, that there have been no writings, or
settlements, I think they call them, drawn up; and so sir Pat
have got all, and he is over head and ears in debt, and my lady is
to pay him out on't!"[51]

At this account, which Adeline feared was a just one, as she
had seen no preparations for a wedding going on, and had observed
no signs of deeds, or any thing of the kind, she started up in an
agony of grief— "Then has my mother given me up, indeed!"
she exclaimed, clasping her hands together, "and the once darling
child may soon be a friend-less outcast!"

"You? want a friend, miss Adeline!" said the kind girl,
bursting into tears. — "Never, while I live or any of my fellow-
servants." And Adeline, whose heart was bursting with a sense
of forlornness and abandonment, felt consoled by the artless
sympathy of her attendant; and, giving way to a violent flood of
tears, she threw her arms round her neck, and sobbed upon her
bosom.

Having thus eased her feelings, she recollected that it was
incumbent on her to exert her fortitude; and that it was a duty
which she owed her mother not to condemn her conduct openly
herself, nor suffer any one else to do it in her presence: still, at
that moment, she could not find in her heart to reprove the
observations by which, in spite of her sense of propriety, she had
been soothed and gratified; but she hastened to dress herself as
became a bridal dinner, and dismissed, as soon as she could, the
affectionate Evans from her presence. She then walked up and
down her chamber, in order to summon courage to enter the
drawing-room.— "But how strange, how cruel it was," said she,
"that my mother did not come to inform me of this important

---

[51] Without a special prenuptial agreement or settlement, on her marriage Mrs.
Mowbray herself and all her wealth become the property of Sir Patrick. Mrs.
Mowbray has behaved foolishly here, making no arrangements for herself or her
daughter either during Sir Patrick's life or after his death when the property will
descend only to his heirs.

event herself!"

In this respect, however, Mrs. Mowbray had acted kindly. Reluctant, even more than she was willing to confess to her own heart, to meet Adeline alone, she had chosen to conclude that she was still asleep, and desired she might not be disturbed; but soon after her return from church, being assured that she was in a sound slumber, she had stolen to her bed-side and put a note under her pillow, acquainting her with what had passed: but this note Adeline in her restlessness had, with her pillow, pushed on the floor, and there unseen it had remained. But, as Adeline was pacing to and fro, she luckily observed it; and, by proving that her mother had not been so very neglectful of her; it tended to fortify her mind against the succeeding interview. The note began:—

> "My *dearest* child! to spare you, in your present weak state, the emotion which you would necessarily feel in attending me to the altar, I have resolved to let the ceremony be performed unknown to you. But, my beloved Adeline, I trust that your affection for me will make you rejoice in a step which you may, perhaps, at present disapprove, when convinced that it was absolutely necessary to my happiness, and can, in no way, be the means of diminishing yours.
> "I remain
> "Your ever affectionate mother."

"She loves me still then!" cried Adeline, shedding her tears of tenderness, "and I accused her unjustly.—O my dear mother, if this event should indeed increase your happiness, never shall I repine at not having been able to prevent it." And then, after taking two or three hasty turns round the room, and bathing her eyes to remove in a degree the traces of her tears, she ventured into the drawing-room.

But the sight of her mother seated by sir Patrick, his arm encircling her waist, in that very room which had so lately witnessed his profligate attempts on herself, deprived her of the little resolution which she had been able to assume, and pale and trembling she sunk speechless with emotion on the first chair near her.

Mrs. Mowbray, or, as we must at present[52] call her, lady O'Carrol, was affected by Adeline's distress, and, hastening to her, received the almost fainting girl in her arms; while even sir Patrick, feeling compassion for the unhappiness which he could more readily understand than his bride, was eager to hide his confusion by calling for water, drops, and servants.

"I want neither medicine nor assistance now," said Adeline, gently raising her head from her mother's shoulder: "the first shock is over, and I shall, I trust, behave in future with proper self-command."

"Better late than never," muttered lady O'Carrol, on whom the word *shock* had not made a pleasant impression; while sir Patrick, approaching Adeline, exclaimed, "If you have not self-command, miss Mowbray, it is the only command which you cannot boast; for your power of commanding others no one can dispute, who has ever had the happiness of beholding you."

"So saying, he took her hand; and, as her mother's husband, claimed the privilege of saluting her,[53] — a privilege which Adeline, though she almost shrunk with horror from his touch, had *self-command* enough not to deny him: immediately after he claimed the same favor from his bride; and they resumed their position on the sopha.

But so embarrassing was the situation of all parties that no conversation took place; and Adeline, unable any longer to endure the restraint to which she was obliged, rose, to return to her own room, in order to hide the sorrow which she was on the point of betraying, when her mother in a tone of reproach exclaimed, "It grieves me to the soul, miss Mowbray, to perceive that you appear to consider as a day of mourning the day which I consider as the

---

[52] I.e., now.
[53] I.e., kissing her.

happiest of my life."

"Oh! my dearest mother!" replied Adeline, returning and approaching her, "it is the dread of your deceiving yourself, only, that makes me sad at a time like this: if this day in its consequences prove a happy one—"

"And wherefore should you doubt that it will, miss Mowbray?"

"Miss Mowbray, do you doubt my honour?" cried sir Patrick hastily.

Adeline instantly fixed her fine eyes on his face with a look which he knew how to *interpret*, but not how to support; and he cast his to the ground with painful consciousness.

She saw her triumph, and it gave her courage to proceed: — "O sir!" she cried, "it is in your power to convert all my painful doubts into joyful certainties; make but my mother happy, and I will love and bless you ever. —Promise me, sir," she continued, her enthusiasm and affection kindling as she spoke, "promise me to be kind and indulgent to her;— she has never known contradiction; she has been through life the darling object of all who surrounded her; the pride of her parents, her husband, and her child: neglect, injury, and unkindness she would inevitably sink under: and I conjure you (here she dropped on her knees and extended her arms in an attitude of entreaty), by all your hopes of happiness hereafter, to give her reason to continue to name this the happiest day of her life."

Here she ceased, overcome by the violence of her emotions; but continued her look and attitude of entreaty, full of such sweet earnestness, that the baronet could hardly conceal the variety of feelings which assailed him; amongst which, passion for the lovely object before him predominated. To make a jest of Adeline's seriousness he conceived to be the best way to conceal what he felt; and while Mrs. Mowbray, overcome with Adeline's expressions of tenderness, was giving way to them by a flood of tears, and grasping in both hers the clasped hands of Adeline, he cried, in an ironical tone,— "You are the most extraordinary motherly young creature that I ever saw in my life, my dear girl!

Instead of your mother giving the nuptial benediction to you, the order of nature is reversed, and you are giving it to her. Upon my soul I begin to think, seeing you in that posture, that you are my bride begging a blessing of mamma on our union, and that I ought to be on my knees too."

So saying, he knelt beside Adeline at lady O'Carrol's feet, and in a tone of mock solemnity besought her to bless both her affectionate children: and as he did this, he threw his arm round the weeping girl, and pressed her to his bosom. This speech, and this action, at once banished all self-command from the indignant Adeline, and in an instant she sprung from his embrace; and forgetting how much her violence must surprise, if not alarm and offend, her mother, she rushed out of the room, and did not stop till she reached her own chamber.

When there, she was alarmed lest her conduct should have occasioned both pain and resentment to lady O'Carrol; and it was with trembling reluctance that she obeyed the summons to dinner; but her fears were groundless. The bride had fallen into one of her reveries during sir Patrick's strange speech, from which she awakened only at the last words of it, viz. "affectionate children:" and seeing sir Patrick at her feet, with a very tender expression on his face, and hearing the words "affectionate children," she conceived that he was expressing his hopes of their being blest with progeny, and that a selfish feeling of fear at such a prospect had hurried Adeline out of the room. She was therefore disposed to regard her daughter with pity, but not with resentment, when she entered the dinner-room, and Adeline's tranquillity in a degree returned: but when she retired for the night she could not help owning to herself, that that day, her mother's wedding-day, had been the most painful day of her existence— and she literally sobbed herself to sleep.

The next morning a new trial awaited her; she had to write a final farewell to Glenmurray. Many letters did she begin, many did she finish, and many did she tear; but recollecting that the longer she delayed sending him one, the longer she kept him in a state of agitating suspense, she resolved to send the last written, even though it appeared to her not quite so strong a transcript of her feelings as the former ones. Whether it were to or not, Glenmurray received it with alternate agony and transport;— with agony, because it destroyed every hope of Adeline's being his,— and with transport, because every line breathed the purest and yet most ardent attachment, and convinced him that, however long their separation, the love of Adeline would experience no change.

Many days elapsed before Glenmurray could bear any companion but the letter of Adeline; and during that time she was on the road with the bride and bridegroom to a beautiful seat in Berkshire, called the Pavilion, hired by sir Patrick, the week before his marriage, of one of his profligate friends. As the road lay through a very fine country, Adeline would have thought the journey a pleasant one, had not the idea of Glenmurray ill and dejected continually haunted her. Sir Patrick appeared to be engrossed by his bride, and she was really wholly wrapt up in him; and at times the beauties of the scenery around had power to engage Adeline's attention: but she immediately recollected how much Glenmurray would have participated in her delight, and the contemplation of the prospect ended in renewed recollections of him.

Chapter IX.

At length they arrived at the place of their destination; and sir Patrick, warmly embracing his bride, bade her welcome to her new abode; and immediately approaching Adeline, he bestowed on her an embrace no less cordial:— or, to say the truth, so ardent seemed the welcome, even to the innocent Adeline, that she vainly endeavored to persuade herself that, as her father-in-law, sir Patrick's tenderness was excusable.

Spite of her efforts to be cheerful she was angry and suspicious, and had an indistinct feeling of remote danger; which though she could not define even to herself, it was new and painful to her to experience. But as the elastic mind of eighteen soon rebounds from the pressure of sorrow, and forgets in present enjoyment the prospect of evil, Adeline gazed on the elegant apartment she was in with joyful surprise; while, through folding doors on either side of it, she beheld a suite of rooms, all furnished with a degree of tasteful simplicity such as she had never before beheld: and through the windows, which opened on a lawn that sloped to the banks of a rapid river, she saw an amphitheatre of wooded hills, which proved that, how great soever had been the efforts of art to decorate their new habitation, the hand of Nature had done still more to embellish it; and all fear of sir Patrick was lost in gratitude for his having chosen such a retirement.

With eager curiosity Adeline hurried from room to room; admired in the western apartments the fine effect of the declining sun shining through rose-coloured window-curtains; gazed with delight on the statues and pictures that every where met the eye, and reposed with unsuspecting gaiety on the couches of eider down which were in profusion around. Every thing in the house spoke it to be the temple of Pleasure: but the innocent Adeline and her unobservant mother saw nothing but elegant convenience in an abode on which the disciples of Epicurus[54] might have delighted; and while aeolian harps[55] in the windows, and perfumes of all kinds, added to the enchantment of the scene, the bride only beheld in the choice of the villa a proof of her husband's desire of making her happy; and Adeline sighed for virtuous love and Glenmurray, as all that was wanting to complete her fascination.

Sir Patrick, meanwhile, was not blind to the impressions made on Adeline by the beauty of the spot which he had chosen, though he was far from suspecting the companion she had pictured to herself as most fitted to enjoy and embellish it; and pleased because she was pleased, and delighted to be regarded

---

[54] Greek philosopher who associated the good with pleasure. Here it indicates a devotion to material and sensual pleasures, particularly sexual ones.

[55] Literally "wind harps," a device that responds to breezes by making musical sounds, particularly important in Romantic poetry as an emblem for poetic inspiration, but here associated more with a kind of "Oriental" luxury and sensuality.

by her with such unusual looks of complacency, he gave himself up to his natural vivacity; and Adeline passed a merry, if not happy, evening with the bride and bridegroom.

But the next morning she arose with the painful conviction as fresh as ever on her mind, that day would succeed to day, and yet she should not behold Glenmurray; and that day would succeed to day, and still should she see O'Carrol, still be exposed to his noisy mirth, to his odious familiarities, which, though she taught herself to believe they proceeded merely from the customs of his country, and the nearness of their relationship, it was to her most painful to endure.

Her only resource, therefore, from unpleasant thoughts was reading; and she eagerly opened the cases of books in the library, which were unlocked. But, on taking down some of the books, she was disappointed to find none of the kind to which she had been accustomed. Mrs. Mowbray's peculiar taste had led her, as we have before observed, to the perusal of nothing but political tracts, systems of philosophy, and Scuderi's and other romances. Scarcely had the works of our best poets found their way to her library; and novels, plays, and works of a lighter kind she was never in the habit of reading herself, and consequently had not put in the hands of her daughter. Adeline had, therefore, read Rousseau's *Contrat Social,* but not his *Julie*; Montesquieu's *Esprit des Loix,* but not his *Lettres Persannes*; and had glowed with republican ardour over the scenes of Voltaire's *Brutus,* but had never had her pure mind polluted by the pages of his *Candide.*[56]

---

[56] Opie is setting up a complex evaluation of literary works and women's self-education by reading: on the one hand, Adeline has been protected from the dangers of light or modern French literature, while on the other hand she has been educated oddly and unrealistically by reading in old-fashioned literature combined with modern philosophy, both of which idealize human behavior and society. Adeline has read sixteenth- and seventeenth-century French Romances (Madeleine de Scudéry), and works of philosophy (Jean-Jacques Rousseau's *Social Contract*, Montesquieu's *Spirit of the Laws*), and the tragedies of Voltaire. She has not read the novels of French *philosophes* like Voltaire (*Candide*) and Rousseau (*Julie or the New Heloise*), nor Montesquieu's *Persian Letters*. In comparison Sir Patrick uses the

Different had been the circumstances, and consequently the practice, of the owner of sir Patrick's new abode. Of all Rousseau's works, he had in his library only the *New Heloise* and his *Confessions*; of Montesquieu, none but the glowing letters above mentioned; and while Voltaire's chaste and moral tragedies were excluded, his profligate tales attracted the eye by the peculiar elegance of their binding; while dangerous French novels of all descriptions met the view under the downy pillows of the inviting sofas around,[57] calculated to inflame the fancy and corrupt the morals.

But Adeline, unprepared by any reading of the kind to receive and relish the poison contained in them, turned with disgust from pages so uncongenial to her feelings; nor did her eye dwell delighted on any of those stores which the shelves contained, till she opened the *Nouvelle Heloise*; and as soon as she had read a few letters in that enchanting work, she seated herself in the apartment but the moment before become disgusting to her; and in a short time she forgot even Glenmurray himself, —or rather, she gave his form to the eloquent lover of Julie.[58] But, unfortunately, the bride came in while her daughter was thus pleasantly engaged; and on being informed what her studies were, she peremptorily forbad her to read a book so pregnant with mischief; and though she had not read it, and consequently could not appreciate its character, she was sure, on the words of

more passionate fictional writings of French philosophers to rouse the passions of his lady friends, but does not provide the more corrective or intellectual works of political philosophy. Adeline's reading has heightened her ideals and expectations of noble behavior, while the reading provided by Sir Patrick emphasizes raising only the passions. See textbox on "Sensibility and Novel Reading" in *Emma Courtney*, this volume, p. 71.

[57] Sofas or sophas are associated with "Oriental" luxury and licentiousness in eighteenth- and early nineteenth-century novels. In *Emma Courtney*, the sofa is where Emma finds her husband with his arm around her servant, and erotic novels frequently feature sofas in the period. John Cleland's *Memoirs of a Woman of Pleasure* (1749) and Crébillon's *Le Sopha* (1742) both feature erotic adventures situated on sofas.

[58] I.e., St. Preux, Rousseu's idealized hero in *Julie, or the New Heloïse*. See textbox on "Sensibility and Novel Reading" in *Emma Courtney*, this volume, p. 71.

others, that such reading was improper for her daughter.

In vain did Adeline venture to say that *Julie*, like the works of Glenmurray, might be, perhaps, condemned by those who had never read a line of it. The book was prohibited; and Adeline, with a reluctant hand, restored it to its place.

Had she read it, the sacrifice which the guilty but penitent Julia makes to filial affection, and the respectable light in which the institution of marriage is held up to view, would have strengthened, no doubt, Adeline's resolution to obey her mother, and give up Glenmurray; and have led her to reconsider those opinions which taught her to think contemptible what ages and nations had been content to venerate. But it was decreed that everything the mother of Adeline did should accelerate the fate of her devoted daughter.

Disappointed in her hopes of finding amusement in reading, Adeline had recourse to walking; and none of the beautiful scenes around remained long unexplored by her. In the rambles she but too frequently saw scenes of poverty and distress, which ill contrasted with the beauty of the house which she inhabited; scenes, which even a small portion of the money expended there in useless decoration would have entirely alleviated: and they were scenes, too, which Adeline had been accustomed to relieve. The extreme of poverty in the cottage did not disgrace, on the Mowbray estate, the well-furnished mansion-house; but Adeline, as we have observed before, was allowed to draw on her mother for money sufficient to prevent dustrious[59] labour from knowing the distresses of want.

"And why should I not draw on her here for money for the same purposes?" cried Adeline to herself, as she beheld one spectacle of peculiar hardships.— "Surely my mother is not dependent on her husband? and even if she were, sir Patrick has not a hard heart, and will not refuse my prayer: and therefore, promising the sufferers instant relief, she left them, saying she

---

[59] The 1834 American edition changes this to the more modern, presumably synonymous "industrious."

should soon reach the Pavilion and be back again; while the objects of her bounty were silent with surprise at hearing that their relief was to come from the Pavilion, a place hitherto closed to the solicitations of poverty, though ever open to the revels and the votaries of pleasure.

Adeline found her mother alone; and with a beating heart and a flushed cheek, she described the scene which she had witnessed, and begged to be restored to her old office of almoner on such occasions.

"A sad scene, indeed, my dear Adeline!" replied the bride in evident embarrassment, "and I will speak to sir Patrick about it."

"Speak to sir Patrick, madam! cannot you follow the impulse of humanity without consulting him?"

"I can't give the relief you ask without his assistance," replied her mother, "for, except a guinea or so, I have no loose cash about me for my own uses.— Sir Patrick's benevolence has long ago emptied his purse, and I gladly surrendered mine to him."

"And shall you in future have no money for the purposes of charity but that you must claim from sir Patrick?" asked Adeline mournfully.

"O dear! yes,—I have a very handsome allowance settled on me; but then at present he wants it himself (Adeline involuntarily clasped her hands together in an agony, and sighed deeply). But, however, child," added the bride, "as you seem to make such a point of it, take this guinea to the cottage you mention, *en attendant!*"[60]

Adeline took the guinea: but it was very insufficient to pay for medical attendance, to discharge the rent due to a clamorous landlord, and to purchase several things necessary for the relief of the poor sufferers: therefore she added another guinea to it, and, not liking to relate her disappointment, sent the money to them, desiring the servant to say that she would see them the next morning, when she resolved to apply to sir Patrick for the relief which her mother could not give; feeling at the same time

---

[60] In expectation of more later, literally "in waiting."

the mournful conviction, that she herself, as well as her mother, would be in future dependent on his bounty.

Though disposed to give way to mournful reflections on her own account, Adeline roused herself from the melancholy abstraction into which she was falling, by reflecting that she had still to plead the cause of the poor cottagers with sir Patrick; and hearing he was in the house, she hastened to prefer her petition.

Sir Patrick listened to her tone of voice, and gazed on her expressive countenance with delight: but when she had concluded her narration a solitary half-guinea was all he bestowed on her, saying, "I am never roused to charity by the descriptions of others; I must always see the distress which I am solicited to relieve."

"Then go with me to the cottage," exclaimed Adeline; but to her great mortification he only smiled, bowed, and disappeared: and when he returned to supper, Adeline could scarcely prevail on herself to look at him without displeasure, and could not endure the unfeeling vivacity of his manner.

Mortified and unhappy she next morning went to the cottage, reluctant to impart to its expecting inhabitants the ill success which she had experienced. But what was her surprise when they came out joyfully to meet her, and told her that a gentleman had been there that morning very early, had discharged their debts, and given them a sum of money for their future wants!

"His name, his name?" eagerly inquired Adeline: but that they said he refused to give; and as he was in a horseman's large coat, and held a handkerchief to his face, they were sure they should not know him again.

A pleasing suspicion immediately came across Adeline's mind that this benevolent unknown might be Glenmurray; and the idea that he was perhaps unseen hovering round her, gave her one of the most exquisite feelings which she had ever known. But this agreeable delusion was soon dissipated by one of the children's giving her a card which the kind stranger had dropped from his pocket; and this card had on it "Sir Patrick O'Carrol."

At first it was natural for her to be hurt and disappointed at finding that her hopes concerning Glenmurray had no foundation in truth; but her benevolence, and indeed regard for her mother's happiness as well as her own, led her to rejoice in this unexpected proof of excellence in sir Patrick.—He had evidently proved that he loved to do good by stealth, and had withdrawn himself even from her thanks.

In a moment, therefore, she banished from her mind every trace of his unworthiness. She had done him injustice, and she sought refuge from the remorse which this consciousness inflicted on her, by going into the opposite extreme. From that hour, indeed, her complaisance to his opinions, and her attentions to him, were so unremitting and evident, that sir Patrick's passion became stronger than ever, and his hopes of a return to it seemed to be built on a very strong foundation.

Adeline had given all her former suspicions to the wind: daily instances of his benevolence came to her knowledge, and threw such a charm over all he said and did, that even the familiarity in his conduct, look, and manner towards her, appeared to her now nothing more than the result of the free manners of his countrymen;—and she sometimes could not help wishing sir Patrick to be known to, and intimate with, Glenmurray. But the moment was now at hand that was to unveil the real character of sir Patrick, and determine the destiny of Adeline.

One day sir Patrick proposed taking his bride to see a beautiful *ferme ornée*[61] at about twelve miles' distance; and if it answered the expectations which he had formed of it, they were determined to spend two or three days in the neighborhood to enjoy the beauty of the grounds;— in that case he was to return in the evening to the Pavilion, and drive Adeline over the next morning to partake in their pleasure.

To this scheme both the ladies gladly consented, as it was impossible for them to suspect the villainous design which it was intended to aid.

---

[61] Literally an "ornamental farm," usually an exercise in both useful and beautiful landscaping.

The truth was, that sir Patrick, having, as he fondly imagined, gained Adeline's affections, resolved to defer no longer the profligate attempt which he had long mediated; and had contrived this excursion in order to insure his wife's absence from home, and a tête-à-tête with her daughter, —not doubting but that opportunity was alone wanting to enable him to succeed in his abandoned wishes.

At an early hour the curricle was at the door, and sir Patrick, having handed his lady in, took leave of Adeline. He told her that he should probably return early in the evening, pressed her hand more tenderly than usual, and, springing into the carriage, drove off with a countenance animated with expected triumph.

Adeline immediately set out on a long walk to the adjoining villages, visited the cottages near the Pavilion, and, having dined at an early hour, determined to pass the rest of the day in reading, provided it was possible for her to find any book in the house proper for her perusal.

With this intention she repaired to an apartment called the library, but what in these times would be denominated a *boudoir*;[62] and this, even in Paris, would have been admired for its voluptuous elegance.—On the table lay several costly volumes, which seemed to have been very lately perused by sir Patrick, as some of them were open, some turned down at particular passages: but as soon as she glanced her eye over their contents, Adeline indignantly threw them down again; and, while her cheek glowed with a blush of offended modesty she threw herself on a sofa, and fell into a long and mournful reverie on the misery which awaited her mother, in consequence of her having madly dared to unite herself for life to a young libertine, who could delight in no other reading but what was offensive to good morals and to delicacy. Nor could she dwell upon this subject without recurring to her former fears for herself; and so lost was she in agonising

---

[62] Literally a "place to pout in," usually "a woman's small private room," often understood as a bedroom where, in the French style, ladies might receive intimate visitors (OED).

reflections, that it was some time before she recollected herself sufficiently to remember that she was guilty of an indecorum, in staying so long in an apartment which contained books that she ought not even to be suspected of having had an opportunity to peruse.

Having once entertained this consciousness, Adeline hastily arose, and had just reached the door when sir Patrick himself appeared at it. She started back in terror when she beheld him, on observing in his countenance and manner evident marks not only of determined profligacy, but of intoxication. Her suspicions were indeed just. Bold as he was in iniquity, he dared not in a cool and sober moment put his guilty purpose in execution; and he shrunk with temporary horror from an attempt on the honour of the daughter of his wife, though he believed that she would be a willing victim. He had therefore stopped on the road to fortify his courage with wine; and, luckily for Adeline, he had taken more than he was aware of; for when, after a vehement declaration of the ardour of his passion, and protestations that she should that moment be his, he dared irreverently to approach her, Adeline, strong in innocence, aware of his intention, and presuming on his situation, disengaged herself from his grasp with ease; and pushing him with violence from her, he fell with such force against the brass edge of one of the sofas, that, stunned and wounded by the fall, he lay bleeding on the ground. Adeline involuntarily was hastening to his assistance: but recollecting how mischievous to her such an exertion of humanity might be, she contented herself with ringing the bell violently to call the servants to his aid. Then, in almost frantic haste, she rushed out of the house, ran across the park, and when she recovered her emotion she found herself, she scarcely knew how, sitting on a turf seat by the road side.

"Great God! what will become of me!" she wildly exclaimed: "my mother's roof is no longer a protection to me;—I cannot absent myself from it without alleging a reason for my conduct, which will ruin her peace of mind for ever. Wretch that I am! whither can I go, and where can I seek for refuge?"

At this moment, as she looked around in wild dismay, and raised her streaming eyes to heaven, she saw a man's face peeping from between the branches of a tree opposite to her, and observed that he was gazing on her intently. Alarmed and fluttered, she instantly started from her seat, and was hastening away, when the man suddenly dropped from his hiding-place, and, running after her, called her by her name, and conjured her to stop; while, with an emotion of surprise and delight, she recognised in him Arthur, the servant of Glenmurray!

Instantly, scarcely knowing what she did, she pressed the astonished Arthur's rough hand in hers; and by this action confused and confounded the poor fellow so much, that the speech which he was going to make faltered on his tongue.

"Oh! where is your master?" eagerly inquired Adeline.

"My master have sent you this, miss," replied Arthur, holding out a letter, which Adeline joyfully received; and, spite of her intended obedience to her mother's will, Glenmurray himself could not have met with a less favourable reception, for the moment was a most propitious one to his love: nor, as it happened, was Glenmurray too far off to profit by it. On his way from Bath he went a few miles out of his road, in order, as he said, and perhaps as he thought, to pay a visit to an old servant of his mother's, who was married to a respectable farmer; but, fortunately, the farm commanded a view of the Pavilion, and Glenmurray could from his window gaze on the house that contained the woman of his affections.

But to return to Adeline, who, while hastily tearing open the letter, asked Arthur where his master was, and heard with indescribable emotion that he was in the neighbourhood.

"Here! so providentially!" she exclaimed, and proceeded to read the letter; but her emotion forbade her to read it entirely. She only saw that it contained bank-notes; that Glenmurray was going abroad for his health; and, in case he should die there, had sent her the money which he had meant to leave her in his will,—lest she should be, in the mean while, any way dependent on sir Patrick.

Numberless conflicting emotions took possession of Adeline's heart while this new proof of her lover's attentive tenderness met her view; and, as she contrasted his generous and delicate attachment with the licentious passion of her mother's libertine husband, a burst of uncontrollable affection for Glenmurray agitated her bosom; and, rendered superstitious by her fears, she looked on him as sent by Providence to save her from the dangers of her home.

"This is the second time," cried she, "that Glenmurray, as my guardian angel, has appeared at the moment when I was exposed to danger from the same guilty quarter! Ah! surely there is more than accident in this! and he is ordained to be my guide and my protector!"

When once a woman has associated with an amiable man the idea of protection, he can never again be indifferent to her; and when the protector happens to be the chosen object of her love, his power becomes fixed on a basis never to be shaken.

"It is enough," said Adeline in a faltering voice, pressing the letter to her lips, and bursting into tears of grateful tenderness as she spoke: "Lead me to your master directly."

"Bless my heart! will you see him then, miss?" cried Arthur.

"See him?" replied Adeline— "see the only friend I now can boast?—But let us be gone this moment, lest I should be seen and pursued."

Instantly, guided by Arthur, Adeline set off full speed for the farm-house, nor stopped till she found herself in the presence of Glenmurray!

"O! I am safe now!" exclaimed Adeline, throwing herself into his arms; while he was so overcome with surprise and joy that he could not speak the welcome which his heart gave her: and Adeline, happy to behold him again, was as silent as her lover. At length Glenmurray exclaimed: "Do we then meet again, Adeline!"

"Yes," replied she; "and we meet to part no more."

"Do not mock me," cried Glenmurray starting from his seat, and seizing her extended hand; "my feelings must not be trifled with."

"Nor am I a woman to trifle with them. Glenmurray, I come to you for safety and protection;—I come to seek shelter in your arms from misery and dishonour. You are ill, you are going into a foreign country: and from this moment look on me as your nurse, your companion;—your home shall be my home, your country my country!"[63]

Glenmurray, too much agitated, too happy to speak, could only press the agitated girl to his bosom, and fold his arms round her, as if to assure her of the protection which she claimed.

"But there is not a moment to be lost," cried Adeline: "I may be missed and pursued: let us be gone directly."

The first word was enough for Glenmurray: eager to secure the recovered treasure which he had thought forever lost, his orders were given, and executed by the faithful Arthur with the utmost dispatch; and even before Adeline had explained to him the cause of her resolution to elope with him they were on their road to Cornwall, meaning to embark at Falmouth for Lisbon.

But Arthur, who was going to marry, and leave Glenmurray's service, received orders to stay at the farm till he had learned how sir Patrick was; and having obtained the necessary information, he was to send it to Glenmurray at Falmouth. The next morning he saw sir Patrick himself driving full speed past the farm; and having written immediately to his master, Adeline had the satisfaction of knowing that she had not purchased her own safety by the sufferings or danger of her persecutor, and the consequent misery of her mother.

CHAPTER X.

BUT Glenmurray's heart needed no explanation of the cause of Adeline's elopement. She was with him—with him, as she said, for ever. True, she had talked of flying far from misery and

---

[63] Ruth, 1:16: "And Ruth said, Intreat me not to leave thee, or to return from following after thee; for where thou goest, I will go; and where thou lodgest, I will lodge: thy people shall be my people, and thy God my God."

dishonour; but he knew they could not reach her in his arms, — not even dishonour according to the ideas of society,— for he meant to make Adeline legally his as soon as they were safe from pursuit, and his illness was forgotten in the fond transport of the present moment.

Adeline's joy was of a much shorter duration. Recollections of a most painful nature were continually recurring. True it was that it was no longer possible for her to reside under the roof of her mother:—but was it necessary for her to elope with Glenmurray? the man whom she had solemnly promised her mother to renounce! Then, on the other side, she argued that the appearance of love for Glenmurray was an excuse sufficient to conceal from her deluded parent the real cause of her elopement.

"It was my sole alternative," said she mentally:— "my mother must either suppose me an unworthy child, or know sir Patrick to be an unworthy husband; and it will be easier for her to support the knowledge of the one than of the other: then, when she forgives me, as no doubt she will in time, I shall be happy: but that I could never be, while convinced that I had made her miserable by revealing to her the wickedness of sir Patrick."

While this was passing in her mind, her countenance was full of such anxious and mournful expression, that Glenmurray, unable to keep silence any longer, conjured her to tell him what so evidently weighed upon her spirits.

"The difficulty that oppressed me is past," she replied, wiping from her eyes the tears which the thought of having left her mother so unexpectedly, and for the first time, produced. "I have convinced myself, that to leave home and commit myself to your protection was the most proper and virtuous step that I could take: I have not obeyed the dictates of love, but of reason."

"I am very sorry to hear it," said Glenmurray mournfully.

"It seems to me so very rational to love you," returned Adeline tenderly, shocked at the sad expression of his countenance, "that what seem to be the dictates of reason may be those of love only."

To a reply like this, Glenmurray could only answer by those incoherent yet intelligible expressions of fondness to the object of them, which are so delightful to lovers themselves, and so uninteresting to other people: nay, so entirely was Glenmurray again engrossed by the sense of present happiness, that his curiosity was still suspended, and Adeline's story remained untold. But Adeline's pleasure was damped by painful recollections, and still more by her not being able to hide from herself the mournful consciousness that the ravages of sickness were but too visible in Glenmurray's face and figure, and that the flush of unexpected delight could but ill conceal the hollow paleness of his cheek, and the sunk appearance of his eyes.

Meanwhile the chaise rolled on,—post succeeded to post; and though night was far advanced, Adeline, fearful of being pursued, would not consent to stop, and they travelled till morning. But Glenmurray, feeling himself exhausted, prevailed on her, for his sake, to alight at a small inn on the road side near Marlborough.

There Adeline narrated the occurrences of the past day; but with difficulty could she prevail on herself to own to Glenmurray that she had been the object of such an outrage as she had experienced from sir Patrick.

A truly delicate woman feels degraded, not flattered, by being the object of libertine attempts; and, situated as Adeline and Glenmurray now were, to disclose the insult which had been offered to her was a still more difficult task: but to conceal it was impossible. She felt that, even to *him*, some justification of her precipitate and unsolicited flight was necessary; and nothing but sir Patrick's attempt could justify it. She therefore, blushing and hesitating, revealed the disgraceful secret: but such was its effect on the weak spirits and delicate health of Glenmurray, that the violent emotions which he underwent brought on a return of his most alarming symptoms; and in a few hours Adeline, bending over the sick bed of her lover, experienced for the first time that most dreadful of feelings, fear for the life of the object of her affection.

Two days, however, restored him to comparative safety, and they reached a small and obscure village within a short distance from Falmouth,[64] most conveniently situated. There they took up their abode, and resolved to remain till the wind should change, and enable them to sail for Lisbon.

In this retreat, situated in air as salubrious as that of the south of France, Glenmurray was soon restored to health, especially as happy love was now his, and brought back the health of which hopeless love had contributed to deprive him. The woman whom he loved was his companion and his nurse; and so dear had the quiet scene of their happiness become to them, that, forgetful there was still a danger of their being discovered, it was with considerable regret that they received a summons to embark, and saw themselves on their voyage to Portugal.

But before she left England Adeline wrote to her mother.

After a pleasant and short voyage, the lovers found themselves at Lisbon; and Glenmurray, pursuant to his resolution, immediately proposed to Adeline to unite himself to her by the indissoluble ties of marriage.

Nothing could exceed Adeline's surprise at this proposal: at first she could not believe that Glenmurray was in earnest; but seeing that he looked not only grave but anxious, and as if earnestly expecting an answer, she asked him whether he had convinced himself that what he had written against marriage was a tissue of mischievous absurdity.

Glenmurray, blushing, with the conceit of an author replied "that he still thought his arguments unanswerable."

"Then, if you still are convinced your theory is good, why let your practice be bad? It is incumbent on you to act up to the principles that you profess, in order to give them their proper weight in society—else you give the lie to your own declarations."

"But it is better for me to do that, than for you to be the sacrifice to my reputation."

[64] English coastal town in Cornwall from which boats would leave for points south.

"I," replied Adeline, "am entirely out of the question: you are to be governed by no other law but your desire to promote general utility, and are not to think at all of the interest of an individual."

"How can I do so, when that individual is dearer to me than all the world beside?" cried Glenmurray passionately.

"And if you but once recollect that you are dearer to me than all the world beside, you will cease to suppose that my happiness can be affected by the opinion entertained of my conduct by others." As Adeline said this, she twisted both her hands in her arms so affectionately, and looked up in his face with so satisfied and tender an expression, that Glenmurray could not bear to go on with a subject which evidently drew a cloud across her brow; and hours, days, weeks, and months passed rapidly over their heads before he had resolution to renew it.

Hours, days, weeks, and months spent in a manner most dear to the heart and most salutary to the mind of Adeline!— Her taste for books, which had hitherto been cultivated in a partial manner, and had led her to one range of study only, was now directed by Glenmurray to the perusal of general literature; and the historian, the biographer, the poet, and the novelist, obtained alternately her attention and her praises.

In her knowledge of the French and Italian languages, too, she was now considerably improved by the instructions of her lover; and while his occasional illnesses were alleviated by her ever watchful attentions, their attachment was cemented by one of the strongest of all ties—the consciousness of mutual benefit and assistance.

CHAPTER XI.

ONE evening, as they were sitting on a bench in one of the public walks, a gentleman approached them, whose appearance bespoke him to be an Englishman, though his sun-burnt complexion showed that he had been for years exposed to a more ardent climate than that of Britain.

As he came nearer, Glenmurray thought his features were

familiar to him; and the stranger, starting with joyful surprise, seized his hand, and welcomed him as an old friend. Glenmurray returned his salutation with great cordiality, and recognised in the stranger a Mr. Maynard, an amiable man, who had gone to seek his fortune in India, and was returned a nabob,[65] but with an irreproachable character.

"So, then," cried Mr. Maynard gaily, "this is the elegant young English couple that my servant, and even the inn-keeper himself, was so loud in praise of! Little did I think the happy man was my old friend,—though no man is more deserving of being happy: but I beg you will introduce me to your lady."

Glenmurray, though conscious of the mistake he was under, had not resolution enough to avow that he was not married; and Adeline, unaware of the difficulty of Glenmurray's situation, received Mr. Maynard's salutation with the utmost ease, though the tremor of her lover's voice, and the blush on his cheek as he said— "Adeline, give me leave to introduce to you Mr. Maynard, an old friend of mine,"—were sufficient indications that the rencontre disturbed him.

In a few minutes Adeline and Mr. Maynard were no longer strangers. Mr. Maynard, who had not lived much in the society of well-informed women, and not at all in that of women accustomed to original thinking, was at once astonished and delighted at the variety of Adeline's remarks, at the playfulness of her imagination, and the eloquence of her expressions. But it was very evident, at length, to Mr. Maynard, that in proportion as Adeline and he became more acquainted and more satisfied with each other, Glenmurray grew more silent and more uneasy. The consequence was unavoidable: as most men would have done on a like occasion, Mr. Maynard thought Glenmurray was jealous of him.

But no thought so vexatious to himself, and so degrading to Adeline, had entered the confiding and discriminating mind of

---

[65] A local, municipal ruler for the British government in India, usually presumed to have accumulated great wealth.

Glenmurray. The truth was, he knew that Mr. Maynard, whom he had seen in the walks, though he had not known him again, had ladies of his party; and he expected that the more Mr. Maynard admired his supposed wife, the more would he be eager to introduce her to his companions.

Nor was Glenmurray wrong in his conjectures.

"I have two sisters with me, madam," said Mr. Maynard, "whom I shall be happy and proud to introduce to you. One of them is a widow, and has lived several years in India, but returned with me in delicate health, and was ordered hither: she is not a woman of great reading, but has an excellent understanding, and will admire you. The other is several years younger; and I am sure she would be happy in an opportunity of profiting by the conversation of a lady, who, though not older than herself, seems to have had so many more opportunities of improvement."

Adeline bowed, and expressed her impatience to form this new acquaintance; and looked triumphantly at Glenmurray, meaning to express—'See, spite of the supposed prejudices of the world, here is a man who wants to introduce me to his sisters.' Little did she know that Maynard concluded she was a wife: his absence from England made him ignorant of the nature of Glenmurray's works, or even that he was an author; so that he was not at all likely to suppose that the moral, pious youth, whom he had always respected, was become a visionary philosopher, and, in defiance of the laws of society, was living openly with a mistress.

"But my sister will wonder what is become of me," suddenly cried Maynard; "and as Emily is so unwell as to keep her room to-day, I must not make her anxious. But for her illness, I should have requested your company to supper."

"And I should have liked to accept the invitation," replied Adeline; "but I will hope to see the ladies soon."

"Oh! Without fail, to-morrow," cried Maynard: "if Emily be not well enough to call on you, perhaps you will come to her apartments."

"Undoubtedly: expect me at twelve o'clock."

Maynard then shook his grave and silent friend by the hand and, departed,—his vanity not a little flattered by the supposed jealousy of Glenmurray.

"There now," said Adeline, when he was out of hearing, "I hope some of your tender fears are done away. You see there are liberal and unprejudiced persons in the world; and Mr. Maynard, instead of shunning me, courts my acquaintance for his sisters."

Glenmurray shook his head, and remained silent; and Adeline was distressed to feel by his burning hand that he was seriously uneasy.

"I shall certainly call on these ladies to-morrow," continued Adeline:— "I really pine for the society of amiable women."

Glenmurray sighed deeply: he dreaded to tell her that he could not allow her to call on them, and yet he knew that this painful task awaited him. Besides, she wished, she said, to know some amiable women; and, eager as he was to indulge all her wishes, he felt but too certainly that in this wish she could never be indulged. Even had he been capable of doing so dishonourable an action as introducing his mistress as his wife, he was sure that Adeline would have spurned at the deception; and silent and sad he grasped Adeline's hand as her arm rested within his, and, complaining of indisposition, slowly returned to the inn.

The next morning at breakfast, Adeline again expressed her eagerness to form an acquaintance with the sisters of Mr. Maynard; when Glenmurray, starting from his seat, paced the room in considerable agitation.

"What is the matter?" cried Adeline, hastily rising and laying her hand in his arm.

Glenmurray grasped her hand, and replied with assumed firmness: "Adeline, it is impossible for you to form an acquaintance with Mr. Maynard's sisters: propriety and honour both forbid me to allow it."

"Indeed!" exclaimed Adeline, "are they not as amiable, then, as he described them? are they improper acquaintances for me? Well then—I am disappointed: but you are the best judge of what is right, and I am contented to obey you."

The simple, ingenuous and acquiescent sweetness with which she said this, was a new pang to her lover:—had she repined, had she looked ill-humoured, his task would not have been so difficult.

"But what reason can you give for declining this acquaintance?" resumed Adeline.

"Aye! there's the difficulty," replied Glenmurray: "pure-minded and amiable as I know you to be, how can I bear to tell these children of prejudice that you are not my wife, but my mistress?"

Adeline started; and, turning pale, exclaimed, "Are you sure, then, that they do not know it already?"

"Quite sure—else Maynard would not have thought you a fit companion for his sisters."

"But surely he must know your principles; he must have read your works?"

"I am certain he is ignorant of both, and does not even know that I am an author."

"Is it possible?" cried Adeline: "is there any one so unfortunate as to be unacquainted with your writings?"

Glenmurray at another time would have been elated at a compliment like this from the woman whom he idolized; but at this moment he heard it with a feeling of pain which he would not have liked to define to himself, and casting his eyes to the ground he said nothing.

"So then," said Adeline mournfully, "I am an improper companion for *them*, not they for *me!*" and spite of herself her eyes filled with tears—— At this moment a waiter brought in a note for Glenmurray;—it was from Maynard, and as follows:

MY DEAR FRIEND,

Emily is better to-day; and both my sisters are so impatient to see, and know, your charming wife, that they beg me to present their compliments to Mrs. Glenmurray and you; and request the honour of your company to a late breakfast:—at eleven o'clock we hope

to see you,
> Ever yours,

> > > G.M.

"We will send an answer," said Glenmurray: but the waiter had been gone some minutes before either Adeline or Glenmurray spoke. At length Adeline, struggling with her feelings, observed, "Mr. Maynard seems so amiable a man, that I should think it would not be difficult to convince him of his errors: surely, therefore, it is your duty to call on him, state our real situation, and our reasons for it, and endeavor to convince him that our attachment is sanctioned both by reason and virtue."

"But not by the church," replied Glenmurray, "and Maynard is of the old school: besides, a man of forty-eight is not likely to be convinced by the arguments of a young man of twenty-eight, and the example of a girl of nineteen."

"If age be necessary to give weight to arguments," returned Adeline, "I wonder that you thought proper to publish four years ago."

"Would to God I never had published!" exclaimed Glenmurray, almost pettishly.

"If you had not, I probably should never have been yours," replied Adeline, fondly leaning her head on his shoulder, and then looking up in his face. Glenmurray clasped her to his bosom; but again the pleasure was mixed with pain. "All this time," rejoined Adeline, "your friends are expecting an answer: you had better carry it in person."

"I cannot," replied Glenmurray, "and there is only one way of getting out of this business to my satisfaction."

"Name it; and rest assured that I shall approve it."

"Then I wish to order horses immediately, and set off on our road to France."

"So soon,—though the air agrees with you so well?"

"O yes;—for when the mind is uneasy no air can be of use to the body."

"But why is your mind uneasy?"

"Here I should be exposed to see Maynard, and—and—he would see you too."

"And what then?"

"What then?—Why, I could not bear to see him look on you with an eye of disrespect."

"And wherefore should he?"

"O Adeline, the name of wife imposes restraint even on a libertine; but that of mistress—— "

"Is Mr. Maynard then a libertine?" said Adeline gravely: and Glenmurray, afraid of wounding her feelings by entering into a further explanation, changed the subject, and again requested her consent to leave Lisbon.

"I have often told you," said Adeline sighing, "that my will is yours; and if you will give strict orders to have letters sent after us to the towns that we shall stop at, I am ready to set off immediately."

Glenmurray then gave his orders; wrote a letter explaining his situation to Maynard, and in an hour they were on their journey to France.

CHAPTER XII.

IN the mean while Mr. Maynard, miss Maynard, and Mrs. Wallington his widowed sister, were impatiently expecting Glenmurray's answer, and earnestly hoping to see him and his lovely companion,—but from different motives. Maynard was impatient to see Adeline because he really admired her; his sisters, because they hoped to find her unworthy of such violent admiration.

Their vanity had been piqued, and their envy excited, by the extravagant praises of their brother; and they had interrupted him by the first questions which all women ask on such occasions,— "Is she pretty?"

And he had answered, "Very pretty."

"Is she tall?"

"Very tall, taller than I am."

"I hate tall women," replied miss Maynard (a little round

girl of nineteen).

"Is she fair?"

"Exquisitely fair."

"I like brown women," cried the widow: "fair people always look silly."

"But Mrs. Glenmurray's eyes are hazel, and her eye-lashes long and dark."

"Hazel eyes are always bold-looking," cried miss Maynard.

"Not Mrs. Glenmurray's; for her expression is the most pure and ingenuous that ever I saw. Some girls, indecent in their dress and very licentious in their manner, passed us as we sat on the walk; and the comments which I made on them provoked from Mrs. Glenmurray some remarks on the behavior and dress of women; and, as she commented on the disgusting expression of vice in women, and the charm of modest dignity both in dress and manners, her own dress, manners, and expression, were such an admirable comment on her words, and she shone so brightly, if I may use the expression, in the graceful awfulness of virtue, that I gazed with delight, and somewhat of apprehension lest this fair perfection should suddenly take flight to her native skies, toward which her fine eyes were occasionally turned."

"Bless me! if our brother is not quite poetical! This prodigy has inspired him," replied the widow with a sneer.

"For my part, I hate *prodigies*," said miss Maynard: "I feel myself unworthy to associate with them."

When one woman calls another a prodigy, and expresses herself as unworthy to associate with her, it is very certain that she means to insult rather than compliment her; and in this sense Mr. Maynard understood his sister's words: therefore, after having listened with tolerable patience to a few more sneers at the unconscious Adeline, he was provoked to say that, ill-disposed as he found they were towards his new acquaintance, he hoped that when they became acquainted with her they would still give him reason to say, as he always had done, that he was proud of his sisters; for, in his opinion, no woman ever looked so lovely as when she was doing justice to the merits and extenuating the faults of a rival.

"A rival!" exclaimed the sisters at once:— "And, pray, what rivalship could there be in this case?"

"My remark was a general one; but since you choose to make it a particular one, I will answer to it as such," continued Mr. Maynard. "All women are rivals in one sense—rivals for general esteem and admiration; and she only shall have my suffrage in her favour, who can point out a beauty or a merit in another woman without insinuating at the same time a counterbalancing defect."

"But Mrs. Glenmurray, it seems, has *no* defects!"

"At least I have not known her long enough to find them out; but you, no doubt, will, when you know her, very readily spare me that trouble."

How injudiciously had Maynard prepared the minds of his sisters to admire Adeline! It was a preparation to make them hate her; and they were very impatient to begin the task of depreciating both her *morale* and her *physique*, when Glenmurray's note arrived.

"It is not Glenmurray's hand," said Maynard (indeed, from agitation of mind the writing was not recognisable). "It must be hers then," continued he, affecting to kiss the address with rapture.

"It is the hand of a sloven," observed Mrs. Wallington, studying the writing.

"But in dress she is as neat as a quaker," retorted the brother, eagerly snatching the letter back, "and her mind seems as pure as her dress."

He then broke the seal, and read out what follows:

DEAR MAYNARD,

"When you receive this, Adeline and I shall be on our road to France, and you,—start not!—are the occasion of our abrupt departure."

"So, so, jealous indeed," said Maynard to himself, and more

impressed than ever with the charms of Adeline; for he concluded that Glenmurray had discovered in her an answering prepossession.

"You the occasion, brother!" cried both sisters.

"Have patience."

"You saw Adeline; you admired her; and wished to introduce her to your sisters—this, honour forbad me to allow"—(the sisters started from their seats) "for Adeline is not my wife, but my companion."

Here Maynard made a full pause—at once surprised and confounded. His sisters, pleased as well as astonished, looked triumphantly at each other; and Mrs. Wallington exclaimed, "So, then, this angel of purity turns out to be a kept lady!" At this remark miss Maynard laughed heartily; but Maynard, to hide his confusion, commanded silence, and went on with the letter:

"But, spite of her situation, strange as it may seem to you, believe me, no wife was ever more pure than Adeline."

At this passage the sisters could no longer contain themselves, and they gave way to loud bursts of laughter, which Maynard could hardly help joining in; but being angry at the same time he uttered nothing but an oath, which I shall not repeat, and retreated to his chamber to finish the letter alone.

During his absence the laughter redoubled;—but in the midst of it Maynard re-entered, and desired they would allow him to read the letter to the end. The sisters immediately begged that he would proceed, as it was so amusing that they wished to hear more.—Glenmurray continued thus:

"You have no doubt yet to learn that some few years ago I commenced author, and published opinions contrary to the established usage of society: amongst other things I proved the absurdity of the institution of marriage; and Adeline, who at an early age read my works, became one of my converts."

"The man is certainly mad," cried Maynard, "and how dreadful it is that this angelic creature should have been his victim."

"But perhaps this *fallen* angel, brother, for such you will allow she is, spite of her *purity*, was as wicked as he. I know people in general only blame the seducer, but I always blame the seduced equally."

"I do not doubt it," said her brother sneeringly, and going on with the letter.

"No wonder then, that, being forced to fly from her maternal roof, she took refuge in my arms."

"Lucky dog!"

"But though Adeline was the victim neither of her own weakness nor of my seductions, but was merely urged by circumstances to act up to the principles which she openly professed, I felt so conscious that she would be degraded in your eyes after you were acquainted with her situation, though in mine she appears as spotless as ever, that I could not bear to expose her even to a glance from you less respectful than those with which you beheld her last night. I therefore prevailed on her to leave Lisbon; nor had I any difficulty in so doing, when she found that your wish of introducing her to your sisters was founded on your supposition of her being my wife, and that all chance of your desiring her acquaintance for them would be over, when you knew the nature of her connection with me. I shall now bid you farewell. I write in haste and agitation, and have not time to say more than God bless you!

F.G."

"Yes, yes, I see how it is," muttered Mr. Maynard to himself when he had finished the letter, "he was jealous of me. I wish (raising his voice) that he had not been in such a confounded hurry to go away."

"Why, brother," replied Mrs. Wallington, "to be sure you would not have introduced us to this piece of angelic purity a little the worse for the wear!"

"No," replied he; "but I might have enjoyed her company myself."

"And perhaps, brother, you might have rivalled the philosophic author in time," observed miss Maynard.

"If I had not, it would have been from no want of good will on my part," returned Maynard.

"Well, then I rejoice that the creature is gone," replied Mrs. Wallington, drawing up.

"And I too," said miss Maynard disdainfully: "but I think we had better drop this subject; I have had quite enough of it."

"And so have I," cried Mrs. Wallington: "but I must observe, before we drop it entirely, that when next my brother comes home and wearies his sisters by exaggerated praises of another woman, I hope he will take care that his goddess, or rather his angel of purity, does not turn out to be a kept mistress."

So saying she left the room, and miss Maynard, tittering, followed her; while Maynard, too sore on this subject to bear to be laughed at, took his hat in a pet, and, flinging the door after him with great violence, walked out to muse on the erring but interesting companion of Glenmurray.

CHAPTER XIII.

WHILE these conversations were passing at Lisbon, Glenmurray and Adeline were pursuing their journey to France; and insensibly did the charm of being together obliterate from the minds of each the rencontre which had so much disturbed them.

But Adeline began to be uneasy on a subject of much greater importance; she every day expected an answer from her mother, but no answer arrived; and they had been stationary at Perpignan some days, to which place they had desired their letters to be addressed, *poste restante*,[66] and still none were forwarded thither from Lisbon.

The idea that her mother had utterly renounced her now took possession of her imagination, and love had no charm to offer her capable of affording her consolation: the care which she had taken of her infancy, the affectionate attentions that had preserved her life, and the uninterrupted kindness which she had shown towards her till her attachment to sir Patrick took place,—all these pressed powerfully and painfully on her memory, till her elopment seemed wholly unjustifiable in her eyes, and she reprobated her conduct in terms of the most bitter self-reproach.

At these moments even Glenmurray seemed to become the object of her aversion. Her mother had forbidden her to think of him; yet, to make her flight more agonizing to her injured parent, she had eloped with *him*. But as soon as ever she beheld him he regained his wonted influence over her heart, and her self-reproaches became less poignant: she became sensible that sir Patrick's guilt and her mother's imprudent marriage were the causes of her own fault, and not Glenmurray; and could she but receive a letter of pardon from England, she felt that her conscience would again be at peace.

But soon an idea of a still more harassing nature succeeded and overwhelmed her. Perhaps her desertion had injured her mother's health; perhaps she was too ill to write; perhaps she was dead:—and when this horrible supposition took possession of her mind she used to avoid even the presence of her lover; and as her spirits commonly sunk towards evening, when the still renewed expectations of the day had been deceived, she used to

[66] I.e., to be left until called for.

hasten to a neighbouring church when the bell called to vespers,[67] and, prostrate on the steps of the altar, lift up her soul to heaven in the silent breathings of penitence and prayer. Having thus relieved her heart she returned to Glenmurray, pensive but resigned.

One evening after she had unburthened her feelings in this manner, Glenmurray prevailed on her to walk with him to a public promenade; and being tired they sat down on a bench in a shady part of the mall. They had not sat long before a gentleman and two ladies seated themselves beside them.

Glenmurray instantly rose up to depart; but the gentleman also rose and exclaimed, "'Tis he indeed! Glenmurray, have you forgotten your old friend Willie Douglas?"

Glenmurray, pleased to see a friend whom he had once so highly valued, returned the salutation with marked cordiality; while the ladies with great kindness accosted Adeline, and begged she would allow them the honour of her acquaintance.

Taught by the rencontre at Lisbon, Adeline for a moment felt embarrassed; but there was something so truly benevolent in the countenance of both ladies, and she was so struck by the extreme beauty of the younger one, that she had not resolution to avoid, or even to receive their advances coldly; and while the gentlemen were commenting on each other's looks, and in an instant going over the occurrences of past years, the ladies, pleased with each other, had entered into conversation.

"But I expected to see you and your lady," said major Douglas; "for Maynard was writing to me from Lisbon when he laid by his pen and took the walk in which he met you; and on his return he filled up the rest of his letter with the praises of Mrs. Glenmurray, and expressions of envy at your happiness."

Glenmurray and Adeline both blushed deeply. "So!" said Adeline to herself, "here will be another letter to write when we got home;" for, though ingenuousness was one of her most striking qualities, she had not resolution enough to tell her new

[67] Evening services.

acquaintance that she was not married: besides, she flattered herself, that, could she once interest these charming women in her favour, they would not refuse her their society when they knew her real situation; for she thought them too amiable to be prejudiced, as she called it, and was not yet aware how much the perfection of the female character depends on respect even to what may be called the prejudices of others.

The day began to close in; but major Douglas, though Glenmurray was too uneasy to answer him except by monosyllables, would not hear of going home, and continued to talk with cheerfulness and interest of the scenes of his and Glenmurray's early youth. He too was ignorant of his friend's notoriety as an author: he had lived chiefly at his estates in the Highlands; nor would he have left them, but because he was advised to travel for his health; and the lovely creature whom he had married, as well as his only sister, was anxious on his account to put the advice in execution. He therefore made no allusions to Glenmurray's opinions that could give him an opportunity of explaining his real situation; and he saw with confusion, that every moment increased the intimacy of Adeline and the wife and sister of his friend.

At length his feelings operated so powerfully on his weak frame, that a sudden faintness seized him, and supported by Adeline and the major, and followed by his two kind companions, he returned to the inn: there, to get rid of the Douglases and avoid the inquiries of Adeline, who suspected the cause of his illness, he immediately retired to bed.

His friends also returned home, lamenting the apparently declining health of Glenmurray, and expatiating with delight on the winning graces of his supposed wife: for these ladies were of a different class of women to the sisters of Maynard.—Mrs. Douglas was so confessedly a beauty, so rich in acknowledged attractions, that she could afford to do justice to the attractions of another; and miss Douglas was so decidedly devoid of all pretensions to the lovely in person, that the idea of competition with the beautiful never entered her mind, and she was always eager to admire what she knew that she was incapable of rivalling. Unexposed, therefore, to feel those petty jealousies, those paltry competitions which injure the character of women in general, Emma Douglas's mind was the seat of benevolence and candour,—as was her beautiful sister's from a different cause; and they were both warmer even than the major in praise of Adeline.

But a second letter from Mr. Maynard awaited major Douglas at the inn, which put a fatal stop to their self-congratulations at having met Glenmurray and his companion.

Mr. Maynard, full of Glenmurray's letter, and still more deeply impressed than ever with the image of Adeline, could not forbear writing to the major on the subject; giving as a reason, that he wished to let him know the true state of affairs, in order that he might avoid Glenmurray.... The letter came too late.

"And I have seen him, have welcomed him as a friend, and he has had the impudence to introduce his harlot to my wife and sister!"

So spoke the major in the language of passion,—and passion is never accurate.—Glenmurray had *not* introduced Adeline; and this was gently hinted by the kind and candid Emma Douglas; while the younger and more inexperienced wife sat silent with consternation, at having pressed with the utmost kindness the hand of a kept mistress.

Vain were the representations of his sister to sooth the wounded pride of major Douglas. Without considering the difficulty of such a proceeding, he insisted upon it that Glenmurray should have led Adeline away instantly, as unworthy to breathe the same air with his wife and sister.

"You find by that letter, brother," said miss Douglas, "that this unhappy Adeline is still an object of respect in his eyes, and he could not wound her feelings so publicly, especially as she seems to be more ill-judging than vicious."

She spoke in vain.—The major was a soldier, and so delicate in his ideas of the honour of women, that he thought his wife and sister polluted from having, though unconsciously, associated with Adeline: being violently irritated therefore at the supposed insult offered him by Glenmurray, he left the room, and, having dispatched a challenge to him, told the ladies he had letters to write to England till bed-time arrived: then, after having settled his affairs in case he should fall in the conflict, he sat brooding alone over the insolence of his former friend.

There was a consciousness too which aggravated his resentment. Calumny had been busy with his reputation; and, though he deserved it not, had once branded him with the name of coward. Besides, his elder sister had been seduced by a man of very high rank, and was then living with him as his mistress. Made still more susceptible therefore of affront by this distressing consciousness, he suspected that Glenmurray, from being acquainted with these circumstances, had presumed on them, and dared to take a liberty with him, situated as he then was, which in former times he would not have ventured to offer.

As Adeline and Glenmurray were both retired for the night when the major's note arrived, it was not delivered till morning,— nor then, luckily, till Adeline, supposing Glenmurray asleep, was gone to take her usual walk to the post-office: Glenmurray, little aware of its contents, opened it, and read as follows:

> "SIR,
>
> "For your conduct in introducing your mistress to my wife and sister, I demand immediate satisfaction. As you may possibly not have recovered your indisposition of last night, and I wish to take no unfair advantages, I do not desire you to meet me till evening; but at six o'clock, a mile out of the north side of the town, I shall expect you.—I can lend you pistols if you have none."

"There is only one step to be taken," said Glenmurray mentally, starting up and dressing himself: and in a few moments he was at major Douglas's lodgings.

The major had just finished dressing, when Glenmurray was

announced. He started and turned pale at seeing him; then, dismissing his servant and taking up his hat and his pistols, he desired Glenmurray to walk out with him.

"With all my heart," replied Glenmurray. But, recollecting himself, "No no," said he: "I come hither now, merely to talk to you; and if, after what has passed, the ladies should see us go out together, they would be but too sure of what was going to happen, and might follow us."

"Well, then sir," cried the major, "we had better separate till evening."

"I shall not leave you, major Douglas," replied Glenmurray solemnly, "whatever harsh things you may say or do, till I have made you listen to me."

"How can I listen to you, when nothing you can say can be a justification of your conduct?"

"I do not mean to offer any.—I am only come to tell you my story, with that of my companion, and my resolutions in consequence of my situation; and I conjure you, by the recollections of our early days, of our past pleasures and fatigues, those days when fatigue itself was a pleasure, and I was not the weak emaciated being that I am now, unable to bear exertion, and overcome even to female weakness by agitation of mind such as I experienced last night——"

"For God's sake sit down," cried the major, glancing his eye over the faded form of Glenmurray.—Glenmurray sat down.

"I say, I conjure you by these recollections," he continued, "to hear me with candour and patience. Weakness will render me brief." Here he paused to wipe the damps from his forehead; and Douglas, in a voice of emotion, desired him to say whatever he chose, but to say directly.

"I will," replied Glenmurray; "for indeed there is one at home who will be alarmed at my absence."

The major frowned; and, biting his lip, said, "Proceed, Mr. Glenmurray," in his usual tone.

Glenmurray obeyed. He related his commencing author,— the nature of his works,—his acquaintance with Adeline,—its consequences,—her mother's marriage,—sir Patrick's villany,—Adeline's elopement, her refusal to marry him, and the grounds on which it was founded.

"And now," cried Glenmurray when his narration was ended, "hear my firm resolve. Let the consequences to my reputation be what they may, let your insults be what they may, I will not accept your challenge; I will not expose Adeline to the risk of being left without a protector in a foreign land, and probably without one in her own. I fear that, in the natural course of things, I shall not continue with her long; but, while I can watch over her and contribute to her happiness, no dread of shame, no fear for what others may think of me, no selfish consideration whatever shall induce me to hazard a life which belongs to her, and on which at present her happiness depends. I think, Douglas, you are incapable of treating me with indignity; but even to that I will patiently submit, rather than expose my life; while, consoled by my motive, I will triumphantly exclaim—'See, Adeline, what I can endure for thy sake!'"

Here he paused; and the major, interested and affected, had involuntarily put out his hand to him; but, drawing it back, he said, "Then I may be sure that you meant no affront to me by suffering my wife and sister to converse with miss Mowbray?"

Glenmurray having put an end to these suspicions entirely, by a candid avowal of his feelings, and of his wish to have escaped directly if possible, the major shook him affectionately by the hand, and told him that though he firmly believed too much learning had made him mad, yet, that he was as much his friend as ever. "But what vexes me is," said he, "that you should have turned the head of that sweet girl. The opinion of the world is every thing to a woman."

"Aye, it is indeed," replied Glenmurray; "and, spite of ridicule, I would marry Adeline directly, as I said before, to guaranty her against reproach.—I wish you would try to persuade her to be mine legally."

"That I will," eagerly replied the major; "I am sure I shall prevail with her. I am sure I shall soon convince her that the opinions she holds are nothing but nonsense."

"You will find," replied Glenmurray, blushing, "that her arguments are unanswerable notwithstanding."

"What, though taken from the cursed books you mentioned?"

"You forget that I wrote these books."

"So I did; and I wish she could forget it also: and then they would appear to her, as they must do no doubt to all people of common sense, and that is, abominable stuff."

Glenmurray bit his lips,—but the author did not long absorb the lover, and he urged the major to return with him to his lodgings.

"Aye, that I will," cried he: "and what is more, my sister Emma, who writes admirably, shall write her a letter to convince her that she had better be married directly."

"She had better converse with her," said Glenmurray.

The major looked grave, and observed that they would do well to go and consult the women on the subject, and tell them the whole story. So saying, he opened the door of a closet leading to their apartment: but there, to their great surprise, they found Mrs. Douglas and Emma, and as well informed of every thing as themselves;—for, expecting that a duel might be the consequence of the major's impetuosity, and hearing Mr. Glenmurray announced, they resolved to listen to the conversation, and, if it took the turn which they expected, to rush in and endeavor to mollify the disputants.

"So, ladies! this is very pretty indeed! Eaves-droppers, I protest," cried major Douglas: but he said no more; for his wife, affected by the recital which she had heard, and delighted to find that there would be no duel, threw her arms round his neck, and burst into tears. Emma, almost equally affected, gave her hand to Glenmurray, and told him nothing on her part should be omitted to prevail on Adeline to sacrifice her opinions to her welfare.

"I said so," cried the major. "You will write to her."

"No; I will see her, and argue with her."

"And so will I," cried the wife.

"That you shall not," bluntly replied the major.

"Why not? I think it my duty to do all I can to save a fellow creature from ruin; and words spoken from the heart are always more powerful than words written."

"But what will the world say, if I permit you to converse with a kept mistress?"

"The world here to us, as we associate with none and are known to none, is Mr. Glenmurray and miss Mowbray; and of their good word we are sure."

"Aye," cried Emma, "and sure of succeeding with this interesting Adeline too; for if she likes us, as I think she does—"

"She adores you," replied Glenmurray.

"So much the better:–then, when we shall tell her that we cannot associate with her, much as we admire her, unless she consents to become a wife, surely she will hear reason."

"No doubt," cried Mrs. Douglas; "and then we will go to church with her, and you, Emma, shall be bride's maid."

"I see no necessity for that," observed the major gravely.

"But I do," replied Emma. "She will repeat her vows with more heartfelt reverence, when two respectable women, deeply impressed themselves with their importance, shall be there to witness them."

"But there is no protestant church here," exclaimed Glenmurray: "however, we can go back to Lisbon, and you are already resolved to return thither."

This point being settled, it was agreed that Glenmurray should prepare Adeline for their visit; and with a lightened heart he went to execute his commission. But when he saw Adeline he forgot his commission and every thing but her distress; for he found her with an open letter in her hand, and an unopened one on the floor, in a state of mind almost bordering on phrensy.

END OF THE FIRST VOLUME.

Adeline Mowbray
Or the
Mother and Daughter:
A Tale,
In Three Volumes
By Mrs. Opie

Vol. II.

Adeline Mowbray
Chapter I.

As soon as Adeline beheld Glenmurray, "See!" she exclaimed in a hoarse and agitated tone, "there is my letter to my mother, returned unopened, and here is a letter from Dr. Norberry which has broken my heart:–however, we must go to England directly."

The letter was as follows:

> "You have made a pretty fool of me, deluded but still dear girl! for you have made me believe in forebodings, and be hanged to you. You may remember with what a full heart I bade you adieu, and I recollect what a devilish queer sensation I had when the park-gates closed on your fleet carriage. I swore a good oath at the postillions for driving so fast, as I wished to see you as long as I could; and now I protest that I believe I was actuated by a foreboding that at that house, and on that spot I should never behold you again. (Here a tear had

fallen on the paper, and the word *'again'* was nearly blotted out.) Dear, lost Adeline, I prayed for you too! I prayed that you might return as innocent and happy as you left me. Lord have mercy on us! who should have thought it!—But this is nothing to the purpose, and I suppose you think you have done nought but what is right and clever."

He then proceeded to inform Adeline, who had written to him to implore his mediation between her and her mother, "that the latter had sent express for him on finding, by the hasty scrawl which came the day after Adeline's departure from the farm-house, that she had eloped, and who was the companion of her flight; that he found her in violent agitation, as sir Patrick, stung to madness at the success of his rival, had with an ingenuousness worthy a better cause avowed to her his ardent passion for her daughter, his resolution to follow the fugitives, and by every means possible separate Adeline from her lover; and that, after having thanked lady O'Carrol for her great generosity to him, he had taken his pistols, mounted his horse, attended by his groom also well armed, and vowed that he would never return unless accompanied by the woman whom he adored."

"No wonder therefore," continued the doctor, "that I was an unsuccessful advocate for you,— especially as I was not inclined to manage the old bride's self-love; for I was so provoked at her cursed folly in marrying the handsome profligate, that, if she had not been in distress, I never meant to see her again. But, poor silly soul! she suffers enough for her folly, and so do you;—for, her affections and her self-love, being equally wounded by sir Patrick's confession, you are at present the object of her aversion. To you she attributes all the misery of having lost the man on whom she still dotes; (an old blockhead!) and when she found from your last

388

letter to me that you are not the wife but the mistress of Glenmurray, (by the bye, your letter to her from Lisbon she desires me to return unopened,) and that the child once her pride is become her disgrace, she declared her solemn resolution never to see you more, and to renounce you for ever—(Terrible words, Adeline, I tremble to write them). But a circumstance has since occurred which gives me the hopes that she may yet forgive, and receive you on certain conditions. About a fortnight after sir Patrick's departure, a letter from Ireland, directed to him in a woman's hand, arrived at the Pavilion. Your mother opened it, and found it was from a wife of her amiable husband, whom he had left in the north of Ireland, and who, having heard of his second marriage, wrote to tell him that, unless he came quickly back to her, she would prosecute him for bigamy, as he knew very well that undoubted proofs of the marriage were in her possession. At first this new proof of her beautiful spouse's villany drove your mother almost to phrensy, and I was again sent for; but time, reflection, and perhaps my arguments, convinced her, that to be able to free herself from this rascal for ever, and consequently her fortune, losing only the ten thousand pounds which she had given him to pay his debts, was in reality a consoling circumstance. Accordingly, she wrote to the real lady O'Carrol, promising to accede quietly to her claim, and wishing that she would spare her and herself the disgrace of a public trial; especially as it must end in the conviction of sir Patrick. She then, on hearing from him that he had traced you to Falmouth, and was going to embark for Lisbon when the wind was favourable, enclosed him a copy of his wife's letter, and bade him an eternal farewell!—But be not alarmed lest this insane profligate should overtake and distress you. He is gone to his final account. In his hurry to get on board, overcome as he was with the great quantity of liquor which he had drunk to banish care, he sprung from the boat before it was near enough to reach the vessel; his foot slipped against the side, he fell into the water, and, going under the ship, never rose again. I leave you to imagine how the complicated distresses of the last three months, and this awful climax to them, have affected your mother's mind; even I cannot scold her, now, for the life of me: she is not yet, I believe, disposed in your favor; but were you here, and were you to meet, it is impossible that, forlorn, lonely, and deserted as she now feels, the tie between you might be once more cemented; and much as I resent your conduct, you may depend on my exertions — O Adeline, child of my affection, why must I blush to subscribe myself

Your sincere friend,
J.N.?"

Words cannot describe the feelings of anguish which this letter excited in Adeline: nor could she make known her sensations otherwise than by reiterated requests to be allowed to set off for England directly,—requests to which Glenmurray, alarmed for her intellects, immediately assented. Therefore, leaving a hasty note for the Douglases, they soon bade farewell to Perpignan; and after a long laborious journey, but a short passage, they landed at Brighton.

It was a fine evening; and numbers of the gay and fashionable of both sexes were assembled on the beach, to see the passengers land. Adeline and Glenmurray were amongst the first: and while heart-sick, fatigued, and melancholy, Adeline took the arm of her lover, and turned disgusted from the brilliant groups before her, she saw, walking along the shore, Dr. Norberry, his wife, and his two daughters.

Instantly, unmindful of every thing but the delight of seeing old acquaintances, and of being able to gain some immediate tidings of her mother, she ran up to them; and just as they turned round, she met them, extending her hand in friendship as she was wont to do.—But in vain;—no hand was stretched out to meet hers, nor tongue nor look proclaimed a welcome to her; Dr. Norberry himself coldly touched his hat, and passed on, while his wife and daughters looked scornfully at her, and, without deigning to notice her, pursued their walk.

Astonished and confounded, Adeline had not power to articulate a word; and, had not Glenmurray caught her in his arms, she would have fallen to the ground.

"Then now I am indeed an outcast! even my oldest and best friend renounces me," she exclaimed.

"But I am left to you," cried Glenmurray.

Adeline sighed. She could not say, as she had formerly done, "and you are all to me." The image of her mother, happy as the wife of a man she loved, could not long rival Glenmurray; but the image of her mother, disgraced and wretched, awoke all the habitual but dormant tenderness of years; every feeling of filial gratitude revived in all its force; and, even while leaning on the shoulder of her lover, she sighed to be once more clasped to the bosom of her mother.

Glenmurray felt the change, but, though grieved, was not offended:— "I shall die in peace," he cried, "if I can but see you restored to your mother's affection, even though the surrender of my happiness is to be the purchase."

"You shall die in peace!" replied Adeline shuddering. The phrase was well-timed, though perhaps undesignedly so. Adeline clung close to his arm, her eyes filled with tears, and all the way to the inn she thought only of Glenmurray with an apprehension which she could not conquer.

"What do you mean to do now?" said Glenmurray.

"Write to Dr. Norberry. I think he will at least have humanity enough to let me know where to find my mother."

"No doubt; and you had better write directly."

Adeline took up her pen. A letter was written,—and as quickly torn. Letter succeeded to letter; but not one of them answered her wishes. The dark hour arrived, and the letter remained unwritten.

"It is too soon to ring for candles," said Glenmurray, putting his arm around her waist and leading her to the window. The sun was below the horizon, but the reflection of his beams still shown beautifully on the surrounding objects. Adeline, reclining her cheek on Glenmurray's arm, gazed in silence on the scene before her; when the door suddenly opened, and a gentleman was announced. It was now so dark that all objects were indistinctly seen, and the gentleman had advanced close to Adeline before she knew him to be Dr. Norberry: and, before she could decide how she should receive him, she felt herself clasped to his bosom with the affection of a father.

Surprised and affected, she could not speak; and Glenmurray had ordered candles before Adeline had recovered herself sufficiently to say these words,

"After your conduct on the beach, I little expected this visit."

"Pshaw!" replied the doctor: "when a man out of regard to society has performed a painful task, surely he may be allowed out of regard to himself, to follow the dictates of his heart.—I obeyed my head when I passed you so cavalierly, and I thought I should never have gone through my task as I did;—but then for the sake of my daughters, I gave a gulp, and called up a fierce look. But I told madam that I meant to call on you, and she insisted, very properly, that it should be in the dark hour."

"But what of my mother?"

"She is a miserable woman, as she deserves to be—an old fool."

"Pray do not call her so; to hear she is miserable is torment sufficient to me:—where is she?"

"Still at the Pavilion: but she is going to let Rosevalley, retire to her estate in Cumberland, and live unknown and unseen."

"But will she not allow me to live with her?"

"What? As Mr. Glenmurray's mistress? Receive under her

roof the seducer of her daughter?"

"Sir, I am no seducer."

"No," cried Adeline: "I became the mistress of Mr. Glenmurray from the dictates of my reason, not my weakness or his persuasions."

"Humph!" replied the doctor, "I should expect to find such reason in Moorfields:[68] besides, had not Mr. Glenmurray's books turned your head, you would not have thought it pretty and right to become the mistress of any man: so he is your seducer, after all."

"So far I plead guilty," replied Glenmurray; "but whatever my opinions are, I have ever been willing to sacrifice them to the welfare of miss Mowbray, and have, from the first moment that we were safe from pursuit, been urgent to marry her."

"Then why the devil are you not married?"

"Because I would not consent," said Adeline coldly.

"Mad, certainly mad," exclaimed the doctor: "but you, 'faith, you are an honest fellow after all," turning to Glenmurray and shaking him by the hand; "weak o' the head, not bad in the heart: burn your d——d books, and I am your friend for ever."

"We will discuss that point another time," replied Glenmurray: "at present the most interesting subject to us is the question whether Mrs. Mowbray will forgive her daughter or not?"

"Zounds, man, if I may judge of Mrs. Mowbray by myself, one condition of her forgiveness will be your marrying her daughter."

"O blest condition!" cried Glenmurray.

"I should think," replied Adeline coldly, "my mother must have had too much of marriage to wish me to marry; but if she should insist on my marrying, I will comply, and on no other account."

---

[68] The hospital of St. Mary of Bethlehem— better known as Bedlam, an institution for the mentally ill—had been located in the Moorfields section of London since the seventeenth century.

"Strange infatuation! To me it appears only justice and duty. But your reasons, girl, your reasons?"

"They are few, but strong. Glenmurray, philanthropically bent on improving the state of society, puts forth opinions counteracting its received usages, backed by arguments which are in my opinion incontrovertible."

"In your opinion!—Pray, child, how old are you?"

"Nineteen."

"And at that age you set up for a reformer? Well,—go on."

"But though it be important to the success of his opinions, and indeed to the respectability of his character, that he should act according to his precepts, he, for the sake of preserving to me the notice of persons whose narrowness of mind I despise, would conform to an institution which both he and I think unworthy of regard from a rational being.—And shall not I be as generous as he is? shall I scruple to give up for his honour and fame the petty advantages which marriage would give me? Never—his honour and fame are too dear to me; but the claims which my mother has on me are in my eyes so sacred that, for her sake, though not for my own, I would accept the sacrifice which Glenmurray offers. If, then, she says that she will never see or pardon me till I am become a wife, I will follow him to the altar directly; but till then I must insist on remaining as I am. It is necessary that I should respect the man I love; and I should not respect Glenmurray were he not capable of supporting with fortitude the consequences of his opinions; and could he, for motives less strong than those he avows, cease to act up to what he believes to be right. For, never can I respect or believe firmly in the truth of those doctrines, the followers of which shrink from a sort of martyrdom in support of them."

"O Mr. Glenmurray!" cried the doctor shaking his head, "what have you to answer for! What a glorious champion would that creature have been in the support of truth, when even error in her looks so like to virtue!—And then the amiable disinterestedness of you both!—Zounds! What a powerful thing must true love be, when it can make a speculative philosopher indifferent to the interests of his system, and ready to act in direct opposition to it, rather than injure the respectability of the woman he loves! Well, well, the Lord forgive you, young man, for having taken it into your head to set up for a great author."

Glenmurray answered by a deep drawn sigh; and the doctor continued: "Then there is that girl again, with a heart so fond and true that her love comes in aid of her integrity, and makes her think no sacrifice too great, in order to prove her confidence in the wisdom of her lover,—urging her to disregard all personal inconveniences rather than let him forfeit, for her sake, his pretensions to independence and consistency of character! 'Sdeath, girl! I can't help admiring you. But no more I could a Malabar widow, who with fond and pious enthusiasm, from an idea of duty, throws herself on the funeral pile of her husband.[69] But still I should think you a cursed fool, notwithstanding, for professing the opinions that led to such an exertion of duty. And now here are you, possessed of every quality both of head and heart to bless others and to bless yourself—owing to your foolish and pernicious opinions—here you are, I say, blasted in reputation in the prime of your days, and doomed perhaps to pine through existence in——Pshaw!—by the Lord I can't support the idea!" added he, gulping down a sob as he spoke, and traversing the room in great emotion.

Adeline and Glenmurray were both of them deeply and painfully affected; and the latter was going to express what he felt, when the doctor, seizing Adeline's hand, affectionately exclaimed, "Well, my poor child! I will see your mother once more; I will go to London tomorrow—by this time she is there—and you had better follow me; you will hear of me at the Old

---

[69] A reference to colonial India and the practice of "suttee" or widow burning, reportedly expected of high caste Hindu wives on the death of their husbands. The practice was outlawed under British rule as a sign of British benevolence and moral authority. Like references to "Turks" disbelieving that women had souls, suttee was commonly invoked to exemplify the higher status of women under British law and tradition.

Hummums;[70] and here is a card of address to an hotel near it, where I would advise you to take up your abode."

So saying, he shook Glenmurray by the hand; when, starting back, he exclaimed

"Odzooks, man! Here is a skin like fire, and a pulse like lightning. My dear fellow, you must take care of yourself."

Adeline burst into tears.

"Indeed, doctor, I am only nervous."

"Nervous!.... What, I suppose you think you understand my profession better than I do. But don't cry, my child: when your mind is easier, perhaps, he will do very well; and, as one thing likely to give him immediate ease, I prescribe a visit to the altar of the next parish church."

So saying he departed; and all other considerations were again swallowed up in Adeline's mind by the idea of Glenmurray's danger.

"Is it possible that my marrying you would have such a blessed effect on your health?" cried Adeline after a pause.

"It certainly would make my mind easier than it is now'" replied he.

"If I thought so," said Adeline: "but no—regard for my supposed interest merely makes you say so; and indeed I should not think so well of you as I now do, if I imagined that you could be made easy by an action by which you forfeited all pretensions to that consistency of character so requisite to the true dignity of a philosopher."

A deep sigh from Glenmurray, in answer, proved that he was no philosopher.

In the morning the lovers set off for London, Dr. Norberry having preceded them by a few hours. This blunt but benevolent man had returned the evening before slowly and pensively to his lodgings, his heart full of pity for the errors of the well-meaning enthusiasts whom he had left, and his head full of plans for their

---

[70] A coffee-house, an establishment where gentlemen met for conversation and which offered bed as well as board.

assistance, or rather for that of Adeline. But he entered his own doors again reluctantly—he knew but too well that no sympathy with his feelings awaited him there. His wife, a woman of narrow capacity and no talents or accomplishments, had, like all women of that sort, a great aversion to those of her sex who united to feminine graces and gentleness, the charms of a cultivated understanding and pretensions to accomplishments or literature.

Of Mrs. Mowbray, as we have before observed, she had always been peculiarly jealous, because Dr. Norberry spoke of her knowledge with wonder, and of her understanding with admiration; not that he entertained one moment a feeling of preference towards her, inconsistent with an almost idolatrous love of his wife, whose skill in all the domestic duties, and whose very pretty face and person, were the daily themes of his praise. But Mrs. Norberry wished to engross all his panegyrics to herself, and she never failed to expatiate on Mrs. Mowbray's foibles and flightiness as long as the doctor had expatiated on her charms.

Sometimes, indeed, this last subject was sooner exhausted than the one which she had chosen; but when Adeline grew up, and became as it were the rival of her daughters in the praises of her husband, she found it difficult, as we have said before, to bring faults in array against excellencies.

Mrs. Norberry could with propriety observe, when the doctor was exclaiming, "What a charming essay Mrs. Mowbray has just written!"

"Aye,—but I dare say she can't write a market bill."

When he said, "How well she comprehends the component parts of the animal system!"

She could with great justice reply, "But she knows nothing of the component parts of a plum pudding."[71]

But when Adeline became the object of the husband's

---

[71] Elizabeth Hamilton's parodic novel, *Memoirs of Modern Philosophers*, similarly mocks the lack of practical female knowledge in "modern philosophers" when the "philosophess" Bridgetina Botherim insists that she refuses to learn to make puddings, preferring metaphysics.

admiration and the wife's enmity, Mrs. Norberry could not make these pertinent remarks, as Adeline was as conversant with all branches of house-wifery as herself; and, though as learned in all systems as her mother, was equally learned in the component parts of pudding and pies. She was therefore at a loss what to say when Adeline was praised by the doctor; and all she could observe on the occasion was, that the girl might be clever, but was certainly very ugly, very affected, and very conceited.

It is not to be wondered at, therefore, that Mrs. Mowbray's degrading and unhappy marriage, and Adeline's elopement, should have been sources of triumph to Mrs. Norberry and her daughters; who, though they liked Mrs. Mowbray very well, could not bear Adeline.

"So, Dr. Norberry, these are your uncommon folks!"— exclaimed Mrs. Norberry on hearing of the marriage and of the subsequent elopement;— "I suppose you are now well satisfied at not having a genius for your wife, or geniuses for your daughters?"

"I always was, my dear," meekly replied the mortified and afflicted doctor, and dropped the subject as soon as possible; nor had it been resumed for some time when Adeline accosted them on the beach at Brighton. But her appearance called forth their dormant enmity; and the whole way to their lodgings the good doctor heard her guilt expatiated upon with as much violence as ever: but just as they got home he coldly and firmly observed, "I shall certainly call on the poor deluded girl this evening."

And Mrs. Norberry, knowing by the tone and manner in which he spoke, that this was a point which he would not give up, contented herself with requiring only that he should go in the dark hour.

CHAPTER II.

IT was to a wife and daughters such as these that he was returning, with the benevolent wish of interesting them for the guilty Adeline.

"So, Dr. Norberry, you are come back at last!" was his first salutation, "and what does the creature say for herself?"

"The creature?—Your *fellow*-creature, my dear, says very little—grief is not wordy."

"Grief!—So then she is unhappy, is she?" cries miss Norberry: "I am monstrous glad of it."

The doctor started; and an oath nearly escaped his lips. He did say, "Why, zounds, Jane!— " but then he added in a softer tone, "Why do you rejoice in the poor girl's afflictions?"

"Because I think it is for the good of her soul."

"Good girl!" replied the father: — "but God grant, Jane, (seizing her hand) that your soul may not need such a medicine!"

"It never will," said her mother proudly: "she has been differently brought up."

"She has been well brought up, you might have added," observed the doctor, "had modesty permitted it. Mrs. Mowbray, poor woman, had good intentions; but she was too flighty. Had Adeline, my children, had such a mother as yours, she would have been like you."

"But not half so handsome," interrupted the mother in a low voice.

"But as our faults and our virtues, my dear, depend so much on the care and instruction of others, we should look with pity as well as aversion on the faults of those less fortunate in instructors than we have been."

"Certainly;—very true," said Mrs. Norberry, flattered and affected by this compliment from her husband: "but you know, James Norberry," laying her hand on his, "I always told you you over-rated Mrs. Mowbray; and that she was but a dawdle,[72] after all."

"You always did, my good woman," replied he, raising her hand to his lips.

"But you men think yourselves so much wiser than we are!"

"We do so," replied the doctor.

The tone was equivocal—Mrs. Norberry felt it to be so, and

[72] I.e., a dawdler, one who wastes time, usually female (OED).

looked up in his face.—The doctor understood the look: it was one of doubt and inquiry; and, as it was his interest to sooth her in order to carry his point, he exclaimed, "We men are, indeed, too apt to pride ourselves in our supposed superior wisdom: but I, you will own, my dear, have always done your sex justice; and you in particular."

"You have been a good husband, indeed, James Norberry," replied his wife in a faltering voice; "and I believe you to be, to every one, a just and honourable man."

"And I dare say, dame, I do no more than justice to you, when I think you will approve and further a plan for Adeline Mowbray's good, which I am going to propose to you."

Mrs. Norberry withdrew her hand; but returning it again:— "To be sure, my dear," she cried. "Any thing you wish; that is, if I see right to——"

"I will explain myself," continued the doctor gently.

"I have promised this poor girl to endeavour to bring about a reconciliation between her and her mother: but though Adeline wishes to receive her pardon on any terms, and even, if it be required, to renounce her lover, I fear Mrs. Mowbray is too much incensed against her, to see or forgive her."

"Hard-hearted woman!" cried Mrs. Norberry.

"Cruel, indeed!" cried her daughters.

"But a mother ought to be severe, very severe, on such occasions, young ladies," hastily added Mrs. Norberry: "but go on, my dear."

"Now it is but too probable," continued the doctor, "that Glenmurray will not live long, and then this young creature will be left to struggle unprotected with the difficulties of her situation; and who knows but that she may, from poverty and the want of a protector, be tempted to continue in the paths of vice?"

"Well, Dr. Norberry, and what then?—Who or what is to prevent it?—You know we have three children to provide for; and I am a young woman as yet."

"True, Hannah," giving her a kiss, "and a very pretty woman

too."

"Well, my dear love, any thing we can do with prudence I am ready to do; I can say no more."

"You have said enough," cried the doctor exultingly; "then hear my plan: Adeline shall, in the event of Glenmurray's death, which though not certain seems likely....to be sure, I could not inquire into the nature of his nocturnal perspirations, his expectoration, and so forth...."

"Dear papa, you are so professional!" affectedly exclaimed his youngest daughter.

"Well, child, I have done; and to return to my subject:—if Glenmurray lives or dies, I think it advisable that Adeline should go into retirement to lie-in.[73] And where can she be better than in my little cottage now empty, within a four-miles ride of our house? If she wants protection, I can protect her; and if she wants money before her mother forgives her, you can give it to her."

"Indeed, papa," cried both the girls, "we shall not grudge it."

The doctor started from his chair, and embraced his daughters with joy mixed with wonder; for he knew they had always disliked Adeline.—True; but then, she was prosperous, and their superior. Little minds love to bestow protection; and it was easy to be generous to the fallen Adeline Mowbray; had her happiness continued, so would their hatred.

"Then it is a settled point, is it not, dame?" asked the doctor, chucking his wife under the chin; when, to his great surprise and consternation, she threw his hand indignantly from her, and vociferated, "She shall never live within a ride of our house, I can assure you, Dr. Norberry."

The doctor was petrified into silence, and the girls could only articulate "La! mamma!" But what could produce this sudden and violent change? Nothing but a simple and natural operation of the human mind. Though a very kind husband, and an

---

[73] I.e., to give birth.

indulgent father, Dr. Norberry was suspected of being a very gallant man;[74] and some of Mrs. Norberry's good-natured friends had occasionally hinted to her their sorrow at hearing such and such reports; reports which were indeed destitute of foundation: but which served to excite suspicioun in the mind of the tenacious Mrs. Norberry. And what more likely to reawaken them than the young and frail Adeline Mowbray living in a cottage of her husband's, protected, supported, and visited by him! The moment this idea occurred, its influence was unconquerable; and with a voice and manner of determined hostility she made known her resolves in consequence of it.

After a pause of dismay and astonishment the doctor cried, "Zounds, dame, what have you gotten in your head? What, all on a sudden, has had such a cursed ugly effect on you?"

"Second thoughts are best, doctor; and I now feel that it would be highly improper for you, with daughters grown up, to receive with such marked kindness a young woman at a cottage of yours, who is going to lie-in of a bastard child."

"But, 'sdeath, my dear, it is a different case, when I do it to keep her out of the way of having any more."

"That is more than I know, Dr. Norberry," replied the wife bridling, and fanning herself.

"Whew!" whistled the doctor; and then addressing his daughters," Girls, you had better go to bed; it grows late."

The young ladies obeyed; but first hung round their mother's neck, as they bade her good night, and hoped she would not be so *cruel* to the poor deluded Adeline.

Mrs. Norberry angrily shook them off, with a peevish— "Get along, girls." The doctor cordially kissed, and bade God bless them; while the door closed and left the loving couple alone.

What passed, it were tedious to repeat; suffice that after a long altercation, continued even after they were retired to rest, the doctor found his wife, on this subject, incapable of listening to reason, and that, as a finishing stroke, she exclaimed "It does

[74] I.e., one fond of women, likely to womanize.

not signify talking, Dr. Norberry," (pushing her pillow vehemently towards the valance as she spoke,) "while I have my senses, and can see into a mill-stone[75] a little, the hussey shall never come near us."

The doctor sighed deeply; turned himself round, not to sleep but to think, and rose unrefreshed the next morning to go in search of Mrs. Mowbray, dreading the interview which he was afterwards to have with Adeline; for he did not expect to succeed in his application to her mother, and he could not now soften his intelligence with a 'but,' as he intended.

"True," he meant to have said to her, "your mother will not receive you; but if you ever want a home or a place of retirement, I have a cottage, and so forth."

"Pshaw!" cried the doctor to himself, as these thoughts came across him on the road, and made him hastily let down the front window of the post-chaise for air.

"Did your honour speak?" cried the post-boy.

"Not I. But can't you drive faster and be hanged to you?"

The boy whipped his horses.—The doctor then found that it was up hill—down went the glass again:— "Zounds, you brute, why do you not see it is up hill?"— For find fault he must; and with his wife he could not, or dared not, even in fancy.

"Dear me! Why, your honour bade me put on."

"Devilishly obedient," muttered the doctor: "I wish every one was like you in that respect." —And in a state of mind not the pleasantest possible the doctor drove into town, and to the hotel where Mrs. Mowbray was to be found.

Dr. Norberry was certainly now not in a humour to sooth any woman whom he thought in the wrong, except his wife; and, whether from carelessness or design, he did not, unfortunately for Adeline, manage the self-love of her unhappy mother.

---

[75] Common expression claiming insight, usually ironic. A mill-stone is a large circular stone with a hole in the center, used to grind grain. Because of the hole, "seeing into a mill-stone" is not particularly difficult.

He found Mrs. Mowbray with her heart shut up, not softened by sorrow. The hands once stretched forth with kindness to welcome him, were now stiffly laid one upon the other; and "How are you, sir?" coldly articulated, was followed by as cold a "Pray sit down."

"Zounds!—Why, how ill you look!" exclaimed the doctor bluntly.

"I attend more to my feelings than my looks," with a deep sigh answered Mrs. Mowbray.

"Your feelings are as bad as your looks, I dare say."

"They are worse, sir," said Mrs. Mowbray, piqued.

"There was no need of *that*, " replied the doctor: "but I am come to point out to you one way of getting rid of some of your unpleasant feelings: —see, and forgive your daughter."

Mrs. Mowbray started, changed colour, and exclaimed with quickness, "Is she in England?" but added instantly, "I have no daughter.—she, who was my child, is my most inveterate foe; she has involved me in disgrace and misery."

"With a little of your own help she has," replied the doctor. "Come, come, my old friend, you have both of you something to forget and forgive; and the sooner you set about it the better. Now do write, and tell Adeline, who is by this time in London, that you forgive her."

"Never:—after having promised me not to hold converse with that villain without my consent? Had I no other cause of complaint against her; — had she not by her coquettish arts seduced the affections of the man I loved;—never, never would I forgive her having violated the sacred promise which she gave me."

"A promise," interrupted the doctor, "which she would never have violated, had not you first violated that sacred compact which you entered into at her birth."

"What mean you, sir?"

"I mean, that though a parent does not, at a child's birth, solemnly make a vow to do all in his or her power to promote the happiness of that child,—still, as he has given it birth, he has tacitly bound himself to make it happy. This tacit agreement you broke, when at the age of forty, you, regardless of your daughter's welfare, played the fool and married a pennyless profligate, merely because he had a fine person and a handsome leg."

Mrs. Mowbray was too angry and too agitated to interrupt him, and he want on:

"Well; what was the consequence? The young fellow very naturally preferred the daughter to the mother; and, as he could not have her by fair, was resolved to have her by foul means; and so he——"

"I beg, Dr. Norberry," interrupted Mrs. Mowbray in a faint voice, "that you would spare the disgusting recital."

"Well, well, I will. Now do consider the dilemma your child was in: she must either elope, or by her presence keep alive a criminal passion in her father-in-law, which you sooner or later must discover; and be besides exposed to fresh insults.—Well, Glenmurray by chance happened to be on the spot just as she escaped from that villanous fellow's clutches, and——"

"He is dead, Dr. Norberry," interrupted Mrs. Mowbray; "and you know the old adage, Do not speak ill of the dead."

"And a devilish silly adage it is. I had rather speak ill of the dead than the living, for my part: but let me go on.—Well, love taking the name and habit of prudence and filial piety, (for she thought she consulted your happiness, and not her own,) bade her fly to and with her lover; and now there she is, owing to the pretty books which you let her read, living with him as his mistress, and glorying in it, as if it was a notable praise-worthy action."

"And you would have me forgive her?"

"Certainly: a fault which both your precepts and conduct occasioned. Not but what the girl has been wrong—terribly wrong:—no one ought to do evil that good may come.[76] You had forbidden her to have any intercourse with Glenmurray;

[76] Romans 3:8.

and she therefore knew that disobeying you would make you unhappy—that was a certainty. That fellow's persevering in his attempts, after the fine rebuff which she had given him, was an uncertainty; and she ought to have run the risk of it, and not committed a positive fault to avoid a possible evil. But then hers was a fault which she could not have committed had not you married that d—d dog. And as to her not being married to Glenmurray, that is no fault of his: the good lad looks as ashamed of what he has done as any modest miss in Christendom; and, with your consent, will marry your daughter to-morrow morning. Lord! Lord! That ever so good, cleanly-hearted a youth should have poked his nose into the filthy mess of eccentric philosophy!"

"Have you done, doctor?" cried Mrs. Mowbray haughtily: "have you said all that miss Mowbray and you have invented to insult me?"

"Your *child* send me to insult you!—She! Adeline!—Why, the poor soul came broken-hearted and post haste from France, when she heard of your misfortunes, to offer her services to console you."

"She console me?—she, the first occasion of them?—But for her, I might still have indulged the charming delusion, even if it were delusion, that love of me, not of my wealth, induced the man I doted upon to commit a crime to gain possession of me."

"Why, zounds!" hastily interrupted the doctor, "every one saw that he loved her long before he married you."

The storm, long gathering, now burst forth; and rising, with the tears, high colour, and vehement voice of unbridled passion, Mrs. Mowbray exclaimed, raising her arm and clenching her fist as she spoke, "And it is being the object of that cruel preference, which I never, never will forgive her!"

The doctor, after ejaculating "Whew!" as much as to say "The murder is out," instantly took his hat and departed, convinced his labour was vain. "Zounds!" muttered he as he went down stairs, "two instances in one day! Ah, ah!— that jealousy is the devil." He then slowly walked to the hotel, where he expected to find Adeline and Glenmurray.

They had arrived about two hours before; and Adeline in a frame of mind but ill fitted to bear the disappointment which awaited her. For, with the sanguine expectations natural to her age, she had been castle-building as usual; and their journey to London had been rendered a very short one, by the delightful plans, for the future, which she had been forming and imparting to Glenmurray.

"When I consider," said she, "the love which my mother has always shown for me, I cannot think it possible that she can persist in renouncing me; and however her respect for the prejudices of the world, a world which she intended to live in at the time of her unfortunate connexion, might make her angry at my acting in defiance of its laws——now that she herself, from a sense of injury and disgrace, is about to retire from it, she will no longer have a motive to act contrary to the dictates of reason herself, or to wish me to do so."

"But your ideas of reason and hers may be so different——"

"No. Our practice may be different, but our theory is the same, and I have no doubt but that my mother will now forgive and receive us; and that, living in a romantic solitude, being the whole world to each other, our days will glide away in uninterrupted felicity."

"And how shall we employ ourselves?" said Glenmurray smiling.

"You shall continue to write for the instruction of your fellow-creatures; while my mother and I shall be employed in endeavouring to improve the situation of the poor around us, and perhaps in educating our children."

Adeline, when animated by any prospect of happiness, was irresistible: she was really Hope herself, as described by Collins—

"But thou, oh Hope! With eyes so fair,
What was thy delighted measure!"[77]

and Glenmurray, as he listened to her, forgot his illness; forgot every thing, but what Adeline chose to imagine. The place of

---

[77] William Collins (1720-59), "The Passions: An Ode for Music," lines 29-30.

their retreat was fixed upon. It was to be a little village near Falmouth, the scene of their first happiness. The garden was laid out; Mrs. Mowbray's library planned; and so completely were they lost in their charming prospects for the future, that every turnpike-man had to wait a longer time than he was accustomed to for his money; and the postillion had driven into London in the way to the hotel, before Adeline recollected that she was, for the first time, in a city which she had long wished most ardently to see.

They had scarcely taken up their abode at the hotel recommended to them by Dr. Norberry, when he knocked at the door. Adeline from the window had seen him coming; and sure as she thought herself to be of her mother's forgiveness, she turned sick and faint when the decisive moment was at hand; and, hurrying out of the room, she begged Glenmurray to receive the doctor, and apologize for her absence.

Glenmurray awaited him with a beating heart. He listened to his step on the stairs: it was slow and heavy; unlike that of a benevolent man coming to communicate good news. Glenmurray began immediately to tremble for the peace of Adeline; and, hastily pouring out a glass of wine, was on the point of drinking it when Dr. Norberry entered.

"Gadzooks,[78] give me a glass," cried he: "I want one, I am sure, to recruit my spirits." Glenmurray in silence complied with his desire. "Come, I'll give you a toast," cried the doctor: "Here is——"

At this moment Adeline entered. She had heard the doctor's last words, and she thought he was going to drink to the reconciliation of her mother and herself; and hastily opening the door she came to receive the good news which awaited her. But, at sight of her, the toast died unfinished on her old friend's lips; he swallowed down the wine in silence, and then taking her hand led her to the sofa.

Adeline's heart began to die within her; and before the doctor,

---

[78] I.e., God's hooks, or the nails of the cross, an old-fashioned oath.

after having taken a pinch of snuff, and blowed his nose full three times, was prepared to speak, she was convinced that she had nothing but unwelcome intelligence to receive; and she awaited in trembling expectation an answer to a "Well, sir," from Glenmurray spoken in a tone of fearful emotion.

"No, it is not well, sir," replied the doctor; "it is d—d ill, sir."

"You have seen my mother," said Adeline, catching hold of the arm of the sofa for support; and in an instant Glenmurray was by her side.

"I have seen Mrs. Mowbray, but not your mother: for I have seen a woman dead to every graceful impulse of maternal affection, and alive only to a selfish sense of rivalship and hatred. My poor child! God forgive the deluded woman! But I declare she detests you!"

"Detests me?" exclaimed Adeline.

"Yes; she swears that she can never forgive the preference which that vile fellow gave you, and I am convinced that she will keep her word; and—Lord have mercy upon us!" cried the doctor, turning round and seeing the situation into which his words had thrown Adeline, who was then lying immoveable in Glenmurray's arms. But she did not long remain so, and with a frantic scream kept repeating the words "She detests me!" till, unable to contend any longer with the acuteness of her feelings, she sunk, sobbing convulsively, exhausted on the bed to which they carried her.

"My good friend, my only friend," cried Glenmurray, "what is to be done? Will she scream again, think you, in that most dreadful and unheard-of manner? For, if she does, I must run out of the house."

"What, then, she never treated you in this pretty way before, heh?"

"Never, never. Her self-command has always been exemplary."

"Indeed?—Lucky fellow! My wife and daughters often scream just as loud, on very trifling occasions: but that scream went to my heart; for I well know how to distinguish between the shriek of agony and that of passion."[79]

When Adeline recovered, she ardently conjured Dr. Norberry to procure her an interview with her mother; contending that it was absolutely impossible to suppose, that the sight of a child so long and tenderly loved should not renew a little of her now dormant affection.

"But you were her rival, as well as her child: remember that. However, you look so ill, that now, if ever, she will forgive you, I think: therefore I will go back to Mrs. Mowbray; and while I am there do you come, ask for me, and follow the servant into the room."

"I will," replied Adeline: and leaning on the arm of her lover, she slowly followed the doctor to her mother's hotel.

Chapter III.

"This is the most awful moment of my life," said Adeline.

"And the most anxious one of mine," replied Glenmurray. "If Mrs. Mowbray forgives you, it will be probably on condition that—— "

"Whatever be the conditions, I must accept them," said Adeline.

"True," returned Glenmurray, wiping the cold dews of weakness from his forehead: "but no matter—at any rate, I should not have been with you long."

Adeline, with a look of agony, pressed the arm she held to her bosom.

Glenmurray's heart smote him immediately — he felt he had been ungenerous; and, while the hectic[80] of a moment passed across his cheek, he added, "But I do not do myself justice in saying so. I believe my best chance of recovery is the certainty of your being easy. Let me but see you happy, and so disinterested is my affection, as I have often told you, that I shall cheerfully

---

[79] I.e., temper.
[80] I.e., fever or flush.

assent to any thing that may ensure your happiness."

"And can you think," answered Adeline, "that my happiness can be independent of yours? Do you not see that I am only trying to prepare my mind for being called upon to surrender my inclinations to my duty?"

At this moment they found themselves at the door of the hotel. Neither of them spoke; the moment of trial was come; and both were unable to encounter it firmly. At last Adeline grasped her lover's hand, bade him wait for her at the end of the street, and with some degree of firmness she entered the vestibule, and asked for Dr. Norberry.

Dr. Norberry, meanwhile, with the best intentions in the world, had but ill prepared Mrs. Mowbray's mind for the intended visit. He had again talked to her of her daughter, and urged the propriety of forgiving her; but he had at the same time renewed his animadversions on her own conduct.

"You know not, Dr. Norberry," observed Mrs. Mowbray, "the pains I took with the education of that girl; and I expected to be repaid for it by being styled the happiest as well as best of mothers."

"And so you would, perhaps, had you not wished to be a wife as well as mother."

"No more on that subject, sir," haughtily returned Mrs. Mowbray.— "Yes,—Adeline was indeed my joy, my pride."

"Aye, and pride will have a fall; and a devilish tumble yours has had, to be sure, my old friend. Zounds, it has broke its knees—never to be sound again."

At this unpropitious moment "a lady to Dr. Norberry" was announced, and Adeline tottered into the room.

"What strange intrusion is this?" cried Mrs. Mowbray: "who is this woman?"

Adeline threw back her veil, and, falling on her knees, stretched out her arms in an attitude of entreaty: speak she could not, but her countenance was sufficiently expressive of her meaning; and her pale sunk cheek spoke forcibly to the heart of her mother.—At this moment, when a struggle which might have ended favourably for Adeline was taking place in the mind of Mrs. Mowbray, Dr. Norberry injudiciously exclaimed,

"There,—there she is! Look at her, poor soul! There is little fear, I think, of her ever rivalling you again."

At these words Mrs. Mowbray darted an angry look at the doctor, and desired him to take away that woman; who came, no doubt instigated by him, to insult her.

"Take her away," she cried, "and never let me see her again."

"Oh my mother, hear me, in pity hear me!" exclaimed Adeline.

"As it is for the last time, I will hear you," replied Mrs. Mowbray; "for never, no never will I behold you more! Hear me vow—— "

"Mother, for God's sake, make not a vow so terrible!" cried Adeline, gathering courage from despair, and approaching her: "I have grievously erred, and will cheerfully devote the rest of my life to endeavor, by the most submissive obedience and attention, to atone for my past guilt."

"Atone for it! Impossible; for the misery which I owe to you, no submission, no future conduct can make me amends. Away! I say: your presence conjures up recollections which distract me, and I solemnly swear—— "

"Hold, hold, if you have any mercy in your nature," cried Adeline almost frantic: "this is, I feel but too sensibly, the most awful and important moment of my life; on the result of this interview depends my future happiness or misery. Hear me, O my mother! You, who can so easily resolve to tear the heart of a child that adores you, hear me! reflect that, if you vow to abandon me for ever, you blast all the happiness and prospects of my life; and at nineteen 'tis hard to be deprived of happiness for ever. True, I may not long survive the anguish of being renounced by my mother, whom I love with even enthusiastic fondness; but then could you ever know peace again with the conviction of having caused my death? Oh! no. Save then yourself and me from these miseries, by forgiving my past errors, and deigning sometimes to see and converse with me!"

The eager and animated volubility with which Adeline spoke

made it impossible to interrupt her, even had Mrs. Mowbray been inclined to do so: but she was not; nor, when Adeline had done speaking, could she find in her heart to break silence.

It was evident to Dr. Norberry that Mrs. Mowbray's countenance expressed a degree of softness which augured well for her daughter; and, as if conscious that it did so, she covered her face suddenly with her handkerchief.

"Now then is the time," thought the doctor. "Go nearer her, my child," said he in a low voice to Adeline, "embrace her knees."

Adeline rose and approached Mrs. Mowbray: she seized her hand, she pressed it to her lips. Mrs. Mowbray's bosom heaved violently: she almost returned the pressure of Adeline's hand.

"Victory, victory!" muttered the doctor to himself, cutting a caper behind Mrs. Mowbray's chair.

Mrs. Mowbray took the handkerchief from her face.

"My mother, my dear mother! look on me, look on me with kindness only one moment, and only say that you do not hate me!"

Mrs. Mowbray turned round and fixed her eyes on Adeline with a look of kindness, and Adeline's began to sparkle with delight; when, as she threw back her cloak, which, hanging over her arm, embarrassed her as she knelt to embrace her mother's knees, Mrs. Mowbray's eyes glanced from her face to her shape.

In an instant the fierceness of her look returned: "Shame to thy race, disgrace to thy family!"[81] she exclaimed, spurning her kneeling child from her: "and canst thou, while conscious of carrying in thy bosom the proof of thy infamy, dare to solicit and expect my pardon?—Hence! ere I load thee with maledictions."

Adeline wrapped her cloak round her, and sunk terrified and desponding on the ground.

"Why, what a ridiculous caprice is this!" cried he doctor. "Is it a greater crime to be in a family way, than to live with a man

[81]"Race" is used here in the sense of family and lineage, rather than ethnicity as in modern usage.

as his mistress?—You knew your daughter had done that last: therefore 'tis nonsense to be so affected at the former.—Come, come, forget and forgive!"

"Never: and if you do not leave the house with her this moment, I will not stay in it. My injuries are so great that they cannot admit forgiveness."

"What a horrible, unforgiving spirit yours must be!" cried Dr. Norberry: "and after all, I tell you again, that Adeline has something to forgive and forget too; and she sets you an example of christian charity in coming hither to console and comfort you, poor forsaken woman as you are!"

"Forsaken!" exclaimed Mrs. Mowbray: "aye; why, and for *whom,* was I forsaken? There's the pang! and yet you wonder that I cannot instantly forgive and receive the woman who injured me where I was most vulnerable."

"Oh my mother!" cried Adeline, almost indignantly, "and can that wretch, though dead, still have power to influence my fate in this dreadful manner? And can you still regret the loss of the affection of that man, whose addresses were a disgrace to you?"

At these unguarded words, and too just reproaches, Mrs. Mowbray lost all self-command; and, in a voice almost inarticulate with rage, exclaimed:— "I loved that wretch, as you are pleased to call him. I gloried in the addresses which you are pleased to call my disgrace. But he loved you—he left me for you—and on your account he made me endure the pangs of being forsaken and despised by the man who I adored. Then mark my words: I solemnly swear," dropping on her knees as she spoke, "and I call on God to witness my oath, by all my hopes of happiness hereafter, that until you shall have experienced the anguish of being forsaken and despised as I have been, till you shall be as wretched in love, and as disgraced in the eye of the world, I never will see you more, or pardon your many sins against me— No—not even were you on your death-bed. Yet, no; I am wrong there—Yes; on your death-bed," she added, her voice faltering as she spoke, and passion giving way in a degree to the dictates of returning nature,— "yes, there; there I should—I should forgive you."[82]

"Then I feel that you will forgive me soon," faintly articulated Adeline sinking on the ground; while Mrs. Mowbray was leaving the room, and Dr. Norberry was standing motionless with horror, from the rash oath which he had just heard. But Adeline's fall aroused him from his stupor.

"For God's sake, do not go and leave your daughter dying!" cried he: "your vow does not forbid you to continue to see her now." Mrs. Mowbray turned back, and started with horror at beholding the countenance of Adeline.

"Is she really dying?" cried she eagerly, "and have I killed her?" These words, spoken in a faltering tone, and with a look of anxiety, seemed to recall the fleeting spirit of Adeline. She looked up at her mother, a sort of smile quivered on her lip; and faintly articulating "I am better," she burst into a convulsive flood of tears, and laid her head on the bosom of her compassionate friend.

"She will do now," cried he exultingly to Mrs. Mowbray: "you need alarm yourself no longer."

But alarm was perhaps a feeling of enjoyment, to the sensations which then took possession of Mrs. Mowbray. The apparent danger of Adeline had awakened her long dormant tenderness: but she had just bound herself by an oath not to give way to it, except under circumstances the most unwelcome and affecting, and had therefore embittered her future days with remorse and unavailing regret.—For some minutes she stood looking wildly and mournfully on Adeline, longing to clasp her to her bosom, and pronounce her pardon, but not daring to violate her oath. At length, "I cannot bear this torment," she exclaimed, and rushed out of the room: and when in another apartment, she recollected, and uttered a scream of agony as she did so, that she had seen Adeline probably for the last time; for,

---

[82] Mrs. Mowbray's parental oath significantly resembles the curse Clarissa's father lays on his daughter in Samuel Richardson's 1747 novel, *Clarissa*, in which he prays that she will suffer for her apparent disobedience in this world and the next. Godwin opposed oaths and promises in *Political Justice*, Books VI and VIII respectively.

voluntarily, she was now to see her no more.

The same recollection occurred to Adeline; and as the door closed on her mother, she raised herself up, and looked eagerly to catch the last glimpse of her gown, as the door shut it from her sight.

"Let us go away directly now," said she, "for the air of this room is not good for me."

The doctor, affected beyond measure at the expression of quiet despair with which she spoke, went out to order a coach; and Adeline instantly rose, and kissed with fond devotion the chair on which her mother had sat. Suddenly she heard a deep sigh—it came from the next room—perhaps it came from her mother; perhaps she could still see her again: and with cautious step she knelt down and looked through the key-hole of the door.

She did see her mother once more. Mrs. Mowbray was lying on the bed, beating the ground with her foot, and sighing as if her heart would break.

"O! that I dare go in to her!" said Adeline to herself: "but I can at least bid her farewell here." She then put her mouth to the aperture, and exclaimed, "Mother, dearest mother! since we meet now for the last time— " (Mrs. Mowbray started from the bed) "let me thank you for all the affection, all the kindness which you lavished on me during eighteen happy years. I shall never cease to love and pray for you." (Mrs. Mowbray sobbed aloud.) "Perhaps, you will some day or other think you have been harsh to me, and may wish that you had not taken so cruel a vow." (Mrs. Mowbray beat her breast in agony: the moment of repentance was already come.) "It may therefore be a comfort to you at such moments to know that I sincerely, and from the bottom of my heart, forgive this rash action:—and now, my dearest mother, hear my parting prayers for your happiness!"

At this moment a noise in the next room convinced Adeline that her mother had fallen down in a fainting fit, and the doctor entered the room.

"What have I done?" she exclaimed.

"Go to her this instant."—He obeyed. Raising up Mrs. Mowbray in his arms, he laid her on the bed, while Adeline bent over her in silent anguish, with all the sorrow of filial anxiety. But when the remedies which Dr. Norberry administered began to take effect, she exclaimed, "For the last time! Cruel, but most dear mother!" and pressed her head to her bosom, and kissed her pale lips with almost frantic emotion.

Mrs. Mowbray opened her yes: they met those of Adeline, and instantly closed again.

"She has looked at me for the last time," said Adeline; "and now this one kiss, my mother, and farewell for ever!" So saying she rushed out of the room, and did not stop till she reached the coach, and, springing into it, was received into the arms of Glenmurray.

SENSIBILITY

In eighteenth-century literature, beginning quite early and continuing through the 1790s, a predominant concern was portraying internal, psychological feelings and raising appropriate responses in readers and theater audiences. Novels of sensibility tended to use stock scenes of human suffering such as deserted lovers, deathbed scenes, wrongfully imprisoned victims, and familial estrangement and reconciliation to engage the reader and also to educate him or her in appropriate sentiments and their display. By the 1790s, the vocabulary of the sentimental scene was well developed, and some parodic or excessive versions were also common.

The idea that human beings might be more or less meritorious based not on their social rank by birth, but rather on their internal psychological feelings was developed under the rubric of sensibility. The "cult of sensibility" represents an early concept of psychological selfhood, and was in some ways an inherently liberalizing, humanistic concept. On the one hand, sensibility provided an anti-authoritarian foundation for social and familial order, one opposed to

Hobbesian assumptions about self-interest as the prime motivator for social and national order. Arguments for the better treatment of children, women, slaves, ethnically and racially different people, and animals were made in the name of sensibility. Rather than demanding that daughters obey their parents and particularly their fathers out of a sense of duty alone, sensibility imagined an internalized, psychological relationship which would lead daughters to be more obedient and at the same time, fathers to act with more concern for their daughter's needs and desires. Initially a gesture for expanding human connection beyond one's "race" or family, sensibility developed into the opposite, a tendency to be overly absorbed in taking the temperature of one's own feelings. By 1796, when *Emma Courtney* was published, and even more by 1805 when *Adeline Mowbray* appeared, sensibility was somewhat suspect, both venerated and vulnerable to fraudulent and hypocritical uses.

Sensibility also possessed a gendered aspect. Originally, the increasing value placed on delicacy of feeling gave women a legitimate claim to special knowledge and abilities. If women were not partners in the government of the state or the household, perhaps they should be, since it was believed that they would bring a particularly quick and attentive awareness of human feeling. Very quickly, however, fictional representations of extremely delicate feelings, suffering heroines and heroes, and animal lovers became suspect. Thus, portrayals of ladies who cried over a dead bird or loved their lap dogs passionately, but who beat their servants or neglected their children became a common satirical thread. In addition to making an effort to distinguish between superficial displays of sentimentality and true sensibility, novelists explored the concept of the "man of feeling," a kind of masculinity that reveled in soft feelings, rather than denying them. For women, sensibility represented different challenges. While women were expected to be delicate, sensitive, and specially attuned to fine feelings, they were also cautioned not only against false imitations of sensibility, but against allowing feeling to drive their behavior. The "woman of feeling" ran the risk of being seen as lacking in the self-control and restraint expected of polite ladies. Sensibility represented both the possibility of appreciating an elite and heightened sensitivity to the suffering of others and, on the other hand, an unfeminine tendency to erotic arousal. In short, polite sensibility had to avoid the extremes of passion and eroticized sensitivity *and* of superficial, fashionable pretence to feelings one did not possess. John Gregory in 1774 praised "natural" female delicacy signaled by the blush, thereby assuming a particular connection between femininity and sensibility:

> One of the chief beauties in a female character is that modest reserve, that retiring delicacy, which avoids the public eye, and is disconcerted even at the gaze of admiration. —I do not wish you to be insensible to applause. If you were, you must become, if not worse, at least less amiable women. But you may be dazzled by that admiration, which yet rejoices your hearts.

> When a girl ceases to blush, she has lost the most powerful charm of beauty. That extreme sensibility which it indicates, may be a weakness and incumbrance in our sex, as I have too often felt; but in yours it is peculiarly engaging. Pedants, who think themselves philosophers, ask why a woman should blush when she is conscious of no crime. It is a sufficient answer, that Nature has made you to blush when you are guilty of no fault, and has forced us to love you because you do so. —Blushing is so far from being necessarily an attendant on guilt, that it is the usual companion of innocence. (Gregory, *Legacy*, 13)

On the contrary, in 1792 Mary Wollstonecraft attacked writers who believed that:

> ...the sexes ought not to be compared; man was made to reason, woman to feel: and that together, flesh and spirit, they make the most perfect whole, by blending happily reason and sensibility into one character.

And what is sensibility? "Quickness of sensation; quickness of perception; delicacy." Thus is it defined by Dr. Johnson; and the definition gives me no other idea than of the most exquisitely polished instinct. I discern not a trace of the image of God in either sensation or matter. Refined seventy times seven, they are still material; intellect dwells not there; nor will fire ever make gold. (*Rights of Woman*, 134)

SOURCES

G. J. Barker-Benfield, *The Culture of Sensibility: Sex and Society in Eighteenth-Century Britain* (Chicago: University of Chicago Press, 1992).

John Gregory, *A Father's Legacy to His Daughters*, London, 1774.

Chris Jones, *Radical Sensibility: Literature and Ideas in the 1790s* (NY: Routledge, 1993).

Janet Todd, *Sensibility: An Introduction* (New York: Methuen, 1986).

Mary Wollstonecraft, *Vindication of the Rights of Woman* (1792), in *Works of Mary Wollstonecraft*, ed. Janet Todd and Marilyn Butler, 5 Vols. Vol. 5 (Washington Square, NY: New York University Press, 1989).

"You are my all now," said she. "You have long been mine," replied he: but respecting the anguish and disappointment depicted on her countenance, he forbore to ask for an explanation; and resting her pale cheek on his bosom, they reached the inn in silence.

Adeline had walked up and down the room a number of times, had as often looked out of the window, before Dr. Norberry, whom she had been anxiously expecting and looking for, made his appearance. "Thank God, you are come at last!" said she, seizing his hand as he entered.

"I left Mrs. Mowbray," replied he, "much better both in

mind and body."

"A blessed hearing!" replied Adeline.

"And you, my child, how are you?" asked the doctor affectionately.

"I know not yet," answered Adeline mournfully: "as yet I am stunned by the blow which I have received: but pray tell me what has passed between you and my mother since we left the hotel."

"What has passed?" cried Dr. Norberry, starting from his chair, taking two hasty strides across the room, pulling up the cape of his coat, and muttering an oath between his shut teeth— "Why, this passed:—The deluded woman renounced her daughter; and her friend, her old and faithful friend, has renounced her."

"Oh! My poor mother!" exclaimed Adeline.

"Girl! Girl! Don't be foolish," replied the doctor; "keep your pity for more deserving objects; and, as the wisest thing you can do, endeavor to forget your mother."

"Forget her! Never."

"Well, well, you will be wiser in time; and now you shall hear all that passed. When she recovered entirely, and found that you were gone, she gave way to an agony of sorrow, such as I never before witnessed; for I believe that I never beheld before the agony of remorse."

"My poor mother!" cried Adeline, against bursting into tears.

"What! again!" exclaimed the doctor. (Adeline motioned to him to go on, and he continued.) "At sight of this, I was weak enough to pity her; and, with the greatest simplicity, I told her, that I was glad to see that she felt penitent for her conduct, since penitence paved the way to amendment; when, to my great surprise, all the vanished fierceness and haughtiness of her look returned, and she told me, that so far from repenting she approved of her conduct; and that remorse had no share in her sorrow; that she wept from consciousness of misery, but of misery inflicted by the faults of others, not her own."

"Oh! Dr. Norberry," cried Adeline reproachfully, "I doubt,

by awakening her pride, you destroyed the tenderness returning towards me."

"May be so. However, so much the better; for anger is a less painful state of mind to endure than that of remorse; and while she thinks herself only injured and aggrieved, she will be less unhappy."

"Then," continued Adeline in a faltering voice, "I care not how long she hates me."

Dr. Norberry looked at Adeline a moment with tears in his eyes, and evidently gulped down a rising sob. "Good child! good child!" he at length articulated. "Yet—no. Girl, girl, your virtue only heaps coals of fire on that devoted woman's head."

"For pity's sake, Dr. Norberry!" cried Adeline.

"Well, well, I have done. But she'll forget and forgive all in time, I do not doubt."

"Impossible: remember her oath."

"And do you really suppose that she will think herself bound to keep so silly and rash an oath; an oath made in the heat of passion?"

"Undoubtedly I do; and I know, that were she to break it, she would never be otherwise than wretched all her life after. Therefore, unless Glenmurray forsakes me (she added, trying to smile archly as she spoke), and this I am not happy enough to expect, I look on our separation in this world to be eternal."

"You do?—Then, poor devil, how miserable she will be, when her present resentment shall subside! Well; when that time comes I may perhaps see her again," added the doctor, gulping again.

"Heaven bless you for that intention!" cried Adeline. "But how could you ever have the heart to renounce her?"

"Zounds, girl! you are almost as provoking as your mother. Why, how could I have the heart to do otherwise, when she whitewashed herself and blackened you? To be sure, it did cause me a twinge or two to do it; and had she been an iota less haughty, I should have turned back and said, 'Kiss, and be friends again.' But she seemed so provokingly anxious to get rid of me, and waved me with her hand to the door in such a d——d tragedy queen sort of a manner that, having told her very civilly to go to the devil her own way, I gulped down a sort of a tender choking in my throat, and made as rapid an exit as possible. And now another trial awaits me. I came to town, at some inconvenience to myself, to try to do you service. I have failed, and I have now no further business here: so we must part, and God knows when we shall meet again. For I rarely leave home, and may not see you again for years."

"Indeed." exclaimed Adeline. "Surely," looking at Glenmurray, "we might settle in Dr. Norberry's neighborhood?"

Glenmurray said nothing, but looked at the doctor; who seemed confused, and was silent.

"Look ye, my dear girl," said he at length: "the idea of your settling near me had occurred to me, but— " here he took two hasty strides across the room— "in short, that's an impossible thing; so I beg you to think no more about it. If, indeed, you mean to marry Mr. Glenmurray— "

"Which I shall not do," replied Adeline coldly.

"There again, now!" cried the doctor pettishly: "you, in your way, are quite as obstinate and ridiculous as your mother. However, I hope you will know better in time. But it grows late— 'tis time I should be in my chaise, and I hear it driving up. Mr. Glenmurray," continued he in an altered tone of voice, "to your care and your tenderness I leave this poor child: and, zounds, man! if you will but burn your books before her face, and swear they are d—d stuff, why, 'sdeath, I say, I would come to town on purpose to do you homage.—Adeline, my child, God bless you! I have loved you from your infancy, and I wish, from my soul, that I left you in a better situation. But you will write to me, heh?"

"Undoubtedly."

"Well, one kiss:—don't be jealous, Glenmurray. Your hand, man.—Woons,[83] what a hand! My dear fellow, take care of yourself, for that poor child's sake: get the advice which I

---

[83] A variant of "God's wounds," like "zounds" a mild oath.

recommended, and good air." A rising sob interrupted him— he hemmed it off, and ran into his chaise.

Chapter IV.

"Now, then," said Adeline, her tears dropping fast as she spoke, "now, then, we are alone in the world; henceforward we must be all to each other."

"Is the idea a painful one, Adeline?" replied Glenmurray reproachfully.

"Not so," returned Adeline. "Still I can't yet forget that I had a mother, and a kind one too."

"And may have again."

"Impossible:—there is a vow in heaven against it. No—My plans for future happiness must be laid unmindful and independent of her. They must have you and your happiness for their sole object; I must live for you alone: and you," added she in a faltering voice, "must live for me."

"I will live as long as I can," replied Glenmurray sighing, "and as one step towards it I shall keep early hours: so to rest, dear Adeline, and let us forget our sorrows as soon as possible."

The next morning Adeline's and Glenmurray's first care was to determine on their future residence. It was desirable that it should be at a sufficient distance from London, to deserve the name and have the convenience of a country abode, yet sufficiently near it for Glenmurray to have the advice of a London physician if necessary.

"Suppose we fix at Richmond?"[84] said Glenmurray: and Adeline, to whom the idea of dwelling on a spot at once so classical and beautiful was most welcome, joyfully consented; and in a few days they were settled there in a pleasant but expensive lodging.

But here, as when abroad, Glenmurray occasionally saw old

---

[84] Up river from London and now a far-flung suburb of greater London, Richmond was the location of a royal palace; in the eighteenth century it became a popular residential area for wealthy merchants, poets, and artists.

acquaintances, many of whom were willing to renew their intercourse with him for the sake of being introduced to Adeline: and who, from a knowledge of her situation, presumed to pay her that sort of homage, which, though not understood by her, gave pangs unutterable to the delicate mind of Glenmurray. "Were she my wife, they dared not pay her such marked attention," said he to himself; and again, as delicately as he could, he urged Adeline to sacrifice her principles to the prejudices of society.

"I thought," replied Adeline gravely, "that, as we lived for each other, we might act independent of society, and serve it by our example even against its will."

Glenmurray was silent.—He did not like to own how painful and mischievous he found in practice the principles which he admired in theory—and Adeline continued:

"Believe me, Glenmurray, ours is the very situation calculated to urge us on in the pursuit of truth. We are answerable to no one for our conduct; and we can make any experiments in morals that we choose. I am wholly at a loss to comprehend why you persist in urging me to marry you. Take care, my dear Glenmurray—the high respect I bear your character was shaken a little by your fighting a duel in defiance of your principles; and your eagerness to marry in further defiance of them, may weaken my esteem, if not my love."

Adeline smiled as she said this: but Glenmurray thought she spoke more in earnest than she was willing to allow; and, alarmed at the threat, he only answered, "You know it is for your sake merely that I speak," and dropped the subject; secretly resolving, however, that he would not walk with Adeline in the fashionable promenades, at the hours commonly spent there by the beau monde.

But, in spite of this precaution, they could not escape the assiduities of some gay men of fashion, who knew Glenmurray and admired his companion; and Adeline at length suspected that Glenmurray was jealous. But in this she wronged him; it was not the attention paid her, but the nature of it, that disturbed

him. Nor is it to be wondered at that Adeline herself was eager
to avoid the public walks, when it is known that one of her
admirers at Richmond was the colonel Mordaunt whom she
had become acquainted with at Bath.

Colonel Mordaunt, "curst with every granted prayer," was
just beginning to feel the tedium of life, when he saw Adeline
unexpectedly at Richmond; and though he felt shocked at first,
at beholding her in so different a situation from that in which he
had first beheld her, still that very situation, by holding forth to
him a prospect of being favoured by her in his turn, revived his
admiration with more than its original violence, and he resolved
to be, if possible, the lover of Adeline, after Glenmurray should
have fallen a victim, as he had no doubt but he would, to his
dangerous illness.

But the opportunities which he had of seeing her suddenly
ceased. She no longer frequented the public walks; and him,
though he suspected it not, she most studiously avoided; for she
could not bear to behold the alteration in his manner when he
addressed her, an alteration perhaps unknown to himself. True,
it was not insulting; but Adeline, who had admired him too
much at Bath not to have examined with minute attention the
almost timid expression of his countenance, and the respectfulness
of his manner when he addressed her, shrunk abashed from the
ardent and impassioned expression with which he now met her,—
an expression which Adeline used to call "looking like sir Patrick;"
and which indicated even to her inexperience, that the admiration
which he then felt was of a nature less pure and flattering than
the one which she excited before; and though in her own eyes
she appeared as worthy of respect as ever, she was forced to own
even to herself, that persons in general would be of a contrary
opinion.

But in vain did she resolve to walk very early in a morning
only, being fully persuaded that she should then meet with no
one. Colonel Mordaunt was as wakeful as she was; and being
convinced that she walked during some part of the day, and
probably early in a morning, he resolved to watch near the door

of her lodgings, in hopes to obtain a hour's conversation with her. The consequence was, that he saw Adeline one morning walking pensively and alone, down the shady road that leads from the terrace to Petersham.

This opportunity was not to be over-looked; and he overtook and accosted her with such an expression of pleasure on his countenance, as was sufficient to alarm the now suspicious delicacy of Adeline; and, conscious as she was that Glenmurray beheld colonel Mordaunt's attentions with pain, a deep blush overspread her cheek at his approach, while her eyes were timidly cast down.

Colonel Mordaunt saw her emotion, and attributed it to a cause flattering to his vanity; it even encouraged him to seize her hand; and, while he openly congratulated himself on his good fortune in meeting her alone, he presumed to press her hand to his lips. Adeline indignantly withdrew it, and replied very coldly to his inquiries concerning her health.

"But where have you hidden yourself lately?" cried he.—"O miss Mowbray! loveliest, and, I may add, most beloved of women, how have I longed to see you alone, and pour out my whole soul to you!"

Adeline answered this rhapsody by a look of astonishment only—being silent from disgust and consternation,—while involuntarily she quickened her pace, as if wishing to avoid him.

"O hear me, and hear me patiently!" he resumed. "You must have noticed the effect which your charms produced on me at Bath; and may I dare to add that my attentions then did not seem displeasing to you?"

"Sir!" interrupted Adeline, sighing deeply, "my situation is now changed; and——"

'It is so, I thank Fortune that it is so," replied colonel Mordaunt; "and I am happy to say, it is changed by no crime of mine." (Here Adeline started and turned pale.)

"But I were unworthy all chance of happiness, were I to pass by the seeming opportunity of being blest, which the alteration to which you allude holds forth to me."

Here he paused, as if in embarrassment, but Adeline was unable to interrupt him.

"Miss Mowbray," he at length continued, "I am told that you are not on good terms with your mother; nay, I have heard that she has renounced you: may I presume to ask if this be true?"

"It is," answered Adeline trembling with emotion.

"Then, as before long it is probable that you will be without—without a protector——" (Adeline turned round and fixed her eyes wildly upon him.) "To be sure," continued he, avoiding her steadfast gaze, "I could wish to call you mine this moment; but, unhappy as you appear to be in your present situation, I know, unlike many women circumstanced as you are, you are too generous and noble-minded to be capable of forsaking in his last illness the man who in his happier moments you honoured with your love." As he said this, Adeline, her lips parched with agitation, and breathing short, caught hold of his arm; and pressing her cold hand, he went on: "Therefore, I will not venture even to wish to be honored with a kind look from you till Mr. Glenmurray is removed to a happier world. But *then*, dearest of women, you whom I loved without hope of possessing you, and whom now I dote upon to madness, I conjure you to admit my visits, and let my attentions prevail on you to accept my protection, and allow me to devote the remainder of my days to love and you."

"Merciful heaven!" exclaimed Adeline clasping her hands together, "to what insults am I reserved!"

"Insults!" echoed colonel Mordaunt.

"Yes sir," replied Adeline: "you have insulted me, grossly insulted me, and know not the woman whom you have tortured to the very soul."

"Hear me, hear me, miss Mowbray!" exclaimed colonel Mordaunt, almost as much agitated as herself: "by heaven I meant not to insult you! and perhaps I—perhaps I have been misinformed—No!—Yes, yes, it must be so; —your indignation proves that I have—You are, no doubt—and on my knees I implore your pardon—you are the wife of Mr. Glenmurray."

"And suppose I am *not* his wife," cried Adeline, "is it then given to a wife only to be secure from being insulted by offers horrible to the delicacy, and wounding to the sensibility, like those which I have heard from you?" But before colonel Mordaunt could reply, Adeline's thoughts had reverted to what he had said of Glenmurray's certain danger; and, unable to bear this confirmation of her fears, with the speed of phrensy she ran towards home, and did not stop till she was in sight of her lodging, and the still closed curtain of her apartment met her view.

"He is still sleeping, then," she exclaimed, "and I have time to recover myself, and endeavour to hide from him the emotion of which I could not tell the reason." So saying, she softly entered the house, and by the time Glenmurray rose she had regained her composure. Still there was a look of anxiety on her fine countenance, which could not escape the penetrating eye of love.

"Why are you so grave this morning?" said Glenmurray, as Adeline seated herself at the breakfast table:— "I feel much better and more cheerful to-day."

"But are you, indeed, better?" replied Adeline, fixing her tearful eyes on him.

"Or I much deceive myself," said Glenmurray.

"Thank God!" devoutly replied Adeline. "I thought—I thought—" Here tears choked her utterance, and Glenmurray drew from her a confession of her anxious fears for him, though she prudently resolved not to agitate him by telling him of the rencontre with colonel Mordaunt.

But when the continued assurances of Glenmurray that he was better, and the animation of his countenance, had in a degree removed her fears for his life, she had leisure to revert to another source of uneasiness, and to dwell on the insult which she had experienced from colonel Mordaunt's offer of protection.

"How strange and irrational," thought Adeline, "are the prejudices of society! Because an idle ceremony has not been muttered over me at the altar, I am liable to be thought a woman of vicious inclinations, and to be exposed to the most daring insults."

As these reflections occurred to her, she could scarcely help regretting that her principles would not allow her delicacy and virtue to be placed under the sacred shelter bestowed by that ceremony which she was pleased to call idle. And she was not long without experiencing still further hardships from the situation in which she had persisted so obstinately to remain. Their establishment consisted of a footman and a maid servant; but the latter had of late been so remiss in the performance of her duties, and so impertinent when reproved for her faults, that Adeline was obliged to give her warning.

"Warning, indeed!" replied the girl: "a mighty hardship, truly! I can promise you I did not mean to stay long; it is no such favour to live with a kept miss;—and if you come to that, I think I am as good as you."

Shocked, surprised, and unable to answer, Adeline took refuge in her room. Never before had she been accosted by her inferiors without respectful attention; and now, owing to her situation, even a servant-maid thought herself authorised to insult her, and to raise herself to her level!

"But surely," said Adeline mentally, "I ought to reason with her, and try to convince her that I am in reality as virtuous as if I were Glenmurray's wife, instead of his mistress."

Accordingly she went back into the kitchen: but her resolution failed her when she found the footman there, listening with a broad grin on his countenance to the relation which Mary was giving him of the "fine trimming" which she had given "madam."

Scarcely did the presence of Adeline interrupt or restrain her; but at last she turned round and said, "And, pray, have you got any thing to say to me?"

"Nothing more now," meekly replied Adeline, "unless you will follow me to my chamber."

"With all my heart," cried the girl; and Adeline returned to her own room.

"I wish, Mary, to set you right," said Adeline, "with respect to my situation. You called me, I think, a kept miss, and seemed to think ill of me."

"Why, to be sure, ma'am," replied Mary, a little alarmed—"every body say you are a kept lady, and so I made no bones of saying so; but I am sure if so be you are not so, why I ax pardon."[85]

"But what do you mean by the term kept lady?"

"Why, a lady who lives with a man without being married to him, I take it; and that I take to be your case, an't it, I pray?"

Adeline blushed and was silent:—it certainly was her case. However, she took courage and went on:

"But mistresses, or kept ladies in general, are women of bad character, and would live any man; but I never loved, nor ever shall love, any man but Mr. Glenmurray. I took on myself as his wife in the sight of God; nor will I quit him till death shall separate us."

"Then if so be that you don't want to change, I think you might as well be married to him."

Adeline was again silent for a moment, but continued—

"Mr. Glenmurray would marry me to-morrow, if I chose."

"Indeed! Well, if master is inclined to make an honest woman of you, you had better take him at his word, I think."

"Gracious heaven!" cried Adeline, "what an expression! Why will you persist to confound me with those deluded women who are victims of their own weakness?"

"As to that," replied Mary, "you talk too fine for me; but a fact is a fact—are you or are you not my master's wife?"

"I am not."

"Why then you are his mistress, and a kept lady to all intents and purposes: so what signifies argufying the matter? I lived with a kept madam before, and she was as good as you, for aught I know."

---

[85] Mary's speech is purposefully rendered as dialect in an imitation of the speech of the servant class, just as Savanna's speech is an effort to render Black Caribbean speech patterns.

Adeline, shocked and disappointed, told her she might leave the room.

"I am going," pertly answered Mary, "and to seek for a place: but I must beg that you will not own you are no better than you should be, when a lady comes to ask my character; for then perhaps I should not get any one to take me. I shall call you Mrs. Glenmurray."

"But I shall not call *myself* so," replied Adeline. "I will not say what is not true, on any account."

"There now, there's spite! And yet you pertend to call yourself a gentlewoman, and to be better than other kept ladies! Why, you are not worthy to tie the shoestrings of my last mistress—she did not mind telling a lie rather than lose a poor servant a place; and she called herself a married woman rather than hurt me."

"Neither she nor you, then," replied Adeline gravely, "were sensible of what great importance a strict adherence to veracity is, to the interests of society. I am;—and for the sake of mankind I will always tell the truth."

"You had better tell one innocent lie for mine," replied the girl pertly. "I dare to say the world will neither know nor care any thing about it: and I can tell you I shall expect you will."

So saying she shut the door with violence, leaving Adeline mournfully musing on the distresses attending on her situation, and even disposed to question the propriety of remaining in it.

The inquietude of her mind, as usual, showed itself in her countenance, and involved her in another difficulty: to make Glenmurray uneasy by an avowal of what had passed between her and Mary was impossible; yet how could she conceal it from him? And while she was deliberating on this point, Glenmurray entered the room, and tenderly inquired what had so evidently disturbed her.

"Nothing of any consequence," she faltered out, and burst into tears.

"Could 'nothing of consequence' produce such emotion?" answered Glenmurray.

"But I am ashamed to own the cause of my uneasiness."

"Ashamed to own it to me, Adeline? To be sure, you have a great deal to fear from my severity!" said he, faintly smiling.

Adeline for a moment resolved to tell him the whole truth; but, fearful of throwing him into a degree of agitation hurtful to his weak frame, she, who had the moment before so nobly supported the necessity of a strict adherence to truth, condescended to equivocate and evade; and turning away her head, while a conscious blush overspread her cheek, she replied, "You know that I look forward with anxiety and uneasiness to the time of my approaching confinement."

Glenmurray believed her; and overcome by some painful feelings, which fears for himself and anxiety for her occasioned him, he silently pressed her to his bosom; and, choked with contending emotions, returned to his own apartment.

"And I have stooped to the meanness of disguising the truth!" cried Adeline, clasping her hands convulsively together: "surely, surely, there must be something radically wrong in a situation which exposes one to such a variety of degradations!"

Mary, meanwhile, had gone in search of a place; and having found the lady to whom she had been advised to offer herself, at home, she returned to tell Adeline that Mrs. Pemberton would call in half an hour to inquire her character. The half-hour, an anxious one to Adeline, having elapsed, a lady knocked at the door, and inquired, in Adeline's hearing, for Mrs. Glenmurray.

"Tell the lady," cried Adeline immediately from the top of the staircase, "that miss Mowbray will wait on her directly." The footman obeyed, and Mrs. Pemberton was ushered into the parlour: and now, for the first time in her life, Adeline trembled to approach a stranger; for the first time she felt that she was going to appear before a fellow-creature as an object of scorn, and, though an enthusiast for virtue, to be considered as a votary of vice. But it was a mortification which she must submit to undergo; and hastily throwing a large shawl over her shoulders, to hide her figure as much as possible, with a trembling hand she opened the door, and found herself in the dreaded presence of Mrs. Pemberton.

Nor was she at all re-assured when she found that lady dressed in the neat, modest garb of a strict quaker—a garb which creates an immediate idea in the mind, of more than common rigidness of principles and sanctity of conduct in the wearer of it.[86] Adeline curtsied in silence.

Mrs. Pemberton bowed her head courteously; then, with a countenance of great sweetness, and a voice calculated to inspire confidence, said, "I believe thy name is Mowbray; but I came to see Mrs. Glenmurray: and as on these occasions I always wish to confer with the principal, wouldst thou, if it be not inconvenient, ask the mistress of Mary to let me see her?"

"I am myself the mistress of Mary," replied Adeline in a faint voice.

"I ask thine excuse," answered Mrs. Pemberton, re-seating herself: "as thou art Mrs. Glenmurray, thou art the person I wanted to see."

Here Adeline changed colour, overcome with the consciousness that she ought to undeceive her, and the sense of the difficulty of doing so.

"But thou are very pale, and seemest uneasy," continued the gentle quaker— "I hope thy husband is not worse?"

"Mr. Glenmurray, but not my husband," said Adeline, "is better to-day."

"Art thou not married?" asked Mrs. Pemberton with quickness.

"I am not."

"And yet thou livest with the gentleman I named, and art the person whom Mary called Mrs. Glenmurray?"

"I am," replied Adeline, her paleness yielding to a deep crimson, and her eyes filling with tears.

Mrs. Pemberton sat for a minute in silence; then rising with an air of cold dignity, "I fear thy servant is not likely to suit me,"

---

[86] Amelia Opie herself converted to Quakerism in 1825 after both her husband's and father's deaths. She had long been close friends with an important Norwich Quaker family, the Gurneys.

she observed. "and I will not detain thee any longer."

"She can be an excellent servant," faltered out Adeline.

"Very likely—but there are objections." So saying she reached the door: but as she passed Adeline she stopped, interested and affected by the mournful expression of her countenance, and the visible effort she made to retain her tears.

Adeline saw, and felt humbled at the compassion which her countenance expressed: to be an object of pity was as mortifying as to be an object of scorn, and she turned her eyes on Mrs. Pemberton with a look of proud indignation: but they met those of Mrs. Pemberton fixed on her with a look of such benevolence, that her anger was instantly subdued; and it occurred to her that she might make the benevolent compassion visible in Mrs. Pemberton's countenance serviceable to her discarded servant.

"Stay, madam," she cried, as Mrs. Pemberton was about to leave the room, "allow me a moment's conversation with you."

Mrs. Pemberton, with an eagerness which she suddenly endeavoured to check, returned to her seat.

"I suspect," said Adeline, (gathering courage from the conscious kindness of her motive,) that your objection to take Mary Warner into your service proceeds wholly from the situation of her present mistress."

"Thou judgest rightly," was Mrs. Pemberton's answer.

"Nor do I wonder," continued Adeline, "that you make this objection, when I consider the present prejudices of society."

"Prejudices!" softly exclaimed the benevolent quaker.

Adeline faintly smiled, and went on— "But surely you will allow, that in a family quiet and secluded as ours, and in daily contemplation of a union uninterrupted, faithful, and virtuous, and possessing all the sacredness of marriage, though without the name, it is not likely that the young woman in question should have imbibed any vicious habits or principles."

"But in contemplating thy union itself, she has lived in the contemplation of vice; and thou wilt own, that, by having given it an air of respectability, thou hast only made it more dangerous."

"On this point," cried Adeline, "I see we must disagree—I

shall therefore, without further preamble, inform you, madam, that Mary, aware of the difficulty of procuring a service, if it were known that she had lived with a kept mistress, as the phrase is (here an indignant blush overspread the face of Adeline), desired me to call myself the wife of Glenmurray: but this, from my abhorrence of all falsehood, I peremptorily refused."

"And thou didst well," exclaimed Mrs. Pemberton, "and I respect thy resolution."

"But my sincerity will, I fear, prevent the poor girl's obtaining other reputable places; and I, alas! am not rich enough to make her amends for the injury which my conscience forced me to do her. But if you, madam, could be prevailed upon to take her into your family, even for a short time only, to wipe away the disgrace which her living with me has brought upon her— "

"Why can she not remain with thee?" asked Mrs. Pemberton hastily.

"Because she neglected her duty, and, when reproved for it, replied in very injurious language."

"Presuming probably on thy way of life?"

"I must confess that she has reproached me with it."

"And this was all her fault?"

"It was:—she can be an excellent servant."

"Thou hast said enough; thy conscience shall not have the additional burden to bear, of having deprived a poor girl of her maintenance—I will take her."

"A thousand thanks to you," replied Adeline: "you have removed a weight off my mind: but my conscience, I bless God, has none to bear."

"No?" returned Mrs. Pemberton: "dost thou deem thy conduct blameless in the eyes of that Being whom thou has just blessed?"

"As far as my connexion with Mr. Glenmurray is concerned I do."

"Indeed!"

"Nay, doubt me not—believe me that I never wantonly violate the truth; and that even an evasion, which I, for the first time in my life, was guilty of to-day, has given me a pang to which I will not again expose myself."

"And yet, inconsistent beings as we are," cried Mrs. Pemberton, "straining at a gnat, and swallowing a camel,[87] what is the guilt of the evasion which weighs on thy mind, compared to that of living, as thou dost, in an illicit commerce? Surely, surely, thine heart accuses thee; for thy face bespeaks uneasiness, and thou wilt listen to the whispers of penitence, and leave, ere long, the man who has betrayed thee."

"The man who has betrayed me! Mr. Glenmurray is no betrayer—he is one of the best of human beings. No, madam: if I had acceded to his wishes, I should long ago have been his wife; but, from a conviction of the folly of marriage, I have preferred living with him without the performance of a ceremony which, in the eye of reason, can confer neither honor nor happiness."

"Poor thing!" exclaimed Mrs. Pemberton, rising as she spoke, "I understand thee now—Thou are one of the enlightened, as they call themselves—Thou are one of those wise in their own conceit, who, disregarding the customs of ages, and the dictates of experience, set up their own opinions against the hallowed institutions of men and the will of the Most High."

"Can you blame me," interrupted Adeline, "for acting according to what I think right?"

"But hast thou well studied the subject on which thou hast decided? Yet, alas! to thee how vain must be the voice of admonition! (she continued, her countenance kindling into strong expression as she spoke)—From the poor victim of passion and persuasion, penitence and amendment might be rationally expected; and she, from the path of frailty, might turn again to that of virtue; but for one like thee, glorying in thine iniquity, and erring, not from the too tender heart, but the vain-glorious head,—for thee there is, I fear, no blessed return to the right

---

[87] St. Matthew 26:24: "Ye blind guides, which strain at a gnat, and swallow a camel."

way; and I, who would have tarried with thee even in the house of sin, to have reclaimed thee, penitent, now hasten from thee, and for ever—firm as thou art in guilt."

As she said this she reached the door; while Adeline, affected by her emotion, and distressed by her language, stood silent and almost abashed before her.

But with her hand on the lock she turned round, and in a gentler voice said, "Yet not even against a wilful offender like thee, should one gate that may lead to amendment be shut. Thy situation and thy fortunes may soon be greatly changed; affliction may subdue thy pride, and the counsel of a friend of thine own sex might then sound sweetly in thine ears. Should that time come, I will be that friend. I am now about to set off for Lisbon with a very dear friend, about whom I feel as solicitous as thou about thy Glenmurray; and there I shall remain some time. Here then is my address; and if thou shouldest want my advice or assistance write to me, and be assured that Rachel Pemberton will try to forget thy errors in thy distresses."

Anti-Jacobinism

Adeline Mowbray has often been identified as an "Anti-Jacobin novel," or a novel showing the faults and dangers of ideas associated with British radicals and reformers. Mrs. Pemberton's argument with Adeline here—her suggestion that rather than excusing her actions Adeline's advanced ideas and education the more obligate her to adhere to the strictest principles of moral behavior as an example to her social inferiors—is congruent with arguments often identified as anti-Jacobin. However, Quakers like Mrs. Pemberton, were themselves common targets in the influential *The Anti-Jacobin,* and *The Anti-Jacobin Review and Magazine* where loyalty to both the Church of England and the King were explicitly linked. *Adeline Mowbray* is then, in particularly complex conversation with the public debates that raged through the 1790s and into the early 1800s.

The so-called "pamphlet wars" of the 1790s, in which radical principles were disseminated through not only formal and expensive books, but cheap, quickly printed broadsides, popular journalism, political cartoons, and magazines, were begun as the loyalist and "Church and King" factions also began publishing their views. Among the most famous and influential publications on the more conservative, loyalist side was the *Anti-Jacobin, or Weekly Examiner* (1797-98) and its sequel, the *Anti-Jacobin Review and Magazine* (1798-1821). Secretly funded by Prime Minister William Pitt's government, the *Anti-Jacobin* more than perhaps any other publication was responsible for misnaming the English radicals "Jacobins" and so permanently associating them with the more reactionary and violent aspects of the French Revolution's Jacobin party. (See textbox on "English Jacobins and Jacobinism," p. 100.) Posing as the product of moral, well-meaning, and loyal Englishmen, and actually authored by recognized literary talents and government officials, the *Anti-Jacobin* announced its creation and purpose as a response to the new fashion for political radical ideas in 1797, declaring that:

> IN MORALS We are equally old-fashioned. We have not yet learned the modern refinement of referring in all considerations upon human conduct, not to any settled and preconceived principles of right or wrong, not to any general and fundamental rules which experience, and wisdom, and justice, and the common consent of mankind have established, but to the internal admonitions of every man's judgement or conscience in his own particular instance.

> ...We reverence LAW, —We acknowledge USAGE, —We look even upon PRESCRIPTION without hatred or horror. And we do not think these, or any of them, less safe guides for the moral actions of men, than that new and liberal system of ETHICS, whose operation is not to bind but to loosen the bands of

social order; whose doctrine is formed not on a system of reciprocal duties, but on the supposition of individual, independent, and unconnected rights; which teaches that all men are pretty equally honest, but that some have different notions of honesty from others, and that the most received notions are for the greater part the most faulty.

We do not subscribe to the opinion, that a sincere conviction of the truth of no matter what principle, is a sufficient defence for no matter what action; and that the only business of moral enquiry with human conduct is to ascertain that in each case the principle and the action agree. ... It is not in our creed, that ATHEISM is as good a faith as CHRISTIANITY, provided it be professed with equal sincerity....

Of all these and the like principles, in one word, of JACOBINISM in all its shapes, and in all its degrees, political and moral, public and private, whether as it openly threatens the subversion of the States, or gradually saps the foundations of domestic happiness, We are the avowed, determined, and irreconcilable enemies. (Prospectus of *The Anti-Jacobin or Weekly Examiner*, November, 1797, pp. 1-6)

The fear that "Jacobinism" might impact the "private" and "moral" realm, the British family as well as the British state, opened the critique of radical politics to women writers, engaging them in political debate in defense of home and family. In 1797 the *Anti-Jacobin* published a letter purportedly written by a lady, detailing the dangers English Jacobinism posed to domestic peace and homelife. She begins by arguing that domestic issues are just as significant (and political) as those of the nation:

What I find most fault with you for, is, that you confine your Remarks chiefly to Public Matters, as if Jacobinism and the Principles, which you set up to oppose, did not disturb domestic Felicity and

Comfort as much as it does Kingdoms and Empires, though, in your Preface or Prospectus, you mention it in that light....

The letter continues, documenting the sad story of how the writer's father was seduced by reading Thomas Paine's *Rights of Man*, and in becoming a radical, has destroyed the family's happiness, even forbidding her marriage to a young soldier on the grounds that he will not have his daughter marry a professional murderer.

Alas! Sir, it is since that period that he has been growing every day bitterer and bitterer, and unkinder and unkinder; ever since the very month after...when he came from hearing a lecturer who went about the country reading history and philosophy, and, as my father said, "kindling a holy enthusiasm of freedom." —I remember the words as if it were but yesterday. I am sure I have reason, and so have we all, for from that moment his whole temper and manner changed so, that our house, from being the pleasantest in the village for chearful society and kindness to one another, is become gloomy disconsolate to us all....

But to return to my Father—who is now reading Books and Pamphlets that seem quite wicked and immoral to my mind and my poor Mother's, whom it vexes sadly to hear my Father talk before company, that Marriage is good for nothing, and ought to be free to be broken by either party at will. It was but the other day that he told her, that if he were to choose again, by the New Law in the only Free Country in the world, he would prefer Concubinage—so he said in my hearing.

He used to be compassionate to the Poor and to Beggars even—but now he drives the latter from his door, saying if they are oppressed, why do they not right themselves? and that the good things of the world are divided unequally, and the moment is at hand when those who have nothing will bear it no longer; and that he will not, for his part, be guilty of making the evil less felt, and so keep off the remedy....

He used to go to church too, regularly every Sunday—but of late he has left it off entirely, though professing at the same time to be more religious than ever, and to adore the Supreme Being in his works. –So he makes me walk in the open air during the service time, and bids me gaze up and look around, and overflow with divine sensation—which he says is *natural* religion, and better than all the preaching and saying printed prayers, in the world. ... I am afraid these particulars may seem tiresome and uninteresting; and I feel that I have not half described the uneasiness which this new temper and principles of my father occasion, and the change that has been in him, nor how surprizing it seems to me that the more he has liberty and independence in his mouth, the more he should be a tyrant ... in his conduct to his family. (*Anti-Jacobin Magazine*, No. 6, Dec 18, 1797, pp.195 &197)

Mrs. Pemberton's debate with Adeline participates in the moral, Christian-based objections to ideas associated with the new philosophy, but is more earnest, less polemical than the supposed "letter from a lady" (probably written by one of the magazine's regular male writers). In the sense that there is a critique of ideas associated with philosophical radicalism and an affirmation of the special duties of ladies such as Adeline to behave irreproachably, the novel appears to participate in an anti-Jacobin critique. However, using the Quaker Mrs. Pemberton as the voice of reason and compassion situates the novel outside the mainstream of anti-Jacobin propaganda in which non-conforming dissenters were politically suspect.

SOURCES
The Anti-Jacobin or Weekly Examiner, No. 1, November 1797.
Anti-Jacobin Magazine and Review, No. 6, December 1797.

So saying she left the room, but returned again, before Adeline had recovered herself from the various emotions which she had experienced during her address, to ask her christian name. But when Adeline replied, "My name is Adeline Mowbray," Mrs. Pemberton started, and eagerly exclaimed, "Art thou Adeline Mowbray of Gloucestershire—the young heiress, as she was called, of Rosevalley?"

"I was once," replied Adeline, sinking back into a chair, "Adeline Mowbray of Rosevalley."

Mrs. Pemberton for a few minutes gazed on her in mournful silence: "And art thou," she cried, "Adeline Mowbray? Art thou that courteous, blooming, blessed being, (for every tongue that I heard name thee blessed thee) whom I saw only three years ago bounding over thy native hills, all grace, and joy, and innocence?"

Adeline tried to speak, but her voice failed her.

"Art thou she," continued Mrs. Pemberton, "whom I saw also leaning from the window of her mother's mansion, and inquiring with the countenance of a pitying angel concerning the health of a wan labourer who limped past the door?"

Adeline hid her face with her hands.

Mrs. Pemberton went on in a lower tone of voice,— "I came with some companions to see thy mother's grounds, and to hear the nightingales in her groves; but—(here Mrs. Pemberton's voice faltered) I have seen a sight far beyond that of the proudest mansion, said I to those who asked me of thy mother's seat; I have heard what was sweeter to my ear than the voice of the nightingale; I have seen a blooming girl nursed in idleness and prosperity, yet active in the discharge of every christian duty; and I have heard her speak in the soothing accents of kindness and of pity, while her name was followed by blessings, and parents prayed to have a child like her.—O lost, unhappy girl! such *was*

Adeline Mowbray: and often, very often, has thy graceful image recurred to my remembrance: but, how art thou changed! Where is the open eye of happiness? Where is the bloom that spoke a heart at peace with itself? I repeat it, and I repeat it with agony.— Father of mercies! is this thy Adeline Mowbray?"

Here, overcome with emotion, Mrs. Pemberton paused; but Adeline could not break silence: she rose, she stretched out her hand as if going to speak, but her utterance failed her, and again she sunk on a chair.

"It was thine," resumed Mrs. Pemberton in a faint and broken voice, "to diffuse happiness around thee, and to enjoy wealth unhated, because thy hand dispensed nobly the riches which it had received bounteously: when the ear heard thee, then it blessed thee; when the eye saw thee, it gave witness to thee; and yet— "

Here again she paused, and raised her fine eyes to heaven for a few minutes, as if in prayer; then, pressing Adeline's hand with an almost convulsive grasp, she drew her bonnet over her face, as if eager to hide the emotion which she was unable to subdue, and suddenly left the house; while Adeline, stunned and overwhelmed by the striking contrast which Mrs. Pemberton had drawn between her past and present situation, remained for some minutes motionless on her seat, a prey to a variety of feelings which she dared not venture to analyse.

But, amidst the variety of her feelings, Adeline soon found that sorrow, sorrow of the bitterest kind, was uppermost. Mrs. Pemberton had said that she was about to be visited by affliction— alluding, there was no doubt, to the probable death of Glenmurray—And was his fate so certain that it was the theme of conversation at Richmond? Were only *her* eyes blind to the certainty of his danger?

On these ideas did Adeline chiefly dwell after the departure of her monitress; and in an agony unspeakable she entered the room where Glenmurray was sitting, in order to look at him, and form her own judgement on a subject of such importance. But, alas! she found him with the brilliant deceitful appearance that attends his complaint—a bloom resembling health on his cheek, and a brightness in his eye rivaLling that of the undimmed lustre of youth. Surprised, delighted, and overcome by these appearances, which her inexperience rendered her incapable of appreciating justly, Adeline threw herself on the sofa by him; and, as she pressed her cold cheek to his glowing one, her tearful eye was raised to heaven with an expression of devout thankfulness.

"Mrs. Pemberton paid you a long visit," said Glenmurray, "and I thought once, by the elevated tone of her voice, that she was preaching to you."

"I believe she was," cheerfully replied Adeline, "and now I have a confession to make; the Season of reserve shall be over, and I will tell you all the adventures of this day without *evasion.*"

"Aye, I thought you were not ingenuous with me this morning," replied Glenmurray: "but better late than never."

Adeline then told him all that had passed between her and Mary and Mrs. Pemberton, and concluded with saying, "But the surety of your better health, which your looks give me, has dissipated every uneasiness; and if you are but spared to me, sorrow cannot reach me, and I despise the censure of the ignorant and the prejudiced.—The world approve! What is the world to me?—

"The conscious mind is its own awful world!"[88]

Glenmurray sighed deeply as she concluded her narration.

"I have only one request to make," said he— "Never let that Mary come into my presence again; and be sure to take care of Mrs. Pemberton's address."

Adeline promised that both his requests should be attended to. Mary was paid her wages, and dismissed immediately; and a girl being hired to supply her place, the ménage[89] went on quietly again.

---

[88] James Thomson, *Tancred and Sigismunda. A Tragedy.* 1745. V.iv.98-99: "The World approve!—What is the World to me?/ The conscious mind is its own awful World."

[89] I.e.,household or housework.

But a new mortification awaited Glenmurray and Adeline. In spite of Glenmurray's eccentricities and opinions, he was still remembered with interest by some of the female part of his family; and two of his cousins, more remarkable for their beauty than their virtue, hearing that he was at Richmond, made known to him their intention of paying him a morning visit on their way to their country-seat in the neighborhood.

"Most unwelcome visitors indeed!" cried Glenmurray, throwing the letter down; "I will write to them and forbid them to come."

"That's impossible," replied Adeline, "for by this time they must be on the road, if you look at the date of the letter: besides, I wish you to receive them; I should like to see any relations or friends of yours, especially those who have liberality of sentiment enough to esteem you as you deserve."

"You!—you see them!" exclaimed Glenmurray, pacing the room impatiently: "O Adeline, that is *impossible!*"

"I understand you," replied Adeline, changing colour: "they will not deem me worthy," forcing a smile, "to be introduced to them."

"And therefore would I forbid their coming. I cannot bear to *exclude* you from my presence in order that I may receive them. No: when they arrive, I will send them word that I am unable to see them."

"While they will attribute the refusal to the influence of the *creature* who lives with you! No, Glenmurray, for my sake I must insist on your not being denied to them; and, believe me, I should consider myself as unworthy to be the choice of your heart, if I were not able to bear with firmness a mortification like that which awaits me."

"But you allow it to be a mortification?"

"Yes; it is mortifying to a woman who knows herself to be virtuous, and is an idolater of virtue, to pay the penalty of vice, and be thought unworthy to associate with the relations of the man whom she loves."

"They shall not come, I protest," exclaimed Glenmurray.

But Adeline was resolute; and she carried her point. Soon after this conversation the ladies arrived, and Adeline shut herself up in her own apartment, where she gave way to no very pleasant reflections. Nor was she entirely satisfied with Glenmurray's conduct:—true, he had earnestly and sincerely wished to refuse to see his unexpected and unwelcome guests; but he had never once expressed a desire of combating their prejudices for Adeline's sake, and an intention of requesting that she might be introduced to them; but, as any common man would have done under similar circumstances, he was contented to do homage to "things as they are,"[90] without an effort to resist the prejudice to which he was superior.

"Alas!" cried Adeline, "when can we hope to see society enlightened and improved, when even those who see and strive to amend its faults in theory, in practice tamely submit to the trammels which it imposes?"

An hour, a tedious hour to Adeline, having elapsed, Glenmurray's visitors departed; and by the disappointment that Adeline experienced at hearing the door close on them, she felt that she had had a secret hope of being summoned to be presented to them; and, with a bitter feeling of mortification, she reflected, that she was probably to the man whom she adored a shame and a reproach.

"Yet I should like to see them," she said, running to the window as the carriage drove up, and the ladies entered it. At that moment they, whether from curiosity to see her, or accident, looked up at the window where she was. Adeline started back indignant and confused; for, thrusting their heads eagerly forward, they looked at her with the bold unfeeling stare of imagined superiority; and Adeline, spite of her reason, sunk abashed and conscious from their gaze.

"And this insult," exclaimed she, clasping her hands and

---

[90] Phrase associated with social critique and the reformers, from Godwin's novel *Things As They Are, or Caleb Williams* (1794) to Elizabeth Inchbald's play *Such Things Are* (1788).

bursting into tears, "I experience from Glenmurray's *relations!* I think I could have borne it better from any one else."

She had not recovered her disorder when Glenmurray entered the room, and, tenderly embracing her, exclaimed, "Never, never again, my love, will I submit to such a sacrifice as I have now made;" when seeing her in tears, too well aware of the cause, he gave way to such a passionate burst of tenderness and regret, that Adeline, terrified at his agitation, though soothed by his fondness, affected the cheerfulness which she did not feel, and promised to drive the intruders from her remembrance.

Had Glenmurray and Adeline known the real character of the unwelcome visiters, neither of them would have regretted that Adeline was not presented to them. One of them was married, and to so accommodating a husband, that his wife's known gallant was his intimate friend; and under the sanction of his protection she was received every where, and visited by every one, as the world did not think proper to be more clearsighted than the husband himself chose to be. The other lady was a young and attractive widow, who coquetted with many men, but intrigued with only one at a time; for which self-denial she was rewarded by being allowed to pass unquestioned through the portals of fashionable society. But these ladies would have scorned to associate with Adeline; and Adeline, had she known their private history, would certainly have returned the compliment.

The peace of Adeline was soon after disturbed in another way. Glenmurray finding himself disposed to sleep in the middle of the day, his cough having kept him waking all night, Adeline took her usual walk, and returned by the church-yard. The bell was tolling; and as she passed she saw a funeral enter the church-yard, and instantly averted her head.

In so doing her eyes fell on a decent-looking woman, who with a sort of angry earnestness was watching the progress of the procession.

"Aye, there goes your body, you rogue!" she exclaimed indignantly, "but I wonder where your soul is now?—where I would not be for something."

Adeline was shocked, and gently observed, "What crime did the person of whom you are speaking, that you should suppose his soul so painfully disposed of?"

"What crime?" returned the woman; "crime enough, I think:—why, he ruined a poor girl here in the neighbourhood; and then, because he never chose to make a will, there is she lying-in of a little by-blow,[91] with not a farthing of money to maintain her or the child, and the fellow's money is gone to the heir at law, scarce of kin to him, while his own flesh and blood is left to starve."

Adeline shuddered:—if Glenmurray were to die, she and the child which she bore would, she knew, be beggars.[92]

"Well, miss, or madam, belike, by the look of you," continued the woman, glancing her eye over Adeline's person, "what say you? Don't you think the fellow's soul is where we should not like to be? However, he had his hell here too, to be sure: for, when speechless and unable to move his fingers, he seemed by signs to ask for pen and ink, and he looked in agonies; and there was the poor young woman crying over him, and holding in her arms her poor destitute baby, who would as he grew up be taught, he must think, to curse the wicked father who begot him, and the naughty mother who bore him!"

Adeline turned very sick, and was forced to seat herself on a tomb-stone. "Curse the mother who bore him!" she inwardly repeated,— "and will my child curse me? Rather let me undergo the rites I have despised!" and instantly starting from her seat she ran down the road to her lodgings, resolving to propose to Glenmurray their immediate marriage.

"But is the possession of property, then," she said to herself as she stopped to take breath, "so supreme a good, that the want

[91] Since the late sixteenth century, an illegitimate child (OED).
[92] Glenmurray's money comes from a life-interest in his familial estate. After his death his mistress and even his wife would have no legal claim on his property or the income it produced, though a legal heir would.

of it, through the means of his mother, should dispose a child to curse that mother?—No: my child shall be taught to consider nothing valuable but virtue, nothing disgraceful but *vice*.—Fool that I am! a bugbear frightened me; and to my foolish fears I was about to sacrifice my own principles, and the respectability of Glenmurray. No—Let his property go to the heir at law—let me be forced to labour to support my babe, when its father—" Here a flood of tears put an end to her soliloquy, and slowly and pensively she returned home.

But the conversation of the woman in the church-yard haunted her while waking, and continued to distress her in her dreams that night; and she was resolved to do all she could to relieve the situation of the poor destitute girl and child, in whose fate she might possibly see an anticipation of her own: and as soon as breakfast was over, and Glenmurray was engaged in his studies, she walked out to make the projected inquiries.

The season of the year was uncommonly fine; and the varied scenery visible from the terrace was, at the moment of Adeline's approach to it, glowing with more than common beauty. Adeline stood for some minutes gazing on it in silent delight; when her reverie was interrupted by the sound of boyish merriment, and she saw, at one end of the terrace, some well-dressed boys at play.

"Alas! regardless of their doom,
The little victims play!"[93]

immediately recurred to her: for, contemplating the probable evils of existence, she was darkly brooding over the imagined fate of her own offspring, should it live to see the light; and the children at their sport, having no care of ills to come, naturally engaged her attention.

But those happy children ceased to interest her, when she saw standing at a distance from the group, and apparently looking at it with an eye of envy, a little boy, even better dressed than the rest; who was sobbing violently, yet ardently trying to conceal

---

[93] Thomas Gray, "Ode on a Distant Prospect of Eton College," 1747, lines 51-2.

his grief. And while she was watching the young mourner attentively, he suddenly threw himself on a seat; and, taking out his handkerchief, indignantly and impatiently wiped away the tears that would no longer be restrained.

"Poor child!" thought Adeline, seating herself beside him; "and has affliction reached thee so soon!"

The child was beautiful: and his clustering locks seemed to have been combed with so much care; the frill of his shirt was so fine, and had been so very neatly plaited; and his sun-burnt neck and hands were so very very clean, that Adeline was certain he was the darling object of some fond mother's attention. "And yet he is unhappy!" she inwardly exclaimed. "When my fate resembled his, how happy I was!" But from recollections like these she always hastened; and checking the rising sigh, she resolved to enter into conversation with the little boy.

"What is the matter?" she cried.—No answer.— "Why are you not playing with the young gentlemen yonder?'

She had touched the right string:—and bursting into tears, he sobbed out, "Because they won't let me."

"No? and why will they not let you?" To this he replied not; but sullenly hung his blushing face on his bosom.

"Perhaps you have made them angry?" gently asked Adeline. "Oh! no, no," cried the boy; "but—— " "But what?" Here he turned from her, and with his nail began scratching the arm of the seat.

"Well; this is very strange, and seems very unkind," cried Adeline: "I will speak to them." So saying, she drew near the other children, who had interrupted their play to watch Adeline and their rejected playmate. "What can be the reason," said she, "that you will not let that little boy play with you?" The boys looked down, and said nothing.

"Is he ill-natured?"

"No."

"Does he not play fair?"

"Yes."

"Don't you like him?"

"Yes."

"Then why do you make him unhappy, by not letting him join in your sport?"

"Tell the lady, Jack," cries one; and Jack, the biggest boy of the party, said: "Because he is not a gentleman's son like us, and is only a little bastard."

"Yes," cried one of the other children; "and his mamma is so proud she dresse him finer than we are, for all he is base-born: and our papas and mammas don't think him fit company for us."

They might have gone on for an hour—Adeline could not interrupt them. The cause of the child's affliction was a dagger in her heart; and, while she listened to the now redoubled sobs of the disgraced and proudly afflicted boy, she was driven almost to phrensy: for "Such," she exclaimed, "may one time or other be the pangs of my child, and so to him may the hours of childhood be embittered!"—Again she seated herself by the little mourner—and her tears accompanied his.

"My dear child, you had better go home," said she, struggling with her feelings; "your mother will certainly be glad of your company."

"No, I won't go to her; I don't love her: they say she is a bad woman, and my papa a bad man, because they are not married."

Again Adeline's horrors returned.— "But, my dear, they love you, no doubt; and you ought to love them," she replied with effort.

"There, there comes your papa," cried one of the boys; "go and cry to him;—go."

At these words Adeline looked up, and saw an elegant-looking man approaching with a look of anxiety.

"Charles, my dear boy, what has happened?" said he, taking his hand; which the boy sullenly withdrew. "Come home directly," continued his father, "and tell me what is the matter, as we go along." But again snatching his hand away, the proud and deeply wounded child resentfully pushed the shoulder next him forward, whenever his father tried to take his arm, and elbowed him angrily as he went.

Adeline felt the child's action to the bottom of her heart. It was a volume of reproach to the father; and she sighed to think what the parents, if they had hearts, must feel, when the afflicted boy told the cause of his grief. "But, unhappy boy, perhaps my child may live to bless you!" she exclaimed, clasping her hands together: "never, never will I expose my child to the pangs which you have experienced to-day." So saying, she returned instantly to her lodgings; and having just strength left to enter Glenmurray's room, she faintly exclaimed: "For pity's sake, make me your wife to-morrow!" and fell senseless on the floor.

On her recovery she saw Glenmurray pale with agitation, yet with an expression of satisfaction in his countenance, bending over her. "Adeline! my dearest life!" he whispered as her head lay on his bosom, "blessed be the words you have spoken, whatever be their cause! To-morrow you shall be my wife."

"And then our child will be legitimate, will he not?" she eagerly replied.

"It will."

"Thank God!" cried Adeline, and relapsed into a fainting fit. For it was not decreed that the object of her maternal solicitude should ever be born to reward it. Anxiety and agitation had had a fatal effect on the health of Adeline; and the day after her rencounter on the terrace she brought forth a dead child.

As soon as Adeline, languid and disappointed, was able to leave her room, Glenmurray, whom anxiety during her illness had rendered considerably weaker, urged her to let the marriage ceremony be performed immediately. But with her hopes of being a mother vanished her wishes to become a wife, and all her former reasons against marriage recurred in their full force.

In vain did Glenmurray entreat her to keep her lately formed resolution: she still attributed his persuasions to generosity, and the heroic resolve of sacrificing his principles, with the consistency of his character, to her supposed good, and it was a point of honour with her to be as generous in return: consequently the subject was again dropped; nor was it likely to be soon renewed; an anxiety of a more pressing nature disturbed their peace and engrossed their attention. They had been three months at Richmond, and had incurred there a considerable debt; and Glenmurray, not having sufficient money with him to discharge it, drew upon his banker for half the half-year's rents from his estate, which he had just deposited in his hands; when to his unspeakable astonishment he found that the house had stopped payment, and that the principal partner was gone off with the deposits!

Scarcely could the firm mind of Glenmurray support itself under the stroke. He looked forward to the certainty of passing the little remainder of his life not only in pain but in poverty, and of seeing increase as fast as his wants the difficulty of supplying them; while the woman of his heart bent in increased agony over his restless couch; for he well knew that to raise money on his estate, or to anticipate the next half-year's rents, was impossible, as he had only a life interest in it; and, as he held the fatal letter in his hand, his frame shook with agitation.

"I could not have believed," cried Adeline, "that the loss of any sum of money could have so violently affected you."

"Not the loss of my all! my support during the tedious scenes of illness!"

"Your all!" faltered out Adeline; and when she heard the true state of the case she found her agitation equalled that of Glenmurray, and in hopeless anguish she leaned on the table beside him.

"What is to be done," said she, "till the next half-year's rents become due? Where can we procure money?"

"Till the next half-year's rents become due!" replied he, looking at her mournfully: "I shall not be distressed for money then."

"No?" answered Adeline (not understanding him): "our expenses have never yet been more than that sum can supply."

Glenmurray looked at her, and, seeing how unconscious she was of the certainty of the evil that awaited her, had not the courage to distress her by explaining his meaning; and she went on to ask him what steps he meant to take to raise money.

"My only resource," said he, "is dunning a near relation of

mine who owes me three hundred pounds: he is now, I believe, able to pay it. He is in Holland, indeed, at present; but he is daily expected in England, and will come to see me here. —I have named him to you before, I believe. His name is Berrendale."

It was then agreed that Glenmurray should write to Mr. Berrendale immediately; and that, to prevent the necessity of incurring a further debt for present provisions and necessaries, some of their books and linen should be sold: —but week after week elapsed, and no letter was received from Mr. Berrendale.

Glenmurray grew rapidly worse;—and their landlord was clamorous for his rent;—advice from London also became necessary to quiet Adeline's mind,—though Glenmurray knew that he was past cure: and after she had paid a small sum to quiet the demands of the landlord for a while, she had scarcely enough left to pay a physician: however, she sent for one, recommended by Dr. Norberry, and by selling a writing-desk inlaid with silver, which she valued because it was the gift of her father, she raised money sufficient for the occasion.

Dr. —— arrived, but not to speak peace to the mind of Adeline. She saw, though he did not absolutely say so, that all chance of Glenmurray's recovery was over: and though with the sanguine feelings of nineteen she could "hope though hope were lost," when she watched Dr. ——'s countenance as he turned from the bed-side of Glenmurray, she felt the coldness of despair thrill through her frame; and, scarcely able to stand, she followed him into the next room, and awaited his orders with a sort of desperate tranquillity.

After prescribing alleviations of the ill beyond his power to cure, Dr. —— added that terrible confirmation of the fears of anxious affection.— "Let him have whatever he likes; nothing can hurt him now; and all your endeavours must be to make the remaining hours of his existence as comfortable as you can, by every indulgence possible: and indeed, my dear madam," he continued, "you must be prepared for the trial that awaits you."

"Prepared! did you say?" cried Adeline in the broken voice of tearless and almost phrensied sorrow.— "O God! if he must die, in mercy let me die with him. If I have sinned, (here she fell on her knees,) surely, surely the agony of this moment is atonement sufficient."

Dr. ——, greatly affected, raised her from the ground, and conjured her for the sake of Glenmurray, and that she might not make his last hours miserable, to bear her trial with more fortitude.

"And can you talk of his 'last hours,' and yet expect me to be composed?—O sir! say but that there is one little little gleam of hope for me, and I will be calm."

"Well," replied Dr. ——, "I *may* be mistaken; Mr. Glenmurray is young, and—and— " here his voice faltered, and he was unable to proceed; for the expression of Adeline's countenance, changing as it instantly did from misery to joy,— joy of which he knew the fallacy,—while her eyes were intently fixed on him, was too much for a man of any feeling to support; and when she pressed his hand in the convulsive emotions of her gratitude, he was forced to turn away his head to conceal the starting tear.

"Well, I may be mistaken—Mr. Glenmurray is young," Adeline repeated again and again, as his carriage drove off; and she flew to Glenmurray's bed-side to impart to him the satisfaction which he rejoiced to see her feel, but in which he could not share.

Her recovered security did not, however, last long: the change in Glenmurray grew every day more visible; and to increase her distress, they were forced, to avoid disagreeable altercations, to give the landlord a draft on Mr. Berrendale for the sum due to him, and remove to very humble lodgings in a closer part of the town.

Here their misery was a little alleviated by the unexpected receipt of twenty pounds, sent to Glenmurray by a tenant who was in arrears to him, which enabled Adeline to procure Glenmurray every thing that his capricious appetite required; and at his earnest entreaty, in order that she might sometimes venture to leave him, lest her health should suffer, she hired a nurse to assist her in her attendance upon him.

A hasty letter too was at length received from Mr. Berrendale, saying, that he should very soon be in England, and should hasten to Richmond immediately on his landing. The terror of wanting money, therefore, began to subside: but day after day elapsed, and Mr. Berrendale came not; and Adeline, being obliged to deny herself almost necessary sustenance that Glenmurray's appetite might be tempted, and his nurse, by the indulgence of hers, kept in good humour, resolved, presuming on the arrival of Mr. Berrendale, to write to Dr. Norberry and solicit the loan of twenty pounds.

Having done so, she ceased to be alarmed, though she found herself in possession of only three guineas[94] to defray the probable expenses of the ensuing week; and, in somewhat less misery than usual, she, at the earnest entreaty of Glenmurray, set out to take a walk.

Scarcely conscious what she did, she strolled through the town, and seeing some fine grapes at the window of a fruiterer, she went in to ask the price of them, knowing how welcome fruit was to the feverish palate of Glenmurray. While the shopman was weighing the grapes, she saw a pine-apple on the counter, and felt a strong wish to carry it home as a more welcome present; but with unspeakable disappointment she heard that the price of it was two guineas—a sum which she could not think herself justified in expending, in the present state of their finances, even to please Glenmurray, especially as he had not expressed a wish for such an indulgence: besides, he liked grapes; and, as medicine, neither of them could be effectual.

It was fortunate for Adeline's feelings that she had not overheard what the mistress of the shop said to her maid as she left it.

"I should have asked another person only a guinea; but as those sort of women never mind what they give, I asked two,

---

[94] A monetary unit coined in gold originally for use in West Africa or "Guinea," worth about 21 shillings, or just over one pound sterling, and strongly associated with the African slave trade.

and I dare say she will come back for it."

"I have brought you some grapes," cried Adeline as she entered Glenmurray's chamber, "and I would have brought you a pine-apple, but that it was too dear."

"A pine-apple!" said Glenmurray languidly turning over the grapes, and with a sort of distaste putting one of them in his mouth, "a pine-apple!—I wish you had bought it with all my heart! I protest that I feel as if I could eat a whole one."

"Well," replied Adeline, "if you would enjoy it so much, you certainly ought to have it."

"But the price, my dear girl!"—what was it?"

"Only two guineas," replied Adeline, forcing a smile.

"Two guineas!" exclaimed Glenmurray: "No,—that is too much to give—I will not indulge my appetite at such a rate—but, take away the grapes—I can't eat them."

Adeline, disappointed, removed them from his sight; and, to increase her vexation, Glenmurray was continually talking of pine-apples, and in a way that showed how strongly his diseased appetite wished to enjoy the gratification of eating one. At last, unable to bear to see him struggling with an ungratified wish, she told him that she believed they could afford to buy the pine-apple, as she had written to borrow some money of Dr. Norberry, to be paid as soon as Mr. Berrendale arrived. In a moment the dull eye of Glenmurray lighted up with expectation; and he, who in health was remarkable for self-denial and temperance, scrupled not, overcome by the influence of the fever which consumed him, to gratify his palate at a rate the most extravagant.

Adeline sighed as she contemplated this change effected by illness; and, promising to be back as soon as possible, she proceeded to a shop to dispose of her lace veil, the only ornament which she had retained; and that not from vanity, but because it concealed from the eye of curiosity the sorrow marked on her countenance. But she knew a piece of muslin would do as well; and for two guineas she sold a veil worth treble the sum; but it was to give a minute's pleasure to Glenmurray, and that was enough for Adeline.

In her way to the fruiterer's she saw a crowd at the door of a mean-looking house, and in the midst of it she beheld a mulatto woman, the picture of sickness and despair, supporting a young man who seemed ready to faint every moment, but whom a rough-featured man, regardless of his weakness, was trying to force from the grasp of the unhappy woman; while a mulatto boy, known in Richmond by the name of the Tawny Boy, to whom Adeline had often given halfpence in her walks, was crying bitterly, and hiding his face in the poor woman's apron.

Adeline immediately pressed forward to inquire into the cause of a distress only too congenial to her feelings; and as she did so, the tawny boy looked up, and, knowing her immediately, ran eagerly forward to meet her, seeming, though he did not speak, to associate with her presence an idea of certain relief.

"Oh! it is only a poor man," replied an old woman in answer to Adeline's inquiries, "who can't pay his debts,—and so they are dragging him to prison—that's all." "They are dragging him to his death too," cried a younger woman in a gentle accent; "for he is only just recovering from a bad fever: and if he goes to jail the bad air will certainly kill him, poor soul!"

"Is that his wife?" said Adeline. "Yes, and my mammy," said the tawny boy, looking up in her face, "and she so ill and sorry."

"Yes, unhappy creatures," replied her informant, "and they have known great trouble; and now, just as they had got a little money together, William fell ill, and in doctor's stuff Savanna (that's the mulatto's name) has spent all the money she had earned, as well as her husband's; and now she is ill herself, and I am sure William's going to jail will kill her. And a hard-hearted, wicked wretch Mr. Davis is, to arrest him—that he is—not but what it is his due, I cannot say but it is—but, poor souls! he'll die, and she'll die, and then what will become of their poor little boy?"

The tawny boy all this time was standing, crying, by Adeline's side, and had twisted his fingers in her gown, while her heart sympathized most painfully in the anguish of the mulatto woman. "What is the amount of the sum for which he is taken up?" said Adeline.

"Oh! trifling: but Mr. Davis owes him a grudge, and so will not wait any longer. It is in all only six pounds; and he says if they will pay half he will wait for the rest; but then he knows they could as well pay all as half."

Adeline, shocked at the knowledge of a distress which she was not able to remove, was turning away as the woman said this, when she felt that the little boy pulled her gown gently, as if appealing to her generosity; while a surly-looking man, who was the creditor himself, forcing a passage through the crowd, said, "Why, bring him along, and have done with it; here is a fuss to make indeed about that idle dog, and that ugly black b—h!"

Adeline till then had not recollected that she was a mulatto; and this speech, reflecting so brutally on her colour,—a circumstance which made her an object of greater interest to Adeline,—urged her to step forward to their joint relief with an almost irresistible impulse; especially when another man reproached the fellow for his brutality, and added, that he knew them both to be hard-working, deserving persons. But to disappoint Glenmurray of his promised pleasure was impossible; and having put sixpence in the tawny boy's hand, she was hastening to the fruiterer's, when the crowd, who were following William and the mulatto to the jail, whither the bailiffs were dragging rather than leading him, fell back to give air to the poor man, who had fainted on Savanna's shoulder, and seemed on the point of expiring—while she, with an expression of fixed despair, was gazing on his wan cheek.

ABOLITION LITERATURE

Alderson Opie was a life-long supporter of the British anti-slavery movement. Late in her life, in 1840, she served as a delegate to the Anti-Slavery Convention in London. After she gave up writing fiction and converted to Quakerism, she continued to write didactic and moral stories and poetry.

Two such poems, "The Negro Boy's Tale" (1824) and the long illustrated narrative poem *The Black Man's Lament; Or How To Make Sugar* (1826) are particularly overt efforts to elicit the sympathy of white readers in favor of changing the practice of African slavery in the British colonies. "The Negro Boy's Tale" is written in dialect similar to that of Savanna and the Tawny Boy in *Adeline*, while *The Black Man's Lament* is not. In all three works, the central enslaved figure speaks for him or herself, though the final message may be one of Christian resignation. Here is an excerpt from *The Black Man's Lament; Or, How To Make Sugar*:

Negro speaks.

"First to our own dear Negro land,
His ships the cruel White man sends;
And there contrives, by armed band,
To tear us from our homes and friends;

"From parents, brethren's fond embrace;
From tender wife, and child to tear;
Then in a darksome ship to place,
Pack'd close, like bales of cotton there.

"Oh! happy those, who, in that hour,
Die from their prison's putrid breath!
Since they escape from White man's pow'r,
From toils and stripes, and lingering death!

...

"Sometimes, 'tis true, when Sabbath-bell
Calls White man to the house of pray'r,
And makes poor blacks more sadly feel
'Tis thought *slaves* have no *business* there:

"Then Negroes try the earth to till,
And raise their food on Sabbath-day;
But Envy's pangs poor Negroes fill,
That we must *work* while others *pray*.

"Then, where have we *one* legal right?
White men may bind, whip, torture slave.
But oh! if we but strike one White,
Who can poor Negro help or save?

"There are, I'm told, upon some isles,
Masters who gentle deign to be;
And there, perhaps, the Negro *smiles*,
But *smiling* Negroes *few* can see.

"Well, I must learn to bear my pain;
And, lately, I am grown more calm;
For Christian men come o'er the main,
To pour in Negro souls a balm.

"They tell us there is one above
Who died to save both bond and free;
And who, with eyes of equal love,
Beholds White man, and *humble me.*

"They tell me if, with patient heart,
I bear my wrongs from day to day,
I shall at death, to realms depart,
Where God wipes every tear away!

"Yet still, at times, with fear I shrink;
For, when with sense of injury prest,
I burn with rage! and *then* I think
I ne'er can *gain* that place of rest." (pp. 3-6, 23-25)

SOURCES

Amelia Alderson Opie, *The Black Man's Lament; Or, How To Make Sugar,* London, 1826.

THE BLACK MAN'S LAMENT.   7

THE LANDING OF NEGROES.

———

For what awaited us on shore,
   Soon as the ship had reach'd the strand,
Unloading its degraded store
   Of freemen, forc'd from Negro land?

B

Illustration to *The Black Man's Lament*, artist unknown, 1826. Each page of this book is illustrated, often graphically portraying the disciplinary methods and planting methods used on West Indian sugar plantations. (By permission of the British Library.)

Adeline thought on Glenmurray's danger, and shuddered as she beheld the scene; she felt it but a too probable anticipation of the one in which she might soon be an actor.

At that moment a man observed, "If he goes to prison he will not live two days, that every one may see;" and the mulatto uttered a shriek of agony.

Adeline felt it to her very soul; and, rushing forward, "Sir, sir," she exclaimed to the unfeeling creditor, "if I were to give you a guinea now, and promise you two more a fortnight hence, would you release this poor man for the present?"

"No: I must have three guineas this moment," replied he. Adeline sighed, and withdrew her hand from her pocket. "But were Glenmurray here, he would give up his own indulgence, I am sure, to save the lives of, probably, two fellow-creatures," thought Adeline; "and he would not forgive me if I were to sacrifice such an opportunity to the sole gratification of his palate."— But then again, Glenmurray eagerly expecting her with the promised treat, so gratifying to the feverish taste of sickness, seemed to appear before her, and she turned away: but the eyes of the mulatto, who had heard her words, and had hung on them breathless with expectation, followed her with a look of such sad reproach for the disappointment which she had occasioned her, and the little boy looked up so wistfully in her face, crying, "Poor fader, and poor mammy!" that Adeline could not withstand the force of the appeal; but almost exclaiming "Glenmurray would upbraid me if I did not act thus," she gave the creditor the three guineas, paid the bailiffs their demand, and then made her way through the crowd, who respectfully drew back to give her room to pass, saying, "God bless you, lady! God bless you!"

But Williams was too ill, and Savanna felt too much to speak; and the surly creditor said, sneeringly, "If I had been you, I would, at least, have thanked the lady." This reproach restored Savanna to the use of speech; and (but with a violent effort) she uttered in a hoarse and broken voice, "*I* tank her! God tank her! I never can:" and Adeline, kindly pressing her hand, hurried away from her in silence, though scarcely able to refrain exclaiming, "You know not the sacrifice which you have cost me!" The tawny boy still followed her, as loth to leave her. "God bless you, my dear!" said she kindly to him: "there, go to your mother, and be good to her." His dark face glowed as she spoke to him, and holding up his chin, "Tiss me!" cried he, "poor tawny boy love you!" She did so; and then, reluctantly, he left her, nodding his head, and saying "Dood bye" till he was out of sight.

With him, and with the display of his grateful joy, vanished all that could give Adeline resolution to bear her own reflections at the idea of returning home, and of the trial that awaited her. In vain did she now try to believe that Glenmurray would applaud what she had done.—He was now the slave of disease, nor was it likely that even his self-denial and principled benevolence could endure with patience so cruel a disappointment—and from the woman whom he loved too!—and to whom the indulgence of his slightest wishes ought to have been the first object.

"What shall I do?" cried she: "what will he say?—No doubt he is impatiently expecting me; and, in this weak state, disappointment may——" Here, unable to bear her apprehensions, she wrung her hands in agony; and when she arrived in sight of her lodgings she dared not look up, lest she should see Glenmurray at the window watching for her return. Slowly and fearfully did she open the door; and the first sound she heard was Glenmurray's voice from the door of his room, saying, "So, you are come at last!—I have been so impatient!" And, indeed he had risen and dressed himself, that he might enjoy his treat more than he could do in a sick-bed.

"How can I bear to look him in the face!" thought Adeline, lingering on the stairs.

"Adeline, my love! why do you make me wait so long?" cried Glenmurray. "Here are knives and plates ready; where is the treat I have been so long expecting?"

Adeline entered the room and threw herself on the first chair, avoiding the sight of Glenmurrray, whose countenance, as she hastily glanced her eyes over it, was animated with the expectation of a pleasure which he was not to enjoy. "I have not brought the pine-apple," she faintly articulated. "No!" replied Glenmurray, "how hard upon me!—the only thing for weeks that I have wished for, or could have eaten with pleasure! I suppose you were so long going that it was disposed of before you got there?"

"No," replied Adeline, struggling with her tears at this first instance of pettishness in Glenmurray.

"Pardon me the supposition," replied Glenmurray, recovering himself: "more likely you met some dun on the road, and so the two guineas were disposed of another way—If so, I can't blame you. What say you? Am I right?"

"No." "Then how was it?" gravely asked Glenmurray. "You must have had a very powerful and sufficient reason, to induce you to disappoint a poor invalid of the indulgence which you had yourself excited him to wish for."

"This is terrible, indeed!" thought Adeline, "and never was I so tempted to tell a falsehood."

"Still silent! You are very unkind, miss Mowbray," said Glenmurray; "I see that I have tired even *you* out."

These words, by the agony which they excited, restored to Adeline all her resolution. She ran to Glenmurray; she clasped his burning hands in hers; and as succinctly as possible she related what had passed. When she had finished, Glenmurray was silent; the fretfulness of disease prompted him to say, "So then, to the relief of strangers you sacrificed the gratification of the man whom you love, and deprived him of the only pleasure he may live to enjoy!" But the habitual sweetness and generosity of his temper struggled, and struggled effectually, with his malady; and while Adeline, pale and trembling, awaited her sentence, he caught her suddenly to his bosom, and held her there a few moments in silence.

"Then you forgive me?" faltered out Adeline.

"Forgive you! I love and admire you more than ever! I know your heart, Adeline; and I am convinced that depriving yourself of the delight of giving me the promised treat, in order to do a benevolent action, was an effort of virtue of the highest order;

and never, I trust, have you known, or will you know again, such bitter feelings as you this moment experienced."

Adeline, gratified by his generous kindness, and charmed with his praise, could only weep her thanks. "And now," said Glenmurray, laughing, "you may bring back the grapes—I am not like Sterne's dear Jenny; if I cannot get pine-apple, I will not insist on eating crab."[95]

The grapes were brought; but in vain did he try to eat them. At this time, however, he did not send them away without highly commending their flavour, and wishing that he dared give way to his inclinations, and feast upon them.

"O God of mercy!" cried Adeline, bursting into an agony of grief as she reached her own apartment, and throwing herself on her knees by the bed-side, "Must that benevolent being be taken from me for ever, and must I, must I survive him!"

She continued for some minutes in this attitude, and with her heart devoutly raised to heaven; till every feeling yielded to resignation, and she arose calm, if not contented; when, on turning round, she saw Glenmurray leaning against the door, and gazing on her.

"Sweet enthusiast!" cried he smiling: "so, thus, when you are distressed, you seek consolation."

"I do," she replied: "Sceptic, wouldst thou wish to deprive me of it?"[96]

"No, by heaven!" warmly exclaimed Glenmurray; and the evening passed more cheerfully than usual.

The next post brought a letter not from Dr. Norberry, but from his wife; it was as follows, and contained three pound-

---

[95] Laurence Sterne, *Life and Opinions of Tristram Shandy, Gentleman*, 1760, Vol. 1, Chapter XVIII, page 100. Tristram observes that when we cannot have the thing we want, we usually refuse to take the next best thing. His example is his "dear, dear Jenny," who, realizing that she cannot afford one kind of silk, in a fit of pique turns around and buys a much cheaper sort. Crab, like oysters, was plentiful and inexpensive at this time.

[96] While "enthusiast" denotes a religious enthusiast, "sceptic" here designates religious scepticism or doubt associated with the New Philosophy of Godwin and his associates.

notes:

> "Mrs. Norberry's compliments to miss Mowbray, having opened her letter, poor Dr. Norberry being dangerously ill of a fever, find her distress; of which shall not inform the Dr., as he feels so much for his friend's misfortunes, specially when brought on by misconduct. But, out of respect for your mother, who is a good sort of woman, though rather particular, as all learned ladies are, have sent three pound-notes; the miss Norberrys giving one a-piece, not to lend, but a gift, and they join Mrs. Norberry in hoping miss Mowbray will soon see the error of her ways; and, if so be, no doubt Dr. Norberry will use his interest to get her into the Magdalen."[97]

This curious epistle would have excited in Glenmurray and Adeline no other feelings save those of contempt, but for the information it contained of the doctor's being dangerously ill; and, in fear for the worthy husband, they forgot the impertinence of the wife and daughters.

The next day, fortunately, Mr. Berrendale arrived, and with him the 300£. Consequently, all Glenmurray's debts were discharged, better lodgings procured, and the three pound notes returned in a blank cover to Mrs. Norberry. Charles Berrendale was first-cousin to Glenmurray, and so like him in face, that they were, at first, mistaken for brothers: but to a physiognomist they must always have been unlike; as Glenmurray was remarkable for the character and expression of his countenance, and Berrendale for the extreme beauty of his features and complexion. Glenmurray was pale and thin, and his eyes and

---

[97] A Magdalen Home or Hospital was an institution for reclaiming prostitutes and fallen women (OED). Mrs. Norberry and her daughters are treating Adeline as a charity case, rather than an old friend in trouble.

hair dark. Berrendale's eyes were of a light blue; and though his eye-lashes were black, his hair was of a rich auburn: Glenmurray was thin and muscular; Berrendale, round and corpulent: still they were alike; and it was not ill observed of them, that Berrendale was Glenmurray in good health.

But Berrendale could not be flattered by the resemblance, as his face and person were so truly what is called handsome, that, partial as our sex is said to be to beauty, any woman would have been excused for falling in love with him. Whether his mind was equal to his person we shall show hereafter.

The meeting between Berrendale and Glenmurray was affectionate on both sides; but Berrendale could scarcely hide the pain he felt on seeing the situation of Glenmurray, whose virtues he had always loved, whose talents he had always respected, and to whose active friendship towards himself he owed eternal gratitude.

But he soon learnt to think Glenmurray, in one respect, an object of envy, when he beheld the constant, skilful and tender attentions of his nurse, and saw in that nurse every gift of heart, mind, and person, which could make a woman amiable.

Berrendale had heard that his eccentric cousin was living with a girl as odd as himself; who thought herself a genius, and pretended to universal knowledge: great then was his astonishment to find this imagined pedant, and pretender, not only an adept in every useful and feminine pursuit, but modest in her demeanour, and gentle in her manners: little did he expect to see her capable of serving the table of Glenmurray with dishes made by herself, not only tempting to the now craving appetite of the invalid but to the palate of an epicure,—while all his wants were anticipated by her anxious attention, and many of the sufferings of sickness alleviated by her inventive care.

Adeline, mean while, was agreeably surprised to see the good effect produced on Glenmurray's spirits, and even his health, by the arrival of his cousin; and her manner became even affectionate to Berrendale, from gratitude for the change which his presence seemed to have occasioned.

Adeline had now a companion in her occasional walks;— Glenmurray insisted on her walking, and insisted on Berrendale's accompanying her. In these tête-à-têtes Adeline unburthened her heart, by telling Berrendale of the agony she felt at the idea of losing Glenmurray; and while drowned in tears she leaned on his arm, she unconsciously suffered him to press the hand that leaned against him; nor would she have felt it a freedom to be reproved, had she been conscious that he did so. But these trifling indulgences were fewel to the flame that she had kindled in the heart of Berrendale; a flame which he saw no guilt in indulging, as he looked on Glenmurray's death as certain, and Adeline would then be free.

But though Adeline was perfectly unconscious of his attachment, Glenmurray had seen it even before Berrendale himself discovered it; and he only waited a favourable opportunity to make the discovery known to the parties. All he had as yet ventured to say was, "Charles, my Adeline is an excellent nurse!— You would like such an one during your fits of the gout;" and Berrendale had blushed deeply while he assented to Glenmurray's remarks, because he was conscious that, while enumerating Adeline's perfections, he had figured her to himself warming his flannels, and leaning tenderly over his gouty couch.

One day, while Adeline was reading to Glenmurray, and Berrendale was attending not to what she read, but to the beauty of her mouth while reading, the nurse came in, and said that "a mulatto woman wished to speak to miss Mowbray."

"Show her up," immediately cried Glenmurray; "and if her little boy is with her, let him come too."

In vain did Adeline expostulate—Glenmurray wished to enjoy the mulatto's expressions of gratitude; and, in spite of all she could say, the mother and child were introduced.

"So!" cried the mulatto, (whose looks were so improved that Adeline scarcely knew her again) "So! me find you at last; and, please God! we not soon part more." As she said this, she pressed the hem of Adeline's gown to her lips with fervent emotion.

"Not part from her again!" cried Glenmurray: "What do

you mean, my good woman?"

"Oh! when she gave tree guinea for me, metought she mus be rich lady, but now dey say she be poor, and me mus work for her."

"And who told you I was poor?"

"Dat cross man where you live once—he say you could not pay him, and you go away—and he tell me dat your love be ill; and me so sorry, yet so glad! for my love be well aden, and he have got good employ; and now I can come and serve you, and nurse dis poor gentleman, and all for noting but my meat and drink; and I know dat great fat nurse have gold wages, and eat and drink fat beside,—I knowd her well."

All this was uttered with great volubility, and in a tone between laughing and crying.

"Well, Adeline," said Glenmurray when she had ended, "you did not throw away your kindness on an unworthy and ungrateful object; so I am quite reconciled to the loss of the pine-apple; and I will tell your honest friend here the story,—to show her, as she has a tender heart herself, the greatness of the sacrifice you made for her sake."

Adeline begged him to desist; but he went on; and the mulatto could not keep herself quiet on her chair while he related the circumstance.

"And did she do dat to save me?" she passionately exclaimed; "Angel woman! I should have let poor man go to prison, before disappoint my William!"

"And did you forgive her immediately?" said Berrendale.

"Yes, certainly."

"Well, that was heroic too," returned he.

"And no one but Glenmurray would have been so heroic, I believe," said Adeline.

"But, lady, you break my heart," cried the mulatto, "if you not take my service. My William and me, too poor to live togedder of some year perhaps. Here, child, tawny boy, down on knees, and vow wid me to be faithful and grateful to this our mistress, till our last day; and never to forsake her in sickness or in sorrow! I swear dis to my great God:—and now say dat after me." She then clasped the little boy's hands, bade him raise his eyes to heaven, and made him repeat what she had said, ending it with "I swear dis, to my great God."

There was such an affecting solemnity in this action, and in the mulatto such a determined enthusiasm of manner incapable of being controlled, that Adeline, Glenmurray, and Berrendale observed what passed in respectful silence: and when it was over, Glenmurray said, in a voice of emotion, "I think, Adeline, we must accept this good creature's offer; and as nurse grows lazy and saucy, we had better part with her: and as for your young knight there," (the tawny boy had by this time nestled himself close to Adeline, who, with no small emotion, was playing with his woolly curls,) "we must send him to school; for, my good woman, we are not so poor as you imagine."

"God be thanked!" cried the mulatto.

"But what is your name?"

"I was christened Savanna," replied she.

"Then, good Savanna," cried Adeline, "I hope we shall both have reason to bless the day when first we met; and to-morrow you shall come home to us." Savanna, on hearing this, almost screamed with joy, and as she took her leave Berrendale slipped a guinea into her hand: the tawny boy meanwhile slowly followed his mother, as if unwilling to leave Adeline, even though she gave him halfpence to spend in cakes: but on being told that she would let him come again the next day, he tripped gaily down after Savanna.

The quiet of the chamber being then restored, Glenmurray fell into a calm slumber. Adeline took up her work; and Berrendale, pretending to read, continued to feed his passion by gazing on the unconscious Adeline.

While they were thus engaged, Glenmurray, unobserved, awoke; and he soon guessed how Berrendale's eyes were employed, as the book which he held in his hand was upside down; and through the fingers of the hand which he held before his face, he saw his looks fixed on Adeline.

The moment was a favourable one for Glenmurray's purpose: and just as he raised himself from his pillow, Adeline had discovered the earnest gaze of Berrendale; and a suspicion of the truth that instant darting across her mind, disconcerted and blushing, she had cast her eyes on the ground.

"That is an interesting study which you are engaged in, Charles," cried Glenmurray smiling.

Berrendale started; and, deeply blushing, faltered out, "Yes."

Adeline looked at Glenmurray, and, seeing a very arch and meaning expression on his countenance, suspected that he had made the same discovery as herself: yet, if so, she wondered at his looking so pleasantly on Berrendale as he spoke.

"It is a book, Charles," continued Glenmurray, "which the more you study the more you will admire; and I wish to give you a clue to understand some passages in it better than you can now do."

This speech deceived Adeline, and made her suppose that Glenmurray really alluded to the book which lay before Berrendale: but it convinced *him* that Glenmurray spoke metaphorically; and as his manner was kind, it also made him think that he saw and did not disapprove his attachment.

For a few minutes, each of them being engrossed in different contemplations, there was a complete silence; but Glenmurray interrupted it by saying, "My dear Adeline, it is your hour for walking; but, as I am not disposed to sleep again, will you forgive me if I keep your walking companion to myself to-day?—I wish to converse with him alone."

"Oh! most cheerfully," she replied with quickness: "you know I love a solitary ramble of all things."

"Not very flattering that to my cousin," observed Glenmurray.

"I did not wish to flatter him," said Adeline gravely; and Berrendale, fluttered at the idea of the coming conversation with Glenmurray, and mortified by Adeline's words and manner, turned to the window to conceal his emotion.

Adeline, then, with more than usual tenderness, conjured Glenmurray not to talk too much, nor do any thing to destroy the hopes on which her only chance of happiness depended, viz. the now possible chance of his recovery, and then set out for her walk; while, with a restraint and coldness which she could not conquer, she bade Berrendale farewell for the present.

The walk was long, and her thoughts perturbed:— "What could Glenmurray want to say to Mr. Berrendale?"—Why did Mr. Berrendale sit with his eyes so intently and clandestinely, as it were, fixed on me?" were thoughts perpetually recurring to her: and half impatient, and half reluctant, she at length returned to her lodgings.

When she entered the apartment, she saw signs of great emotion in the countenance of both the gentlemen; and in Berrendale's eyes the traces of recent tears. The tone of Glenmurray's voice too, when he addressed her, was even more tender than usual, and Berrendale's attentions more marked, yet more respectful; and Adeline observed that Glenmurray was unusually thoughtful and absent, and that the cough and other symptoms of his complaint were more troublesome than ever.

"I see you have exerted yourself and talked too much during my absence," cried Adeline, "and I will never leave you again for so long a time."

"You never shall," said Glenmurray. "I must leave *you* for so long a time at last, that I will be blessed with the sight of you as long as I can."

Adeline, whose hopes had been considerably revived during the last few days, looked mournfully and reproachfully in his face as he uttered these words.

"It is even so, my dearest girl," continued Glenmurray, "and I say this to guard you against a melancholy surprise:—I wish to prepare you for an event which to me seems unavoidable."

"Prepare me!" exclaimed Adeline wildly. "Can there be any preparation to enable one to bear such a calamity? Absurd idea! However, I shall derive consolation from the severity of the stroke: I feel that I shall not be able to survive it." So saying, her head fell on Glenmurray's pillow; and, for some time, her sorrow almost suspended the consciousness of suffering.

From this state she was aroused by Glenmurray's being attacked with a violent paroxysm of his complaint, and all selfish distress was lost in the consciousness of his sufferings: again he struggled through, and seemed so relieved by the effort, that again Adeline's hopes revived; and she could scarcely return, with temper, Berrendale's "good night," when Glenmurray expressed a wish to rest, because his spirits had not risen in any proportion to hers.

The nurse had been dismissed that afternoon; and Adeline, as Savanna was not to come home till the next morning, was to sit up alone with Glenmurray that night; and, contrary to his usual custom, he did not insist that she should have a companion.

For a few hours his exhausted frame was recruited by a sleep more than usually quiet, and but for a few hours only. He then became restless, and so wakeful and disturbed, that he professed to Adeline an utter inability to sleep, and therefore he wished to pass the rest of the night in serious conversation with her.

Adeline, alarmed at this intention, conjured him not to irritate his complaint by so dangerous an exertion.

"My mind will irritate it more," replied he, "if I refrain from it; for it is burthened, my Adeline, and it longs to throw off its burthen. Now then, ere my senses wander, hear what I wish to communicate to you, and interrupt me as little as possible."

Adeline, oppressed and awed beyond measure at the unusual solemnity of his manner, made no answer; but, leaning her cheek on his hand, awaited his communication in silence.

"I think," said Glenmurray, "I shall begin with telling you Berrendale's history: it is proper that you should know all that concerns him."

Adeline, raising her head, replied hastily,— "Not to satisfy any curiosity of mine; for I feel none, I assure you."

"Well then," returned Glenmurray, sighing, "to please me, be it.—Berrendale is the son of my mother's sister, by a merchant in the neighborhood of the 'Change,[98] who hurt the family pride

---

[98] The Royal Exchange, where merchants conducted financial business.

so much by marrying a tradesman, that I am the only one of the clan who has noticed her since. He ran away, about four years ago, with the only child of a rich West Indian from a boarding-school.[99] The consequence was, that her father renounced her; but, when, three years ago, she died in giving birth to a son, the unhappy parent repented of his displeasure, and offered to allow Berrendale, who from the bankruptcy and sudden death of both his parents had been left destitute, an annuity of 300£ for life, provided he would send the child over to Jamaica, and allow him to have all the care of his education. To this Berrendale consented.

"Reluctantly, I hope," said Adeline, "and merely out of pity for the feelings of the childless father."

"I hope so too," continued Glenmurray; "for I do not think the chance of inheriting all his grandfather's property a sufficient reason to lead him to give up to another, in a foreign land too, the society and education of his child: but, whatever were his reasons, Berrendale acceded to the request, and the infant was sent to Jamaica; and ever since the 300£ has been regularly remitted to him: besides that, he has recovered two thousand and odd hundred pounds from the wreck of his father's property; and with œconomy, and had he a good wife to manage his affairs for him, Berrendale might live very comfortably."

"My dear Glenmurray," cried Adeline impatiently, "what is this to me? and why do you weary yourself to tell me particulars so little interesting to me?"

Glenmurray bade her have patience, and continued thus: "And now, Adeline, (here his voice evidently faltered) I must open my whole heart to you, and confess that the idea of leaving you friendless, unprotected, and poor, your reputation injured, and your peace of mind destroyed, is more than I am able to bear, and will give me, in my last moments, the torments of the damned." Here a violent burst of tears interrupted him; and

[99] I.e., the daughter of an English landowner and merchant of the Caribbean colonies, here Jamaica.

Adeline, overcome with emotion and surprise at the sight of the agitation which his own sufferings could never occasion in him, hung over him in speechless woe.

"Besides," continued Glenmurray, recovering himself a little, "I—O Adeline!" seizing her cold hand, "can you forgive me for having been the means of blasting all your fair fame and prospects in life?"

"For the sake of justice, if not of mercy," exclaimed Adeline, "forbear thus cruelly to accuse yourself. You know that from my own free, unbiassed choice I gave myself to you, and in compliance with my own principles."

"But who taught you these principles?—who led you to a train of reasoning, so alluring in theory, so pernicious, in practice? Had not I, with the heedless vanity of youth, given to the world the crude conceptions of four-and-twenty, you might at this moment have been the idol of a respectable society; and I, equally respected, have been the husband of your heart; while happiness would perhaps have kept that fatal disease at bay, of which anxiety has facilitated the approach."

He was going on: but Adeline, who had till now struggled successfully with her feelings, wound up almost to phrensy at the possibility that anxiety had shortened Glenmurray's life, gave way to a violent paroxysm of sorrow, which, for a while, deprived her of consciousness; and when she recovered she found Berrendale bending over her, while her head lay on Glenmurray's pillow.

The sight of Berrendale in a moment roused her to exertion;—his look was so full of anxious tenderness, and she was at the moment so ill disposed to regard it with complacency, that she eagerly declared she was quite recovered, and begged Mr. Berrendale would return to bed; and Glenmurray seconding her request, with a deep sigh he departed.

"Poor fellow!" said Glenmurray, "I wish you had seen his anxiety during your illness!"

"I am glad I did *not*," replied Adeline: "but how can you persist in talking to me of any other person's anxiety, when I am tortured with yours? Your conversation of to-night has made me even more miserable than I was before. By what strange fatality do you blame yourself for the conduct worthy of admiration?—for giving to the world, as soon as produced, opinions which were calculated to enlighten it?"

"But," replied Glenmurray, "as those opinions militated against the experience and custom of ages, ought I not to have paused before I published, and kept them back till they had received the sanction of my maturer judgement?"

"And does your maturer judgement condemn them?"

"Four years cannot have added much to the maturity of my judgement," replied Glenmurray: "but I will own that some of my opinions are changed; and that, though I believe those which are unchanged are right in theory, I think, as the mass of society could never at *once* adopt them, they had better remain unacted upon, than that a few lonely individuals should expose themselves to certain distress, by making them the rules of their conduct.[100] You, for instance, you, my Adeline, what misery—!" Here his voice again faltered, and emotion impeded his utterance.

"Live—do but live," exclaimed Adeline passionately, "and I can know of misery but the name."

"But I cannot live, I cannot live," replied Glenmurray, "and the sooner I die the better;—for thus to waste your youth and health in the dreadful solitude of a sick-room is insupportable to me."

"O Glenmurray!" replied Adeline, fondly throwing herself

---

[100] Compare Godwin's comments on his positive representation of marriage in his 1805 novel, *Fleetwood, or the New Man of Feeling*: "A thousand things might be found excellent and salutary, if brought into general practice, which would in some cases be attended with tragical consequences, if prematurely acted upon by a solitary individual. The author of *Political Justice*... is the last man in the world to recommend a pitiful attempt, by scattered examples to renovate the face of society, instead of endeavouring by discussion and reasoning, to effect a grand and comprehensive improvement in the sentiments of its members" (Ed. Gary Handwerk and A. A. Markley. (Petersborough, Ontario: Broadview Press, 2001), p. 49).

on his neck, "could you but live free from any violent pain, and were neither you nor I ever to leave this room again, believe be, I should not have a wish beyond it. To see you, to hear you, to prove to you how much I love you, would, indeed it would, be happiness sufficient for me!" After this burst of true and heartfelt tenderness, there was a pause of some moments: Glenmurray felt too much to speak, and Adeline was sobbing on his pillow. At length she pathetically again exclaimed, "Live; only live! and I am blest!"

"But I *cannot* live, I *cannot* live," again replied Glenmurray; "and when I die, what will become of you?"

"I care not," cried Adeline: "if I lose you, may the same grave receive us!"

"But it *will* not, my dearest girl;—grief does not kill; and, entailed as my estate is, I have nothing to leave you: and though richly qualified to undertake the care of children, in order to maintain yourself, your unfortunate connection, and singular opinions, will be an eternal bar to your being so employed. O Adeline! these cutting fears, these dreadful reflections, are indeed the bitterness of death: but there is one way of alleviating my pangs."

"Name it," replied Adeline with quickness.

"But you must promise then to hear me with patience.— Had I been able to live through my illness, I should have conjured you to let me endeavour to restore you to your place in society, and consequently to your usefulness, by making you my wife: and young, and I may add innocent and virtuous, as you are, I doubt not but the world would at length have received you into its favour again."

"But you must, you will, you shall live," interrupted Adeline, "and I shall be your happy wife."

"Not *mine*," replied Glenmurray, laying an emphasis on the last word.

Adeline started, and, fixing her eyes wildly on his, demanded what he meant.

'I mean," replied he, "to prevail on you to make my last

moments happy, by promising, some time hence, to give yourself a tender, a respectable, and a legal protector."

"O Glenmurray!" exclaimed Adeline, "and can you insult my tenderness for you with such a proposal? If I can even survive you, do you think that I can bear to give you a successor in my affection? or, how can you bear to imagine that I shall?"

"Because my love for you is without selfishness, and I wish you to be happy even though another makes you so. The lover, or the husband, who wishes the woman of his affection to form no second attachment, is, in my opinion, a selfish, contemptible being.[101] Perhaps I do not expect that you will ever feel, for another man, an attachment like that which has subsisted between us—the first affection of young and impassioned hearts; but I am sure that you may again feel love enough to make yourself and the man of your choice perfectly happy; and I hope and trust that you will be so."

"And forget you, I suppose?" interrupted Adeline reproachfully.

"Not so: I would have you remember me always, but with a chastized and even a pleasing sorrow; nay, I would wish you to imagine me a sort of guardian spirit, watching your actions, and enjoying your happiness."

"I have *listened* to you," cried Adeline in a tone of suppressed anguish, "and, I trust, with tolerable patience: there is one thing yet for me to learn—the *name* of the object whom you wish me to marry, for I suppose *he* is found."

"He is," returned Glenmurray. "Berrendale loves you; and he it is whom I wish you to choose."

"I thought so," exclaimed Adeline, rising and traversing the room hastily, and wringing her hands.

"But wherefore does his name," said Glenmurray, "excite

---

[101] Late eighteenth-century novels frequently engage the question of whether a second passion is possible, or a sign of a lack of delicacy. Marianne in Jane Austen's *Sense and Sensibility* (1811) must learn to accept a second love. Compare Emma Courtney's marriage to her passion for Augustus Harley.

such angry emotion? Perhaps self-love makes me recommend him," continued he, forcing a smile, "as he is reckoned like me, and I thought that likeness might make him more agreeable to you."

"Only the more odious," impatiently interrupted Adeline. "To look like you, and not *be* you, Oh! insupportable idea!" she exclaimed, throwing herself on Glenmurray's pillow, and pressing his burning temples to her cold cheek.

"Adeline," said Glenmurray solemnly, "this is, perhaps, the last moment of confidential and uninterrupted intercourse that we shall ever have together;" Adeline started, but spoke not; "allow me, therefore, to tell you it is my *dying request*, that you would endeavour to dispose your mind in favour of Berrendale, and to become in time his wife. Circumstanced as you are, your only chance for happiness is becoming a wife: but it is too certain that few men worthy of you, in the most essential points, will be likely to marry you after your connection with me."

"Strange prejudice!" cried Adeline, "to consider as my disgrace, what I deem my glory!"

"Glenmurray continued thus: "Berrendale himself has a great deal of the old school about him, but I have convinced him that you are not to be classed with the frail of your sex; and that you are one of the purest as well as loveliest of human beings."

"And did he want to be convinced of this?" cried Adeline indignantly; "and *yet* you advise me to marry him?"

"My dearest love," replied Glenmurray, "in all cases the most we can expect is, to choose the best *possible* means of happiness. Berrendale is not perfect; but I am convinced that you would commit a fatal error in not making him your husband; and when I tell you it is my *dying request* that you should do so— "

"If you wish me to retain my senses," exclaimed Adeline, "repeat that dreadful phrase no more."

"I will not say any more at all now," faintly observed Glenmurray, "for I am exhausted:—still, as morning begins to dawn, I should like to sit up in my bed, and gaze on it, perhaps for— " Here Adeline put her hand to his mouth: Glenmurray kissed it, sighed, and did not finish the sentence. She then opened the shutters to let in the rising splendor of day, and, turning round towards Glenmurray, almost shrieked with terror at seeing the visible alteration a night had made in his appearance; while the yellow rays of the dawn played on his sallow cheek, and his dark curls, once cripsed and glossy, hung faint and moist on his beating temples.

"It is strange, Adeline," said Glenmurray (but with great effort), "that, even in my situation, the sight of morning, and the revival as it were of nature, seems to invigorate my whole frame. I long to breathe the freshness of its breeze also."

Adeline, conscious for the first time that all hope was over, opened the window, and felt even her sick soul and languid frame revived by the chill but refreshing breeze. To Glenmurray it imparted a feeling of physical pleasure, to which he had long been a stranger: "I breathe freely," he exclaimed, "I feel alive again!"—and, strange as it may seem, Adeline's hopes began to revive also.— "I feel as if I could sleep now," said Glenmurray, "the feverish restlessness seems abated; but, lest my dreams be disturbed, promise me, ere I lie down again, that you will behave kindly to Berrendale."

"Impossible! The only tie that bound me to him is broken:—I thought he sincerely sympathized with me in my wishes for your recovery; but now that, as he loves me, his wishes must be in direct opposition to mine,—I cannot, indeed I cannot, endure the sight of him."

Glenmurray could not reply to this natural observation: he knew that, in a similar situation, his feelings would have been like Adeline's; and, pressing her hand with all the little strength left him, he said "Poor Berrendale!" and tried to compose himself to sleep; while Adeline, lost in sad contemplation, threw herself in a chair by his bed-side, and anxiously awaited the event of his reawaking.

But it was not long before Adeline herself, exhausted both in body and mind, fell into a deep sleep; and it was mid-day before she awoke: for no careless, heavy-treading, and hired nurse now watched the slumbers of the unhappy lovers; but the mulatto, stepping light as air, and afraid even of breathing lest she should disturb their repose, had assumed her station at the bed-side, and taken every precaution lest any noise should awake them. Hers was the service of the heart; and there is none like it.

At twelve o'clock Adeline awoke; and her first glance met the dark eyes of Savanna kindly fixed upon her. Adeline started, not immediately recollecting who it could be; but in a moment the idea of the mulatto, and of the service which she had rendered her, recurred to her mind, and diffused a sensation of pleasure through her frame. "There is a being whom I have served," said Adeline to herself, and, extending her hand to Savanna, she started from her seat, invigorated by the thought: but she felt depressed again by the consciousness that she, who had been able to impart so much joy and help to another, was herself a wretch for ever; and in a moment her eyes filled with tears, while the mulatto gazed on her with a look of inquiring solicitude.

"Poor Savanna!" cried Adeline in a low and plaintive tone.

There are moments when the sound of one's own voice has a mournful effect on one's feelings—this was one of those moments to Adeline; the pathos of her own tone overcame her, and she burst into tears: but Glenmurray slept on; and Adeline hoped nothing would suddenly disturb his rest, when Berrendale opened the door with what appeared unnecessary noise, and Glenmurray hastily awoke.

Adeline immediately started from her seat, and, looking at him with great indignation, demanded why he came in in such a manner, when he knew Mr. Glenmurray was asleep.

Berrendale, shocked and alarmed at Adeline's words and expression, so unlike her usual manner, stammered out an excuse. "Another time, sir," replied Adeline coldly, "I hope you will be more *careful*."

"What is the matter?" said Glenmurray, raising himself in the bed. "Are you scolding, Adeline? If so, let me hear you: I like novelty."

Here Adeline and Berrendale both hastened to him, and

Adeline almost looked with complacency on Berrendale; when Glenmurray, declaring himself wonderfully refreshed by his long sleep, expressed a great desire for his breakfast, and said he had a most voracious appetite.

But to all Berrendale's attentions she returned the most forbidding reserve; nor could she for a moment lose the painful idea, that the death of Glenmurray would be to him a source of joy, not of anguish. Berrendale was not slow to observe this change in her conduct; and he conceived that, as he knew Glenmurray had mentioned his pretensions to her, his absence would be of more service to his wishes than his presence; and he resolved to leave Richmond that afternoon,—especially as he had a dinner engagement at a tavern in London, which, in spite of love and friendship, he was desirous of keeping.

He was not mistaken in his ideas: the countenance of Adeline assumed less severity when he mentioned his intention of going away, nor could she express regret at his resolution, even though Glenmurray with anxious earnestness requested him to stay. But Glenmurray entreated in vain: used to consider his own interest and pleasure in preference to that of others, Berrendale resolved to go; and resisted the prayers of a man who had often obliged him with the greatest difficulty to himself.

"Well, then," said Glenmurray mournfully, "if you must go, God bless you! I wish you, Charles, all possible earthly happiness; nay, I have done all I can to ensure it to you: but you have disappointed me. I hoped to have joined your hand, in my last moments, to that of this dear girl, and to have bequeathed her in the most solemn manner to your care and tenderness; but, no matter, farewell! we shall probably meet no more."

Here Berrendale's heart failed him, and he almost resolved to stay: but a look of angry repugnance which he saw on Adeline's countenance, even amidst her sorrow, got the better of his kind emotions, by wounding his self-love; and grasping Glenmurray's hand, and saying, "I shall be back in a day or two," he rushed out of the room.

"I am sorry Mr. Berrendale is forced to go," said Adeline

involuntarily when the street-door closed after him.

"Had you condescended to tell him so, he would undoubtedly have staid," replied Glenmurray rather peevishly. Adeline instantly felt, and regretted, the selfishness of her conduct. To avoid the sight of a disagreeable object, she had given pain to Glenmurray; or, rather, she had not done her utmost to prevent his being exposed to it.

"Forgive me," said Adeline, bursting into tears: "I own I thought only of myself, when I forbore to urge his stay. Alas! with you, and you alone, I believe, is the gratification of self always a secondary consideration."

"You forget that I am a philanthropist," replied Glenmurray, "and cannot bear to be praised, even by you, at the expense of my fellow-creatures. But come, hasten dinner; my breakfast agreed with me so well, that I am impatient for another meal."

"You certainly are better to-day," exclaimed Adeline with unwonted cheerfulness.

"My feelings are more tolerable, at least," replied Glenmurray: and Adeline and the mulatto began to prepare the dinner immediately. How often during her attendance on Glenmurray had she recollected the words of her grandmother, and blessed her for having taught her to be *useful!*

As soon as dinner was over, Glenmurray complained of being drowsy: still he declared he would not go to bed till he had seen the sun set, as he had that day, for the second time since his illness, seen it rise; and therefore, when it was setting, Adeline and Savanna led him into a room adjoining, which had a western aspect. Glenmurray fixed his eyes on the crimson horizon with a peculiar expression; and his lips seemed to murmur, "For the last time! Let me breathe the evening air, too, once more," said he.

"It is too chill, dear Glenmurray."

"It will not hurt me," replied Glenmurray; and Adeline complied with his request.

"The breeze of evening is not refreshing like that of morning," he observed; "but the beauty of the setting is, perhaps, superior to that of the rising sun:—they are both glorious sights, and I have enjoyed them both to-day, nor have I for years experienced so strong a feeling of devotion."

"Thank God!" cried Adeline. "O Glenmurray! there has been one thing only wanting to the completion of our union; and that was, that we should worship together."

"Perhaps, had I remained longer here," replied Glenmurray, "we might have done so; for, believe me, Adeline, though my feelings have continually hurried me into adoration of the Supreme Being, I have often wished my homage to be as regular and as founded on immutable conviction as it once was: but it it too late now for amendment, though, alas! not for *regret, deep* regret: yet He who reads the heart knows that my intentions were pure, and that I was not fixed in the stubbornness of error."

"Let us change this discourse," cried Adeline, seeing on Glenmurray's countenance an expression of uncommon sadness, which he, from a regard to her feelings, struggled to cover. He did indeed feel sadness—a sadness of the most painful nature; and while Adeline hung over him with all the anxious and soothing attention of unbounded love, he seemed to shrink from her embrace with horror, and, turning away his head, feebly murmured, "O Adeline! this faithful kindness wounds me to the very soul. Alas! alas! how little have I deserved it!"

If Glenmurray, who had been the means of injuring the woman he loved, merely by following the dictates of his conscience, and a love of what he imagined to be truth, without any view to his own benefit or the gratification of his personal wishes, felt thus acutely the anguish of self-upbraiding,—what ought to be, and what must be, sooner or later, the agony and remorse of that man, who, merely for the gratification of his own illicit desires, has seduced the woman whom he loved from the path of virtue, and ruined for ever her reputation and her peace of mind!

"It is too late for you to sit at an open window, indeed it is," cried Adeline, after having replied to Glenmurray's self-reproaches by the touching language of tears, and incoherent expressions of confiding and unchanged attachment; "and as you are evidently better to-day, do not, by breathing too much cold air, run the risk of making yourself worse again."

"Would I were really better! would I could live!" passionately exclaimed Glenmurray: "but indeed I do feel stronger to-night than I have felt for many months." In a moment the fine eyes of Adeline were raised to heaven with an expression of devout thankfulness; and, eager to make the most of a change so favourable, she hurried Glenmurray back to his chamber, and, with a feeling of renewed hope, sat by to watch his slumbers. She had not sat long before the door opened, and the litle tawny boy entered. He had watched all day to see the good lady, as he called Adeline; but, as she had not left Glenmurray's chamber except to prepare dinner, he had been disappointed: so he was resolved to seek her in her own apartment. He had bought some cakes with the penny which Adeline had given him, and he was eager to give her a piece of them.

"Hush!" cried Adeline, as she held out her hand to him; and he in a whisper crying "Bite," held his purchase to her lips. Adeline tasted it, said it was very good, and, giving him a halfpenny, the tawny boy disappeared again: the noise he made as he bounded down the stairs woke Glenmurray. Adeline was sitting on the side of the bed; and as he turned round to sleep again he grasped her hand in his, and its feverish touch dampened her hopes, and re-awakened her fears. For a short time she mournfully gazed on his flushed cheek, and then, gently sliding off the bed, and dropping on one knee, she addressed the Deity in the language of humble supplication.

Insensibly she ceased to pray in thought only, and the lowly-murmured prayer became audible. Again Glenmurray awoke, and Adeline reproached herself as the cause.

"My rest was uneasy," cried he, "and I rejoice that you woke me: besides, I like to hear you—Go on, my dearest girl; there is something in the breathings of your pious fondness that sooths me," added he, pressing the hand he held to his parched lips.

Adeline obeyed: and as she continued, she felt ever and anon, by the pressure of Glenmurray's hand, how much he was affected by what she uttered.

"But must he be taken from me!" she exclaimed in one part of her prayer. "Father, if it be possible, permit this cup to pass by me untasted."[102] Here she felt the hand of Glenmurray grasp hers most vehemently; and, delighted to think that he had pleasure in hearing her, she went on to breathe forth all the wishes of a trembling yet confiding spirit, till overcome with her own emotions she ceased and arose, and leaning over Glenmurray's pillow was going to take his hand:—but the hand which she pressed returned not her pressure; the eyes were fixed whose approving glance she sought; and the horrid truth rushed at once on her mind, that the last convulsive grasp had been an eternal farewell, and that he had in that grasp expired.

Alas! what preparation however long, what anticipation however sure, can enable the mind to bear a shock like this! It came on Adeline like a thunder-stroke: she screamed not; she moved not; but, fixing a dim and glassy eye on the pale countenance of her lover, she seemed as insensible as poor Glenmurray himself; and hours might have elapsed—hours immediately fatal both to her senses and existence—ere any one had entered the room, since she had given orders to be disturbed by no one, had not the tawny boy, encouraged by his past success, stolen in again, unperceived, to give her a piece of the apple which he had bought with her last bounty.

The delighted boy tripped gaily to the bed-side, holding up his treasure; but he started back, and screamed in all the agony of terror, at the sight which he had beheld—the face of Glenmurray ghastly, and the mouth distorted as if in the last agony, and Adeline in the stupor of despair.

The affectionate boy's repeated screams soon summoned the whole family[103] into the room, while he, vainly hanging on

---

[102] St. Matthew, 26:39. Before the crucifixion, Jesus prays "If it be possible, let this cup pass from me."
[103] "Family" in this context signifies the extended household, rather than the more modern concept of a "nuclear family" related only by consanguinity.

Adeline's arm, begged her to speak to him: But nothing could at first rouse Adeline, not even Savanna's loud and extravagant grief. When, however, they tried to force her from the body, she recovered her recollection and her strength; and it was with great difficulty she could be carried out of the room, and kept out when they had accomplished their purpose.

But Savanna was sure that looking at such a sad sight would kill her mistress; for she should die herself if she saw William dead, she declared; and the people of the house agreed with her. They knew not that grief is the best medicine for itself; and that the overcharged heart is often relieved by the sight which standers-by conceive likely to snap the very threads of existence.

As Adeline and Glenmurray had both of them excited some interest in Richmond, the news of the death of the latter was immediately abroad; and it was told to Mrs. Pemberton, with a pathetic account of Adeline's distress, just as the carriage was preparing to convey her and her sick friend on their way to Lisbon. It was a relation to call forth all the humanity of Mrs. Pemberton's nature. She forgot Adeline's crime in her distress; and knowing she had no female friend with her, she hastened on the errand of pity to the abode of vice. Alas! Mrs. Pemberton had learnt but too well to sympathize in grief like that of Adeline. She had seen a beloved husband expire in her arms, and had afterwards followed two children to the grave. But she had taken refuge from sorrow in the active duties of her religion, and in becoming a teacher of those truths to others, by which she had so much benefited herself.

Mrs. Pemberton entered the room just as Adeline, on her knees, was conjuring the persons with her to allow her to see Glenmurray once more.

Adeline did not at all observe the entrance of Mrs. Pemberton, who, in spite of the self-command which her principles and habits gave her, was visibly affected when she beheld the mourner's tearless affliction: and the hands which, on her entrance, were quietly crossed on each other, confining the modest folds of her simple cloke, were suddenly and involuntarily separated by the irresistible impulse of pity; while, catching hold of the wall for support, she leaned against it, covering her face with her hands. "Let me see him! only let me see him once more!" cried Adeline, gazing on Mrs. Pemberton, but unconscious who she was.

"Thou shalt see him," replied Mrs. Pemberton with considerable effort; "give me thy hand, and I will go with thee to the chamber of death." Adeline gave a scream of mournful joy at this permission, and suffered herself to be led into Glenmurray's apartment. As soon as she entered it she sprang to the bed, and, throwing herself beside the corpse, began to contemplate it with an earnestness and firmness which surprised every one. Mrs. Pemberton also fixedly gazed on the wan face of Glenmurray: "And art thou fallen!" she exclaimed, "thou, wise in thine own conceit, who presumedst, perhaps, sometimes to question even the existence of the Most High, and to set up thy vain chimeras of yesterday against the wisdom and experience of centuries? Child of the dust! child of error! what art thou now, and whither is thy guilty spirit fled? But balmy is the hand of affliction; and she, thy mourning victim, may learn to bless the hand that chastizes her, nor add to the offences which will weigh down thy soul, a dread responsibility for hers!"

Here she was interrupted by the voice of Adeline; who, in a deep and hollow tone, was addressing the unconscious corpse. "For God's sake, speak! for this silence is dreadful—it looks so like death."

"Poor thing! said Mrs. Pemberton, kneeling beside her, "and is it even thus with thee? Would thou couldst shed tears, afflicted one!"

"It is very strange," continued Adeline: "he loved me so tenderly, and he used to speak and look so tenderly, and now, see how he neglects me! Glenmurray, my love! for mercy's sake, speak to me!" As she said this, she laid her lips to his: but, feeling on them the icy coldness of death, she started back, screaming in all the violence of phrensy; and, recovered to the full consciousness of her misfortune, she was carried back to her room in violent convulsions.

"Would I could stay and watch over thee!" said Mrs. Pemberton, as she gazed on Adeline's distorted countenance; "for thou, young as thou art, wert well known in the chambers of sorrow and of sickness; and I should rejoice to pay back to thee part of the debt of those whom thy presence so often soothed; but I must leave thee to the care of others."

"You leave her to my care," cried Savanna reproachfully,—who felt even her violent sorrow suspended while Mrs. Pemberton spoke in accents at once sad yet soothing,— "you leave her to my care, and who watch, who love her more than me?"

"Good Savanna!" replied Mrs. Pemberton, pressing the mulatto's hand as she returned to her station beside Adeline, who was fallen into a calm slumber, "to thy care, with confidence, I commit her. But perhaps there may be an immediate necessity for money, and I had better leave this with thee," she added, taking out her purse: but Savanna assured her that Mr. Berrendale was sent for, and to him all those concerns were to be left. Mrs. Pemberton stood for a few moments looking at Adeline in silence, then slowly left the house.

When Adeline awoke, she seemed so calm and resigned, that her earnest request of being allowed to pass the night alone was granted, especially as Mrs. Pemberton had desired that her wish, even to see Glenmurray again, should be complied with: but the faithful mulatto watched till morning at the door. No bed that night received the weary limbs of Adeline. She threw herself on the ground, and in alternate prayer and phrensy passed the first night of her woe: towards morning, however, she fell into a perturbed sleep. But when the light of day darting into the room awakened her to consciousness; and when she recollected that he to whom it usually summoned her existed no longer; that the eyes which but the preceding morning had opened with enthusiastic ardour to hail its beams, were now for ever closed; and that the voice which used to welcome her so tenderly, she should never, never hear again; the forlornness of her situation, the hopelessness of her sorrow burst upon her with a violence too powerful for her reason: and when Berrendale arrived, he found Glenmurray in his shroud, and Adeline in a state of insanity. For six months her phrensy resisted all the efforts of medicine, and the united care which Berrendale's love and Savanna's grateful attachment could bestow; while with Adeline's want[104] of their care seemed to increase their desire of bestowing it, and their affection gathered new strength from the duration of her helpless malady. So true is it, that we become attached more from the aid which we give than that which we receive; and that the love of the obliger is more apt to increase than that of the obliged by the obligation conferred. At length, however, Adeline's reason slowly yet surely returned; and she, by degrees, learnt to contemplate with firmness, and even calmness, the loss which she had sustained. She even looked on Berrendale and his attentions not with anger, but gratitude and complacency; she had even pleasure in observing the likeness he bore Glenmurray; she felt that it endeared him to her. In the first paroxysms of her phrensy, the sight of him threw her into fits of raving; but as she grew better she had pleasure in seeing him: and when, on her recovery, she heard how much she was indebted to his persevering tenderness, she felt for him a decided regard, which Berrendale tried to flatter himself might be ripened into love.

But he was mistaken; the heart of Adeline was formed to feel violent and lasting attachments only. She had always loved her mother with a tenderness of a most uncommon nature; she had felt for Glenmurray the fondest enthusiasm of passion: she was now separated from them both. But her mother still lived; and though almost hopeless of ever being restored to her society, all her love for her returned; and she pined for that consoling fondness, those soothing attentions, which, in a time of such affliction, a mother on a widowed daughter can alone bestow.

"Yet, surely," cried she in the solitude of her own room, "her oath cannot now forbid her to forgive me; for, am I not as WRETCHED IN LOVE, nay more, far more so, than *she* has been? Yes—yes; I will write to her: besides, HE wished me to do so"

---

[104] I.e., need.

(meaning Glenmurray, whom she never named); and she did write to her, according to the address which Dr. Norberry sent soon after he returned to his own house. Still week after week elapsed, and month after month, but no answer came.

Again she wrote, and again she was disappointed; though her loss, her illness in consequence of it, her pecuniary distress, and the large debt which she had incurred to Berrendale, were all detailed in a manner calculated to move the most obdurate heart. What then could Adeline suppose? Perhaps her mother was ill; perhaps she was dead: and her reason was again on the point of yielding to this horrible supposition, when she received her two letters in a cover, directed in her mother's hand-writing.

At first she was overwhelmed by this dreadful proof of the continuance of Mrs. Mowbray's deep resentment; but, ever sanguine, the circumstance of Mrs. Mowbray's having written the address herself appeared to Adeline a favourable symptom; and with renewed hope she wrote to Dr. Norberry to become her mediator once more: but to this letter no answer was returned; and Adeline concluded her only friend had died of the fever which Mrs. Norberry had mentioned in her letter.

"Then I have lost my only friend!" cried Adeline, wringing her hands in agony, as this idea recurred to her. "Your only friend?" repeated Berrendale, who happened to be present, "O Adeline!"

Her heart smote her as he said this. "My oldest friend I should have said," she replied, holding out her hand to him; and Berrendale thought himself supremely happy.

But Adeline was far from meaning to give the encouragement which this action seemed to bestow: wholly occupied by her affliction, her mind had lost its energy, and she would not have made an effort to dissipate her grief by employment and exertion, had not that virtuous pride and delicacy, which in happier hours had been the ornament of her character, rebelled against the consciousness of owing pecuniary obligations to the lover whose suit she was determined to reject, and urged her to make some vigorous attempt to maintain herself.

Women and Work II

The problem of earning her own living becomes more and more pressing for Adeline as she moves from being the wealthy heiress to the unmarried companion to Glenmurray, to the destitute and indebted mistress of a dead lover. The novel here engages an ongoing debate about the increasing problem of unmarried or unmarriageable women who lack families to support them. Responding to earlier arguments on appropriate paid work for women, the Quaker and moralist Priscilla Wakefield wrote *Reflections on the Present Condition of the Female Sex* in 1798. She offers detailed suggestions on women's work at all social levels, including those which pertain to Adeline's and Emma's situation as genteel, educated, literate, and without substantial capital for investment:

[A] few remarks upon the nature of those employments, which are best adapted to the higher classes of the sex, when reduced to necessitous circumstances, may, perhaps, afford useful hints to those, who are languishing under the pressure of misfortune....

Numerous difficulties arise in the choice of occupations for the purpose. They must be such as are neither laborious nor servile, and they must of course, be productive, without requiring a capital.

For these reasons, pursuits which require the exercise of intellectual, rather than bodily powers, are generally the most eligible.

Literature affords a respectable and pleasing employment, for those who possess talents, and an adequate degree of mental cultivation. For although the emolument is precarious, and seldom equal to a maintenance, yet if the attempt be tolerably successful, it may yield a comfortable assistance in narrow circumstances, and beguile many hours, which might otherwise be passed in solitude or unavailing regret. The fine arts offer a mode of

subsistence, congenial to the delicacy of the most
refined minds, and they are peculiarly adapted by
their elegance, to the gratification of taste. The
perfection of every species of painting is attainable
by women, from the representation of historic facts,
to the minute execution of the miniature portrait,
if they will bestow sufficient time and application
for the acquisition of the principles of the art, in
the study of those models, which have been the
means of transmitting the names and character of
so many men, to the admiration of posterity. The
successful exercise of this imitative art requires
invention, taste, and judgement: in the two first
the sex are allowed to excel, and the last may be
obtained by perserverance in examining, comparing,
and reflecting upon the works of those masters,
who have copied nature in her most graceful forms.
(124-7)

Wakefield then considers other careers related to the fine
arts: completing backgrounds or drapery as a studio assistant
to a master painter, creating designs for ornamental needlework, hand-coloring prints, doing fine work such as
miniatures and enameling jewelry, making botanical drawings
for books on natural history, creating patterns for fabric or
paper, and engraving. Wakefield then considers the plastic
arts such as sculpting in soft materials, musical composition,
and ornamental gardening. She continues:

The stage is a profession, to which many women
of refined manners, and a literary turn of mind have
had recourse....[the stage] is not mentioned for the
purpose of recommending it, but of proving that the
abilities of the female sex are equal to nobler labours
than are usually undertaken by women. The
profession of actress is indeed most unsuitable to the
sex in every point of view, whether it be considered
with respect to the courage requisite to face an
audience, of the variety of situations incident to it,

which expose moral virtue to the most severe trials....

The presiding over seminaries for female education, is likewise a suitable employment for those, whose minds have been enlarged by liberal cultivation, whilst the under parts of the profession may be more suitably filled by persons whose early views have been contracted within narrower limits. (Wakefield, 130-138)

Mary Wollstonecraft was less optimistic in 1788, when she initially raised the problem of work available to middling women, seeing a more limited and largely demeaning set of possibilities:

Few are the modes [for women] of earning a subsistence, and those very humiliating. Perhaps to be a humble companion to some rich old cousin, or what is still worse, to live with strangers, who are so intolerably tyrannical, that none of their own relations can bear to live with them, though they should even expect a fortune in reversion. It is impossible to enumerate the many hours of anguish such a person must spend....

A teacher at a school is only a kind of upper servant, who has more work than the menial ones.

A governess to young ladies is equally disagreeable. It is ten to one if they meet with a reasonable mother; and if she is not so, she will be continually finding fault to prove she is not ignorant, and be displeased if her pupils do not improve, but angry if the proper methods are taken to make them do so. The children treat them with disrespect, and often with insolence. ... 'and when youth and genial years are flown,' they have nothing to subsist on; or, perhaps, on some extraordinary occasion, some small allowance may be made for them, which is thought a great charity.

The few trades which are left, are now gradually falling into the hands of the men, and certainly they are not very respectable....

A woman, who has beauty without sentiment, is in great danger of being seduced; and if she has any, cannot guard herself from painful mortifications. It is very disagreeable to keep up a continual reserve with men she has been formerly familiar with; yet if she places confidence, it is ten to one but she is deceived. Few men seriously think of marrying an inferior; and if they have honor enough not to take advantage of a woman who loves, and thinks not of the difference of rank, they do not undeceive her until she has anticipated happiness, which, contrasted with her dependant situation, appears delightful. The disappointment is severe; and the heart receives a wound which does not easily admit of a compleat cure, as the good that is missed is not valued according to its real worth: for fancy drew the picture, and grief delights to create food to feed on.

If what I have written should be read by parents, who are now going on thoughtless extravagance, and anxious only that their daughters may be *genteelly educated*, let them consider to what sorrows they expose them; for I have not over-coloured the picture. (Wollstonecraft, 'Unfortunate Situation of Females, Fashionably Educated, and Left without a Fortune,' pp. 25-7)

Note that both Wakefield and Wollstonecraft name forms of education as an acceptable profession for genteel women. Underlying Wakefield's hopeful suggestions and Wollstonecraft's pessimistic assessment are the limited marketable skills possessed by politely educated Englishwomen: needlecraft, French, dancing, drawing, and the more amorphous "taste." These are the set of skills shared by both Adeline and Emma Courtney in these novels.

SOURCES

Priscilla Wakefield, *Reflections on the Present Condition of the*

> *Female Sex, with Suggestions for Its Improvement*, London, 1798.
> Mary Wollstonecraft, *Thoughts on the Education of Daughters: with Reflections on Female Conduct, in the more Important Duties of Life.* (1788) In *Works*, eds. Janet Todd and Marilyn Butler. Vol 4, 'Unfortunate Situation of Females, Fashionably Educated, and Left without a Fortune,' pp. 25-7.

Many were the schemes which occurred to her; but none seemed so practicable as that of keeping a day-school in some village near the metropolis.—True, Glenmurray had said, that her having been his mistress would prevent her obtaining scholars; but his fears, perhaps, were stronger than his justice in this case. These fears, however, she found existed in Berrendale's mind also, though he ventured only to hint them with great caution.

"You think, then, no prudent parents, if my story should be known to them, would send their children to me?" said Adeline to Berrendale.

"I fear—I—that is to say, I am sure they would not."

"Under such circumstances," said Adeline, "you yourself would not send a child to my school?"

"Why—really—I—as the world goes,"—replied Berrendale.

"I am answered," said Adeline with a look and tone of displeasure; and retired to her chamber, intending not to return till Berrendale was gone to his own lodging. But her heart soon reproached her with unjust resentment; and, coming back, she apologized to Berrendale for being angry at his laudable resolution of acting according to those principles which he thought most virtuous, especially as she claimed for herself a similar right.

Berrendale, gratified by her apology, replied, "that he saw no objection to her plan, if she chose to deny him the happiness of sharing his income with her, provided she would settle in a village where she was not likely to be known, and change her name."

"Change my name! Never. Concealment of any kind almost always implies the consciousness of guilt; and while my heart does not condemn me, my conduct shall not seem to accuse me. I will go to whatever place you shall recommend; but I beg your other request may be mentioned no more."

Berrendale, glad to be forgiven on any terms, promised to comply with her wishes; and he having recommended to her to settle at a village some few miles north of London, Adeline hired there a small but commodious lodging, and issued immediately cards of advertisement, stating what she meant to teach, and on what terms; while Berrendale took lodgings within a mile of her, and the faithful mulatto attended her as a servant of all-work.

Fortunately, at this time, a lady at Richmond, who had a son of the age of the tawny boy, became so attached to him, that she was desirous of bringing him up to be the play-fellow and future attendant on her son; and the mulatto, pleased to have him so well disposed of, resisted the poor little boy's tears and reluctance at the idea of being separated from her and Adeline: and before she left Richmond she had the satisfaction of seeing him comfortably settled in the house of his patroness.

Adeline succeeded in her undertaking even beyond her utmost wishes. Though unknown and unrecommended, there was in her countenance and manner a something so engaging, so strongly inviting confidence, and so decisively bespeaking the gentlewoman, that she soon excited in the village general respect and attention: and no sooner were scholars intrusted to her care, than she became the idol of her pupils; and their improvement was rapid in proportion to the love which they bore her.

This fortunate circumstance proved a balm to the wounded mind of Adeline. She felt that she had recovered her usefulness;—that desideratum in morals, and life, spite of her misfortunes, acquired a charm in her eyes. True it was, that she was restored to her capability of being useful, by being where she was unknown; and because the mulatto, unknown to her, had described her as reduced to earn her living, on account of the death of the man to whom she was about to be married: but she did not revert to the reasons of her being so generally esteemed; she contented herself with the consciousness of being so; and for some months she was tranquil, though not happy. But her tranquillity was destined to be of short duration.

END OF SECOND VOLUME.

ADELINE MOWBRAY
OR THE
MOTHER AND DAUGHTER:
A TALE,
IN THREE VOLUMES
BY MRS. OPIE

VOLUME III.

ADELINE MOWBRAY
CHAPTER I.

The village in which Adeline resided happened to be the native place of Mary Warner, the servant whom she had been forced to dismiss at Richmond; and who having gone from Mrs. Pemberton to another situation, which she had also quitted, came to visit her friends.

The wish of saying lessening things of those of whom one hears extravagant commendations, is, I fear, common to almost every one, even where the object praised comes in no competition with oneself:—and when Mary Warner heard from every quarter of the grace and elegance, affability and active benevolence of the new comer, it was no doubt infinitely gratifying to her to be able to exclaim,— "Mowbray! did you say her name is? La! I dares to say it is my old mistress, who was kept by one Mr. Glenmurray!" But so greatly were her auditors prepossessed in favour of Adeline, that very few of them could be prevailed upon to believe Mary's supposition was just; and so much was she piqued at the disbelief which she met with, that she declared she would go to church the next Sunday to shame the hussey, and go up and speak to her in the church-yard before all the people.

"Ah! do so, if you ever saw our miss Mowbray before," was the answer: and Mary eagerly looked forward to the approaching Sunday. Mean while, as we are all of us but so apt to repeat stories to the prejudice of others, even though we do not believe them, this strange assertion of Mary was circulated through the village even by Adeline's admirers; and the next Sunday was expected by the unconscious Adeline alone with no unusual eagerness.

Sunday came; and Adeline, as she was wont to do, attended the service: but, from the situation of her pew, she could neither see Mary nor be seen by her till church was over. Adeline then, as usual, was walking down the broad walk of the church-yard, surrounded by the parents of the children who came to her school, and receiving from them the customary marks of respect, when Mary, bustling through the crowd, accosted her with— "So!— your sarvant, miss Mowbray, I am glad to see you here in such a respectable situation."

Adeline, though in the gaily-dressed lady who accosted her she had some difficulty in recognizing her quondam servant, recollected the pert shrill voice and insolent manner of Mary immediately; and involuntarily starting when she addressed her, from painful associations and fear of impending evil, she replied, "How are you, Mary?" in a faltering tone.

"Then it is Mary's miss Mowbray," whispered Mary's auditors of the day before to each other; while Mary, proud of her success, looked triumphantly at them, and was resolved to pursue the advantage which she had gained.

"So you have lost Mr. Glenmurray, I find!" continued Mary.

Adeline spoke not, but walked hastily on:—but Mary kept pace with her, speaking as loud as she could.

"And did the little one live, pray?"

Still Adeline spoke not.

"What sort of a getting-up had you, miss Mowbray?"[105]

---

[105] Mary apparently refers to Adeline's preparations for the birth and post-birth of

At this mischievously-intended question Adeline's other sensations were lost in strong indignation; and resuming all the modest but collected dignity of her manner, she turned round, and, fixing her eyes steadily on the insulting girl, exclaimed aloud, "Woman, I never injured you either in thought, word, or deed:— whence comes it, then, that you endeavour to make the finger of scorn point at me, and make me shrink with shame and confusion from the eye of observation?"

"Woman! indeed!" replied Mary—but she was not allowed to proceed; for a gentleman hastily stepped forward, crying, "It is impossible for us to suffer such insults to be offered to miss Mowbray;—I desire, therefore, that you will take your daughter away (turning to Mary's father); and, if possible, teach her better manners." Having said this, he over-took the agitated Adeline; and, offering her his arm, saw her home to her lodgings: while those who had heard with surprise and suspicion the strange and impertinent questions and insolent tone of Mary, resumed in a degree their confidence in Adeline, and turned a disgusted and deaf ear to the hysterical vehemence with which the half-sobbing Mary defended herself, and vilified Adeline, as her father and brother-in-law, almost by force, led her out of the church-yard.

The gentleman who had so kindly stepped forward to the assistance of Adeline was Mr. Beauclerc, the surgeon of the village, a man of considerable abilities and liberal principles; and when he bade Adeline farewell, he said, "My wife will do herself the pleasure of calling on you this evening:" then, kindly pressing her hand, he with a respectful bow took his leave.

Luckily for Adeline, Berrendale was detained in town that day; and she was spared the mortification of showing herself to him, writhing as she then was under the agonies of public shame, for such it seemed to her. Convinced as she then was of the light in which she must have appeared to the persons around her from the malicious interrogatories of Mary;—convinced too, as

her child by Glenmurray.

she was more than beginning to be, of the fallacy of the reasoning which had led her to deserve, and even to glory in, the situation which she now blushed to hear disclosed;—and conscious as she was, that to remain in the village, and expect to retain her school, was now impossible—she gave herself up to a burst of sorrow and despondence; during which her only consolation was, that it was not witnessed by Berrendale.

It never for a moment entered into the ingenuous mind of Adeline, that her declaration would have more weight than that of Mary Warner; and that she might, with almost a certainty of being believed, deny her charge entirely: on the contrary, she had no doubt but that Mrs. Beauclerc was coming to inquire into the grounds for Mary's gross address; and she was resolved to confess to her all the circumstances of her story.

After church in the afternoon Mrs. Beauclerc arrived, and Adeline observed, with pleasure, that her manner was even kinder than usual; it was such as to ensure the innocent of the most strenuous support, and to invite the guilty to confidence and penitence.

"Never, my dear miss Mowbray," said Mrs. Beauclerc, "did I call on you with more readiness than now; as I come assured that you will give me not only the most ample authority to contradict, but the fullest means to confute, the vile calumnies which that malicious girl, Mary Warner, has, ever since she entered the village, been propagating against you: but, indeed, she is so little respected in her rank of life, and you so highly in yours, that your mere denial of the truth of her statement will, to every candid mind, be sufficient to clear your character."

Adeline never before was so strongly tempted to violate the truth; and there was a friendly earnestness in Mrs. Beauclerc's manner, which proved that it would be almost cruel to destroy the opinion which she entertained of her virtue. For a moment Adeline felt disposed to yield to the temptation, but it was only for a moment,—and in a hurried and broken voice she replied, "Mary Warner has asserted of me nothing but——— " Here her voice faltered.

"Nothing but falsehoods, no doubt," interrupted Mrs. Beauclerc triumphantly,— "I thought so."

"Nothing but the TRUTH!" resumed Adeline.

"Impossible!" cried Mrs. Beauclerc, dropping the cold hand which she held: and Adeline, covering her face, and throwing herself back in the chair, sobbed aloud.

Mrs. Beauclerc was herself for some time unable to speak; but at length she faintly said— "So sensible, so pious, so well-informed, and so pure-minded as you seem!—to what strange arts, what wicked seductions, did you fall a victim?"

"To no arts—to no seductions"—replied Adeline, recovering all her energy at this insinuation against Glenmurray.

"My fall from virtue, as you would call it, was, I may say, from love of what I thought virtue; and if there be any blame, it attaches merely to my confidence in my lover's wisdom and my own too obstinate self-conceit. But you, dear madam, deserve to hear my whole story; and, if you can favor me with an hour's attention, I hope, at least, to convince you that I was worthy of a better fate than to be publicly disgraced by a malicious and ignorant girl."

Mrs. Beauclerc promised the most patient attention; and Adeline related the eventful history of her life, slightly dwelling on those parts of it which in any degree reflected on her mother, and extolling most highly her sense, her accomplishments, and her maternal tenderness. When she came to the period of Glenmurray's illness and death, she broke abruptly off, and rushed into her own chamber; and it was some minutes before she could return to Mrs. Beauclerc, or before her visitor could wish her to return, as she was herself agitated and affected by the relation which she had heard;—and when Adeline came in she threw her arms round her neck, and pressed her to her heart with a feeling of affection that spoke consolation to the wounded spirit of the mourner.

She then resumed her narration;—and, having concluded it, Mrs. Beauclerc, seizing her hand, exclaimed, "For God's sake, marry Mr. Berrendale immediately; and abjure for ever, at the foot of the alter, those errors in opinion to which all your misery has been owing!"

"Would I could atone for them some other way!" she replied.

"Impossible! and if you have any regard for me you will become the wife of your generous lover; for then, and not till then, can I venture to associate with you."

"I thought so," cried Adeline; "I thought all idea of remaining here, with any chance of keeping my scholars, was now impossible."

"It would not be so," replied Mrs. Beauclerc, "if every one thought like me: I should consider your example as a warning to all young people; and to preserve my children from evil I should only wish them to hear your story, as it inculcates most powerfully how vain are personal graces, talents, sweetness of temper, and even active benevolence, to ensure respectability and confer happiness, without a strict regard to the long-established rules for conduct, and a continuance in those paths of virtue and decorum which the wisdom of ages has pointed out to the steps of every one.—But others will, no doubt, consider, that continuing to patronise you, would be patronizing vice; and my rank in life is not high enough to enable me to countenance you with any chance of leading others to follow my example; while I should not be able to serve you, but should infallibly lose myself. But some time hence, as the wife of Mr. Berrendale, I might receive you as your merits deserve: till then—" here Mrs. Beauclerc paused, and she hesitated to add, "we meet no more."

Indeed it was long before the parting took place. Mrs. Beauclerc had justly appreciated the merits of Adeline, and thought she had found in her a friend and companion for years to come: besides, her children were most fondly attached to her; and Mrs. Beauclerc, while she contemplated their daily improvement under her care, felt grateful to Adeline for the unfolding excellencies of her daughters. Still, to part with her was unavoidable; but the pang of separation was in a degree soothed to Adeline by the certainty which Mrs. Beauclerc's sorrow gave her, that, spite of her errors, she had inspired a real friendship in the bosom of a truly virtuous and respectable woman; and this idea gave a sensation of joy to her heart to which it had long been a stranger.

The next morning some of the parents, whom Mary's tale had not yet reached, sent their children as usual. But Adeline refused to enter upon any school duties, bidding them affectionately farewell, and telling them that she was going to write to their parents, as she was obliged to leave her present situation, and, declining keeping school, meant to reside, she believed, in London.

The children on hearing this looked at each other with almost tearful consternation; and Adeline observed, with pleasure, the interest which she had made to herself in their young hearts. After they were gone she sent a circular letter to her friends in the village, importing that she was under the necessity of leaving her present residence; but that, whatever her future situation might be, she should always remember, with gratitude, the favors which she had received at ———.

The necessity that drove her away was, by this time, very well understood by every one; but Mrs. Beauclerc took care to tell those who mentioned the subject to her, the heads of Adeline's story; and to add always, "and I have reason to believe that, as soon as she is settled in town, she will be extremely well married."

To the mulatto the change in Adeline's plans was particularly pleasing, as it would bring her nearer her son, and nearer William, from whom nothing but a sense of grateful duty to Adeline would so long have divided her. But Savanna imagined that Adeline's removal was owing to her having at last determined to marry Mr. Berrendale; an event which she, for Adeline's sake, earnestly wished to take place, though for her own she was undecided whether to desire it or not, as Mr. Berrendale might not, perhaps, be as contented with her services as Adeline was.

While these thoughts were passing in Savanna's mind, and her warm and varying feelings were expressed by alternate smiles and tears, Mr. Berrendale arrived from town: and as Savanna opened the door to him, she, half whimpering half smiling, dropped him a very respectful curtsey, and looked at him with eyes full of unusual significance.

"Well, Savanna, what has happened?"—Any thing new or extraordinary since my absence?" said Berrendale.

"Me tink not of wat have appen, but wat will appen," replied Savanna.

"And what is going to happen?" returned Berrendale, seating himself in the parlour, "and where is your mistress?"

"She dress herself, that dear missess," replied Savanna, lingering with the door in her hand, "and I,—I ope to ave a dear massa too."

"What" cried Berrendale, starting wildly from his seat, "what did you say?"

"Why, me ope my missess be married soon."

"Married! to whom?" cried Berrendale, seizing her hand, and almost breathless with alarm.

"Why, to you, sure," exclaimed Savanna, "and den me hope you will not turn away poor Savanna!"

"What reason you have, my dear Savanna, for talking thus, I cannot tell; nor dare I give way to the sweet hopes which you excite: but, if it be true that I may hope, depend on it you shall cook my wedding dinner, and then I am sure it will be a good one.

"Can full joy eat?" asked the mulatto thoughtfully.

"A good dinner is a good thing, Savanna," replied Berrendale, "and ought never to be slighted."

"Me good dinner day I marry, but I not eat it.—O sir, pity people look best in dere wedding clothes, but my William look well all day and every day, and perhaps you will too, sir; and den I ope to cook your wedding dinner, next day dinner, and all your dinners."

"And so you shall, Savanna," cried Berrendale, grasping her hand, "and I— " Here the door opened, and Adeline appeared; who, surprised at Berrendale's familiarity with her servant, looked gravely, and stopped at the door with a look of cold surprise. Berrendale, awed into immediate respect—for what is so timid and respectful as a man truly in love?—bowed low, and lost in an instant all the hopes which had elevated his spirits to such an unusual degree.

Adeline with an air of pique observed, that she feared she interrupted them unpleasantly, as something unusually agreeable and enlivening seemed to occupy them as she came in, over which her entrance seemed to have cast a cloud.

The mulatto had by this time retreated to the door, and was on the point of closing it, when Berrendale stammered out, as well as he could, "Savanna was, indeed, raising my hopes to such an unexpected height, that I felt almost bewildered with joy; but the coldness of your manner, miss Mowbray has sobered me again."

"And what did Savanna say to you?" cried Adeline.

"I—I say," cried Savanna returning, "dat is, he say, I should be let cook de wedding dinner."

Adeline, turning even paler than she was before, desired her coldly to leave the room; and, seating herself at the greatest possible distance from Berrendale, leaned for some time in silence on her hand—he not daring to interrupt her meditations. But at last she said, "What could give rise to this singular conversation between you and Savanna I am wholly at a loss to imagine: still I—I must own that it is not so ill-timed as it would have been some weeks ago. I will own, that since yesterday I have been considering your generous proposals with the serious attention which they deserve."

On hearing this, which Adeline uttered with considerable effort, Berrendale in a moment was at her side, and almost at her feet.

"I—I wish you to return to your seat," said Adeline coldly: but hope had emboldened him, and he chose to stay where he was.

"But, before I require you to renew your promises, or make any on my side, it is proper that I should tell you what passed yesterday; and if the additional load of obloquy which I have acquired does not frighten you from continuing your addresses—" Here Adeline paused:—and Berrendale, rather drawing back, then pushing his chair nearer her as he spoke, gravely answered, that his affection was proof against all trials.

Adeline then briefly related the scene in the church-yard, and her conversation with Mrs. Beauclerc, and concluded thus:— "In consequence of this, and of the recollection of HIS advice, and HIS decided opinion, that by becoming the wife of a respectable man, I could alone expect to recover my rank in society, and, consequently, my usefulness, I offer you my hand; and promise, in the course of a few months, to become yours in the sight of God and man."

"And from no other reason?—from no preference, no regard for me?" demanded Berrendale reproachfully.

"Oh! pardon me; from decided preference; there is not another being in the creation whom I could bear to call husband."

Berrendale, gratified and surprised, attempted to take her hand; but, withdrawing it, she continued thus:— "Still I almost scruple to let you, unblasted as your prospects are, take to wife a beggar, blasted in reputation, broken in spirits, with a heart whose best affections lie buried in the grave, and which can offer you in return for your faithful tenderness nothing but cold respect and esteem; one too who is not only despicable to others, but also self-condemned."

While Adeline said this, Berrendale, almost shuddering at the picture which she drew, paced the room in great agitation; and even the gratification of his passion, used as he was to the indulgence of every wish, seemed, for a moment, a motive not sufficiently powerful to enable him to unite his fate to that of a woman so degraded as Adeline appeared to be; and he would, perhaps, have hesitated to accept the hand she offered, had she not added, as a contrast to the picture which she had drawn— "But if, in spite of all these unwelcome considerations, you persist in your resolution of making me yours, and I have resolution enough to conquer the repugnance that I feel to make a second connection, you may depend on possessing in me one who will study your happiness and wishes in the minutest particulars;—one who will cherish you in sickness and in sorrow;—(here a twinge of the gout assisted Adeline's appeal very powerfully;) and who, conscious of the generosity of your attachment, and her own unworthiness, will strive, by every possible effort, not to remain your debtor even in affection."

Saying this, she put out her hand to Berrendale; and that hand, and the arm belonging to it, were so beautiful, and he had so often envied Glenmurray while he saw them tenderly supporting his head, that while a vision of approaching gout, and Adeline bending over his restless couch, floated before him, all his prudent considerations vanished; and, eagerly pressing the proffered hand to his lips, he thanked her most ardently for her kind promise; and, putting his arm round her waist, would have pressed her to his bosom.

But the familiarity was ill-timed;—Adeline was already surprised, and even shocked, at the lengths which she had gone; and starting almost with loathing from his embrace, she told him it grew late, and it was time for him to go to his lodgings. She then retired to her own room, and spent half the night at least in weeping over the remembrance of Glenmurray, and in loudly apostrophizing his departed spirit.

The next day Adeline, out of the money which she had earned, discharged her lodgings; and having written a farewell note to Mrs. Beauclerc, begging to hear of her now and then, she and the mulatto proceeded to town, with Berrendale, in search of apartments; and having procured them, Adeline began to consider by what means, till she could resolve to marry Berrendale, she should help to maintain herself, and also contrive to increase their income if she became his wife.

The success which she had met with in instructing children, led her to believe that she might succeed in writing little hymns and tales for their benefit; a method of getting money which she looked upon to be more rapid and more lucrative than working plain or fancy works:[106] and, in a short time, a little volume was

---

[106] I.e., needlework, plain sewing, or the fancy, decorative needlework taught gentlewomen to pass the time productively.

ready to be offered to a bookseller;—nor was it offered in vain.[107] Glenmurray's bookseller accepted it; and the sum which he gave, though trifling, imparted a balsam to the wounded mind of Adeline: it seemed to open to her the path of independence; and to give her, in spite of her past errors, and the means of serving her fellow-creatures.

But month after month elapsed, and Glenmurray had been dead two years, yet still Adeline could not prevail on herself to fix a time for her marriage.

But next to the aversion she felt to marrying at all, was that she experienced at the idea of having no fortune to bestow on the disinterested Berrendale; and so desirous was she of his acquiring some little property by his union with her, that she resolved to ask counsel's opinion on the possibility of her claiming a sum of money which Glenmurray had bequeathed her, but without, as Berrendale had assured her, the customary formalities.

The money was near 300£, but Berrendale had allowed it to go to Glenmurray's legal heir, because he was sure that the writing which bequeathed it would not hold good in law. Still Adeline was so unwilling to be under so many pecuniary obligations to a man whom she did not love, that she resolved to take advice on the subject, much against the will of Berrendale, who thought the money for fees might as well be saved; but as a chance for saving the fee he resolved to let Adeline go to the lawyer's chambers alone, thinking it likely that no fee would be accepted from so fine a woman. Accordingly, more alive to œconomy than to delicacy or decorum, Berrendale, when Adeline, desiring a coach to be called, summoned him to accompany her to the Temple,[108] pleaded terror of an impending fit of the gout, and begged her to excuse his attendance; and Adeline, unsuspicious of the real cause

---

[107] Poetry, hymns, children's stories, and moral tales were appropriate genres for women. Moral novels, such as those of Amelia Opie were also considered appropriate, though a more problematic genre. See textboxes on "Women and Work," pp. 238 and 494.

[108] One of the Inns of Court, the site of English Law practice.

of his refusal, kindly expressing her sorrow for the one he feigned, took the counsellor's address, and got into the coach, Berrendale taking care to tell her, as she got in, that the fare was but a shilling.

The gentleman, Mr. Langley, to whom Adeline was going, was celebrated for his abilities as a chamber counsellor, and no less remarkable for his gallantries: but Berrendale was not acquainted with this part of his history; else he would not, even to save a lawyer's fee, have exposed his intended wife to a situation of such extreme impropriety; and Adeline was too much a stranger to the rules of general society, to feel any great repugnance to go alone on an errand so interesting to her feelings.

The coach having stopped near the entrance of the court to which she was directed, Adeline, resolving to walk home, discharged the coach, and knocked at the door of Mr. Langley's chambers. A very smart servant out of livery answered the knock; and Mr. Langley being at home, Adeline was introduced into his apartment.

Mr. Langley, though surprised at seeing a lady of a deportment so correct and of so dignified an appearance enter his room unattended, was inspired with so much respect at sight of Adeline, whose mourning habit added to the interest which her countenance never failed to excite, that he received her with bows down to the ground, and, leading her to a chair, begged she would do him the honour to be seated, and impart her commands.

Adeline embarrassed, she scarcely knew why, at the novelty of her situation, drew the paper from her pocket, and presented it to him.

"Mr. Berrendale recommended me to you, sir," said Adeline faintly.

"Berrendale, Berrendale, O, aye,—I remember—the cousin of Mr. Glenmurray: you know Mr. Glenmurray too, ma'am, I presume; pray how is he?"—Adeline, unprepared for this question, could not speak; and the voluble counsellor went on— "Oh!—I ask your pardon, madam, I see;—pray, might I presume so far, how long has that extraordinarily clever man been lost to the world?"

"More than two years, sir," replied Adeline faintly.

'You are,—may I presume so far,—you are his widow?"—Adeline bowed. There was a something in Mr. Langley's manner and look so like sir Patrick's that she could not bear to let him know she was only Glenmurray's mistress.

"Gone more than two years, and you still in deep mourning!—Amiable susceptibility!—How unlike the wives of the present day! But I beg pardon.—Now to business." So saying, he perused the paper which Adeline had given him, in which Glenmurray simply stated, that he bequeathed to Adeline Mowbray the sum of 260£ in the 5 per cents, but it was signed by only one witness.

"What do you wish to know, madam?" asked the counsellor.

"Whether this will be valid, as it is not signed by two witnesses, sir?"

"Why,—really not," replied Langley, "though the heir at law, if he have either equity or gallantry, could certainly not refuse to fulfil what evidently was the intention of the testator:—but then, it is very surprising to me that Mr. Glenmurray should have wished to leave any thing from the lady who I have the honor to behold. Pray, madam,—if I may presume to ask,—Who is Adeline Mowbray?"

"I—I am Adeline Mowbray," replied Adeline in great confusion.

"You, madam! Bless me, I presumed;—and pray, madam,—if I may make so bold,—what was your relationship to that wonderfully clever man?—his niece,—his cousin,—or—?"

"I was no relation of his," said Adeline still more confused; and this confusion confirmed the suspicions which Langley entertained, and also brought to his recollection something which he had heard of Glenmurray's having a very elegant and accomplished mistress.

'Pardon me, dear madam," said Mr. Langley, "I perceive now my mistake; and I now perceive why Mr. Glenmurray was so much the envy of those who had the honour of visiting at his house. 'Pon my soul," taking her hand, which Adeline indignantly withdrew, "I am grieved beyond words at being unable to give you a more favourable opinion."

"But you said, sir," said Adeline, "that the heir at law, if he had any equity, would certainly be guided by the evident intention of the testator."

"I did, madam," replied the lawyer, evidently piqued by the proud and cold air which Adeline assumed;— "but then,—excuse me,—the applicant would not stand much chance of being attended to, who is neither the *widow* nor *relation* of Mr. Glenmurray."

"I understand you, sir," replied Adeline, "and need trouble you no longer."

"Trouble! my sweet girl!" returned Mr. Langley, "call it not trouble; I— " Here his gallant effusions were interrupted by the sudden entrance of a very showy woman, highly rouged, and dressed in the extremity of fashion; and who in no very pleasant tone of voice exclaimed,— "I fear I interrupt you."

"Oh! Not in the least," replied Langley, blushing even more than Adeline, "my fair client was just going. Allow me, madam, to see you to the door," continued he, attempting to take Adeline's hand, and accompanying her to the bottom of the first flight of stairs.

"Charming fine woman upon my soul!" cried he, speaking through his shut teeth, and forcibly squeezing her fingers as he spoke; "and if you ever want advice I should be proud to see you here; at present I am particularly engaged, (with a significant smile;) but— " Here Adeline, too angry to speak, put the fee in his hand, which he insisted on returning, and, in the struggle, he forcibly kissed the ungloved hand which was held out, praising its beauty at the same time, and endeavouring to close her fingers on the money: but Adeline indignantly threw it on the ground, and rushed down the remaining staircase; over-hearing the lady, as she did so, exclaim, "Langley! Is not that black mawkin[109] gone yet? Come

---

[109] Demon or specter, a scarecrow, or an unfashionable figure (OED).

up this moment, you devil!" while Langley obsequiously replied, "Coming this moment, my angel!"

Adeline felt so disappointed, so ashamed, and so degraded, that she walked on some way without knowing whither she was going; and when she recollected herself, she found that she was wandering from court to court, and unable to find the avenue to the street down which the coach had come: while her very tall figure, heightened colour, and graceful carriage, made her an object of attention to every one whom she met.

At last she saw herself followed by two young men; and as she walked very fast to avoid them, she by accident turned into the very lane which she had been seeking: but her pursuers kept pace with her; and she overheard one of them say to the other, "A devilish fine girl! Moves well too,—I cannot help thinking that I have seen her before."

"And so do I.—O zounds! by her height, it must be that sweet creature who lived at Richmond with that crazy fellow, Glenmurray."

Here Adeline relaxed in her pace: the name of Glenmurray—that name which no one since his death had ventured to pronounce in her presence,—had, during the last half-hour, been pronounced several times; and, unable to support herself from a variety of emotions, she stopped, and leaned for support against the wall.

"How do you do, my fleet and sweet girl?" said one of the gentlemen, patting her on the back as he spoke:—and Adeline, roused at the insult, looked at him proudly and angrily, and walked on. "What! angry! If I may be so bold (with a sneering smile,) fair creature, may I ask where you live now?"

"No, sir," replied Adeline; "you are wholly unknown to me."

"But were you to tell me where you live, we might cease to be strangers; but, perhaps your favours are all bespoke.—Pray who is your friend now?"

"O! I have but few friends," cried Adeline mournfully.

"Few! the devil!" replied the young templar;[110] "and how

---

[110] A law student or lawyer with chambers in the Inner or Middle Temple in

many would you have?" Here he put his arm around her waist: and his companion giving way to a loud fit of laughter, Adeline clearly understood what he meant by the term "friend:" and summoning up all her spirit, she called a coach which luckily was passing; and, turning round to her tormentor, with great dignity said,— "Though the situation, sir, in which I once was, may, in the eyes of the world and in yours, authorise your present insulting address, yet, when I tell you that I am on the eve of marriage with a most respectable man, I trust that you will feel the impropriety of your conduct, and be convinced of the fruitlessness and impertinence of the questions which you have put to me."

"If this be the case, madam," cried the gentleman, "I beg your pardon, and shall take my leave, wishing you all possible happiness, and begging you to attribute my impertinence wholly to my ignorance." So saying, he bowed and left her, and Adeline was driven to her lodgings.

"Now," said Adeline, "the die is cast:—I have used the sacred name of wife to shield me from insult; and I am therefore pledged to assume it directly. Yes, HE was right—I find I must have a legal protector."

She found Berrendale rather alarmed at her long absence; and, with a beating heart, she related her adventures to him: but when she said that Langley was not willing to take the fee, he exclaimed, "Very genteel in him, indeed! I suppose you took him at his word?"

"Good Heavens!" replied Adeline, "Do you think I would deign to owe such a man a pecuniary obligation!—No, indeed; I threw it with proud indignation on the floor."

"What madness!" returned Berrendale: "you had much better have put it in your pocket."

"Mr. Berrendale," cried Adeline gravely, and with a look bordering on contempt, "I trust that you are not in earnest: for if these are your sentiments,—if this is your delicacy, sir— "

London (OED).

"Say no more, dearest of women" replied Berrendale pretending to laugh, alarmed at the seriousness with which she spoke: "How could you for one moment suppose me in earnest? Insolent coxcomb!—I wish I had been there."

"I wish you had," said Adeline, "for then no one would have dared to insult me:" and Berrendale, delighted at this observation, listened to the rest of her story with a spirit of indignant knight-errantry which he never experienced before; and at the end of her narration he felt supremely happy; for Adeline assured him that the next week she would make him her protector for life:—and this assurance opened his heart so much, that he vowed he would not condescend to claim of the heir at law the pitiful sum which he might think proper to withhold.[111]

To be brief.—Adeline kept her word; and resolutely struggling with her feelings, she became the next week the wife of Berrendale.

For the first six months the union promised well. Adeline was so assiduous to anticipate her husband's wishes, and contrived so many dainties for his table, which she cooked with her own hands, that Berrendale, declaring himself completely happy for the first time in his life, had not a thought or a wish beyond his own fire-side; while Adeline, happy because she conferred happiness, and proud of the name of wife, which she had before despised, began to hope that her days would glide on in humble tranquillity.

It was natural enough that Adeline should be desirous of imparting this change in her situation to Mrs. Pemberton, whose esteem she was eager to recover, and whose kind intentions towards her, at a moment when she was incapable of appreciating them, Savanna had, with great feeling, expatiated upon. She therefore wrote to her according to the address which Mrs. Pemberton had left for her, and received a most friendly letter in

---

[111] Although Berrendale would be well-placed as Adeline's husband to demand the inheritance as her legal right, were he to gain it, the money would in fact be his, not hers after their marriage.

return. In a short time Adeline had again an expectation of being a mother; and though she could not yet entertain for her husband more than cold esteem, she felt that as the father of her child he would insensibly become more dear to her.

But Berrendale awoke from his dream of bliss, on finding to what a large sum of bills for the half-year's house-keeping amounted. Nor was he surprised without reason. Adeline, more eager to gratify Berrendale's palate than considerate as to the means, had forgotten that she was no longer at the head of a liberal establishment like her mother's, and had bought for the supply of the table many expensive articles.

In consequence of this terrible discovery Berrendale remonstrated very seriously with Adeline; who meekly answered, "My dear friend, good dinners cannot be had without good ingredients, and good ingredients cannot be had without money."

"But, madam," cried Berrendale, knitting his brows, but not elevating his voice, for he was one of those soft-speaking beings who in the sweetest tones possible can say the most heart-wounding things, and give a mortal stab to your self-love in the same gentle manner in which they flatter it:— "there must have been great waste, great mismanagement here, or these expenses could not have been incurred."

"There may have been both," returned Adeline, "for I have not been used to œconomize, but I will try to learn;—but I doubt, my dear Berrendale, you must endeavor to be contented with plainer food; for not all the œconomy in the world can make rich gravies and high sauces cheap things."

"Oh! care and skill can do much," said Berrendale;— "and I find a certain person deceived me very much when he said you were a good manager."

"He only said," replied Adeline sighing deeply, "that I was a good cook, and you yourself allow that: but I hope in time to please your appetite at less expense: as to myself, a little suffices me, and I care not how plain that food is."

"Still, I think I have seen you eat with a most excellent appetite," said Berrendale, with a very significant expression.

Adeline, shocked at the manner more than at the words, replied in a faltering voice, "As a proof of my being in health, no doubt you rejoiced in the sight."

"Certainly; but less robust health would suit our finances better."

Adeline looked up, wishing, though not expecting, to see by his face that he was joking: but such serious displeasure appeared on it, that the sordid selfishness of his character was at once unveiled to her view; and clasping her hands in agony, she exclaimed, "Oh, Glenmurray!" and ran into her own room.

It was the first time that she had pronounced his name since the hour of his death, and now it was wrung from her by a sensation of acute anguish; no wonder, then, that the feelings which followed completely overcame her, and that Berrendale had, undisputed and solitary possession of his supper.

But he, on his side, was deeply irritated. The "Oh, Glenmurray!" was capable of being interpreted two ways:—either it showed how much she regretted Glenmurray, and preferred him to his successor in spite of the superior beauty of his person, of which he was very vain; or it reproached Glenmurray for having recommended her to marry him. In either case it was an unpardonable fault; and this unhappy conversation laid the foundation of future discontent.

Adeline rose the next day dejected, pensive, and resolved that her appetite should never again, if possible, force a reproach from the lips of her husband. She therefore took care that whatever she provided for the table, besides the simplest fare, should be for Berrendale alone; and she flattered herself that he would be shamed into repentance of what he had observed, by seeing her scrupulous self-denial:—she even resolved, if he pressed her to partake of his dainties, that she would, to show that she forgave him, accept what he offered.

But Berrendale gave her no such opportunity of showing her generosity;—busy in the gratification of his own appetite, he never observed whether any other persons ate or not, except when by eating they curtailed his share of good things:—besides, to have an exclusive dish to himself was to him *tout simple*;[112] he had been a pampered child; and, being no advocate for the equality of the sexes, he thought it only a matter of course that he should fare better than his wife.

Adeline, though more surprised and more shocked than ever, could not help laughing internally, at her not being able to put her projected generosity in practice; but her laughter and indignation soon yielding to contempt, she ate her simple meal in silence: and while her pampered husband sought to lose the fumes of indigestion in sleep, she blessed God that temperance, industry and health went hand in hand; and, retiring to her own room, sat down to write, in order to increase, if possible, her means of living, and consequently her power of being generous to others.

APPETITE AND TEMPERANCE

Berrendale's appetite for highly seasoned and rich food signifies more than just his tendency to gourmandize. Likewise, Adeline's ability to deny herself in the interests of her loved Glenmurray and as an economizing measure for Berrendale indicates her internal moral qualities of rationality, sensitivity to the needs of others, and her own social usefulness. Temperance, the concept of restraining one's appetites, was importantly valued in late eighteenth century British culture at large, and was particularly lauded among the Rational Dissenters. Restraint in public entertainment, by evading and minimizing opportunities for public display of clothing and talents, was advised. Modest dress and behavior was particularly recommended to young ladies, who were advised in countless conduct manuals that by seeming to shun attention and avoiding displays of wit, they would actually attract more admiration and attention, and those of the right sort, from men. The largely unspoken implication

---

[112] Literally "apparent" or "expected," in the normal course of things.

of this advice for young women was to control and moderate their appetite for male sexual attention. Young women were to be chosen by, rather than to choose their lovers (although they were usually permitted to reject proposals for themselves). The assumption was that restraint in other appetites would carry over into a larger self-restraint. Thus, young ladies were advised to moderate their presumed "natural" desire for beautiful and rich dress, to control their indulgence in food and drink, to avoid addictive entertainments such as gambling, masquerade balls, operas, and pleasure grounds like Vauxhall and Ranelagh. They were to cultivate taste in music, literature, and philosophy only so far as made them better and fitter companions for educated men, but not competitors for public attention with such men. Moderation of appetites carried over into early Romanticism as well, inculcating a preference for more rustic landscapes, presumably more "natural" entertainment such as long walks in the country, and in some cases (most famously that of Percy Bysshe Shelly), vegetarianism. The notion that eating only certain foods or restraining one's consumption could impact sexual desire is alluded to in Laurence Sterne's *Life and Opinions of Tristram Shandy, Gentleman*, where Tristram attempts to calm and cool himself by eating only "cold seeds" or vegetables. Idealized novelistic heroines such as Samuel Richardson's Pamela and Clarissa had been notably light eaters, often nibbling only at the wing of cooked fowl or drinking dishes of tea. When Lovelace drugs Clarissa, he is able to do so only in dishes of tea, and then when the drugs make Clarissa unusually thirsty, in some small beer, rather than heavy wines, which are more often associated with dangerous potions.

Women's role as consumers of luxury goods, from rare fabrics to fashionable entertainment, exotic and imported colonial goods and foods, increased cultural anxiety about controlling women's behavior. Moral tracts and conduct literature urged women to restrain and restrict their role as consumers, associating excessive consumption of fashionable and exotic goods and foods with aristocratic excesses. As the middling sort grew in power and voice through the century, suspicion toward the hereditary aristocracy also grew. By the 1790s, the association between aristocrats, excess, effeminacy or "unmanliness" and particularly "Frenchness" was well established, and was countered by an ideal of middling gentry and mercantile families as restrained, rational, modest, and ruled by common sense. John Gregory, in *A Legacy to His Daughters*, warns explicitly against gourmandizing:

> There is a species of refinement in luxury, just beginning to prevail among the gentlemen of this country, to which our ladies are yet as great strangers as any women upon earth; I hope, for the honour of the sex, they may ever continue so: I mean, the luxury of eating. It is a despicable selfish vice in men, but in your sex it is beyond expression indelicate and disgusting. (18)

Highly seasoned, sauced, and rare foods were associated more strongly with French aristocratic excess and cuisine than with homey English beef. Gregory's warning to his daughters suggests that some English women were perceived as developing a dangerous interest in both eating and keeping a fine table. Mary Wollstonecraft's *Rights of Woman* addressed the problem of appetite, associating lack of self-control more with men than women:

> Men are certainly more under the influence of their appetites than women; and their appetites are more depraved by unbridled indulgence and the fastidious contrivances of satiety. Luxury has introduced a refinement in eating, that destroys the constitution; and a degree of gluttony which is so beastly, that a perception of seemliness of behavior must be worn out before one being could eat immoderately in the presence of another, and afterwards complain of the oppression that his intemperance naturally produced. Some women, particularly French

women, have also lost a sense of decency in this respect; for they will talk very calmly of an indigestion. (Chapter VIII, p. 207)

Appetite always carried sexual overtones, just as temperance carried the implication of chastity and rational control. While men were expected occasionally to indulge such appetites by "the world," women were expected rigorously to combat them. Moreover, concerns about female excesses gained an added moral imperative because women were viewed most importantly as the bearers and early educators of children. Thus, the sins of the mother were likely to be carried over to the next generation, either as inappropriate behavior or even in "degenerate" offspring. As the vogue for "natural" motherhood grew, women came under particular pressures, including an increased belief in breastfeeding one's own children rather than sending them out to wet-nurse:

> The mind and dispositions of an infant, as well as the constitution, are probably much influenced by those of the mother, especially during pregnancy, a period in which, for that reason, tumultuous pleasures, violent passions, and an irregular life, should be resolutely avoided. The manners of our women of fashion, are but ill calculated to prevent the degeneracy of the species; an object of great importance to the public welfare: crowded rooms, late hours, luxurious tables, and slothful inactivity, must contribute to the production of a puny offspring, inadequate to the noble energies of patriotism and virtue.

> The same causes, combined with the injudicious mode in which they have been brought up, deprive the greater part of females in high life of the capacity of discharging the first maternal office, from which no rank, however elevated, can exempt them. The evils consequent upon this defect, are of sufficient magnitude to awaken the most strenuous endeavours

to protect it. That which strikes the imagination with the most forcible impression, is the destruction, or at least the diminution of that sympathy between the mother and the child, for the promotion of which, nature has, in a thousand ways, so wisely provided; but others, equally pernicious and more extensive, are the frequent attendants of an inability to perform this sacred task, or a voluntary neglect of it. The helpless infant is not only banished from the arms of its mother, but is consigned to the care of a substitute, who is tempted, by the expectation of large gains, to abandon her husband and her family, to turn a deaf ear to the piteous cries of her own offspring, for that nourishment, which she bestows upon a stranger. Too frequently the life of this deserted babe is sacrificed; the husband is rendered profligate; and the woman herself so much corrupted by her new mode of living, as to be unfitted to return to her humble station.

The effeminate mode of educating young ladies at present in vogue, is the source from whence this defect in the rearing of children in the higher ranks of life originates; an imperfection to which they are almost exclusively subject, for there is a very small proportion of the labouring poor, who are unable to suckle their children; whereas a judicious writer asserts, that the converse of this proposition is true, with respect to the girls brought up at boarding schools, which he attributes chiefly to confinement and want of exercise (Wakefield, 15-18).

Sources

John Gregory. *A Father's Legacy to His Daughters.* London, 1774.

Priscilla Wakefield. *Reflections on the Present Condition of the Female Sex with Suggestions for Its Improvement.* London, 1798.

Mary Wollstonecraft. *Vindication of the Rights of Woman*
(1792), in *Works of Mary Wollstonecraft*, Ed. Janet Todd
and Marilyn Butler, 5 Vols. Vol. 5 (Washington Square,
NY: New York University Press, 1989).

But though Adeline resolved to forget, if possible, the petty
conduct of Berrendale,—the mulatto, who, from the door's being
open, had heard every word of conversation which had so
disturbed Adeline, neither could nor would forget it; and though
she did not vow eternal hatred to her master, she felt herself very
capable of indulging it, and from that moment it was her
resolution to thwart him.

Whenever he was present, she was always urging Adeline to
eat some refreshments between meals, and drink wine or
lemonade, and tempting her weak appetite with some pleasant
but expensive sweetmeats. In vain did Adeline refuse them;
sometimes they were bought, sometimes only threatened to be
bought; and once when Adeline had accepted some, rather than
mortify Savanna by a refusal, and Berrendale, by his accent and
expression, showed how much he grudged the supposed
expense,—the mulatto, snapping her fingers in his face, and
looking at him with an expression of indignant contempt,
exclaimed, "I buy dem, and pay for dem wid mine nown money;
and my angel lady sall no be obliged to you!"

This was a declaration of war against Berrendale, which
Adeline heard with anger and sorrow, and her husband with
rage. In vain did Adeline promise that she would seriously reprove
Savanna (who had disappeared) for her impertinence; Berrendale
insisted on her being discharged immediately; and nothing but
Adeline's assurances that she, for slender wages, did more work
than two other servants would do for enormous ones, could pacify
his displeasure: but at length he was appeased. And as Berrendale,
from a principle of œconomy, resumed his old habit of dining
out amongst his friends, getting good dinners by that means
without paying for them, family expenses ceased to disturb the

quiet of their marriage; and after she had been ten months a wife Adeline gave birth to a daughter.

That moment, the moment when she heard her infant's first cry, seemed to repay her for all she had suffered; every feeling was lost in the maternal one; and she almost fancied that she loved, fondly loved, the father of her child: but this idea vanished when she saw the languid pleasure, if pleasure it could be called, with which Berrendale congratulated her on her pain and danger being past, and received his child in his arms.

The mulatto was wild with joy: she almost stifled the babe with her kisses, and talked even the next day of sending for the tawny boy to come and see his new mistress, and vow to her, as he had done to her mother, eternal fealty and allegiance.

But Adeline saw on Berrendale's countenance a mixed expression,—and he had mixed feelings. True, he rejoiced in Adeline's safety; but he said within himself, "Children are expensive things, and we may have a large family;" and, leaving the bed-side as soon as he could, he retired, to endeavor to lose in an after-noon's nap his unpleasant reflections.

"How different," thought Adeline, "would have been HIS expressions of them at such a time! Oh!—" but the name of Glenmurray died away on her lips; and hastily turning to gaze on her sleeping babe, she tried to forget the disappointed emotions of the wife in the gratified feelings of the mother.

Still Adeline, who had been used to attentions, could not but feel the neglect of Berrendale. Even while she kept her room he passed only a few hours in her society, but dined out; and when she was well enough to have accompanied him on his visits, she found that he never even wished her to go with him, though the friends whom he visited were married; and he met, from his own confession, other ladies at their tables. She therefore began to suspect that Berrendale did not mean to introduce her as his wife; nay, she doubted whether he avowed her to be such; and at last she brought him to own that, ashamed of having married what the world must consider as a kept mistress, he resolved to keep her still in the retirement to which she was habituated.

This was a severe disappointment indeed to Adeline: she longed for the society of the amiable and accomplished of her own sex; and hoped that, as Mr. Berrendale's wife, that intercourse with her own sex might be restored to her which she had forfeited as the mistress of Glenmurray. Nor could she help reproaching Berrendale for the selfish ease and indifference with which he saw her deprived of those social enjoyments which he daily enjoyed himself, convinced as she was that he might, if he chose, have introduced her at least to his intimate friends.

But she pleaded and reasoned in vain. Contented with the access which he had to the tables of his friends, it was of little importance to him that his wife ate her humble meal alone. His habits of enjoyment had ever been solitary: the pampered school-boy, who had at school eaten his tart and cake by stealth in a corner, that he might not be asked to share them with another, had grown up with the same dispositions to manhood: and as his parents, though opulent, were vulgar in their manners and low in their origin, he had never been taught those graceful self-denials inculcated into the children of polished life, which, though taught from factitious and not real benevolence, have certainly a tendency, by long habit, to make that benevolence real which at first was only artificial.

Adeline had both sorts of kindness and affection, those untaught of the heart, and those of education;—she was polite from the situation into which the accident of birth had thrown her, and also from the generous impulse of her nature. To her, therefore, the uncultivated and unblushing *personnalité,* as the French call it, of Berrendale, was a source of constant wonder and distress: and often, very often did she feel the utmost surprise at Berrendale's having appeared to Glenmurray a man likely to make her happy. Often did she wonder how the defects of Berrendale's character could have escaped his penetrating eyes.

Adeline forgot that the faults of her husband were such as could be known only by an intimate connection, and which cohabitation could alone call forth;[113]—faults, the existence of which such a man as Glenmurray, who never considered himself in any transaction whatever, could not suppose possible;—and, which, though they inflicted the most bitter pangs on Adeline, and gradually untwisted the slender thread which had begun to unite her heart with Berrendale's, were of so slight a fabric as almost to elude the touch, and of a nature to appear almost too trivial to be mentioned in the narration of a biographer.

But though it has been long said that trifles make the sum of human things, inattention to trifles continues to be the vice of every one; and many a conjugal union which has never been assailed by the battery of crime, has fallen a victim to the slowly undermining power of petty quarrels, trivial unkindnesses and thoughtless neglect; —like the gallant officer, who, after escaping unhurt all the rage of battle by land and water, tempest on sea and earthquake on shore, returns perhaps to his native country, and perishes by the power of a slow fever.

But Adeline, who, amidst all the chimæras of her fancy and singularities of her opinions, had happily held fast her religion, began at this moment to entertain a belief that soothed in some measure the sorrows which it could not cure. She fancied that all the sufferings she underwent were trials which she was doomed to undergo, as punishments for the crime she had committed in leaving her mother and living with Glenmurray; and as expiations also. She therefore welcomed her afflictions, and lifted up her meek eyes to heaven in every hour of her trials, with the look of tearful but grateful resignation.

Meanwhile her child, whom, after her mother, she called Editha, was nursed at her own bosom, and thrived even beyond her expectations. Even Berrendale beheld its growing beauty with delight, and the mulatto was wild in praise of it; while Adeline, wholly taken up all day in nursing and in working for it, and every evening in writing stories and hymns to publish, which would, she hoped, one day be useful to her own child as

---

[113] See Godwin on Cohabitation from *The Enquirer*, Appendix 1.

well as to the children of others, soon ceased to regret her seclusion
from society; and by the time Editha was a year old she had
learnt to bear with patience the disappointment she had
experienced in Berrendale. Soon after she became a mother she
again wrote to Mrs. Pemberton, as she longed to impart to her
sympathizing bosom those feelings of parental delight which
Berrendale could not understand, and the expression of which
he witnessed with contemptuous and chilling gravity. To this
letter she anticipated a most gratifying return; but month after
month passed away, and no letter from Lisbon arrived. "No doubt
my letter miscarried," said Adeline to Savanna, "and I will write
again:" but she never had resolution to do so; for she felt that her
prospects of conjugal happiness were obscured, and she shrunk
equally from the task of expressing the comfort which she did
not feel, or unveiling to another the errors of her husband. The
little regard, mean while, which she had endeavoured to return
for Berrendale soon vanished, being unable to withstand a new
violence offered to it.[114]

Editha was seized with the hooping-cough: and as Adeline
had sold her last little volume to advantage, Berrendale allowed
her to take a lodging at a short distance from town, as change of
air was good for the complaint. She did so, and remained there
two months. At her return she had the mortification to find that
her husband, during her absence, had intrigued with the servant
of the house:[115]—a circumstance of which she would probably
have remained ignorant, but for the indiscreet affection of Savanna,
who, in the first transports of her indignation on discovering the
connection, had been unable to conceal from her mistress what
drove her almost frantic with indignation.

But Adeline, though she felt disgust and aversion swallowing

---

[114] Compare Adeline's loss of affection for her husband with the more extreme case
of Wollstonecraft's Maria in *Wrongs of Woman*, who considers her marriage dissolved
when her profligate husband offers his wife's sexual favors in payment of a gambling
debt.

[115] Compare Emma Courtney's discovery of her husband's similar behavior, p. 256.

up the few remaining sparks of regard for Berrendale which she felt, had one great consolation under this new calamity.— Berrandale had not been the choice of her heart: "But, thank God! I never loved this man," escaped her lips as she ran into her own room; and pressing her child to her bosom, she shed on its unconscious cheeks the tears which resentment and a deep sense of injury wrung from her.— "Oh! had I loved him," she exclaimed, "this blow would have been mortal!"

She, however, found herself in one respect the better for Berrendale's guilt. Conscious that the mulatto was aware of what had passed, and afraid lest she should have mentioned her discovery to Adeline, Berrendale endeavoured to make amends for his infidelity by attention such as he had never shown her since the first weeks of his marriage: and had she not been aware of the motive, the change in his behaviour would have reawakened her tenderness. However, it claimed at least complaisance and gentleness from her while it lasted: which was not long; for Berrendale, fancying from the apparent tranquillity of Adeline (the result of indifference, not ignorance) that she was not informed of his fault, and that the mulatto was too prudent to betray him, began to relapse into his old habits; and one day, forgetting his assumed liberality, he ventured, when alone with Savanna, who was airing one of Editha's caps, to expatiate on the needless extravagance of his wife in trimming her child's caps with lace.

This was enough to rouse the quick feelings of the mulatto, and she poured forth all her long concealed wrath in a torrent of broken English, but plain enough to be well understood.— "You man!" she cried at last, "you will kill her; she pine at your no kindness;—and if she die, mind me, man! never you marry aden.—You marry, forsoot! You marry a lady! true bred lady like mine! No, man!—You best get a cheap miss from de street and be content—— "

As she said this, and in an accent so provoking that Berrendale was pale and speechless with rage, Adeline entered the room; and Savanna, self-condemned already for what she had uttered, was terrified when Adeline, in a tone of voice unusually severe, said, "Leave the room; you have offended me past forgiveness."

These words, in a great measure, softened the angry feelings of Berrendale, as they proved that Adeline resented the insult offered to him as deeply as he could wish; and with some calmness he exclaimed, "Then I conclude, Mrs. Berrendale, that you will have no objection to discharge your mulatto directly."

That conclusion, though a very natural one, was both a shock and a surprise to Adeline; nor could she at first reply.

"You are *silent*, madam," said Berrendale; "what is your answer? Yes, or No?"

"Ye,—yes,—certainly," faltered out Adeline; "she—she ought to go—I mean that she has used very improper language to you."

"And, therefore, a wife who resents as she ought to do, injuries offered to her husband, cannot hesitate for a moment to discharge her."

"True, very true in some measure," replied Adeline; "but——"

"But what?" demanded Berrendale.

"Oh Berrendale,!" cried Adeline, bursting into an agony of frantic sorrow, "if she leaves me, what will become of me! I shall lose the only person now in the world, perhaps, who loves me with sincere and faithful affection!"

Berrendale was wholly unprepared for an appeal like this; and, speechless from surprise not unmixed with confusion, staggered into the next chair. He was conscious, indeed, that his fidelity to his wife had not been proof against a few weeks' absence; but then, being, like most men, not over delicate in his ideas on such subjects, as soon as Adeline returned he had given up the connection which he had formed, and therefore he thought she had not much reason to complain. In all other respects he was sure that he was an exemplary husband, and she had no just grounds for doubting his affection. He was sure that she had no reason to accuse him of unkindness; and, unless she wished him to be always tied to her apron-string, he was certain he had never omitted to pay her all proper attention.

Alas! he felt not the many wounds he had inflicted by
> "The word whose meaning kills; yet, told,
> The speaker wonders that you thought it cold:"[116]

and he had yet to learn, that in order to excite or testify affection, it is necessary to seem to derive exclusive enjoyment from the society of the object avowed to be beloved, and to seek its gratification in preference to one's own, even in the most trivial things. He knew not that opportunities of conferring large benefits, like bills for 1000£ rarely come into use; but little attentions, friendly participations and kindnesses, are wanted daily, and, like small change, are necessary to carry on the business of life and happiness.

A minute, and more perhaps, elapsed, before Berrendale recovered himself sufficiently to speak; and the silence was made still more awful to Adeline, by her hearing from the adjoining room the sobs of the mulatto. At length, "I cannot find words to express my surprise at what you have just uttered," exclaimed Berrendale. "My conscience does not reproach me with deserving the reproof it contained."

"Indeed!" replied Adeline, fixing her penetrating eyes on his, which shrunk downcast and abashed from her gaze. Adeline saw her advantage, and pursued it. "Mr. Berrendale," continued she, "it is indeed true, that the mulatto has offended both of us; for in offending *you* she has offended *me*; but, have you committed no fault, nothing for *me* to forgive? I know that you are too great a lover of truth, too honourable a man, to declare that you have not deserved the just anger of your wife: but you know that I have never reproached you, nor should you ever have been aware that I was privy to the distressing circumstance to which I allude, but for what has just passed: and, now, do but forgive the poor mulatto, who sinned only from regard for me, and from supposed

---

[116] Hannah More (1745-1833), "Sensibility: An Epistle to the Honourable Mrs. Boscawen: "The guarded phrase, whose meaning kills, yet told,/ The list'ner wonders how you thought it cold" (lines 330-4).

slight offered to her mistress, and I will not only assure you of my forgiveness, but, from this moment, will strenuously endeavour to blot from my remembrance every trace of what has passed."

Berrendale, conscious and self-condemned, scarcely knew what to answer; but, thinking that it was better to accept Adeline's offer even on her own conditions, he said, that if Savanna would make a proper apology, and Adeline would convince her that she was seriously displeased with her, he would allow her to stay; and Adeline, having promised every thing which he asked, peace was again restored.

"But what can you mean, Adeline," said Berrendale, "by doubting my affection? I think I gave a sufficient proof of that, when, disregarding the opinion of the world, I married you, though you had been the mistress of another: and I really think that, by accusing me of unkindness, you make me a very ungrateful return." To this indelicate and unfeeling remark Adeline vainly endeavoured to reply; but, starting from her chair, she paced the room in violent agitation.— "Answer me," continued Berrendale, "name one instance in which I have been unkind to you." Adeline suddenly stopped, and, looking steadfastly at him, smiled with a sort of contemptuous pity, and was on the point of saying, "Is not what you have now said an instance of unkindness?" But she saw that the same want of delicacy, and of that fine moral *tact* which led him to commit this and similar assaults on her feelings, made him unconscious of the violence which he offered.

Finding, therefore, that he could not understand her causes of complaint, even if it were possible for her to define them, she replied, "Well, perhaps I was too hasty, and in a degree unjust: so let us drop the subject; and, indeed, my dear Berrendale, you must bear with my weakness: remember, I have always been a spoiled child."

Here the image of Glenmurray and that of *home*, the home she once knew, the home of her childhood, and of her *earliest* youth, pressed on her recollection. She thought of her mother, of the indulgences which she had once known, of the advantages of opulence, the value of which she had never felt till deprived of them; and, struck with the comparative forlornness of her situation—united for life to a being whose sluggish sensibilities could not understand, and consequently not sooth, the quick feelings and jealous susceptibility of her nature—she could hardly forbear falling at the feet of her husband, and conjuring him to behave, at least, with forbearance to her, and to speak and look at her with kindness.

She did stretch our her hand to him with a look of mournful entreaty, which, though not understood by Berrendale, was not lost upon him entirely. He thought it was a confession of her weakness and his superiority; and, flattered by the thought into unusual softness, he caught her fondly to his bosom, and gave up an engagement to sup at an oyster club, in order to spend the evening tête-à-tête with his wife. Nay, he allowed the little Editha to remain in the room for a whole hour, though she cried when he attempted to take her in his arms, and, observing that it was a cold evening, allowed Adeline her due share of the fire-side.

These circumstances, trivial as they were, had more than their due effect on Adeline, whose heart was more alive to kindness than unkindness; and those paltry attentions of which happy wives would not have been conscious, were to her a source of unfeigned pleasure——As sailors are grateful, after a voyage unexpectedly long, for the muddy water which at their first embarking they would have turned from with disgust.

That very night Adeline remonstrated with the mulatto on the impropriety of her conduct; and, having convinced her that in insulting her husband she failed in respect to her, Savanna was prevailed upon the next morning to ask pardon of Berrendale; and, out of love for her mistress, she took care in future to do nothing that required forgiveness.

As Adeline's way of life admitted of but little variety, Berrendale having persisted in not introducing her to his friends, on the plea of not being rich enough to receive company in return, I shall pass over in silence what occurred to her till Editha was two years old; premising that a series of little injuries on the part of Berrendale, and a quick resentment of them on the part of Adeline, which not even her habitual good humour could prevent, had, during that time, nearly eradicated every trace of love for each other from their hearts.

One evening Adeline as usual, in absence of her husband, undressed Editha by the parlour fire, and, playing with the laughing child, was enjoying the rapturous praises which Savanna put forth of its growing beauty; while the tawny boy, who had spent the day with them, built houses with cards on the table, which Editha threw down as soon as they were built, and he with good-humoured perseverance raised up again.

Adeline, alive only to the maternal feeling, at this moment had forgotten all her cares; she saw nothing but the happy group around her, and her countenance wore the expression of recovered serenity.

At this moment a loud knock was heard at the door, and Adeline, starting up, exclaimed, "It is my husband's knock!"

"O! no:—he never come so soon," replied the mulatto running to the door; but she was mistaken—it was Berrendale: and Adeline, hearing his voice, began instantly to snatch up Editha's clothes, and to knock down the tawny boy's newly-raised edifice: but order was not restored when Berrendale entered; and, with a look and tone of impatience, he said, "So! fine confusion indeed! Here's a fire-side to come to! Pretty amusement too, for a literary lady—building houses of card! Shame on your extravagance, Mrs. Berrendale, to let that brat spoil cards in that way!"

The sunshine of Adeline's countenance on hearing this vanished: to be sure, she was accustomed to such speeches; but the moment before she had felt happy, for the first time, perhaps, for years. She, however, replied not: but, hurrying Editha to bed, ordering the reluctant tawny boy into the kitchen, and setting Berrendale's chair, as usual, in the warmest place, she ventured in a faint voice to ask, what had brought him home so early.

"More early than welcome," replied Berrendale, "if I may

judge from the bustle I have occasioned."

"It is very true," replied Adeline, "that, had I expected you, I should have been better prepared for your reception; and then you, perhaps, would have spoken more kindly to me."

"There—there you go again.—If I say but a word to you, then I am called unkind, though, God knows, I never speak without just provocation: and, I declare, I came home in the best humour possible, to tell you what may turn out of great benefit to us both:—but when a man has an uncomfortable home to come to, it is enough to put him out of humour."

The mulatto, who was staying to gather up the cards which had fallen, turned herself round on hearing this, and exclaimed, "Home was very comfortable till you come;" and then with a look of the most angry contempt she left the room, and threw the door to with great violence.

"But what is this good news, my dear?" said Adeline, eager to turn Berrendale's attention from Savanna's insolent reply.

"I have received a letter," he replied, "which, by the by, I ought to have had some weeks ago, from my father-in-law in Jamaica, authorizing me to draw on his banker for 900£, and inviting me to come over to him; as he feels himself declining, and wishes to give me the care of his estate, and of my son, to whom all his fortune will descend; and of whose interest, he properly thinks, no one can be so likely to take good care as his own father."[117]

"And do you mean that I and Editha should go with you?" said Adeline turning pale.

"No, to be sure not," eagerly replied Berrendale; "I must first see how the land lies. But if I go—as the old man no doubt will make a handsome settlement on me—I shall be able to remit you a very respectable annuity."

Adeline's heart, spite of herself, bounded with joy at this discovery; but she had resolution to add—and if duplicity can

---

[117] Berrendale's first wife was the daughter of this man and mother of his child, raised by the grandfather's family in Jamaica.

ever be pardonable, this was,— "So then the good news which you had to impart to me was, that we were going to be separated!" But as she said this, the consciousness that she was artfully trying to impress Berrendale with an idea of her feeling a sorrow which was foreign to her heart, overcame her; and affected also at being under the necessity of rejoicing at the departure of that being who ought to be the source of her comfort, she vainly struggled to regain composure, and burst into an agony of tears.

Bur her consternation cannot be expressed, when she found that Berrendale imputed her tears to tender anguish at the idea of parting with him: and when, his vanity being delighted by this homage to his attractions, he felt all his fondness for her revive, and, overwhelming her with caresses, he declared that he would reject the offer entirely if by accepting it he should give her a moment's uneasiness; Adeline, shocked at his error, yet not daring to set him right, could only weep on his shoulder in silence: but, in order to make real the distress which he only fancied so, she enumerated to herself all the diseases incident to the climate, and the danger of the voyage. Still the idea of Berrendale's departure was so full of comfort to her, that, though her tears continued to flow, they flowed not for his approaching absence. At length, ashamed of fortifying him in so gross an error, she made an effort to regain her calmness, and found words to assure him, that she would no longer give way to such unpardonable weakness, as she could assure him that she wished his acceptance of his father-in-law's offer, and had no desire to oppose a scheme so just and so profitable.

But Berrendale, to whose vanity she had never before offered such a tribute as her tears seemed to be, imputed these assurances to disinterested love and female delicacy, afraid to own the fondness which it felt; and the rest of the evening was spent in professions of love on his part, which, on Adeline's, called forth at least some grateful and kind expressions in return.

Still, however, she persisted in urging Berrendale to go to Jamaica: but, at the same time, she earnestly begged him to remember, that temperance could alone preserve his health in such a climate:— "or the use of pepper in great quantities," replied he, "to counteract the effects of good living!"—and Adeline, though convinced temperance was the *best* preservative, was forced to give up the point, especially as Berrendale began to enumerate the number of delicious things for the table which Jamaica afforded.[118]

To be brief: Berrendale, after taking a most affectionate leave of his wife and child, a leave which almost made the mulatto his friend, and promising to allow them 200£, a year till he should be able to send over for them, set sail for Jamaica; while Adeline, the night of his departure, endeavoured, by conjuring up all the horrors of a tempest at sea on his passage, and of a hurricane and an earthquake on shore when he arrived, to force herself to feel such sorrow as the tenderness which he had expressed at the moment of parting seemed to make it her duty to feel.

But morning came, and with it a feeling of liberty and independence so delightful, that she no longer tried to grieve on speculation as it were; but giving up her whole soul to the joys of maternal fondness, she looked forward with pious gratitude to days of tranquil repose, save when she thought with bitter regret of the obdurate anger of her mother, and with tender regret of the lost and ever lamented Glenmurray.

Berrendale had been arrived at Jamaica some months, when Adeline observed a most alarming change in Savanna. She became thin, her appetite entirely failed, and she looked the image of despondence. In vain did Adeline ask the reason of a change so apparent: the only answer she could obtain was, "Me better soon;" and, continuing every day to give this answer, she in a short time became so languid as to be obliged to lie down half the day.

Adeline then found that it was necessary to be more serious in her interrogatories; but the mulatto at first only answered, "No, me die, but me never break my duty vow to you: no, me die, but never leave you."

These words implying a wish to leave her, with a resolution

[118] See textbox on "Appetite and Temperance," p. 521.

not to do so how much soever it might cost her, alarmed in a moment the ever disinterested sensibility of Adeline; and she at length wrung from her a confession that her dear William, who was gone to Jamaica as a servant to a gentleman, was, she was credibly informed, very ill and like to die.

"You therefore wish to go and nurse him, I suppose, Savanna?"

"O! me no wish; me only tink dat me like to go to Jamaica, see if be true dat he be so bad; and if he die I den return, and die wid you."

"Live with me, you mean, Savanna; for, indeed, I cannot spare you. Remember, you have given me a right to claim your life as mine; nor can I allow you to throw away my property in fruitless lamentations, and the indolent indulgence of regret. You shall go to Jamaica, Savanna: God forbid that I should keep a wife from her duty! You shall see and try to recover William if he be really ill," (Savanna here threw herself on Adeline's neck,) "and then you shall return to me, who will either warmly share in your satisfaction or fondly sooth your distress."

"Den you do love poor Savanna?"

"Love you! Indeed I do, next to my child, and, and my mother," replied Adeline, her voice faltering.

'Name not dat woman," cried Savanna hastily; "me will never see, never speak to her even in heaven."

"Savanna, remember, she is my mother."

"Yes, and Mr. Berrendale be your husban; and yet, who dat love you can love dem?"

"Savanna," replied Adeline, "these proofs of your regard, though reprehensible, are not likely to reconcile me to your departure; and I already feel that in losing you—— " here she paused, unable to proceed.

"Den me no go—me no go:—yet, dearest lady, you have love yourself."

"Aye, Savanna, and can feel for you: so say no more. The only difficulty will be to raise money enough to pay for your passage, and expenses while there."

"Oh! me once nurse the captain's wife who now going to Jamaica, and she love me very much; and he tell me yesterday that he let me go for noting, because I am good nurse to his wife, if me wish to see William."

"Enough," replied Adeline: "then all I have to do is to provide you with money for your maintenance when you arrive; and I have no doubt but that what I cannot supply the tawny boy's generous patroness will."

Adeline was not mistaken. Savanna obtained from her son's benefactress a sum equal to her wants; and almost instantly restored to her wonted health, by her mind's being lightened of the load which oppressed it, she took her passage on board her friend's vessel, and set sail for Jamaica, carrying with her letters from Adeline to Berrendale; while Adeline felt the want of Savanna in various ways, so forcibly, that not even Editha could, for a time at least, console her for her loss. It had been so grateful to her feelings to meet every day the eyes of one being fixed with never-varying affection on hers, that, when she beheld those eyes no longer, she felt alone in the universe—nor had she a single female friend to whom she could turn for relief or consolation.

Mrs. Beauclerc, to whose society she had expected to be restored by her marriage, had been forced to give up all intercourse with her, in compliance with the peremptory wishes of a rich old maid, from whom her children had great expectations, and who threatened to leave her fortune away from them, if Mrs. Beauclerc persisted in corresponding with a woman so bad in principle, and so wicked in practice, as Adeline appeared to her to be.[119]

But, at length, from a mother's employments, from writing, and, above all, from the idea that by suffering she was making atonement for her past sins, she derived consolation, and became resigned to every evil that had befallen, and to every evil that might still befall her.

---

[119] Compare Mrs. Beauclerc's original argument for Adeline's marriage, pp. 505-6, this volume.

Perhaps she did not consider as an evil what now took place: increasing coldness in the letters of Berrendale, till he said openly at last, that as they were, he was forced to confess, far from happy together, and as the air of Jamaica agreed with him, and as he was resolved to stay there, he thought she had better remain in England, and he would remit her as much money occasionally as his circumstances would admit of.

But she thought this was a greater evil than it at first appeared; when an agent of Berrendale's father-in-law in England, and a friend of Berrendale himself, called on her, pretending that he came to inquire concerning her health, and raised in her mind suspicions of a very painful nature.

After the usual compliments:— "I find, madam," said Mr. Drury, "that our friend is very much admired by the ladies in Jamaica."

"I am glad to hear it, sir," coolly answered Adeline.

"Well, that's kind and generous now," replied Drury, "and very disinterested."

"I see no virtue, sir, in my rejoicing at what must make Mr. Berrendale's abode in Jamaica pleasant to him."

"May be so; but most women, I believe, would be apt to be jealous on the occasion."

"But it has been the study of my life, sir, to endeavour to consider my own interest, when it comes in competition with another's, as little as possible;—I doubt I have not always succeeded in my endeavours; but, on this occasion I am certain that I have expressed no sentiment which I do not feel."

"Then, madam, if my friend should have an opportunity, as indeed I believe he has, of forming a most agreeable and advantageous marriage, you would not try to prevent it?"

"Good heavens! sir," replied Adeline; "What can you mean? Mr. Berrendale form an advantageous marriage when he is already married to me?"

"Married to you, ma'am!" answered Mr. Drury with a look of incredulity. "Excuse me, but I know that such marriages as yours may be easily dissolved."

At first Adeline was startled at this assertion; but recollecting that it was impossible any form or ceremony should have been wanting at the marriage, she recovered herself, and demanded, with an air of severity, "what Mr. Drury meant by so alarming and ill-founded a speech."

"My meaning, ma'am," replied he, "must be pretty evident to you: I mean that I do not look upon you, though you bear Mr. Berrendale's name, to be his lawful wife; but that you live with him on the same terms on which you lived with Mr. Glenmurray."

"And on what, sir, could you build such an erroneous supposition?"

"On Mr. Berrendale's own words, madam; who always spoke of his connection with you, as of a connection which he had formed in compliance with love and in defiance of prudence."

"And is it possible that he could be such a villain?" exclaimed Adeline. "Oh my child! and does thy father brand thee with the stain of illegitimacy?—But, sir, whatever appellation Mr. Berrendale might choose to give his union with me to his friends in England, I am sure he will not dare to incur the penalty attendant on a man's marrying one wife while he has another living; for, that I am his wife, I can bring pretty sufficient evidence to prove."

"Indeed, madam! You can produce a witness of the ceremony, then, I presume?"

"No, sir; the woman who attended me to the altar, and the clergyman who married us, are dead; and the only witness is a child now only ten years old."

"That is unfortunate!" (with a look of incredulity) "but, no doubt, when you hear that Mr. Berrendale is married to a West Indian heiress, you will come forward with incontrovertible proofs of your prior claims; and if you do that, madam, you may command my good offices:—but, till then, I humbly take my leave." Saying this, with a very visible sneer on his countenance he departed, leaving Adeline in a state of distress—the more painful to endure from her having none to participate in it,—no one to whom she could impart the cause of it.

That Mr. Drury did not speak of the possible marriage of Berrendale from mere conjecture, was very apparent; and Adeline resolved not to delay writing to her husband immediately, to inform him of what had passed, and to put before his eyes, in the strongest possible manner, the guilt of what he was about to do; and also the utter impossibility of its being successful guilt, as she was resolved to assert her claims for the sake of her child, if not for her own. This letter she concluded, and with truth too, with protestations of believing all Mr. Drury said to be false: for, indeed, the more she considered Berrendale's character, she more she was convinced that, however selfish and defective his disposition might be, it was more likely Mr. Drury should be mistaken, than Berrendale be a villain.

But, where a man's conduct is not founded on virtuous motives and immutable principles, he may not err while temptation is absent; but once expose him to her presence, and he is capable of falling into the very vices the most abhorrent to his nature: and though Adeline knew it not, such a man was Berrendale.

Adeline, having relieved her mind by this appeal to her husband, and being assured that Berrendale could not be married before her letter could reach him, as it was impossible that he should dare to marry while the mulatto was in the very town near which he resided, felt herself capable of attending to her usual employments again, and had recovered her tranquillity, when an answer to her letter arrived; and Adleine, being certain that the letter itself would be a proof of the marriage, had resolved to show it, in justification of her claims, to Mr. Drury.

What then must have been her surprise, to find it exactly such a letter as would be evidence against a marriage between her and Berrendale having ever taken place! He thanked her for the expressions of fond regret which her letter contained, and for the many happy hours which he owed to her society; but hoped that, as Fate had now separated their destinies, she could be as happy without him as she had been with him; and assuring her that he should, according to his promise, regularly remit her 150£ a year if possible, but that he could at present only inclose a draft for 50£.

Adeline was absolutely stupefied with horror at reading this apparent confirmation of the villany of her husband and the father of her child; but roused to indignant exertion by the sense of Berrendale's baseness, and of what she owed her daughter, she resolved to take counsel's opinion in what manner she should proceed to prove her marriage, as soon as she was assured that Berrendale's (which she had no doubt was fixed upon) should have taken place; and this intelligence she received a short time after from the mulatto herself, who, worn out with sorrow, sickness and hardship, one day tottered into the house, seeming as if she indeed only returned to die with her mistress.

At first the joy of seeing Savanna restored to her swallowed up every other feeling; but tender apprehension for the poor creature's health soon took possession of her mind, and Adeline drew from her a narrative, which exhibited Berrendale to her eyes as capable of most atrocious actions.

CHAPTER II.

IT is very certain that when Berrendale left England, though he meant to conceal his marriage entirely, he had not even the slightest wish to contract another; and had any one told him that he was capable of such wicked conduct, he would have answered like Hazael, "Is thy servant a dog that he should do this thing?"[120] But he was then unassailed by temptations:— and habituated as he was to selfish indulgence, it was impossible that to strong temptation he should not fall an immediate victim.

This strong temptation assailed him soon after his arrival, in the person of a very lovely and rich widow, a relation of his first wife, who, having no children of her own, had long been very fond of his child, then a very fine boy and with great readiness transferred to the father the affection which she bore the son.

[120] Kings, 8:13.

For some time conscience and Adeline stood their ground against this new mistress and her immense property; but at length, being pressed by his father-in-law, who wished the match, to assign a sufficient reason for his coldness to so fine a woman, and not daring to give the true one, he returned the lady's fondness; and though he had not yet courage enough to name the marriage day, it was known that it would some time or other take place.

But all his scruples soon yielded to the dominion which the attractions of the lady, who was well versed in the arts of seduction, obtained over his senses, and to the strong power which the sight of the splendor in which she lived, acquired over his avarice; when, just as every thing was on the point of being concluded, the poor mulatto, who had found her husband dead, arrived almost broken-hearted at the place of Berrendale's abode, and delivered to him letters from Adeline.

Terrified and confounded at her presence, he received her with such evident marks of guilty confusion in his face, that Savanna's apprehensive and suspicious attachment to her mistress took the alarm; and, as she had seen a very fine woman leave the room as she entered, she, on pretence of leaving Berrendale alone to read his letters, repaired to the servants' apartments, where she learnt the intended marriage. Immediately forgetting her own distresses in those of Adeline, she returned to Berrendale, not with the languid, mournful pace with which she had first entered, but with the firm, impetuous and intrepid step of conscious integrity going to confound vice in the moment of its triumph.

Berrendale read his doom, the moment he beheld her, in her dark and fiery eye, and awaited in trembling silence the torrent of reproaches that trembled on her lip. But I shall not repeat what passed. Suffice that Berrendale pretended to be moved by what she said, and promised to break off the marriage,—only exacting from Savanna, in return, a promise of not imparting to the servants, or to any one, that he had a wife in England.

In the mean while he commended her most affectionately to the care of the steward; and confessing to his intended bride that he had a mistress in England, who had sent the mulatto over to prevent the match if possible, by persuading her he was already married, he conjured her to consent to a private marriage; and to prevent some dreadful scene, occasioned by the revenge of disappointed passion, should his mistress, as she had threatened, come over in person, he entreated her to let every splendid preparation for their nuptials be laid aside, in order to deceive Savanna, and induce her to return quietly to England.

The credulous woman, too much in love to believe what she did not wish, consented to all he proposed: but Berrendale, still fearful of the watchful jealousy of Savanna, contrived to find out the master to whom she belonged before she had escaped, early in life, with her first husband to England; and as she had never been made free, as soon as he arrived, he, on a summons from Berrendale, seized her as his property; and poor Savanna, in spite of her cries and struggles, was conveyed some miles up the country.

At length, however, she found means to escape to the coast; and, having discovered an old acquaintance in an English sailor on board a vessel then ready to sail, and who had great influence with the captain, she was by him concealed on board, with the approbation of the commander, and was on her way to England before Berrendale was informed of her escape.

I will not endeavour to describe Adeline's feelings on hearing this narration, and on finding also that Savanna before she left the island had been assured that Berrendale was really married, though privately, but that the marriage could not long be attempted to be concealed, as the lady even before it took place was likely to become a mother; and, that as a large estate depended on her giving birth to a son, the event of her confinement was looked for with great anxiety.

Still, in the midst of her distress, a sudden thought struck Adeline, which converted her anger into joy, and her sorrow into exultation. "Yes, my mother may now forgive me without violating any part of her oath," she exclaimed.— "I am now forsaken, despised and disgraced!"—and instantly she wrote to

Mrs. Mowbray a letter, calculated to call forth all her sympathy and affection. Then, with a mind relieved beyond expression, she sat down to deliberate in what manner she should act to do herself justice as a wife and a mother, cruelly aggrieved in both these intimate relations. Nor could she persuade herself that she should act properly by her child, if she did not proceed vigorously to prove herself Berrendale's wife, and substantiate Editha's claim to his property; and as Mr. Langley was, she knew, a very great lawyer, she resolved, in spite of his improper conduct to her, to apply to him again.

Indeed she could not divest herself of a wish to let him know that she was become a wife, and no longer liable to be treated with that freedom with which, as a mistress, he had thought himself at liberty to address her. However, she wished that she had not been obliged to go to him alone: but, as the mulatto was in too weak a state of health to allow of her going out, and she could not speak of business like hers before any one else, she was forced to proceed unaccompanied to the Temple; and on the evening of the day after Savanna's return, she, with a beating heart, repaired once more to Mr. Langley's chambers.

Luckily, however, she met the tawny boy on her way, and took him for her escort. "Tell your master," said she to the servant, "that Mrs. Berrendale wishes to speak to him:" and in a few minutes she was introduced.

"Mrs. Berrendale!" cried Langley with a sarcastic smile; "pray be seated, madam! I hope Mr. Berrendale is well."

"He is in Jamaica, sir," replied Adeline.

"Indeed!" returned Langley. "May I presume so far as to ask,—hem, hem—whether your visit to me be merely of a professional nature?"

"Certainly, sir" replied Adeline: "of what other nature should it be?"

Langley replied to this only by a significant smile. At this moment the tawny boy asked leave to walk in the Temple gardens; and Adeline, though reluctantly, granted his request.

"Oh! à propos, John," cried Langley to the servant, "let Mrs.

Montgomery know that her friend miss Mowbray, Mrs. Berrendale I mean, is here—she is walking in the garden."

"My friend Mrs. Montgomery, sir! I have no friend of that name."

"No, my sweet soul? You may not know her by that name; but names change, you know. You, for instance, are Mrs. Berrendale now, but when I see you again you may be Mrs. somebody else."

"Never, sir," cried Adeline indignantly; "but, though I do not exactly understand your meaning, I feel as if you meant to insult me, and therefore— "

"Oh no—sit down again, my angel; you are mistaken, and so apt to fly off in a tangent! But—so—that wonderfully handsome man, Berrendale, is off—heh? Your friend and mine, heh! pretty one!"

"If, sir, Mr. Berrendale ever considered you as his friend, it is very strange that you should presume to insult his wife."

"Madam," replied Langley with a most provoking sneer, "Mr. Berrendale's wife shall always be treated by me with proper respect."

"Gracious Heaven!" cried Adeline, clasping her hands and looking upwards with tearful eyes, "when shall my persecutions cease! and how much greater must my offences be than even my remorse paints them, when their consequences still torment me so long after the crime which occasioned them has ceased to exist! But it is Thy will, and I will submit even to indignity with patience."

There was a touching solemnity in this appeal to heaven, an expression of truth, which it was so impossible for art to imitate, that Langley felt in a moment the injustice of which he had been guilty, and an apology was on his lips, when the door opened, and a lady, rouged like a French countess of the ancien régime, her hair covered with a profusion of brown powder, and dressed in the height of the fashion, ambled into the room; and saying, "How d'ye do, miss Mowbray?" threw herself carelessly on the sofa, to the astonishment of Adeline, who did not recollect her, and to the confusion of Langley, who now, impressed with involuntary respect for Adeline, repented of having exposed her to the scene that awaited her: but to prevent it was impossible; he was formed to be the slave of women, and had not courage to protect another from the insolence to which he tamely yielded himself.

Adeline at first did not answer this soi-disant[121] acquaintance of hers; but, in looking at her more attentively, she exclaimed, "What do I see? Is it possible that this can be Mary Warner!"

"Yes, it is, my dear, indeed," replied she with a loud laugh, "Mary Warner, alias Mrs. Montgomery; as you, you know, are miss Mowbray, alias Mrs. Berrendale."

Adeline, incapable of speaking, only gazed at her silence, but with a countenance more in sorrow than in anger.

"But, come, sit down, my dear," cried Mary; "no ceremony, you know, among friends and equals, you know; and you and I have been mighty familiar, you know, before now. The last time we met you called me *woman,* you know—yes 'woman!' says you—and I have not forgotten it, I assure you," she added with a sort of loud hysterical laugh, and a look of the most determined malice.

"Come, come, my dear Montgomery," said Langley, "you must forget and forgive;—I dare say miss Mowbray, that is to say Mrs. Berrendale, did not mean— "

"What should you know about the matter, Lang.?" replied Mary; "I wish you would mind your own business, and let me talk to my dumb friend here. Well, I suppose you are quite surprised to see how smart I am!—seeing as how I once overhard you say to Glenthingymy, 'How very plain Mary is!' though, to be sure, it was never a barrel the better herring, and 'twas the kettle in my mind calling the pot—heh, Lang.?"

Here was the clue to the inveterate dislike which this unhappy girl had conceived against Adeline. So true is it that little wounds inflicted on the self-love are never forgotten or forgiven, and that

[121] I.e., so-called.

it is safer to censure the morals of acquaintances than to ridicule them on their dress, or laugh at a defect in their person. Adeline, indeed, did not mean that her observation should be over-heard by the object of it,—still she was hated: but many persons make mortifying remarks purposely, and yet wonder that they have enemies!

Motionless and almost lifeless Adeline continued to stand and to listen, and Mary went on—

"Well, but I thank you for one thing. You taught me that marriage was all nonsense, you know; and so thought I, miss Mowbray is a learned lady, she must know best, and so I followed your example—that's all you know."

This dreadful information roused the feelings of Adeline even to phrensy, and with a shriek of anguish she seized her hand, and conjured her by all her hopes of mercy to retract what she had said, and not to let her depart with the horrible consciousness of having been the means of plunging a fellow-being into vice and ignominy.

A loud unfeeling laugh, and an exclamation of "the woman is mad," was all the answer to this.

"This then is the completion of my sufferings," cried Adeline,— "this only was wanted to complete the misery of my remorse."

"Good God! this is too much," exclaimed Langley. "Mary, you know very well that— "

"Hold your tongue, Lang.; you know nothing about the matter: it is all nothing, but that miss Mowbray, like a lawyer, can change sides, you see, and attack one day what she defended the day before, you know; and she have made you believe that she think now being kept a shameful thing."

"I do believe so," hastily replied Adeline; "and if it be true that my sentiments and my example led you to adopt your present guilty mode of life,—oh! save me from the pangs of remorse which I now feel, by letting my present example recall you from the paths of error to those of virtue."

"Well pleaded," cried the cold-hearted Mary— "Lang., you

could not have done't so well—not up to that."

"Mrs. Montgomery," said Langley with great severity, "if you cannot treat Mrs. Berrendale with more propriety and respect, I must beg you to leave the room; she is come to speak to me on business, and— "

"I sha'n't stir, for all that: and mark me, Lang., if you turn me out of the room, you know, curse me if ever I enter it again!"

"But your little boy may want you; you have left him now some time."

"Aye, that may be true, to be sure, poor little dear! Have you any family, miss Mowbray?"—when, without waiting for an answer, she added, "My little boy have got the small-pox very bad, and has been likely to die from convulsion fits, you know. Poor dear! I had been nursing it so long that I could not bear the stench of the room, and so I was glad, you know, to come and get a little fresh air in the gardens."

At this speech Adeline's fortitude entirely gave way. *Her* child had not had the small-pox, and she had been for some minutes in reach of the infection; and with a look of horror, forgetting her business, and every thing but Editha, she was on the point of leaving the room, when a servant hastily entered, and told Mary that her little boy was dead.

At hearing this, even her cold heart was moved, and throwing herself back on the sofa she fell into a strong hysteric; while Adeline, losing all remembrance of her insolence in her distress, flew to her assistance; and, in pity for a mother weeping the loss of her infant, forgot for a moment that she was endangering the life of her own child.

Mr. Langley, mean time, though grieved for the death of the infant, was alive to the generous forgiving disposition which Adeline evinced; and could not help exclaiming, "Oh, Mrs. Berrendale! forgive us! we deserved not such kindness at your hands:" and Adeline, wanting to loosen the tight stays of Mary, and not choosing to undress her before such a witness, coldly begged him to withdraw, advising him at the same time to go and see whether the child was really dead, as it might possibly only appear so.

Revived by this possibility, Mr. Langley left Mary to the care of Adeline, and left the room. But whether it was that Mary had a mind to impress her lover and the father of her child with an idea of her sensibility, or whether she had overheard Adeline's supposition, certain it is, that as soon as Langley went away, and Adeline began to unlace her stays, she hastily recovered, and declared her stays should remain as they were: but still exclaiming about her poor dear Benny, she kept her arms closely clasped around Adeline's waist, and reposed her head on her bosom.

Adeline's fears and pity for her being thus allayed, she began to have leisure to feel and fear for herself; and the idea, that, by being in such close contact with Mary, she was imbibing so much of the disease as must inevitably communicate it to Editha, recurred so forcibly to her mind, that, begging for God's sake she would loose her hold, she endeavoured to break from the arms of her tormentor.

But in vain.—As soon as Mary saw that Adeline wished to leave her, she was the more eager to hold her fast; and protesting she should die if she had the barbarity to leave her alone, she only hugged her the closer. "Well, then, I'll try to stay till Mr. Langley returns," cried Adeline: but some minutes elapsed, and Mr. Langley did not return; and then Adeline, recollecting that when he did return he would come fresh fraught with the pestilence from the dead body of his infant, could no longer master her feelings, but screaming wildly,— "I shall be the death of my child; for God's sake let me go,"—she struggled with the determined Mary. "You will drive me mad if you detain me," cried Adeline.

"You will drive me mad if you go," replied Mary, giving way to a violent hysterical scream, while with successful strength she parried all Adeline's endeavours to break from her. But what can resist the strength of phrensy and despair? Adeline, at length worked up to madness by the fatal control exercised over her, by one great effort threw the sobbing Mary from her, and, darting down stairs with the rapidity of phrensy, nearly knocked down Mr. Langley in her passage, who was coming to announce the restoration of the little boy.

She soon reached Fleet-street, and was on her road home before Langley and Mary had recovered their consternation: but she suddenly recollected that homewards she must not proceed; that she carried death about her; and wholly bewildered by this insupportable idea, she ran along the Strand, muttering the incoherencies of phrensy as she went, till she was intercepted in her passage by some young men of *ton*,[122] who had been dining together, and, being half intoxicated, were on their way to the theatre.

Two of these gentlemen, with extended arms, prevented her further progress.

"Where are you going, my pretty girl," cried one, "in this hurry? shall I see you home? heh!"

"Home!" replied Adeline; "name it not. My child! my child! thy mother has destroyed thee."

"So!" cried another, "an actress, by all that's tragical!"

"Unhand me!" exclaimed Adeline wildly. "Do not you know, poor babe, that I carry death and pollution about with me!"

"The devil you do!" returned the gentleman; "then the sooner you take yourself off the better."

"I believe the poor soul is mad," said a third, making way for Adeline to pass.

"But," cried the first who spoke, catching hold of her, "if so, there is method and meaning in her madness; for she called Jaby here a poor babe, and we all know he is little better."

By this time Adeline was in a state of complete phrensy, and was again darting down the street in spite of the gentleman's efforts to hold her, when another gentleman, whom curiosity had induced to stop and listen to what passed, suddenly seized hold of her arm and exclaimed, "Good Heavens! what can this mean? It is—it can be no other than miss Mowbray."

---

[122] Literally "tone," indicating men of fashion.

At the sound of her own name Adeline started: but in a moment her senses were quite lost again; and the gentleman, who was no other than colonel Mordaunt, being fully aware of her situation, after reproving the young men for sporting with distress so apparent, called a coach which happened to be passing, and desired to know whither he should have the honour of conducting her.

But she was too lost to be able to answer the question: he therefore, lifting her into the coach, desired the man to drive towards Dover-street; and when there, he ordered him to drive to Margaret-street Oxford-street; when, not being able to obtain one coherent word from Adeline, and nothing but expressions of agony, terror, and self-condemnation, he desired him to stop at such a house, and, conducting Adeline up stairs, desired the first assistance to be procured immediately.

It was not to his own lodgings that colonel Mordaunt had conducted Adeline, but to the house of a convenient friend of his, who, though not generally known as such, and bearing a tolerably good character in the world, was very kind to the tender distresses of her friends, and had no objection to assist the meetings of two fond lovers.

It is to be supposed, then, that she was surprised at seeing colonel Mordaunt with a companion, who was an object of pity and horror rather than of love: but she did not want humanity; and when the colonel recommended Adeline to her tenderest care, she with great readiness ordered a bed to be prepared, and assisted in prevailing on Adeline to lie down on it. In a short time a physician and a surgeon arrived; and Adeline, having been bled and made to swallow strong opiates, was undressed by her attentive landlady; and though still in a state of unconsciousness, she fell into a sound sleep, which lasted till morning.

But colonel Mordaunt passed a sleepless night. The sight of Adeline, even frantic and wretched as she appeared, had revived the passion which he had conceived for her; and if on her awaking the next morning she should appear perfectly rational, and her phrensy merely the result of some great fright which she had received, he resolved to renew his addresses, and take advantage of the opportunity now offered him, while she was as it were in his power.

But to return to the Temple. Soon after Mr. Langley had entered his own room, and while Mary and he were commenting on the frantic behavior of Adeline, the tawny boy came back from his walk, and heard with marks of emotion, apparently beyond his age, (for though near twelve he did not look above eight years old,) of the sudden and frantic disappearance of Adeline.

"Oh! my dear friend," cried he, "if you are not gone home you will break my poor mother's heart!"

"And who is your mother?"

"Her name is Savanna; and she lived with Mrs. Berrendale."

"Mrs Berrendale!" cried Mary, "miss Mowbray you mean."

"No, I do not;—her name was Mowbray, but is now Berrendale."

"What! is she really married?" asked Langley.

"Yes, to be sure."

"But how do you know that she is?"

"Oh! because I went to church with them, and my mother cooked the wedding-dinner, and I ate plum-pudding and drank punch, and we were very merry,—only my mother cried, because my father could not come."

"Very circumstantial evidence, indeed!" cried Langley, "and I am very sorry that I did not know so much before. So you and your mother love this extraordinary fine woman, Mrs. Berrendale, heh?"

"Love her! To be sure—we should be very wicked if we did not. Did you never hear the story of the pine-apple?" said the tawny boy.

"Not I. What was it?" and the tawny boy, delighted to tell the story, with sparkling eyes sat down to relate it.

"You must know, Mr. Glenmurray longed for a pine-apple."

"Mrs. Glenmurray you mean," said Mary laughing immoderately.

"I know what I say," replied the tawny boy angrily; "and so miss Adeline, as she was then called, went out to buy one;— well, and so she met my poor father going to prison, and I was crying after her, and so— " Here he paused, and bursting into tears exclaimed, "And perhaps she is crying herself now, and I must go and see for her directly."

"Do so, my fine fellow," cried Langley: "you had better go home, tell your mother what has passed, and to-morrow (accompanying him down stairs, and speaking in a low voice) I will either write a note of apology or call on Mrs. Berrendale myself."

The tawny boy instantly set off, running as fast as he could, telling Langley first, that if any harm had happened to his friend, both he and his mother should lie down and die. And this further proof of Adeline's merit did not tend to calm Langley's remorse for having exposed her to the various distresses which she had undergone at his chambers.

Chapter III.

ADELINE awoke early the next morning perfectly sane, though weakened by the exertions which she had experienced the night before, and saw with surprise and alarm that she was not in her own lodging.

But she had scarcely convinced herself that she was awake, when Mrs. Selby, the mistress of the house, appeared at her bed-side, and, seeing what was passing in her mind by her countenance, explained to her as delicately as she could the situation in which she had been brought there.

"And who brought me hither?" replied Adeline, dreadfully agitated, as the remembrance of what had passed by degrees burst upon her.

"Colonel Mordaunt of the life-guards," was the answer; and Adeline was shocked to find that he was the person to whom she was under so essential an obligation. She then hastily arose, being eager to return home; and in a short time she was ready to enter the drawing-room, and to express her thanks to colonel

Mordaunt.

But in vain did she insist on going home directly, to ease the fears of her family. The physician, who arrived at the moment, forbade her going out without having first taken both medicine and refreshment; and by the time that, after the most earnest entreaties, she obtained leave to depart, she recollected that, as her clothes were the same, she might still impart disease to her child, and therefore must on no account think of returning to Editha.

"Whither, whither then can I go?" cried she, forgetting she was not alone.

"Why not stay here?" said the colonel, who had been purposely left alone with her. "O dearest of women! that you would but accept the protection of a man who adores you; who has long loved you; who has been so fortunate as to rescue you from a situation of misery and danger, and the study of whose life it shall be to make you happy."

He uttered this with such volubility, that Adeline could not find an opportunity to interrupt him; but when he concluded, she calmly replied, "I am willing to believe, colonel Mordaunt, from a conversation which I once had with you, that you are not aware of the extent of the insult which you are now offering to me. You probably do not know that I have been for years a married woman?"

Colonel Mordaunt started and turned pale at this intelligence; and in a faltering voice replied, that he was indeed a stranger to her present situation;—for that, libertine as he confessed himself to be, he had never yet allowed himself to address the wife of another.

This speech restored him immediately to the confidence of Adeline. "Then I hope," cried she, holding out her hand to him, which in spite of his virtue he passionately kissed, "that, as a friend, you will have the kindness to procure me a coach to take me to a lodging a few miles out of town, where I once was before; and that you will be so good as to drive directly to my lodgings, and let my poor maid know what is become of me. I dread to think," added she bursting into tears, "of the agony that my unaccountable absence must have occasioned her."

The colonel, too seriously attached to Adeline to know yet what he wished, or what he hoped on this discovery of her situation, promised to obey her, provided she would allow him to call on her now and then; and Adeline was too full of gratitude to him for the service which he had rendered her, to have resolution enough to deny his request. He then called a coach for himself, and for Adeline, as she insisted on his going immediately to her lodgings; and also begged that he would tell the mulatto to send for advice, and prepare her little girl for inoculation directly.

Adeline drove directly to her old lodgings in the country, where she was most gladly received; and the colonel went to deliver his commission to the mulatto.

He found her in strong hysterics; the tawny boy crying over her, and the women of the house holding her down on the bed by force, while the little Editha had been conveyed to a neighbour's house, that she might not hear the screams which had surprised and terrified her.

Colonel Mordaunt had opened the door, and was witnessing this distressing scene, before any one was conscious of his presence; but the tawny boy soon discovered him, and crying out—

"Oh! sir, do you bring us news of our friend?" sprang to him, and hung almost breathless on his arm.

Savanna, who was conscious enough to know what passed, though too much weakened from her own sufferings and anxieties to be able to struggle with this new affliction, started up on hearing these words, and screamed out "Does she live? Blessed man! but say so, dat's all," in a tone so affecting, and with an expression of agonized curiosity so overwhelming to the feelings, that colonel Mordaunt, whose spirits were not very high, was so choked that he could not immediately answer her; and when at last he faltered out, "She lives, and is quite well," the frantic joy of the mulatto overcame him still more. She jumped about his neck, she hugged the tawny boy; and her delight was as extravagant as her grief had been; till exhausted and silent she sunk upon the bed, and was unable for some minutes to listen quietly to the story which colonel Mordaunt came to relate.

When she was composed enough to listen to it, she did not long remain so; for as soon as she heard that colonel Mordaunt had met Adeline in her phrensy, and conveyed her to a place of safety, she fell at his feet, embraced his knees, and, making the tawny boy kneel down by her, invoked the blessing of God on him so fervently and so eloquently, that colonel Mordaunt wept like a child, and, exclaiming, "Upon my soul, my good woman, I cannot bear this," was forced to run out of the house to recover his emotion.

When he returned, Savanna said, "Well—now, blessed sir, take me to my dear lady."

"Indeed," replied he, "I must not; you are forbidden to see her."

"Forbidden!" replied she, her eyes flashing fire; "and who dare to keep Savanna from her own missess?—I will see her."

"Not if she forbids it, Savanna; and if her child's life should be endangered by it?"

"O, no, to be sure not," cried the tawny boy, who doted upon Editha, and, having fetched her back from the next house, was lulling her to sleep in his arms.

Colonel Mordaunt started at sight of the child, and, stopping down to kiss its rosy cheek, sighed deeply as he turned away again.

"Well," cried Savanna, "you talk very strange—me no understand."

"But you shall, my excellent creature," replied the colonel, "immediately." He then entered on a full explanation to Savanna; who had no sooner heard that her mistress feared that she had been so much exposed to the infection of the small-pox, as to make her certain of giving it to her child, than she exclaimed, "Oh, my good God! save and protect her own self! She never have it, and she may get it and die!"

"Surely you must be mistaken," replied the colonel, "Mrs.

Berrendale must have recollected and mentioned her own danger if this be the case."

"She!" hastily interrupted the mulatto, "she tink of herself! Never—she only mind others' good.—Do you tink, if she be one selfish beast like her husban, Savanna love her so dear? No, Mr. colonel, me know her, and me know though we may save the child we may lose the mother." Here she began to weep bitterly; while the colonel, more in love than ever with Adeline from these proofs of her goodness, resolved to lose no time in urging her to undergo herself the operation which she desired for Editha.[123]

Then, begging the mulatto to send for a surgeon directly, in spite of tears of the tawny boy, who thought it cruel to run the risk of spoiling miss Editha's pretty face, he took his leave, saying to himself, "What a heart has this Adeline! how capable of feeling affection! for no one can inspire it who is not able to feel it: and this creature is thrown away on a man undeserving her, it seems!"

On this intelligence he continued to muse till he arrived at Adeline's lodgings, to whom he communicated all that had passed; and from whom he learned, with great anxiety, that it was but too true that she had never had the small-pox; and that, therefore, she should probably show symptoms of the disease in a few days: consequently, as she considered it too late for her to be inoculated, she should do all that now remained to be done for her security, by low living and good air.

That same evening colonel Mordaunt returned to Savanna, in hopes of learning from her some further particulars respecting Adeline's husband; as he felt that his conscience would not be much hurt by inducing Adeline to leave the protection of a man who was unworthy of possessing her. Fortunately for his wishes,

---

[123] Immediate inoculation on exposure to smallpox could minimize the severity of the illness. Smallpox inoculation had been brought from Turkey to England early in the eigtheenth century by Lady Mary Wortley Montague (1689-1762), wife of the English ambassador. Although she was mistrusted, she had her own children vaccinated with the live vaccine used in Turkey.

he could not wish to hear more than Savanna wished to tell every thing relating to her adored lady: and colonel Mordaunt heard with generous indignation of the perfidious conduct of Berrendale; vowing, at the same time, that his time, his interest, and his fortune, should all be devoted to bring such a villain to justice, and to secure to the injured Editha her rightful inheritance.

The mulatto was in raptures:—she told colonel Mordaunt that he was a charming man, and infinitely handsomer than Berrendale, though she must own he was very good to look at; and she wished with all her soul that colonel Mordaunt was married to her lady; for then she believed she would have never known sorrow, but been as happy as the day was long.

Colonel Mordaunt could not hear this without a secret pang. "Had I followed," said he mentally, "the dictates of my heart when I saw Adeline at Bath, I might now, perhaps, instead of being a forlorn unattached being, have been a happy husband and father; and Adeline, instead of having been the mistress of one man, and the disowned wife of another, might have been happy and beloved, and as respectable in the eyes of the world as she is now in those of her grateful mulatto."

However, there was some hope left for him yet.—Adeline, he thought, was not a woman likely to be over-scrupulous in her ideas; and might very naturally think herself at liberty to accept the protection of a lover, when, from no fault of hers, she had lost that of her husband.

It is natural to suppose that, while elevated with these hopes, he did not fail to be very constant in his visits to Adeline; and that at length, more led by passion than policy, he abruptly, at the end of ten days, informed Adeline that he knew her situation, and that he trusted that she would allow him to hope that in due time his love, which had been proof against time, absence, and disdain, would meet with reward; and that, on his settling a handsome income on her and her child for their joint lives, she should allow him to endeavour to make her as happy as she, and she only, could make him.

To this proposal, which was in form of a letter, colonel Mordaunt did not receive an immediate answer; nor was it at first likely that he should ever receive an answer to it at all, as Adeline was at the moment of its arrival confined to her bed, according to her expectations, with the disease which she had been but too fearfully imbibing: while the half-distracted mulatto was forced to give up to others the care of the sickening Editha, to watch over the delirious and unconscious Adeline.

But the tawny boy's generous benefactress gave him leave to remain at Adeline's lodgings, in order to calm his fears for Editha, and assist in amusing and keeping her quiet; and if attention had any share in preserving the life and beauty of Editha, it was to the affectionate tawny boy that she owed them; and he was soon rewarded for all his care and anxiety by seeing his little charge able to play about as usual.

Colonel Mordaunt and the mulatto meanwhile did not obtain so speedy a termination to their anxieties; Adeline's recovery was for a long time a matter of doubt; and her weakness so great after the crisis of the disorder was past, that none ventured to pronounce her, even then, out of danger.

But at length she was in a great measure restored to health, and able to determine what line of conduct it was necessary for her to pursue.—To return an answer to colonel Mordaunt's proposals was certainly her first business; but as she felt that the situation in which he had once known her made his offer less affronting than it would have been under other circumstances, she resolved to speak to him on the subject with gentleness, not severity; especially as during her illness, to amuse the anxiety that had preyed upon him, he had taken every possible step to procure evidence of the marriage, and gave into Savanna's hands, the first day that he was permitted to see her, an attested certificate of it.

Chapter IV.

THE first question which Adeline asked on her recovery was, Whether any letter had come by the general post during her illness; and Savanna gave one to her immediately.

It was the letter so ardently desired; for the direction was in her mother's handwriting! and she opened it full of eager expectation, while her whole existence seemed to depend on the nature of its contents. What then must have been her agony on finding that the *enveloppe* contained nothing but her own letter returned! For some time she spoke not, she breathed not; while Savanna mixed with expressions of terror, at sight of her mistress's distress, execrations on the unnatural parent who had so cruelly occasioned it.

After a few day's incessant struggle to overcome the violence of her sorrow, Adeline recovered the shock, in appearance at least: yet to Savanna's self-congratulations she could not help answering (laying her hand on her heart), "The blow is here, Savanna, and the wound incurable."

Soon after she thought herself well enough to see colonel Mordaunt, and to thank him for the recent proof of his attention to her and her interest. But no obligation, however great, could shut the now vigilant eyes of Adeline to the impropriety of receiving further visits from him, or to the guilt of welcoming to her house a man who made open professions to her of illicit love.

She however thought it her duty to see him once more, in order to try to reconcile him to the necessity of the rule of conduct which she was going to lay down for herself; nor was she without hope that the yet recent traces of the disease, to which she had so nearly fallen a victim, would make her appearance so unpleasing to the eyes of her lover, that he would be very willing to absent himself from the house, for some time at least, and probably give up all thoughts of her.

But she did neither herself nor colonel Mordaunt justice.—She was formed to inspire a real and lasting passion—a passion that no external change could destroy—since it was founded on the unchanging qualities of the heart and mind: and colonel Mordaunt felt for her such an attachment in all its force. He had always admired the attractive person and winning graces of Adeline, and felt for her what he denominated love; but that rational though enthusiastic preference, which is deserving of the name of true love, he never felt till he had an opportunity to appreciate justly the real character of Adeline: still there were times when he felt almost gratified to reflect that she could not legally be his; for, whatever might have been the cause and excuse of her errors, she had erred, and the delicacy of his mind revolted at the idea of marrying the mistress of another.

But when he saw and heard Adeline this repugnance vanished; and he knew that, could he at those moments lead her to the altar, he should not have hesitated to bind himself to her for ever by the sacred ties which the early errors of her judgement had made her in his opinion almost unworthy to form.

At length a day was fixed for his interview with Adeline, and with a beating heart he entered the apartment; nor was his emotion diminished when he beheld not only the usual vestiges of her complaint, but symptoms of debility, and a death-like meagreness of aspect, which made him fear that though one malady was conquered, another, even more dangerous, remained. The idea overcame him; and he was forced to turn to the window to hide his emotion: and his manner was so indicative of ardent yet respectful attachment, that Adeline began to feel in spite of herself that her projected task was difficult of execution.

For some minutes neither of them spoke: Mordaunt held the hand which she gave him to his heart, kissed it as she withdrew it, and again turned away his head to conceal a starting tear; while Adeline was not sorry to have a few moments in which to recover herself, before she addressed him on the subject at that time nearest to the heart of both. At length she summoned resolution enough to say:—

"Much as I have been mortified and degraded, colonel Mordaunt, by the letter which I received from you, still I rejoice that I did receive it:—in the first place, I rejoice, because I look on all the sufferings and mortifications which I meet with as latent blessings, as expiations required of me in mercy by the Being whom I adore, for the sins of which I have been guilty; and, in the second place, because it gives me an opportunity of proving, incontrovertibly, my full conviction of the fallacy of my past opinions, and that I became a wife, after my idle declamations against marriage, from change of principle, on assurance of error, and not from interest, or necessity."

Here she paused, overcome with the effort which she had made; and colonel Mordaunt would have interrupted her, but, earnestly conjuring him to give her a patient hearing, she proceeded thus:—

"Had the change in my practice been the result of any thing but rational conviction, I should now, unfortunate as I have been in the choice of a husband, regret that ever I formed so foolish a tie, and perhaps be induced to enter into a less sacred connection, from an idea that that state which forced me to drag out existence in hopeless misery was contrary to reason, justice, and the benefit of society; and that, the sooner its ties were dissolved, the better it would be for individual happiness and for the world at large."

"And do you not think so?" cried colonel Mordaunt; "cannot your own individual experience convince you of it?"

"Far from it," replied Adeline; "and I bless God that it does not: for thence, and thence only, do I begin to be reconciled to myself. I have no doubt that there is a great deal of individual suffering in the marriage state, from contrariety of temper and other causes; but I believe that the mass of happiness and virtue is certainly increased by it. Individual suffering, therefore, is no more an argument for the abolition of marriage, than the accidental bursting of a musquet would be for the total abolition of fire-arms."

"But, surely, dear Mrs. Berrendale, you would wish divorce to be made easier than it is?"

"By no means," interrupted Adeline, understanding what he was going to say: "to BEAR and FORBEAR I believe to be the grand secret of happiness, and ought to be the great study of life: therefore, whatever would enable married persons to separate on the slightest quarrel or disgust, would make it so much the less necessary for us to learn this important lesson; a lesson so needful in order to perfect the human character, that I believe the difficulty of divorce to be one of the greatest blessings of society."

"What can have so completely changed your opinions on this subject?" replied colonel Mordaunt.

"Not my own experience," returned Adeline; "for the painful situations in which I have been placed, I might attribute, not to the *fallacy* of the system on which I have acted, but to those existing prejudices in society which I wish to see destroyed."

"Then, to what else is the change in your sentiments to be attributed?"

"To a more serious, unimpassioned, and unprejudiced view of the subject than I had before taken: at present I am not equal to expatiate on matters so important: however, some time or other, perhaps, I may make known to you my sentiments on them in a more ample manner: but I have, I trust, said enough to lead you to conclude, that though Mr. Berrendale's conduct to me has been atrocious, and that you are in many respects entitled to my gratitude and thanks, you and I must henceforward be strangers to each other."

Colonel Mordaunt, little expecting such a total overthrow to his hopes, was, on receiving it, choked with contending emotions; and his broken sentences and pale cheek were sufficiently expressive of the distress which he endured. But I shall not enter into a detail of all he urged in favour of his passion; nor the calm, dignified, and feeling manner in which Adeline replied. Suffice that, at last, from a sort of intuitive knowledge of the human heart, as it were, which persons of quick talents and sensibilities possess, however defective their experience, Adeline resolved to try to sooth the self-love which she had wounded, knowing that self-love is scarcely to be distinguished in its effects from love itself; and that the agony of disappointed passion is always greater when it is inflicted by the coldness or falsehood of the beloved object, than when it proceeds from parental prohibition, or the cruel separation enjoined by conscious poverty. She therefore told colonel Mordaunt that he was once very near being the first choice of her heart: when she first saw him, she said, his person, and manners, and attentions, had so strongly prepossessed her in his favour, that he himself, by ceasing to see and converse with her, could alone have saved her from the pain of the hopeless attachment.

"For God's sake, spare me," cried Mordaunt, "the contemplation of the happiness I might have enjoyed!"

"But you know you were not a marrying-man, as it is called; and forgive me if I say, that men who can on system suppress the best feelings of their nature, and prefer a course of libertine indulgence to a virtuous connection, at that time of life when they might become happy husbands and fathers, with the reasonable expectation of living to see their children grown up to manhood, and superintending their education themselves— such men, colonel Mordaunt, deserve, in the decline of life, to feel that regret and that self-condemnation which you this moment anticipate."

"True—too true!" replied the colonel; "but, for mercy's sake, torture me no more."

"I would not probe where I did not intend to make a cure," replied Adeline.

"A cure!—what mean you?"

"I meant to induce you, ere it be yet too late, to endeavour to form a virtuous attachment, and to unite yourself for life with some amiable young woman who will make you as happy as I would have endeavoured to make you, had it been my fortunate lot to be yours: for, believe me, colonel Mordaunt," and her voice faltered as she said it, "had *he*, whom I still continue to love with unabated tenderness, though years have elapsed since he was taken from me,—had he bequeathed me to you on his death-bed, the reluctance with which I went to the altar would have been more easily overcome."

Saying this, she suddenly left the room, leaving colonel Mordaunt surprised, gratified, and his mind struggling between hopes and fears; for Adeline was not conscious that she imparted hope as well as consolation by the method which she pursued; and though she sent Savanna to tell the colonel she could see him no more that evening, he departed in firm expectation that Adeline would not have resolution to forbid him to see her again.

In this, however, he was mistaken: Adeline had learnt the best of all lessons,—distrust of her own strength;—and she resolved to put it out of her power to receive visits which a regard to propriety forbade, and which might injure her reputation, if not her peace of mind. Therefore, as soon as colonel Mordaunt was gone, she summoned Savanna, and desired her to proceed to business.

"What!" cried the delighted mulatto, "are we going to prosecu massa?"

"No," replied Adeline, "we are going into the country: I am come to a determination to take no legal steps in this affair, but leave Mr. Berrendale to the reproaches of his own conscience."

"A fiddle's-end!" replied Savanna, "he have no conscience, or he no leave you: better get him hang; if you can den you marry de colonel."

"I had better hang the father of my child, had I, Savanna?"

"Oh! no, no, no, no,—me forget dat."

"But I do not, nor can I even bear to disgrace the father of Editha: therefore, trusting that I can dispose of her, and secure her interest better than by forcing her father to do her justice, and bastardize the poor innocent whom his wife will soon bring into the world, I am going to bury myself in retirement, and live the short remainder of my days unknowing and unknown."

CHAPTER V.

SAVANNA was going to remonstrate, but the words "short remainder of my days" distressed her so much, that tears choked her words; and she obeyed in silence her mistress's orders to pack up, except when she indulged in a few exclamations against her lady's cruelty in going away without taking leave of colonel Mordaunt, who, sweet gentleman, would break his heart at her departure, especially as he was not to know whither she was going. A post-chaise was at the door the next morning at six o'clock; and as Adeline had not much luggage, having left the chief part of her furniture to be divided between the mistresses of her two lodgings, in return for their kind attention to her and her child, she took an affectionate leave of her landlady, and desired the post-boy to drive a mile on the road before him; and when he had done so, she ordered him to go on to Barnet; while the disappointed mulatto thanked God that the tawny boy was gone to Scotland with his protectress, as it prevented her having the mortification of leaving him behind her, as well as the colonel.— "Oh! had I had such a lover," cried she, (her eyes filling with tears,) "me never leave him, nor he me!" and for the first time she thought her angel-lady hard-hearted.

For some miles they proceeded in silence, for Adeline was too much engrossed to speak; and the little Editha, being fast asleep in the mulatto's arms, did not draw her mother out of the reverie into which she had fallen.

"And where now?" said the mulatto, when the chaise stopped.

"To the next stage on the high north road." And on they went again: nor did they stop, except for refreshments, till they had travelled thirty miles; when Adeline, worn out with fatigue, staid all night at the inn where the chaise stopped, and the next morning they resumed their journey, but not their silence. The mulatto could no longer restrain her curiosity; and she begged to know whither they were going, and why they were to be buried in the country?

Adeline, sighing deeply, answered, that they were going to live in Cumberland; and then sunk into silence again, as she could not give the mulatto her true reasons for the plan that she was pursuing without wounding her affectionate heart in a manner wholly incurable. The truth was, that Adeline supposed herself to be declining: she thought that she experienced those dreadful langours, those sensations of internal weakness, which, however veiled to the eye of the observer, speak in forcible language to the heart of the conscious sufferer. Indeed, Adeline had long struggled, but in vain, against feelings of a most ovewhelming nature; amongst which, remorse and horror, for having led by her example and precepts an innocent girl into a life of infamy, were the most painfully predominant: for, believing Mary Warner's assertion when she saw her at Mr. Langley's chambers, she looked upon that unhappy girl's guilt as the consequence of her own; and mourned, incessantly mourned, over the fatal errors of her early judgement, which had made her, though an idolater of virtue, a practical assistant to the cause of vice. When Adeline imagined the term of her existence to be drawing nigh, her mother, her obdurate but still dear mother, regained her wonted ascendancy over her affections; and to her, the approach of death seemed fraught with satisfaction. For that parent, so long, so repeatedly deaf to her prayers, and to the detail of those sufferings which she had made one of the conditions of her forgiveness, had promised to see and forgive her on her *death-bed*; and her heart yearned, fondly yearned, for the moment when she should be pressed to the bosom of a relenting parent.

To Cumberland, therefore, she was resolved to hasten, and into the very neighbourhood of Mrs. Mowbray; while, as the chaise wheeled them along to the place of their destination, even the prattle of her child could not always withdraw her from the abstraction into which she was plunged, as the scenes of her early years thronged upon her memory, and with them the recollection of those proofs of a mother's fondness, for a renewal of which, even in the society of Glenmurray, she had constantly and despondingly sighed.

As they approached Penrith, her emotions redoubled, and she involuntarily exclaimed— "Cruel, but still dear, mother, you little think your child is so near!"

"Heaven save me!" cried Savanna; "are we to go and be near dat woman?"

"Yes," replied Adeline. "Did she not say she would forgive me on my death-bed?"

"But you not there yet, dear mistress," sobbed Savanna; "you not there of long years!"

"Savanna," returned Adeline, "I should die contented to purchase my mother's blessing and forgiveness."

Savanna, speechless with contending emotions, could not express by words the feelings of mixed sorrow and indignation which overwhelmed her; but she replied by putting Editha in Adeline's arms; then articulating with effort, "Look there!" she sobbed aloud.

"I understand you," said Adeline, kissing away the tears gathering in Editha's eyes, at sight of Savanna's distress: "but perhaps I think my death would be of more service to my child than my life."

"And to me too, I suppose," replied Savanna reproachfully. "Well,—me go to Scotland; for no one love me but the tawny boy."

"You first will stay and close my eyes, I hope!" observed Adeline mournfully.

In a moment Savanna's resentment vanished. "Me will live and die vid you," she replied, her tears redoubling, while Adeline again sunk into thoughtful silence.

As soon as they reached Penrith, Adeline inquired for lodgings out of the town, on that side nearest to her mother's abode; and was so fortunate, as she esteemed herself, to procure two apartments at a small house within two miles of Mrs. Mowbray's.

"Then I breathe once more the same air with my mother!" exclaimed Adeline as she took possession of her lodging. "Savanna, methinks I breathe freer already!"

"Me more choked," replied the mulatto, and turned sullenly away.

"Nay, I—I feel so much better, that to-morrow I will—I will take a walk," said Adeline hesitatingly.

"And where?" asked Savanna eagerly.

"Oh, to-night I shall only walk to bed," replied Adeline smiling, and with unusual cheerfulness she retired to rest.

The next morning she arose early; and being informed that a stile near a peasant's cottage commanded a view of Mrs. Mowbray's house, she hired a man and cart to convey her to the bottom of the hill, and with Editha by her side, she set out to indulge her feelings by gazing on the house which contained her mother.

When they alighted, Editha gaily endeavoured to climb the hill, and urged her mother to follow her; but Adeline, rendered weak by illness and breathless by emotion, felt the ascent so difficult, that no motive less powerful than the one which actuated her could have enabled her to reach the summit.

At length, however, she did reach it:—and the lawn before Mrs. Mowbray's white house, her hay-fields, and the running stream at the bottom of it, burst in all their beauty on her view.— "And this is my mother's dwelling!" exclaimed Adeline; "and there was I born: and near here— " shall I die, she would have added but her voice failed her.

"Oh! what a pretty house and garden!" cried Editha in the unformed accents of childhood;— "how I should like to live there!"

This artless remark awakened a thousand mixed and overpowering feelings in the bosom of Adeline; and, after a pause of strong emotion, she exclaimed, catching the little prattler to her heart— "You *shall* live there my child!—yes, yes, you *shall* live there!"

"But when?" resumed Editha.

"When I am in my grave," answered Adeline.

"And when shall you be there?" replied the unconscious child, fondly caressing her: "pray, mamma—pray be there soon!"

Adeline turned away, unable to answer her.

"Look—look, mamma!" resumed Editha: "there are ladies.— Oh! do let us go there now!—why can't we?"

"Would to God we could!" replied Adeline; as in one of the ladies she recognized Mrs. Mowbray, and stood gazing on her till her eyes ached again: but what she felt on seeing her she will herself describe in the succeeding pages; and I shall only add, that, as soon as Mrs. Mowbray returned into the house, Adeline, wrapped in a long and mournful reverie, returned, full of a new plan, to her lodgings.

There is no love so disinterested as parental love; and Adeline had all the keen sensibilities of a parent. To make, therefore, "assurance doubly sure" that Mrs. Mowbray should receive and should love her orphan when she was no more, she resolved to give up the gratification to which she had looked forward, the hope, before she died, of obtaining her forgiveness—that she might not weaken, by directing any part of them to herself, those feelings of remorse, fruitless tenderness, and useless regret in her mother's bosom, which she wished should be concentrated in her child.

"No," said Adeline to herself, "I am sure that she will not refuse to receive my orphan to her love and protection when I am no more, and am become alike insensible of reproaches and of blessings; and I think that she will love my child the more tenderly, because to me she will be unable to express the compunction which, sooner or later, she will feel from the recollection of her conduct towards me: therefore, I will make no demands on her love for myself; but, in a letter to be given her after my decease, bequeath my orphan to her care;"—and with this determination she returned from her ride.

"Have you see her?" said Savanna, running out to meet her.

'Yes—but not spoken to her; nor shall I see her again."

"What—I suppose she see you, and not speak?"

"Oh, no; she did not see me, nor shall I urge her to see me: my plans are altered," replied Adeline.

"And we go back to town and colonel Mordaunt?"

"No," resumed Adeline, sighing deeply, and preparing to write to Mrs. Mowbray.

But it is necessary that we should for a short time go back to Berrendale, and relate that, while Adeline and Editha were confined with the small-pox, Mr. Drury received a summons from his employer in Jamaica to go over thither, to be intrusted with some particular business: in consequence of this he resolved to call again on Adeline, and inquire whether she still persisted in styling herself Mrs. Berrendale; as he concluded that Berrendale would be very glad of all the information relative to her and her child which he could possibly procure, whether his curiosity on the subject proceeded from fear or love.

It so happened, that as soon as Editha, as well as her mother, was in the height of the disorder, Mr. Drury called; and finding that they were both very bad, he thought that his friend Berrendale was likely to get rid of both his incumbrances at once; and being eager to communicate good news to a man whose influence in the island might be of benefit to him, he every day called to inquire concerning their health.

The second floor in the house where Adeline lodged was then occupied by a young woman in indigent circumstances, who, as well as her child, had sickened with the distemper the very day that Editha was inoculated: and when Drury, just as he was setting off for Portsmouth, ran to gain the latest intelligence of the invalids, a char-woman, who attended to the door, not being acquainted with the name of the poor young woman and her little girl, concluding that Mr. Drury, by Mrs. Berrendale and miss who were ill with the small-pox, meant them, replied to his inquiries,— "Ah, poor things! it is all over with them, they died last night."

On which, not staying for any further intelligence, Drury set off for Portsmouth, and arrived at Jamaica just as Berrendale was going to remit to Adeline a draft for a hundred pounds. For Adeline, and the injury which he had done her, had been for some days constantly present to his thoughts. He had been ill; and as indigestion, the cause of his complaints, is apt to occasion disturbed dreams, he had in his dreams been haunted by the image of Glenmurray, who, with a threatening aspect, had reproached him with cruelty and base ingratitude to him, in deserting in such a manner the wife whom he had bequeathed to him.

The constant recurrence of these dreams had depressed his spirits and excited his remorse so much, that he could calm his feelings in no other way than by writing a kind letter to Adeline, and inclosing her a draft on his banker. This letter was on the point of being sent when Drury arrived, and, with very little ceremony, informed him that Adeline was dead.

"Dead!" exclaimed Berrendale, falling almost senseless on

his couch:— "Dead!—Oh! for God's sake, tell me of what she died!—Surely, surely, she— " Here his voice failed him.

Drury coolly replied, that she and her child both died of the small-pox.

"But *when*? my dear fellow!—when? Say that they died nine months ago (that was previous to his marriage), and you make me your friend for life!"

Drury, so *bribed*, would have said *any thing*; and, with all the coolness possible, he replied, "Then be my friend for life:— they died rather better than nine months ago."

Berrandale, being then convinced that bigamy was not likely to be proved against him, soon forgot, in the joy which this thought occasioned him, remorse for his conduct to Adeline, and regret for her early fate: besides, he concluded that he saved 100£ by the means; for he knew not that the delicate mind of Adeline would have scorned to owe pecuniary obligations to the husband who had basely and unwarrantably deserted her.

But he was soon undeceived on this subject, by a letter which colonel Mordaunt wrote in confidence to a friend in Jamaica, begging him to inquire concerning Mr. Berrendale's second marriage; and to inform him privately that his injured wife had zealous and powerful friends in England, who were continually urging her to prosecute him for bigamy.

This intelligence had a fatal effect on the health of Berrendale; for though the violent temper and overbearing disposition of his second wife had often made him regret the gentle and compliant Adeline, and a separation from her, consequently, would be a blessing, still he feared to encounter the disgrace of a prosecution, and still more the anger of his West Indian wife; who, it was not improbable, might even attack his life in the first moment of ungoverned passion.

And to these fears he soon fell a sacrifice: for a frame debilitated by intemperance could not support the assaults made on it by the continued apprehensions which colonel Mordaunt's friend had excited in him; and he died in that gentleman's presence, whom in his last moments he had summoned to his apartment to witness a will, by which he owned Adeline Mowbray to be his lawful wife, and left Editha, his acknowledged and only heir, a very considerable fortune.

But this circumstance, an account of which, with the will, was transmitted to colonel Mordaunt, did not take place till long after Adeline took up her abode in Cumberland.

Chapter VI.

But to return to colonel Mordaunt. Though Adeline had said that he must discontinue his visits, he resolved to disobey her; and the next morning, as soon as he thought she had breakfasted, he repaired to her lodgings; where he heard, with mixed sorrow and indignation, that she had set off in a post-chaise at six o'clock, and was gone no one knew whither.

"But, surely she has left some note or message for me!" exclaimed colonel Mordaunt.

"Neither the one nor the other," was the answer; and he returned home in no very enviable state of mind.

Various, indeed, and contradictory were his feelings: yet still affection was uppermost; and he could not but respect in Adeline the conduct which drove him to despair. Nor was self-love backward to suggest to him, that had not Adeline felt his presence and attentions to be dangerous, she could not so suddenly have withdrawn from them; and this idea was the only one on which he could at all bear to dwell: for, when he reflected that day after day might pass without his either seeing or hearing from her, existence seemed to become suddenly a burthen, and he wandered from place to place with joyless and unceasing restlessness.

At one time he resolved to pursue her; but the next, piqued at not having received from her even a note of farewell, he determined to endeavour to forget her: and this was certainly the wiser plan of the two: but the succeeding moment he determined to let a week pass, in hopes of receiving a letter from her, and, in case he did not, to set off in search of her, being assured of succeeding in his search, because the singularity of Savanna's appearance, and the traces of the small-pox visible in the face of Adeline, made them liable to be observed, and easy for him to describe.

But before the week elapsed, from agitation of mind, and from having exposed himself unnecessarily to cold, by lying on damp grass at midnight, after having heated himself by immoderate walking, colonel Mordaunt became ill of a fever; and when, after a confinement of several weeks, he was restored to health, he despaired of being able to learn tidings of the fugitives; and disappointed with dejection, he sought in the gayest scenes of the metropolis and its environs to drown the remembrances, from which in solitude he had vainly endeavoured to fly. At this time a faded but attractive woman of quality, with whom he had formerly been intimate, returned from abroad, and, meeting colonel Mordaunt at the house of mutual friend, endeavoured to revive in him his former attachment: but it was a difficult task for a woman, who, though capable of charming the senses, had never been able to touch the heart, to excite an attachment in a man already sentimentally devoted to another.

Her advances, however, flattered colonel Mordaunt, and her society amused him, till, at length, their intimacy was renewed on its former footing: but soon disgusted with an intercourse in which the heart had no share, tired of his mistress, and displeased with himself, he took an abrupt leave of her, and, throwing himself into his post-chaise, retired to the seat of a relation in Herefordshire.

Near this gentleman's house lived Mr. Maynard and his two sisters, who had taken up their abode there immediately on their return from Portugal. Major Douglas, his wife, and Emma Douglas, were then on a visit to them. Mordaunt had known major Douglas in early life; and as soon as he found that he was in the neighbourhood, he rode over to renew his acquaintance with him; and received so cordial a welcome, not only from the major, but the master of the house and his sisters, that he was strongly induced to repeat his visits, and not a day passed in which he was not, during some part of it, a guest at Mr. Maynard's.

Mrs. Wallington and miss Maynard, indeed, received him with such pointed marks of distinction and preference, as to make it visible to every observer that it was not as a friend only they were desirous of considering colonel Mordaunt; while, by spiteful looks and acrimonious remarks directed to each other, the sisters expressed the jealousy which rankled in their hearts, whenever he seemed by design or inadvertency to make one of them a particular object of his attention.

Of Emma Douglas's chance for his favour, they were not at all fearful:—they thought her too plain, and too unattractive, to be capable of rivalling them; especially in the favour of an officer, a man of fashion; and therefore they beheld without emotion the attention which colonel Mordaunt paid to her whenever she spoke, and the deference which he evidently felt for her opinion, as her remarks on whatever subject she conversed were formed always to interest, and often to instruct.

One evening, while major Douglas was amusing himself in looking over some magazines which had lately been bound up together, and had not yet been deposited in Mr. Maynard's library, he suddenly started, laid down the book, and turning to the window, with an exclamation of— "Poor fellow!"—passed his hand across his eyes, as if meaning to disperse an involuntary tear.

"What makes you exclaim 'Poor fellow?'" asked his lovely wife: "have you met with an affecting story in those magazines?"

"No, Louisa," replied he, "but I met in the obituary with a confirmation of the death of an old friend, which I suspected must have happened by this time, though I never knew it before; I see by this magazine that poor Glenmurray died a few months after we saw him at Perpignan."

"Poor fellow!" exclaimed Mrs. Douglas.

"I wish I knew what is become of his interesting companion, miss Mowbray," said Emma Douglas.

"I wish I did too," secretly sighed colonel Mordaunt: but his heart palpitated so violently at this unexpected mention of the woman for whom he still pined in secret, that he had not resolution to say that he knew her.

"Become of her!" cried miss Maynard sneeringly: "you need not *wonder,* I think, what her fate is: no doubt Mr. Glenmurray's *interesting companion* has not lost her companionable qualities, and is a companion still."

"Yes," observed Mrs. Wallington; "or, rather, I dare say that angel of purity is gone upon the town."

It was the dark hour, else colonel Mordaunt's agitation, on hearing these gross and unjust remarks, must have betrayed his secret to every eye; while indignation now impeded his utterance as much as confusion had done before.

"Surely, surely," cried the kind and candid Emma Douglas, "I must grossly have mistaken miss Mowbray's character, if she was capable of the conduct which you attribute to her!"

"My dear creature!" replied Mrs. Wallington, "how should you know any thing of her character, when it was gone long before you knew her?—*Character,* indeed! you remind me of my brother...Mr. Davenport," continued she to a gentleman present, "did you ever hear the story of my brother and an angel of purity whom he met with abroad?"

"No—never."

"Be quiet," said Maynard; "I will not be laughed at."

However, Mrs. Wallington and miss Maynard, who had not yet forgiven the deep impression which Adeline's graces had made on their brother, insisted on telling the story; to which colonel Mordaunt listened with eager and anxious curiosity. It received all the embellishments which female malice could give it; and if it amused any one, certainly that person was neither Mordaunt, nor Emma Douglas, nor her gentle sister.

"But how fortunate it was," added miss Maynard, "that we were not with my brother! as we should unavoidably have walked and talked with this angel."

Mordaunt longed to say, "I think the good fortune was all on miss Mowbray's side."

But Adeline and her cause were in good hands: Emma Douglas stood forth as her champion.— "We feel very differently on that subject," she replied. "I shall ever regret, not that I saw and conversed with miss Mowbray, but that I did not see and converse with her again and again."

At this moment Emma was standing by colonel Mordaunt, who involuntarily caught her hand and pressed it eagerly; but tried to disguise his motive by suddenly seating her in a chair behind her, saying, "You had better sit down; I am sure you must be tired with standing so long."

"No; really, Emma," cried major Douglas, "you go too far there; though to be sure, if by seeing and conversing with miss Mowbray you could have convinced her of her errors, I should not have objected to your seeing her once more or so."

"Surely," said Mrs. Douglas timidly, "we ought, my love, to have repeated our visits till we had made a convert of her."

"A *convert* of her!" exclaimed Mr. Maynard's sisters, "a convert of a kept mistress!" bursting into a violent laugh, which had a most painful effect on the irritable nerves of colonel Mordaunt, whose tongue, parched with emotion, cleaved to the roof of his mouth whenever he attempted to speak.

"Pray, to what other circumstance, yet untold, do you allude?" said Mr. Davenport.

"Oh, we too had a rencontre with the philosopher and his charming friend," said major Douglas, "and—but, Emma, do you tell the story.—'Sdeath!—Poor fellow!—Well, but we parted good friends," added the kind-hearted Caledonian,[124] dispersing a tear; while Emma, in simple but impressive language, related all that passed at Perpignan between themselves, Adeline, and Glenmurray; and concluded with saying, that, "from the almost idolatrous respect with which Glenmurray spoke and apparently thought of Adeline, and from the account of her conduct and its motives, which he so fully detailed, she was convinced that, so far from being influenced by depravity in connecting herself with Glenmurray, Adeline was the victim of a romantic, absurd, and false conception of virtue; and she should have thought it her

[124] I.e., one from Caledonia, a Scot.

duty to have endeavoured, assisted by her sister, to have prevailed on her to renounce her opinions, and, by becoming the wife of Glenmurray, to restore to the society of her own sex, a woman formed to be its ornament and its example. Poor thing!" she added in a faltering voice, "would that I knew her fate!"

"I can guess it, I tell you," said Mrs. Wallington.

"We had better drop the subject, madam," replied Emma Douglas indignantly, "as it is one that we shall never agree upon. If I supposed miss Mowbray happy, I should feel for her, and feel interest sufficient in her fate to make me combat your prejudices concerning her; but now that she is perhaps afflicted, poor, friendless, and scorned, though unjustly, by every 'virtuous she that knows her story,'[125] I cannot command my feelings when she is named with sarcastic disrespect, nor can I bear to hear an unhappy woman supposed to be plunged in the lowest depths of vice, whom I, on the contrary, believe to be at this moment atoning for the error of her judgement by a life of lonely penitence, or sunk perhaps already in the grave, the victim of a broken heart."

Colonel Mordaunt, affected and delighted, hung on Emma Douglas's words with breathless attention, resolving when she had ended her narration to begin his, and clear Adeline from the calumnies of Mrs. Wallington and miss Maynard; but after articulating with some difficulty— "Ladies,—I—miss Douglas,—I— " he found that his feelings would not allow him to proceed: therefore, suddenly raising Emma's hand to his lips, he imprinted on it a kiss, at once fervent and respectful, and, making a hasty bow, ran out of the house.

Every one was astonished; but none so much as Emma Douglas.

"Why, Emma!" cried the major, "who should have thought it? I verily believe you have turned Mordaunt's head;—I protest that he kissed your hand:—I suppose he will be here tomorrow, making proposals in form."

---

[125] Not found.

"I wish he may!" exclaimed Mrs. Douglas.

"It is not very likely, I think," cried miss Maynard.

Mrs. Wallington said nothing; but she fanned herself violently.

"How do you know that?" said Maynard. "He kissed your hand very tenderly—did he not, miss Douglas? and took advantage of the dark hour: that looks very lover-like."

Emma Douglas, who, in spite of her reason, was both embarrassed and flattered by colonel Mordaunt's unexpected mode of taking leave, said not a word; but Mrs. Wallington, in a voice hoarse with angry emotion, cried:

"It was very free in him, I think, and very unlike colonel Mordaunt; for he was not a sort of man to take liberties but where he met with encouragement."

"Then I am sure he would be free with *you*, sister, sometimes," sarcastically observed miss Maynard.

"Nay, with both of you, I think," replied Maynard, who had not forgiven the laugh at his expense which they had tried to excite; on which an angry dialogue took place between the brother and sisters: and the Douglases, disgusted and provoked, retired to their apartment.

"There was something very strange and uncommon," said Mrs. Douglas, detaining Emma in her dressing-room, "in colonel Mordaunt's behaviour—Do you not think so, Emma?—If it should have any meaning!"

"Meaning!" cried the major: "what meaning should it have? Why, my dear, do you think Mordaunt never kissed a woman's hand before?"

"But it was so *particular.*—Well, Emma, if it should lead to consequences!"

"Consequences!" cried the major: "my dear girl, what can you mean?"

"Why, if he should *really love* our Emma?"

"Why then I hope our Emma will really love him.—What say you, Emma?"

"I say?—I— " she replied: "really I never thought it possible that colonel Mordaunt should have any thoughts of me, nor do I now;—but it is very strange that he should kiss my hand!"

The major could not help laughing at the *naïveté* of this reply, and in a mutual whisper they agreed how much they wished to see their sister so happily disposed of: while Emma paced up and down her own apartment some time before she undressed herself; and after seeming to convince herself, by recollecting all colonel Mordaunt's conduct towards her, that he could not possibly *mean* any thing by his unusual adieu, she went to sleep, exclaiming, "But it is very strange that he should kiss my hand!"

Chapter VII.

THE next morning explained the mystery: for breakfast was scarcely over, when colonel Mordaunt appeared; and his presence occasioned a blush, from different causes, on the cheeks of all the ladies, and a smile on the countenances of both the gentlemen.

"You left us very abruptly last night," said major Douglas.

"I did so," replied Mordaunt with a sort of grave smile.

"Were you taken ill?" asked Maynard.

"I—I was not quite easy," answered he: "but, miss Douglas, may I request the honour of seeing you alone for a few minutes?"

Again the ladies blushed, and the gentlemen smiled. But Emma's weakness had been temporary; she had convinced herself that colonel Mordaunt's action had been nothing more than a tribute to what he fancied her generous defence of an unfortunate women, and with an air of unembarrassed dignity she gave him her hand to lead her into an adjoining apartment.

"This is very good of you," cried colonel Mordaunt: "but you are all goodness!—My dear miss Douglas, had I not gone away as I did last night, I believe I should have fallen down and worshipped you, or committed some other extravagance."

"Indeed!—What could I say to excite such enthusiasm?" replied Emma, deeply blushing.

"What!—Oh, miss Douglas!"—Then after a few more ohs, and other exclamations, he related to her the whole progress of his acquaintance with and attachment to Adeline, adding as he concluded, "Now then judge what feelings you must have excited in my bosom:—yes, miss Douglas, I reverenced you before for your own sake, I now adore you for that of my lost Adeline."

"So!" thought Emma, "the kiss of the hand is explained,"—and she sighed as she thought it; nor did she much like the word *reverenced*: but she had ample amends for her mortification by what followed.

"Really," cried colonel Mordaunt, gazing very earnestly at her, "I do not mean to flatter you, but there is something in your countenance that reminds me very strongly of Adeline."

"Is it possible?" said Emma, her cheeks glowing and her eyes sparkling as she spoke: "you may not mean to flatter me, but I assure you I am flattered; for I never saw any woman whom in appearance I so much wished to resemble."

"You do resemble her indeed," cried colonel Mordaunt, "and the likeness grows stronger and stronger."

Emma blushed deeper and deeper.

"But come," exclaimed he, "let us go; and I will—no, *you* shall—relate to the party in the next room what I have been telling you, for I long to shame those d— "

"Fye!" said Emma smiling, and holding up her hand as if to stop the coming word. And she did stop it; for colonel Mordaunt conveyed the reproving hand to his lips; and Emma said to herself, as she half-frowning withdrew it, "I am glad my brother was not present."

Their return to the breakfast-room was welcome to every one, from different causes, as colonel Mordaunt's motives for requesting a tête-à-tête had given rise to various conjectures. But all conjecture was soon lost in certainty: for Emma Douglas, with more than usual animation of voice and countenance, related what colonel Mordaunt had authorised her to relate; and the envious sisters heard, with increased resentment, that Adeline, were she unmarried, would be the choice of the man whose affections they were eagerly endeavouring to captivate.

"You can't think," said colonel Mordaunt when Emma had

concluded, leaving him charmed with the manner in which she had told his story, and with the generous triumph which sparkled in her eyes at being able to exhibit Adeline's character in so favourable a point of view, "you can't think how much miss Douglas reminds me of Mrs. Berrendale!"

"Lord!" said miss Maynard with a toss of the head, "my brother told us that she was handsome!"

"And so she is," replied the colonel, provoked at this brutal speech: "she has one of the finest countenances that I ever saw,—a countenance never distorted by those feelings of envy, and expressions of spite, which so often disfigure some women,—converting even a beauty into a fiend; and in this respect no one will doubt that miss Douglas resembles her:

'What's female beauty—but an air divine,
Thro' which the mind's all gentle graces shine?'[126]

says one of our first poets: therefore, in Dr. Young's opinion, madam" continued Mordaunt, turning to Emma, "you would have been a perfect beauty."

This speech, so truly gratifying to the amiable girl to whom it was addressed, was a dagger in the heart of both the sisters. Nor was Emma's pleasure unalloyed by pain; for she feared that Mordaunt's attentions might become dangerous to her peace of mind, as she could not disguise to herself, that his visits at Mr. Maynard's had been the chief cause of her reluctance to return to Scotland whenever their journey home was mentioned. For, always humble in her ideas of her own charms, Emma Douglas could not believe that Mordaunt would ever entertain any feeling for her at all resembling love, except when he fancied that she looked like Adeline.

But however unlikely it seemed that Mordaunt should become attached to her, and however resolved she was to avoid his society, certain it is that he soon found he could be happy in the society of no other woman, since to no other could he talk

---

[126] Edward Young, "Satire VI. On Women," lines 151-4. Cited also in *Emma Courtney*, see p. 137.

on the subject nearest his heart; and Emma, though blaming herself daily for her temerity, could not refuse to receive Mordaunt's visits: and her patient attentions to his conversation, of which Adeline was commonly the theme, seemed to have a salutary effect on his wounded feelings.

But the time for their departure arrived, much to the joy of Mrs. Wallington and her sister, who hoped when Emma was gone to have a chance of being noticed by Mordaunt.

What then must have been their confusion and disappointment, when colonel Mordaunt begged to be allowed to attend the Douglases on their journey home, as he had never seen the Highlands, and wished to see them in such good company! Major Douglas and his charming wife gave a glad consent to this proposal: but Emma Douglas heard it with more alarm than pleasure; for, though her heart rejoiced at it, her reason condemned it.

A few days, however, convinced her apprehensive delicacy, that, if she loved colonel Mordaunt, it was not without hope of a return.

Colonel Mordaunt declared that every day seemed to increase her resemblance to Adeline in expression and manner; and in conduct his reason told him that she was her superior; nor could he for a moment hesitate to prefer as a wife, Emma Douglas who had never erred, to Adeline who had.

Colonel Mordaunt felt, to borrow the words of a celebrated female writer,[127] that "though it is possible to love and esteem a woman who has expiated the faults of her youth by a sincere repentance; and though before God and man her errors may be obliterated; still there exists one being in whose eyes she can never hope to efface them, and that is her lover or her husband." He felt that no man of acute sensibility can be happy with a

---

[127] Madam de Staël, *Recueil de Morceaux Dé-tachés*, page 208. [AAO]. Mme de Staël (1766-1817), born Germaine Necker, was the daughter of an important architect of the French Revolution and herself a well-educated and reform-minded literati. The *Recueil* was translated as *Collection of Detached Pieces* in 1796.

woman whose recollections are not pure: she must necessarily be jealous of the opinion which he entertains of her; and he must be often afraid of speaking, lest he utter a sentiment that may wound and mortify her. Besides, he was, on just grounds, more desirous of marrying a woman whom he "admired, than one whom he forgave;"[128] and therefore, while he addressed Emma, he no longer regretted Adeline.

In short, he at length ceased to talk of Emma's resemblance to Adeline, but seemed to admire her wholly for her own sake; and having avowed his passion, and been assured of Emma's in return, by major Douglas, he came back to England in the ensuing autumn, the happy husband of one of the best of women.

Chapter VIII.

We left Adeline preparing to address Mrs. Mowbray and recommend her child to her protection:—but being deeply impressed with the importance of the task which she was about to undertake, she timidly put it off from day to day; and having convinced herself that it was her duty to endeavour to excite her husband to repentance, and make him acknowledge Editha as his legitimate child, she determined to write to him before she addressed her mother, and also to bid a last farewell to colonel Mordaunt, whose respectful attachment had soothed some of the pangs which consciousness of her past follies had inflicted, and whose active friendship deserved her warmest acknowledgements.—Little did she think the fatal effect which one instance of his friendly zeal in her cause had had on Berrendale; unconscious was she that the husband, whose neglect she believed to be intentional, great as were his crimes against her, was not guilty of the additional crime of suffering her to pine in poverty without making a single inquiry concerning her, but was convinced that both she and her child were no longer in existence.

In her letter to him, she conjured him by the love which he

128 Not found.

always bore Glenmurray, by the love he *once* bore her, and by the remorse which he would sooner or later feel for his conduct towards her and her child, to acknowledge Editha to be his lawful heir, but to suffer her to remain under that protection of which she meant to bequeath her; and on these conditions she left him her blessing, and her pardon.

The letter to colonel Mordaunt was long, and perhaps diffuse: but Adeline was jealous of his esteem, though regardless of his love; and as he had known her while acting under the influence of a fatal error of opinion, she wished to show him that on conviction she had abandoned her former way of thinking, and was candid enough to own that she had been wrong.

"You, no doubt," she said, "are well acquainted with the arguments urged by different writers in favour of marriage. I shall therefore only mention the argument which carried at length full conviction to *my* mind, and conquered even my deep and heartfelt reverence for the opinions of one who long was, and ever will be, the dearest object of my love and regret. But *he*, had he lived, would I am sure have altered his sentiments; and had he been a parent, the argument I allude to, as it is founded on a consideration of the interest of children, would have found its way to his reason, through his affections.

"It is evident that on the education given to children must depend the welfare of the community; and, consequently, that whatever is likely to induce parents to neglect the education of their children must be *hurtful* to the welfare of the community. It is also certain, that though the agency of the *passions* be necessary to the existence of all society, it is on the cultivation and influence of the *affections* that the happiness and improvement of social life depend.

"Hence it follows that marriage must be more beneficial to society in its consequences, than connections capable of being dissolved at pleasure; because it has a tendency to call forth and exercise the affections, and control the passions.—It has been said, that, were we free to dissolve at will a connection formed by love, we should not wish to do it, as constancy is natural to us, and there is in all of us a tendency to form an exclusive attachment. But though I believe, from my own experience, that the few are capable of unforced constancy, and could love for life one dear and honoured object, still I believe that the many are given to the love of change;—that, in men especially, a new object can excite new passion; and, judging from the increasing depravity of both sexes, in spite of existing laws, and in defiance of shame,—I am convinced, that if the ties of marriage were dissolved, or it were no longer to be judged infamous to act in contempt of them, unbridled licentiousness would soon be in general practice.—What then, in such a state of society, would be the fate of the children born in it?—What would their education be?—Parents continually engrossed in the enervating but delightful egotism of a new and happy love, lost in selfish indulgence, the passions awake, but the affections slumbering, and the sacred ties of parental feeling not having time nor opportunity to fasten on the heart,—their offspring would either die the victims of neglect, and the very existence of the human race be threatened; or, without morals or instruction, they would grow up to scourge the world by their vices, till the whole fabric of civilized society was gradually destroyed.

"On this ground, therefore, this strong ground, I venture to build my present opinion, that marriage is a wise and ought to be a sacred institution; and I bitterly regret the hour when, with the hasty and immature judgement of eighteen, and with a degree of presumption scarcely pardonable at any time of life, I dared to think and act contrary to this opinion and the reverend experience of ages, and became in the eyes of the world an example of vice, when I believed myself the champion of virtue."

She then went on to express the following sentiments. "You will think, perhaps, that I ought to struggle against the weakness which is hurrying me to the grave, and live for the sake of my child.—Alas! it is for her sake that I most wish to die.

"There are two ways in which a mother can be of use to her daughter: the one is by instilling into her mind virtuous principles, and by setting her a virtuous example: the other is, by being to her in her own person an awful warning,—a melancholy proof of the dangers which attend a deviation from the path of virtue. But, oh! how jealous must a mother be of her child's esteem and veneration! and how could she bear to humble herself in the eyes of the beloved object, by avowing that she had committed crimes against society, however atoned for by penitence and sorrow! I can never, now, be a correct example for my Editha, nor could I endure to live to be a warning to her.— Nay, if I lived, I should be most probably a dangerous example to her; for I should be (on my death-bed I think I may be allowed the boast) respected and esteemed; while the society around me would forget my past errors, in the sincerity of my repentance.

"If then a strong temptation should assail my child, might she not yield to it from an idea that 'one false step may be retrieved,' and cite her mother as an example of this truth? while, unconscious of the many secret heart-aches of that repentant mother, unconscious of the sorrows and degradations she had experienced, she regarded nothing but the present respectability of her mother's life, and contented herself with hoping one day to resemble her.

"Believe me, that were it possible for me to choose between life and death, for my child's sake, the choice would be the latter. Now, when she shall see in my mournful and eventful history, written as it has been by me in moments of melancholy leisure, that all my sorrows were consequent on one presumptuous error of judgement in early youth, and shall see a long and minute detail of the secret agonies which I have endured,—those agonies wearing away my existence, and ultimately hurrying me to an untimely grave; she will learn that the woman who feels justly, yet has been led even into the practice of vice, however she may be forgiven by others, can never forgive herself; and though she may dare to lift an eye of hope to that Being who promises pardon on repentance, she will still recollect with anguish the fair and glorious course which she might have run; and that, instead of humbly imploring forbearance and forgiveness, she might have demanded universal respect and esteem.

"True it is, that I did not act in defiance of the world's opinion, from any depraved feelings, or vicious inclinations: but the world could not be expected to believe this, since motives are known only to our own hearts, and the great Searcher of hearts: therefore, as far as example goes, I was as great a stumbling block to others as if the life I led had been owing to the influence of lawless desires; and society was right in making, and in seeing, no distinction between me and any other woman living in an unsanctioned connection.

"But methinks I hear you say, that Editha might never be informed of my past errors. Alas! wretched must that woman be whose happiness and respectability depend on the secrecy of others! Besides, did I not think the concealment of crime in itself a crime, how could I know an hour of peace while I reflected that a moment's malice, or inadvertency, in one of Editha's companions might cause her to blush at her mother's disgrace?— that, while her young cheek was flushed perhaps with the artless triumphs of beauty, talent, and virtue, the parent who envied me, or the daughter who envied her, might suddenly convert her joy into anguish and mortification, by artfully informing her, with feigned pity for my sorrows and admiration of my penitence, that I had once been a *disgrace* to that family of which I was now the pride?—No—even if I were not for ever separated in this world from the only man whom I ever loved with passionate and well-founded affection, united for life to the object of my just aversion, and were I not conscious (horrible and overwhelming thought!) of having by my example led another into the path of sin,—still, I repeat it, for my child's sake I should wish to die, and should consider, not early death, but lengthened existence, as a curse."

So Adeline reasoned and felt in her moments of reflection: but the heart had sometimes dominion over her; and as she gazed on Editha, and thought that Mrs. Mowbray might be induced to receive her again to her favour, she wished even on any terms to have her life prolonged.

Chapter IX.

Having finished her letter to colonel Mordaunt and Berrendale, she again prepared to write to her mother; a few transient fears overcoming every now and then those hopes of success in her application, which, till she took up her pen, she had so warmly encouraged.

Alas! little did she know how erroneously for years she had judged of Mrs. Mowbray. Little did she suspect that her mother had long forgiven her; had pined after her; had sought, though in vain, to procure intelligence of her, and was then wearing away her existence in solitary woe, a prey to self-reproach, and to the corroding fear that her daughter, made desperate by her renunciation of her, had, on the death of Glenmurray, plunged into a life of shame, or sunk, broken-hearted, into the grave! for not one of Adeline's letters had ever reached Mrs. Mowbray; and the mother and the daughter had both been the victims of female treachery and jealousy.

Mrs. Mowbray, as soon as she had parted with Adeline for the last time, had dismissed all her old servants, the witnesses of her sorrows and disgrace, and retired to her estate in Cumberland,—an estate where Adeline had first seen the light, and where Mrs. Mowbray had first experienced the transports of a mother. This spot was therefore ill calculated to banish Adeline from her mother's thoughts, and to continue her exclusion from her affections. On the contrary, her image haunted Mrs. Mowbray:—whithersoever she went, she still saw her in an attitude of supplication; she still heard the plaintive accents of her voice;—and often did she exclaim, "My child, my child! wretch that I am! must I never, never see thee more!"

These ideas increased to so painful a degree, that, finding her solitude insupportable, she invited an orphan relation in narrow circumstances to take up her abode with her.

This young woman, whose ruling passion was avarice, and whose greatest talent was cunning, resolved to spare no pains to keep the situation which she had gained, even to the exclusion of Adeline, should Mrs. Mowbray be weak enough to receive her again. She therefore intercepted all the letters which were in or like Adeline's hand-writing; and having learnt to imitate Mrs. Mowbray's, she enclosed them in a blank cover to Adeline; who, thinking the direction was written in her mother's hand, desisted, as the artful girl expected she would do, from what appeared to her a hopeless application.

And she exulted in her contrivance;—when Mrs. Mowbray, on seeing in a magazine that Glenmurray was dead, (full a year after his decease,) bursting into a passion of tears, protested that she would instantly invite Adeline to her house.

"Yes," cried she, "I can do so without infringement of my oath.—She is disgraced in the eye of the world by her connection with Glenmurray, and she is wretched in love; nay, more so, perhaps, than I have been; and I can, I will invite her to lose the remembrance of her misfortunes in my love!"

Thus did her ardent wish to be reunited to Adeline deceive her conscience; for, by the phrase "wretched in love," she meant, forsaken by the object of her attachment,—and that Adeline had not been: therefore her oath remained in full force against her. But where could she seek Adeline?—Dr. Norberry could, perhaps, give her this information; and to him she resolved to write—though he had cast her from his acquaintance: "but her pride," as she said, "fell with her fortunes;" and she scrupled not to humble herself before the zealous friend of her daughter. But this letter would never have reached him, had not her treacherous relation been ill at the time when it was written.

Dr. Norberry had recovered the illness of which Adeline supposed him to have died: but as her letter to him, to which she received no answer, alluded to the money transaction between her and Mrs. Norberry; and as she commented on the insulting expressions in Mrs. Norberry's note, that lady thought proper to suppress the second letter as well as the first; and when the doctor, on his recovery, earnestly demanded to know whether any intelligence had been received of miss Mowbray, Mrs. Norberry, with pretended reluctance, told him that she had written to him in great distress, while he was delirious, to borrow money; that she had sent her *ten pounds,* which Adeline had returned, reproaching her for her parsimony, and saying that she had found a friend who would not suffer her to want.

"But did you tell her that you thought me in great danger?"
"I did."

"Why, zounds, woman! did she not, after that, write to know how I was?"

"Never."

"Devil take me if I could have thought it of her!" answered the doctor who could not but believe this story for the sake of his own peace, as it was less destructive to his happiness to think Adeline in fault, than his wife or children guilty of profligate falsehood he therefore, with a deep sigh, begged Adeline's name might never be mentioned to him again; and though he secretly wished to hear of her welfare, he no longer made her the subject of conversation.

But Mrs. Mowbray's letter recalled her powerfully both to his memory and affections, while, with many a deep-drawn sigh, he regretted that he had no possible means of discovering where she was;—and with a heavy heart he wrote the following letter, which miss Woodville, Mrs. Mowbray's relation, having first contrived to open, and read it, ventured to give into her hands, as it contained no satisfactory information concerning Adeline.

"'I look on the separation of my mother and me in this world to be eternal,' said the poor dear lost Adeline to me, the last time we met. 'You do!' replied I: 'then, poor devil! how miserable will your mother be when her present resentment subsides!—Well, when that time comes, I may perhaps see her again,' added I, with a d——d queer something rising in my throat as I said it, and your poor girl blessed me for the kind attention.— (Pshaw! I have blotted the paper: at my years it is a shame to be so watery-eyed.) Well,—the time above mentioned is come—you are miserable, you are repentant—and you ask me to forget and forgive.—I do forget, I do forgive:

some time or other, too, I will tell you so in person; and were the lost Adeline to know that I did so, she would bless me for the act, as she did before for the intention. But, alas! where she is, what she is, I know not, and have not any means of knowing. To say the truth, her conduct to me and mine has been devilish *odd*, not to say *wrong*. But, poor thing! she is either dead or miserable, and I forgive her:—so I do you, as I said before, and the Lord give you all the consolation which you so greatly need!

Yours once more,
In true kindness of spirit,
JAMES NORBERRY."

This letter made Mrs. Mowbray's wounds bleed afresh, at the same time that it destroyed all her expectations of finding Adeline; and the only hope that remained to cheer her was, that she might perhaps, if yet alive, write sooner or later, to implore forgiveness. But month after month elapsed, and no tidings of Adeline reached her despairing mother.

She then put an advertisement in the paper, so worded that Adeline, had she seen it, must have known to whom it alluded; but it never met her eyes, and Mrs. Mowbray gave herself up to almost absolute despair; when accident introduced her to a new acquaintance, whose example taught her patience, and whose soothing benevolence bade her hope for happier days.

One day as Mrs. Mowbray, regardless of a heavy shower, and lost in melancholy reflections, was walking with irregular steps on the road to Penrith, with an unopened umbrella in her hand, she suddenly raised her eyes from the ground, and beheld a quaker-lady pursued by an over-driven bullock, and unable any longer to make an effort to escape its fury. At this critical moment Mrs. Mowbray, from a sort of irresistible impulse, as fortunate in its effects as presence of mind, yet scarcely perhaps to be denominated such, suddenly opened her umbrella; and, approaching the animal, brandished it before his eyes. Alarmed at this unusual appearance, he turned hastily and ran towards the town, where she saw that he was immediately met and secured.

"Thou hast doubtless saved my life," said the quaker, grasping Mrs. Mowbray's hand, with an emotion which she vainly tried to suppress; "and I pray God to bless thine!"

Mrs. Mowbray returned the pressure of her hand, and burst into tears; overcome with joy for having saved a fellow-creature's life; with terror, which she was now at leisure to feel for the danger to which she had herself been exposed; and with mournful emotion from the consciousness how much she needed the blessing which the grateful quaker invoked on her head.

"Thou tremblest even more than I do," observed the lady, smiling, but seeming ready to faint; "I believe we had better, both of us, sit down on the bank: but it is so wet that perhaps we had better endeavour to reach my house, which is only at the end of yon field." Mrs. Mowbray bowed her assent; and, supporting each other, they at length arrived at a neat white house, to which the quaker cordially bade her welcome.

"It was but this morning," said Mrs. Mowbray, struggling for utterance, "that I called upon Death to relieve me from an existence at once wretched and useless."—Here she paused:—and her new acquaintance, cordially pressing her hand, waited for the conclusion of her speech;— "but now," continued Mrs. Mowbray, "I revoke, and repent my idle and vicious impatience of life. I have saved your life, and something like enjoyment now seems to enliven mine."

"I suspect," replied the lady, "that thou hast known deep affliction; and I rejoice that at this moment, and in so providential a manner, I have been introduced to thy acquaintance:—for I too have known sorrow, and the mourner knows how to speak comfort to the heart of the mourner. My name is Rachel Pemberton; and I hope that when I know thy name, and thy story, thou wilt allow me to devote to thy comfort some hours of the existence which thou hast preserved." She then hastily withdrew, to pour forth in solitary prayer the breathings of devout gratitude:—while Mrs. Mowbray, having communed with her own thoughts, felt a glow of unwonted satisfaction steal over her mind; and by the time Mrs. Pemberton returned, she was able to meet her with calmness and cheerfulness.

"Thou knowest my name," said Mrs. Pemberton as she entered, seating herself my Mrs. Mowbray, "but I have yet to learn thine."

"My name is Mowbray," she replied, sighing deeply.

"Mowbray!—The lady of Rosevalley in Gloucestershire; and the mother of Adeline Mowbray?" exclaimed Mrs. Pemberton.

"What of Adeline Mowbray? What of my child?" cried Mrs. Mowbray, seizing Mrs. Pemberton's hand. "Blessed woman! tell me,—Do you indeed know her?—can you tell me where to find her?"

"I will tell thee all that I know of her," replied Mrs. Pemberton in a faltering voice; "but thy emotion overpowers me.—I—I was once a mother, and I can feel for thee." She then turned away her head to conceal a starting tear; while Mrs. Mowbray, in incoherent eagerness, repeated her questions, and trembling awaited her answer.

"Is she well? Is she happy?—say but that!" she exclaimed, sobbing as she spoke.

"She was well and contented when I last heard from her," replied Mrs. Pemberton calmly.

"Heard from her? Then she writes to you! Oh, blessed, blessed woman! show me her letters, and tell me only that she has forgiven me for all my unkindness to her—." As she said this, Mrs. Mowbray threw her arms round Mrs. Pemberton, and sunk half-fainting on her shoulder.

"I will tell thee all that has ever passed between us, if thou wilt be composed," gravely answered Mrs. Pemberton; "but this violent expression of thy feelings is unseemly and detrimental."

"Well—well—I will be calm," said Mrs. Mowbray; and Mrs. Pemberton began to relate the interview which she had with Adeline in Richmond.

"How long ago did this take place?" eagerly interrupted Mrs. Mowbray.

"Full six years."

"Oh, God!" exclaimed she, impatiently,— "Six years! By this time then she may be dead—she may—— "

"Thou art incorrigible, I fear," said Mrs. Pemberton, "but thou art afflicted, and I will bear with thy impatience:—sit down again and attend to me, and thou wilt hear much later intelligence of thy daughter."

"How late?" asked Mrs. Mowbray, with frantic eagerness;— and Mrs. Pemberton, overcome with the manner in which she spoke, could scarcely falter out, "Within a twelvemonth I have heard of her."

"Within a twelvemonth!" joyfully cried Mrs. Mowbray: but, recollecting herself, she added mournfully— "but in that time what—what may not have happened!"

"I know not what to do with thee nor for thee," observed Mrs. Pemberton; "but do try, I beseech thee, to hear me patiently!"

Mrs. Mowbray then re-seated herself; and Mrs. Pemberton informed her of Adeline's premature confinement at Richmond; of her distress on Glenmurray's death, and of her having witnessed it.

"Ah! you acted a mother's part—you did what I ought to have done," cried Mrs. Mowbray, bursting into tears,— "but, go on—I will be patient."

Yet that was impossible; for, when she heard of Adeline's insanity, her emotions became so strong that Mrs. Pemberton, alarmed for her life, was obliged to ring for assistance.

When she recovered,— "Thou hast heard the worst now," said Mrs. Pemberton, "and all I have yet to say of thy child is satisfactory."

She then related the contents of Adeline's first letter, informing her of her marriage:—and Mrs. Mowbray, clasping her hands together, blessed God that Adeline was become a wife. The next letter Mrs. Pemberton read informed her that she was the mother of a fine girl.

"A mother!" she exclaimed, "Oh, how I should like to see her child!"—But at the same moment she recollected how bitterly she had reviled her when she saw her about to become a mother, at their last meeting; and, torn with conflicting emotions, she was again insensible to aught but her self-upbraidings.

"Well—but where is she now? where is the child? and when did you hear from her last?" cried she.

"I have not heard from her since," hesitatingly replied Mrs. Pemberton.

"But can't you write to her?"

"Yes;—but in her last letter she said she was going to change her lodgings, and would write again when settled in a new habitation."

Again Mrs. Mowbray paced the room in wild and violent distress: but her sorrows at length yielded to the gentle admonitions and soothings of Mrs. Pemberton, who bade her remember, that when she rose in the morning she had not expected the happiness and consolation which she had met with that day; and that a short time might bring forth still greater comfort.

"For," said Mrs. Pemberton, "I can write to the house where she formerly lodged, and perhaps the person who keeps it can give us intelligence of her."

On hearing this, Mrs. Mowbray became more composed, and diverted her sorrow by a thousand fond inquiries concerning Adeline, which none but a mother could make, and none but a mother listen to with patience.

While this conversation was going on, a knock at the door was heard, and miss Woodville entered the room in great emotion; for she had heard, on the road, that a mad bullock had attacked a lady; and also that Mrs. Mowbray, scarcely able to walk, had been led into the white house in the field by the road side.

Miss Woodville was certainly as much alarmed as she pretended to be: but there was a somewhat in the expression of her alarm which, though it gratified Mrs. Mowbray, was displeasing to the more penetrating Mrs. Pemberton. She could not indeed guess that miss Woodville's alarm sprung merely from apprehension lest Mrs. Mowbray should die before she had provided for her in her will: yet, notwithstanding, she felt that her expressions of concern and anxiety had no resemblance to those of real affection; and in spite of her habitual candour, she beheld miss Woodville with distrust.

But this feeling was considerably increased on observing, that when Mrs. Mowbray exultingly introduced her, not only as the lady whose life she had been the means of preserving, but as the friend and correspondent of her daughter, she evidently changed colour; and, in spite of her habitual plausibility, could not utter a single coherent sentence of pleasure or congratulation:—and it was also evident, that, being conscious of Mrs. Pemberton's regarding her with a scrutinizing eye, she was not easy till, on pretence of Mrs. Mowbray's requiring rest after her alarm, she had prevailed on her to return home.

But she could not prevent the new friends from parting with eager assurances of meeting again and again: and it was agreed between them, that Mrs. Pemberton should spend the next day at the Lawn.[129]

Mrs. Pemberton, who is thus again introduced to the notice of my readers, had been, as well as Mrs. Mowbray, the pupil of adversity. She had been born and educated in fashionable life; and she united to a very lovely face and elegant form, every feminine grace and accomplishment.

When she was only eighteen, Mr. Pemberton, a young and gay quaker, fell in love with her; and having inspired her with a mutual passion, he married her, notwithstanding the difference of their religious opinions, and the displeasure of his friends. He was consequently disowned by the society: but being weaned by the happiness which he found at home from those public amusements which had first lured him from the strict habits of his sect, he was soon desirous of being again admitted a member of it; and in process of time he was once more received into it; while his amiable wife, having no wish beyond her domestic

[129] The lawn at Mrs. Mowbray's Cumberland estate seems to stand as a synecdoche for the estate itself and is the name by which the estate itself is known.

circle, and being disposed to think her husband's opinions right, became in time a convert to the same profession of faith, and exhibited in her manners the rare union of the easy elegance of a woman of the world with the rigid decorum and unadorned dress of a strict quaker.

But in the midst of her happiness, and whilst looking forward to a long continuance of it, a fever, caught in visiting the sick bed of a cottager, carried off her husband, and next two lovely children; and Mrs. Pemberton would have sunk under the stroke, but for the watchful care and affectionate attentions of the friend of her youth, who resided near her, and who, in time, prevailed on her to receive with becoming fortitude and resignation the trials which she was appointed to undergo.

During this season of affliction, as we have before stated, she became a teacher in the quaker's society: but at the time of her meeting Adeline at Richmond, she had been called from the duties of her public profession to watch over the declining health of her friend and consoler, and to accompany her to Lisbon.

There, during four long years, she bent over her sick couch, now elated with hope, and now sunk into despondence; when, at the beginning of the fifth year, her friend died in her arms, and she returned to England, resolved to pass her days, except when engaged in the active duties of her profession, on a little estate in Cumberland, bequeathed to her by her friend on her death-bed. But ill health and various events had detained her in the west of England since her return; and she had not long taken possession of her house near Penrith, when she became introduced in so singular a manner to Mrs. Mowbray's acquaintance—an acquaintance which would, she hoped, prove of essential service to them both; and as soon as her guest departed, Mrs. Pemberton resolved to inquire what character Mrs. Mowbray bore in the neighbourhood, and whether her virtues at all kept pace with her misfortunes.

Her inquiries were answered in the most satisfactory manner; as, fortunately for Mrs. Mowbray, with the remembrance of her daughter had recurred to her that daughter's benevolent example.

She remembered the satisfaction which used to beam from Adeline's countenance when she returned from her visits to the sick and the afflicted; and she resolved to try whether those habits of charitable exertion which could increase the happiness of the young and light-hearted Adeline, might not have power to alleviate the sorrows of her own drooping age, and broken joyless heart.

"Sweet are the uses of adversity!"[130]—She who, while the child of prosperity, was a romantic, indolent theorist, an inactive speculator, a proud contemner of the dictates of sober experience, and a neglecter of that practical benevolence which can in days produce more benefit to others than theories and theorists can accomplish in years—this erring woman, awakened from her dreams and reveries to habits of useful exertion by the stimulating touch of affliction, was become the visitor of the sick, the consoler of the sorrowful, the parent of the fatherless, while virtuous industry looked up to her with hope; and her name, like that of Adeline in happier days, was pronounced with prayers and blessings.

But, alas! she felt that blessing could reach her only in the shape of her lost child: and, though she was conscious of being useful to others, though she had the satisfaction of knowing that she had but the day before been the means of preserving a valuable life, she met Mrs. Pemberton, when she arrived at the lawn, with a countenance of fixed melancholy, and was at first disposed to expect but little success from the project of writing to Adeline's former lodgings in order to inquire.

The truth was, that miss Woodville had artfully insinuated the improbability of such an inquiry's succeeding; and, though Mrs. Mowbray had angrily asserted her hopes when miss Woodville provokingly asserted her *fears*, the treacherous girl's insinuations had sunk deeply into her mind, and Mrs. Pemberton saw, with pain and wonder, an effect produced of which the cause was wholly unseen. But she at length succeeded in

---

[130] William Shakespeare, *As You Like It*, II.i.12.

awakening Mrs. Mowbray's hopes; and in the letter written by Mrs. Pemberton to the mistress of the house whence Adeline formerly dated, she inclosed one to her daughter glowing with maternal tenderness, and calculated to speak peace to her sorrows.

These letters were sent, as soon as written, to the post by Mrs. Mowbray's footman; but miss Woodville contrived to meet him near the post-office, and telling him she would put the letter in the receiver, she gave him a commission to call at a shop in Penrith for her, at which she had not time to call herself.

Thus was another scheme for restoring Adeline to her afflicted mother frustrated by the treachery of this interested woman;[131] who, while Mrs. Pemberton and Mrs. Mowbray looked anxiously forward to the receipt of an answer from London, triumphed with maligned pleasure in the success of her artifice.—But, spite of herself, she feared Mrs. Pemberton, and was not at all pleased to find that, till the answer from London could arrive, that lady was to remain at the Lawn.

She contrived, however, to be as little in her presence as possible; for, contrary to Mrs. Pemberton's usual habits, she felt a distrust of miss Woodville, which her intelligent eye could not help expressing, and which consequently alarmed the conscious heart of the culprit. Being left therefore, by miss Woodville's fears, alone with Mrs. Mowbray, she drew from her, at different times, ample details of Adeline's childhood, and the method which Mrs. Mowbray had pursued in her education.

"Ah! 'tis as I suspected," interrupted Mrs. Pemberton during one of these conversations. "Thy daughter's *faults* originated in thee! her education was cruelly defective."

"No!" replied Mrs. Mowbray with almost angry eagerness, "whatever my errors as a mother have been, and for the rash marriage which I made I own myself culpable in the highest degree, I am sure that I paid the greatest attention to my daughter's education. If you were but to see the voluminous

---

[131] I.e., self-interested. Miss Woodville stands to inherit much if Adeline remains alienated.

manuscript on the subject, which I wrote for her improvement——"

"But where was thy daughter; and how was she employed during the time that thou wert writing a book by which to educate her?"

Mrs. Mowbray was silent; she recollected that, while she was gratifying her own vanity in composing her system of education, Adeline was almost banished her presence; and, but for the humble instruction of her grandmother, would, at the age of fifteen, have run a great risk of being both an ignorant and useless being.

"Forgive me, friend Mowbray," resumed Mrs. Pemberton, aware in some measure of what was passing in Mrs. Mowbray's mind—"forgive me if I venture to observe, that till of late years, a thick curtain of self-love seems to have been dropped between thy heart and maternal affection. It is now, and now only that thou hast learned to feel like a true and affectionate mother!"

"Perhaps you are right," replied Mrs. Mowbray mournfully, "still, I always meant well; and hoped that my studies would conduce to the benefit of my child."

"So they might, perhaps, to that of thy second, third, or fourth child, hadst thou been possessed of so many; but, in the mean while, thy first-born must have been fatally neglected. A child's education begins almost from the hour of its birth; and the mother who understands her task, knows that the circumstances which every moment calls forth, are the tools with which she is to work in order to fashion her child's mind and character.—What would you think of the farmer who was to let his fields lie fallow for years, while he was employed in contriving a method of cultivating land to increase his gains ten-fold?"

"But I did not suffer Adeline's mind to lie fallow.—I allowed her to read, and I directed her studies."

"Thou didst so; but what were those studies? and didst thou acquaint thyself with the deductions which her quick mind formed from them? No—thou didst not, as parents should do, inquire into the impressions made on thy daughter's mind by the books which she perused. Prompt to feel, and hasty to decide, as Adeline was, how necessary was to her the warning voice of judgement and experience!"

"But how could I imagine that a girl so young should dare to act, whatever her opinions might be, in open defiance of the opinions of the world?"

"But she had not lived in the world; therefore, scarcely knew how repugnant to it her opinions were; nor, as she did not mix in general society, could she care sufficiently for its good opinion, to be willing to act contrary to her own ideas of right, rather than forfeit it: besides, thou ownest that thou didst openly profess thy admiration of the sentiments which she adopted; nor, till they were confirmed irrevocably her's, didst thou declare, that to set up to them was, in thy opinion, vicious. And then it was too late: she thought thy timidity, and not thy wisdom, spoke, and she set thee the virtuous example of acting up to the dictates of conscience. But Adeline and thou are both the pupils of affliction and experience; and I trust that, all your errors repented of, you will meet once more to expiate your past follies by your future conduct."

"I hope so too," meekly replied Mrs. Mowbray, whose pride had been completely subdued by self-upbraidings and distress: "Oh! when—when will an answer arrive from London?"

CHAPTER X.

ALAS! day after day elapsed, and no letter came; but while Mrs. Mowbray was almost frantic with disappointment and anxiety, Mrs. Pemberton thought that she observed in miss Woodville's countenance a look of triumphant malice, which ill accorded with the fluent expressions of sympathy and regret with which she gratified her unsuspicious relation, and she determined to watch her very narrowly; for she thought it strange that Adeline, however she might respect her mother's oath, should never, in the bitterness of her sorrows, have unburthened her heart by imparting them to her: one day, when, as usual, the post had been anxiously expected, and, as usual, had brought no

Adeline Mowbray • 607

letter from London concerning Adeline; and while miss Woodville was talking on indifferent subjects with ill suppressed gaiety, though Mrs. Mowbray, sunk into despondence, was lying on the sofa by her; Mrs. Pemberton suddenly exclaimed— "There is only one right way of proceeding, friend Mowbray,—thou and I must go to London, and make our inquiries in person, and then we shall have a great chance of succeeding." As she said this, she looked steAdfastly at miss Woodville, and saw her turn very pale, while her eye was hastily averted from the penetrating glance of Mrs. Pemberton; and when she heard Mrs. Mowbray, in a transport of joy, declare that they had better set off that very evening, unable to conceal her terror and agitation, she hastily left the room.

Mrs. Pemberton instantly followed her into the apartment to which she had retired, and the door of which she had closed with great violence.—She found her walking to and fro, and wringing her hands, as if in agony. On seeing Mrs. Pemberton, she started, and sinking into a chair, she complained of being very ill, and desired to be left alone.

"Thou art ill, and thy illness is of the worst sort, I fear," replied Mrs. Pemberton; "but I will stay, and be thy physician."

"*You*, my physician?" replied miss Woodville, with fury in her looks; "*You*?"

"Yes—*I*—I see that thou art afraid lest Adeline should be restored to her paternal roof."

"Who told you so, officious, insolent woman?" returned miss Woodville.

"Thy own looks—but all this is very natural in thee: thou fearest that Adeline's favour should annihilate thine."

"Perhaps I do;" cried miss Woodville, a little less alarmed, and catching at this plausible excuse for her uneasiness; "for, should I be forced to leave my cousin's house, I shall be reduced to comparative poverty, and solitude again."

"But why shouldest thou be forced to leave it? Art thou not Adeline's friend?"

"Ye—yes," faltered out, miss Woodville.

"But it is uncertain whether we can find Adeline—still we shall be very diligent in our enquiries; yet it is so strange that she should never have written to her mother, if alive, that perhaps—"

"Oh, I dare say she is dead," hastily interrupted miss Woodville.

"Has she been dead long? thinkest thou."

"No—not long—not above six months, I dare say."

"No!—Hast thou any reason then for knowing that she was alive six months ago?" asked Mrs. Pemberton, looking steadily as miss Woodville, as she spoke.

"I?—Lord—no—How should I know?" she replied, her lip quivering, and her whole frame trembling.

"I tell thee how.—Art thou not conscious of having intercepted letters from thy cousin, to her relenting parent?"

Mrs. Pemberton had scarcely uttered these words, when miss Woodville fell back nearly *insensible* in her chair—a proof that the accusation was only too well founded. As soon as she recovered, Mrs. Pemberton said, with great gentleness, "Thou art ill,—ill indeed, but, as I suspected, thy illness is of the mind; there is a load of guilt on it; throw it off then by a full confession, and be the sinner that repenteth."

In a few moments miss Woodville, conscious that her emotion had betrayed her, and suspecting that Mrs. Pemberton had by some means or other received hints of her treachery, confessed that she had intercepted and destroyed letters from Adeline to her mother; and also owned, to the great joy of Mrs. Pemberton, that Adeline's last letter, the letter in which she informed Mrs. Mowbray that all the conditions were then fulfilled, without which alone she had sworn never to forgive her, had arrived only two months before; and that it was dated from such a street, and such a number, in London.

"My poor friend will be so happy!" said Mrs. Pemberton; and, her own eyes filling with tears of joy, she hastened to find Mrs. Mowbray.

"But what will become of *me*?" exclaimed miss Woodville, detaining her— "*I* am ruined—ruined for ever!"

"Not so," replied Mrs. Pemberton, "thou art *saved,*—saved, I trust, *for ever.*—Thou hast confessed thy guilt, and made all the atonement now in thy power. Go to thine own room, and I will soon make known to thee thy relation's sentiments towards thee."

So saying, she hastened to Mrs. Mowbray, whom she found giving orders, with eager impatience, to have post horses sent for immediately.

"Then thou art full of expectation, I conclude, from the event of our journey to town?" said Mrs. Pemberton smiling.

"To be sure I am," replied Mrs. Mowbray.

"And so am I," she answered— "for I think that I know the present abode of thy daughter."

Mrs. Mowbray started—her friend's countenance expressed more joy and exultation than she had ever seen on it before; and, almost breathless with new hope, she seized her hand and conjured her to explain herself.

The explanation was soon given; and Mrs. Mowbray's joy, in consequence of it, unbounded.

"But what is thy will," observed Mrs. Pemberton, "with regard to thy guilty relation?"

"I cannot—cannot see her again now, if ever;—and she must immediately leave my house."

"Immediately?"

"Yes,—but I will settle on her a handsome allowance; for my conscience tells me, that, had I behaved like a mother to my child, no one could have been tempted to injure her thus.—I put this unhappy woman into a state of temptation, and she yielded to it:—but I feel only too sensibly, that no one has been such an enemy to my poor Adeline as I have been; nor, conscious of my own offences towards her, dare I resent those of another."

"I love, I honour thee for what thou hast now uttered," cried Mrs. Pemberton with unusual animation.— "I see that thou art now indeed a christian; such are the breathings of a truly contrite spirit; and, verily, she who can so easily forgive the crimes of others may hope to have her own forgiven."

Mrs. Pemberton then hastened to speak hope and comfort to the mind of the penitent offender, while Mrs. Mowbray ran to meet her servant, who, to her surprise, was returning without horses, for none were to be procured; and Mrs. Mowbray saw herself obliged to delay her journey till noon the next day, when she was assured of having horses from Penrith. But when, after a long and restless night, she arose in the morning, anticipating with painful impatience the hour of her departure, Mrs. Pemberton entered her room, and informed her that she had passed nearly all night at miss Woodville's bed-side, who had been seized with a violent delirium at one o'clock in the morning, and in her ravings was continually calling on Mrs. Mowbray, and begging to see her once more.

"I will see her directly," replied Mrs. Mowbray, without a moment's hesitation; and hastened to miss Woodville's apartment, where she found the medical attendant whom Mrs. Pemberton had sent for just arrived. He immediately declared the disorder to be an inflammation on the brain, and left them with little or no hope of her recovery.

Mrs. Mowbray, affected beyond measure at the pathetic appeals for pardon addressed to her continually by the unconscious sufferer, took her station at the bed-side; and, hanging over her pillow, watched for the slightest gleam of returning reason, in order to speak the pardon so earnestly implored: and while thus piously engaged, the chaise that was to convey her and her friend to London, and perhaps to Adeline, drove up to the gate.

"Art thou ready?" said Mrs. Pemberton, entering the room equipped for her journey.

At this moment the poor invalid reiterated her cries for pardon, and begged Mrs. Mowbray not to leave her without pronouncing her forgiveness.

Mrs. Mowbray burst into tears; and though sure that she was not even conscious of her presence, she felt herself almost unable to forsake her:—still it was in search of her daughter that she was going—nay, perhaps, it was to her daughter that she was hastening; and, as this thought occurred to her, she hurried to the door of the chamber, saying she should be ready in a moment.

But the eyes of the phrensied suffereR followed her as she did so, and in a tone of unspeakable agony she begged, she entreated that she might not be left to die in solitude and sorrow, however guilty she might have been.—Then again she implored Mrs. Mowbray to speak peace and pardon to her drooping soul; while, unable to withstand these solicitations, though she knew them to be the unconscious ravings of the disorder, she slowly and mournfully returned to the bedside.

"It is late," said Mrs. Pemberton— "we ought ere now to be on the road."

"How can I go, and leave this poor creature in such a state?— But then should we find my poor injured child at the end of the journey! Such an expectation as that!—— "

"Thou must decide quickly," replied Mrs. Pemberton gently.

"Decide! Then I will go with you.—Yet still, should Anna recover her senses before her death, and wish to see me, I should never forgive myself for being absent—it might sooth the anguish of her last moments to know how freely I pardon her.—No, no:—after all, if pleasure awaits me, it is only delaying it a few days; and this, this unhappy girl is on her *death-bed*.—You, you must go *without* me."

As she said this, Mrs. Pemberton pressed her hand with affectionate eagerness, and murmured out in broken accents, "I honour thy decision, and may I return with comfort to thee!"

"Yet though I wish you to go," cried Mrs. Mowbray, "I grieve to expose you to such fatigue and trouble in your weak state of health, and—— "

"Say no more," interrupted Mrs. Pemberton, "I am only doing my duty; and reflect on my happiness if I am allowed to restore the lost sheep to the fold again!"—So saying she set off on her journey, and arrived in London only four days after Adeline had arrived in Cumberland.

Mrs. Pemberton drove immediately to Adeline's lodgings,

but received the same answer as colonel Mordaunt had received; namely, that she was gone no one knew whither. Still she did not despair of finding her: she, like the colonel, thought that a mulatto, a lady just recovered from the small-pox, and a child, were likely to be easily traced; and having written to Mrs. Mowbray, owning her disappointment, but bidding her not despair, she set off on her journey back, and had succeeded in tracing Adeline as far as an inn on the high North road,—when an event took place which made her further inquiries needless.

CHAPTER XI.

ADELINE, after several repeated trials, succeeded in writing the following letter to her mother:

"Dearest of Mothers,

"WHEN this letter reaches you, I shall be no more; and however I may hitherto have offended you, I shall then be able to offend you no longer; and that child, whom you bound yourself by oath never to see or forgive but on the most cruel of conditions while living, dead you may perhaps deign to receive to your pardon and your love.—Nay, my heart tells me that you will do more,—that you will transfer the love which you once felt for me, to my poor helpless orphan; and in full confidence that you will be thus indulgent, I bequeath her to you with my dying breath.—O! look on her, my mother, nor shrink from her with disgust, although you see in her my features; but rather rejoice in the resemblance, and fancy that I am restored to you pure, happy, and beloved as I once was.—Yes, yes,—it will be so: I have known a great deal of sorrow—let me then indulge the little ray of pleasure that breaks in upon me when I think that you will not resist my dying prayer, but bestow on my child the long arrears of tenderness due to me.

"Yes, yes, you will receive, you will be kind to her;

and by so doing you will make me ample amends for all
the sorrow which your harshness caused me when we
met last.—That was a dreadful day! How you frowned
on me! I did not think you could have frowned so
dreadfully—but then I was uninjured by affliction,
unaltered by illness. Were you to see me now, you would
not have the heart to frown on me: and yet my letters,
being repeatedly returned, and even the last unnoticed
and unanswered, though it told you that even on your
own conditions I could now claim your pardon, for that
I had been "wretched in love," and had experienced "the
anguish of being forsaken, despised, and disgraced in
the eye of the world," proves but too surely that the
bitterness of resentment is not yet past!—But on my
death-bed you promised to see and forgive me—*and I
am there, my mother!!* Yet will I not claim that promise;—
I will not weaken, by directing it towards myself, the
burst of sorrow, of too late regret, of self-upbraidings,
and long-restrained affection, which must be directed
towards my child when I am not alive to profit by it.
No:—though I would give worlds to embrace you once
more, for the sake of my child I resign the gratification.

"Oh, mother! you little think that I saw you, only a
few days ago, from the stile by the cottage which overlooks
your house: you were walking with a lady, and my child
was with me (my Editha, for I have called her after you).
You seemed, methought, even cheerful, and I was so
selfish that I felt shocked to think I was so entirely
forgotten by you; for I was sure that if you thought of me
you could not be cheerful. But your companion left
you; and then you looked so very sad, that I was wretched
from the idea that you were then thinking too much of
me, and I wished you to resume your cheerfulness again.

"*I* was not cheerful, and Editha by her artless prattle
wounded me to the very soul.—She wished, she said, to
live in that sweet house, and asked why she should not

live there? I *could* have told her why, but dared not do it; but I assured her, and do not for mercy's sake prove that assurance false! that she *should* live there *one day*.

"'But when—when?' she asked.

"'When I am in my grave,' replied I: and, poor innocent! throwing herself into my arms with playful fondness, she begged me to go to my grave directly. I feel but too sensibly that her desire will soon be accomplished.

"But must I die unblest by you? True, I am watched by the kindest of human beings! but then she is not my mother—that mother, who, with the joys of my childhood and my home, is so continually recurring to my memory. Oh! I forget all your unkindness, my mother, and remember only your affection. How I should like to feel your hand supporting my head, and see you perform the little offices which sickness requires.—And must I never, never see you more? Yes! you will come, I am sure you will, but come, come quickly, or I shall die without your blessing.

"I have had a fainting fit—but I am recovered, and can address you again.—Oh! teach my Editha to be humble, teach her to be slow to call the experience of ages contemptible prejudices; teach her no opinions that can destroy her sympathies with general society and make her an alien to the hearts of those amongst whom she lives.

"Be above all things careful that she wanders not in the night of scepticism. But for the support of religion, what, amidst my various sorrows, what would have become of *me*?

"There is something more that I would say. Should my existence be prolonged even but a few days, I shall have to struggle with poverty as well as sickness; and the anxious friend (I will not call her servant) who is now my all of earthly comfort, will scarcely have money sufficient to pay me the last sad duties; and I owe her, my mother, a world of obligation! She will make my last moments easy, and *you* must reward her. From her you will receive this letter when I am no more, and to your care and protection I bequeath her. She is—my eyes grow dim, and I must leave off for the present."

On the very evening in which Adeline had written this address to her mother, Mrs. Mowbray had received Mrs. Pemberton's letter; and as miss Woodville had been interred that morning, she felt herself at liberty to join Mrs. Pemberton in her search after Adeline, while various plans for this purpose presented themselves to her mind, and each of them was dismissed in its turn as fruitless or impracticable. Full of these thoughts she pensively walked along the lawn before her door, till sad and weary she leaned on a little gate at the bottom of it; which, as she did so, swung slowly backwards and forwards, responsive as it were to her feelings.

But, as she continued to muse, and to recall the varied sorrows of her past life, the gate on which she leaned began to vibrate more quickly; till, unable to bear the recollections which assailed her, she was hastening with almost frantic speed towards the house, when she saw a cottager approaching, to whose sick daughter and helpless family she had long been a bountiful benefactress.

"What is the matter, John?" cried Mrs. Mowbray, hastening forward to meet him— "you seem agitated."

"My poor daughter, madam!" replied the man, bursting into tears.

At the sight of his distress, his *parental* distress, Mrs. Mowbray sighed deeply, and asked if Lucy was worse.

"I doubt she is dying,"[132] said the afflicted father.

"God forbid!" exclaimed Mrs. Mowbray, throwing her shawl over her shoulders; "I will go and see her myself."

[132] I.e., fear or suspect she is dying.

"What, really?—But the way is so long, and the road so miry!"

"No matter—I must do my duty."

"God bless you, and reward you!" cried the grateful father—"that is so like you! Lucy said you would come!"

Mrs. Mowbray then filled a basket with medicine and refreshments, and set out on her charitable visit.

She found the poor girl in a very weak and alarming state; but the sight of her benefactress, and the tender manner in which she supported her languid head, and administered wine and other cordials to her, insensibly revived her; and while writhing under the feelings of an unhappy parent herself, Mrs. Mowbray was soothed by the blessings of the parent whom she comforted.

At this moment they were alarmed by a shriek from a neighbouring cottage, and a woman who was attending on the sick girl ran out to inquire into the cause of it.

She returned, saying that a poor sick young gentlewoman, who lodged at the next house, was fallen back in a fit, and they thought she was dead.

"A young gentlewoman," exclaimed Mrs. Mowbray, "at the next cottage!" rising up.

"Aye sure," cried the woman, "she looks like a lady for certain, and she has the finest child I ever saw."

"Perhaps she is not dead," said Mrs. Mowbray:— "let us go see."

Chapter XII.

Little did Mrs. Mowbray think that it was her own child whom she was hastening to relieve; and that, while meditating a kind action, recompense was so near.

Adeline, while trying to finish her letter to her mother, had scarcely traced a few illegible lines, when she fell back insensible on her pillow; and at the moment of Mrs. Mowbray's entering the cottage, Savanna, who had uttered the shriek which had excited her curiosity, had convinced herself that she was gone for ever.

The woman who accompanied Mrs. Mowbray entered the house first; and opening a back chamber, low-roofed, narrow, and lighted only by one solitary and slender candle, Mrs. Mowbray beheld through the door the lifeless form of the object of her solicitude, which Savanna was contemplating with loud and frantic sorrow.

"Here is a lady come to see what she can do for your mistress," cried the woman, while Savanna turned hastily round:— "Here she is—here is good madam Mowbray."

"Madam Mowbray!" shrieked Savanna, fixing her dark eyes fiercely on Mrs. Mowbray, and raising her arm in a threatening manner as she approached her: then snatching up the letter which lay on the bed,— "Woman!" she exclaimed, grasping Mrs. Mowbray's arm with frightful earnestness, "read dat—'tis for you!"

Mrs. Mowbray, speechless with alarm and awe, involuntarily seized the letter—but scarcely had she read the first words, when uttering a deep groan she sprung forward, to clasp the unconscious form before her, and fell beside it equally insensible.

But she recovered almost immediately to a sense of her misery; and while, in speechless agony, she knelt by the bedside, Savanna, beholding her distress, with a sort of dreadful pleasure exclaimed, "Ah! have you at last learn to feel?"

"But is she, is she *indeed* gone?" cried Mrs. Mowbray, "is there *no* hope?" and instantly seizing the cordial which she had brought with her, assisted by the woman, she endeavoured to force it down the throat of Adeline.

Their endeavours were for some time vain: at length, however, she exhibited signs of life, and in a few minutes more she opened her sunk eye, and gazed unconsciously around her.

"My God! I thank you!" exclaimed Mrs. Mowbray, falling on her knees; while Savanna, laying her mistress's head on her bosom, sobbed with fearful joy.

"Adeline! my child, my dear, dear child!" cried Mrs. Mowbray, seizing her clammy hand.

That voice, those words which she had so long wished to

hear, though hopeless of ever hearing them again, seemed to recall the fast fading recollection of Adeline; she raised her head from Savanna's bosom, and, looking earnestly at Mrs. Mowbray, faintly smiled, and endeavoured to throw herself into her arms,— but fell back again exhausted on the pillow.

But in a few minutes she recovered so far as to be able to speak; and while she hung round her mother's neck, and gazed upon her with eager and delighted earnestness, she desired Savanna to bring Editha to her immediately.

"Will you, will you—," said Adeline, vainly trying to speak her wishes, as Savanna put the sleeping girl in Mrs. Mowbray's arms: but she easily divined them; and, clasping her to her heart, wept over her convulsively— "She shall be dear to me as my own soul!" said Mrs. Mowbray.

"Then I die contented," replied Adleine.

"Die!" exclaimed Mrs. Mowbray hastily: "no, you must not, shall not die; you must live to see me atone for— "

"It is in vain," said Adeline faintly. " I bless God that he allows me to enjoy this consolation—say that you forgive me."

"Forgive you! Oh, Adeline! for years have I forgiven and pined after you: but a wicked woman intercepted all your letters; and I thought you were dead, or had renounced me for ever."

"Indeed!" cried Adeline. "Oh! had I suspected that!"— "Nay more, Mrs. Pemberton is now in London, in search of you, in order to bring you back to happiness!" As Mrs. Mowbray said this, Savanna, drawing near, took her hand and gently pressed it.

Adeline observed the action, and seeing by it that Savanna's heart relented towards her mother, said, "I owe that faithful creature more than I can express; but to your care I bequeath her."

"I will love her as my child," said Mrs. Mowbray, "and behave to her better than I did to— "

"Hush!" cried Adeline, putting her hand to Mrs. Mowbray's lips.

"But you *shall* live! I will send for Dr. Norberry; you shall be moved to my house, and all will be well—all our past grief be forgotten," returned Mrs. Mowbray with almost convulsive eagerness.

Adeline faintly smiled, but repeated that every hope of that kind was over, but that her utmost wish was gratified in seeing her mother, and receiving her full forgiveness.

"But you must live for my sake!" cried Mrs. Mowbray: "and for mine," sobbed out Savanna.

"Could you not be moved to my house?" said Mrs. Mowbray. "There every indulgence and attention that money can procure shall be yours. Is this a place,—is this poverty—this—" here her voice failed her, and she burst into tears.

"Mother, dearest mother," replied Adeline, "I see you, I am assured of your love again, and I have not a want beside. Still, I could like, I could wish, to be once more under a *parent's roof.*"

In a moment, the cottager who was present, and returning with usury to Mrs. Mowbray's daughter the anxious interest which she had taken in his, proposed various means of transporting Adeline to the Lawn; a difficult and a hazardous undertaking; but the poor invalid was willing to risk the danger and the fatigue; and her mother could not but indulge her. At length the cottager, as it was for the *general benefactress,* having with care procured even more assistance than was necessary, Adeline was conveyed on a sort of a litter, along the valley, and found herself once more in the house of her mother; while Savanna, sharing in the joy which Adeline's countenance expressed, threw herself on Mrs. Mowbray's neck, and exclaimed, "Now I forgive you!"

"Mother, dear mother," cried Adeline, after having for some minutes vainly endeavoured to speak— "I am so happy! no more an outcast, but under my mother's roof!—Nay, I even think I *can* live now," added she with a faint smile.

Had Adeline risen from her bed in complete health and vigour, she would scarcely have excited more joy in her mother, and in Savanna, than she did by this expression.

"Can live!" cried Mrs. Mowbray, "O! you shall, you must live."—And an express was sent off immediately to Dr. Norberry too, who was removed to Kendal, to be near his elder daughter, lately married in the neighbourhood.

Dr. Norberry arrived in a few hours. Mrs. Mowbray ran out to meet him; but a welcome died on her tongue, and she could only speak by her tears.

"There, there, my good woman, don't be foolish," replied he: "it is cursed silly to blubber, you know: besides, it can do no good,"—giving her a kiss, while tears tricked down his rough cheek.— "So, the lost sheep is found?"

"But, O! she will be lost again," faltered Mrs. Mowbray; "I doubt nothing can save her!"

"No!" cried the old man, with a gulp, "no! not my coming so many miles on purpose?—Well, but where is she?"

"She will see you presently, but begged to be excused for a few minutes."— "You see," said he, "by my dress, what has happened," gulping as he spoke. "I have lost the companion of thirty years!—and—and—" here he paused, and after an effort went on to say, that his wife in her last illness had owned that she had suppressed Adeline's letters, and had declared the reason of it— "But, poor soul!" continued the doctor, "it was the only sin against me, I believe, or any one else, that she ever committed—so I forgave her; and I trust that God will."

Soon after they were summoned to the sick room, and Dr. Norberry beheld with a degree of fearful emotion, which he vainly endeavoured to hide under a cloak of pleasantry, the dreadful ravages which sorrow and sickness had made in the face and form of Adeline.

"So, here you are at last!" cried he, trying to smile while he sobbed audibly, "and a pretty figure you make, don't you?—But we have you again, and we will not part with you soon, I can tell you, (almost starting as the faint but rapid pulse met his fingers,) that is, I mean," added he, "unless it please God."—Mrs. Mowbray and Savanna, during this speech, gazed on his countenance in breathless anxiety, and read in it a confirmation of their fears.— "But who's afraid?" cried the doctor, forcing a laugh, while his tone and his looks expressed the extreme of apprehension, and his laugh ended in a sob.

Mrs. Mowbray turned away in a sort of desperate silence; but the mulatto still kept her penetrating eye fixed upon him, and with a look so full of woe!

"I'll trouble you, mistress, to take those formidable eyes of yours off my face," cried the doctor, pettishly; "for, by the Lord, I can't stand their inquiry!—But who the devil are you?"

"She is my nurse, my consoler, and my friend," said Adeline.

"Then she is mine of course," cried the doctor, "though she has a devilish terrible stare with her eyes:—but give me your hand, mistress. What is your name?"

"Me be name Savanna," replied the mulatto; "and me die and live wid my dear mistress," she added, bursting into tears.

"Zounds!" cried the doctor, "I can't bear this—here I came as a physician, and these blubberers melt me down into an old woman.—Adeline, I must order all these people out of the room, and have you to myself, or I can do nothing."

He was obeyed; and on inquiring into all Adeline's symptoms, he found little to hope and every thing to fear— "But your mind is relieved, and you have youth on your side; and who knows what good air, good food, and good nurses may do for you!"

"Not to mention a good physician," added Adeline, smiling, "and a good friend in that physician."

"This it be to have money," said Savanna, as she saw the various things prepared and made to tempt Adeline's weak appetite:— "poor Savanna mean as well—her heart make all these, but her hand want power."

During this state of alarming suspense Mrs. Pemberton was hourly expected, as she had written word that she had traced Adeline into Lancashire, and suspected that she was in her mother's neighbourhood.—It may be supposed that Mrs. Mowbray, Adeline, and Savanna, looked forward to her arrival with eager impatience; but not so Dr. Norberry—he said that no doubt she was a very good sort of woman, but that he did not like pretensions to righteousness over much, and had a particular aversion to a piece of formal drab-coloured morality.

Adeline only laughed at these prejudices, without attempting to confute them; for she knew that Mrs. Pemberton's appearance and manners would soon annihilate them. At length she reached the Lawn; and Savanna, who saw her alight, announced her arrival to her mistress, and was commissioned by her to introduce her immediately into the sick chamber.—She did so; but Mrs. Pemberton, almost overpowered with joy at the intelligence which awaited her, and ill fortified by Savanna's violent and mixed emotions against the indulgence of her own, begged to compose herself a few moments before she met Adeline: but Savanna was not to be denied; and seizing her hand she led her up to the bed-side of the invalid.—Adeline smiled affectionately when she saw her; but Mrs. Pemberton started back, and, scarcely staying to take the hand which she offered her, rushed out of the room, to vent in solitude the burst of uncontroulable anguish which the sight of her altered countenance occasioned her.—Alas! her eye had been but too well tutored to read the characters of death in the face, and it was some time before she recovered herself sufficiently to appear before the anxious watchers by the bed of Adeline with that composure which on principle she always endeavoured to display.—At length, however, she re-entered the room, and, approaching the poor invalid, kissed in silence her wan yet flushed cheek.

"I am very different now, my kind friend, to what I was when you *first* saw me," said Adeline, faintly smiling.

To the moment when they *last* met, Adeline had not resolution enough to revert, for then she was mourning by the dead body of Glenmurray.

Mrs. Pemberton was silent for a moment; but, making an effort, she replied, "Thou art now more like what thou wert in *mind,* when I *first* saw thee at Rosevalley, than when I first met thee at Richmond. At Rosevalley I beheld thee innocent, at Richmond guilty, and here I see thee penitent, and, I hope, resigned to thy fate."—She spoke the word *resigned* with emphasis, and Adeline *understood* her.

"I am indeed resigned," replied Adeline in a low voice: "nay,

I feel that I am much favoured in being spared so long. But there is one thing that weighs heavily on my mind: Mary Warner is leading a life of shame, and she told me when I last saw her, that she was corrupted by my precept and example: if so— "

"Set thy conscience at rest on that subject," interrupted Mrs. Pemberton: "while she lived with me, I discovered, long before she ever saw thee, that she had been known to have been faulty."

"Oh! what a load have you removed from my mind!" replied Adeline. "Still it would be more relieved, if you would promise to find her out; and she may be heard of at Mr. Langley's chambers in the Temple. Offer her a yearly allowance for life, provided she will quit her present vicious habits; I am sure my mother will gladly fulfil my wishes in this respect."

"And so will I," replied Mrs. Pemberton. "Is there any thing else that I can do for thee?"

"Yes: I have two pensioners at Richmond,—a poor young woman, and her orphan boy,—an illegitimate child," she added, deeply sighing, as she recollected what had interested her in their fate. "I bequeath them to your care; Savanna knows where they are to be found. And now, all that disturbs my thoughts at this awful moment is, the grief which my poor mother and Savanna will feel;—nay, they will be quite unprepared for it; for they persist to hope still, and I believe that even Dr. Norberry allows his wishes to deceive his judgement."

"They will suffer, indeed!" cried Mrs. Pemberton: "but I give thee my word, that I will never leave thy mother, and that Savanna shall be our joint care."

"It is enough—I shall now die in peace," said Adeline; and Mrs. Pemberton turned away to meet Mrs. Mowbray, who with Dr. Norberry at that moment entered the room. Mrs. Mowbray met her, and welcomed her audibly and joyfully: but Mrs. Pemberton, aware of the blow which impended over her, vainly endeavoured to utter a congratulation; but throwing herself into Mrs. Mowbray's extended arms, she forgot her usual self-command, and sobbed loudly on her bosom.

Dr. Norberry gazed at the benevolent quaker with

astonishment. True, she was *"drab-coloured;"* but where was the repulsive formality that he had expected? "Zounds!" thought he, "this woman can feel like other women, and is as good a hand at a crying-bout as myself." But Mrs. Pemberton did not long give way to so violent an indulgence of her feelings; and gently withdrawing herself from Mrs. Mowbray's embrace, she turned to the window, while Mrs. Mowbray hastened to the bedside of Adeline. Mrs. Pemberton then turned round again, and, seizing Dr. Norberry's hand, which she fervently pressed, said in a faltering voice, "Would thou couldst *save* her!" "And— and *can't* I? can't I?" replied he, gulping. Mrs. Pemberton looked at him with an expression which he could neither mistake nor endure; but muttering in a low tone, "No! dear, sweet soul! I doubt I can't, I doubt I can't, by the Lord!" he rushed out of the room.

From that moment he never was easy but when he could converse with Mrs. Pemberton; for he knew that she, and she only, sympathized in his feelings, as she only knew that Adeline was not likely to recover. The invalid herself observed his attention to her friend, nor could she forbear to rally him on the total disappearance of his prejudices against the fair quaker; for, such was the influence of Mrs. Pemberton's dignified yet winning manners, and such was the respect with which she inspired him, that, if he had his hat on, he always took it off when she entered the room, and never uttered any thing like an oath, without humbly begging her pardon; and he told Adeline, that were all quakers like Mrs. Pemberton, he should be tempted to cry, "Drab is your only wear."

Another, and another day elapsed, and Adeline still lived.— On the evening of the third day, as she lay half-slumbering with her head on Savanna's arm, and Mrs. Mowbray, lulling Editha to sleep on her lap, was watching beside her, glancing her eye alternately with satisfied and silent affection from the child to the mother, whom she thought in a fair way of recovery; while Dr. Norberry, stifling an occasional sob, was contemplating the group, and Mrs. Pemberton, her hands clasped in each other, seemed lost in devout contemplation, Adeline awoke, and as she gazed on Editha, who was fondly held to Mrs. Mowbray's bosom, a smile illuminated her sunk countenance. Mrs. Mowbray at that moment eagerly and anxiously pressed forward to catch her weak accents, and inquire how she felt. "I have seen that fond and anxious look before," she faintly articulated, "but in happier times! and it assures me that you love me still."

'Love you still!" replied Mrs. Mowbray with passionate fondness:— "never, never were you so dear to me as now!"

Adeline tried to express the joy which flushed her cheek at these words, and lighted up her closing eyes: but she tried in vain. At length she grasped Mrs. Mowbray's hand to her lips, and in imperfect accents exclaiming "I thank thee, gracious Heaven!" she laid her head on Savanna's bosom, and expired.

THE END.

Appendix I
Godwin on Marriage and Cohabitation

William Godwin wrote in *An Enquiry Concerning Political Justice* (1793) about his vision for a rational world in which legal and religious marriage—with no possibility for divorce except on very limited grounds—would no longer be either legally or socially requisite. (See textbox on "Female Sexuality and Desire," and Introduction for excerpts.) He, perhaps naively, believed that in an entirely enlightened, rational society, men and women would find social communion richer and more varied than that permitted under a system of strict monogamy based on a husband's sexual property in his wife. Many scholars believe that Godwin's original assessment of adult sexual relations as rather insignificant in *Political Justice* changed after his romantic relationship with Mary Wollstonecraft began in 1796. Nevertheless, this section of *Political Justice* was cited and paraphrased repeatedly in *The Anti-Jacobin Review* and other anti-reformist propaganda through the 1790s as an example of the dangerous and promiscuous threat to the social fabric and the British nation posed by English "Jacobins."

However, Godwin remained concerned about the likelihood that conventional marriage and cohabitation could degrade an adult relationship and lead a husband to tyrannize over his wife. Even after William Godwin and Mary Wollstonecraft were legally married and no longer merely lovers, they each kept a separate residence and wrote daily letters to each other arranging to meet for dinner. Both of them believed it important to separate their daily work from their domestic, romantic lives out of mutual respect. Godwin explained his rationale for the maintenance of separate households in his essay "Of Cohabitation" in 1797:

But we treat adults of either sex, when upon a footing of undue familiarity, our wife or our comrade, in a great degree as we do children. We lay aside the arts of ingenuous persuasion; we forsake the mildness of expostulation; and we expect them to bow to the despotism of command or the impatience of anger. No sooner have we adopted this conduct, than in this case, as in the case of education, we are perfectly ready to prove that it has every feature of wisdom, profound judgement and liberal virtue.

The ill humour which is so prevalent through all the different walks of life, is the result of familiarity. If we did not see each other too frequently, we should accustom ourselves to act reasonably and with urbanity. But, according to a well known maxim, familiarity breeds contempt. The first and most fundamental principle in the intercourse of man with man, is reverence; but we soon cease to reverence what is always before our eyes. Reverence is a certain collectedness of the mind, a pause during which we involuntarily impress ourselves with the importance of circumstances and the dignity of persons. In order that we may properly exercise this sentiment, the occasions calling it forth towards any particular individual, should be economised and rare. It is true, that genuine virtue requires of us a certain frankness and unreserve. But it is not less true that it requires of us a quality in some degree contrasted with this, that we set a guard upon the door of our lips, that we carefully watch over our passions, that we never forget what we owe to ourselves, and that we maintain a vigilant consciousness strictly animadverting and commenting upon the whole series of our actions. (Godwin, "Of Cohabitation," *The Enquirer: Reflections on Education, Manners, and Literature*, (1797) New York: Garland, 1971, 91-92)

Reviews of *Emma Courtney*

From *The Analytical Review* 25 (1797): 174–78.
Art. XV. Memoirs of Emma Courtney. By Mary Hays. 2 Vols.
12 mo. 404 pages. Price 6s. in boards.
Robinsons. 1796.

It is with pleasure that we divert our attention from the loose lascivious scenery, which imparts so dangerous a fascination to the pages of many a modern novel, and devote it to the chaste and simple beauties which the pencil of miss Hays has sketched. The character of Emma Courtney, an insulated unprotected orphan at nineteen, exhibits, in the progress of an imperious passion, an example, that sensibility, if it be the parent of our most refined enjoyments, may also give birth to the keenest anguish and the deepest distress. The dangerous consequences, which may result from the early unrestrained indulgence of this too exquisite feeling, are displayed with additional effect from the strong philosophic mind of her who bends under its influence; with an understanding highly cultivated, with powers for deep reflection, and a soul accustomed to contemplate the fine characters which existed "in those glorious times of Greece and Rome, when wisdom, virtue, and liberty, formed the only triumvirate,"[1] ...

The tale which these volumes contain is extremely simple, and is enriched with several affecting scenes; we cannot however give an unqualified approbation of the characters as entirely natural. We scarcely believe the possibility of an attachment existing unabated for so many years as that of Emma Courtney for Augustus Harley, chilled with such indifference and almost aver-

---

[1] See Chesterfield's preface to Hammond's elegies. [M.H.]

sion on his part, as hers was. If it were natural, with such strong emotions, at first to avow the passion, it was certainly much otherwise to tease him with her neglected love; and, after the appeal to his passions had proved ineffectual, to attack his principles, and argue, on the ground of utility, that it was incumbent on him to return the attachment. Nor do we see any reason why Augustus should keep secret his marriage from her, who could claim his confidence, though she could not wring from him an avowal of his love. We were hurt at Emma's marriage with Montague; gratitude is hardly a principle sufficiently powerful to sanction it; and, however necessary it might be for the catastrophe which succeeds, is by no means natural; neither indeed are we informed of any motive which Montague could have for the murder of his bastard babe. Notwithstanding these objections, which after all may be of questionable validity, we are much pleased with the performance.

The authoress has made it the vehicle of much good sense and much liberal principle. In this novel — if we may be allowed the allusion — like the library in Mr. Harley's cottage, "nothing seems costly, yet neatness, order, and taste, appear through the whole apartment, bespeaking the elegant and cultivated mind of the owner." L.M.S.

From *The Critical Review; or, Annals of Literature*; 19 (1797): 109–11.
Memoirs of Emma Courtney. 2 vols 12mo. 6s. sewed. Robinsons. 1796.

Emma Courtney is designed to represent a character, who, though loving virtue, is enslaved by passion, liable to the errors and weaknesses of our fragile nature. This passion, not love at *first sight*, but even *before* first sight (for Emma Courtney's affection for Mrs. Harley is conveyed to her son Augustus Harley, even before she sees him), will perhaps, to some readers, appear to savour of extravagance; and in its consequences, after Emma Courtney's acquaintance with Harley, to produce eccentricity of character and conduct; but her errors are represented as the off-spring of extreme sensibility; and the result of an *hazardous* experiment, Miss Hays tells us, is made to operate as a *warning*, rather than as an example. ...

It may be proper to observe that this work is a course of letters addressed to Augustus Harley, the son of Mr. Harley, the idol of Emma Courtney's passion.

We conclude by observing that we do not hold up Emma Courtney as a character for general imitation, any more than, we presume, the authoress herself would. Whenever great passions break out, or a strong bias inclines, there reason should direct its more immediate attention; and our conduct must, in a great measure, be regulated by the welfare and good order of society. Strong sensibilities require more than ordinary management: the passions, the source of personal enjoyment and of public utility, may easily become our own tormentors, and the spring of injustice to others.

From *The Anti-Jacobin Review and Magazine; or, Monthly Political Literary Censor*, No. 3 (1799): 54–7.

The Reviewers Reviewed[2]

Art. 1. *Memoirs of Emma Courtney*. By Mary Hays. 12 mo. 2 vols. Price 6s. Robinsons, London. 1796.

Art. II. *The Victim of Prejudice. A Novel.* By Mary Hays. 12 mo. 2 vols. Price 6s. Johnson, London. 1799.

"EMMA Courtney" the first of these productions appeared about three years ago. The Monthly Review of April, 1797, thus speaks of it: —

"These memoirs rise above the class of vulgar novels, which aspire only to divert the unoccupied mind, by occasional illusion, from an irksome attention to the daily

---

[2] This section reviews not just literary works but reviews of those works in competing periodicals, particularly those with liberal political affiliations, in an effort to control their impact.

occurrences and trivial incidents of real life."

Meaning, as we suppose, to praise this attempt of the "fair writer" to find other employment for the female mind, than that which nature, situation, and sex, have designed it.

"This author," they proceed "attempts the solution of a moral problem which is eminently important, viz. whether it be prudent in minds of a *superior mould*, whether it will bring to them a greater balance of happiness, in the whole account, to exempt themselves from the common *delicacies and hypocrises* of life, and, on all occasions, to give vent to their *wildest feelings* with *conscientious sincerity*, or patiently to submit to the *incumbent mountains* of circumstances, without one *volcanic effort to shatter the oppressive load* into ruin."

Setting aside this slang of modern philosophy, the plain question is — Whether it is most for the advantage of society that women should be so brought up as to make them dutiful daughters, affectionate wives, tender mothers, and good Christians, or, by a corrupt and vicious system of education, fit them for revolutionary agents, for heroines, for Staels, for Talliens, for Stones,[3] setting aside all the decencies, the softness, the gentleness, of the female character, and enjoying indiscriminately every envied privilege of man?

The aim of this novel is to claim for the female sex the rights of the latter character. The heroine for such she is literally meant to be, is, even in early years, described——

"—as active, blythsome, bounding, sporting, romping, light, gay, alert, and full of glee; as offending all the pious ladies at church by her gamesome tricks."

[3] Mme de Stael, writer and daughter of French revolutionary Necker; Jean Lambert Tallien (1769-1820), French revolutionary Jacobin; John Hurford Stone (1763-1818), a dissenter and member of the Society of the Friends of the Revolution living and working in Revolutionary France. He is referenced here as the married lover of Helen Maria Williams, a famous writer and poet whose multivolume *Letters Written in France* report on the progress of the French Revolution in generally supportive terms.

She is next pourtrayed in still stronger terms: —

> "My desires were impetuous, and brooked no delay; my affections were warm, ... I now remember with shuddering."

An excellent beginning this, and fully calculated to produce the fruit intended. The next advance of her mind is effected by the perusal of Plutarch: —

> "I went down into the dining-room, my mind pervaded with *republican ardour*, my sentiments elevated by a *high-toned philosophy*, and my bosom glowing with the *virtues* of patriotism."

Does not this out-Helen even the wife or mistress of Stone? Not less alive does she appear to have been to the softer affections — let her speak for herself: —

> "In the course of my researches, the Heloise of Rousseau fell into my hands. — ah! with what transport, with what enthusiasm, did I peruse this dangerous, enchanting, work! — How shall I paint the sensations that were excited in my mind! — the pleasure I experienced approached the limits of pain — it was *tumult* — all the *ardour* of my character was excited."

That the mind here displayed should run into errors of no inferior enormity, was naturally to be expected, and, of course, we all along find her disdaining all those holy restraints which the wisdom and virtue of ages have esteemed necessary for the controul of human passions. But, lest we should be supposed *prejudiced* against her, we will quote her own sentiments on some important points: —

> "The wildest speculations are less mischievous than the torpid state of error: he, who tamely resigns his understanding to the guidance of another, sinks at once, from the dignity of a rational being, to a mechanical puppet, moved at pleasure on the wires of the artful operator. — Imposition is the principle and support of every varied description of tyranny, whether civil or ecclesiastical, moral or mental; its baneful consequence is to degrade

both him who is imposed on, and him who imposes—
obedience is a word, which ought *never to have had existence,*" &c. &c.

What stuff is here! — but a little more, and we have done with
the filthy labour: —

"To the professions my objections are still more serious. — The study of law, is the study of chicanery —
The church, is the school of hypocrisy and usurpation!
You could only enter the universities by a moral degradation, that must check the freedom, and contaminate
the purity, of the mind, and, entangling it in an inexplicable maze of error and contradiction, *poisoning virtue at
its source,*" &c. &c.

On the subject of female chastity she is consistent with herself, in her defence for offering her honour to a man who avoided
her. "*Individuality of affection,*" she says, "*constitutes chastity;*" or,
in other words, the mistress is, in all respects, as honourable as
the wife, provided she hath but one lover. If such a sentiment
does not strike at the root of every thing that is virtuous, that is
praise-worthy, that is valuable, in the female character, we are at
a loss to discover by what wickedness they are to fall.

The tale of this novel is not at variance with the opinions we
have extracted. That it is in all points reprehensible, in the highest degree, would be doubted by none, but the Monthly Reviewers, and their liberal fellow-labourers. Their concluding remarks upon it [*Emma Courtney*] is worthy of them: —

"Many remarkable and several *excellent* reflections (precious guardians of a nation's literature) are interspersed,
and the whole displays great intellectual powers. There
are also sentiments which are open to attack, (indeed!)
and opinions which require serious discussion: but we
leave every reader to form his or her own judgement."

Had the tendency of this novel been favourable to virtue,
honour, religion, morality, the liberality of these critics would
have been less conspicuous. But we have already bestowed, perhaps, too much notice on this performance. [The review here

turns to Hays's 1799 novel, *The Victim of Prejudice*.] ...

To the very last she is true to her principles. – Our opinion of these two novels is now clearly known, and we have said more of them than their intrinsic merit could possibly entitle them to expect. We have noticed them merely to guard the female world against the mischievousness of their tendency, "lest the venom of the shaft should be mistaken for the vigour of the bow." —As *usefulness* seems to be the watchword of this author and her friends, we will tell her how she may be much more useful than she can possibly make herself by devoting her time to literary labours—*to your distaff, Mary, to your distaff.* —On the *style* of her writings it is needless to remark; who stays to admire the workmanship of a dagger wrenched from the hand of an assassin?

Appendix III
Reviews of *Adeline Mowbray*

From *The Lady's Monthly Museum* 14 (May 1805): 343.
Adeline Mowbray; or, the Mother and Daughter: a Tale, in Three
Vols. By Mrs. Opie. 13s. 6d.

We always feel great satisfaction in taking up a work which
has employed the ingenuity and talents of Mrs. Opie, and it is
but justice to confess, that our expectations have never been disappointed. What we have looked for from her invention, we have
rarely missed; and what we have thought due from her powers of
description and pathos, has almost invariably been meted to us
in a measure overflowing. Adeline Mowbray abounds in all these
desirable qualities, and will be read with infinite interest and no
small degree of instruction.

From the *European Magazine,* 47 (February 1805): 129-30.
Adeline Mowbray; or, The Mother and Daughter. A Tale. Three
Volumes. 12mo. 1805.

Mrs. Mowbray is a learned lady, and a widow, devoted altogether to abstruse and metaphysical speculations. While this ill-
judging mother is occupied in preparing a voluminous system
of education, Adeline her daughter, for whom she entertains
nevertheless the most parental and tender regard, remains in the
meantime neglected and uninstructed; and had she not found
in Mrs. Woodville, the mother of Mrs. Mowbray, a teacher after
"the old fashion," her mind at fifteen would have been without
improvement and without knowledge; the important system of
Mrs. M. being still imperfect and incomplete. Adeline, who has
the highest respect for her mother's literary talents, about this
period, and after Mrs. Woodville's death, becomes emulous of

similar pursuits. Totally inexperienced, and without any proper director of her studies, she obtains the perusal of her mother's books, and unfortunately, in the writings of an author who is called Glenmurray, she discovers objections which she deems invincible against the institution of marriage. Upon the strength of this conviction, she forms a solemn compact with herself, and resolves never to marry. At Bath she meets with this Glenmurray, and, of course, they are mutually enamoured. He is reasonable enough, notwithstanding the public avowal of her sentiments, to offer her marriage; but this she disclaims, and in defiance of a parent's command, of the sense of the world, and the solicitation of Glenmurray himself, she unites herself to him, on her own baneful and absurd principles "of love and honour:" —a step this, it must be admitted, not consistent with that delicate feeling, and those exalted notions of filial affection and duty, which she is represented to possess; and although her conduct, with this single exception, be considered faultless, yet such an obstinate pertinacity of opinion must be conceived as belonging rather to the bold and lawless innovator, than to the submissive, the gentle, the benevolent, Adeline Mowbray.

This unlicensed union could only produce misery, shame, and disgrace; and of this Adeline is an eminent, and, it may be hoped, a useful example. By no means so much can be said for Glenmurray; a man without any fixed notions of religion, or indeed of any thing else, "for he doubts of all things," who dies without any renunciation of his errors, and yet is exhibited in the fascinating colours of splendid talents and attractive excellence and virtue. On the death of Glenmurray, Adeline is brought to some acknowledgment of her great mistake; and, in obedience to his dying request, resolutely struggling with her feelings, she marries his relation, Mr. Berrendale. By him she is deserted; and at length, after some additional evidences, she relinquishes, *on conviction,* her former way of thinking; —she is convinced, that if the ties of marriage were dissolved, or it were no longer to be judged infamous to act in contempt of them, unbridled licentiousness would soon be in general practice. The remainder of the tale is short. Mrs. M., by a wild sort of conditional oath, had renounced her daughter; and after many mutual attempts at reconciliation, which were frustrated by a malicious *Miss Woodville*, Adeline, in a declining state, retires with her child, an only daughter, by Mr. Berrendale, to a cottage within two miles of her native place, where her mother resides.

Here they casually meet; Adeline in a dying condition, and Mrs. Mowbray full of unabated affection: the former is conveyed, at her particular entreaty, to the shelter of a parent's roof; and the whole concludes, "in the German stile," at the moment of her death.

Mrs. Opie is well known as "a mighty mistress of pathetic song," and though the above outlines seem unpromising, because the sufferings of Adeline are deserved; yet so many affecting incidents, so many little circumstances, are skilfully introduced, that this tale cannot be perused without strong emotion, even by those "unused to the melting mood."

The character of Mrs. Pemberton, a quaker, merits unqualified praise; and Dr. Norberry, a physician, blunt, and rather vulgar, is well drawn.

The language of Mrs. Woodville, the early instructress of Adeline, is rather overcharged; it is "downright vulgar;" and therefore scarcely correct enough for "the sole surviving daughter of an opulent merchant of London."

To conclude with a specimen of the work: on the subject of Mrs. Mowbray's early and abstracted pursuits Mrs. O. thus ably observes:—

"Fatal and unproductive studies! While, rapt in philosophical abstraction, she was trying to understand a metaphysical question on the mechanism of the human mind, or what the true nature of virtue, she suffered day after day to pass in the culpable neglect of positive duties; and while imagining systems for the good of society, and the furtherance of general philanthropy, she allowed individual suffering in her neighbourhood to pass unobserved and unrelieved; while professing her unbounded love for the great family of the world, she suffered her own family to pine under the consciousness of her neglect, and viciously devoted those hours to the vanity of abstruse and solitary study, which might have been better spent in amusing the declining age of her venerable parents, whom affection had led to take up their abode with her." — V. I.

From *The Monthly Review*, 1806. 51 (1806): 320-1.
Art. 22. Adeline Mowbray, or the Mother and Daughter, a Tale. By Mrs. Opie. 12mo. 3 Vols. 13s.6d. Boards. Longman and Co.

These volumes are, both in their design and execution, so superior to those which we usually encounter under the title of novels, that we can safely recommend them to the perusal of our readers. We wish, nevertheless, to hint to Mrs. Opie, that her work would be improved by a more strict attention to the proprieties of some of her expressions, which at times are affected, and at others inelegant: but we forbear to point out instances, under the persuasion that our caution is already sufficient to a writer who possesses so much good sense.

It is the intention of this work to portray the lamentable consequences, which would result from an adoption of some lax principles relative to a rejection of matrimonial forms, which have been inculcated by certain modern writers.

From *The Literary Journal* 5 (1805): 171-5.
Adeline Mowbray: or the Mother and Daughter - A Tale. By Mrs. Opie. 3 vols. 12mo. 13s.6d. Longman & Co. 1805.

[The review begins with an extensive summary of the novel's plot.] Such is the substance of the story before us. It will readily appear that its object is to point out the consequences of opinions that have been propagated by certain persons calling themselves philosophers, especially respecting the institution of marriage. The tale itself is simple, elegant, and highly interesting throughout. The style is perspicuous, and though it cannot be said to be always pure and correct, yet it does not deserve the epithets of harsh and unpleasant. The characters are ably drawn and well preserved. Adeline is represented with all those qualities that can command our esteem, or gain our affection. Her faults arise from the want of an enlightened instructor, a circumstance over which she herself had no controul. She is young and beautiful, possessed of the most benevolent heart and of the most pleasing manners. Her mind is invigorated by exertion. Having once adopted erroneous principles, she acts upon them with ardour and decision. While we condemn her conduct, we pity her as a martyr to mistaken notions of virtue. The fortitude with which she bears her distresses is exemplary. The change in her sentiments is sufficiently accounted for, and the sincerity of her repentance consistent with her character. It may perhaps be supposed that such a character as this must be prejudicial to the interests of morality, by giving vice the appearance of respectability. Here the address of our authoress is conspicuous. The error in Adeline's education is constantly kept in view, and all her miseries are clearly exhibited as its natural consequence. By its operation we find a being, formed to adorn society, rejected as an outcast; and our abhorrence of the vice almost rises in proportion to our esteem for her virtues, and our pity for her misfortunes. The character next in importance is Glenmurray, a young man who is also formed to adorn society, but whose opinions have rendered him an isolated and useless being. He had published one of the works which had perverted the mind of Adeline. His mind is constantly tormented with the idea of the miseries which his opinions brought upon the object of his affection. When we find him blaming his own rashness and youthful presumption, and brought by anxiety to an early grave, we are forced to confess that his punishment is adequate to his offence.

The character of Mrs. Mowbray is also well drawn, but her continued affection for a man who deceived and married her, while he had another wife alive, does not seem to be altogether natural. Her virulent hatred against her daughter for having been an object of preference to such a wretch, is equally objectionable. Instances, however, are not wanting that might at first view appear to justify such a departure from probability. But unless all the circumstances could be brought under our view that contributed to produce such instances, they cannot be considered as decisive in favour of our authoress. Doctor Norberry is represented as a man of the highest benevolence, with a dash of eccentricity, which adds considerably to the effect of his character.

The moral of the story is unobjectionable. It points out the fatal consequences of an improper education, and the danger of acting upon principles contrary to the established rules of society. It shews the folly of forming rash and presumptuous opinions in our youth, and propagating them before they have received the sanction of our maturer years. The tale is throughout a lively representation of the incompatibility of a disregard of the institution of marriage with the happiness of the individual and the good of society.

Upon the whole this work must be allowed to rank considerably higher than the ordinary productions of the same kind. The interest of the story is well preserved to the end. The incidents in general follow naturally from the causes assigned, and are wrought up with uncommon skill. The tale is for the most part close and connected. We only recollect one instance of what appeared an unnecessary digression from the principal story. It is the rise and progress of Colonel Mordaunt's love for the sister of Major Douglas. But this digression, though it detracts from the uniformity of the tale, is in itself so agreeable that we cannot wish it away. (174-5)

From *The Annual Review and History of Literature* Edited by Arthur Aikin. 4 (1805): 653.
Art. IV. - Adeline Mowbray; or the Mother and Daughter: a Tale. In Three Volumes. By Mrs. Opie. 8vo.

NOVELS in former days were nothing but love stories, or works professing, often indeed falsely enough, to exhibit pictures of real life and manners. The importance that they have lately been allowed to usurp in the republic of letters, is at once a curious and an alarming symptom of the frivolity of the age. There was a time when a person wishing to inform himself in the higher branches of literature or philosophy, would have been obliged to undergo the labour of perusing dry crabbed treatises, written professedly on serious and important subjects. Now, happy revolution! he may luxuriantly imbibe, in the tempting form of a novel, the beauties of history embellished with all the eloquence of fiction, encumbered by no dates, and perplexed with no documents. Through the same medium he may see the happy effects of a new scheme of education, illustrated by the example of children who were never born; or the advantages of a new system of morals displayed, or its evil consequences exposed, on the unexceptionable authority of characters that have never existed. The work before us undertakes to shew, from the example of miss Adeline Mowbray, that a young lady who ventures to ridicule and condemn the marriage-tie, will expose herself to insult; that if she consents, though from the purest motives imaginable, to live with a man as his mistress, she will assuredly be driven out of decent company; that her children, being illegitimate, will be destitute of the right of inheritance, and subject to a thousand affronts; and that she cannot do better, if deprived of her lover by death, than to accept the first legal protector that offers. From the adventures of the mother is taught, the folly of neglecting all the duties of life for the study of metaphysics and politics; the ill consequences attendant on a complete ignorance of the world in the mother of a grown up daughter; and the madness of a rich widow's falling in love with and marrying a profligate young Irishman overwhelmed with debt, from whom she forgets to demand a settlement. It must be confessed that these great truths are sufficiently familiar; and in spite of the rage for experiment in moral conduct, which some years ago prevailed to a considerable extent, we hope there are few ladies "so to seek in virtue's lore," as to be inclined to put in practice the extravagances of poor Adeline. As for the faults and follies of her mother, we fear the causes of most of them are too deeply wrought into the con-

stitution of the human race, to be removed by the united eloquence of all moralists, novelists, and divines, who have ever
written, preached, or taught. If, therefore, it was Mrs. Opie's
wish, by the present work, to establish her name among the
great guides of female conduct and promoters of practical wisdom, she has assuredly failed of her object; but if she has adopted
the vehicle of system only for the sake of placing interesting
characters in new and striking situations, contenting herself with
the more appropriate task of amusing the fancy and touching
the heart, she may certainly lay claim to a pretty large portion of
applause. In drawing characters indeed we do not think she has
been very successful, for both Adeline and her mother appear to
us considerably out of nature; but there are situations and incidents of great effect. Glenmurray, the hero, is a most interesting
being; and several well-imagined circumstances serve to set in a
strong light the native benevolence and sensibility of his mind,
triumphing first over the stoical pride of system, and afterwards
over the fretful selfishness produced by lengthened sickness. The
account of Adeline's meeting with the illegitimate child at Richmond is natural and striking, and the speech of the quaker over
the body of the misguided Glenmurray is quite in character.
There are other passages of considerable merit interspersed
throughout, and some of deep pathos; but we should have been
better pleased if the tale had ended with the death of the hero,
before the odious Berrendale had appeared to put us out of love
with husbands.

From *The Critical Review* 4 (1805): 219-21.
Art. 37. —*Adeline Mowbray; or the Mother and Daughter: a Tale,
in 3 Volumes. By Mrs Opie. 12mo. 3s.6d.* 1805.

We opened with great pleasure a new novel from the entertaining pen of Mrs. Opie, a lady whose uncommon talents do
honour to her sex and country. She displayed, in her pathetic
tale of 'the Father and Daughter,' a power of working upon the
passions we think unrivalled (perhaps with the single exception

of Mrs. Inchbald,) by any writer of the present day. Nor has she failed to affect her readers with many heart-rending scenes in the work before us.

The story of 'the Mother and Daughter' may be comprised in few words. The former imbibes and supports *in theory* the principles of the new code of morality; the latter carries them into *practice*, and becomes the mistress of one of the authors who broached them to the world. Upon this her mother, inconsistently, but naturally, renounces her; and by the death of her lover she is driven to seek support in the exercise of those accomplishments her education had bestowed upon her. But her course of virtuous industry is interrupted by the scandalous reports of those who remembered her in her former vicious situation; and she is awakened to a sense of her misguided conduct. She is in consequence married; but her husband using her ill, after much misery she is restored to her mother, and dies contented.

But this scanty outline Mrs. Opie has most ably filled up with a variety of characters and incidents, well conceived, and adroitly introduced. She keeps up the attention of her readers to the end. The moral of her work is declared in the following passage: (Vol. iii. p. 13.)

The example of Adeline is held up 'as a warning to all young people; for her story inculcates most powerfully how vain are personal graces, talents, sweetness of temper, and even active benevolence, to ensure respectability, and confer happiness, without a strict regard to the long established rules for conduct, and a continuance in those paths of virtue and decorum which the wisdom of ages has pointed out to every one' (see p. 506)

But we cannot avoid remarking that the effect of this moral does not seem to have been consulted, when the state in which Adeline and Glenmurray lived was represented as perfectly happy, as far as their happiness rested in themselves; but the instant that Adeline marries, she becomes miserable from the conduct of her husband. Rightly considered, this reflects nothing upon the marriage state; but what we have to object to are the fascinating colours thrown over the erroneous virtues of

Adeline and Glenmurray, 'making' (as the benevolent quaker observes, Vol. ii. page 109) 'vice more dangerous by giving it an air of respectability.'

We have to remark a few inaccuracies in Mrs. Opie's style: solely from a regard to her reputation as a writer, for we doubt not her good sense will profit by our hints. 'Gulping down sobs and sighs' is an expression that occurs too often throughout the three volumes; 'a fine moral tact' we cannot help thinking a silly and affected phrase; 'it was the dark hour' means nothing but 'it was dark;' and why should 'the maternal feeling' be substituted for the feelings of a mother?

The interesting interview between the mother of Adeline and the benevolent quaker, in which the latter gives the former tidings of her daughter, is successfully imitated from the scene between Lady Randolph and the Stranger, in the play of Douglas.

But the description of the death of Adeline may bear a comparison with that of Richardson's Clarissa, or Rousseau's Heloise. Her last letter to her mother, where she bequeaths her infant daughter to her care, must move every reader to tears who can melt at the recital of unmerited distress; and that to colonel Mordaunt, recanting her false principles, and strongly contending in favour of marriage for the sake of the children and their education, is an honourable proof of Mrs. Opie's powers of argument in the defence of the good old cause.

We shall conclude our observations on the present work, with an extract from the second volume, page 116, which we conceive to be a very beautiful specimen of Mrs Opie's eloquent and interesting flow of language. Mrs. Pemberton (the benevolent quaker) thus addresses Adeline; whom she had heard of in her days of innocence, and now met with in disgrace.

> "And art *thou*," she cried "Adeline Mowbray? art *thou*
> that courteous, blooming, blessed being, (for every
> tongue that I heard name thee blessed thee) whom I
> saw only three years ago bounding over thy native hills,
> all grace, and joy, and innocence?" Adeline tried to speak,

but her voice failed her. "Art *thou* she," continued Mrs. Pemberton, "whom I saw leaning from the window of her mother's mansion, and inquiring with the countenance of a pitying angel concerning the health of a wan labourer who limped past the door?" Adeline hid her face with her hands. Mrs. Pemberton went on in a lower tone of voice. "I came with some company to see thy mother's grounds; and to hear the nightingales in her groves; but" (here Mrs. Pemberton's voice faltered) "I have seen a sight far beyond that of the proudest mansion, said I to those who asked me of thy mother's seat; I have heard what was sweeter to my ear than the voice of the nightingale; I have seen a blooming girl, nursed in idleness and prosperity, yet active in the discharge of every christian duty; and I have heard her speak in the soothing accents of kindness and of pity, while her name was followed by blessings, and parents prayed to have a child like her. Oh! lost, unhappy girl! Such *was* Adeline Mowbray: and often, very often, has thy graceful image recurred to my remembrance; but how art thou changed! Where is the open eye of happiness? where is the bloom that spoke a heart at peace with itself? I repeat it, and I repeat it with agony, Father of mercies! is this thy Adeline Mowbray?"